This is Our Generation Calling

Tony Beesley

Photo copyright: Steve Parkin 2010 steve@steveparkinphotography.com

Other titles in this trilogy

Volume 1 - Our Generation: The Punk and Mod children of Sheffield, Rotherham and Doncaster 1976 – 1985

Volume 2 - Out of Control: Punk Rock at the Doncaster Outlook and Rotherham Windmill 1976 - 1978

ISBN: 978-0-9565727-1-4

First Published 2010 by
Days like Tomorrow books

Cover designed by Dave Spencer

Layout and design by Tony Beesley

Printed on FSC approved paper by

FASTPRINT PUBLISHING

PETERBOROUGH, ENGLAND

www.printondemand-worldwide.com

This is Our Generation calling!

Contents

Our Generation

"Our Generation has been passionately put together: Packed with reminiscences from over 150 fans, Beesley's comprehensive oral history lifts the lid on the mish mash of local scenes that emerged during punk's first wave" (**Ross Bennett – MOJO magazine**)

"Fascinating reading and a right trip down memory lane" (**Jo Callis -The Rezillos**)

"As more and more Punk tomes cram the shelves, it's books like this, telling of the experiences of ordinary kids miles away from the King's Road, that are proving to be the most interesting and revealing" (**Shane Baldwin - Record Collector magazine**)

"Beesley's enthusiasm is infectious" (**Rachael Clegg - Sheffield Telegraph**)

"A true Punk Rock book: honest, vibrant and passionate: Highly recommended. My book of the year so far" (**Phil Singleton - God save the Sex Pistols website**)

"It pulls you in from the first paragraph. I can't recommended this book enough (**Sally Burton" - South Yorkshire Times**)

"Great stuff: A must for anyone who was there of course, but also a good insight into the whole era. I thoroughly enjoyed it" (**Arturo Bassick - The Lurkers/999**)

"I love this book. Such passion!" (**Tim Downes - TV Smith/The Adverts website**)

"In the book (Our Generation) we follow Tony and his punk 'cast' as they share some of their humorous anecdotes, and by the second chapter you really begin to feel like you are friends with these people; it's almost as if you are reliving their youth with them" (**Trudy Duffin– Rotherham News**)

"It is AWESOME!!! For those hours of reading sessions, I am back there... Thanks for doing this book and giving me something I can hopefully use to explain one day to my Grandkids what all the fuss was about" (**Wayne Kenyon - Doncaster Punk/skinhead and musician - Skin Deep**)

"Captures the spirit of an era totally spot on; A great read" (**Micky Geggus - Cockney Rejects**)

Out of Control

"This lad certainly knows some serious stuff about Punk" (**Barry Crabtree – Doncaster Free Press**)

"Tony crafts his book skilfully. It's a strong account – an easy but powerful read" (**Sally Burton – South Yorkshire Times**)

"Tony would make a good detective with his persistence in uncovering treasure troves of anecdotes and interesting accounts and photos" (**John Quinn – Sheffield Star**)

"An absolute gold mine of fans photos, posters, fanzines & fliers: a massively informative and entertaining read" (**Den Browne – Mudkiss online fanzine**)

Where to now?

Foreword by Paul Bower

Now the Freak Show's over

Dateline: SS Marko Polo off the Coast of Croatia August 2010

I have not had a glass of wine this cheap since Mr. Kite's in 1979. The weather is certainly better than it was on Division Street 31 years ago when it seemed to rain perpetually. Northern skies wept for the hopes shattered and jobs lost as the recession began to bite. After the raw energy and optimism of Punk, the early 80s in South Yorkshire felt like someone had turned off the lights. 30 years later off the Croatian coast the sun is shining and I am eating a cheese toastie on the top deck bar of an old car ferry. Phil Oakey's baritone bursts from the ship's PA.

"I'm only human, of flesh and blood are made. Human. Born to make mistakes"

A piece of Sheffield via Minneapolis echoes down the years and across the sparkling Adriatic. I begin to wonder what cosmic forces had conspired to catapult some of our old friends to fame but not always contentment, whilst others were consigned to a serene obscurity. So, I pull up a chair order another £1.30 glass of wine and let my mind drift back to the point where Callaghan gave way to Thatcher and Punk gave way to New Wave and Electro.

Phil had always been a star of sorts, even when he was a hospital porter at the Fulwood NHS plastic surgery clinic that specialised in treating chronic acne. His shoulder length hair with a blonde streak, black nail varnish, eye shadow and biker leathers certainly made him stand out at Pinestone Street's top night spot - the Crazy Daizy. Women loved him. Teddy Boys, Skins and Townies hated him. I don't think he ever took a beating, though. This was probably because at 6' 3" he looked like he might be able to handle himself despite the high heeled women's boots on his feet. At times he could seem distant and aloof but that was because his mind was elsewhere, not because he was ignoring you. He could also be very kind... in a strange way.

When my first serious girlfriend dumped me, he took me out for a lunch time ride down winding Derbyshire lanes on his 500 cc Kawasaki. Corners were taken at 70 mph but Phil really put his foot down on the straights. "IT WILL HELP YOU GET OVER THE EMOTIONAL PAIN!" he shouted through the roaring wind. The terror I felt being Phil's pillion passenger reminded me that I did not want to die of a broken heart and that in fact I really wanted to survive this perilous journey. He pulled into a pub car park in Hathersage and I begged him to drive more slowly. He agreed and asked for a drink. "I'll have a snowball... with a cocktail cherry on top. Don't forget the cherry."

I ordered a pint and then his snowball... with a cocktail cherry on top. Remembering that he was wearing nail varnish and eyeliner I asked Phil in a very loud voice how his girlfriend was. The locals stared. Two years later Phil was on the front cover of NME with Martyn Ware and Ian Marsh. Four years later he was a permanent fixture on Top of the Pops with Susan Ann Sulley and Joanne Catherall. We had all predicted that Heaven 17 would be first into the charts and that Phil would struggle with the new Human League.

But what of the other South Yorkshire stars for whom great things were predicted but never materialised?

The Negatives may have been turned out in sharp mod gear but above all else they were a superb pop band with well crafted songs. This stuck in my throat at the time because I had been trying to do the same thing for years with 2.3. Then these young upstarts came along and did it much better. The Limit Club on West Street (I went there so often that I should have just slung up a hammock behind the bar) – was a loyal supporter of local bands. Every couple of months they would stage a 50p gig with up to eight bands a night. At one of these gigs Cabaret Voltaire took their special brand of noise terrorism to the masses and miraculously they were well received despite not playing any songs. At the front of the stage a bunch of Skins made threatening gestures and Cabaret Voltaire's Richard Kirk reciprocated by goading them to come and have a go it they thought they were hard enough. The Skins had come to see Molodoy, an angular punk outfit who dressed as the Droogs from A Clockwork Orange. Kirk was not bothered. Harking back to his 1968 skinhead days growing up in Pitsmoor he had equipped himself with a crowbar to fend off a stage invasion. Cabaret Voltaire went on to shape the sound of countless industrial hard core and dance records. They even helped New Order with their first demos but Cabaret Voltaire never achieved the recognition they deserved.

The three chord Punk thrash of local bands who penned songs with titles like "I Don't Care About Your Abortion" had thankfully died away by the early 80s. A more intelligent but no less passionate approach had taken its place. I'm So Hollow created strange, tuneful and haunting songs such as "Touch". Their synth player and backing vocalist Jane Wilson was an unforgettable figure. Petite and stick-thin she had a dress sense half way between Cabaret and Diamond Dogs. She was certainly one of Sheffield' originals and very glamorous in a dangerous way... One night at the Crazy Daizy back in 1975 I remember her wearing a neatly tailored black bin liner held together with safety pins. A bunch of Townies took offence at the way she looked and started gobbing at her. She leapt off the raised dance floor and laid into one of the startled beer monsters, with fists and feet flailing. Jane was a kind and pleasant young woman but she was not going to be pushed around by bigots. The bouncers evicted the Townies and Jane resumed her dancing. Five years later it was good to see her making music with Rod, Joe and Gary. They split after one album and three well crafted singles.

There were also friends who never made it past their early twenties and into the 1990s thanks to the wave of cheap lethal heroin that arrived in South Yorkshire around the same time as mass unemployment. First, but not the last in this list of rock and roll casualties was Judd (Stephen Turner), the original bass player with Clock DVA. They were a giant band who managed to harness Cabaret Voltaire's innovation with driving rhythms and mesmerising bass vocals from Adi Newton (Gary Coates late of Parsons Cross). DVA made three fabulous records "White Souls in Black Suits", "Thirst" and "Advantage" and were constantly splitting up acrimoniously over money and unpaid bills... Adi always managed to recruit new members from the willing pool of young bohemians who were keen to be part of the nearest thing South Yorkshire had to the Velvet Underground. Early in their career the band outgrew Judd's limited musical abilities and there was no place for him in the new line up. It would be too simplistic to say he took an overdose because he was out of the band. It is always more complicated than that. However, it is a measure of the bleakness of those times that hopelessness and readily available smack could take a young man from energetic optimism to despair and an overdose in his council flat in the space of a few months. At Judd's funeral some of his mates droned on "*This is the way he would have wanted it. He never wanted to get old*" To that I repeat what I said back then "*Bollocks! It was a meaningless waste of a young man's life and we still miss him*" In fact I wish he was on this boat with me now. I still owe him a fiver and I could buy the wine and toasties. He'd like that.

Then there were other bands who were so clearly either rubbish or so out of step with the Zeitgeist that they had no chance of reaching a wider audience. We wondered why some of them even bothered.

"OH *MY GOD NOT BLOODY PULP AGAIN!!! I have more chance of playing for Wednesday than that gormless twat from Walkley ... whatsisname? Jarvis Cocker... has of being a pop star*", was a sentiment shared by many, including me. The only loyal Pulp fans that I can remember from that era were Mick and Laura Deeley. It took Jarvis another 15 years but he and the band went on to make one of the finest pop albums of the 1990s.

Then there was the technically competent bands who were just too old fashioned to ever sell any records. I mean *Rock Is Dead* so what chance have a bunch of long hairs from Firth Park with a stupid name like Def Leppard got? Scottish Pete who ran Revolution Records in Castle Market and helped them get their first EP released thought differently. He was sure that that Def Leppard were going to be huge in America. I smiled knowingly. No chance Pete. No chance at all.

The music drifting out of the PA is interrupted by an announcement...

"The ferry will dock in Dubrovnik harbour in approximately 15 minutes" Time to grab my rucksack, wake up my brother who is having a siesta on a sun lounger and head for the exit. Then more glorious proof of South Yorkshire's musical wealth pours from the ferry's PA system. It is The Arctic Monkeys' "Bet You Look Good on the Dance Floor."

Thirty years after the first South Yorkshire Punk bands had thrashed out their crude songs a group came along that combined everything we were looking to do but never managed. Great tunes, humour, manic energy, intelligent lyrics and not a fake cockney or American accent to be heard. Did any of us think that we would live to see words like mardy, scumbag and some'ut rhymed with stomach on prime time radio? Alex Turner I want to hug you and buy you a pint.

Walking out into the late afternoon sunshine touts hassle us with offers of the best cheap hotel rooms in Dubrovnik. I wonder to myself what it was that drove me and thousands of other kids in South Yorkshire to form bands and dream that we could make a new life for ourselves from playing music and writing fanzines. I think that we were unified by the incendiary desire to make some noise and escape jobs that felt like a prison sentence with no remission until you were 65. Then you would draw your meagre pension and retire to the allotment shed plagued by regrets for what might have been. Most of all we were looking to lead a life less ordinary. We still are.

And South Yorkshire? What of her? She is still making great music and producing great women and men. 2010 feels very like 1980 to me. But not to worry. We've been here before. We can take it.

Paul Bower Camden Town August 2010

Introduction

Our Generation the Punk and Mod children of Sheffield, Rotherham and Doncaster told the story of many of the local music fans and their lives revolving around the late 70's to early 80's Punk revolution and it's following Post-Punk era, Mod Revival and 1980's Futurist scene. The book's pages closed around the middle of that decade, book-ending the whole era as told in roughly chronological order by a varied selection of voices; be it musicians who never made it past the local venues and dance halls or those who ventured world-wide to play their music... also fanzine writers, snotty school kid Punk Rockers, ardent gig-going band followers, parka-clad Mods, make up smeared New Romantics and grey Mac-wearing Post-Punk intellectuals. They were all represented and captured in print: the hopes, spirit and dreams of a generation.

This is Our Generation calling revisits those days and beyond but also challenges the participants to reveal the paths taken immediately after the 1985 closing date of the first volume. Again, roughly in sequence of events, the story takes in left field-thinking Punks, Mods who evolved into scooter boys, Psychobilly loving ex-Punk kids, Goths, Casuals, musicians made good after years of hard work and little success, musicians who disappeared into obscurity: also Ravers and Punk kids who left the scene around the closing of its first chapters to later return to embrace the whole ideology, excitement and fun of the music and its scene. This is also a story of friendships re-discovered, mid-life crisis's and change - all of it joined together with a starting point - the love of music... the music of Our Generation!

How did we get to this point? How did we arrive in the year 2010... 34 years after the year Punk truly began and the nation sat up and took notice- a Punk motivated generation of Sheffielders, Rotherhamites and Donny and Barnsley pals, we almost to a man and woman began our journeys back in the early to mid 70's, musically at least! Inspired and learning from Glam Rock, Soul and a diet of cheesy 70's pop that served to initiate us into the world of Pop culture and its highs and lows, we were also, unanimously, a mixed up, frustrated and anxious little gang of kids who didn't quite know what we wanted or what we were searching for. With the arrival of Punk in our generation's lives, between the years 1976 – 1979, we were kick-started into being a part of a *new teenage rampage* that was served up as anything but sweet: from Punk Rock to the Mod revival and its 2-Tone cousin through to the New Romantic zeitgeist, we were all captivated and entranced within a fresh world of excitement, creativity and a new sense of belonging!

Our diary-esque chronicles told in the first volume's account and the experiences of 'Out of Control' could not include every single experience that needed to be told. They did not contain some of the many unheard voices that have joined the fold since and also – just as importantly – did not tell the coming of age years of the post-1985 years. What routes did we all take once the so called golden period of our youth, the formative years of 76 – 85, had passed our way? How did we cope with the shallowness of the mid 1980's when it seemed as though the revolution had been fought for nothing and our dreams and rebellions had all been forgotten! What did we make of all the scenes that sprung from Punk and grew from Mod along with the 90's Britpop explosion and the best of all the Punk inspired bands of recent years? How did we all cope with reaching our 30's and 40's and furthermore how did we continue to hold onto the ideals of our youth?

Here in these pages, we revisit the original Punk era with new captivating voices of rebellion told in even greater depth than the original volume had space or scope to explore; we jump into the lives of Mods and 2-Tone fans who were just as intoxicated by their scenes as the Punk Rock kids before them. We listen to the youngest voices of Punk and Mod yet, and how they came to terms with being just a couple of years too young to fully enjoy the scenes they obsessively embraced themselves to, yet often their experiences displaying far more human and interesting accounts than some of the older Punks and Mods they were hanging onto the straps of bondage trousers and fishtail parkas of!

Here within this conclusion to the 'Our Generation' trilogy, we can hear, and in some characters visually experience, the changes faced and frustrations felt of being a part of a generation lucky enough to have been part of the most anti-establishment and evocative era of any teenagers lives. From the starting point of the late 70's through to the present day, here are the voices of that generation: This is Our Generation calling!

Chapter One
Out of Control: The Story of a Rotherham Punk Rock lass (1976 - 1978)

"What I loved about Punk was the bands were no longer untouchable and seemed just like us. I ligged around watching Punk bands - covering everywhere around the region and met many of them. Those times were fantastic. I wish I could live them out again!" - **Julie Longden**

Above: Julie Longden at right on both photos with Punk friends in 1977

Living in Rotherham in 1976 could prove to be extremely hard if you aimed to be different and self expressive. Admittedly it wasn't easy anywhere in the UK during the dark days of the formative year of Punk Rock, but in a Northern Pit town such as Rotherham, the going could not get much tougher for anyone Punk inclined. If you wore bell bottoms from local jeanster shop Sexy Rexy's in the town centre, wore your hair long (Farah Fawcett style) and listened to David Essex and the Real Thing, then you were fine and in good company. Maybe, if you took to rocking out with the long-haired greasers at the local youth club or a Sheffield discothèque, then you would still be pretty safe. As a girl if you decided to slap on the black eye liner with extra zeal in new improvised shapes, ripped your fishnets and old school blazer and stencilled the word 'Anarchy' in bright-bold ransom note lettering on once fashionable girly tops and stuck two fingers up to all and sundry... then you could be walking a very fine line. One Rotherham lass did take this path with an uncontrollable agenda to be different and non-conformist, kicking the system in the bollocks and having as much fun as is humanly possible whilst doing so. Julie Longden was one of an extremely small number of early Punk Rock girls in the Rotherham area of 1976.

While most of the localities youth were still entranced with the glitzy Pop of the day, watching Bobby Knutt in 'The Price of Coal' on TV, waiting to start work either down the coal mines, British Steel or on the checkout at Boots and Woolworths - depending on your sex, Julie was on the Punk front line of gigs in the area and beyond. From 1976 to 1978, she lived the life with a truly hedonistic Punk Rock attitude and outlook. She hung out with - and was known on first name terms with - almost all of the main players of the Punk scene including key bands such as the Boys and the Stranglers. She hitchhiked all over the place to see some of the most exciting performances ever seen by anyone during their teenage years: she even knew the girl Johnny Rotten wrote about in their song 'Bodies'. Julie loved being a Punk Rocker and truly lived the life. This is a part of her story!

Julie Longden: "I had been going to gigs from the age of 13 in the early to mid 70's. I would go and see all of the big bands of the day and hang around the backstage door afterwards. I saw and met Queen, Yes, the who I

Sensational Alex Harvey Band, Thin Lizzy and Deep Purple – blame for partial deafness in my left ear – having been leant up against their speaker stack. I was also a massive 'Bowie' freak and loved all of his records. I remember a local lad called Paul Clarkson. He was a big Bowie fan and he used to model himself on him. He used to run a record stall on the Rotherham outside market, and I remember me and my mate would go there and try and think of interesting things to say to him, but actually all we wanted to do was just look at him. They were good times, but I sensed that a lot of the bands of the day were becoming far too big and more and more removed from us - the fans. I was ready for something new to come along... and it did!

"It would be around November 76 when I saw the Sex Pistols on TV for the first time. When I saw them and how they looked, with the attitude, I decided there and then, that this new form of raw Rock music was for me. I was so excited and immediately made up my mind - I'm gonna be a Punk Rocker! I quickly pulled out the old school blazer and adorned it with safety pins, tears and painted badges and tied a nice striped Top's dish cloth around my neck and went out and bought my first Punk single - 'New Rose' by The Damned. My family despaired of me and simply did not understand. I remember at one point having my hair cut extremely short and my Mum's disgusted reply was *'Julie, you look like a boy!'* I got rid of the old clothes, managed to get myself a pair of drainpipe jeans - which were so very hard to get a hold of in those days. I would go out with an old gas mask or a kettle for a handbag... anything just to be different. Of course, the attention was not always good. We had to put up with hassle and sometimes violence from Teddy Boys, Skinheads and would you believe it Rastafarians! That side of it could be terrifying. But, this was it... a new start for me. I soon began to lose friends who simply could not understand or get on with my new look, but I made lots of new friends on the Punk scene.

"It was early 1977 when I started to look out for Punk gigs to go to. To begin with there was hardly anything going off at all. Then over in Doncaster there was a club called the Outlook that started to put on Punk gigs, so with my like-minded friends, I set off attending lots of gigs there. I loved the Outlook. It was grubby and dingy, but the atmosphere was great and there was hardly ever any trouble. Also they put on some fantastic Punk bands and I would try and get to them all.

"One of my favourites was The Boys. I loved that band, especially their singer Duncan Reid - bless him! When they played the Outlook after their set, I went to the backstage door and knocked on it and when it opened I just said *'Hello!'* I ended up following them on all of their tour and we all became friends. Honest John Plain was great, they all were. Duncan once showed me a magazine article ... a kind of ode to how far you would go to get to see your favourite bands that he had seen somewhere. He said it was about me and wouldn't let me keep it, so I copied it down. I still have it as well. I saw some fabulous Boys gigs. They were one of the very best and I will always have a soft spot for them.

"A lot of the time after the Outlook gigs we would scrounge lifts from the newspaper delivery van that was heading towards Rotherham with the next day's papers. I once got mistaken for Fay Fife who was the singer with the Rezillos. I signed quite a few photos as her ha ha! We would drink a lot back in those days too and the drug of choice was amphetamines; don't let anyone tell you otherwise.

"Next up were the Stranglers, who were also great

The Boys copyright © Julie Longden

guys. I saw them at the Gaumont cinema in Doncaster with Punk group London supporting, featuring a young pre-Culture Club Jon Moss on Drums. I had met the Stranglers a few days earlier over in Sheffield at the Top Rank. In Donny, I was alone but swept past the whole queue to get in. The security asked us *'Who are you'* and I replied *'I am on the guest list'.* *'Wait a minute'* they said but before you knew it I was in there for free. I went over to the dressing room and could hear 'Happy Birthday' being sung inside. Stranglers' singer and guitarist Hugh Cornwell answered the door and straight away he said *'Sheffield yeah... c'mon on in.'* It turns out it was one of the road crew's birthday. They ended up throwing cake all over the place and J.J Burnel wiped his cake-smothered nose on my T-Shirt...cheers J.J! We took lots of photos of the Stranglers and they were all great with us. One thing I noted about the Stranglers was that they were very intelligent and articulate. Hugh stated to me that *'We are not a Punk band, we are a Rock band.'* When they next played Sheffield at the Top Rank with the Drones supporting we had another great night with them. After one gig, over at the hotel, J.J Burnel had to be talked out of walking across the fourth floor outside window ledge by myself and everyone else present. He was confident he could do it, but managed to be persuaded otherwise.

"When The Jam went out on their first nationwide tour for their 'In the City' LP, we went along to see them at the Top Rank in Sheffield. We had been to the Outlook that many times by now that it was a change of scenery. The Jam were great and amazing to see live, but when we met them afterwards they were a bit stand-offish. They signed stuff for us and everything and spoke to the fans, but they were just that bit aloof, especially Paul Weller. Bruce Foxton was much friendlier and a bit more willing to talk to the fans."

Stranglers by Jools

As 1977 progressed ... clubs and live venues up and down the country began to see that this new Punk Rock phenomenon was a potential money earner. Whereas early on (and in some cases continuing a lot longer) the venues were banning Punk Rock, now there was an element of places willing to give Punk a chance. Locally around Sheffield and Rotherham, there had only been a few places to book Punk and new wave bands... hence the popularity of the Outlook club in Doncaster. To begin with, though, gigs in Sheffield were sporadic...the odd one at the Top Rank, University or the new Punk nights at the Penthouse and occasional Crazy Daizy outing being the most one could expect.

The Adverts TV Smith and the late Howard Pickup by Jools

Over in Rotherham a new Punk night began in August with Doctors of Madness supported by Penetration playing the opening night. The venue continued to book Punk and related bands for the rest of the year and a little into 1978 and Julie attended almost all of these new wave nights: one of these bookings was garage band Punks the Adverts.

At one Adverts gig that Julie attended, in a classic rendition of the famous *'playing the right notes but in the wrong order'* Morecambe and Wise' sketch, TV Smith realised that Gaye had been playing the right notes... BUT! On the wrong string!

Julie Longden: "I liked the Adverts, especially Tim (TV Smith - singer). We went to see them play all over the place, as well as Rotherham. I can remember once watching in amazement when, after their set, TV Smith was yelling at bass player Gaye Advert. He was shouting *'You have been playing the wrong notes all the way through on every song'* to which she replied, shrugging her shoulders *'Well it's the guitar strap that's too short'.* We took the mickey out of them for that all night."

During the Punk era, the notorious serial killer the Yorkshire Ripper was still on the loose and there was no serious lead as to catching him. The thought of being followed and being a victim to this barbaric monster must have been present in most females' minds, let alone the garish and often explicitly dressed Punk girls of the time.

Julie Longden: "This was the Ripper era you have to remember, so when we were going out dressed as we were it was also a risk on that point as well. We went over to Leeds to see The Boys at the F-club, which was situated almost right at the heart of where some of the Rippers murders had taken place and the place itself was not very pleasant either. We met future Soft Cell singer Marc Almond at that gig. He was in the ladies toilets and was trying to borrow make up from us. He asked us for our lipstick and we told him to fuck off! Apparently he was supposed to be one of the Punk faces in Leeds.

Above – Phil Spalding and Bernie Torme
Left – Their road manager Mark (Jools photos)

"After the gig, The Boys had two estate cars for them and the Bernie Torme band (who had been supporting) and a van for their equipment. There was four of us girls and Bernie's drummer all waiting for one of the cars, so they had to do a shuttle service to get us all back to the hotel. As we were stood around with our Punk gear and make up on, the cars passing by started to slow down, wind the windows down and ask us *'How much then?'.*

"Clearly they thought we were all hookers on the biz! When we got to the hotel, we carried the guitars in and the receptionist asked us who we were. For some reason we told them that we were the Radio Stars and they waved us in. I was later told that unfortunately (for the Radio Stars), the band was actually staying there that very night and the receptionist did not believe them when they arrived there to get in. As for us, like true rock n' roll stars, we trashed the hotel room and the next morning we followed the chamber maid around and stole the food from her trolley each time she went into a room.

"The next time we went to Leeds was to see the Boomtown Rats. We were having problems getting in as it was on their student tour of 1977 where they played all the Universities and Polytechnics and to get in you had to either be a student yourself or get one to sign you in as a guest. We were arguing with the student union boy and we saw Boomtown Rat Pete Briquette who, when hearing us shout over, shouted back *'All right girls'.* Next thing we were in the venue.

Boomtown Rats promo photo given to Jools by Bob Geldof which is fully-autographed to her on the back.

"We had recently been to the Sheffield Polytechnic to try and see the Rats and had been turned away by the same type of studenty git who said we weren't allowed in cos we were not students. As we were sat on a wall outside the venue, the Boomtown Rats passed by and saw us. They asked us what we were doing and how come we weren't in the venue. So we told 'em that we weren't allowed in. After we had been for a couple of beers, they saw us again and took us along to the door. Bob Geldof told the student git on the door that if we can't come in then they wouldn't be coming in either and there would be no gig. In we went!

"Inside the place, Bob Geldof asked me what I thought of their first album that had just been released. When I told him I didn't have it, he replied *'What... we have got you in for free and you haven't even bought our album yet!'* I told him I would buy it once I had heard it. He started to beat me playfully with a towel. The gig was great, the new songs from the album were great and I bought the album. Bob had told me that the next time he sees me I had better have bought the record. I loved the Boomtown Rats.

"Around this time, I managed to meet two of the Sex Pistols when they arrived to do a signing and promotion for their new 'Never mind the Bollocks' LP that had just been released. Steve Jones and Paul Cook were really chatty and friendly and were proper diamond geezers. My Mum and Dad's paper shop sold records back then so I bought the LP through the shop. Not many shops were stocking the record back then cos of the title."

One of the songs on the Sex Pistols one and only album was called 'Bodies'. The song caused outrage with its tale of 'a girl from Birmingham who had just had an abortion'. The girl that the song is based on was someone Julie had crossed paths with; briefly and sadly.

Julie Longden: "I actually met the girl that the 'Bodies' song was written about. She was called Polly and she really did have an abortion. She had been raped by two or three men and it had affected her mind. That much is true, though the story follows that she (allegedly) self-aborted the baby, so I am told. When the Pistols played at Barbabarellas they met Polly and heard her story. Johnny Rotten took her story and turned it into the song 'Bodies'. I later saw Polly again at a gig and the song was played. Bless her; she skipped around the dance floor to it. She wasn't right and was a damaged and sad little girl. Bless her...she just needed a cuddle and to be loved. I wonder what ever happened to her?

"Back then me and my mate would buy the NME on a Thursday and go straight to the gig guide. We would go through it and pinpoint all the interesting Punk gigs coming up in the coming week and make our plans on which ones to attend. It might be Hull on Friday, Leeds on Saturday and Manchester the next day and then there were also the gigs closer to home. We must have covered all of the North of England, but never ventured that far south. By hook or crook we hitchhiked all over and never ever paying to get into the gigs, just blagging our way in one way or another.

"One heavy experience we had was when we went to Birmingham Barbarellas to see a new Punk band called Sham 69. There was such a bad atmosphere at that place. We were told by the regulars there, to not hang around outside afterwards and, when we went to the train station, to steer clear of the Rastas. We said to them *'But we are girls they won't hit us?'* But they told us that didn't matter and it made no difference to the Rastas if we were boy or girl. The Rasta's would be waiting and hanging around the train station waiting for Punks to beat up. Following the gig we ran straight through the station and got onto the train, pulling the blinds down so they couldn't see us. They did get on the train, though, and we could hear their voices getting nearer. I was absolutely terrified, huddled up, shaking and waiting for them to find us. Luckily the train set off and they got off. As the train pulled out and we lifted up the blinds they spotted us and were giving it some verbal... disappointed they hadn't got us. That was a very scary experience and we never went back to Birmingham again.

"When the Clash played the Top Rank we went backstage and met the band. Mick Jones was the friendliest: Topper just looked so out of it even then - he looked like a zombie and dreadful. The Clash told us they didn't really like all the Punk girls 'Painted up' and who tried too hard to be Punk. They preferred the more natural looking ones: Punk girls who  looked like the Slits. Clearly, they weren't taken in by all of the Punk fashion thing. We swiped one of their shirts too and took some great photos that night. On one of the photos we took, Paul has his head on Joe's lap and Joe was laughing saying *'Fuck me, that photo will be in the papers saying Paul gives Joe a blow job.'*

"A good gig was a Punk all dayer in Keighley at the Nikkers club with Buzzcocks, the Skunks and John Cooper Clarke performing. We got there about late afternoon and it was an open bar, which we hit with a vengeance.

"Another few we went to were at the newly opened Sheffield Limit club. The following year we saw Adam and the Ants (amongst others) there. I can remember trying to get near Adam Ant and she was there - Jordan. Straight away she said *'What do you want, what you after.'* Her manner was very abrupt and she was not keen on anyone getting too close to Adam Ant. She was quite scary actually.

"Back to the Boys, when we went to see them at the Sheffield Penthouse after the gig we all went back to their digs, which was the Howard Hotel near Pond Street. Me and my mate got sneaked in by the band. The Boys shared rooms and the next morning when they went down for breakfast, we hid in the room. The chambermaid came banging on the door and we threw the dirty sheets out. Of course, she went down and told Gordon (the tour manager) and he made The Boys pay for us. So that's why he barred us from their hotels forever. But we still went along... making our own way between gigs.

THE DRONES
24-hour punkerama
THE DRONES, the Skunks, Dawn Watcher, Rudi And The Zips, Rouge, V2 and John Cooper Clark all appear at a special 24-hour punk festival at Keighley Nikkers starting at 1pm on Tuesday, December 27 and continuing until 1pm on Wednesday.

"Back nearer to home I decided to go for a drink at the Dickens Bar in Rotherham town centre (During this period the Dickens bar was a Heavy Rock drinking hole). As soon as I stepped into the place, I was told to get out! It was clear that punks would not be allowed in there. That night every pub in Rotherham threw us out, because of the way we were dressed and we ended up at the Grapes in Dalton. When we walked into the Grapes, there was a stripper on and we got much more attention than she did. She was working so hard at it, bless her, but no one was paying her a blind bit of notice as they were all staring at us."

Ironically, the very same Dickens venue Julie recalls in relation to this story that was banning Punks and Punk music is now promoting all styles of Rock and Punk related gigs. Julie herself had been a regular at the pub prior to her Punk transformation, but it had been a Heavy Rock themed bar. After many years as a typical town centre pub, the venue has now reverted to its old name of the Dickens bar and is now putting on name Punk Rock bands. What goes around comes around.

Julie Longden: "My Mum and Dad hate it (Punk Rock). They think I'm a moron. We have big rows about it, them asking me why I do dress like this and why I am ruining my life. But I don't think I am." (Sheffield Star - 8/11/77)

The end of Julie's Punk Rock journey was almost coming to a close by 1978 following her pregnancy. Interestingly, a new wave outsider showed gentle concern for her, each time she arrived to see him perform.

Julie Longden: "I loved Ian Dury. In fact, I was also a big fan of Elvis Costello and loved the Stiffs tour that these two did with Wreckless Eric. By early to mid 1978, I was at that point very heavily pregnant. Each time I went along to see Ian Dury and the Blockheads and would meet up with them, Ian's tender concern would increase. He was so kind and considerate and would show great care towards me. I have to say, that out of all the many bands I saw in those days, Ian Dury and the Blockheads were the friendliest, warmest and well humoured of them all. They would always make a fuss of me and make me feel important. They had a big hulky roadie guy called

Fred and he was the same. One of their associates was a bloke called Kosmo Vinyl (He later went on to work with the Clash), and after the City Hall gig, he offered to marry me. He was going on non-stop all the way back to the Hotel. I told him strictly *'No I won't marry you, I'm pregnant and not by you!'* In September 1978 my first child was born and that put paid to the Punk thing for me. I would return to gigging later on, but the Punk scene had almost died by then."

Julie's return to the gigging scene saw momentous early gigs such as the legendary Specials/Madness/Selecter line up at the Sheffield Top Rank, which occurred right at the middle of the 2-Tone and Mod Revival: the sixties thing, though, being quite familiar to her.

Julie Longden: "Quite a few of my friends went into the Mod revival and 2-tone scene and I kind of went along and bought into it a little. The thing is, though, my older brother had grown up during the original Mod era, so the new Mod sounds were nothing new to me. I was already familiar with The Who, Small Faces etc and I felt that a lot of the Mod revival was really just a watered down version."

The reality of Punk's necessity had changed and for Julie, the Punk era now belonged to the past, and the rebellion was treading shallow water.

Sharon and Julie Longden prior to embarking on their Punk Rock rampage around Rotherham Town centre (right)

Julie Longden: "For me, Punk died when all of the bands became too big and started to become superstars. They soon became just like the ones they had come along to replace. They were now the bands being held on a pedestal and there was a kind of backlash forming against that. The closeness of the whole scene was now gone and it wasn't possible to go and do what we used to do back in the earlier days...meeting the bands and sharing a drink with them and all that kind of thing: Punk just simply stopped being accessible.

"To me, Punk is like a bubble of when it all happened within that time frame, everything changed afterwards socially and economically so the need for it was different too. These bands that come along nowadays and say that they are a Punk band, Green Day for example; well they aren't Punk at all. They are just another rock band that may be influenced by Punk."

New styles came and went as Julie sampled most of the seemingly cutting edge scenes.

Julie Longden: "The New Romantics came along and I went to see Duran Duran. Again it was a case of *'I've seen it all before'* as in when I met up with Nick Rhodes of the band and noticed he had four times as much make up on as I had. I had been a Bowie fan since I was 11 years old and to my mind nobody does pampered and powdered better than Bowie. The New Romantics was just a Peacock thing and I had seen it all before."

During the two years that Julie embraced the Punk Rock scene, she saw countless bands, met most of them and photographed some of the best of them. Her notebook contains messages from the Rich Kids, XTC, Generation X (Billy Idol's scribbled comment being *'They offered me a part in Blake's 7, but I wanted to play guitar* – Love Billy Idol'), The Boys, Ian Dury ('1 x dead dog, animals rule free' is his comment), Graham Parker, the Stranglers and Bernie Torme band. Her photos, also, have messages from the bands on the back – Stranglers drummer Jet Black proclaiming *'Jet Black woz ere' too'*... but it is the actual photos themselves that tell the real stories: that being into Punk Rock and hanging out with some of the key-players of the scene could be a welcoming and unpretentious experience... but just as importantly it could also be fun. Captured here, in the next few pages are snap-shots in time... of 1977 Punk Rock from the backstage area and from a fan's eyes view.

Some of Jool's Punk friends including Honest John Plain of The Boys, M.J Drone (Drones singer) and a Billy Connolly look-alike grabbing a handful Top photo: courtesy of Sheffield newspapers

Jools Punk Rock Gallery

Stranglers tour including Sheffield 1977

The Stranglers photos copyright © Julie Longden

The Clash Backstage at Sheffield Top Rank 1977

All Clash photos copyright © Julie Longden

The Boys on tour 1977 - Sheffield and Doncaster

The Boys album cover image courtesy of Cherry Red Records. www.cherryred.co.uk

The Boys 1977 line up - Honest John Plain, Casino Steele, Duncan 'Kid' Reid, Matt Dangerfield and Jack Black

The Boys photos copyright © Julie Longden

The Boys album cover image courtesy of Cherry Red Records. www.cherryred.co.uk

The Drones backstage (Stranglers support at Sheffield Top Rank

Drones photos copyright © Julie Longden

ALL PUNK GALLERY PHOTOS COURTESY OF JULIE 'JOOLS' LONGDEN

Chapter Two
Punk Rock voices! 1976-1978

"The shame of it all! I had to go to the magistrates and I got a 12-month conditional discharge and Andy got a £50 fine. Yes, the pinching stopped - for a little while after that. I was a PUNK...and a nasty little thieving one at that: One thing is for certain; by 1977 I was developing quickly into an Anarchist and was very anti-establishment" – **Steve Marshall** (Sheffield Punk Rocker)

The Punk Rock voices of 1976 – 78 are not all fully formed ones, with all the right retrospectively informed insight to paint the perfect picture of Punk rebellion: Rather they are honest, direct, funny, sometimes awkward and always individual. These stories create a true account of how it felt to be dragged along with something as adventurous and non-conformist as Punk. How each individual reacted to his or her first taste of the revolution is as unique as the next one and far better for it.

Leading the way throughout this gallery of Punk-intoxicated kids of late 70's Sheffield and its bus-ride away rebels is Steve 'Mushroom' Marshall (so named Mushroom after a strange hat that he once wore and the saying...*"I'm a mushroom...they keep me in the dark and feed me bullshit!")* ... The Punk with a cause! The cause being 'whatever you got' – to paraphrase old style rebel Marlon Brando as the Wild one! Anarchy and freedom being the motives here: and Punk Rock music being the soundtrack... press the start button; the tapes ready to run!

Sheffield music fan Steve Marshalls' life crossed paths with Punk Rock during the chaotic Punk year of 1977. His sister Debs (Rocka Debs) was already well on the chosen path of Punk by that time, having already chalked up a more than credible list of gigs and Punk Rock experiences. During the summer Steve, for reasons he is not quite totally sure of himself, made journeys to Manchester to witness the polar opposites of Punk – Canadian M.O.R rockers Rush. His gig experiences prior to that had been Glam Rock and amongst a series of City Hall gatecrashed and rarely ticket paid gigs – a Marc Bolan and T-Rex concert. Though Bolan was to be accepted and mostly respected amongst the early Punk crowd, the meanderings of Rush and all the other long haired hairies of the time were enough to turn any good music fan to something like – Punk Rock! Steve was no exception!

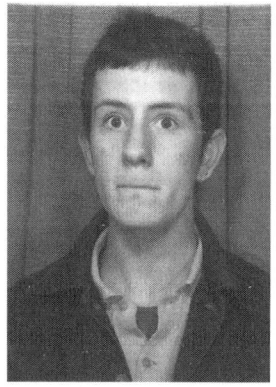

Steve's anti-authoritarian pre-Punk habits, a sign of the anarchic attitude and dislike for the system to come included 'nicking Airfix kits from Redgates toy shop in the City centre 'until *we got caught'* and bunking into Glam Rock concerts at the City Hall. His story starts before Punk right in the middle of the Glam Rock era, a more than common starting off point for many future Punk Rockers!

Steve Marshall: "What I remember mostly (pre-Punk) is that when I was 14 or 15 in 1974/5...I tagged on with my older sister Debs and her mate Sarah going to a lot of the concerts that were then being held at the City Hall...the BIG venue in Sheffield at the time. The thing is, apart from a few that we really wanted to see, we never had tickets. So we would hang out outside the City Hall, talking and messing around with a few regular kids that always used to go. After 7.30pm when the doors closed we would be led by Specky (who was about 15 or 16) and dressed a bit like Bowie and try to get into the concerts for free.

"The wooden City Hall doors at the side and the back were not patrolled by bouncers as they were upstairs on the circle or balcony and showing the *paying people* to their seats, etc. The trick for us was to somehow push at the outside doors until we reached the silver fire door bar inside which could then be somehow lifted and then we were in. When we got in we went up quietly in little groups so the doormen wouldn't hear: we would have to creep up loads of concrete stairs to either the circle or balcony entrances and then, if the inside doors weren't covered by doormen, we would all scamper in the dark to find a spare seat anywhere and make out that we had just arrived late.

"The concerts would have already started so the dark often helped, but my strong memory is that my heart really raced and thumped away during that last climb of the stairs and then the dash inside for a seat trying NOT to get caught out. Sometimes we would get to the top of the stairs and the bouncers would come out and we would have to scramble and run like fuck right back down again with hearts racing and us laughing and scattering when we got out. If we failed once, we would try again and again for half and hour or more until we mostly got in, sitting on the balcony, circle or even sometimes downstairs if we were very lucky and sneaky... which you had to be really.

"This way, at 14 or 15, I saw some major groups of the time absolutely for free. I remember seeing Queen, Be-Bop Deluxe, Dr. Feelgood, Sensational Alex Harvey Band, 10CC and other notables of the time... all with a teen kid's excitement. I was into Slade, Sweet, Sparks and T.Rex... so I actually PAID to go and see these at the City Hall - just to be double sure of getting in! For the other gigs there were about a dozen or so of us regular gatecrashers, though we had another name for ourselves, which I have now forgotten. It was fun, but I often got into bother when I got back home late...at 10pm or after when the concerts had ended.

"The bouncers got used to us and sometimes, when the concert was crap - and not many tickets sold - like Pilot for instance, instead of having us running round and bashing doors, they just came out of the front when we walked up to the City Hall and said come on in you lot!! Ha! I have forgotten who all the little gang were but it was the start of a life of sneakiness and mischief for me! Looking back I apologise to all those paying customers, we were just kids!"

Steve's early pre-Punk experiences also led him to a venue that he would later re-visit right in the middle of Punk; and in turn attain employment of sorts there.

Steve Marshall:
"I was really into heavy(ish) rock back then. Queen were considered heavy at the time and Slade and Sweet were rocking, so I had long straggly hair which was grown to deliberately cover my big ears so the birds at school wouldn't notice! Ha. I bought clothes in the market at Harrington's in Sheffield. The trendy stuff... two-tone trousers, star jumpers, etc! And on Saturday mornings a lot of our schoolmates would all go to the Sheffield Top Rank, which had a 2 or 3-hour disco dance session for the teeny kids every week. It was all the usual kids stuff of snogging the best birds if you could, dancing around and shouting football chants... remember 'Hi Ho Sheffield Wednesday'."

By 1976 and into 1977 Steve's journey into Punk Rock had already begun: the days of mischief still being a part of the experience.

Steve Marshall: "I was pretty smart at school and did well, so I stayed on to do O levels and A levels in 6th Form where you could dress down on one or two days a week. Sometime in 1976 my sister Debs, older than me by a year and a half, had progressed into Punk via Bowie and T.Rex; so I followed a bit sheep-like. One day, on the school notice board I saw this ad for a Clash and a Damned concert or a record (I forget which) and I was a bit amazed: I thought I was the only one who even knew about Punk at school then!

"I was mostly too young - and definitely too young looking - to go to 18's and over concerts and the only job I had was a paper round and a few savings from that, but I started to buy Sounds and NME when I could afford it and listen to John Peel on the radio at night. I suppose the main appeal of Punk was its difference and rebellion, which suited me because, although I was quiet and a bit introvert, I was also a rebel. I had been going out with one or two mates since I was 14 or 15 in the town on a Saturday...pinching or trying to pinch Airfix models or subbuteo teams (I was into both!!), from places like Redgates in town.

"Usually, I could afford to buy some of them and sometimes did; but the nicking was a bit of excitement...a buzz! It was such a great embarrassment when, with my mate Andy, one Saturday morning in W.H.Smiths in Sheffield, we both got caught – him nicking a felt-tip pen and me trying to cover for him: we played it wrong and tried to act cool so we got caught when we went out onto Fargate. Man, the embarrassment – in the MIDDLE OF TOWN! Worst still, this was cup final day in 1977 and they sent two police women in a car to put us in and take us both back home (we lived on the same street) to our surprised and very angry parents. The shame of it all! I had to go to the magistrates and got a 12 month conditional discharge. Andy got a £50 fine. Yes, the pinching stopped - for a little while after that. I was a PUNK...and a nasty little thieving one at that!"

Punk entered into many young teenagers lives in that year zero of 1977: most of those being drawn to its allure... being of the rebellious nature. But, once the step was taken to wear your rebellion on your sleeves, the revolt was made public.

Steve Marshall: "I suppose that Punk and the press it was already getting (at the time), led me to think that I should be deliberately different and obnoxious....and so I was. My teenage anger and rebellion led me to changing from a fairly smart, quiet, long haired T.Rex teen to a shorter haired, bizarrely-dressed 17 year old bloke. I can't remember my first Punk clothes...but, since I was then working part-time shelf-filling, I had money and I soon bought a leather jacket and some jeans to go with my Doc Marten boots. But at times I had to cross the road, if I saw my current or old school mates, because of my radical change to being one of these 'disreputable Punks'. Of course, in the hot summer of 1977 when the Sex Pistols brought out 'God Save the Queen', I not only bought it straight away but I was also on the local Radio Sheffield programme, defending the Pistols against attack from unbelievers and the mainstream masses. I was sort of 'proud' of that...at the time.

"The first records and groups I heard were due both to my sister Deb's music and to John Peel. I was much influenced by John Peel and, apart from at my mates, or through my own sister's records, that was the only place I could hear Punk records. I was straight into the Sex Pistols and The Clash, Wire, Adverts, Damned, Generation X. I can't remember where I got my first Punk records from... but it was probably Revolution records on the Sheffield Market gallery, as nowhere else really had them in stock in the early days. Maybe Bradley's down the Moor in Sheffield might have had them – but I can't remember now. It all seemed so subversive in the early days as Punk was unknown, dirty and nasty and got a bad press everywhere.

"I am not exactly sure how my parents reacted. I expect my Dad was pretty disappointed and thought I would go down hill into drugs and all that. My parents were going through a lot of arguments and disagreement in their marriage anyway, so myself, my older and younger sister were, I think, just doing our own thing anyway. I played golf a lot with my good school pal Andy. I remember his look of horror as I proudly told him in the summer of 1977 that I was going to get part of my hair dyed blue and start wearing a Punk leather jacket... and maybe start up a group!! "I had some family support as I said...my sister Debra and my younger sister Christine, plus their friends, Sarah and Donna were all into Punk Rock, Gen X, The Clash and what have you... so it gave me a bit of encouragement; that I wasn't a freak or a weirdo. One thing is for certain though; by 1977 I was developing quickly into an Anarchist and anti-establishment hero!!

"I think I first went to gigs by mates from school in local bands (EXIT, Black Rainbow...and then, before long... the Stunt Kites). I was working part-time at a supermarket so I had money when I was 17 and I remember getting changed downstairs in the staff room from a respectable supermarket boy to loud and snotty (black blazer and jeans wearing) Punk with my Punk mate Julian - a middle class kid from Gleadless who also worked there and was well into Punk too. I remember getting tickets in 1977 for Boomtown Rats, the Damned, and The Jam, Stranglers, Clash and others at the Sheffield Top Rank. I also went once with our Debs and her then boyfriend Slonk and his mate Mick D and Sarah Bod to the Windmill club at Rotherham. We saw the Adverts and a local support group 2.3. Slonk was good mates with Paul Bower who sang with 2.3. I was always a bit wary, partly because of my young looking face and maybe not being able to get into concerts sometimes, and partly because I knew I might get picked on because of my weird, Punky type appearance. Mind you, I was 16/17 that year, and I really soon became very attracted to Punkettes... and plenty of 'em too!

"In 1977 the two LPs I do remember the most were 'Never Mind the Bollocks' which I bought on release after all the pre-release fuss... and it was, and still is... a very good LP. The other one was The Clash first LP. To this day, in my opinion, that is one of the very best Punk LP's out of all the hundreds of em. It was raw, fast (except 'Police and Thieves') and fucking brill. I learned all the songs and words off by heart within a few weeks.

"At the Top Rank I felt a lot better when I did get in i.e....not being picked out by the door staff for being too young or looking too obnoxious. The Top Rank was huge downstairs – with two coatrooms as you went in and you paid on the left - then at least four bars and three lots of downstairs toilets. It had a similar layout upstairs too...with two different flights of stairs going up or down and some seats alongside the fronts of the glass parapet overlooking the top balcony. When Punk bands were on in 1977 and 1978 there were big queues outside of weird and wonderful Punks and students - most of them probably too young like me. Inside it was a melee of colour and fashion and I just wandered round and round upstairs and down before the bands came on with a plastic pint glass of watered down beer or lager *looking up* all the strange and glamorous Punkette birds and wondering where the HELL THEY ALL CAME FROM!!

"For the major bands' gigs, downstairs was usually mostly packed on the large square dance floor with idiots like me, jumping, pogoing and sweating away in the thick of it all; dancing to these so called idiot thug Punk groups playing loud music through those huge amps at us. It was all an experience I suppose; just something you did when you were that age. The pre-bands disco of course was brilliant... Dancing around on the dance floor to early Punk classics and just enjoying myself with my mates. It was mostly good times there; there were occasional fights and bits of trouble but the bouncers usually sorted it out and threw out the culprits. I was picked on once (at the Stiff Little Fingers Top Rank one) on the dancefloor when two Skinheads felled me from behind. I got up to sort of tackle it when another kid I knew jumped in and stopped any further bother. They probably took exception to my purple and blue silky checked trousers, which were a bit unique and weird. Usually me and my mates would just drink, dance about, pose for/with the Punkettes and sometimes - like the Boomtown Rats - talk to the groups after the gig: Geldof came upstairs to talk to a gang of us after the Boomtown Rats gig there in 1977.

A special Christmas present for 1977 arrived for Steve: one that would later be notable for the last UK performance of the band that kick-started the whole Punk explosion!

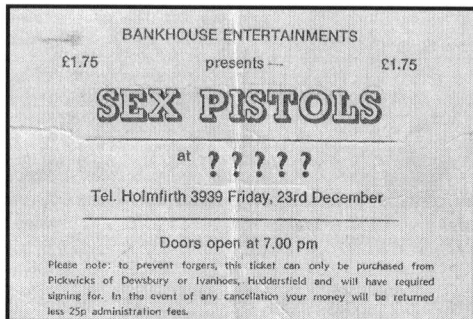

BANKHOUSE ENTERTAINMENTS

£1.75 —— presents —— £1.75

SEX PISTOLS

at ? ? ? ? ?

Tel. Holmfirth 3939 Friday, 23rd December

Doors open at 7.00 pm

Please note: to prevent forgers, this ticket can only be purchased from Pickwicks of Dewsbury or Ivanhoes, Huddersfield and will have required signing for. In the event of any cancellation your money will be returned less 25p administration fees.

"Thanks to my older sister passing her driving test at the first go, we were able to go to Huddersfield Ivanhoe's on Christmas Day 1977 for the Sex Pistols evening gig. Debra had bought an orange mini saloon, and being a Rich Kids follower; she went up to Dewsbury on the 21st December for their gig and was able to get four or five tickets for the Sex Pistols gig. On the afternoon of Christmas Day, about 4 or 5 o'clock, we set out from Sheffield for Huddersfield in her mini: she had two or three pick ups to do on the way and we ended up with six crammed in this little mini car. It was Debs, Sarah, Slonk, Mick Denton, me and Nigel Lockwood. My main worry, despite having a ticket, was that I was only just turned 17 and might not get let in; so I think I had false ID on me - just in case I got asked. Thankfully (on arrival) we found a burger bar, had some food, and then queued up for an hour or so outside Ivanhoe's. Despite one or two of our lot not having tickets, we all managed to get let in and then dispersed inside.

"I managed to get served with a drink at the bar and remember seeing Sid Vicious standing right alongside of me before the gig. I think he was topless - apart from that chain with the lock thing he wore - and he had some leather Punk trousers on. I was pretty amazed – as you don't expect to see the group really before they come on stage!

"I can't remember that much about the gig itself; they weren't too bad live, just chaotic and manic - as their reputation described. For some reason Rotten got his hair and jacket covered in talcum powder by a kid at the front, but he didn't give a shit. I was about halfway back in the crowd, a full crowd of several hundred, and Rotten's glare seemed to go right through you. It was a great experience and it turned out to be the last British gig the Pistols played before they split and Sid Vicious died a little over a year later.

"Seeing the Sex Pistols live on Christmas Day was a big moment for me and one of my favourite Punk memories: the other one being when I went to see The Clash in Derby with my then girlfriend Cheryl (from Brixham in Devon). That gig was heaving and Strummer was immense and on the train back, I was a part of the many Sheffielders who had gone over to Derby and I was just buzzing with good vibes; talking to all the mates and girlfriends and having a real good time in my life. That too, was very special to me as I felt a PART of something really together, strong and exciting called PUNK ROCK!

"I got a temp job/casual as a 'roadie/humper' at the Top Rank. I had met Mick Denton through my sister (Rocka Debs) and he introduced me to some of the early Sheffield Hard core Punks and also got me onto the humping/road crew casuals at Top Rank for the Punk gigs. I had some good times at the Punk gigs with mates like Mick, Tiny (Ian Squires), Alan Squeaky, Mark from the Kitchens, Kev, Sean and others too. We got paid (I think about £8 for the day... which was LOADS in those days), and we mostly got in for free as well; so I used to sell my tickets that I had bought for the gig - just in case. We sometimes got badges and other group freebies like being on the guest list and so on as well.

"We would gather around 12noon/1pm at the Top Rank and wait for those massive trans-am trucks to arrive...then, when the truckers and road crew unloaded, we set up ramps up at the steps and lifted and wheeled in all the groups' gear into the Rank; where the hairies and electricians would then set up on stage. It was a bit hard at times but fun. It would take about two hours to set up and then (after the gigs) we would have to wait until about 11pm until the group were finished and the punters had all left, to take down and unload all the gear again, which took less time, around an hour or more. We sometimes still had time for a few late beers and a bit of left over food from the kitchens too. Then we would have a go on the old space invader machines for free... brilliant! Then I would get a taxi back; I was living in bed-sits at Pitsmoor and Abbeyfield in those days.

"The main gigs I remember doing are the Clash, Undertones, Siouxsie and the Banshees, The Police, Penetration, Albertos y los trios Paranoias and Sham 69 but there were loads more too. Tiny was a good laugh; always larking about but working hard. Well we all did really - it was a good little team. I think we all enjoyed that – we all had a good laugh and got on well with the sound engineer Ron and the other Top Rank staff too: Happy times.

Left: Drones supporting the Stranglers at the Top Rank: one of the gigs Steve attended in 1977

"By 1978 I was still at school (6th form) but well into Punk and football. Working part-time on evenings and Sat mornings, I lived a bit of a double life - part responsible, part obnoxious. I went to as many local Punk things as possible. The Sheffield Penthouse was one place (a third floor club above BHS in Sheffield Centre). It was well dodgy going there as a Punk, even when a Punk group was on, and, from memory, it was mostly hardcore type groups that seemed to play there. The Penthouse was a well known local rockers hang out and there were always plenty of them there when we went - Punks mixing uneasily with hairies and rockers.

"I saw at least two real bad fights in there and the bouncers didn't bother much sometimes too: then other times they would throw the poor aggressors...LITERALLY down the steepish concrete stairs. To a 17/18 year old it was a bit of a tough place to be and I kept fairly close to the group of mates I went there with. I saw the Stunt Kites play there (probably in 1978). I followed the Stunt Kites practically everywhere as all of them were good mates from my school, and they were actually quite a good Punk band!

"The Stunt Kites... originally Steve Chapman - guitar, John Allen - vocals, Roger Quail - drums and Nigel Renshaw - guitar were all friends of mine of roughly the same age from Firth Park School. Most of them lived in Firth Park or Fir Vale, Pitsmoor, Burngreave area....and started this Punk band, I think it must have been in 1977. They had various line-up changes. I think there was a guy called Brent on Bass and then another drummer replaced Roger...can't remember all the names....but Ashley Eckhardt played bass for a bit too I do remember.

"John Allen was the Johnny Rotten figure of the band and up to all the usual adolescent nonsense...during and after school I remember. I saw loads of Stunt Kites gigs between 1978 and 1983... or whenever it was they split up, probably 90% of all their gigs I saw I suppose. Steve was a good mate; we used to hang out together in the early Punk days and did a bit of work together after. He had an attic-flat above a beer off/wine bar in Hunters Bar... then, in the early 1980s he went off to Germany with his German girlfriend. I have never seen him since... but there were rumours that, somewhere along the way, they had opened a sex shop in Germany and were doing alright!! John Allen lived, for a while, in a bed-sit, where I lived, down Abbeyfield Road in Sheffield, we went off to loads of mates' parties, and what have you... that must have been 1979 I suppose.

Stunt Kites photos copyright © Steve Marshall)

"Nowadays, I cannot remember any of their songs, but at the time, I was going to all the gigs, helping them to set up and unload, etc and I knew and liked all of their songs. I followed them all over... to pubs, clubs and school halls for gigs and Anarchy and chaos, Sheffield style. I lost touch with the Stunt Kites and haven't seen any of them since those early manic days!

"As for Punk clothes? I went off to Leeds where they had this X-Clothes Punk shop on Call Lane. I bought printed t-shirts, trendy Punk shoes with a buckle and some zip pants. There was a shop run by a guy called Dave at the bottom of Howard Street in Sheffield three floors up. He made and sold wacky and mainstream Punk stuff, so I was in there a lot too. I would buy jeans, badges and studs for my leather jacket. Sometimes when he went out the back of the shop we would nick stuff too. I was also out most nights of the week, meeting up down the local for a beer or two, then off into town or the University Now Soc with Karl Lango or some other mates for the Punk and New Wave gigs.

"In the summer of 1978, I left school a year early – I dropped out because I was bored with study and was working which was more exciting. I then left home in June or July of 1978 to go and live in Plymouth. I found a bed-sit near the town and got two or three supermarket jobs. At night I would go down to the local Punk place (The Metro) and I saw Ultravox (with John Foxx) and the Buzzcocks. I was a bit wacky though and bought these blue plastic/leather type trousers which a lot of the local army types didn't take kindly to when I was out and about. I came back to Sheffield after 3 months around October time.

"The main fanzines I got were NMX – mostly because I knew Martin Russian fairly well. He produced and printed it and also got one or two copies of local fanzines – Home Groan, Gun Rubber and Pink Flag and I joined S.I.S. (Stranglers Information Service in 1978) and got a few copies of the Strangled magazine. Mostly, though, I read the NME and Sounds pretty much every week and got right into all the interviews, listings and articles on Punk and New Wave.

In true Punk attitude, Steve's love of the Punk bands didn't stretch to idolism and the dubious un-punk like pastime of autograph hunting.

"Although I liked most of the Punk and New Wave groups, and got to hear the records and attended the gigs, I wasn't all that fussed or bothered about getting autographs or becoming mates with any of them... apart from the local groups. In Plymouth I did sit talking with Rat Scabies and Captain Sensible before a Damned gig as they came and sat at my table eating their pizzas! I think I bullshitted about how I was from Sheffield – but was following them round on tour because they were good!! HA. I saw the Clash in five different towns (Sheffield, Bridlington, Derby, Birmingham and Newcastle) because they were SO GOOD live. My sisters, Debs and Chris were following the Clash around and became well known to the group along with some of the Sheffield contingent - Delroy, Trigger, Tiny, etc... but I wasn't into all that backstage stuff. The only groups I knew well - like I said before - were The Stunt Kites and They Must be Russians

"I travelled up and down the country as my mate Julian became a student; first in Liverpool then in Birmingham and I would often go and stay with him and his girlfriend taking in the best Punk gigs on the way. I was just enjoying myself the whole time really. In Sheffield, I had mates locally, sharing a beer or two and playing pool – then I would go into town to the Blue Bell, Dove and Rainbow, Golden Ball - meeting up with mates and then go up West Street to the Hallamshire and West Street pubs where local groups were on - followed by the Limit until 2.00am; getting a doner kebab...or 3, before running for the late buses home. Brilliant times: Lots of adventures and lots of boozing, drinking, birding and fun. I was really into Punkette type girlfriends mostly, though I had straight ones who I met when my straight non-Punk mates and me went down to the Crown Pub on Rutland Road. I also had a lot of Punkette/New-

Wave pen-friend/girlfriends from all over the country: we wrote to each other first via ads in Sounds or NME magazines and I would go off to Liverpool, Manchester, Lancaster, London, and Coventry, or wherever, to see and stay with them. Some of them would come up to Sheffield for a few days and stay with me at one of my bed-sits. I knew a few Sheffield girls who went to Punk gigs and I remember Alison (Monkey) and her dark haired mate, Mary (Muriel) from Ecclesall. I went out with both of them, but only fairly briefly. John Allen's sister Heather was also fairly foxy and there were others too who always used to hang out at the Top Rank. It was crazy, chaotic and got a bit manic sometimes."

As the first chapters of Steve's Punk journey's concluded their anarchic tales of excitement, fun and rebellion, the local scene began its next volume of change: the more experimental side of Punk progression advancing steadily up the region of West Street amongst other forays.

Steve Marshall: "Some nights, I would go down West Street where THE (Artery), 2.3, Stunt Kites and others played at the Hallamshire, The West Street Pub and the Beehive...as it was then. So, much of the time, I was out and about, watching tons of local groups... Punk, New Wave, Indie and even Mod. With different sets of mates I also went up to the NOW Society Union Bar 2 at Sheffield University Weston Bank, where a lot of good avant-garde local groups cut their teeth during 1978 to 1980. I saw The Human League play their second ever gig with Phil Oakey on synthesizer! Cabaret Voltaire, Clock DVA, They Must be Russians and loads of others like De Tian, I'm so Hollow, Vice-Versa... all numerous times.

"On a lot of the nights out you had a lot of the regular local Punks/ettes, students turn out such as Pat and Sue, Maxine, Ian Williams, Tealeaf...? (Never knew his real name!) and They must be Russians when they weren't playing along with Martin X Russian, of course, who started and wrote the famous Sheffield NME/NMX Fanzine now known as Martin Lacey.

"Now, the Limit Club was something else... When the Limit started, some weeks I was in there seven nights a week – dancing, drinking and talking to mates. Usually a queue to get in, depending on when you went (the bouncers usually gave you a good looking up and down).It cost 30p to get in some nights and usually with one or two local or national groups on. There was originally a stage to the left of the exit door – by the DJ desk, then later on the (slightly) higher stage at the end of the room. I think, below these, were small shiny surface dance floors (two of em) where you could dance yourself drunkenly silly to a set of the best Punk/Rock/Indie stuff that DJ Paul Unwin played.

"Getting to the bar was ALWAYS A PAIN as it was always chocca-bloc full and when you got there you were so thirsty that you ended up getting two pints of (watered down) lager instead of just one. I spent a lot of the time just wandering round and round the little place; talking to different mates or acquaintances and hardly ever sitting at the back where there were chairs and tables for sitting down and eating - or smoking: what substances I KNOW NOT!! Although crazily sometimes, because I was into wearing badges, I wore a 'Legalise Cannabis' badge on this grey gabardine Oxfam overcoat I had while going there...simply because I liked the colours on the badge; but I dare say the undercover cops would probably have followed me around!! I saw loads there – Generation X, 999, Wayne County, B-52s, Madness, UK Subs etc. I had lots of mates in there - Oliver/Specky (a local student), Duane and his mate, Tiny (large and small ones), Tom (who also worked with us with the Top Rank Humping crew), Mick Denton, Paul Slonks, Julian and his girlfriend Pat, Pat and Sue, Maxine and all their Punk mates too. Again, it was good times... loads of drinking, socializing, seeing and listening to good music.

Penetration at Sheffield Top Rank 1979

Pauline Murray and Neale Floyd

Photos courtesy of: Above – Nick Hawksworth– and Steve Marshall

Those exciting, fun-filled and chaotic punk days lasted the best part of five years for Steve, and like many of that generation, are mostly fondly remembered!

Steve Marshall: "The late 1970s and early 1980s were crazy but great times for me. I was an adolescent teen, fed up of school at A level, so I dropped out because I was working part-time and had money for records, clothes, gigs and eventually beer and football. I tried to look cool - with the leather Punk jacket, t-shirt, jeans or Clash type trousers and Doc Marten boots with various hairstyles from skinhead to coloured hair of blue, yellow and black at the same time. I was ALWAYS dying it black - Jet black - and used to have to clean the dye marks off my face the day after. Dying your hair even at 20 or 21 just seemed like the thing to do back then! Well, to me at least."

Rewind back to 1975, and there's a young rebel kid with a gang of city-wise juveniles: they are fixing to screw the system, won't pay to see their Glam Rock idols and are gonna try to subvert the rules and get inside this establishment City Hall building. Punk is just around the corner and this rebel kid called Steve is awaiting its arrival. It will suite his rebel agenda and carry him onwards as a free-thinking Punk informed individual. Long live the rebels in our midst!

It was not only rebels who felt an affiliation to Punk Rock. In some instances, it could be the open-minded music fan; the intuitive music obsessive who had an unbeatable instinct to suss out the next new and exciting happening music – almost before it had truly begun! One Sheffield music fan would embark upon a truly enviable journey through music which saw him taste many varied styles and genres before and after Punk... taking centre stage to it all being Punk Rock itself!

Nigel Lockwood: (Sheffield Bowie/Punk fan) "Like many others, I too listened to the sounds of the late sixties, on my portable leather bound transistor radio, under the bed sheets: mainly Radio Luxembourg, medium wave 208. Even at junior school, everybody would go up to each other, and ask that classic question, *'mod or rocker?'* (Or mocker, if you were Ringo Starr!!), I always said *'Mod'*, partly because my older cousin had a Lambretta, circa 1966, and was well into the Small Faces. Some years later, he gave me all his Small Faces singles, which I still have to this day. Soul and Motown was also massive at this time, and always on the radio, so I couldn't help but soak it all up, and I also still have that transistor radio!!

"The first three singles I ever bought were after I'd just got my first record player, for Christmas 1969, and were Kenny Rodgers and the first edition 'Ruby don't take your love to town', Arrival 'Friends', and Creedence Clearwater Revival's 'Green river', all from upstairs at Boots on Fargate Sheffield. Soon I started hearing all the classic Trojan reggae singles, all from Jamaica, and gradually, it took over from Motown in my collection. I used to go to Violet Mays (record shop) every week from school with my mate Anthony Thompson to check all the new releases. You should have seen Violet May's face light up when I swapped all my Motown singles for loads of reggae singles! I vividly remember a Jamaican family living near my mates off Ecclesall road; they knew him, and our love of that music, so they called us 'the reggae boys', which we respected. I even ended up subscribing to the Jamaican weekly Gleaner newspaper, which came weekly from Jamaica, which the newsagent ordered for me. I still have a reggae scrapbook, cos the newspaper had a music section. This was 1970/ 1971, and if I'd been old enough, I would have been going to Shades nightclub every week, on Ecclesall Road, loads of Trojan artists played there. I still have loads of Trojan stuff now, mainly on (boring) CD, it still makes me shake a leg and smile...

"1972 was a pivotal year for me; I really got into the suedehead culture at school, being 15 at the time: Levi 2; Sta-Prest two tone trousers; Fred Perry shirts; Slazenger jumpers; loafer shoes; Ben Sherman shirts; crombie coat, and the obligatory Motown Chartbusters LP's tucked under my sleeve. I bought those clothes from Austin's on the Moor, Colvin's on Waingate, and Bunny's in Castle Market.

"At school, two camps had now formed, so far as music was concerned. One camp was the kids into Led Zeppelin, Deep Purple, Black Sabbath etc and the other was the kids into David Bowie, Roxy Music, Lou Reed, Marc Bolan etc: I was firmly into the latter, and suddenly I realised this was it. I then saw Bowie doing 'Starman' on Top of the Pops with Mick Ronson, all in face make up, and my hairs stood on end. My schoolmate, John Richardson, asked me if I wanted to go see him at the Top Rank. This was 6th September 1972, I was 16: I'd only previously seen the Four Tops/Stevie Wonder/Edwin Starr/Jimmy Ruffin at the City Hall and the Fiesta, so this was my indoctrination to rock gigs, and it blew me away: that was it, I was transformed.

"From then on, through 1973/1974/1975, I was obsessed with Bowie/Roxy Music/Lou Reed/ Mick Ronson/Eno/Alice Cooper/the Faces/Mott the Hoople and even Status Quo who were great back then! I bought all the records from Wilson Peck/Bradleys/Canns and not forgetting Rare n' Racy and Violet Mays. Fashions weren't so great then, but trendy shops included Sexy Rexys and another one on King Street near the Castle Market.

"Like the two camps of music fans at school, it was the same with night clubs. Whilst the more traditional clubs included Genevieve, Samantha's, Penny Farthing, Top Rank...my sacred heaven was to be found in the Crazy Daizy, which I ended up going to 108 times, starting August 1975 until early 1978, just before the Limit opened and took its place. Pre-punk, the Daizy had Roxy nights, and that's exactly what it was: They played all great music by Bowie, Roxy, Lou Reed etc. My abiding memory is always of them playing 'Billy Porter' by Mick Ronson. One week in 1975, I went every night, it was that great. Everyone loved it, and no, I never saw the meeting of Phil Oakey and the two Human League girls!!

"The other club I frequented was the Penthouse, sometimes going to both the same night. In the Penthouse, you really could let your inhibitions run wild, as it was dark, dank, and murky and played all the music really really loud: some Heavy Metal, which I didn't like, but also stuff like Thin Lizzy/Free/Hawkwind/Bad Company etc, all great songs. Of course I never came out of there sober. The Penthouse eventually became Rebels.

"1975 saw a need for change in the musical climate, Pub Rock had been bubbling under for a while, mainly on the live gig front. Spearheading this was Dr Feelgood, who I managed to see; also Ian Dury's band Kilburn and the High Roads and the Kursaal Flyers, Ducks Deluxe etc. Most of these came to the Black Swan, who championed the Pub Rock movement, and unbeknown to most of them, apart from one John Mellor, and his band the 101ers, these were all paving the way for the mother of all musical revolutions, in the summer of 1976, which I embraced 100%. Although Bowie still ruled the roost, a massive change was ready to enter rock's rich tapestry, but as usual, it was London that exploded first. However, Sheffield and myself saw an early incarnation of it; at the Black Swan on 4th July 1976 (ironically USA Independence day and some would argue the highly influential American band the New York Dolls, endorsed by the late Malcolm McLaren, were the instigators). After seeing the Dolls on the Old Grey Whistle Test I went out immediately to buy their first single 'Jet Boy' to devour its potency.

"My mate Paul 'Shaft' Sharpe, who went on to form 2.3 and De Tian, suggested we go see a band whose singer had *green teeth and threw chairs at the audience*, called the Sex Pistols, so we went with an open mind, and weren't disappointed. We knew the tides of musical change were in the form of Punk Rock and that this was the much needed musical turning point, not just in Sheffield, but nationwide. Everyone stayed sat down at the gig, and of course the support was the Clash's first ever gig, yes, Joe (ex John Mellor), Strummer, he saw the light! I knew immediately that I wanted to see them again: it felt such a privilege to witness something so fresh and new, especially in Sheffield. Wondering if the Pistols would release any records, me and Paul Sharp didn't have to wait long before we did see them again - on August 21st at Nottingham Boat club, which was full of bikers, and then again on September 27th 1976 at Doncaster Outlook, and still everyone stayed sat down!

Above: Original Sex Pistols at the Black Swan poster, Anarchy tour poster and left Nigel with Kid Strange of Doctors of Madness

"In the meantime I was still going to the Crazy Daizy, wondering if they would play any Punk Rock, but that was a while away yet. At this time, me and Paul Sharpe started going to a like minded club in Manchester called Pips, which had separate rooms, including a Roxy room, so I was in seventh heaven again. Then we found out about another Manchester club, called the Ranch Bar, at the back of Piccadilly station: next to it was a transvestite/gay club, and they all used to drift in. Again, it was all Bowie/Roxy/Cockney Rebel/Lou Reed etc, however Punk had arrived in Manchester before Sheffield, and I remember seeing a bleached-blond Pete Shelley, going round everyone, to sell them the Buzzcocks 'Spiral Scratch' E.P. This was December 1976! Dec 1st 1976 saw me buying 'Anarchy in the UK'. At last, something I could play over and over again, closely followed by the Damned's 'New Rose'. The Pistols had now already gained notoriety on Bill Grundy's show, in essence sealing their fate and fame at the same time.

"A few weeks earlier, I'd been down the London Kings Road in search of Malcolm's 'Sex' shop, and I wasn't disappointed: I bought a pair of grey drainpipe trousers, with green plastic pockets, brilliant!! I later realised I'd been served by Sid Vicious, he told me their changing room was 'Behind *that leather curtain over there'*, brilliant!! Anyway, I asked him if they sold any shoes, they didn't, but Sid had a pair of brothel creepers on, which he told me I could get from another shop round the corner.

"By the time the ill-fated 'Anarchy' tour was announced that December, they ended up only doing three dates, Leeds Poly, and two nights at the Electric Circus in Manchester. I went to the 9th December night, with supports from the Heartbreakers, The Clash, and the Howard Devoto led Buzzcocks. I remember Pete Shelley pogoing furiously throughout the Pistols set. Electric atmosphere indeed, and of course Glen Matlock left the Pistols shortly afterwards.

"The Punk influence had already started. I'd been to Manchester a few nights before, to see Woody Woodmanseys' U-boat, at Salford College, on December 3rd, proudly wearing my 'Sex' trousers. A bloke came up to me, and asked how much Malcolm had ripped me off for selling them to me; they were £20, a fortune then!! The two supports that night were the Count Bishops, a kind of thrusty pub/R&B/early Punky-sounding band and the Punk house gang were the other support. So the name connotations had started early. The bloke who had asked me about Malcolm's trousers was in a band called the Stiff Kittens, who I think were an early version of Joy Division.

"The night after that, Saturday December 4th, me and some mates drove to Derby, hoping to see the Anarchy tour at Derby Kings Hall, but of course it had been cancelled, so we stopped at pubs in Alfreton and Shirland on the way back, me dressed in my 'Sex' trousers, paper clips all round my neck, and a ripped old shirt of my dads. I remember one mate pissing out the car window whilst we were still driving... To top the night off we all went back to our empty house, and preceded to pogo furiously to 'Anarchy', 'New Rose' and Eddie and the Hot Rods several times over in our back room, and no damage, thankfully!

"Punk Rock had started to really affect me by early 77: there had hardly been any more records released so far, but then I realised it was because no major label really knew what to think of it all. I went to London again on Saturday January 8th, with my then girlfriend, Alison Barnes, in search of the Kings Road again, and the *'new fashion'*. I certainly found it... I bought some black leather effect drainpipe trousers, a pair of red winkle pickers, and a red mohair jumper from ACME Attractions, which was the shop Don Letts (Roxy DJ/Big Audio Dynamite) ran. ACME eventually mutated into the infamous 'Boy' brand.

"Although Punk was nearly 100% upon us in the public domain, I was still going to see Be Bop Deluxe/Cockney Rebel/Bryan Ferry/Woody's U-boat etc. I was longing for the next Punk gig, though. By now I'd seen Bowie six times, Roxy Music ten times as well as Lou Reed, the Faces, Alice Cooper, Mott the Hoople, Mick Ronson, Eno, Elton John, Status Quo, Queen etc (all in fair sized venues) so it was great to think I could now see bands in really small stand up venues, with little or no security, although I was soon to realise it wouldn't happen in Sheffield as much as I'd like...So, on March 3rd 1977, the first of my dreams came true, when I went to Manchester Apollo, to see Iggy Pop, who, at the time was very much a Punk hero, despite being already 30 years old: what was the double whammy, was that Bowie (Iggy's mentor at the time) was playing keyboards on this tour !! On the same day, I had bought the Damned's second single 'Neat Neat Neat'. I saw the Iggy/ Bowie show again, at the now defunct London Rainbow, two nights later and the support was the Vibrators.

"A similar double whammy occurred the week after when I saw, also at the Manchester Apollo, Marc Bolan and (a version of) T-Rex and the Damned. I'd seen Bolan four times on one tour, the previous year, and he was awesome, much better than when he was a Glam Rock star and had 14 year old Bay City Rollers fans screaming at him. The Damned gave him back some credibility, and it was the first of many times I'd see the Damned, when they were authentically great. This was when Dave Vanian came out of a coffin on stage and Rat Scabies would set fire to his cymbals.

"Another band I ended up seeing 18 times weren't really a Punk band either: the Doctors of Madness who I'd seen a few times in 76, but they were well ahead of their time, even their stage names were bizarre- Kid Strange, Urban Blitz, Stoner and Pete De Lemma- I loved them!! The next two Punk singles I bought were 'White Riot' and 'I Wanna Be your Boyfriend'. April 77 was when Sheffield really started to see Punk kick into life: I also went to, what many now regard as, the first Punk band to play Sheffield in 77, which was Ultravox! at the Top Rank. Again, they weren't strictly that: singer John Foxx was more steeped in electronic music, but they were great, I loved it, and saw them loads more after that.

"The other Punk manifestation in April was that my beloved Crazy Daizy, which I still went to, started having Punk nights, the first of which I went to on April 6th with Manchester Punk band the Drones playing. The noticeable shift in culture was that a lot of the original Daizy crowd didn't get Punk, and had their noses pushed out of joint, so I stopped going. Me, I embraced it with an obsessional passion, even though the initial excitement didn't last. That same month I was 21; A month that saw President Nixon own up to the Watergate scandal but also (more importantly!) saw the record

releases coming thick and fast: the first LP's from Ultravox, the Damned, the Clash, Blondie and singles by Television, Eddie and the Hot Rods, the Stranglers, The Boys and The Jam. I had a party at the now defunct Brincliffe Oaks pub, at Nether Edge, and all I wanted to play was Punk records, along with Bowie, Motown and Reggae, perfect!!

"Personally speaking, the period from May to December 1977 was the halcyon period for Punk, especially live. The record companies/promoters/venues/PR agencies and A and R men, had all realised Punk was sweeping the nation. Apart from Ultravox at the Top Rank in April, the next name band to play Sheffield was Television, supported by Blondie, at the City Hall, on May 24th. I remember Tom Verlaine had a transparent guitar and they encored with a cover of 'Satisfaction', and Debbie Harry was soooo exquisite but, like Ultravox, neither were really Punk Rock bands in the true sense. The next gig was the following night, at the *oh so difficult to get* in non-student Poly, in the old building, at the top of Howard Street. I always, luckily, managed to get a student to sign me in as a guest. This one was 'the 4 chords wonder tour'... the Damned play 3, the Adverts one. As we got there was already rucking going off in the manic crowd, but it was an electric atmosphere. The Damned doing their then current single 'Neat Neat Neat' twice and the Adverts also doing 'One chord wonders' twice... and I loved it!

"Unfortunately Sheffield didn't have an abundance of Punk gigs (to begin with). The ones that I went to in the ensuing months were the Stranglers, The Jam, Doctors of Madness (with Penetration), Johnny Thunders and the Heartbreakers with Siouxsie and Banshees, the Bunch of Stiffs- Elvis Costello/Ian Dury and Blockheads/Nick Lowe/Wreckless Eric, The Clash and Richard

Hell, the Runaways, Damned and Dead Boys, the Stranglers and The Jam again, the Adverts, Ian Dury and Blockheads: so not that many.

"Luckily, I could borrow my dad's car, so me and various mates managed to get to Leeds, Manchester, and Nottingham etc. The atmosphere was electric at them all. I got to see The Clash on the 'White Riot tour at Leeds Poly, Manchester Electric Circus and Nottingham Palais: the latter was bizarre cos the Buzzcocks, who were supporting, had a bizarre bass player known only as Garth and never to be seen again after his Buzzcocks short career! Also, at that gig, before the Buzzcocks came on, they played, over the PA., a live tape of Subway Sect! I managed to see The Clash six times in 77 and apart from the McLaren spin that surrounded the Pistols, The Clash easily outshone everyone.

 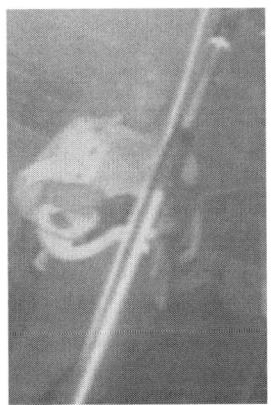 

The Damned Electric Circus, Bruce Foxton at the Electric Circus (In the City tour) (Nigel Lockwood) The Clash on the 'White Riot' tour (Debra Marshall)

"The Manchester Electric Circus was in the middle of a housing estate, in an area called Collyhurst. It seemed that you had to take your life in your own hands when going to the venue and would always be wondering if the car would be in one piece after the gig. Luckily, I had no hassles and having survived the Anarchy and White Riot tour gigs at the Circus, which were both awesome, I got to see - in the space of a few months- the Ramones/Talking Heads, the Stranglers, The Jam, the Damned, Doctors of Madness and the Adverts there: then the venue closed not long after.

"My mate Paul Shaft/Sharpe believed that the true essence of Punk died at the time of the 'White Riot' tour, so I didn't see him a lot after that. Myself, I felt it was, maybe, later in the year around the time of the Clash gig at the Top Rank in November. As for records, I bought all the best releases on a weekly basis, Revolution records in Castle Market always had the weekly new releases, and of course, there was the infamous Jam pa, on Monday July 11th. This was the day after they played the Top Rank on their 'In the City' tour. I got my copy of 'All Around The World' single signed. Another culture that crept into Punk was reggae, the Clash covered Junior Murvin's 'Police and thieves' early on, and other Reggae singles I bought in 77 included Tapper Zukie, Dillinger, Doctor Alimantado, Bob Marley, Steel Pulse etc.

"I kept on going to the Doncaster Outlook (Sex Pistols as Tax Exiles, now of course with Sid - out of tune, looking great and an unbelievable atmosphere), Sheffield Poly/University, Rotherham Windmill, etc, often seeing the same band twice on the same tour. I also went to London again, seeing the Radio Stars and X-Ray Spex, on successive nights at the Marquee, getting on stage with singer Polystyrene for an encore reprise of 'Oh Bondage Up Yours'. Another visit to London was to see Iggy Pop at the Rainbow for two successive nights, September 30th and October 1st, with the Adverts supporting: The first night saw me pulling Iggy's thumb as he sang 'Breaks Out Laughing'. He did a cover version of Bowie's 'Fame', and then he licked and bit my fingers! That same night, I couldn't find my mate I was staying with in London, so having missed the last tube; I latched onto some London Punks. We followed some skins, and then went to see the Wasps at the Roxy club, and then I had to crash out for the night in the basement of Vortex records, with other Punks, after they had vetoed my presence and checked my Punk credentials! The second night I made sure I didn't lose my mate. Iggy sang 'Nightclubbing' in German at this gig!!

"Another eventful night was going to see The Clash at Manchester's Elizabethan Suite on November 15th, which was being filmed for 'So it Goes'. Everybody got in for free, when we should have paid. Siouxsie and the Banshees supported, and it was brilliant, but I never saw it on video until years later, cos it was only shown on Granada TV, which we couldn't get in Sheffield. During all this time, I was still going to the Crazy Daizy, but skirmishes became more regular, so I more or less stopped going: luckily, another saviour and sanctuary beckoned early in 1978 with the Limit!

"Now that I'd seen all the bands live, I realised it was all much better live than on record, as most of the songs were fast and furious, and great to pogo to. The Pistols had truly been immortalised as the band that were billed to play in the UK but very rarely did. In fact, after their August pseudonym tour, they only appeared one more time in the UK. Before that however, they were billed to (unofficially) play at the Wigan Casino on Saturday September 3rd. The night before I'd been to see 2.3 at the Lion pub on the Wicker, and mixed on the sound desk... that was a laugh!! Anyway, we decided to go to Wigan the day after, on the train, via Manchester. It was billed as the Sex Pistols, along with Ed Banger and the Nosebleeds, who Morrissey briefly joined, and included Billy Duffy, who later joined The Cult. Also on the bill were the Drones, Exodus, China Street, and Demolition, all of whom we saw. We made the decision to stay till the end, in the hope the Pistols were still on. Of course, they weren't, and we had now missed the last train to Manchester. When we came out of Wigan Casino, there was a queue of Northern Soul fans waiting to get in for the all nighter, and they were looking at us like we were from another planet or something!! Anyway, as it turned out about fifteen of us had come from Sheffield, but we didn't all know each other. We all started walking, for about five hours managing fifteen miles, and then we all hitched a ride on an open-top lorry, taking the Sunday morning papers into Manchester. After getting back to Piccadilly station, we had to wait another 3 hours for the first train back to Sheffield...

"It wasn't until Christmas day 1977 that I got to see the Sex Pistols one more time, before they split. Just the week before, me and 2 mates went to Huddersfield Ivanhoe's, which was a Bier

Keller, to see Glen Matlock's new band, the Rich Kids, who also included Midge Ure. I loved them... they were a sign of what was to come in 1978 with Power Pop. Anyway, ironically, at that gig, the promoter was selling tickets for Glen Matlock's old band, the Sex Pistols for their Christmas day gig there. This was the only way you could get the tickets so we got them. Following the afternoon slot for the younger kids, as we were queuing to get in, someone from the venue brought round turkey sandwiches!! The gig, of course, was awesome; I stood with Richard Kirk from Cabaret Voltaire. I think they did 'Submission' as an encore, and, again, ironically, Johnny Rotten was wearing a T-Shirt that said 'Never mind the Rich Kids, we're The Sex Pistols'.

"That was pretty much the end of the halcyon period that was called Punk Rock... for me anyway. It had been a whirlwind year and nothing would be the same again, in musical terms, or so we all thought. The gigs were all great, so many bands to go see, so much to do: from going to 45 gigs in 1976, I went to 105 in 1977, not including local bands etc, only 27 of these were not Punk bands. I went to London one more time in 77, for the New Year, and went down the Kings Road again, and Carnaby Street. My diary entry reads *'going through a complete transitional phase, bad vibes at the moment'.* How much things had all changed from when I went there back in January....

"So 1977 was THE year when Punk had revolutionised music. Of course there's always a down side to everything, and what happened in 1978/9 was that it went into the mainstream, all the majors wanted to make a quick buck, yes it was great the original Punk explosion gave young kids the motivation and inspiration to form their own bands, cos they now knew you didn't have to play their instruments that well, or even have meaningful lyrics. The trouble was that most of these bands were simply copying what had gone before, or they really were rubbish. The original bands with the real originality went onto release great singles in 1978, including The Jam, the Clash and the Stranglers: the Pistols had already imploded, and John Lydon was already thinking about Public Image Ltd.

"1978 was just as eventful for me as 1977 was, but for different musical reasons: I mentioned I'd seen the Rich Kids in December 77 at Huddersfield. Of course they weren't a Punk band but had a great visual line up, from different musical genres... what with ex-Pistol Matlock, and ex-teeny-bop band Slik singer Midge Ure, the guitarist Steve New, who had originally auditioned for the Pistols who also looked great, along with style of Rusty Egan. I ended up seeing the Rich Kids 19 times altogether and got to know them quite well, sometimes staying over with them in the same Hotels. I remember when we had seen them at Leeds Polytechnic, this was October 26th 1978, and we stayed at the Merrion Hotel with them after their storming gig: me, Glen Matlock, and Steve New went to see Wayne County at Leeds Brannigans which was originally the F-club. Then when we got back to the Hotel, Matlock was doing impersonations of Nick Kent, Mick Jones and Tony James. Another time we went to see them in Blackpool, at the Imperial Hotel. The gig was actually in the basement, so we were staying in the same hotel as the gig, bizarre!! Anyway, this was on August 6th, the Slits were the support and this was the last night of that tour. The Slits were great, they came on stage with the Rich Kids for the encore of 'Ghosts of Princes in Towers' and then 'Pretty Vacant', with drummer Rusty Egan playing guitar: there was a great party afterwards, and I've still got the photos from that. Just to mention another great Rich Kids gig which was at London Whitechapel City Polytechnic, on Friday 13th! October 1978. I stayed at

Steve New's flat after the gig. The gig was even better, when Billy Idol came on stage with the band for an encore cover of the Stooges 'Shake Appeal'.

Nigel with Rich Kid and ex-Pistol Glen Matlock and Billy Idol... and the Slits join the Rich Kids in Blackpool

"The year 1978 still saw some great Punk and New Wave bands come to the fore: Blondie, Talking Heads, XTC, Television (supported by the mighty Only Ones) Magazine, the Shirts, the Fabulous Poodles and more... my own faves were 999, Sham 69, Generation X, Adam and the Ants and even the Boomtown Rats. I managed to see them all: the first time I saw Sham 69, was at the infamous Doncaster Outlook, but Jimmy Pursey went over the top with his political overtones. I then saw them again on January 14th, at the old Sheffield Poly at which they did a cover of 'White Riot' as one of the encores. I even managed to get on stage, with my arm around Dave Parsons, singing 'Borstal Breakout' and 'What have we got' with him! I remember their influence at the time made me start wearing Doc Marten shoes again. The down side of their impact was that they incited quite a lot of rucking at gigs with the Skinheads. Luckily, for me, I saw little trouble throughout this whole period, although I was still going to the Crazy Daizy. The second half of 1977 had seen occasional flare-ups in there and one night the police were called which was Wednesday July 27th: I was there the week before for a mate's birthday, and there was trouble that night too. I never went again, but it was only a matter of weeks before the Limit opened.

"The only real serious incident I witnessed at a 1978 gig was the Buzzcocks at Bradford St Georges Hall, on Friday May 19th: the police were called halfway through their set, cos someone was waving a knife around in the audience. The P.A. was switched off, the guy was arrested, and Pete Shelley carried on singing through a megaphone and using his stage monitors. We saw Ultravox at Manchester Middleton Civic Hall, on Friday January 27th 1978: the gig was brilliant, but afterwards, the local Punk-hating gangs were waiting to ambush us. I had to hide in a chip shop till it was safe to go, then we went to the Ranch Bar. I lost my great Ultravox badge, and as usual, we caught the 2am train back to Sheffield...

"Although I saw the Clash again in 1978, I missed their summer gig at the Top Rank, as I was literally on the David Bowie tour: I remember one night we saw Bowie in Glasgow, at the now defunct Apollo and Iggy Pop was sat in my seat, mistakenly of course. He was very apologetic, and moved elsewhere... Back to The Clash I could tell that they wanted to move on musically although they were still doing a lot live, in 1978, from the first album. At the November 19th 1978 Top Rank gig, Mick Jones had improved immensely with his stage presence, confidence, and guitarmanship, and I could tell, if the Clash split up, he would have moved on in leaps musically. Of course this proved to be the case in the mid 80s, with B.A.D but that's another decade...

Nigel in New York in Iggy Pop's hotel room with Glen Matlock: also with Rich Kid Steve New after a Rich Kids Blackpool gig

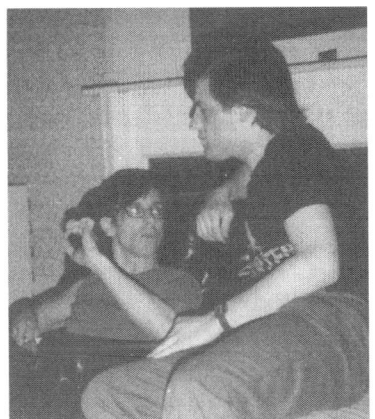

Photo: Debra Marshall

"New York New Wave also made its mark with me in 78; I'd seen Talking Heads make a very nervous live introduction in the UK in May 1977, supporting the Ramones which was a real mismatch really. By the time they did their first headlining tour, in January 78, I went to see them twice, at Doncaster Outlook, on Monday January 23rd, and the Friday before, at the Lower Refectory at Sheffield University, still promoting their first album: David Byrne was far more confident, Tina Weymouth was having sex with her bass guitar, and the support band was a then unknown at the time Dire Straits!

"The Sheffield Limit opened in late March 78: to me it was an immediate sanctuary, after the Crazy Daizy had fizzled out, and a lot of like minded people defected to the Limit. In its first year of opening, it was more of a venue than a club, and I saw loads there- Siouxsie, Adam and the Ants - including Jordan, who was soooo scary!! - also Wire, Cherry Vanilla, Generation X, Ultravox, 999, Wayne County and others. My own fave Limit gig in 78 was David Johansen as he did two sets: the second one he came on at midnight and George Webster struggled to get everyone out after the first set. We managed to stay in. I remember Johansen's band members carrying him over their shoulders and onto the stage... they did a few New York Dolls numbers, and in between sets, the resident Limit DJ played all of Springsteen's 'Darkness on the Edge of Town', in its entirety!!

"The Limit had now established itself just as much as a club as well as a venue, and I went all the time, gigs I saw there included Wreckless Eric, the Undertones, Joe Jackson (twice), the Skids, the Members, the Cure and the B-52s. I loved the Limit, and ended up going 225 times, as far as I can work out: again Sheffield didn't bring every band on their tours, so I still had to travel loads. I had a great Christmas in 78. Me and my mate spent that Christmas in London and saw the first ever gig by Public Image Ltd, doing the entire first album and a cover version of 'Belsen Was a Gas'. Ironically, his band now included Keith Levine, who I saw in that first line up of the Clash at the Black Swan back in July 76. Lydon was still thinking the audience couldn't suss him out, but I loved it anyway, especially them opening with that awesome first single 'Public Image'. Another irony was that this was a year to the day that I'd seen the last Pistols UK gig at Huddersfield, what a difference a year makes - EXACTLY!! By the time the end of 1979 had come, I'd been to nearly 450 gigs since 1973."

Iggy Pop: Punk Rock Icon

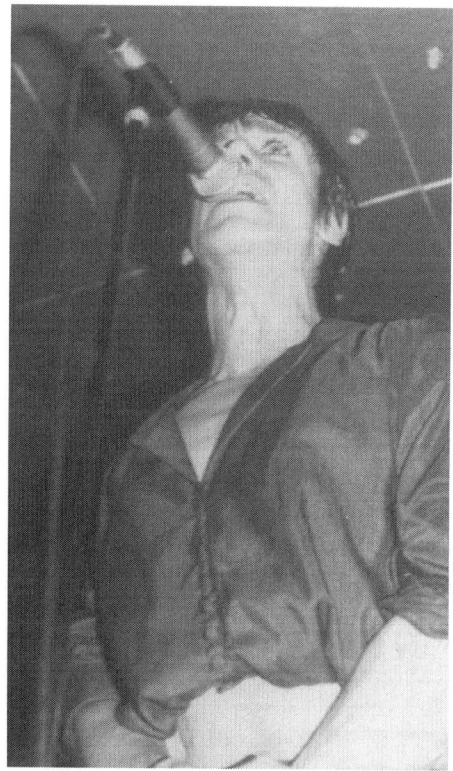

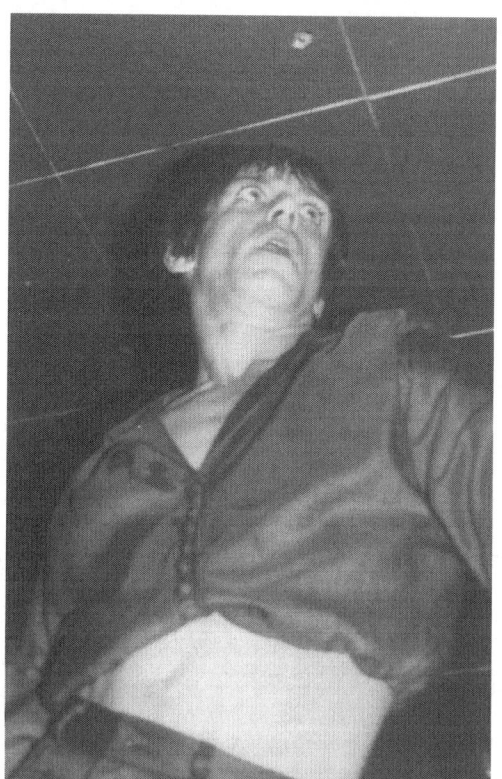

Photos taken by Nigel Lockwood

Iggy Pop (and the Stooges) was a massive and profound influence on the original UK Punk bands of the late 70's as well as contributing greatly to the 'Low' era period of David Bowie: a fact not lost on Bowie fanatic Nigel Lockwood.

The Punk connection was further sealed when ex-Sex Pistol Glen Matlock was invited to join Iggy Pop's touring band. The Punk kid and the Godfather of Punk turned up at Sheffield Top Rank to play a memorable set to the new order! The legendary Nigel Lockwood was around (how could he not be) to take the above snaps along with some others from Iggy Pop gigs.

'Talking bout' Rich Kids' a band before their time

Rich Kids photos all taken by Nigel Lockwood

Steve New R.I.P (May 2010)

Coming soon! 'Talkin' bout Rich kids' the story of the band published by 'Days like Tomorrow' books

A Punk friend of Nigel Lockwoods' was Steve Marshall's older sister Debra, more commonly known as Rocka Debs. She was part of the Sheffield Punk crowd attending many local gigs and tours around the country. Like Nigel, Debs was a great lover of the Rich Kids, touring with them for what seemed, at the time, like a full year... and was also a big fan of the Slits; a band that quite regularly supported, and had romantic links with, Deb's favourite Punk band – The Clash.

Rocka Debs: "I was a Clash fan right from the start: their first album was one of the first Punk ones I bought and I still have it to this day. I liked their music, style and energy as well as the fact that the band were always so easy to approach and talk to at gigs; unlike the Glam bands from the mid 70's like Roxy music and Bowie etc. Me and my friend Sarah would go to lots of Punk gigs in those early days of 76 -79 and beyond. I think the first Clash gig we saw was at the Top Rank in Sheffield in November 1977. We waited outside in the freezing cold and managed to get to see them arrive and go in the place. I took some photos and chatted with them about the tour.

"The next Clash gig was in Manchester near Belle Vue Granada studios. I had a Mini and me and Sarah made the trip over the Pennines and back to see them. I had recently passed my test and we were terrified in the pitch-black, but it was worth it to see The Clash again. I went to see a lot of bands all over the country in that little car. Eventually the brakes just went, we used it that much. I also saw The Clash at the Bridlington Spa with Mandy Lincoln and other mates Ian, Bob and Ian (Sheffield band the Untouchables, later Rolling Thunder). We started to get recognised by the band, by now, and I would take photos along to show them of their previous gigs. Joe would always ask which ones I had got. He was always interested in where they were from, asking loads of questions. I liked Paul Simonon the best, though, and bought a bass guitar 'cos I thought I would like to become a female version of Paul in my own band (Siren) – but it didn't last... I was rubbish at playing, being left handed, so I decided to be a singer instead!

"The next year (1979), we went to France to see the band at 'Le Palais des Sports', I think it was called – we just turned up – no tickets, after

hitching down most of the way. We were tired and hungry and sitting in the park, when a van pulled up and out jumped The Clash roadies followed by Joe and Paul. We went with them and got sandwiches and backstage passes."

Rocka Deb's Punk Gallery

Generation X at the Limit club
(Photo at right – fan Tanya joins the band)
Below:Deb's sister Chris with Joe Strummer and Kleenex at the Penthouse

Above left: and right Déjà Vu (Jules, Rocka Debs, Al and Sue)

'Unless something is done soon we are going to have Anarchy! Proclaimed the notorious Judge Pickles when he addressed the late Ian Williams and his two Punk destructors – Sheffield Punk Rockers Pat and Sue in court following their alleged train wrecking spree on the way back from a Punk Rock concert in Derby. Ian was spared a custodial sentence, but Pat and Sue went down for three months.

Pat and Sue were very well known on the Sheffield Punk Rock scene and were massive Stranglers fans, dressed entirely in pink and blue and were easily recognisable for their shrieks and hysterical laughing. They were also members of Sheffield ramshackle-garage-slits-influenced-punk band Siren!

Siren were formed with the true spirit of Punk noise in mind and epitomised the spirit of D.I.Y punk. Alongside Pat (Bass guitar), Sue (Guitar) were Webby – replacing Mandy – on drums and Rocka Debs (Debra Marshall) also on guitar. They turned out such home-made Punk and reggae gems as 'Reggae-ing' and 'Transvestites and 'Injections', performing at venues such as Wisewood school, the Saddle on West Street and George IV on Infirmary Road. The band had many line-up changes and was consequently known as Shattered Life and Déjà Vu... and eventually Debar!

Above: Siren at play- Pat Hudson, Rocka Debs, guest drummer Joyce Gordon and Sue Berry

Debra Marshall's younger Punk kid brother Steve Marshall was friends with the Stunt Kites and singer John Allen! Colleen Allen was little sister to John Allen and thanks to him, like Steve, Colleen also set out on a Punk Rock journey of her own... one that presented a new focus, escape and a sense of belonging, but also, amongst the many fondly (only just remembered) highlights, some quite unsavoury uninvited moments: luckily the challenges of being a young Punk girl back then only served to reinforce the individual rather than crush the rebel fighting to emerge!

Colleen Allen: (Sheffield Punkette) "The 70's, though somewhat wrung out and bleached, dish-cloth style in my troubled memory, gave to me such a sweet and life saving tonic that I must pay tribute. Not defined by years and dates but moments, 'flavours' and risking on purpose. Punk delivered amongst other things, a special human moment in the reunion with my lost brother.

"So, after horrific young chapters, runaway days and rescue missions, the mid 70's returned me back to my amazing mother, my sister Heather and younger brother David. Primal scream met informal primal therapy for me, in good company of few (but many) others squirming uncomfortably within mainstream shapes, never fitting, marginalised and dying a little bit. Aged

13, debilitated by shyness, brought with it a moment that was to swallow me up and spit me out, a place, a world, a shape that I could slip into with some level of comfort; Punk Rock!

"The scene was 1976, Rotherham, the place 'British Home Stores', on High Street, now boasting the lovely Primark and bargains from hell. Situated at the back of the shop was an unglamorous cafe, grubby little overbite of yet another chain doomed to fail, post miners' strike. Here we waited, tentative, long haired, prettied, numb and 'normal' for the first meeting for a number of years with our big brother and enigma, John.

"The person that met us there was not John, the once little, fossil collecting genius 'big' brother we remembered. This was John the cutting edge front man, vocal carrier and Stunt Kite, tangibility releasing his former shadow.

Punk princess Colleen Allen

Ordering tea, incongruous polite line queuing, I also saw Clive, Steve and Gibb, equating to the original Stunt Kites, plural.

"Sugar-Spiked, safety-pinned, 'fuck me' anti-style, second-hand garb and emaciation beyond size zero, (with 'associations' that few survived,) time stood still and faces dropped like strokes, shocked and confused. Rotherham didn't; wouldn't; couldn't 'do' different. This collection of ugly, pretty boys spread a light that cut like a razor through shit, revealing hope, beauty and discord. Of course me and Heather fell in love; we also had our brother back.

"My first experience of being in a 'band' started (and stayed) at home with my sister and a futuristic looking, second hand reel to reel tape recorder in 1976. Voices well oiled from years of passionate hairbrush harmonies, MJ and Carly Simon renditions; we were primed for any passing record producers. Producers who would naturally make a detour from the Capital and the Kings Road to 'bend ear' in our northern mining village, lured hypnotically, off track to our cul-de-sac to the song of these sister sirens. We were hopeful girls.

"Inspired of course by the Sex Pistols, but more so by those who we could really 'be', our gender, our perspective, our voices; Siouxsie and the Banshees, Penetration, X-Ray Spex, The Slits, girls with bollocks and brains. This period still brings howls of laughter in our reflections, one particularly intense moment saw us alluding to prison, *'brick red walls, ten feet high'* we chorused aggressively, to a sophisticated backing track created solely from our mutual, violent crumpling of crisp packets! It was fantastic, we were very impressed, until we reflected (not on the crisp packet backdrop, no, that worked for us,) but the sudden horror that "10 feet high" was actually not very high at all and urgent lyrical repairs were required so we could breathe again. And so that well known sitting room hit was perfected and complete with the message "brick red walls, God knows how high", pure genius!

"I loved Sid Vicious, but I think me and Heather had struck a deal that Sid Vicious was 'hers' and Johnny Rotten was 'mine'. I marked this relationship with an old watch I strung around my neck, it had a tiny photo of JR placed lovingly on the face, this claimed him as my very own and I

would wear it with as much ownership as a wedding ring. When Sid Vicious died, I was heartbroken (I know Johnny was officially mine, but I did prefer Sid really), I braved school with a black armband demonstrating my loss and respect, the naughty boys at school used their single brain cell to acknowledge positively this mark of uniform rebellion, knowing what it was for was irrelevant, everyone else I imagine, thought I was an absolute prat.

"Siouxsie Sioux always remained my hero, her strength, her angst, her performance style and of course her makeup, she had that ugly beauty I felt was possible. Debbie Harry was a woman I later obsessed over, men loved her probably because she could project Punk/New Wave with aesthetic beauty and women. I think I loved that too, it gave licence to mix rebellion with sex appeal and with the belief that this was something I certainly lacked; it gave me a template of hope. Debs also wrote some catchy tunes it has to be said. Polystyrene was our very own Emmeline Pankhurst; her *fuck you* style was an antidote to Debbie Harry's beauty pressures, her embracing of visual imperfection startling, liberating and perfect! As much as I respected and still do love her 'stuff', I admit that I never particularly wanted to poach her look.

"The Stunt Kites and John specifically were to have the greatest single influence on our lives at that tender age, an influence which we were so grateful for, because they welcomed myself and my sister into a world that was to consume us with a new 'home,' that accepted, protected and loved us. Punk and 13 onwards took me fleetingly to the ultra cool and edgy Sheffield University scene. In these very early days of my Punk career I must have made an amusing sight, stepping in the shadows of my beautiful, popular sister who

was fully entrenched in the scene, living and breathing its highs and horrors. Not much more than a child, I moved in a very grown up, drug riddled world, full of glamorous, intelligent, wild and wonderful people, I willed myself to be at least 16. It didn't work. Punks mingled easily with the intellectual, the eccentric, the drunk and the deviant, they even welcomed into their fold the under-aged without being obviously patronising or exploitative (with one or two exceptions).

"Into Sheffield on the spluttering 206 chariot, whenever begs, bargains and betrayal allowed at home. Risking suburban catcalls and bitching en route, the Stunt Kites gigs were my church and my sister's shadow, my sanctuary. I was so proud of my association with my brother and his band, the reflected glory it brought at a time when their popularity was at the height that saw their name graffitized brazenly on most Sheffield walls. (This graffiti remained for many years, pre-Sheffield regeneration). Hasty fly posting, illegally and strategically placed on walls, bus stops, lamp posts and 'anywhere's', soon to be covered or torn and replaced by more of the same, an exciting collage demonstrating the excitement of the time. Rare and Racy, fanzines, free-hand posters, two pence phone box calls and sometimes fly posting fines.

"Heady memories of the Limit, the Penthouse, numerous youth club gigs in places like Shiregreen, parties, pub back rooms, student flats and near misses, always protected by my brother to a debilitating (where boys were concerned) degree, we wondered why they didn't ever approach us, we discovered they were preserving their lives. Less pleasant memories and getting mixed up with some skinheads; 'mine' Twiggy, Heathers (name?) We believed that beneath their somewhat exciting and dangerous exterior might live a softer side; they seemed quite sweet and nice, if not exactly conjuring up images of puppies and fluffy bunnies.

"We met them in Rotherham a couple of times, I distinctly remember putting car paint spray in my hair as a makeshift, sneaky (from my mum) and rather desperate colourant and the result being a delightfully plastic coated chunk of murdered hair, not clever or pretty or discreet in terms of preventing the ensuing mummy madness, a level of madness that would have been hysterical had she known of the skinhead rendezvous! I have no clue what we did, where we went or what happened in Rotherham, but it was clearly uneventful, perhaps influenced by my charming barnet.

"However, I remember being with 'the skinheads' at some punk night, somewhere obscure in Sheffield, it was misty, outside, something 'kicked off', lots of running, shouting and ugliness in the atmosphere. It was one of those occasions where sinister meets the needs for description, I heard talk I didn't want to hear, 'Paki bashing'. I can't remember by who or where, there was fighting, I don't know if I saw it, sensed it or was simply told it, but violence was certainly thick in the night, fear, confusion, unbelievable sadness. Memory fails me, perhaps mercifully as to the product of this obscene event, but the feeling remains, stunned repulsion, heart plummeting and absolute disgust and shame of unknowingly associating with people who would prey on others simply because of their racial/cultural background. Racists, the evolving, opportunist right-wing skinhead, with little idea of the roots of 'their' soul, ska, rocksteady and reggae influences, their West Indian rude boy and Mod 'brothers' from whom skinhead culture was born. These boys, Pond Street mob etc, latched on to a dangerous sub-cultural opportunity to spread hate, intimidate and steal turf. Thankfully with all extremism comes reaction, the National Front associated skinhead had their left wing opposites, anti-Nazi style with the SHARP (skinheads against racial prejudice) movement backed by the 'original' skinheads, but it didn't help those facing racially motivated violence in the North where tolerance towards change has always been something of a struggle.

"Rotherham was more my domain, perhaps less elite than Sheffield and a little younger in scene. Boys were not warded off with the threat of murder by 'the band', but my shyness worked equally well as a deterrent. I used to throw on my mother's snakeskin trousers, (she had some fantastic 60's clothes), pointed jumble sale shoes painted with red nail varnish spots, blazer given to me by a punk boyfriend, with zips, safety pins et el, only to face the most phenomenal but predictable bullying in my village, halfwit comments and cruel intents hitting coldly to the core, but fading mercifully as I reached my destination, my people, my world.

"Rotherham, though limited in its hardcore of Punks was brilliant for bringing the 'offcuts' into some special homogenous lump, a tribe of youth with a purpose, to defy convention and ward off mainstream infiltration. No one 'type' of socio-economic nest birthed a Punk; the crowd were diverse, yet united. Oh happy days in dusty halls and honed in nights for the rejects, The Co op, The Charade, the Windmill. These Punk nights harvested a well montaged set, courtesy of Boots makeup counter (some actually paid for) and Sheffield 'X Clothes', black eye-lined and nailed, pan stick white faces, hair-sprayed, spiked, greased, abused, crazy coloured for the waged, food coloured for the not, bin bags and back combing.

"Translucent memories of people and faces, the names and context of which it would be brilliant to unite, but to this day remain, 'the guy who wore the trench coat', 'the one with the bleached hair who we met in 'The Sound of music records shop', 'her with the red backcombed hair who did a wee in a kettle once' and 'the two girls, joined at the hip with sunshine hair and sunshine smiles, one small the other a little taller'.

"Rotherham College of Arts and 16, I can relate absolutely no transition memories from the Punk scene, Rotherham RCAT and my previous and completely hated school life. Dinnington Comprehensive school did and still does breed a unique template of vile bully, who although they sidestepped overt hate towards their one remaining Punk, me, (my sister being the other before she left), made life a living hell for 'different' students generally. A mining village environment was a difficult place for a young Punk to live, with an almost feverish hatred of anything different or challenging. RCAT was fantastic and I made some wonderful friends, few if any of whom I know now.

"Rotherham was not exactly Bond Street, however, that was okay, Punks and Yorkshire folk are resourceful souls, and it's in the blood. So, hail to our very own C & A, Wakefield's Army Stores, every second-hand shop and jumble sale in South Yorkshire and my mum's stash of vintage clothing. From a simple mish-mash of resourced 'bits' came forth a cornucopia of cannibalised Punk regalia. Army coats and military jackets, trilbies, berets, fedoras, crass flammable dresses and cheeky fur stoles, 'took up', 'let down', sewn tight - tourniquet, sewn on, ripped out, zipped to death.

"My favourite second hand shop was at the side of the Peace Gardens in Sheffield, only Punks, grannies, oddballs and indeed mothballs went in such places in those days, vintage chic was not really heard of then, unlike now where Punk is the new retro. Often I would go to these charity shop goldmines with my sister and we would buy any pointed shoes we could find regardless of size. Pointed 50's style, Mary Quant-esque square toed 60's stretch patent knee-highs or laced up chunky boots were our passion. We had been known to sellotape our feet to the insole of a desirable pair of jumble shoes, using double-sided tape if feeling flash and stuffing the toes with feverish gusto. By any means necessary we would get those buggers on.

"The village idiots would harass me horribly, poison-tongued bitching and harassment, shouts of 'witch' and 'tramp' falling ugly from uneducated lips, I didn't let them know they hurt me, they could never comprehend that this was the reclaiming of liberty, elective, determined and profound and that I had more class in my 50 pence shoes than they would ever have, hold or know.

"A couple of lads from my village came up to me, swaggering with the usual sarcasm and lack of grace and said, *"Colleen, me and the lads have been discussing it and we have decided to club together and buy you some new shoes because we feel sorry for you having to wear those".* This made me sick to the core, aside from the fact that anti-fashion was my choice, the idea that they dare insinuate I wanted or needed their condescending, barely literate 'sympathy' made me feel murderous. I perceived it as an insult to my mother who was and is the most educated, aware, proud and cool person alive.

"My mother was a superstar, a single parent before it was the norm, with 3 of her four kids expressing themselves via Punk. In an almost wholly bigoted village my mum still allowed us to explore our creativity, make mistakes, be who we wanted to be. She made clothes for us, put up

with the flak and horrified stares from the neighbours and let the whole of the Stunt Kites and many other waifs and strays sleep over as required, a couple of people even lived with us for a while. My mum never judged anyone on how they looked and she is still loved by many of the remaining associates from that period. This was the problem for small sub-cultural groups, we had to go home to our respective far flung abodes and in doing so had to walk the plank in isolation, I am sure I am not alone in being faced with the same bitter contempt from the un-brave."

Nigel Renshaw: (The Stunt Kites guitarist) "I had always been into the Velvet Underground and The Stooges... for me it was a natural progression to Punk and especially when I first heard 'New Rose' and 'Anarchy in the UK', they (almost) literally blew my head off!!!"

A visit to the Outlook in 1977 to see the Damned led to a couple of Punk excursions further afield when Sheffield Punk Barry Bartle managed to take part in celebrations of Punk black sheep the Damned's first year together. He went down to see the wild antics of the Damned at the Marquee. Here he speaks of that event and his earlier Damned moments.

Dave Vanian of the Damned at the Electric Circus (Nigel Lockwood)

Barry Bartle: (Sheffield Punk/Home Groan fanzine writer) – "It was always the Damned for me. I loved the Pistols (even having a ticket to see em that a girlfriend nicked when we split up), but give me the Damned any day. I first saw them on the Marc Bolan tour and then at the University with the Adverts supporting. As well as going to their Outlook gig, which was a superb gig... two classic Punk bands for the price of one, I also went to Manchester to see them around the same time; I cannot remember the exact venue (probably the Electric circus) but there were some high-rise flats nearby and people were throwing bottles down at us Punks. We went in the car and we were amazed to find that it was still around after the gig. We gave Gun-Rubber fanzine writer Paul Bower a lift home that night.

"I went to see them play at the Marquee with a mate. The band were giving their 'Stretcher case'/ 'Sick of Being Sick' single away at the door. While we were queuing up outside the venue, Captain Sensible and Rat Scabies appeared in their car – getting out with crates of beer. We helped them hump the crates in and then Sensible decided he was hungry and invited us along to a local Wimpy bar for some food.

"We got in there, looking forward to some food, but it didn't take long before the Captain and Rat started to squirt their milk shakes all over the place. No one got to eat their food. They were squirting it all over us and everyone else. The cops soon arrived and turfed us all out. So it was back over to the Marquee to continue our Damned party."

Jackie Ineson: (Rotherham Punk) "It was a big shock to everyone who knew me when I became a Punk. I'd always been really shy and quiet, and suddenly there I was wearing outlandish clothes and drawing attention to myself. I think a lot of Punks were like me, misfits who suddenly found an identity and individuality. You could put on the clothes, slap on the make up, and be who you'd always wanted to be, someone bold and brave and different. To me, it was more than clothes or music; it was a way of life.

"Rotherham was a drab, dirty, depressed place in the 70s. It was a town desperately in need of an injection of colour and energy- and boy, did we give it one! Like most people, I'd read the tabloid shock-horror stories about Punks, and thought they were pretty disgusting. I didn't t get it at all. Then the music started to filter through, and when I first heard 'God Save The Queen', I was just blown away. It was like nothing that had gone before- so raw, so energetic, so damned exciting. So then I started getting into Punk music and gradually beginning to dress the part as well. When I was studying for my O' levels, the rules at school became a bit more relaxed, and I'd just about get away with a collarless shirt, badly-taken-in drainpipes, and the odd safety pin on my blazer. My form teacher used to smile indulgently and say *'that s not quite school uniform is it?'*

"I went with my sister Gilly to see Ian Dury at the City Hall. Our mate knew the band a bit so we got to spend the afternoon in the gent's toilets with Ian while he cut the rest of the band's hair! I m afraid I was too awestruck to speak, but he was really nice to me. Gilly was also friends with The Boys, so we went to see them whenever they were touring."

Gary Peacock: (Rotherham Punk) "I left Oakwood School in 1977 and started work as an apprentice at Stanley tools in Sheffield and didn't really get into Punk straight away, but two of my old school mates Alan Sleight (Ronnie Gunge) and Paul Ruddlestone (Vic Vomit) gradually got me into it. Darryl D'silva was also a good mate at this time and a good lad. Most of us didn't really dress as hardcore Punks and we were as much into Talking Heads, Kraftwerk, Television, The Only Ones, Bowie etc as we were into Punk, the exception was The Clash."

Although things were fairly late to get moving in Sheffield for Punk gigs, once the taste for gigs had been sampled the Punks came out in full force.

Left: Gun Rubber ad for Sex Pistols (June 77)

Tim Jones: (Rotherham Punk) "At the Top Rank, the queues went right down the stairs and down the ramp and onto the pavement; all Punks together, hundreds of em. All of a sudden, we were not the odd ones out. I saw the Stranglers at the Top Rank, supported by the Drones and London, the queue was massive and it took ages to get in. As we slowly moved towards the front of the queue, I could see why. The bouncers were searching everyone. What was it with the bouncers? What did they think we were?

"Finally we got into the Top Rank and the Drones were already playing, it had taken that long to get in. The queue outside was still quite big so I wouldn't be surprised if some Punks missed the Drones completely. London were on next who were ok but the Stranglers were awesome.

"I also saw the Damned there and The Clash with first, Richard Hell and later on Chelsea and also the Slits supporting someone, maybe The Clash. I remember there was plenty of spitting which is something I never really liked. I saw Elvis Costello at the Top Rank and couldn't get my head around the fans covering him in spit. Same happened with the Jam. One thing I took notice of was that there was so much power and energy with the Jam's music considering there were only three of them. Punk had arrived and was now here to stay - although not for as long as I thought it would."

Above: Rotherham Punks Tim Jones and the much-missed Jo Brailsford

The journey's to Sheffield and its relative Punk scenes and beyond, also brought along Punk fans from further south: some of them grasping the advantage of becoming students in the steel city and consequently taking advantage of the seemingly abundance of Punk action on the live stage!

Paul Jespersen: (Sheffield student/Punk fan) "Unlike most of the folk in this book, I came to Sheffield as a Polytechnic student in September 1977. I grew up near Lowestoft in Suffolk, where the chances of seeing Punk bands were very slim; the nearest Punk venue was West Runton

Pavilion on the North Norfolk coast, which was over 50 miles away, although I did manage to get there to see the Jam, supported by New Hearts (later to become Secret Affair) in July 1977... the day that 'This Is The Modern World' was released. This gig was a revelation. We had been used to seeing the likes of Fairport Convention at the UEA (University of East Anglia) in Norwich, where the longhaired students would sit cross-legged on the floor throughout the entire gig. At the Jam gig, the crowd were a mix of fledgling Punks and curious 'straights'. Of course, everybody stood up, and there was much pogoing. Weller and Foxton were jumping about all over the stage, and, due in part to their suits and ties, were soon dripping with sweat, as were the crowd. It made a big impression on me that Weller was the same age as me, whereas most of the bands I was into were probably at least ten years older. This Is the Modern World, indeed.

"Coming to Sheffield two months later was mind-blowing. Having been relatively starved of live music, I binged on gigs, seeing thirty bands in my first ten-week term. I had been used to seeing maybe one gig every three months (and travelling at least 30 miles to do so, when I had no means of transport other than lifts from kids with cars or motorbikes), whereas in Sheffield, you could see a gig every night of the week, and usually there was a choice – and I could get there on foot! So, all you Sheffield Rotherham and Chesterfield kids – you were pretty lucky!

Paul's homage to the Mick Jones look

"I remember seeing the Clash twice, Buzzcocks, the Jam at least twice, the Only Ones, the Rich Kids, Talking Heads, XTC, Doctor Feelgood, the Flamin' Groovies, Elvis Costello, the famous Stiff tour with Ian Dury etc, and many more. I teamed up with a kid from Great Ayton in North Yorkshire called Dick Holland. He was a kindred spirit – we would devour the NME every Thursday, and spend spare hours in Sheffield's many record shops buying the latest punk and new wave singles, and cool second-hand albums from Rare N Racy and The Record Collector. Punk's Year Zero meant that all uncool albums were purged from our collections – no Elvis, Beatles or Rolling Stones (and definitely no Emerson Lake and Palmer) in 1977!

"As new students we were warned to be wary of signing non-students in to gigs at the Poly, as you would get grief if you signed in someone as your personal guest who later caused trouble. Again, this was new to me, as there had been an open-door policy at the UEA, and we would often sign local kids in if they looked to be genuine music fans. I can see with hindsight that students might have appeared to be insular and excluding outsiders, but the Polytechnic, with its city centre location, was a great melting pot for hearing new music and meeting new people with new ideas (lots of arty students making their own clothes and wearing second-hand stuff), and loads of Poly students were local Sheffield kids, so there was good integration, more so than at the University where many students lived and studied on campus and had no need to interact with the city itself.

"In my second year I brought my drum kit to Sheffield, and with my housemates Al, Adge and Graeme formed the Agitators, practising in our student house on Sharrow Lane (the neighbours were amazingly tolerant. It was like the Young Ones' house but louder and less clean!). The repertoire included 'It's Too Bad' by the Jam, 'No Dancing' by Elvis Costello, 'The Kid Are Alright' by The Who and 'Shake Some Action' by The Flamin' Groovies. We were pretty tight but had little clue about how to get a gig, and no transport to move our gear about. Then some guys at Poly asked me to join their new band - TV Product."

Julia Reeves: (Rotherham Punk girl) "I hung out with Simon Ellis, Julie Longden and Tim Jones...we were the first generation of Punks in the Rotherham area. Neil McKenzie (Artery) was a founding member of The Prams and he was also one of my friends back then. I saw loads of bands back in the day (many with Julie Longden)...Clash, Damned, Stranglers etc. We wore strange clothes back then too...I remember wearing ball gowns with Doc Marten boots!"

The sounds of Marquee Moon and the sight of Punk's favourite Blonde set the pace here!

Andy Munday: (Sheffield Punk Rocker from Abbeydale Road) "My memories of that time are all a bit fuzzy - beer, fags, a few fights, loud mad music, loud mad people, wonderful clobber etc...But having said all that I went with a pal to Sheffield City Hall one night (mid-week) to a gig just advertised as a PUNK PACKAGE FROM NEW YORK. I bet the place was only one third full if that but the word got round in the downstairs bar that the support act was a real sexy bird with ripped clobber on. The bar rapidly cleared and I'm glad we went up for a look and a listen ... there she was, Debbie Harry in full swing with Blondie, what a treat and the main act that evening turned out to be TELEVISION (Tom Verlaine) who with his see-through Perspex guitar got the crowd in his hand from start to finish and to this day if ever I hear 'Marquee Moon', I drift back to that concert."

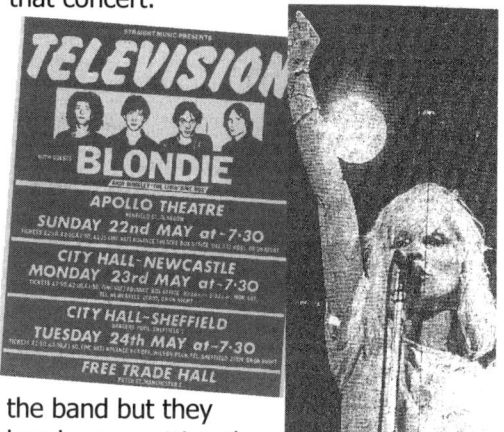

Andy's Punk ventures also centred around one of Sheffield's liveliest drinking spots: one that was, amongst a minority of establishments willing to accommodate Punk Rock in 1977.

Andy Munday: "Most of the bands down the Broadfield in that era were from the Sheffield area cos the music scene was buzzing and everybody wanted a piece of the action, but the majority were just loud, scary, not too talented hopefuls that got stuck in and had a good time, not giving a fuck: but that seemed to be exactly what we all wanted! One night(I forget the band but they had a bit of a following in there that night): this band were getting the crowd going by inviting one or two people up to the microphone to join in the chorus or summat and quickly I think half the pub (including yours truly) were jostling about up the front to scream down the mike cos he said it was being recorded and within 20 seconds the place went up, birds on the floor, beer everywhere, lads chucking punches and pint pots. But I can remember the singer who invited all this on just aimed his mike (while the band kept on playing) at us down the front and just stood there grinning like a cat like that was just what he wanted: it soon stopped but that is all we talked about for a week.

"I was never one to go over the top with clothing, although my Dad would look at me in disgust sometimes and throw the odd comment or two at me before I went out and I wish he'd have been down the Broadfield on this night: another good turn-out for a band and a gang of Punks were in with all the trimmings (Coloured hair, chains, string vests, tartan bum-flaps, plastic beach sandals etc...). One of 'em had a pair of crab claws for earrings and he must have purposely rubbed the rest of the crab meat or whatever all over his clobber as he stunk like hell of rotten fish, this lad had a good view of the band - as ya can imagine! Strange."

Jackie Ineson: "In the summer of 78, I was finally free of the horror that was South Grove Comp. I cropped and spiked my hair, adopted full Siouxsie Sioux make up, and started to develop my own style of dress. I never had any money, but when I was at RCAT I used to get 50p lunch money a day, and that would buy me 3 or 4 carrier bags full of amazing clothes at the old Oxfam shop. Who needed food anyway? That shop, was full of hidden treasures- dozens of pairs of original winkle pickers, fake fur coats, 50's ball gowns, 60's Day-Glo mini dresses- all for about 2p each! Some of the Punks bought their stuff ready ripped and pinned off the rack, but I thought it was better to have your own unique style. My mum was really good at sewing and she'd make me tartan trousers and such like. I once showed her a photo of a jacket of Siouxsie's and she knitted it for me bless her!

"A gang of us used to hang around Sheffield on Saturdays, just mucking about, being naughty, and seeing how many shops we d get thrown out of. Our favourite trick was to go to the café in Rackham's department store. It was very up market, and there used to be these women going round the café modeling very posh and expensive outfits, and carrying cards with the designer's names on them. So we'd write our own cards saying things like 'Scum Fashions' and put on our own fashion show. We d soon be asked to leave, but we thought it was hilarious.

"Punk was now making a huge impact on mainstream music, and we could actually see our favourite groups on Top of the Pops! I was really into The Damned, Siouxsie and the Banshees, The Rezillos, The Buzzcocks, and of course The Sex Pistols. I couldn't afford to buy many records, but you could always go to the Sound of Music and listen to new releases in their booth. A lot of Punks used to go to the Co-op up at the Stag. It was just like a working men's club, but Jock, the DJ, despite looking like an old hippy, was really into new wave music. He was like Rotherham's very own John Peel! There was really a lot going on for Punks in Rotherham. There used to be regular new wave events at the Assembly Rooms and Clifton Hall, with local bands and DJ's playing our music.

"So Punk brought me out of my shell, and I became a complete party animal. But with all the fun and games there was a very dark shadow lurking in the background. When I was 16 and 17 the Yorkshire Ripper was at the height of his sick career, and no woman or girl was safe. He (or the equally sick hoax caller, as it turned out) had said his next victim would be in a South Yorkshire town. Every time I found myself walking home alone, I'd be petrified, and would swear to never, ever go out alone again. But the next day I'd do it all over again, because I was young and daft, and there was too much going on to let that bastard spoil my fun. Then there'd be the walk home again, and the heart-stopping terror. Strange days indeed."

Future Mod (via a Glam initiation and a Punk Rock calling), Pete Skidmore drew his first taste of Punk from the sounds of the street as exposed by Paul Weller at his most vitriolic!

Pete Skidmore: (Sheffield Punk) (Left with best mate John Russell) "The first sort of music I would have heard around home would have probably been Motown and Glam Rock stuff such as T-Rex Sweet, Slade etc, these tended to be my older sister's favourites, who is six years older than myself. We lived in a two bedroom terraced house in the Sheffield suburb of Woodseats living on a street that was a very tight knit community. We had no central heating, no bathroom so bath night was in the tub in front of the fire, and an outside toilet! I came into the world in February 1964: when I was born my parents would have been late 30s early 40s so from day one it was a hell of a generation gap between parents and child, although I tend to look at things differently now as our son was born when I was 39! My sister had a pretty good record collection by the standards of the day; it was also topped up by swapping with her big circle of friends and our next-door neighbour's daughter who worked at Wilson Peck in Sheffield city centre.

"My sister would play her records on a record player we had in the front room of our house which was sort of out of bounds a lot of the time purely down to the fact that it was always freezing cold in there and was used on special occasions only! Or when we had loads of my mum's relatives visiting from Ireland! My sister was also a big Northern Soul fan and on Thursday nights my parents would go to the local workingmen's club and I was off to bed whilst she had her friends round and the settee was pushed to the wall and soul was played whilst they danced in the very small room, songs such as Al Green's 'Let's Stay Together' and Smokey Robinson's 'Tears of a Clown' being played. Around this time my sister came home with a few LP's she had borrowed from a friend, the two that stood out were Alex Harvey Band 'Next' and Deep Purple's 'Machine Head': These where probably the first records I ever put on a turntable. Around June of 1977, we moved house from a two-bedroom terrace to a three-bedroom bungalow about a mile away in the suburb of Greenhill, we were moving to a house where I had my own bedroom! And central heating!

"My friends at the time were mostly into football, so I didn't really know anybody who was that into music. I can remember the newspapers at the time running articles on this new Punk Rock music that was vulgar and shocking and any decent folk should avoid it. Well I took one look at this and fucking Hell! This was for me! The first band I took an interest in would have been The Jam; I liked the look and the short fast songs they played. I can remember watching them on Top of the Pops when all the family would sit and watch it and my Dad banging on about them saying *'Look at these are they on drugs or something?'* It was a complete breath of fresh air watching it as there was all these hippy bands standing playing their instruments, looking completely bored, and then The Jam appeared bouncing around and spitting the words out as they really meant it - eyes out on stalks. It knocked me sideways this new music.

"During this period of 1977, I ventured into Virgin records at the bottom of the Moor on a small precinct. The Moor was still a major road with buses running up and down it back then. I remember getting the bus to town on a Saturday and standing around outside Virgin and watching the youths coming and going. It was an alien environment to me as it just looked like an extension of the sixth form at school, all fucking long hair and those silly afghan coats and flares. I hated the Hippies then and still do to this day. After about 20 minutes, a couple of Punk types approached and went in so I followed. It was like entering a cave complete with the aforementioned cavemen. It was dark and it stunk of that hippy juice. I just stood and looked around: there were records all over, on the walls and racks and everywhere. When entering the shop at the counter there was two hippies with headphones listening to some records and at the side of them was what I was looking for... Punk records!!! I flicked through them and found The Jam 'In the City', The Stranglers 'Grip', the Sex Pistols 'Pretty Vacant' and the Damned's 'New Rose': these were the first Punk records I ever bought and still have them to this day. I remember paying for them and the utter look of disgust I got from the hippy said it all. I then developed a life long hatred of most things prog-rock and hippy.

"I couldn't get home quick enough to play this new music. My parents had splashed out on a music centre so I was in heaven; I could tape records as well. They got played and played and played; I started buying NME and Sounds and, with more pocket money saved up, I bought The Jam's 'Modern World' LP. The next one was Ian Dury's 'New Boots and Panties' for which I got an almighty clip around the ear because of all the swearing at the start of the song 'Plaistow Patricia', which I didn't know about but my mum was stood in the room at the time! Further albums followed in this short period which were Graham Parker's 'Stick to Me', Ramones 'Rocket to Russia', the Stranglers 'Rattus Norvegicus' and the first Clash LP.

"The highlight of my walk to school around 77 was buying the music papers on a Thursday and reading them at school. I tended to spend breaks and dinnertimes reading them rather than playing football with my mates. The first Punks I can remember around this time were a couple of older lads who would have been 18-19 and they had that early Clash look with the leather biker jackets and the drainpipes and Dockers. I would see them hanging around where I lived: they obviously had into Punk really early, but to this day, I never spoke to them or knew any of their names.

"As I mentioned, my sister is 6 years older than me so Punk sort of passed her by as she was a Souly, although I think she did see The Jam the first time they played the Top Rank on the 'In the City' tour. I would listen to Radio Luxemburg with the crackly sound and try to tape records I thought were Punk but I had no one to share my new found love of this crazy adrenalin-fuelled music. I was alone in a great big school full of those fucking hairy Led Zep-loving Muppets; what could I do? Our school didn't have a strict uniform code as such, so I asked my mum to take in a pair of flared jeans I had. Once we had had the usual hour-long argument about it, she did them and after having a very short hair cut done, the look was on the way!

"Going into school my mates laughed at my new attire, the answer was *'fuck off!'* *'He thinks he's a Punk'* was the ribbing I got from them but I didn't care, all I could think about was Thursday for the NME and to see what new records where coming out. Now at the time there was mainstream radio, which was Radio One, and Punk was not played period. For me, it was trial and error by reading music papers and guessing what was Punk. More records followed and bought such as 'Holidays in the Sun', 'White Riot', 'No More Heroes', 'The Modern World' and 'Gary Gilmore's Eyes'. I would venture most Saturdays into Virgin records and get these records. I caught onto the fact that you could pick a record and sit and listen to them in the shop so I would be up early on Saturday and get in there first thing to get a chair and headphones: I remember listening to the Saints first album, which I didn't purchase until the mid 90s. Each Saturday, there seemed to be more and more Punks in the shop; I would look at them and wish I could join them, also making a mental note of what they were wearing and hopefully be able to copy it.

Right: Punk compilation poster from 1977

"One Saturday I was in there and was listening to a Ramones album when I got a shove off the stool by a big hairy rocker *'Fuck off kid and take that shit with you'* were the words I got. Now as he was about 20 year old and I would have been 13 years that was a pretty big thing to do!... there's nowt like a bully - I've always hated bullies and still do even now: over the years I've dished out a few kickings to people such as this hairy bastard who deserved a taste of their own medicine, I've never been a person to start a fight, but one thing is...I will never back down!

"All of a sudden a big hand appeared on the rocker's shoulder *'Leave the kid alone'*. As the rocker turned around, he was confronted by a big black lad around 17 years old, the rocker crumbled and the black lad asked if I was ok to which I answered *'Yes'*. The lad just said *'We have to look after our own'* and walked away. I was shocked... a black Punk Rocker! Enter the legend of Delroy Wellington, Woodseats lad, Wednesday boy and Punk! He was with a lad called John who winked at me and gave me the thumbs up!"

"1977 - Year of punk, Year of violence, disillusionment, disaster, strikes and terrorism- Elvis died, Marc Bolan died and Punk Rock died. London still dominates the scene and whose fault is it? Yours! Punk Rock gave the kid in the street confidence to get on stage and say his piece. But was it his piece he was saying? Was he merely repeating what he'd thought he should, what he's been told or what he'd read in the music press or the Sun, or a fanzine. So you don't wanna conform? You're conforming by saying that dummy! 500,000 Sex Pistols copyists are not what's needed. The Punk bomb was defused by fat men with cigars who dangled the carrots of fame and fortune under the noses of its prime exponents. Who can blame them for selling out? Who says they sold their independence for a steady future? Punk session men/manufactured images/contrived stage pose/package it/sell it/ make it harmless. It is now safe for the Sex Pistols to play in your town; they are now no more than a joke. A dirty joke, but still a joke. The independent labels are just as narrow-minded as the established ones. Their policy is to play safe. These labels and the fanzines could have been put to good use, but they'd rather go on about the Clash's new stage clothes, the colour of Johnny Rotten's hair or where to buy plastic sandals and mohair jumpers." (From Gun Rubber fanzine no.7 December 1977)

1977 Punk fanzines

The initial Punk media exposure and subsequent involvement in Punk rock would, in some cases, be followed by a more left-field approach to tastes in Punk and new wave.

Bryan Bell: (Rotherham Punk) "The national music papers were atrocious... the locals sometimes as well. It was all blown out of proportion: you would be sat on the bus and get all this abuse from the Daily Mirror readers *'Oh you're a Punk, you spit all over and put yer fingers down yer throat to make yerself sick!'... 'No we don't, where did you read all that?'* I mean you could go any weekend and watch all the straights piling out of Tiffany's nightclub in town and puking up all over the place and nowt got said about that did it?

"Once all the outrage and media crap calmed down, there were some great gigs to go to. The Top Rank and later on the Limit were good and some of the support acts were great too. I remember one night at the Top Rank (I think we were watching Buzzcocks?) and I remember kicking Ari Up of the Slits up the arse on the dance floor for not moving when me and my mate Martin tried to get to the front. The Slits were supporting and when they got on stage Ari Up was giving me the glare. Not long into the Punk era, there would be a lot of the so-called electro Punk being played at Punk nights and gigs. I had bought Kraftwerk's 'Autobahn' LP in 1975, just before Punk, so I was open to listen to some new sounds other than the standard Punk stuff. I was into Ultravox and saw them at The Outlook in Donny. They were great with John Foxx; 'Rockwrok' and 'The Man Who Dies Everyday' etc."

The ideals and ethics for Punk's youth were always going to differ between each individual. The expectations, hopes and dreams of a generation had been held to question with the arrival of Punk

Rock in 1976, and as the danger and excitement of the initial bubble of activity burst – spreading its shrapnel and after-effects far and wide, often diluting the original intensity, and then the disillusionment and feelings of betrayal came to the fore. What may have been achieved; what possibilities and ambitions had been dissipated and held to ransom - and there lies the paradox and potential hypocrisy of the whole Punk movement... everyone seized the opportunity to create, to take a slice of the cake, start again and become who they wanted to be and in the process aim to selfishly be the best and become the most noticed of the pack... there in lies Punk's pre-determined destiny to be doomed to failure!! But what can be expected from it all? Youth is only a temporary condition after-all, so why not enjoy it while its there? Punk gave many young people that clarion call and chance to be creative and individual and for a while it all seemed worthwhile! Despite all of its failings and questionable motives, Punk did change lives and have a positive effect on the way of thinking of many individuals... it also gave young people the confidence to try and do something with their lives. Young Punk kid Murray Fenton was later to join one of Sheffield's finest bands Artery; but his first stab at performing was via his 'Do it yourself' intro to Punk!

Murray Fenton: (Sheffield Punk/musician) "My early Punk days living in Parson Cross... well it wasn't particularly a hot bed of Punk Rock back in 1977. There were a couple of Punks on the estate but they were older and not really in a rush to befriend 14 year old oiks. My next-door but one neighbour was Tony Armitage (later to be in the second line-up of the Stunt Kites who still perform to this day). I had a drum kit and a guitar and we used to play together round at my house much to the chagrin of the old couple next door. Tony's dad was a long-distance lorry driver and one day he came home with 'The Good Time Music of the Sex Pistols', a bootleg album recorded at a very early gig in Manchester. Terrible sound quality but we used to play it over and over.

"There were four of us in our little gang of mates and eventually expanded our bedroom jams into forming a full band. Simon Rippon was the next to join and with typical 14-year-old naivety we called our punk band RAF after our three initials. Our other mate Dean eventually got hold of a bass and off we went. Our first gig was at the school concert, which had two shows one in the morning, one in the afternoon. Dean had a massive, scary Alsatian dog which used to go apeshit when it heard the garden gate go. The dog escaped and he had to go out searching for it before it tore people's faces off, so he missed the morning show but we just did it anyway. We only did one real gig, at Lindsey Road Youth Club. We only had twenty minutes or so but we went down so well we ended up playing the songs four times each! Our final gig was the following year's Xmas concert, where we played 'Belsen Was A Gas' after which ironically, the older Punks in the estate poached our singer for their own band who played pubs and stuff so we didn't have a chance! We carried on for a while longer with Tony the drummer handling the vocals but it soon disintegrated without a front man and Tony went on to join the second and still current line-up of the Stunt Kites.

"The first real Punk gig I went to was Siouxsie and the Banshees at the Top Rank, Halloween 1978. Cabaret Voltaire opened, still in their very dark period, then Spizz Oil, a two-piece racket. I'd been to loads of normal gigs but this was something else. John Peel had played 'The Scream' in its entirety so I knew the songs quite well by the time the gig came along and they were just fantastic. I think I went in my school clothes. I remember feeling really self-conscious once I got there. I'd never felt the need to buy into the look of Punk until that night. That was it. I had my hair cut short and within weeks I'd bought some nifty gear from jumble sales. A mixture of army gear and stuff like my favourite shirt - a lurid orange 1950s nylon shirt and dress shirts like Tom Jones would've worn and an old dinner suit and some black suede creepers. My school had a farm attached to it, sheep on the football pitches! In the spring of 1979 when the lambs were born, the Rural Studies teacher had these white overalls he birthed all the lambs in, battered in blood and afterbirth. I snuck one out in my bag and wore it to go see Magazine on the 'Second-hand Daylight' tour. Disgusting really, ha-ha!

"Magazine were another of my favourites. I liked the basic up-and-at-em stuff like The Clash and The Sex Pistols but found myself deeply drawn to the more left-field sounding bands. Howard Devoto wrote really strange lyrics and the musicians in the band were all top drawer without tipping over into being musos. The gig was mesmerising but one of the things I remember most about it – apart from Howard Devoto's disdain and being spat on and threatening to walk off stage – was the fact that the DJ had somehow conspired to forget or be denied access to his records. The pre/in-between/post-band music consisted entirely of the Magazine album interspersed with the A & B side of the support band's debut single, Simple Minds 'Life in a Day', which got on everybody's tits after about the fourth playing!"

The new confidence for producing something musically left of centre also began to make its mark in Sheffield: noted here by one of the earliest of the North's Punk fans.

Nigel Lockwood: "The Human League's first incarnation was in mid 77. I saw the Studs/The Future at the University, in a lecture room, on July 16th, part of a party that night. I remember future Clock DVA singer Adi Newton, the Human League's Martyn Ware and Ian Craig Marsh dabbling with different music: they were influenced by the likes of Kraftwerk, Can etc, but Punk had given them the impetus to form their own bands. I saw Cabaret Voltaire at the Crucible and the Penthouse in the ensuing months, along with 2.3 and the Extras, who also played at the Broadfield and later, in early 78, at the Limit. I knew 2.3 very well, but Paul Shaft/Sharpe and Paul Bower fell out, Paul Sharpe formed a much more electronically influenced band, De Tian, and I went to their first gig, at the small bar downstairs in the old Refectory. They did a first set, which comprised of a 20 minute instrumental 'Sonata' and during the interval; my mate Andy Manton did a 10 minute magic act!

"Bowie had also got into electronic music, with his album 'Low' in 1977 and this also influenced local musicians. Other local bands at the time included Cindy and the New Jets, who I dabbled at managing, along with 2.3 and Artery (who I also knew, Mick Fidler in particular). One particular night I organised a package gig at the Revolution club in York November 24th 1978, with De Tian, Artery and the New Jets. Not many turned up but we had a great night! The only other local band I really liked at the time was Charles Hawtrey and the Deaf Aids, who were really quite rocky and Terry the singer looked good."

Below: 2.3 at Sheffield Weston Park August 5ᵗʰ 1979 (Kristan James Melik)

Nigel Renshaw: "The Stranglers at the Top Rank, fuckin' awesome!!! The Human League supported them and while they were playing Stranglers bassist JJ Burnel (Below) was seated on the floor surrounded by fans asking him for his autograph and telling them all to *'fuck off'* because he wanted to listen to the Human League. He also told them that the only place they would get to hear music like that was in Paris..."

Pete Weston: (Rotherham Punk) (Left) "Punk was totally up my street because it was so different and as I've stated previously certainly changed my life. Its strange that most of the other kids I knew, who were really into the progressive rock, stuck with it and hated all the new Punk stuff but accepted it with Dire Straits and shit like that and developed a retrospective Punk life to be cool in later years (Bitchin over!).

"Punk was all about being different but was turned into loud and fast amateur banging and shouting for the masses: Originally there were some classic Punk bands who played it different and were special for it. Among these were a few bands that stuck with me for years. Scritti Politti - I remember getting a compilation tape from the NME with 'Sweetest Girl' on, which was years before it saw light of day on vinyl. It's an absolute classic track but to me all their early singles were very political and full of big words that I didn't know the meaning of, but pushed me to find out what they meant. Then Green Gartside made a decision to go main stream and I couldn't quite get that but years later looked back and loved all the tracks that didn't fit me at the time they were released.

"Suicide - I remember walking into X Clothes in Leeds and hearing 'Frankie Teardrop' and asking who it was and from then on being hooked into that psycho disco beat, Simple but so much intensity built into the beat. I feel that Suicide paved the way for bands like the Chemical Brothers and Prodigy. I can't say the previous without mentioning the godfathers of Electronic music Kraftwerk and acknowledge their massive influence across all genres whether you like them or not their influence is in some of the music you listen to, guaranteed.

Suicide

"Gloria Mundi -They were one of the bands who took a centre spread of the daily newspapers after the initial Punk shock reporting, and who tried to explain what it was all about. They had story type songs with great music and a great band I was lucky to have seen (Limit club) and a very Arty delivery. I remember Eddie Maelov in a black swimming hat delivering the vocals unmoving in the fixed position. Stood on one leg leaning forwards with your arms outspread and singing for the duration of a song isn't easy but creates an unusual spectacle.

"Rikki and the Last Days of Earth were turned into a bit of a joke band by later Punk documenters but I thought they did some great records mirroring a desolate landscape that was the late 70's. We named our son after Rikki not for any reason more than we like the name with the unusual spelling; our daughter is Sheena for obvious reasons. Reading a lot of the retrospective books about the early days of Punk it appears that Rikki Sylvian had quite a bit of a devil preoccupation going on and that does show in the records especially "Alistair Crowley"; if he'd have stuck to it he could have scooped the Marylyn Manson spot.

"Ultravox! - Classic band with three great albums, yes three that's all Ultravox did! That abomination fronted by Midge Ure wasn't anything to do with Ultravox as far as I'm concerned. John Foxx was the true talent. Midge Ure as front man for the Sex Pistols was an option I'm led to believe. But what kind of a world would it have been without a Sex Pistols fronted by the fantastic Mr John Lydon, We would be listening to a chart propped up with a dodgy TV programme dictating our music by a greed orientated, Headline-grabbing megalomaniac pushing glorified club turns as the new talent. People would be going to see shows in our glorious Capital glorifying dodgy 70's/80's bands like Abba and Queen, Oops! Punk did a great job for a couple of years but it didn't take long for the powers that be to pull the reins back in and stitch it all up again."

Above: Pete Weston – Looking beyond the restrictions of the standard Punk of the day

Early Rotherham Punk Rocker Bryan Bell also found the need to not be held back by a sole diet of Punk by numbers: already having an eclectic taste in music prior to Punk, Bryan found the appeal of the fledgling sounds of futurism being played out at West Street's most dependable cutting edge music venue... the Limit!

Bryan Bell: "Later on I saw Simple Minds at the Limit club after hearing their 'Chelsea Girl' single being played in a record shop and seeing 'em on the Old Grey Whistle Test; OMD at the Limit as well, I think around the time that 'Electricity' was out; Bill Nelson's Red Noise were good too... 'Revolt into Style and 'Furniture Music' were good records. Magazine... I liked some of their stuff. All of this was happening and paving the way for the New Romantics, but we had been listening to a lot of it for some time. There was so much coming out, it was hard to keep a track on it all."

Andi Stevenson (Right) **(Rotherham Punk/Synth fan):** "I was heavily into Punk in the seventies and still am now. I'm also a keyboard player who started out in a Rotherham Punk band called The Grip in 1978. We changed our name to The Frozen Ones as we were heavily influenced by early Ultravox! and Tubeway Army: the name coming from one of Ultravox's! songs on their 'HA Ha Ha' LP."

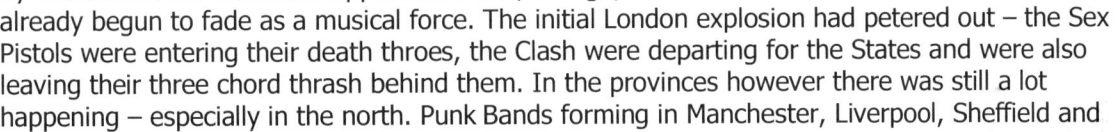

One Rotherham Punk had been turned on by the early sounds of Punk shortly after the initial explosion, but it wasn't long before the appeal of something more diverse being added to the ingredients opened up more Punk possibilities.

Richard Chatterton (Rotherham Punk) (Right on photo below)**:** "The directness, honesty and attitude of Punk appealed to me and I realised I was never going to settle down and have a job in an office and be anything other than true to my beliefs. By the time I had learned to appreciate Punk, though, it had already begun to fade as a musical force. The initial London explosion had petered out – the Sex Pistols were entering their death throes, the Clash were departing for the States and were also leaving their three chord thrash behind them. In the provinces however there was still a lot happening – especially in the north. Punk Bands forming in Manchester, Liverpool, Sheffield and

Leeds were starting to outgrow the Punk manifesto which the fanzine Sideburns had set in 1976, printing diagrams of guitar chords A, E and G and proclaiming *'This is a chord. This is another. This is a third. Now form a band.'* Punk was dying – but more interesting and varied music was beginning to take its place.

"Punk had inspired young people to pick up guitars and many of these people had been in Punk bands and would go on to create sounds with the Punk DIY attitude but with a variety of influences and styles. From the Reggae and Dub grooves of the Clash, The Slits, PiL and the Pop Group to the Industrial Sounds of the Simple Minds, the Fall, Magazine, Throbbing Gristle, Killing Joke and Joy Division, the proto-Goth/suburban meltdown of Siouxsie and the Banshees and the Cure, to the Ska Punk of the Specials and the agit-funk of Scritti Politti and the Gang of Four. I would venture into

Sheffield on the 24 bus from Brinsworth (Rotherham) to the Top Rank, the Sheffield Polytechnic and Sheffield University to catch this exciting music and felt extremely lucky to be in a city which also was starting to grow its own. Sheffield's musical awakening was fuelled not just by the energy of Punk but the revolutionary music created by the German pioneers Neu and Can and especially the repetitive electronica of Kraftwerk.

"After the gigs, if I had missed the last bus, I would walk the six miles home through the Sheffield's industrial area of Attercliffe and hear the thump thump thump of hammers and machinery which was shaping and forming Sheffield steel and think that these must be the same sounds which had inspired Kraftwerk's sonic rhythms. Strangely enough my father worked for 30 years in these hot noisy workshops which I never managed to see properly save for odd glimpses I caught from outside at night on my long walks home. My dad once agreed to take me inside once so that I could make some sketches while I was at Art College but he reneged on the promise after I had dyed my hair pink the night before.

"I had seen Joy Division support the Buzzcocks at the Top Rank in 1979 in what must have been one of the gigs of the decade but only twelve months later the headliners were playing to a less than half full Sheffield City Hall, which illustrates I guess how Punk was going out of fashion. Punk had never really dented the charts – apart from the Sex Pistols Jubilee number one which never was – but in a couple of years some of these experimental art school bands were going to do just that and indeed incredibly go on to form the new pop dynasty."

Paul Bower (Sheffield musician/Gun Rubber fanzine writer): "1977 was the year I moved to London and moved back again – quickly. Like many people I'd expected to join in on the exciting dynamic scene down there. Like many others I expected that the Punk movement was the start of the new age. It wasn't. Despite what anybody says I don't think it was ever very good, not even in the beginning. I visited the Roxy four times during March 77 and on each occasion it was hot, sweaty, cramped and expensive. Upstairs at the Roxy was nothing so much more than a collection of empty-headed fashion dummies staring at each other. Conserving their cool; Doing nothing! More boring than bored. Ok, so I wasn't there at the start, but all I can say is that if a movement can only keep its initial energy for a few months then it can't be much of a movement."

Right: Paul Bower performing with 2.3 in 1977

Paul's disappointment with Punk was not something to be taken light-heartedly: he had been there right at the beginning of Sheffield's immersion into Punk... in fact his Punk ventures had already begun a good couple of years before Punk with Musical Vomit. More importantly, Paul had got up off his backside and actually done something when the call for a new order was heard, first creating Sheffield's very first Punk fanzine Gun-rubber and then his own Punk band 2.3 – both of these projects never blandly participating in the Punk party-line and fashionable train of thought. Always questioning the validity and genuine sentiments of Punks main players, and often his own personal motives and relevance, Paul Bower represented the most honest, wilful and genuine voice of our generation's first wave of Punk thinkers and activists... truly the real face of our Punk and Post-Punk history! He was not alone in wishing to move forward.

Tim Jones: (Below) "Punk had given music a good old kick up the backside and loads of new stuff appeared in the charts. There was the 2-Tone stuff (Selector, Specials, the Beat etc) which was played a lot at the Limit and there was the new wave stuff like Blondie, Talking Heads, Echo and the Bunnymen, Cabaret Voltaire, The Cure to name but a few. I tended to favour this new-

wave stuff. As time went on our interest in music remained, always looking for something new. We started to listen more and more to bands like Gang of Four, the Cramps etc."

Whilst the more studious of the Punk bands were looking at presenting their new vision of what could be created from the ashes of Punk Rock, the beginnings of a new more street welcoming rootsier Punk was being performed by one of the second wave bands who hailed from Sunderland and with one of their early lines-ups visited the newly opened Limit club.

Rob 'Dingo' Dowling: (Sheffield Punk) "Me and my mates (Daisy & Becky) had heard a single called 'Who killed Liddle Tower's' by the Angelic Upstarts and thought it was awesome. So we decided to go and see them at the Limit club, but we didn't know them from Adam. On the way, we went into a dive of a pub called the Saddle on West Street where all the Punks and Skinheads at that time used to hangout (circa 78). We were the only people in the pub apart from a few regulars and four strangers, so we struck up a conversation with them. It turned out to be Mensi, Mond, Steve Forston and Decca who were the Angelic Upstarts. We ended up going on a pub-crawl with them and took 'em to all the local dive's 'the Cannon', 'the Marples' etc... We got absolutely hammered on spirits and cider.

"Mensi had got a plastic carrier bag with him that he wouldn't let go of and was holding onto it for dear life. Becky (Paul Beighton) kept on asking him what he had in the bag and eventually he showed him. It was a Pig's head that he had bought from the Castle Market in Sheffield earlier that day and said it was a surprise for somebody. Anyway, after copious amounts of alcohol, we staggered our way back to the Limit for the gig and they got us in for nowt and even shared their retainer with us (24 Stella's), so you can imagine the tangle they were in when they took to the stage? Mensi wobbled on and in his hands he'd got a big stick with the pig's Head with a policeman's hat on stuck on it. '*Good Evening Sheffield*' he slurred '*WHO KILLED LIDDLE TOWERS*' fuckin' awesome and when they'd finished we got even more hammered - what a fucking night!!"

The Punk Rock voices of our generation would continue to make themselves heard and be announced as loud as need be for another couple of years after the late 70's first wave. Their stories and experiences travelled a path that would take them through the years of the Limit club – where a whole host of Punk loving characters with coats of many colours would branch out into the Post-Punk years with their own ideals and dreams; the last of the great Sunday night classic Punk nights at Steeleys (the Top Rank); the new aggression and speed of the post 1980 Punk bands who would draw the last paying members of the local Punk tribe to its hailstorm of metallic apocalyptic mayhem and the new decade that would also herald many more options to push the Punk ideals further onwards and many well-worn miles away from the starting point of the original care free rebels of the class of 76. By the end of 1978, and certainly as the following year progressed, a shift backwards to the sixties became more evident... often as a result of disillusioned Punks wanting to smarten up from the increasingly duller uniformed fashion apathy of modern Punk! The late 70's were still a very tribal orientated time, however, and socialising between the two cults could vary.

Julia Reeves: "Punks and Mods got along as I remember. I worked at The Charade when I was about 16 (1978) and we had a Punk night and later a Mod night...but they played both kinds of music."

Gary Peacock: "As the Mod thing started there'd be loads of people asking you to sign them in (over at the Co op), in the full knowledge that they'd try and batter you later on. My worst incident was having two Mods quizzing me about me carrying a knife and then being chased over the sports fields by three scooters, never caught me though.

"Other memories include getting on the Maltby bus on Wellgate (in Rotherham) and going upstairs with my girlfriend, there were two seats left that didn't have a parka, 10 minutes of *'uh uh'* until we got off and received various threats and gob. Some of the Mod lads went on to be good friends of mine including Glyn Teasdale, Ian Hill, Trev? Shammy, Bake and Neil Green: how I giggled when they used to recount stories of the chasings at the Stag roundabout and surroundings. Another lad doing the rounds then was John Moore who together with Jake ran a tailors shop at the top of the High Street. They used to make Mod suits, but their claim to fame was making the spangly suits for ABC's Top of the Pops appearance (now that's rock and roll)."

Nigel Lockwood: "The Jam had come to be regarded as some sort of mod leaders within the new wave: Weller's heroes included Steve Marriott and Pete Townshend, and that whole mid to late sixties Soul and Mod period, so much so, it spawned a new generation of Mod bands, most of whom I saw at the Limit. The best of these new bands were Secret Affair – I thought that their 'Time for Action' single was awesome. The Limit Mod nights became regular, so I saw Merton Parkas, Small Hours and the Chords amongst others there. Around this time was the mutation from some of the Punk ethos into 2-Tone and ska. Again, the Limit championed it all... again, I loved it all and saw the Specials/ Madness/Selecter there reminding me of my original love of Trojan reggae back in the early 70s."

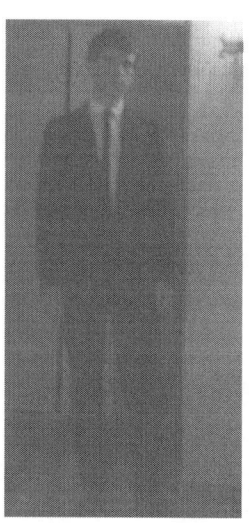
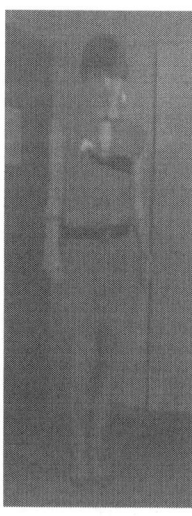

Tim Jones and Jo Brailsford moving to the style of Mod from Punk

Before Punk Rock, and well before the long haired over-fed rock stars of the pre-Punk era rock idol scene, there was another time when another short, sharp pop music with a style all of its own had existed: before the dinosaurs of the sixties rock scene had started to even pay tax... never mind dodge the dearly loved tax man to live in tax-free zones out of the country... before then a short haired aggressive and immaculately presented youth cult had taken a hold of the reins and dictated the way the world of fashion, music, attitude and the way young people could live their lives would be... In addition, that very British phenomenon would also re-emerge alongside, and more noticeably after, the first high tide of UK Punk over a decade later. The Mod was back and once again, it was time to love the weekend!

Chapter Three
Young Mods' forgotten voices!

"I was just 15 and it was truly awesome to be part of something like Mod; we just knew there was a big change about to take place" – **Pete Skidmore** (Sheffield Mod)

"There must have been over a hundred scooters flying past the queue of traffic that we were stuck in and a sea of parkas and boating blazers speeding past my transfixed eyes. I had no real idea what I was witnessing apart from a vague notion that they were Mods, but I knew from that moment on, that that was what I had to be" – **Lee Radforth** (Sheffield Mod)

Lee Radforth

Paul Morton

'*The Punk* and the Godfather'– Pete Townshend's 1973 'Quadrophenia' LP track almost gave the game away: Something was on the cards as far as street level music was concerned. The prog-Rockers, the filthy rich Rock stars: the jaded left overs from the sixties were soon gonna be on the way out. Townshend knew it, a very small minority of tuned in Rock fans knew it and by early 1976, the music weeklies were crying out for it!

When Punk Rock came along in the UK, short hair returned, thinner lapels were back, the 3 minute back to basics Rock n' Roll pop song was re-acclaimed and the music was once more being made by the young for the young: the adrenalin was flowing again and the over 25's hated it. Punk Rock also opened the doors for another short-haired, thin lapelled, short, fast and to the point up-tempo music fan: the Mod!

Without Punk, it's quite possibly debatable if there would have ever been a Mod re-visitation. True, the Northern Soul scene (Mod's direct descendent) and the scooter clubs were still around, but Mod as the iconic epitome of cool that we know it was barely anywhere to be seen pre-Punk - a certain Paul Weller and the odd diehard aside that is. When The Jam cut through the Punk wave with a maximum speed to rival any of the frenetic energy of the more Punk-by-numbers bands, the scene was set in motion: as sure as Punk had to make a clean sweep of the hairy brigade of 1976, then a generation of (often Punk-inspired) kids would seek to emulate the look and music of a cleaner and much sharper youth cult. From the smouldering ashes of Punk, whilst its flame was still burning, a new Mod generation was ready to stand up and be recognised.

The taste for all things Mod spread much quicker to the North this time around and by 1978, Huddersfield, Sheffield and Barnsley had a distinct ever growing number of Mods. By mid 79, with the parallel explosion of 2-Tone and the saturation of 'Quadrophenia', the Mod revival was in full force. Sheffield, Rotherham, Doncaster, Barnsley, Chesterfield and every other Northern town along with the rest of the country became intoxicated with the whole Mod scene and its many musical and fashion associations.

The Mods of this region were a mix of post-Quadrophenia obsessed parka-clad kids with a thirst for the 1960's and a fixation with the new mod sounds being created, along with more Soul & Rn'B addicted, tailored-clothes-wearing stylists who had more in common with George Fame and the Blue Flames than the Purple Hearts! Along with Rude Boys and scooterists, the whole Mod umbrella spread out as far as any youth cult possibly could. Be it the love of Soul, Ska, and the new Punk/ska hybrid of 2-Tone, the revival bands, and the classic Mod sounds of the 60's or the sound of a Lambretta kicking in: the crombie or the tonic suit, the parka or the Harrington... or most of these in equal turns - the Mod was here and although the media would help to kick it back to its underground roots in no time at all, the Mod has never truly gone away; constantly evolving and digesting the past and the present with a healthy nod to the future. And to the uninitiated to the Mod cause, the tasty retort is *'It's a Mod thing you wouldn't understand'*!

The Scooterist

Paul Morton: (Rotherham Mod) "My first real knowledge of Mods and scooters came in 1969. I was 10 years old and I had just changed schools from High Greave to Doncaster Road. On the first day, the teacher sat me next to a lad called Steven and we became instant friends. Every now and then the teacher would let us bring games into school and Steve would always bring in a battery powered record player along with some really great records; mostly Ska- not that we knew it at the time. I remember him bringing in 'Double Barrel' and 'the Israelites' as well as Judge Dredd, which the teacher took off him. It turned out all these records were his older sisters who was about five years older than us. One day I was at Steve's house when his sister's boyfriend turned up; he was riding a blue series 2 Lambretta with lights, mirrors, whip aerial, and had a full-length sheepskin coat on. I thought he was the coolest guy I had ever seen. In about 1971, he bought a mustard colour G.P. and the series 2 stayed in Steve's shed: sometimes we would sneak out on it, me on the back and we would have a ride round the East Dene and Clifton areas of Rotherham.

"In 73/74 I was at Spurley Hey School. One of the teachers was called Mr Cox, he would tell us stories of his days as a mod, plus a lot of the older lads were into Northern Soul and so was he. We thought he was really old but he was probably only in his early 30s. The, music that was around at this time was dire with bands like 10cc and Rick Wakeman: there was nothing of any merit. Most of the girls were into the Bay City Rollers or the Osmonds.

"I left school in May 1976, just the right age and when the Punk scene exploded it was a total revelation, I was still knocking about with Steve and we would go to some great pubs and gigs, we would spend a lot of our time in Retford. We had met some girls in Skegness who lived in Retford and we would go and stay with them. There was a place called the Porterhouse and we saw some great bands there. Mansfield was another haunt we spent a lot of time in.

"In 1977 the Jam were on TV with 'In the City' and I thought they were fantastic. The Punk scene wiped the board clean of what I thought was tired boring 70s music. By 1978 the beginnings of the Mod revival had started, I had gone to see the family in Great Yarmouth and while there I saw half a dozen scooters riding past, it all came flooding back and so I bought my first scooter, a Vespa 90. A year or so later Quadrophenia was released and the rest is history.

"One of the biggest moments for Mods in Rotherham was the first night at the Assembly Rooms. Word got around that all the Mods from East Dene would meet at the top of Far Lane to go into town together. I went into the Eastwood for a pint or two first with a couple of lads and after a while my mate Terry came in and said everyone was waiting outside so we finished our drinks and left. I was amazed, I expected to see about a dozen lads at most but there must have been 30 or 40 of us. The bus went straight past so we all walked through the park into town.

"The late 70s and 80s were quite violent. The National Front were parading everywhere and the Socialist Workers party would turn up for a fight. The unions were clashing with the police and there were riots in a lot of the major cities, this was the climate of the times and the Mods were part of this. The different tribes would get stuck into each other at the drop of a hat. The Punks would fight with the Teddy boys, the Mods would fight with both, along with the Skinheads who would fight with anybody.

"One of our hangouts was Strad's cafe on Mansfield road. It had a very mod juke box and there were always Mods in there whilst gangs of Teddy boys would hang around outside the Rockingham cafe, outside the bus station. The Dickens was a proper biker pub and just opposite the pub there is a set of traffic lights. One night on my way back from Sheffield, I pulled up at the lights on my Lambretta; all of a sudden I was showered with pint glasses and bottles being thrown at me from across the road by groups of Heavy Rockers.

"The Mods were up for it as much as anyone else, though. One Saturday, about 20 of us went to Sheffield to get stuck into the Punks. We chased about half a dozen into a record shop on Fargate and gave them a good hiding, we then came back up the Moor all singing 'Tom Hark', when we bumped into a big gang of Skinheads near the Peace gardens and it was now our turn to take a right pasting. There was trouble at the Peace gardens quite often after that. Another evening we got about a dozen scooters together and charged through Rotherham bus station, air horns blaring, but the – usually resident - Teds had gone.

"The seaside rallies were amazing in the early 80s and there were clashes with bikers in Scarborough, amongst other towns. One night we came out of the Harbour Lights pub straight into a big crowd of bikers, they were called Satan's Slaves, it was such a big ruck, I never did find out who won.

"The Lambrettas were a big Mod band and one day Radio Hallam announced that they would be appearing on the road show at the Hilltop pub in Kimberworth, so I threw a sickie and rode up for the afternoon. When I got there I was surprised to see lots of other mods had the same idea. A lot of people missed work that day, it was a great show. The Lambrettas had just recorded a song called 'Page 3', but when the crowd chanted for it, we were told they could not perform it because the Sun newspaper were suing them over the lyrics. Still I got my parka signed by the lead singer.

"We would travel miles to a party or scooter club do, if it meant an over night stay we would hire a van and all sleep in it. We once went to a scooter do held by the Burnley and Pendle scooter club in Lancashire. We would get hammered and sleep it off in the van, but when we came out no one could find the keys, so we were out in the cold till someone managed to break in. North or South we would set off on our scoots with a couple of pounds in our pockets, no rescue van, and no R.A.C. cover at all and in all weathers. I was once stopped by the police in Torquay who thought I was mad when they realised how far we had travelled.

"By the mid 80s people had started to drift away from the Mod scene, the mirrors and lights were coming off and custom paint jobs and engine tuning was the in thing. People were wearing flat top hair cuts and the music on the rallies was becoming more varied. Punk and Psychobilly records were being played, lads started wearing leather bike jackets and boxing boots. Some were giving up scooters altogether. A lot of the lads were miners and now they had bigger things to fight for. New clubs were being formed as others broke up.

"In 1986, Rotherham S.C held a big do at the Clifton Hall; as usual we were all having a good few beers when we got into a bit of banter with some Skinheads from Worksop. We were drinking with them when one of them dared me to jump off the balcony 'Jimmy style': not willing to back down I climbed onto the balcony and looked down, it suddenly seemed a long way down but when you are young and drunk you do daft things, so I jumped. I landed really badly and was wearing Brogues. I broke four vertebrae, two ribs and my right heel. I spent seven weeks in hospital.

"Rallies became more organised which in some respects was better, with organised camp sites etc, but I think it was losing its Mod roots. The people attending these gatherings were becoming more diverse and venues would have two or three different rooms to cater for the different types of music. In the 90s I stopped attending national rallies altogether, the numbers were dwindling and most had nothing in common with the Mod scene at all. I started going on *Mod only* rallies, which were where I felt I belonged. I still had lights and mirrors as this is my way of things and my roots. Another thing was that people were also getting married and having kids, me included.

"Towards the end of the 90s things started to pick up a little and people started turning up at rallies, the numbers were increasing into the new century with people turning up who I had not seen for years. There was a renewed interest in scooters; they were being featured in adverts, on TV and in films. The downside to this was a very steep rise in the cost of scooters, which has continued to this day. I am still riding my scooters with lights, mirrors and whip aerial and I am not alone, with a good proportion of mod scooters showing up: when we are at the seaside people will often ask if they can have their photo taken on my scooter, especially kids. To me, Mod is a very British thing. It means beat and Ska music, nice clothes and full Mod scooters. To other people it means something else. Like they say *'it's a Mod thing, you wouldn't understand'".

The Jam fan

Sheffield Mod Pete Skidmore had, like Paul Morton, been introduced to the coolness of Mod by the first waves of 1977 Punk. His total immersion into the music of The Jam and the coolness, clothes and hairstyle of Paul Weller would lead him scootering into the path of the Modern world!

Pete Skidmore: "I started wanting to dress like my hero Mr Weller, but when you are 14 you have to make do and get by adapting your style. Now one thing I was lucky with was my older sister had been a skinhead and my good fortune was that she had kept a lot of the clothes which she had worn, and as they had been men's clothes even better!! A few original Ben Sherman's; a couple of Fred Perry's; some Levi 501s: I was well and truly fucking sorted! All of this topped off with Doc Martens shoes, the suede boots came later. I didn't know what a mod truly was in 1978; all I knew was that I wanted to dress like my hero- as you do when you are 14 and into music. I had no idea of The Who being Mods or the Small Faces; that all came later.

"Now the straight jeans were not a problem, but the trousers were. Harrington's in the Castle Market started doing straight leg trousers but they were something like 22 inch bottoms so were maybe a bit wide: I wanted drainpipes! Around March/April 1978, we had a trip from school to the steelworks in the East End of Sheffield; nowadays its possible Meadowhall stands on the same bit of land. Anyway in we trooped; a class of 14 year olds all hell-bent on having a laugh and messing about. We walked into a massive marble-floored reception and were met by two or three young receptionists; we assembled and then were taken down a corridor by one of the girls. Now I was walking behind her and she had the hour-glass figure and the big knockers to go with it, what a bird! She was probably only about 18 or 19 but to me she was a woman, probably giving me my first hard on! The second hard I had was when we went into a room and a young lad came to show us around... it was a Mod!

"This lad had an ice-blue Mod suit just like Weller wore and black slip on shoes and a polka dot tie. My mate shoved me in the back *'fucking hell Pete look at him! He's got to be into The Jam'.* We followed him around the steelworks checking out all the time what he was wearing; the lad obviously noticed and started making eye contact with us. Now in these parts Maggie Thatcher is hated, when she dies there will be so many parties going on it will be like New Years Eve all over again but one thing I've got to thank her for is getting me out of having to work in the steel works as she managed to shut most of them down chucking mates and family etc on the rock and roll. Our careers teacher thought it was a great place to work, *'well you go and fucking work there then you fucking hippie'* I thought!'

"Anyway at the end of our little trip we collared the lad with the neat suit *'Are you into The Jam?'* I piped up, *'Err not really sonny, I'm more into sixties and Northern Soul why?'* My mate John jumped in *'Well we thought you were as you've got a suit same as Paul Weller wears';* the lad with the suit replied *'Well there's more to wearing a suit then The Jam, it's a sixties thing you know'.* We looked at each other stunned; how the fuck can you wear stuff like Weller and not like The Jam? So big daft lad here asks him where he got his suit, it turns out there was a Teddy boy shop on Park Hill flats

that sold all that stuff; really cool drainpipes and the odd sixties 3-button jackets but it catered mainly for the cavemen with the grease and the quiffs. One thing was - he warned us not to go on Saturdays as basically we would get a good kicking from the Teds. Looking back we knew fuck all, and mod culture still had maybe another year to wait for us to join it: we carried on through 1978 following The Jam and watching other bands and trying to chase down stuff that Weller was wearing. I managed to track down some Ben Sherman's in a shop in Sheffield. I had the bright idea of wagging school one day and go and visit the Teds shop on Park Hill. This area I knew of, but it seemed like another world away, having only seen it as I went past on a bus or from the town centre. The next day nobody was having it so I got register out of the way and was off for the bus to town: *'oh fuck'* the next stop down my mum was getting on and I'm sat upstairs trying to hide. Luckily she sat downstairs and trouble was avoided.

"So anyway I gets off in Pond Street and makes my way down Pond Hill and across the road to Park Hill flats, to quote the great Jarvis Cocker, *'Councillors from Moscow came and looked at them and decided to build a better version in the suburbs of Moscow'* is an understatement... it was

Dickensian and here's me, a 14 year old, wagging school and entering a place such as this? The things we did to look different and stylish! So big breath and I entered the Teds shop. It was small but incredibly well stocked... there was a Ted behind the counter probably about 30ish who gave me the once over *'You should be in school kid! Where you from?' 'Err Woodseats pal' 'what you after'* ... so I blurted it out *'I want some drainpipes in black or blue'*. Two minutes, later there they are on the counter: I tried em on and they were awesome! At £14, which was a lot of money then and cleared me out, but they were mine!! I ran back down to Pond Street - careful that there was no work-dodging skinheads around - and was on the first bus back to our little mod corner of Sheffield.

"Looking for mod clothes was probably a full time occupation around this time, but thinking back we always found what we wanted. There was a hell of a lot of gentleman's outfitters type shops who still had the old stuff which was perfect, I even raided my Dad's wardrobe and came out with a nice 3-button checked jacket which certainly got some wear for a couple of years. I remember a few of us wearing Adidas, Samba or Bamba around this time as well. I can also remember a shop on the corner of Barker's Pool; it was a music shop and I think it closed down and turned into a Burtons and they had some wicked black and white halved Ben Sherman's.

"So there I was at the local youth club in my blue straight leg trousers, and pink button-down shirt looking like the fucking dogs

bollocks at 14 years old. John and Steve were well impressed. Probably like most youth clubs around that time, you had to wait for your 15 mins of fame whilst the usual Motown and disco was being played, one record that stands out from that time was 'The Bottle' by Gil Scott Heron which at the time never bothered me until a few years

later when I heard it and thought it was awesome, in fact its one of my favourite records of all time now, just shows you what time can do!

"So anyway it was a quick 15 minutes of the best The Jam and Clash etc could offer! Then it was back to the usual stuff. We had been to see a few bands by this time mainly at Sheffield Poly and Top Rank plus a local band called The Push at the drama hall at school; a gig that was organised by the youth club leader (a certain Mr Howard Holmes who championed some of us young Punks/Mods). I bought records when I had the money saved up, and it was usually around at my house where we would gather, mainly Steve, John and Jimmy and later on a lad called Simon - all being school friends. Looking back now, I think we were the only Punks/Mods in our year at school; although a few became Punks later on and there was a hell of a lot of Mods come the revival that happened the following year.

Autumn 78 saw The Jam arrive at the student infected Polytechnic on Pond Street: perfect timing for a Jam gig eager Pete Skidmore!

"On scanning the NME, The Jam were touring! and yes Sheffield was on the tour! That's it; all we could talk about was The Jam coming to Sheffield: on seeing that it was the Polytechnic we debated for days about if we could get in or not, due to the student entrance policy. It did prove to be a nightmare trying to get signed in, there were people coming and going but nobody would sign us in. We sat outside on the wall trying our hardest; I was with Jimmy and maybe Steve and who comes walking down Pond Street in a green parka? Yes Mr Paul Weller! Fucking Hell! we asked him to get us in but the apprentice student Hitler on the door was having none of it. Eventually we made it in and could hear the sounds of Patrik Fitzgerald upstairs, *'Got a safety pin stuck in my heart for you!'* it was awesome... a packed and sweaty concert hall, we stood at the back. Next up were the Dickies, I had never heard of them but I was knocked sideways at the speed they played, next up The Jam!!!!!!!!!We decided to go to the front when they came on: I can honestly hold my hands up here and say I can't remember one thing about this gig! But what I do know is that I went in a big Jam fan and came out an absolutely huge die hard fan.

"After that gig, I tried to get anything and everything on The Jam that appeared in magazines books newspapers etc. I got 'All Mod Cons' when it came out and played it for a solid week, I studied the inside sleeve with the collage of mod and sixties related stuff and the breakdown of the scooter for hours and hours. I actually wrote to Paul Weller and one of the many things in it was where could I get the *'who the fuck is David Watts'* badges and the long pin type metal badge. It must have been a while later when I got a letter: I had forgotten about writing it by this time, wondering who it was from, I quickly opened it to find a letter from Paul Weller wrote on paper from a hotel in Germany. Over the last 30 years or so I've asked my parents every now and again if they still have this letter anywhere and the answer is always no, and I'm not sure that if I threw it away along with the scrapbooks I had of The Jam. What I can remember was him writing saying that the items I had asked for were promo items and had all gone; however he had found a couple of the long pin badges and hoped I liked them! What an understatement of the year! I couldn't wait to show my mates; I was on cloud 9 for a long time and got loads of mileage out of that one!

In conjunction with the onset of Sheffield's Mod revival stirrings came a second visit to the City in less than eight months, of Pete's favourite new wave band... this time moving up to the University

"1979 arrived and early in that year another Jam tour was announced, the success of 'All Mod Cons' had brought new fans and The Jam were due to play two nights at Sheffield University Lower Refectory on the 'Strange Town' tour. The gig was on a Friday night and we were all dressed up ready to go. I can't remember much about it but what I do remember was it was 29p for a pint of lager! As well as The Jam playing, this day will go down in history as when Maggie Thatcher got in power, a very unwanted memory indeed. I can vaguely remember standing near the front to the right hand side of the stage. Over the years there have been quite a few photos of these concerts knocking about however I just can't seem to be able to pick our gang out! Although a girl from Woodseats, whose name I can't remember, is clearly on them (she was even younger than us). What I do remember was a hell of a lot more people dressed in The Jam uniform since the last time. It must have been 75% full of Mods: you could not move for lads in Fred Perry's, Levis, Ben Sherman's, suede boots and parkas - it was really taking off.

"I was just 15 and it was truly awesome to be part of something like that; we just knew there was a big change about to take place. The NME seemed to be, all of a sudden, full of articles on Jam look-alike bands such as the Purple Hearts, Secret Affair, the Chords and Merton Parkas. We started following these bands as well and an unsuccessful attempt to gain entry to the Secret Affair gig at the Limit failed to dampen our spirits. Throughout 1979 we did loads of gigs at the Top Rank seeing the Damned, Stiff little Fingers, Undertones, Stranglers and later on the 2-Tone tour with the Specials, Madness and the Selecter.

"At school, Mods started appearing - probably a dozen in my year - and further down the years a certain now famous Sheffield artist whose great works have captured the memories of these generations far more then a million words could - Mr Pete McKee as well as Jason Frost - a lad who has been at the front of the scooter scene in Sheffield for over 25 years: glad I had an influence on somebody!

"We got to see the Merton Parkas at the Limit; it may have been a matinee performance. We all had their single ('You Need Wheels') with the free patch! I had a parka, and if my memory serves me correctly, it cost £12 from an army stores in Attercliffe/Darnall. I was in my element and wearing it for school, I got really slaughtered by the older lads: it got quite nasty and I took a few kicks and punches from certain sixth formers over the weeks, but as they say *what goes around comes around* and 3 of them got their come-uppance a couple of years later on Woodseats, and I'm still not sorry for what I did to them!

"When 'Setting Sons' came out, we went crackers on it; it was played non-stop but the tour didn't come to Sheffield this time, so we missed out. That year, we went to see Quadrophenia about a dozen times and I got the soundtrack for Xmas. Every time we went to see Quadrophenia, there were always loads of Mods - all kids our age, faces that I would get to know over the next couple of years following The Jam tours. One of the other bands we followed was a Sheffield band called the Negatives who came from the Gleadless area of Sheffield. I saw them two or three times; we went to see them at the old George IV pub on Langsett Road: a whole crowd of us from school went along with John's brother plus Shaun whose brother knew them well as he was in a band called Short Circuit. We got the single they had out (all signed by the band) which I still have to this day.

"By this time I had a part time job collecting glasses at a local working men's club a couple of nights a week so I had cash to spend on records or clothes. One thing I remember from that time was me and John were hardly ever in school; we would get registered and then either go to his house or mine depending on what days our mums were working! As 1980 arrived I would be leaving school... what did I want to do? No idea? All my time was spent on music and following The Jam. I had made friends all over Sheffield, you would see lads in town on Saturdays on Fargate or the Hole in the Road, or the many record shops we had, hanging around and you would check them out and you would give 'em the nod and them returning it and gradually we got on speaking terms with them: lads such as Fraser whose brother was in the Negatives and a lad called

Siddy and his mates from Heeley Green - plus we had in our ranks now a lad called Phil Grant who had been a Ted ... the ranks were growing!

"Early 1980 and The Jam went to no1 with 'Going Underground'. John and myself celebrated by going for a pint in one of the pubs in Greenhill village! I think we had 3 pints and were hammered! My clothes around this time were still Ben Sherman's plus I had a couple of Fred Perry jumpers mainly in brown and a red one, Levis and another pair of drainpipes from the Ted shop! Around that time we got chased by some Rockers in town and they were mad for it; we got chased up the Moor, me running across the road dodging buses, when I tripped up and fell. By this time they were on me but nothing happened... I looked around and there was a great big bear of a man around 40 or so stood over me telling these rockers to either fuck off or take a good beating! They crapped themselves and ran off! Turns out the guy had been a Mod in the sixties... I was saved!

"We all had exams and had to write for jobs, check up on history and 1980 was the worst year yet for leaving school with jobs being very few: I had loads of letters sent out I didn't know what I wanted to do, I still don't! I had an interview for a job at Sheffield Council as a gardener. The night before I had took a left hook to my face and had a huge black eye which didn't go down well at my interview and needless to say I didn't get the job. On leaving school I had dole money plus glass collecting money and I did some fiddle for a neighbour labouring on the building sites so I had quite a lot of cash. Stuff I wore at the time was Raleigh cycling shirts with the pockets on the back cut off, bleached Levis and some slip-ons which were rather cool. Places we went to were the local youth club - which now played loads of 2-Tone and Mod stuff - and we started

venturing to the KGB club on Abbeydale road, which played mostly Soul records. I would also wear t-shirts of The Jam and had quite a few... I just wish I still had them now!

"The Sound Affects tour! The Jam played Sheffield Top Rank on a Sunday night and it was packed: we had knocked around in the day and my mate Jimmy took all his Jam singles and albums to be autographed which he managed to get sorted! He even had all those Japanese imports signed, which must be worth a fortune now. It was a great gig although spoiled after by the gangs of Pond

Street Skinheads who were hell-bent on beating every young Mod up, although a few of the older Mods who had scooters gave them a good kicking. I also went to Leeds on this tour as well.

"I had toyed with the idea of a scooter for a while (against my dad's wishes as his brother had killed himself on a motorbike years ago). I had a job at the post office and worked shifts, sometimes till 9 at night, but it never stopped me getting changed and out up West Street and the Limit four or five nights a week. Within a few months of being a schoolboy I was working and things are different when you have some money, although it would be gone by Friday as I was

always going to a concert or buying clothes. The NME had an advert for the Carnaby Cavern in London; so I got a catalogue and got a pair of grey drainpipes and some blue ones plus a yellow and blue polka dot shirt along with a Paisley button down.

"I had the Jam shoes already from early in the year, and the bowling shoes which I had done a great swap at the Bowling Alley at Firth Park: I had some old plimsolls which I handed in and then walked out with a nice size 8 bowling shoe!

"Records were also high on the list and every week I bought all the latest releases, from shops such as Revolution, K&D in the market and Virgin. When 'Start' by The Jam came out I loved it and it also put me on to the Beatles, who I had never shown much interest in before. I was well impressed by the 'Revolver' album and also started listening to Small Faces and The Who: over the next couple of years I went to loads of Jam gigs, 1981 seemed to be Jam gigs non-stop going to Skegness, Leicester, and Stafford Bingley Hall, Bridlington, Preston and London. 'Funeral Pyre' was now out and this single I loved.

"I was now knocking about with a couple of lads from Gleadless namely Phil (Wright) and Jon plus a lad from Parson Cross called Neil who went on to be a concert photographer. I would go to gigs with these lads as well as to the Limit club and most of the pubs on West Street; starting in the Three Tuns in Paradise square then the Mailcoach, Beehive, Hallamshire, the West Street Hotel and the Saddle before descending the stairs to the Limit. It was this summer that I went to the big scooter rally in Scarborough: I went in a van with a few lads from Woodseats - around this time Woodseats

had a big mod scene - older lads such as ACE and Tony. There were always a dozen or so scooters parked up outside the Woodseats Hotel or the Big tree. I had a small frame Vespa bought for £100 which I must have done at least 50 miles on during the entire time I had it! I would go to the Woodbourn hotel and Staniforth Arms scooter clubs with a lad from work called Paul: Also to the Travellers pub on Barnsley Road near the bottom past Lane Top.

"Scarborough was mad: various figures have been mentioned about 10,000 scooters being there which is possible! Lads were throwing scooters off the cliffs at the time. I slept in the van one night (and under a hedge the other)... it was absolutely mad, the town was a sea of green; it was what being young was all about. There were fights and all sorts of crazy stuff going on; I think every youth under 20 from Yorkshire was there! There were various scooter clubs in Sheffield at the time (there was also a girl's scooter club called something like Queen of Fools?) I think the first club in Sheffield was Scorpions SC, although I'm not 100% on that, plus Alcoholic Maniacs, which is still running although I think somebody just took the name and re-launched it - plus Northern Line of which I was a member when it reformed in the mid 90s.

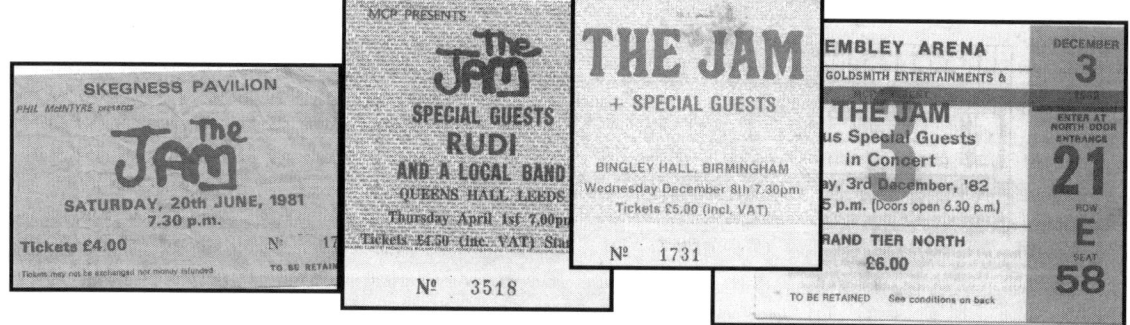

"1982 was a big year for The Jam: The Gift album was a mixture of styles - basically Paul Weller laying the foundations for what would become the Style Council. The first gig of the year I went to was Birmingham Bingley hall, all of us in Jim's car: I had my first proper girlfriend around this time so I was getting a bit sidetracked like you do. She was younger then me and was in her last year of school; we had been friends for two years or so and it just happened - my first love! What a great feeling, still I had loads of concerts to get to. I had passed my driving test and was driving vans at work. On the Gift tour we went to Birmingham, Leicester, Manchester and the 2 nights at Sheffield Top Rank: we also went to Leeds Queens Hall where we played football at the back of the hall whilst The Jam were on! Little did we know this was the Jam's final year and a split was on the cards.

"Now don't ask me why, but I was sporting a moustache around this time, and was wearing Adidas boots similar to the Converse ones and Levis. The parka had gone with loads of kids knocking on my parents door wanting to buy it, my mum every now and again will tell the story of having to turn kids away who had heard I was selling it! I was also wearing a red jean jacket with a medal on, just like Weller! Plus white moccasins and blue socks, remember the Lonsdale tops? The Jam started wearing these and everybody was into them, but you couldn't get them in Sheffield at all... WRONG!

Paul Weller by Neil Kitson

"Now I worked for the Post Office and one day I was delivering a telegram on the Arbourthorne estate. In the centre of it there is a square of shops, the usual ones such as a chippy, Co-op, post office, pub etc, and a sports shop. So here's me parked outside and I just

looked in the window and spotted a Lonsdale shirt hung up. So in I go and there was a complete rack of Lonsdale t-shirts and sweatshirts - fucking hell!

"I came out with a green short-sleeved sweatshirt, a grey short-sleeved sweatshirt and a long-sleeved white sweatshirt! And... another six white long-sleeved sweatshirts! Ready to sell on! I got the lads around to mine and *'here you go boys what about these'!* A nice profit of £20! I cleared that shop out over the next few weeks and I made a mint! I reckon 50% of the Mods in

Paul Weller by Jim Gatus

Sheffield had a Lonsdale from me! Sam (my girlfriend) was wearing all my old Jam t-shirts now and she was well into it, her uncle was and still is a very well known singer.

"Come September, me and the lads had a trip planned to see The Jam in Belgium? Or France? Not sure which now? It was me, Jimmy, a lad called Shaun who had knocked about with us for over a year and a lad called Steve who I had known since I was 6 years old. Also another lad called John who was deaf in one ear. We were all ready to go and Jim had a phone call saying it was off, Weller had shingles and it was cancelled; we were gutted, even more gutted when we heard Weller was splitting the band! Everything was crumbling around me... my girlfriend Sam had given me the boot, my favourite band was splitting so there was nowt else to live for! Everybody knows the story of the split so I'm not going into it. Dates were arranged for a farewell tour; we had tickets for Stafford, one of the Wembley Arena dates, Bridlington and Birmingham. I tried and tried to take everything in on these last gigs and, making the most of it, we went to Bridlington and I took a camera. At Birmingham I was getting intimate with a Mod girl from Greenhill who was a bit younger then me which was nice! Whilst at Wembley we stayed in a B&B in Kings Cross which was full of hookers. My band, our band, our voice of our generation had split!

I hated Weller, I hated music: The Clash were going downhill fast, The Jam had split... I didn't have owt now!"

The frustration and disappointment for Pete, and a nation of Jam fans in 1982, would, in many ways continue through the best part of the decade... not much, if anything, on offer could compensate for the loss of one of the greatest bands of the whole Punk era!

**Pete deciding which direction to take after The Jam's split
The Jam at Bridlington Spa 1982 on their last tour (Pete Skidmore)**

"The Birmingham gig was probably one of the last concerts I went to for a long time. I lost interest in music, records and gigs altogether. I went to see Bauhaus in 1983 at the Top Rank and was bored stiff. I changed all my mates; I was going to football more and was making new mates who followed Sheffield Wednesday and were more into fashion and drinking. I did do a few scooter rallies from 83-86 but nowt big: I sold my small frame Vespa to a lad from Chesterfield for £50 or something and stopped buying records. There was a lot of lads who had followed music from 77 onwards and had lost interest in it once The Jam split, I went to a few gigs at the Marples but for me it was the Limit 4 nights a week.

"On West Street and the Limit, a lot of the Mods and Punks I knew from the early 80s were now Casuals and football lads; the live bands had stopped at the Limit, it was just music. I was always chasing girls and it was just about the shagging; I didn't want to get tied down. I went to see the Style Council a few times with a footballing mate. They were good and it was nice to see a lot of girls at these gigs, a lot more than there were at Jam gigs as it wasn't as laddish. I went to Donington Park scooter rally; I think Bad Manners were on and I remember seeing Edwin Starr at a rally but my Mod roots had died; I was more into designer clothes and was always spending a lot of cash in a shop called Direction on Woodseats which is still there now and with the same owner!

"That final Jam concert (back in 82)...I had cried my eyes out, it seems daft now but at the time that's how it felt. Looking back now- Weller was right to do it, music had to move on: Jam concerts had got just like standing on the terraces at football, it was too much... it all just had to end!"

The end of the Jam years had come for Pete and many other fans and with it the Mod association too. It would take a good few more years for Pete to return to the world of scooters, Soul and Ben Sherman's and once again it would be his hero Mr Weller who would be partly responsible!

All Jam photos (unless stated otherwise) Courtesy of Pete Skidmore

The 79 Mod

Kevin Munday: (Rotherham Mod) "I got into the Mod scene like most, copying the older kids and being into Quadrophenia. I bought a Vespa 50 special and my cousin Simon did too, I got blue, and he had the red one. They had a top speed of about 38mph. We soon personalised

'em, racks, mirrors, lights n' crash bars, whippy aerial and of course a back-rest for the bird...top speed now 30mph with tail wind! Most of it now seems to have been just a booze-fuelled blur. I was hardly ever sober. There were sobering moments though. One such occasion was when I turned onto Middle Avenue (Rawmarsh) followed by some greasers on bikes. They caught up instantly and were trying to hoof me off. One was grabbing at my aerial n' trying to whip me with it whacking the foxtail I had on it into my face...twat!

"Buzzin around Rawmarsh on the scoot got me in with the older kids and some were in a club called Easy Beats SC in Rotherham. I met Paul Morton there and remember setting off for Bridlington with him one Saturday. I broke down and was sat in this lay-by when down the road came loads of scooters. There were fucking hundreds of 'em all waving pointing laughing and giving' me the wanker sign... not one of 'em stopped!

"The do's in 1979 - 1980 were the school youthy, other school youthy's (for a scrap) and Mod nights being held anywhere and everywhere or later the Assembly Rooms Clifton Hall and Tiffany's

Kevin Munday and Cousin Simon - 1979

nightclub. The most popular nights out though by far, though, were house parties mainly held at somebody's bird's house. I remember one on Quarry Street (Rawmarsh): It was in full swing and I was upstairs waiting for a piss. This bird's step dad came home unexpected and went ape, kicking (literally) everyone out. I could see him coming upstairs just as his daughter came out of the bog and was standing on the landing with me!! The only part I haven't mentally blocked out is how steep those fucking terraced house stairs are when you're going down em' head first!

"I got back into scooters mid 90's - talked into it by my brother in law Tony Lound. He was riding around with a club from Barnsley so I went along. I was amazed that yet again we were the younger ones with a few exceptions. Everywhere we went we bumped into the kids from the 80's all trying to relive it, including my cousin Simon and old mate Paul Morton. It was ok for a ride out n' a piss up but (for me) the heyday had gone."

The Mod stylist

Lee Radforth: (Sheffield Mod) "It must have been the six weeks holiday back in '79, a rather pivotal time for more reasons than one as I was 11 years old and about to move from junior school to comprehensive. I'd always been fascinated by music and at the start of the holiday was still mainly into rock and roll, Elvis, Eddie Cochran and Buddy Holly, which was probably a bit odd for an 11 year old at the time but the film Grease had a big impact on me (mainly due to Olivia Newton John) and even then I never really got the current chart music but I did love something in the sound of those 50's records. But all of that was about to change.

"I started to become aware of, and like, records being played on the radio, but at this time was unaware that there was any kind of link between them. Madness, The Specials, The Beat and The Jam all lodging somewhere in my subconscious mind... and then it happened! We'd also just moved house and my parents were skint so couldn't afford to take us on holiday that summer. My grandparents stepped in and rented a caravan in Skegness from someone in the local club and offered to take myself and my brother away for the week. As fate would have it the week they booked was the week of the August bank holiday. Well, off we set, completely oblivious of the impact this journey would have on the rest of my life.

"About forty minutes into the journey something caught my attention, perhaps the glint of sun off chrome, and I looked out of the car window to see a vision that had an effect upon me that I'm not sure anything since has ever quite matched. There must have been over a hundred scooters flying past the queue of traffic that we were stuck in and a sea of parkas and boating blazers speeding past my transfixed eyes. I had no real idea what I was witnessing apart from a vague notion that they were Mods, but I knew from that moment, that that was what I had to be.

"Well the rest of the holiday was spent with me noting what clothes these amazingly cool people were wearing, Sta-Prest trousers, Fred Perrys, button down shirts, knitted square end ties, Gibson shoes, bowling shoes and the music they were listening to, soul, ska, 60's influenced power pop; I was hooked.

"So that September I went up to Aston Comprehensive and everyone there seemed to have been cast under the same spell as myself. Every school disco was a sea of Sta-Prest trousers, Fred Perrys and market crombies with the red lining pulled out of the breast pocket, moon stomping to ska and declaring that this was indeed a *time for action*. Well it was for about a year, and then it was all New Romantic foppery, except for me and a handful of others who truly had been touched by the hand of Mod. Every waking moment now was spent trying to discover more about the greatest youth cult there will ever be (I Know I'm over 40 now but it isn't a youth cult anymore- it really is a way of life encompassing art, design, music, clothes and a distinct mind set.)

"Saturdays over the next few years were spent in Sheffield trawling the amazing second hand shops that existed then - selling original vintage sixties clothes (it seemed like the sixties were a million years ago to me then but it was in fact only around a decade since they had ended – a lifetime though to someone as young as me at the time) and shops like Impulse, Rebina Shoes,

Harry Webb on the Moor market who always had a good stock of bowling shoes, and Hickory Dickory Shock that sold new Mod and Punk gear and in the case of Hickory Dickory Shocks had a fantastic juke box in the actual shop. Special mention in the very early days has to go to Harrington's in Sheffield market though. Sta-Prest of every colour imaginable were available along with, of course Harrington jackets, which at the time I assumed were named after the shop!! (Rodney Harrington of Peyton Place you may spin in your grave). All of these tried on in the attic of the shop which was reached by climbing up a ladder, to emerge to the sight of 30 other Mods and Skinheads in various states of undress. Each one leaving with, along with the Sta-Prest trousers, a roll of free wonder web which was used to turn and stick (with the aid of an iron) the hem to the correct length.

"Back then there was also a fantastic amount of record shops, Bradley's Records (three in the centre of town), HMV, a pre pubescent Virgin Records at the bottom of the Moor so dimly lit that you could barely read the 45 sized cardboard that the record details were scrawled on that had to be taken to the counter to exchange for the real thing, Amazing Records, Kenny's on the Wicker, later Hitsville off Division St, Spin City scarily sited above the market and run by my good friend and font of Soul knowledge Andy, and the legend that was Violet Mays (if I had a time machine that is the place that I would travel back to, the stock that she had would be worth a fortune now).

"The camaraderie of the time is what still makes me look back with such great affection though. Any like minded (dressed) soul you spied would be approached and spoken to, and friendships made. I still have friends from way back then. Everyone was writing or trying to write fanzines and all the record shops had hundreds of them for sale spread around the shop telling of local bands, local scenes, local do's and all the bands you were into would write back (handwritten replies) if you made the effort. I regularly used to write to and get letters back from Eddie Pillar ('Extraordinary Sensations' Fanzine – later the man behind Acid Jazz Records), Ed Ball of The Times (later Alan McGee of Creation Records and discoverer of Oasis) right hand man, Anthony Meynell of Squire... the list is endless.

"But it was also a dangerous time... each sojourn down Fargate took your life into your hands. Skinheads, Flat tops, casuals, Punks, Rockers, this was the era of youth cults and they all seemed to hate Mods. Being rather skinny and only 5 foot 6 ish I've lost count of the amount of times that I was chased or hit during this period but a few occasions spring to mind. Perhaps the most memorable (with a happy ending) was the time I'd ventured into the market to buy a pair of Sta-Prest from Harrington's and foolishly decided to stop off and have a mug of tea and a chip butty in the upstairs cafe (Granelli's if memory serves me right). There was myself, my younger brother and a couple of his friends all bedecked in our finest Mod clobber enjoying our butties when up the stairs walked around ten of the hardest looking Skinheads I had ever had the misfortune to set eyes upon. Well they saw us straight away and didn't bother to go through the formalities of buying anything but came straight across and sat at the next table to us. To say my heart sank would be an understatement, I really thought my life was about to end. Well we sat there for about thirty minutes trying to summon up the courage to get up and walk past them when a saviour appeared at the top of the cafe stairs in the shape of a Parka-clad brick shithouse! The widest person I have seen to this day surveyed the scene and wandered over to our table grinning at the skinheads on the next table. *'Are you alright lads?'* he said to us. I explained that as far as I was concerned we weren't exactly alright, to which he

Ian Page of Secret Affair at the Limit club 1979 – Kristan James Melik

laughed and said *'don't worry'.* He explained that he was on leave from the Navy and liked a spot of bother. With that he produced a metal chain with a padlock on the end from his parka pocket and began to swing it round his head while asking the skinheads on the adjacent table if they cared to step outside! Suffice to say they wanted to go outside and get as far away from this seafaring mad man as their legs would take them. After buying him a full English breakfast and thanking him profusely we too left and headed off to Pond St Bus station as fast as we could.

"I guess the Mod scene at this time was centred around bands, first of all the '79 revival bands spearheaded by The Jam and followed in the rear guard by the criminally under-rated Secret Affair, The Chords, The Purple Hearts and the whole 2-Tone thing. But still being at school I was a bit young to get to see any of them live so I had to make do with my weekly trips to Sheffield on Saturdays to meet up with like-minded souls and once a week trips to Tiffany's in Rotherham for an under eighteens night where the DJ played a fair amount of 60's pop (The Kinks, The Who, The Small Faces), some Northern Soul and Motown and a smattering of revival tunes.

"Over the next few years there would be a number of people from Sheffield and Rotherham that would stay true to the faith and shun the passing fads and fashions and become something of a nucleus to the scene in South Yorkshire. Bell, Steve Parkes, Steve Parlett, Alison, Damian, Janine and Maria, Mutley, Chris Blackburn (not a Mod but he introduced us to American garage and had a fantastic record collection, a dandy sense of dress and plays a mean guitar – he formed and still fronts the legendary British garage band The Mourning After), Roy Mason, Wayne Dearman, Sean Phillips, Nick Parry and a host of others with which many a top night and adventure would be had.

"As the second wave of revival bands hit the scene in the early 80's (The Moment, Makin' Time, The Rage, Small World) there was something of a division in the Mod scene taking place, with those who wanted to watch a live band, and those who were delving more into the movement's roots and starting to collect and want to dance and listen to obscure 60's Soul and Rhythm and

Blues. For the time being an uneasy truce was held and some great nights were had; especially at Rotherham Assembly Rooms with a whole host of bands playing there (the highlight being The Prisoners), a few Londoners venturing up North (Eddie Pillar and Derwent seemed to be there every other month), and a good mix of music being played to a very enthusiastic crowd. Friday nights would be spent at the Woodbourn pub where the City Limits scooter club met or The Hallamshire Hotel on West St for a beer and chat to discuss where to meet up in town the next day. Upstairs at The Hallamshire hosted gigs, with The Moment playing one of the most memorable there. I've never seen the place as packed and I seriously thought the floor below us (the pubs ceiling) was going to collapse- such was the sheer exuberance of the crowd that night. Clint Boon (later to become the Inspiral Carpets main man) hosted some Psych nights there on Sundays and taught Chris the intro to? and the Mysterians '96 Tears' on his Farfisa one night. Wednesdays would be 60's night at The Leadmill with the usual mix of 60's pop, soul and the odd rarer tune, I seem to recall Wynder K Frog's version of 'Green Door' being a fave at the time. There was also the annual Mojo reunion night with Peter Stringfellow returning to his home town (somewhat ironic ,as it was at The Leadmill which in the 60's had been The Esquire- his biggest rival): Memorable, also, because there was always a free bar courtesy of Peter for about 30 minutes.

"Talking of Chris, my abiding memory of him round about this time involved a scooter club/Northern Soul night at The Staniforth Arms in Attercliffe. It had been a pretty good night when everyone set off home, around 30-40 scooters heading off into the night when what seemed like an army of casuals came running out of the shadows

swinging chains and knocking people off their scooters. Chris resplendent in Cuban heeled Chelsea boots, and a beautiful Paisley shirt running frantically down Staniforth Road with a piss pot helmet the wrong way round on his head, Stella bottles raining down on him trying desperately to catch up Nigel Owen who was riding the Vespa Chris had been thrown from.

"By around 1986 we'd decided that Sheffield needed a regular Mod night so off Bell went and located the best venue that money could buy! The upstairs function room of The Queens Head, Attercliffe, and the weekly club night, Upstairs at The Attic was born. Every week it was packed (well around 20 of us) and occasionally a group of gypsies trying to nick the measly takings or cadge a beer off you. It might not have been The Scene Club or The Mojo but we were a serious hardcore Modernist crowd all extremely competitive on the clothes and record collecting front. Hats off to Nick Parry and Sean Phillips who always managed to unearth some great sounds and played the sort of late 50's and early 60's Rn'B' that would later become a staple of Manchester's legendary Hideaway club. Trousers and suits were now all tailor-made (Colin Starsmore or Barney Goodman in the main for the Sheffield Mods, Keith Mallinson or George for the Rotherham lot) and the music policy was now a strict diet of Soul, Rhythm and Blues, Ska and 60's Beat.

"It was round this time that we all started going to do's further afield and forging friendships all around the country. The CCI Mod rallies at coastal resorts like Scarborough, Blackpool and Great

Yarmouth were attracting huge crowds of Mods from all four corners of Britain and myself, Steve Parlett and Carney found ourselves heading off in my mini most Friday nights for a weekend of Modernist hedonism. Well, all night dancing, drinking, and sleeping three to a mini unless some kind soul would let you crash at theirs, which more times than not they would.

"Trips to Coventry for The Hip Citizen nights at The Polish club, Mansfield for The Athenian all-dayers with Speed and Ivan, all-nighters in Peterborough, Loughborough, Derby (at a fantastic club full of Rasta's and old boy Jamaicans downstairs smoking weed and a packed upstairs full of Mods), monthly trips to Leeds and Manchester to meet up with Ralston (travelling down from Blackpool), Steve Millington (Lord Dunsby) who is now living in Sheffield (and like loads of people from then still into the scene), Si and Steve and regular sojourns over to Stoke where Mace (still dealing in records) would put do's on. I'm certain I couldn't stand the pace now and even then almost nodded off on occasion whilst driving back the next day, oh the folly of youth. The whole scene round this period was buzzing with some fantastic DJ's (Paul Hallam and Dom Bassett in particular) spinning some great tunes ('Shmon' – Mr Dynamite, 'The Pain Just Gets a little Deeper' - Darrow Fletcher, 'Black Cat' - Brian Auger, 'Stomach Ache' - Jnr Wells, '98 Cents Plus Tax' - Detroit City Limits to name but a few) and matters sartorial going into overdrive. It was commonplace for people to take 2/3 tailored suits to a nighter and remiss to wear the same outfit all night.

"Now while I said seeing bands had somewhat fallen out of favour by now there was an exception to the rule, The James Taylor Quartet. Formed by the ex Prisoners Hammond maestro they captured the mood of the time perfectly playing instrumental covers of 60's theme tunes and were hugely popular. Myself, Steve and Carney made the journey down to London for the launch of their debut LP.

"Not long after this my best buddy Steve Parlett went off to study at Salford University and we branched off (as did many others) into (as it later became named but wasn't then) the Acid Jazz scene. More and more danceable jazz and Latin tunes had started being played and certain individuals started changing their dress. Trouser waists started getting higher, pleats and turn ups appeared, as did braces, blazers and (God forbid) hair gel. To some of us it seemed a natural progression of the Mod aesthetic; to others it was heresy.

"Weekends now were spent in Manchester at Ganders go South and Band on the Wall to watch the like of The Tommy Chase Quartet or The Jazz Renegades (Paul Weller's new young drummer Steve White's project), and the occasional foray to Camden for the Dingwalls Jazz alldayers, a Style Council inspired trip to Paris, and I (along with my now brother in law, and Sheffield musical legend Richard Hawley) was about to start a regular club at The Leadmill. Goatees grown, Vout oroonie was born. Named after the hipster slang of Slim Gaillard, we played Hammond grooves, late 60's and early 70's funk, Latin, and Jazz of the Blue Note and prestige variety. We also brought some top live acts to the city, Big John Patten, Jimmy McGriff, and an embryonic Brand New Heavies among many others. The night lasted just over two years, got reviewed in the NME, voted in the top ten club nights ever at The Leadmill and its flyers (courtesy of Designers Republic) got featured in a design book and exhibited at an art show in Japan. We also DJ'd in the chill out room at a house night at Mona Lisa's in Charter Square who had some of the country's top dance DJ's of the time- some of whom used to pop upstairs and sit in the sound booth with us between sets talking music, a lot of them were really into rare 60's Soul and Jazz.

"It was around this time that I started getting into bands again with the likes of The Charlatans (featuring ex Makin' Time bassist Martin Blunt), The Stone Roses, The Inspiral Carpets, The Happy Mondays, Galliano and The Young Disciples being particular favourites. The early 90's also saw Paul Weller re-enter my life as he tried to kick-start his career, after being dropped by Polydor, by playing low-key gigs watched by only a couple of hundred people at most. It was an exciting time watching him slowly regain his confidence and forge a new direction that would eventually see him become the most successful and gifted songwriter of his generation. He's also now really good mates with my old DJ partner in crime Richard Hawley and even got on stage with Rich to sing one of his songs 'Just like the Rain' at a festival in Spain, now if you'd told me that 20 years ago I'd have thought you were mad.

"By now I'd dropped out of the Mod Scene and only attended the occasional rally, but still considered myself a Mod and most of my mates were into the same music and clothes as myself. Saturday nights were spent in The Washington pub with Mick Marston (a renowned Graphic Designer) and Tim McCall (Jarvis Cocker's guitarist – who sadly passed away in 2010) talking football, music and matters sartorial.

"By early 2000 the kernel of a new Sheffield scene began to take shape revolving around that legendary Sheffield boozer The Washington. A monthly night called Moke had been started by Darren Williamson and Graham Wright playing rare sixties Soul, Rn'B, British beat, ska and a smattering of American 60's garage. It acted as something of a magnet for forty-something Sheffield Modernists and after a while myself and wife Rebecca, Mick Marston and Liz, Nick and Rachel Pearson, Darren and Dot and Graham were heading off to Manchester's Hideaway club, rallies in Scarborough and Skegness, and nights in Leeds with old friend Nick Brady who like myself had been around the scene since the early eighties (in fact I regularly kipped on his Dad's floor, along with about 20 others, after nights out in Leeds in the mid 80's.)

"So what of now? Well I'm still obsessed with the whole Mod philosophy. Still wearing only bespoke suits and trousers made by 'now good friend' Colin Starsmore, still buying vinyl records, riding (when the weathers good!) a 1965 Lambretta and living for music both live and recorded: Which brings me back to where we began. The scene at present is dominated by late 50's early 60's Rn'B which crosses over with the Rocking scene and indeed a good many people from that scene can now be found at Mod nights, and vice versa. So perhaps my early love of Rock and Roll was not that misplaced after all, it is after all only white boys playing Rn'B with a hint of country. I've even had something of a reliving of my youth this last 18 months having been to see Secret Affair and The Purple Hearts in London and Manchester with Mani of The Stone Roses and Primal Scream getting up on stage with The Purple Hearts, and Squire up in Liverpool with my brother Mark who slowly but surely is returning to his Mod roots!. My best friends are all cut from the same cloth and share the same passions, so to paraphrase Weller 'You'll bury me a Mod!'"

Another Way – The Mod musicians!

Terry Sutton: (Mexborough Mod) "My first experience of anything 'Mod-related' was probably listening to 'The Story of The Who' on the '8-track' in my Dad's Volvo on the way to a holiday in Skegness. I was pretty much obsessed from that day. Not just the music but the clothes, hair, drugs and girls.This became heightened after reading the Quadrophenia tie-in book when I was in the fourth-year at Junior school. I wanted to try those Purple Hearts and Black Bombers NOW.! I couldn't wait to grow up a bit and get shagging/dancing/riding a scooter - just like any good Mod. Now I'm completely the opposite. I hate 'codes' and 'trends' and 'scenes'."

Left: Terry and a Mod icon!

Ian Deakin: (Mexborough Mod) "I didn't have anything that could be described as 'Mod' before meeting Tony Beesley and John Harrison. I was well aware of all the bands involved in the Post-Punk Mod scene, and their records, but always found myself drifting towards Punk (I include The Jam in this as I always thought of them as a Punk outfit). The first piece of Mod clothing I bought was when Tony was ordering something from Cavern and asked if I would like to take the hint and buy something to fit in a bit more. I could tell he was serious about our dress code as a band. When Terry came along he fitted right in as he already had the complete Mod wardrobe."

Terry Sutton: "Yes. I'd go down with my mates on the bus to London after saving for ages and just go mad at Cavern/Shellys. The intention was always to look good in the Youth Club disco or (when it was open) The Empress in Mexborough. It could be quite hazardous going in the Mod get-up though. I once got crowbarred by a gang of skinheads coming out of The Trinity in Wath-Upon-Dearne and another time on The Moor in Sheffield. That time, a few of them chased me into a shop and the merchandise was flying everywhere. I HATED Skinheads. You know, the neo-Nazi kind, a bit like Tim Roth in 'Made In Britain'. Around this time (the end of 83) I'd formed my first proper band doing original songs, 'The Way' (Mk I), with my friends Dick and Johnny. We were a true 'garageband' and loads of our schoolmates would come to have a gander. As a musician, I have an orchestral background having played double bass from the age of seven, so I always found the shouting and lack of finesse in our little band pretty grating. I was the only proper musician among them and you could tell. It wasn't long before I was looking for some new bandmates."

Ian Deakin: "We had a mutual Mod friend, Mark Ely, and one day he told me that Terry Sutton was asking about whether we need a bass player. I knew of him because my dad was caretaker at the school near Tel's house and my dad would always be chasing him off the grounds for taking a short cut. Anyway, I told Mark that we needed a singer/guitarist and luckily Tel had been practising guitar for about six months and, best of all, his dad had bought him a Rickenbacker for his birthday. Essential for our Mod image!"

Terry Sutton: "Mark arranged a meeting at Ian's house and right from the start we got on famously. He's just very funny. An eternal optimist. Sadly, Mark Ely passed away from meningitis within a year of me joining. Without him, 'The Way', and the tale we're telling now, probably wouldn't have existed. His death became a big driving force for me personally. The Clifton Hall gig we did was great. I've never forgotten walking through the Mods afterwards and thinking to myself, '*I aaam onea da Faces!*'. But Scarborough was special. I'll never forget it. No amount of money can bring you the feeling that an audience is possibly enjoying your performance."

The Way quickly attracted a local Mod following and for a while that Spring, everything seemed to be taking shape.

Ian Deakin: "Within a few months the demos were garnering good reviews in some of the Mod fanzines and the gigs just seemed to get better and better till it all peaked at the Scarborough Scooter Rally in June 1985."

Ian Deakin: "The reality was - that gig was such a high that the following gig at the Mexborough Civic was akin to entering Dante's Ninth Circle of Hell. Great fun though, watching Tony and

John storming off the stage mid-song, whilst I played along to the DJ who had struck up 'Material Girl' after John had exclaimed, at utmost lung capacity, '*Maybe you'd rather listen to WHAM or some fucking SHIT LIKE THAT!!! YOU'RE JUST A SET OF FUCKING WANKERS!*"

Terry Sutton: "I couldn't show my face in school the next day. Someone spat on the back of my parka. This is what one might refer to as 'the down side of being in a band'. The following Friday I watched a compilation of The Tube on CH4. On it there was a performance by The Redskins ('Keep On Keepin' On') and, immediately, I knew where I was going, musically, next. Something harder, overtly political (the Miners' Strike had affected me deeply), looser than the Mod-R'n'B four-piece format we currently had. We soldiered on through those last months of '85 with a Live Aid-style gig in Rotherham and a final performance at the Arts Centre but it was obvious we were about to split. Tony and John arranged a meeting at which Ian and I were told they wanted to leave (and when you're 16 you don't argue with 20/22year olds). And then I realised, like I was shot, like I was shot with a diamond - I might end up stranded, so sure was I that they'd ask Ian to stay. Which they did. And when Ian said, *'No, I'm staying with Terry'*, I was so elated. It was time for a new start and, as anyone who knows me will tell you, I relish 'the new'. We've been recording together twenty-five years now. I don't think we'll ever run out of ideas and I know we both enjoy the thrill of hearing a track coming together. THAT'S what being a Mod was about to me. The future. Revision. Ian and I were listening to Big Audio Dynamite's first album all the time and we wanted a more modern sound. Conversely, I was really sad about Tony's departure at the time, and the nature of it, because I really looked up to Tony. He'd turned me on to a lot of music in that short time and taught me a lot about attitude and principles. He'd seen Punk first hand and here was I, only just discovering the thrill and direct hit of the first Clash LP."

Above left: Terry in reflective mood and at right, the new line up of 1986

Below: Ian Deakin, Terry Sutton and John Harrison (Johnny Ache)

Ian Deakin: "However, we couldn't find a bassist. Revolver's Russ Weaver lasted a week I think. Terry had a huge party for his 17th birthday and I came along with the soon-to-be re-christened 'Johnny Ache'. We asked how things were going with Tony's project and he said it *'doesn't seem to be happening'*. Well, at that moment we pounced and asked Johnny to come back and rehearse. Tel bought a brand new H+H bass amp from 'Keyboards Plus' to entice him back I think."

Terry Sutton: "This is when we started rehearsing in the attic my dad had kitted out for us to use. We're still using the same space to record drums on our new album and it's seen many-a-famous Z-list musician pass through that hallowed trapdoor. Following The Jam and Redskins lead, I decided it was essential to have a brass section so I asked my classmate, Andy Probert, if he fancied having a blow. Cough! A few months later we had a pretty decent three piece section and it enabled us to add a few soul covers to the set (e.g. Move On Up) though I was still trying to hone my songwriting chops. The worst part was having to teach Johnny the basslines note-by-note. It just seemed to take forever bless 'im.

"By a curious twist of fate my double bass teacher (a one Mr.Lawrence Gray, the biggest musical inspiration in MY life) asked me to phone a pupil of his who was 'extremely talented' but lacked the motivation to play double bass, preferring bass guitar instead. Why? I don't know. What was I meant to say? Give up bass guitar! Anyway, I called this kid called Jonathan White and got chatting. Strangely, he was well aware of The Way and had heard our most recent demo tape that was doing the rounds amongst the brass section of the Doncaster Youth Jazz Orchestra, to whom we had gone for saxophonists. He said he liked our stuff and did we need a bassist...? Well, I told him that Johnny was our bassist and that if anything came up I'd give him a call. Suffice to say, after our Christmas '86 gig at Rotters in Doncaster, Johnny decided he'd had enough and departed by shoving a letter into my hand and running off into the distance. He'd quit. I've only seen him twice since. I've got many fond memories of Johnny. We had a great holiday together on the Norfolk Broads that summer and I always missed his dry sense of humour."

The Way with Brass section and minus John Harrison (replaced by Jonathan White – far right)

Ian Deakin: "Me too, though I've seen him around Rotherham many times as I still live in the town centre. For years I had a few tapes of me, Tel and John when they stayed over at my Mum's house for the weekend. Just us talking and fucking around. I wish I still had them because it showed just how close we were at one time. By the way, I remember the last Mod-themed gig was at the Rotherham Assembly Rooms with 'The Moment'. You could tell that scene was on its arse by then."

The Mod years were now behind The Way, but a new journey, away from that starting point, was soon to begin! (More accounts of The Way's Mod years are included in 'Our Generation' Volume 1)

The Way photos courtesy of Terry Sutton

The Modette

The Mod scene was always very male orientated- from its early Jazz beginnings, the original stylists and Dandies of the pre-swinging sixties London scene and onwards through the Hard Mods of 64 to the 1979 revival and beyond: The zest for the right clothes – perfect to every inch of detail, short and neat haircuts, sportsman-like competitiveness and extreme detail in every aspect of a Mod's life was something unforgivably attractive and obsessive that it was almost perfectly designed for any prospective individual male wanting to aspire to be the best, the coolest and the most respected face around town. True the classic male Mod was not your average 'ton up boy' heading straight for the boozer with his self interests merely stretching as far as the next pint, girl or win at the horses: he was and is something much more refined and articulate than that... and was/is vain, self-respecting, intuitive and very focused. He is an ever-changing anachronism, impossible to pin down and stands high above his peers... the ultimate icon of male cool!

The first Mod girls wanted to look like their male Mod mates. They wanted to emulate their French crop hair cuts and boyish looks along with their Italian-knitted polo tops, two-tone jackets and

Peyton place Harringtons. They followed the boys; they hung around with them, copied them and fell in love with the Mod look, borrowing their ever evolving enthusiasm for Rhythm and Blues, Blue Beat and the new Soul sounds from the USA. In time though, they would come to gradually prepare and create their own style and identity... being as much influenced by Cathy McGowan, Diana Rigg, Mary Quant and Jean Shrimpton as they were as intoxicated with the sounds and stylings of classic Mod. As the sixties and the Mod look progressed a classic Mod girl look also evolved: one that is forever identified as the look of the swinging sixties fashion girl, but in truth was in itself almost just as detailed, pre-meditated and articulate as the male counterpart.

When the Post-Punk era Modernist revival came to the City of Sheffield during the late 1970's, the original Mod era was something that could be borrowed from at any stage of its development... hence its many hybrids of styles and spin off looks. Sheffield Mod girl Heather Quinn began her Mod story in exactly the same way as many of her 1960's Mod girl relations would have done. It would not take long, though, for Heather to strike out and soak up the very best of Mod clothes, music and culture from all of its incarnations and whilst doing so live a true Mod obsessive's life.

Photo: Courtesy of Heather Quinn

Heather Quinn: (Sheffield Modette) "It started around '79 when I was listening to the likes of the Specials, Madness, the Beat and other 2-Tone bands, plus Mod revival stuff. From that, I started to become interested in the roots of this music. I discovered a market stall in Sheffield City Centre which sold second-hand 45s. I remember flicking through hundreds of singles, reading the name of the artist and song, seeing if I recognised anything, but with the exception of famous names like the Beatles, most of the time I had absolutely no idea what I was looking at. My rule of thumb was if the name sounded cool, then I bought it - and of course if it had a picture-sleeve, all the better!

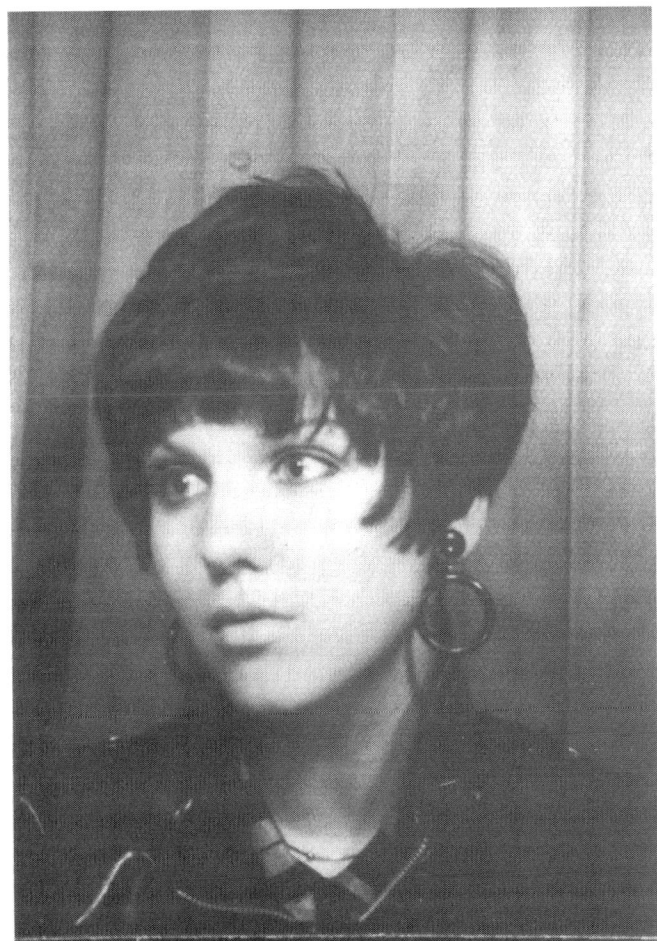

"My record collection started with the Hollies, Moody Blues, Amen Corner and the Animals etc. I think I have my mum to thank for suggesting I try listening to the Who, Kinks and Small Faces. Around this time, I came across Violet May's record shop on Matilda Street. I remember the first time I went in; it was wall to wall records. I was very nervous; everyone in the shop seemed much older and looked like they knew what they were looking for.

"There was a guy behind the counter and I asked him if he had any Small Faces records. I seem to remember him getting down a long, heavy wooden box full of 45s. He pulled out one of the singles and it was an original Small Faces' 'Hey Girl' on Decca. It cost £1.35. 'Hey Girl' isn't necessarily one of the Small Faces best songs; it's typically commercial for the times. I thought it was good, but it was Marriott's vocals which caught my attention. I played the 'B' side instrumental, 'Almost Grown' - now I *really* liked this. I had to hear more. I took a trip to Bradley's Records and bought a Small Faces Greatest Hits LP. There was a branch of Bradley's on Fargate, and also one on Chapel Walk. I later bought a copy of the Who's 'Meaty Beaty Big and Bouncy', together with a Kinks Greatest Hits LP. I loved (and still do) all three bands, but Steve Marriott will always be my personal favourite.

"I just couldn't buy records fast enough. Every penny I saved went on music - records, posters, magazines. I discovered Record Collector magazine and from that discovered record fairs. I was fuelling my addiction by reading up on anything and everything about records - labels; 45s, EPs, LPs; foreign pressings... and the *pièce de résistance*, I discovered Small Faces French EPs, which came complete with picture sleeves. The first French EP I bought was 'All or Nothing' and it cost £12, which was an arm and a leg in those days. The picture-sleeve was superb; the Small Faces looked immaculate. The EP was especially expensive considering I had managed to get hold of a copy of an original Small Faces Decca LP for a fiver! It's difficult to choose a favourite track from that album, but I think it would possibly be 'You Need Loving'. Marriott's vocals on the LP are just so raw and brilliant.

"As well as being into 60s British bands, I was also listening to lots of 60s Soul, Motown, Stax, Blues, and original Ska and Reggae. I couldn't really pick a favourite artist, I just loved it all. I became a regular punter at record fairs. In Sheffield, I would still go to what was Violet May's, plus Windmill Records in the Wicker, where I remember I found a mint copy of The Who's 'My Generation' single. Amazing Records opened up on Cambridge Street - they also had a shop in Leeds. The ace Mod who worked in there really knew his stuff and used to recommend excellent records.

"For new records I loved Virgin, when it was just a pokey little shop at the bottom of the Moor. Inside was so dark and cramped, especially on a Saturday when it was packed full of music lovers of all kinds. I used to hassle the staff to let me have used cardboard shop displays. I'm sure they must have been really sick of me. When the Jam split, Virgin had an impressive wall display of Jam singles from Japan, plus the entire re-released UK back-catalogue. Heaven!

"Without consciously setting out to become a mod, I had started to dress like the bands I was listening to. At first I was quite masculine in my tastes - short hair with a Stevie Marriott centre parting; button-down collar shirts - possibly Paisley, or spots (I used to buy these by mail order from Melandi's of Carnaby Street.

"I bought a fish-tail parka with the regulation fur on the hood and a cringingly embarrassing Small Faces logo painted on the back. I had a green and navy boating blazer which I bought from a 'Mod' stall in Leeds market. My shoes were usually from Rebina's, which had a shop just off High Street, Sheffield and a stall in Sheffield's Castle Market. I managed to get hold of a pair of black and white Jam shoes which were made for girls. I was so proud of them and wore them until they fell to pieces.

Above: Ian Page of Secret Affair at the Limit 1979 (Kristan James Melik) Paul Weller sound-checking at Sheffield Top Rank March 1982 (Pete Skidmore)

"I remember going with a couple of other girls from school to see Secret Affair at Sheffield City Hall. We all wore a uniform of trousers, braces and Fred Perry polo shirts - mine was black with yellow tipped collar. We thought we looked like Terry Hall and were *the* business.

"As well as seeing Secret Affair, I remember going to see Madness at Sheffield City Hall which was a fantastic gig - in the days before health & safety, stage barriers or a pit. I went with a group of school friends and was right at the front; being pushed so much from the crowd behind that the next day I had ribs that were black and blue. I didn't care though – I was still in heaven re-living Chas reaching out to hold my hand. I also saw the Kinks at the Lyceum and the Truth at the Limit.

And, of course, there was the Jam who played two nights at Sheffield Top Rank. I went with my friend Penny and we were lucky enough to be able to go both nights. I remember wearing a navy and white boating blazer, a shirt, a red mini-skirt and matching red shoes. It was at the stage where I was wearing my hair like Marriott's and I truly believed I looked liked him too!

**Madness at the City Hall in 1981 and below
The Truth at the Limit club (by Heather Quinn)**

"As the obsession for records continued, so did the clothes. My style of dress became more extreme. I dressed less like a guy. As I started to find a style of my own I grew my hair and had it styled in a typical, Sassoon inverted bob, with two V shapes cut into the neckline at the back. In those days, charity shops and jumble sales were brilliant for finding original label clothes. In one charity shop in town, I found a virtually unworn black and white, op-art Mac. I still have it, but am far too old to get away with wearing it today!

"Somehow I managed to convince my parents that it was okay for me to go down to London on my own. I don't think I'd even left school at this stage. Naturally, I had to visit Carnaby Street, which had various shops coining in on the Mod revival. There used to be an indoor market up above the shops; many of the stalls sold original 60s/Mod related clothes. London was full of 'alternative' shops, plus fantastic markets like Portobello Road. Second-hand record shops were also in abundance. I discovered a fantastic shop which sold 60s magazines like Rave, Fab208, Vogue etc.

"I found buying new clothes quite difficult in Sheffield. Sometimes you could find nice items which looked ok, but mostly it was typical 80's fashions with big shoulder pads and ruffles. X Clothes in town was good. It was mainly Punky, but at least it wasn't mainstream. What I couldn't buy in clothes, I used to try to make. I would trawl through the 60s mags I'd bought and try to recreate the fashions. I was not too bad at dress making and even turned my hand to making accessories such as bags and jewellery. From trying to be Steve Marriott, I was now morphing into Mary Quant.

The Truth supporting the Kinks at Sheffield Lyceum Dec 17th 1982 (Heather Quinn)

"I never had a particular club night that I went to - sometimes I'd go to the Leadmill and the Limit, but as I was still at school it was not always easy getting out to places. As the '80s progressed, the mod revival waned; the Jam were no more and there seemed to be less and less good bands around to go and see. Around '83/84, Steve Marriott with his delicately named band "Packet of Three", were playing the pub circuit around London. I managed to go down and see him play in Camden Lock.

"I wasn't sure what to expect from the night. Everyone hung around at the bar waiting for the gig to start. The audience was a mixed bunch. Ages ranged from teenage mods to 40 something's. Marriott walked through the main door just as if he was a regular punter. He was much more petite than I had imagined - he had gained quite a few pounds, but his frame was still slender. His

hair was short and spiky on top, with a dreadful mullet at the back. Although he didn't look at all the 'star' he used to be; he still had that *something* which set him apart from us mere mortals. As he walked through the place, people parted like a wave to let him through. Everyone was straining to get a look in, as he headed backstage.

"When Marriott and the band first came on stage, they could have been any other pub band, but when Marriott started to play his guitar and sing, my God it was incredible. How could a voice like that come from someone so slight? He belted his way through old standards like 'Five Long Years' and 'I Don't Need No Doctor'. Quite a few people at the front of the audience shouted for Small Faces stuff, which Marriott refused to play. He didn't appear best pleased at the chants and shouted back, *'I'm no fucking juke box, y'know!'*

"After the gig, Marriott came out into the pub for a drink. He mingled with everyone and had all the time in the world for fans. I was really nervous about talking to him, but eventually braved it and approached him. Being born and bred in Sheffield, it was obvious that I wasn't local and Marriott asked me where I was from. I explained how I'd come down from Sheffield. He appeared quite touched. He told me how he had an affection for Sheffield - something which I never expected him to say in a million years!

"Back around '65, when the Small Faces were first starting out, they were packed off 'up North' to Sheffield - I think to appear at the (famous) Mojo Club. Steve told me how dreadful the journey was and how - when they arrived in Sheffield - everything just went horribly wrong, including the band having nowhere to sleep that night. He said that some 'old girl' offered them her spare room for the night, gave them some warm food and so saved the day. He said he would always remember her generosity at taking in four unknown, young men into her home. Steve was so down to earth, no rock star behaviour. He seemed genuinely pleased how well the audience had received him and how everyone wanted to talk to him afterwards. A good night was had by all and I returned home to Sheffield the next day.

"Whenever I had the chance, I would follow Steve and the band from gig to gig. I have watched him play live so many times I've lost track. Even my honeymoon was spent in London and revolved around going from gig to gig. (My other half, by the way, is extremely tolerant, plus it helps that he is also into all things Mod.) Marriott's band went through various line-up and name changes over the years - Packet of Three; DT's; Official Receivers and the Next Band.

"In the late 80's I saw an ad in The Star newspaper that Steve was appearing at The Pheasant pub, Sheffield Lane Top. This was unbelievable. Maybe he really did have affection for Sheffield? This was one of his many appearances at The Pheasant. Marriott also played Cubley Hall, in Penistone and the Jug, in Doncaster.

"The time we went to the Jug, we had to catch the train from Sheffield to Doncaster and then rely on the last train to get us back home. Going in the Jug was one of those scary moments where the place was full of bikers, heavy-metal fans and aging Hell's Angels... and in the middle was us two mods, looking completely out of place. At the bar, there were crates of Newcastle Brown being served by the bottle and the crate - bottle caps left on. Me being a bit naïve wondered how I was meant to open the cap. The bikers standing next to me soon showed me how - with your teeth! I felt really uncomfortable being there and wondered what the rest of the night was going to be like. There was no trouble by anyone and actually, the others in the pub were really friendly. When Marriott came on with his band, he looked better than before. He had lost weight, looked healthier, dressed better and had got rid of the mullet hair. He sang his lungs out that night. I think he must have been on stage about two hours.

"The pub was packed and the audience knew every word to every song. They shouted, cheered, and treated Marriott like a god. The adulation was incredible; the most I'd seen at any Marriott gig. At the end, Marriott left the stage and walked through the crowd. It was a strange sight to see this diminutive idol being patted on the back and congratulated by fans twice his size. Marriott, as always, appeared genuinely touched by the thanks."

Like all fellow Mods, the tragic and unsuspecting news that arrived in the spring of 1991 really hit hard for Heather and the author included!

Tony Beesley: "Steve was booked and due to play the local working men's club literally just around the corner from my house a week or two after he died. I was gutted. I had been a great fan of Steve for some time and was really looking forward to seeing him, and maybe even meeting him. What a truly tragic loss."

Heather Quinn: "It was late morning on 20 April 1991 and I remember having the radio on in the background when it was announced that Steve had died in a fire at his home. It didn't seem real and I was heartbroken. I still love the Small Faces. It's sad now that both Steve and Ronnie [Lane] have gone. On the brighter side, it's wonderful that Mac (Ian McLagan) is still touring with the Bump Band. He occasionally tours the UK, even though he lives in Austin, Texas. I have seen him a couple of times at the Boardwalk - the first time in 2004 and then in 2008. Both gigs were laid back affairs."

Ian Mclagan Sheffield Boardwalk 2008 (Heather Quinn)

"The songs played were a mix of everything, spanning over 40 years. My particular favourites were tracks from Mac's tribute album to Ronnie – 'Spiritual Boy' and also some from his 'Never Say Never' album. Ian's voice has grown more like Rod Stewart's over the years. His keyboard playing is second to none and he still uses the same Hammond organ from years ago - with that huge, funny old Leslie speaker - the sound is just superb. Mac likes to give out plenty of banter during a gig. He has a great sense of humour, tells a good story and gives each song that personal touch. At both gigs, he talked about Steve with fondness and in particular Ronnie, who he was obviously very close to. After both gigs, Mac came out to talk to fans and to sign merchandise. He was willing to talk to everyone and was very generous with his time. It would be great to see him again in Sheffield.

"In recent times, I love many of the bands to come out of Sheffield. My favourites being Arctic Monkeys and Reverend and the Makers, together with (RIP) The Harrisons and Milburn. I like their energy, enthusiasm and attitude and many, just like Brit pop bands, cite their influences in Mod and Punk bands gone by. Ironically, I also like The Violet May - a great up-and-coming band who have taken their name from the infamous record shop of all those years ago!"

The much loved and admired Mod favourite Steve Marriott at various venues including Sheffield 84 – 89 (Heather Quinn)

Above: Mod legend and former Small Face Ian Mclagen with Heather Quinn at Sheffield Boardwalk 2008

The Mod photographer!

The Mod scene, be it nationwide or local has always been a very visual phenomenon: and Mods have always loved that element; hence the great emphasis on clothes (down to the very last detail), the neatness and clean look as well as its iconography – Pop Art influences included along with the Mod accessory – the scooter. The need to document this visual side of things was something that Barnsley Mod girl Louise Mckenning aimed to do. Luckily with more than a passing interest in the art of photography already at her disposal, Louise managed to capture numerous Mod rallies she attended during the 1980's, the results of some of which are displayed within these pages. Before the photos, though, and not surprisingly, came the love of Mod music.

Louise Mckenning: (Barnsley Mod girl) "I already had some early influences of photography from my Dad: I would watch him take pictures of my Mother and us with his Pracktica camera, pacing up and down, getting the settings just right with his light metre. I also loved album covers, especially the early Elvis ones. The combination of the pictures, with the typography and graphics influenced my choice in career, when I became a graphic designer years later. I was gutted when the CD replaced vinyl albums and the artwork was no longer as tactile and fun to collect.

"At Barnsley Art College, I was introduced to early black and white cinematography from the 1920's and 30's. The images from the silent movie Pandora's box (1929) starring Louise Brooks (whose hairstyle I later copied) the first Dracula film, Nosferatu (1922) and Battleship Potemkin (1925). At college, I also had access to a darkroom. The process of taking the photos and actually developing the negatives and seeing your images appearing in front of you under the red light is magical. Around that time, I also discovered Eve Arnold. She was an American photographer who took many iconic pictures of the 60's including people such as Marilyn Monroe and Malcolm X. An American photographer and photojournalist called Arthur Fellig, but better known as Weegee, was a massive influence too. His stark black and white photography depicted realistic scenes from the streets of New York from the 30's: My favourite photograph of his being 'The Bathers at Coney Island'.

"When I left Art College, I got a job as a paste-up artist with a magazine publisher in London, where I loved watching the airbrush artists weave their magic over the wonky eyes and wrinkles on photographs of models and the famous people of the 1980's. Later, with the advent of computers I went on to do the same, but with my photographic computer packages.

"In the early days of my photographic addiction, I used a disk camera. It was easy to transport, but produced dreadful grainy pictures due to the tiny negatives. So my parents bought me a Pracktica camera, which was my pride and joy. It produced fantastic quality pictures but was really big and heavy. I used to sit pillion, travelling on scooters to Mod rallies with it hanging round my neck like a lead weight, worried sick that I would drop it."

Louise's early connections with music gave only a small clue as to where her future tastes would emerge.

Louise Mckenning: "Apart from the odd big band track and a smattering of Elvis and Nat King Cole, my parents record collection and musical taste left much to be desired: I had to endure 'Sing Something Simple' by the Adams singers, whilst my pleas to listen to the Sunday charts run down usually fell upon deaf ears! I can credit my Dad with turning me on to Elvis though, which was a start! This sad life continued until I was 11, when I started Wombwell High school. My friend's big brother and his mates were Mods and certainly stood out from the crowd. I watched the film 'Quadrophenia' with them and I was absolutely blown away by it all. The clothes, the music and the lifestyle; just everything about it all made a massive impact on me.

"Through my new Mod friends, I then discovered The Jam, Selecter, the Specials and Madness: The 'One step beyond' album by Madness led me down the path to discover Prince Buster and the original ska sounds. The school Disco and Rebecca's under18's Disco in Barnsley were the places to be at the time. My clothes mostly came from checking out Barnsley second hand market, charity shops and Rebina shoe shop in Sheffield... etc etc.

"Most Saturdays were spent trawling round the charity shops for clothes, followed by a visit to Casa Disco or the record stall upstairs in the market at Barnsley where I loved to spend my hard earned money on anything that caught my eye or should I say ear. 2-Tone was my first choice, followed by random purchases of 1960's stuff that I'd never heard of and which I usually got rid of after a while. Then there was the occasional visit to London and my favourite record shop, 'Out on the Floor', just across from the tube station in Camden. I could spend hours there looking at all the Ska, Rock Steady and Blue Beat imports on the Studio 1 and Trojan labels. Clancy Eccles was one of my favourites along with Alton Ellis, The Maytals and The Wailers.

"Camden used to be heaven for clothes shopping too. Down on the market you could pick up some fantastic stuff at reasonable prices, unlike today with the ridiculously inflated prices for the Japanese tourists! One of the stalls I visited on a regular basis had a massive selection of original Levi Sta-Prest trousers and big 'E' Levi jeans that I had an obsession for, as well as Fred Perry tops and checked shirts with Button Down collars. All these things I wore, with my favourite shoes, Bass Weejun penny loafers: The best dancing shoes in the world and only recently replaced in favour, by a pair of Jeffery West brogues. Leather soles were a must for my soul stomping...because I love to dance. I remember one time at a soul do, a friend brought in a bag of white powder he said he had purchased from the chemist. We sat there with raised eyebrows while he enthused about how fantastic this stuff was, only to burst out laughing as he sprinkled it on the dance floor. No idea what it was, but it certainly wasn't talc and boy did it make the floor slippy! Bloody hell! None of us could stand up straight and we stood there on the dance floor holding each other up, crying with laughter and unable to move. It was like standing on ice. Dance...we couldn't even walk!

"Eventually, most of the Mods I knew moved on to the next fashion trend – Casuals, trendies, Pringle Boys or whatever you

City Limits
Present
"FOR A FEW PENNIES MORE!"

AT
ASSEMBLY ROOMS
Effingham St., Rotherham
ON
NOVEMBER 14th
7:30 - 12

Latin, Soul,
Jazz & R'n'B

DJs - DOM, DAMIAN,
JON KELLY, RALSTON
+ GUESTS

Tickets £2·00
(£2·50 on the door)
Please make cheques
payable to:-
City Limits
101 Cemetery Road
Sheffield
S. Yorks.

Hip Dress Essential

want to call them; but I carried
on as I was, getting deeper into Mod culture. After leaving school, I started Barnsley Art College and also got a Saturday job. The job gave me the freedom to get to mod dos all over the area: places like The Queens Head and the Ska night at the Take Two in Attercliffe and the Assembly Rooms in Rotherham. Around this time, I also got my first car – a lovely aqua Mini 1000. My wheels gave me the freedom to get to do's all over the area and I soon became the required means of transport for my mates all to come along. As well as these Mod nights, I would also see local bands like The Gents, who at the time were really the main local band we all loved; as they were our band... so to speak. Another band was the 100 Men (who featured Mik Whitnal later of Babyshambles).

"I started going to Mod rallies with my, then, boyfriend Tom, usually on his PX125; mainly to Scarborough, Bridlington, Blackpool and Great Yarmouth. Most of the time we went on the scooter and the journey there was usually the most eventful part of the weekend. I can only remember 3 occasions where we managed to arrive without breaking down on some scooter or another. One trip to Blackpool for a Mod weekend, on an LI150, we ground to a halt somewhere near Huddersfield. We had to push the scooter up a hill... Tom was yelling at me to push harder and I was yelling back at him that I was bloody pushing.

"As It turned out, the brakes had seized up so we weren't going anywhere fast! A friend came and picked us up in his van; took us to a mate's (John Slater) garage, where Tom retrieved his PX and off we went again. We had a great weekend until we came home to find the LI and a friends Vega had been stolen from the garage. Another time, we nearly came a cropper on a 50 Special in Scarborough. Going over the cobbles was bad enough, but we had to stop when the back wheel started to wobble. It turns out there was only one bolt left holding the wheel on!

"As for the Mod scene, I later moved on from the Mod rallies and headed more towards Northern Soul and a smattering of Acid Jazz. But I still go to the occasional scooter do and my love of Ska, 2-Tone and Mod remains; especially with the recent Specials reunion gigs still ringing in my ears and the likes of local ska influenced band Barmy Surplus keeping the sounds alive."

Louise's Mod photo gallery

Rotherham Assembly rooms

City Limits
Present
"A NICE LITTLE EARNER"
AT
ASSEMBLY ROOMS
Effingham St., Rotherham
ON
DECEMBER
Thirteenth
Tickets £1·50
(£2·on the door)
7·30-12
Hip Dress Essential

Blackpool Jan 1987

THE NEIGHBOURHOOD PRESENTS A

R+B SOUL SKA
All Nighter (8pm to 8am)

at the
RICHMOND HOTEL
Hornby Road, Central Blackpool
SATURDAY 10th JANUARY 1987
Admission by ticket only   Ticket £3
D.Js Ralston, Steve with Special Guest
Paul Hallam

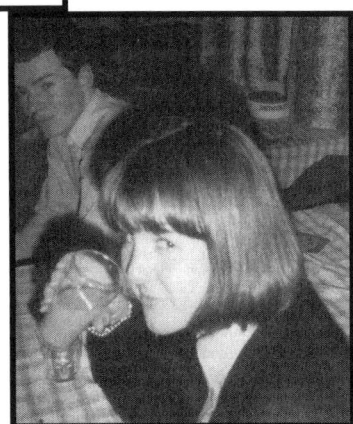

Scarborough 1987

C.C.I. PRESENTS ON THE

SCARBOROUGH

MOD RALLY '87

at

THE LEMON TREE CLUB
HUNTRISS ROW

on

SUNDAY, 24th MAY, 7 p.m. — 12 midnight.

MOD KNEES-UP PARTY

D.J.s Tony Class, Dom, Wayne
& Guests

SMART DRESS ESSENTIAL

STRICTLY MEMBERS ONLY

ADMISSION BY THIS TICKET ONLY

Blackpool 1987

Scarborough 1988

CLASS Presents on the

SCARBOROUGH

MOD RALLY '88

A WELCOMING ALLNIGHTER

at the SALISBURY HOTEL, HUNTRISS ROW
FRIDAY, 29th APRIL
8 p.m. — 8 a.m.

D.J.s Tony Class, Ian Jackson, Dom, 2 Toby's
Mark Bailey, Rob Cox, Tony Schokman
Phil Whelan and Guests

STRICTLY CCI MEMBERS ONLY
SMART MOD DRESS ONLY

Blackpool 1988

TONY CLASS PRESENTS

NATIONAL MOD MEETING ALLNIGHTER '88
on
SATURDAY, 5th NOVEMBER
at
SPANISH HALL, WINTER GARDENS
BLACKPOOL

Live on Stage

THE SECOND GENERATION & THE CLIQUE
FEATURING
D.J.s Tony Class, Rob Cox, Phil Whelan, Toby Fosh,
Rob Bailey, Mark Bailey, Ian Jackson & Tony Schokman

8 pm TILL 8 am
SMART DRESS ONLY

CLASS Presents on the

BLACKPOOL
MOD RALLY '88

Live on Stage

SECOND GENERATION + RED HOT & THE SUN SPOTS
at the
SPANISH HALL, WINTER GARDENS
on
SATURDAY, 6th AUGUST
8 p.m. — 2 a.m.

D.J.s Tony Class, Dom, Phil Whelan,
Rob Cox, Tony Schokman, Mark Bailey,
Toby Fosh, and Rob Bailey.

STRICTLY CCI MEMBERS ONLY

Scarborough 1989

CLASS PRESENTS
THE
SCARBOROUGH
ALLNIGHTER
on
SATURDAY, 21st JANUARY, 1989
at
THE LEMONTREE CLUB
HUNTRISS ROW
8 p.m. — 8 p.m.

D.J.s Tony Class, Tony Schokman
Phil Whelan, Ian Jackson & Rob Bailey,

STRICTLY CCI MEMBERS ONLY

**All Mod scene photographs from pages 108 -119
copyright and courtesy of Louise Mckenning**

Coming soon from 'Days Like Tomorrow books'
'Mods at the Coast'

The Chesterfield Mod

Julian Leusby: (Chesterfield Mod) "Well my time as a Mod was probably the best time of my life. The scene around my area (Chesterfield) and the years 1984 to 1986 were about the best ones: There were something happening almost every week... God all my mates were doing fanzines, Face to Face and Immediate Reaction were the best two, but there were others like Teenage Beat, Stop-Go, Win or Lose, The Enthusiast, A taste of Pink, Me and the Face etc - and remember most of these editors where still at school.

"The Chesterfield scene was really compact and everyone seemed to know one another,the whole scene being an extremely healthy one. I think Chesterfield at the time was one of the most mod populated areas, not in the same league as London or Coventry but we were up there. There was always something to do; the lads were going off everywhere around the country. I must also give credit to the Chesterfield scene for the Fakers Modernist society(which I was a member of) and also the Chesterfield urchins (Andy Bull's lot). Also I have to mention the Mansfield Athenians; they did some good alldayers especially the one with Yeh-Yeh and Five Thirty, great memories.

"Going back to the Fakers Mod society,the organisation was brought together to try and improve the Mod scene in our area; we use to meet every Sunday to discuss and organise gigs, transport to gigs and the local situation in general. We were named after the Gents' song who most of us liked and followed.

Julian and Mod mates (Left at Rotherham Assembly Rooms)

"We were even mentioned on Radio One by Mike Read and also looking through the old Phoenix lists you will see us mentioned all the time. We use to go everwhere for gigs; my favourite venue was the Assembly Rooms in Rotherham, and the best band I saw there was the Prisoners who were an amazing band. Every time we went to the Assembly Rooms there was always a shout of *'The Casuals are waiting outside'*, but to tell you the truth I never bloody saw any.

"Now Sheffield: we used to go every other Saturday to search for clothes and records; I bought some bloody great records from Sheffield. The only downfall to going to Sheffield was the

Casuals... a bloody dangerous place Sheffield was in those days. I remember getting my head smashed against a wall at Sheffield train station, and what got me about that was that I was the smallest in my whole group. Another time in Sheffield we went to see the Gents at a Radio Hallam roadshow; can't remember whereabouts but I think it was a large park. I remember this gig because the Gents were on the same bill as Black Lace and they got so much stick from the Mods. I bet it sounded great on the radio as the Gents were brilliant as usual: they were a great band until Mark Johnson got hold of them. Those days as a mod were truly the best times of my life and to be honest the Mod thing has never left me to this day!"

Photos by Louise Mckenning

These local Mods and Modettes all have stories to tell; tales of an obsession with a scene so exciting, unique and when sussed out correctly – the most individualistic of all music cults. However, more Mod stories would arrive - often directly – from the spurrings of Punk; others as a result of being fans of the new 2-Tone sounds (themselves springing out of the fusion of Ska with Punk energy and lyricism). The Mods favourite method of transport – the scooter – would also be much more prevalent in the ensuing years, and it is with these influences and starting points that these Mod experiences would unfold; along with their Punk cousins – living a life encompassing too much too young!

The Negatives: Sheffield's premier Mod band

The Negatives' line up was Pete Eason (Vocals), Fraser 'Snapper' Charles (Guitar/Piano), Steve Wilmot (Drums/Backing Vocals) Brad Martini (Bass/Vocals)

The Negatives single 'Money Talk'/'Electric Waltz' was released in 1980 on Steal records

Negatives photos courtesy of Pete Eason and Kristan James Melik

The Mod Icon

Photo: Pete Skidmore

Paul Weller chatting to fans outside the Sheffield Top Rank March 1982

"What is the connection between Punk and Mod? I don't really have the straight answers to that one, but as much as there was a tide of on-going indifference towards each other at the time, with Mods chasing Punks around and vice versa, and both being hounded by skinheads and Teddy boys, there was - and still is, as far as I am concerned - a very close affinity between a Mod and his Punk Rock cousin. One thing is for sure, in my opinion, there wouldn't have been either of them doing the rounds during the late seventies without the influence of the other." – **Tony Beesley**

Chapter Four
Too much too young!
(Part 1 - The Punk years)

"While the older Punk kids were watching The Jam and The Clash at the Top Rank in 1977, me and my mate Andy Goulty were lapping up the Goodies Punk special on the telly. We thought it was hilarious... in fact in 1977 – can you believe – Punk wasn't something we even took that seriously: amazing really, considering the effect it had on our lives in the long run!" – **Tony Beesley**

 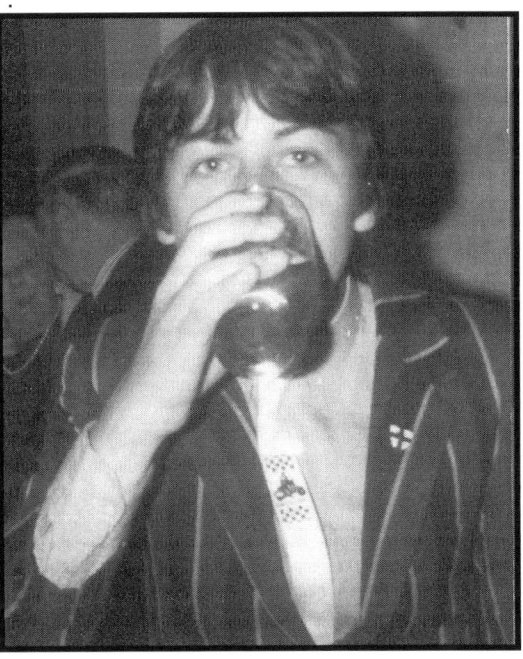

While local Punks and Mods over the age of 16 had the advantage of being able to decide which bands and club events to attend at venues like the Outlook, Windmill, Top Rank, Limit club, Penthouse and the student affiliated homes of live music - the Sheffield Polytechnic and University (with the signature of a long-haired hippy of course), the situation was far more limited for a younger generation of *hip to the music* local fans. The Comprehensive and Grammar school upstarts of the 13 to 15 year old local gangs had to make do with their musical kicks at the local youth club disco and a host of other adaptable sources: though often in some cases the infiltration of the 18's only venues was rampant for some brave kids... Throughout the region of South Yorkshire, much like the many out of town places up and down the country, a thousand front rooms were alive with the sound of the 'Sound of the Suburbs', 'Too Much Too Young' and 'Time for Action'. The often direct result would be an array of smashed ornaments and lampshades, graffitied settee cushions and Adidas sports bags; logo emblazoned leather jackets, donkey jackets and parkas as the new revolutionary sounds of Punk, Mod Revival and 2-Tone Ska infiltrated the homes of a whole generation of spotty, rebellious and intoxicated kids: their lives changed forever!

The invasion of Punk for the generation below the originators and the pro-active Punk participants came mostly throughout the days of mid 77 to late 1978; with a few late comers joining the fray when they realised that something interesting was going on down the school corridors. Two years or so later the very same thing would be happening with the Mod revival and the 2-Tone movement. For now though, let's explore the formative days of the school jotter generation of Punk kids!

Tony Beesley: "First it was Glam Rock and Wings, then Disco, plastic Soul, an Elvis, Mud And Showaddywaddy obsession, Rod Stewart, Queen and The Who: then between the few of us we started buying The Jam, Stranglers, Boomtown Rats and Sex Pistols (as well as some of the chart crap of the time for a while) and before you knew it we were proper little Punk Rockers; or so we thought we were. While the older lads were going down to the Windmill and Outlook clubs and truly experiencing Punk Rock, we were waiting for 'No More Heroes' and 'Mary of the Fourth Form' to come on Top of the Pops on the portable telly down at the school youth club disco on a Thursday night! While the hardcore Punks at the Sheffield gigs were dispensing bottles and gob at Richard Hell and hanging out with The Clash we were winning conker competitions and listening to 'Do Anything You Wanna Do' by Eddie and the Hot Rods. With our bog-brush make-do spiky hair dos and Dennis the Menace jumpers, we didn't take it all that seriously, but we thought we were quite cool. I suppose at the side of the rest of the kids knocking about, that were our age at the time, we actually were."

Which dodgy Punk T-Shirt would you have chosen in 1977?

Dave Burkinshaw: (Rotherham Punk fan) "Before Punk the music scene was shit. I thought '*This is just what music needs- a kick up the arse.*' My first memory of the Punk era was seeing (one of Rawmarsh's first Bell walking up the street

713 SLITS

272. NEW STRANGLERS

Punk Rockers) Bryan with a pair of boots covered in fur and wearing a pair of tight jeans and ripped t shirt. This must have been about 1977. I didn't think how daft he looked like some did, I thought what style he had."

John Quinn: (Sheffield Punk fan) "I hated Punk. It horrified me: At first anyway. Before I'd heard any of the records I knew it was bad and dangerous. Punks swore at people, wore weird clothes and hated everything on earth. How could anyone like something like that? Or be like that? I had only recently moved to Sheffield and wanted nothing more than to just blend in. Alienation was not on my agenda.

"Like a good little pre-teen tabloid reader I swallowed all the stuff about them - and especially the Sex Pistols - being a threat to society if not civilisation itself. I can even remember the first time I saw real life Punks. It was on a Sunday afternoon and I was sitting alone in my dad's car outside his place of work on Division Street near the city centre. I cowered terrified as they spat on the car and then reached in through the window and grabbed and destroyed the radio which was playing Elton John or suchlike. Actually, they just walked past but that's what I imagined Punks would do. My dad's car at the time didn't even have a radio. And incidentally I didn't have a record player either. My elder sister had taken the family one when she left home and I didn't manage to persuade my parents to buy me one until my 14th birthday in 1979.

"Unlike those cool characters - otherwise known as 'liars' - who you hear claiming that they were really into Dylan and the Velvet Underground when still at junior school, I have no shame nowadays in admitting that my favourite band at the time Punk broke was rock n' roll revivalists Showaddywaddy. I also liked the doo-wop of Darts, and their deep-voiced vocalist Den Hegarty later appeared on 'Sandinista' by The Clash, which must prove...something.

"Things started to change as I went to secondary school. As the only Scottish kid in the entire place and also having ginger hair and a limp it became obvious that I wasn't going to quite fit in no matter how I tried. Punk seemed to appeal to those who were outsiders, either by inclination or accident, so I fell under its spell, helped by the fact that 1978 saw some fantastic slices of what I had come to know as Punk - basically speedy guitars, witty or heartfelt lyrics and lots of nervous energy and attitude - The Rezillos' 'Top Of The Pops', Buzzcocks' 'Ever Fallen In Love' and 'Promises', The Jam's 'David Watts' and 'Down In The Tube Station At Midnight', Jilted John's eponymous one-hit wonder and even 'She's So Modern' and 'Like Clockwork' by the Boomtown Rats. Even better, you could hear these songs on daytime Radio One and see the bands perform them on television. It didn't seem dangerous to me anymore. It seemed great.

"And then there were The Undertones. They were my favourites. Still are. Apart from the fact that 'Teenage Kicks' was originally released the very month I became a teenager, there was something about them that hit me in the right place. I think it was the combination of great songwriting, a unique voice and the fact that their mums obviously still bought their clothes - a problem I was all-too familiar with

"As well as the re-release of their debut album being the first one I bought on vinyl (I already had Blondie's 'Parallel Lines' - owned by every member of my generation - on cassette) they were one of the first bands I saw live, beaten only by Echo and the Bunnymen and Kraftwerk. However while those two were at Sheffield City Hall, which anyone could get in to provided they paid, the Top Rank - which is now the O2 Academy - was open to over 18s only. I was 15, looked about nine and turned up on the day hoping to buy a ticket while still wearing my school uniform. Bad move. Not only would they not sell me one, they told me not to bother coming back and trying to get in later. Then I saw the band themselves - minus Feargal - coming out of the venue and explained my situation, to which Billy the drummer wrote my name on his hand and said he'd put me on the guest list. They then asked for directions, not to the nearest drug den or house of ill-repute, but to a sweet shop. You couldn't make it up.

"On my return that evening after a costume change - although still wearing my - flared! - School trousers - I was recognised on the door and told to go home. My name may have been down but I still wasn't getting in. I hung around though, along with two equally underage-looking girls - rather implausibly arguing about which one of the band was most fanciable - and then just as they came on stage, the bouncer beckoned to us and said he'd let us in as long as we didn't touch any alcohol. As my chances of getting served at any bar in Britain were non-existent anyway, I readily agreed and was in. The show was magnificent even though I got stopped by the police on the way home who quite rightly wondered what a 15-year-old-who-looked-about-nine was doing walking down The Moor on his own late at night. Not that I went to every show on my own. I soon discovered kindred souls, some at school, and some elsewhere. Adrian and Simon AKA Sid and Salt, from the year below me at school had some similar tastes while another Simon from a different school, who I first met when he attempted to amputate my leg during a game of football, became a close mate and a regular concert companion - at the ones I could get into anyway - occasionally accompanied by characters like Ernie and Gav.

"It was with Sid and Salt that I went to see UK Subs, when what was then just known as the Polytechnic but is now the Nelson Mandela Building, hosted a series of free concerts for the unemployed (and obviously schoolboys pretending to be unemployed). That remains in the memory as the only time in my life I've got up on stage with a band, on the grounds that most of the rest of the crowd was up there already and I didn't want to stand out by being on a lower level. I also saw The Fall for the first of many times the same week. No-one would dare get up on the stage during that and face Mark E Smith's wrath, even though he did spend most of the show with his back to the audience, turning round only to issue retorts to a couple of Siouxsie look-alikes in the audience who were baiting him endlessly. The Damned also played in this series of shows but for some reason lost in the mists of time I didn't go.

"When I wasn't going to concerts I was hanging around record shops for hours on end, staring at the sleeves and occasionally even purchasing something, pocket money and paper round cash permitting, Since my birthday treats to myself (first singles bought: 'Gangsters' by The Specials, 'Reasons To Be Cheerful' by Ian Dury and the Blockheads, 'Money' by The Flying Lizards, 'Harmony In My Head' by Buzzcocks, 'Rock Lobster' by the B52s, and 'Up The Junction' by Squeeze - not that I'm anally retentive or anything), I had built up quite a collection of Punk and New Wave vinyl. To my utter horror my dad had started learning the bagpipes and practising them in the bathroom, which was next to my bedroom, so we regularly had competitions to see whose sound could drown the others out. Connie and Vin, the elderly couple next door, must have loved us. Even nowadays I still listen to a lot of the music that Punk enticed me into. I wonder if Billy from The Undertones still has my name written on his hand."

Perhaps one of the greatest prizes to be cashed in from the scattered lottery ashes of the Sheffield Post-Punk scene was Pulp. Formed a little after the birth of the era, it would take the emergence of Britpop many years later before the rest of the nation finally caught up with the talents of Jarvis Cocker and the band. Drummer Nick Banks hailed from Rotherham and as an associate of local Punks Dave Spencer and Graham Torr and gang, became aware of Punk Rock at the very earliest side of his teens.

Nick Banks: (Pulp drummer from Rotherham) " I have only hazy recollections of some strange thing called 'Punk' that was stirring across the country. Probably thru' parents mutterings I had a vague idea that there were groups of young people that seemed to take their pleasure in spitting at each other, gratuitous swearing and general yobbery. I was 11 in '76 and can remember thinking *'urgh, don't fancy that much!!* School life carried on as much as normal, music/youth culture didn't figure much in my life. Although I had bought my first single a couple of years earlier - 'Bohemian Rhapsody' - still a classic in my book - my main music experience was wonderful radio 1 and my Mam n' dad's annual Christmas disco, James Last and Boney M were popular if I recall. My main enjoyment until about late '78 would be mucking about in the woods, cycling, and reading war comics.

"Music started to become more interesting around 1978. I had bought ELO's LP 'Out of the Blue' – 'Mr Blue Sky's' yer man here - so a 'rock' interest had begun. At school, Oakwood Comp, some of the lads that I kind of knew started talking about this new music, 'Punk'. These were Dom Wood, Dave Spencer, Lawrence Major, Graham Torr, Adrian Carver, John Wheaton, Darryl Huggup etc. they started looking different. I guess it was a case of get with the program or get left behind. Having an elder brother seemed to be an advantage in hearing this new stuff, mine was not bothered one jot. I had to find out for myself. The Pistols were an obvious first choice, with the singles from the 'Great Rock n' Roll Swindle' being about. Top of the Pops was viewed avidly for any Punk groups appearing. The Stranglers and The Clash being the ones that started doing it for me. (They were doing it for everybody else so they must be good, right?)."

Talking about Top of the Pops, how about Top of the Punk tots!

Craig Chatterton: (Rotherham Punk) "Me and some school mates set about getting a Punk band together sometime around 1978: the thing is we had no instruments so made our own ... using cardboard boxes and biscuit tins. Our Phil provided the artwork design on the biscuit tin drum kit. We were called – the very Punk-sounding – The Rib and made a right row"

Left: Craig Chatterton's first school boy make-shift Punk band 'The Rib' complete with cardboard guitars and biscuit tins for drums

Mandy Taylor: (Sheffield Punk girl) "The first time I heard of the Sex Pistols was on our way to a family holiday in the South of France (we weren't loaded but my mum had got these vouchers out of Woman's Weekly magazine and her Persil vouchers had paid for the return fare to London to pick up the coach!!) I was 11 and I remember running down tiled tube corridors in London trying to get to Victoria station and seeing the Sex Pistols posters on the walls in various states of wear and tear. I was intrigued and almost hooked straight away, but as it was it was the Boomtown Rats that got to be the first Punk band I truly got into.

"I got into the Boomtown Rats later that year, when my Nan and Granddad took me and my brother away to Ingoldmells near Skegness. My Nan always let me and my brother have a first couple of bingo wins to pick what we wanted so I picked a square Boomtown Rats mirrored badge because I thought it looked cool. It was about two inches square and I thought it was so great and never took it off. I don't know what happened to it, but recently Andy (Morton) gave me a similar non-mirrored badge which I have since worn- How old am I????

"When I think back now to the Rats I can remember learning all the lyrics from their album sleeves and there used to be a small newspaper type little magazine with lyrics in. I used to sit in front of the stereogram every Sunday afternoon (for the Top Twenty) with this magazine singing along to what I thought was the cool stuff and it used to make my Sunday if the Rats were in the top twenty (along with some poor northern sod winning a speedboat on Bulls eye). I can still do the entire lyrics word perfect to 'Rat Trap' and know most of the words to their other stuff!"

Tony Beesley: "I bought the first two Boomtown Rats LP's and their first run of singles. I know they were not well liked by the hardcore Punk crowd but at our ages their rules didn't apply to us. I remember buying 'Mary of the Fourth Form' from Sound of Music in December 77 and I didn't get the pic sleeve. Picture covers were the essential thing with our singles back then and to see the single you had asked for getting put into the bag in those horrible plain white sleeves was a major let down. In fact a lot of the time, I would say *'Don't bother if no pic sleeve'.* Most of the time we would peer over the counter at the stacks of singles filed away on the shelves and try and figure out if the pic covers were still with the records. Anyway, this time I was without the desired article, but I knew that the lad next door to me had it in the cover.

"Stevie was a good many years older than me and into the 70's Rock stuff. He had a fairly extensive collection of albums - Bad Company, Boston, Wishbone Ash etc. But, he did have the Stranglers 'No More heroes' LP and 'Mary of the Fourth Form' in a cover. I hounded him until he gave it to me that December month and added it to my sparse little collection of Punk and New Wave 45's. Stevie was a great lad and a real funny guy. I had known him all my life. Years later, he suffered a severe brain haemorrhage and although he partially recovered, he was never the same and became dependent on being looked after full time.

"Like a lot of us young 'uns, I knew most of the words to both the Boomtown Rats and The Jam songs: though I found great difficulty in trying to decipher the words to 'The Day the World turned Day-Glo' by X-Ray Spex' when that came on Top of the Pops. When I look through my record boxes nowadays it's amazing how many of the records we went out and bought were not what you would term proper Punk. Sure, we had all the Clash records and between us a good selection of the tougher stuff, but you would just as likely catch us listening to Jilted John, 'Take me I'm Yours' by Squeeze and 'Sweet Gene Vincent' by Ian Dury and the Blockheads as 'Pretty Vacant' and 'White Riot'. It was much more of a learning curve for us lot. We had no real guidelines to go by at all. The cynical and intellectual crap spouted in the NME went straight over our heads; all we were interested in was listening to this new and dangerous music, sticking two fingers up to our elders and having a good time at the same time."

Gary Stables: (Rotherham Punk) "Punk? It's all your fault Tony. Being an old school friend of Tony's we would hang around at his house in the evenings and weekends (his Mom was a saint putting up with us lot!) we were all dabbling in and listening to Punk/New Wave stuff but this particular evening Tony had got a copy of 'Never mind the Bollocks' and from the moment he put it on I was blown away, the sheer energy & power was amazing and from that moment on I was hooked: it was out with sewing kit and on with the zips."

Front room Punk rackets aplenty for the young upstarts of our story!

Mandy Taylor: "After I'd started getting into the Rats I started to get into The Clash and other bands. Every Friday night we used to go over to my Auntie's and my Dad and Uncle would go to the pub while my Mum and Aunty would gossip in the front room, leaving me and my cousin (Aidy) to play our Clash albums on their stereogram whilst being pestered by our younger brothers! We would compare records that we'd bought that week, and Aidy used to convince me to swap any picture records I had for a black vinyl one then he'd throw in another record to seal the deal. A few years ago I found out how what a big mistake that was, I can't remember how many rare and picture discs I'd swapped, but you live and learn.

"I know lots of the bands were well established before I got into them, but you have to remember I was a young Punk, we didn't have the net or text then, (I can't imagine what the scene would have been like had we got Facebook and the like!) so everything was word of mouth: a friend of a friend would recommend something, or you would read or see something in a weekly magazine or TV programme. There's no way your parents would have taken you to a gig like they do now, the corporate Arena scene wasn't even a twinkle in anyone's eye, although I can't think of anything worse as a teenager then going to see a gig with your parents – Punk was my music back then not theirs.

"When I think back to some of the stuff I used to wear – usually from the army stores and then tweaked with accessories pinned, bleached and tied on. Apart from my plastic sandals I used to love my winkle pickers from Ravel on High Street Sheffield. One of my favourite outfits used to be my killer winkle pickers, Army PJ bottoms (sewn into skinny legs) with a army t shirt and a big belt with the obligatory spiky hair, I remember once getting into a trendy club and being asked what I'd come as (I think it was Isabella's) I wasn't bothered all the girls looked like they'd dressed for Princess Di's wedding!"

A teenage Punks' school years Rebellion!

Tony Beesley: "One of the big LP's for me and Andy Goulty during the summer of 1978 was the Stranglers 'Black and White' LP: the sounds of Prog-Punk exemplified by the records closing track 'Toiler on the Sea', would be blaring out of Andy's bedroom window as we spun our daily record sessions. Now don't get me wrong, I can't stand Prog-Rock nor Genesis - the band quite possibly the absolute antithesis of Punk Rock (and yes I do know some Punk did come out of Prog) – but, along with the usual batch of weekly New Wave singles bought on a Saturday afternoon - I did sadly buy 'Follow You Follow Me' by the hairy-custard-faced-prog-poppers as it climbed the charts in Spring 78. It wasn't so much of a love of the record, but more of a case of all the lasses at the youth club disco loved it and maybe if I bought the damned thing they might follow me too!

"That was what it was like for us spotty faced young Punk wannabes during our first year of Punk loving excitement: we would buy all sorts of stuff. Me and Andy Goulty would buy five or six Punk singles and maybe two or three shitty chart ones too. He would be buying Buzzcocks 'Love you more' and Ian Dury's 'What a Waste' on their release at the same time as something like 'Wild West Hero' by ELO. Behind him, I may be stood at the Sound of Music record shop counter with The Jam's 'News of the World' and 'I don't want to go to Chelsea' by Elvis Costello and the Attractions along with 'Don't Fear the Reaper by Blue Oyster Cult'. Great times, but by the end of summer of 78 we would have ditched this innocent pop kid approach to music and be racing to the counter with masses of proper Punk and New Wave records, or at least what we thought were the proper stuff anyhow! Quite literally, I had gone from buying Scalextric track and Airfix model tanks from Redgates in Sheffield at the very start of 1977 to trekking down to the bottom of the Moor to pester the Hippy sales assistants for the latest Clash, Jam, Stranglers or Lurkers singles.

"I can remember, quite embarrassingly now, when me and my mates re-enacted the 'Anarchy in the UK' tour in my Mum's front room. We had missed those legendary early Punk tours, so through our over-exuberant Punk imaginations we mimed, shouted, scratched at tennis rackets and dived about to the relevant records as though we were on tour. My kid acoustic guitar had been smashed when I did a 'Townshend' on it not long after me and Andy Goulty wrote our first Punk song 'The Tramps' in 1978, so the accompaniment was spared my rudimentary idea of what a chord looked and sounded like! Johnny Thunders and the Heartbreakers LP 'L.A.M.F' (bought for a quid from Virgin records from one of the Hippy lot) was played as loud as my old Alba music centre's volume slide would go as we escaped into the world of 1976, which in 1978-79 seemed a lifetime away to us. 'Damned, Damned Damned', the Clash first LP and the Pistols 'Spunk' bootleg followed as we completed the Punk package tour date. The Leeds University date (encores included) honoured, it was time to take our well earned rest and listen to the John Peel show, before the next gig down in Caerphilly ... err umm my mate Dean 'Beanz' Stables house the night after.

"Other great times were had at parties arranged by some of our crowd at selected houses when the parents were otherwise conveniently disposed of, where we would take a bottle of cider (from Ernie's the only place that would serve under-aged kids alcohol) and a good selection of our new wave records. I can remember one particular Christmas period party at my fellow Punk-loving pal Andy Goulty's house... Other great parties were held at Shaun Angells' house. Anyway after being fended off by the lasses (wishful thinking!) we had invited, and a night full of bellyaching laughs, come ons, taking the piss and choice new wave music played on Andy's Dansette record player, I made my way home after the 11.30 watershed to be met by both my Mum and Dad sat eating late-night chips that my brother had brought in from after a few bevies at the local. Their faces and shaking heads at my furious attempts at trying to create a persona of sobriety were hilarious. They had no idea I had been drinking... I mean we were all mostly not quite 13 years old yet, so the confusion written on their faces was something that amused me even more. The Old Grey Whistle Test was on the telly and my grey face finally managed to pass the test as I carefully slipped off to retire to my bed with the sound in my head of Ian Dury's opening rant of 'Plastow Patricia – 'Arseholes, Bastards, Fuckin' Cunts and Pricks.' Ian Dury records were always popular at our Punk parties!

"But it was at school where us young aspiring Punk Rockers unfortunately had to be forced to spend most of our time; unless you were like my mate John Harrison who had taken the rebellion a step further and dodged school like the plague. He could often be spotted being chased around the local park by the school bobby, but he still didn't turn up for school the next day.

"I went to Rawmarsh Comprehensive (also known as Haugh Road)... I was a relatively quiet and unassuming kid and knocked about with all the hard kids at school... although often quiet, I was a clown; a joker and just a little bit fucked up I suppose – especially after my Dad died ... most of all though - I was an out and out Punk Rock rebel!!

"Every single teacher that taught me ended up giving me the cane, a belt around the lug-hole or the slipper (except one, more of which later), I never did homework, I did not wear a full, or even a half-way resemblance of a uniform, I never wore the regulation tie to school once; but ironically wore the one I had out of school to go to the half-Punk disco at the Cricket club; I produced fuck all out of a two year term of Metalwork (instead I chose to dodge the creative 'er' building of a desk lamp and disrupt the rest of the class and generally piss around)... My world of Technical Drawing, General Science and Mathematical equations beginning and ending with useless Algebra was a mirage meaning absolutely nothing and only vaguely hiding the world I lived in... of the Jam, Stranglers, Boomtown Rats and the Clash!!

"My first acts of visible rebellion, apart from *getting done,* was via the art of trying to infiltrate, as much as possible, my D.I.Y Punk look into my everyday school part-uniform. Trainers were banned, so I wore Doc Martin boots. Denim was banned, so I wore my Donkey Jacket with 'Hate and War', 'The Clash' and 'Ignore Alien Orders' chalked/painted on the back. When long hair was acceptable and the norm for school kids (and most of the Hippy throwback teachers) a lawnmowered messed up crop was achieved... and when spiky hair became too common-place for me, I reverted to a longer hair style... unkempt and Mick Jones(ish). One particular teacher gave me a right roughing up for ignoring his request of removing my denim jacket and calling him something choicely obscene!

"Speaking of the teachers and their pep talk and misty-eyed conversations of the old days when they had graduated into the big wide world of a few years earlier and all their talk of sixties idealism and radicalisation!!! In memory, this was all condensed into one single early morning

Assembly when two of these ex-sixties-free-thinking-radicals who had been with the hip crowd (actually the Deputy Head and a cohort I think?) introduced us to the delights of the Beatles 'Hey Jude' as our Monday morning wake up call! I was almost physically fucking sick, I can tell you. Rambling on about what all of the songs sentiments and memories created meant... all the changes they had seen in the Education system and society and that this was their soundtrack to all that initial optimism they had once embraced... as I say I was almost physically sick!! Ironically I now have all the Beatles records (including 'Hey Jude') and find myself feeling and talking in pretty similar lines to how they reminisced, with less misty-eyed nostalgia I am sure and much more cynicism I am convinced.

"As mentioned earlier, there was one kind teacher who did not need to raise a hand to me throughout my two years of European Studying with her and her class... Miss Taylor was a Stranglers fan (she waved at us diving around below from her balcony position at a Stranglers gig); she was always interested in reading my new wave poetic rants that barely disguised my inner demons and anger at the adult world and would listen intently and converse (without any condescending platform of opinion) to my views and dreams of an alternative future. Miss Taylor was a proper teacher and she was in touch with us kids... if both sides were willing to meet halfway. I wonder what happened to her and how much of her Post-New Wave ideology she managed to take along with her through her life.

A donkey's ear for a microphone anyone? Me in 1978 ➡

"School Art lessons were, for me, a chance to try and express some of my new wave leanings via a series of Pop-Art looking paintings and sketches. I wanted to go to art school, despite the Leyton Buzzards telling me not to! All of those hopes were dashed when the so-called powers that be *that apparently know best*, decided to take me out of my Art lessons and merge me into the pleasurable delights of Technical Drawing. Did they not realise Art offered me some hope! Some slight possibility of self expression that may lead to something more solid, creative and worthwhile than sniffing glue, chewing rubber erasers and throwing compasses at the cork-board on the wall? I had enjoyed painting and sketching all of my life up to that point. My Mother had proudly framed my depiction of a farmer's field and the Battle of Isandlwana and placed them on the living room wall, until I took them down, smashed the frames and tore up the inner works of what I now classed useless and irrelevant art, now that I had been rejected from that class! I firmly believed back then... that all but a minor few teachers knew very little more than us... self education was the key and learning more that way. Being an individual ruled... The whole system sucked!!!

"One particular night during the summer of 78, me and the lads got the blame for having loud music blaring out from my Mothers front room by the next door neighbour and she reported us to the council: official warning letter n' all. Now every other time, it would have been us, but this time we weren't to blame as we were throwing buckets of water all over my oil-drenched dog while my brother played Wishbone Ash's 'Running Free' on his much lauded 'Bang n' Olufsen' state of the art hi/fi set up. Neither us nor the Clash were to blame for that one.

"Back to Punk Rock... that cause for Monday mornings off school after a night out at Steely's the night before. Kids would tell the form teacher *'Beesley's not coming in today sir, he went to see The Jam last night'* Teachers sending letters to my Mother about this and other indiscretions never really bothered her. Of course I would get a telling off, I wasn't fucking spoilt or disregarded by my Mother. She was a fantastic parent and did her best to hold things together for us when the pit killed my dad at the very start of 1978. What did bother her, though, was when anything involved the police, although she didn't mind my 'Roxanne' single! Her face drained of all colour and tears drowned around her eyes, bless her, when she turned round to me, from the door, one school lunchtime and said *'Tony, the police are at the door for you'.* It turns out that the windows we had been smashing, whilst conducting our bike-riding evening crab-apple-slinging raids had belonged to some poor old lady and we had been spotted by a neighbour. That was one of the very few times us Punk partisans got caught: we were threatened, given a cautionary scare and told to pay the bill... we ended up paying nothing and carried on our raids, but carefully avoided that old lady's house and any others we knew may be unfair game due to retirement policy and fragility. Other nights of rampage included smashing every window of the garden sheds in the back gardens of the houses up the road and when one set of the parents came home, the aggression caught on and escalated into each of them fencing furiously with each other on the street with the ornamental swords they had dragged off their imitation wood-panelled wall. A year or so later, the Damned apparently wrote one of their Punk anthems 'Smash it up' devoted to us lot ha ha!!

"The school discos and youth club nights are amongst the greatest times of my life. Everything was crammed into three hours or so each weekday night at whichever school's disco we attended, usually our own, but now and again other ones. We would piss about, talk music, swap Punk badges, gobble cans of Tizer and coke, try and chat up the lasses (usually failing miserably) and most importantly bring our own personal records to the occasion.

"We would turn up in our ill-informed attempts at the new wave look: myself (to begin with) in baggy Bowie-type pegs and pointed shoes, mohair sweater and mug-sized badges topped off with a fly-away Sweeny Todd spiked-hair-do. To begin with, there was maybe four or five of us in our own exclusive Punk club: there were two other lads a year older than us – Sugar and Paul Maiden – who were much more hardcore (and with it more cynical) than us: us kids who thought that Rezillos 'Top of the Pops' record could compete with 'The Drones 'I Just Want To Be Myself' 1977 Punk anthem. We were young and impressive, unknowledgable of what the rules were with Punk (and thankfully so)... we were unsure, a little scared and a lot more confused: but we meant it maaan and this was our generation and we were loving every minute of it... school-kid-mini-punk kids all - rebels to the very last...!!!"

Parents' disgust and indifference to the new sounds coming our generation of kids' way would sometimes result in them unwittingly letting their guard down.

John Quinn: "The first ever 12" single I bought was Lene Lovich's 'Say When', the follow-up to 'Lucky Number'. It wasn't even an extended version. The song lasted about two minutes. Also, my dad, who didn't like pop music in general and Punk in particular, thought X Ray Spex 'Germ Free Adolescents' was excellent. I think he had a crush on Poly Styrene. The next pop record he even remotely liked was 'Dub Be Good to Me' by Beats International in 1990. I was watching Top of the Pops and he went: *'That's really good. What was that other one I liked? Germ free something?'* I was like: *'Dad, that was a dozen years ago...'* I also tried to teach him to play 'Teenage Kicks' on the bagpipes. My parents just didn't get my musical taste in general, but my mum did knit me a mohair jumper which was nice. She even reattached one of the arms after I managed to somehow rip it off while spectacularly pissed on my 18th birthday."

Anon: (Rotherham Punk fan) "I guess I was a bit late getting into Punk but I tried my best to make up for it and think I have since earned my stripes over the past 30 years! The first Punk album I bought was Tonic for the Troops by The Boomtown Rats and the first Punk single was 'Angels with Dirty Faces' by Sham 69. These were probably inspired by energetic appearances on Top of the Pops. I'd been listening to the music for maybe a year or so with a mate and we'd been doing the usual taping off the Top 40 on a Sunday along with surreptitious listens to John Peel when I could stay awake after a hard day at school and an evening out roaming the streets.

"I remember going on holiday with my mum and watching Top of the Pops in the hotel because I knew The Damned would be on doing 'Love Song'. I loved it while all these older folks just tut-tutted in disgust and being a stroppy teenager I wouldn't let them swap channels. This was my music. I went out next day and bought the single. I wanted the Captain Sensible cover but had to settle for Algy Ward...ah well it was the music that mattered eh! I also bought 'Can't Stand the Rezillos' album. Seeing as I was in Scotland I thought it only fair!

The Clash on Tiswas - 1979

"I remember seeing Tony Beesley walking through school with The Clash scrawled on his blazer in chalk and carrying 'Give 'Em Enough Rope' under his arm and thinking 'cool cover'. I pestered my mum to send for it from Grattan's catalogue of all places...so what if it cost 20 weeks to pay for it, I'd probably worn it out by then! I think that's when my lifetime love of The Clash and all of its incarnations began.

"I used to get most of my Punk gear from the local army stores and put my own studs and badges on and get my mum to stitch patches on, usually purchased from Pandora's Box. I sent for some Clash jeans from the back of the NME and a Clash armband which I always wore round my leg (why?). I also used to spend hours taking in my flared school trousers and customising T-shirts. Docs were the footwear of choice though I did buy a pair of second hand creepers from the Ted shop on the Wicker in Sheffield. They were ace for pogoing in! I loved those shoes. To be honest, though, I was more into the music and the gigs so never went for the 100% Punk look 24/7.

"They used to have dinner time discos in the common room at school when you got into the fourth year. They'd sometimes play the Punk singles brought in by the Punks. I remember Sugar, Paul Maiden, Tony Beesley, Pete Roddis and a few others getting up to pogo in the arena like room – all the settee like chairs used to get lined up in a circle to form a kind of dance floor. You used to get grebo's or skins trying to trip them up. I got up a few times with my mates, Mark Lee, Steely, Balford and a couple of others to throw ourselves about to the Pistols or the Damned. We didn't have as eclectic taste in those days! All eyes used to be on Barney Rubble (Mark Barnet), when he arrived on the Punk scene, and his mocking of all things non-Punk. He never meant any harm; it's just that some people didn't see it that way. Ask the Modern Romance fans! That was Rubble at his finest.

"Some of my mates had been to see The Damned at the Top Rank just before Christmas and the day after they never shut up about this special place they'd been to and all the punks who were there and the great music that was played. A few of us decided we needed to go and three gigs were on offer to us just after Christmas- 999, The Clash and the Ramones (supported by The Boys): I chose 999 and that started my love affair with live music and it carries on to this day. I still remember walking up that slope and seeing loads of Punks milling around, walking up those steps, handing over my ticket and entering the club. It smelt like nowhere on earth, was sort of posh but well shabby and seemed huge. There were gangs of Punks and kids hanging around all over sharing pints of snakebites in plastic glasses. The music was brilliant, just like the best Punk disco ever. The bands were awesome and I grabbed like half a poster that they threw out at the end – I've still got it! I woke up next day with that now familiar buzzing in my ears and a 20,000 kilowatt grin on my face. School was brilliant; we were all reliving the night and planning our next gig. It was fair to say I'd got the bug! I just lived for Punk gigs for the next year or so.

"Back at school, around this time, Mod revivalists were just starting to don their parkas and would be Rude Boys were leaving school at lunchtime with centre partings and coming back with suedeheads in the afternoon. It was a good time to be into music with all the youth cults jostling for position in the common room and the youth clubs after school. I used to mix with most of them but found some of the heavy rockers a bit narrow minded. If I did get any grief over my choice of music it was usually from these smelly Herberts! It was a lot to do with their monotonous blend of pompous stadium drivel that Punk was created, so I could always take the moral high ground anyway. When we left school we all drifted apart a bit and that's when I got more into Oi and the faster Punk stuff, mainly because the gigs were cheap, plentiful and lively. After a couple of years of that I got more into football and the casual scene."

Two future Rotherham musicians Phil and Craig Chatterton had been introduced to Punk Rock unwittingly by their elder Punk loving brother Richard back in the late 70's. Following the short-lived school boy band of Craig's, both brothers set about getting down to some serious Punk indulgence.

Phil Chatterton: (Rotherham Punk) "Our Rich was buying all those Punk LP's back at the time: the Stranglers, Clash and Damned amongst others were his great loves, but he would throw a fit when we went out and bought anything... it was his own thing this Punk music and he didn't want us getting in on it. He would be taping the John Peel show and then playing the tapes back the next day and we would hear all this unknown Punk music that would often be getting somewhere six months or so later. We were really influenced by all of this. Our Rich did give in and let us go out and buy a Ramones LP as he wasn't that bothered about them."

Craig Chatterton: "The defining moment was when our Rich came home with two singles – 'Mr Blue Sky' by ELO and 'Five Minutes' by the Stranglers. That same week the Stranglers were on Top of the Pops and I remember thinking *'Who are these scary dudes looking so mean'.* The next big thing was when the 'Black and White LP came out. I loved that LP. At school there were a couple of other kids who were into Punk, but we had the upper hand on them with us having an older brother who was actually going along to see these Punk bands and stuff. The very first Punk LP that I went out and bought was 'Scared to Dance' by the Skids early in 1979. Our Phil bought 'It's Alive' by the Ramones."

Phil Chatterton: "I went to see the Damned at the Sheffield Top Rank in mid 1979 for my first Punk gig. I had been to a few Rock gigs before that: UFO at the City Hall was one of em I went to, being dragged along by a mate and I was never so bored in my life. When I got to the Top Rank, I remember standing outside the place waiting to go in and being shocked and in complete awe of all these massive (to me at my age) Punks. I mean I had been listening to the records, but this was the real thing. Artery were one of the supports, but it was the other one the Ruts who I was more into.

Phil Chatterton The face of Punk ➡️
defiance in flares

"I went in there pogoing to them with my Punk badges pinging off one by one. They had just released 'Babylon's Burning' and not long before that 'In a Rut' and I loved those two records, so enjoyed them a lot. After a while I went to the back of the place and stood around just taking it all in. This gig was followed by some more local ones at the Rotherham Arts Centre and the next big ones – the Ramones and the Boys again at the Top Rank. I also went along to see the Members there. By this time the Punk crowd was decreasing a bit as a lot of the Punk kids were moving into the Mod Revival and Ska thing. When we got dropped off there by one of my mates Dads in the car, as we got out of the car outside the venue, I saw our Rich shaking his head and he said *'Well that's not very Punk Rock is it!'*"

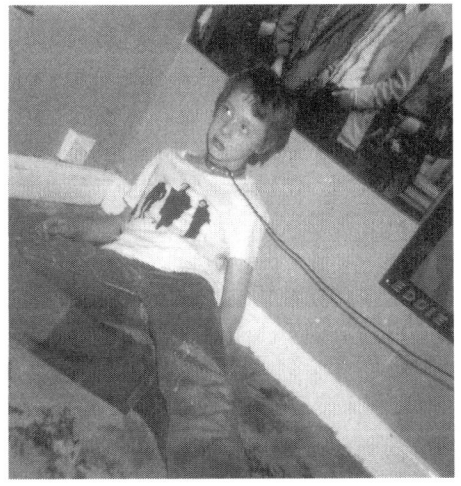

Craig Chatterton: "My first Punk gig was Devo at the City Hall who I thought were brilliant. There were plant pots being thrown around and it was a great gig. Not long after I saw Pulp play their first gig at the Arts Centre, followed by the Cockney Rejects at the Limit club afternoon matinee gig – which was quite scary as it had already been cancelled and as the small stage filled with skinheads I was thinking it would all kick off and get cancelled again... also the Dead Kennedys at the Leadmill: that was a great one. Our Phil took me to these as I was only 11 year old. I also saw my first Stranglers gig at the Polytechnic. Unbelievably being so young, we were in the bar area and the keyboard player Dave Greenfield was in there sat at a table playing a space invader game. He got chatting to us all too."

"I wore black bondage Clash style canvas trousers that almost stuck to my legs and I never took them off. We used to go and buy Punk t-shirts from a Punk clothes shop on Howard Street in Sheffield called Promoter Print. You could also get Punk t-shirts from the Showboat amusement arcade up on the balcony on Pond Street, but I was often too scared to go up there cos of all the skinheads gobbing at us from up there. I did get a good Clash first album front cover t-shirt from there but it was one of those prints that peeled off after a bit."

Phil Chatterton: "We weren't really as outrageous clothes wise as our Rich. I wore a biker jacket and Punk t-shirts. I also bought an Ultravox T-shirt from the Promoter Print shop for 50p.

They were cheap trial ones for 50p and mine had AC/DC on the back of the shirt would you believe! I actually saw Ultravox in Doncaster (Rotters) at the same time when Midge Ure first joined them: Can't really say I was a fan though."

Tony Beesley: "The clothes were as ill-informed as our knowledge of what real Punk was. It was all mohair looking baggy sweaters: my Mum even knitted me a lime green one and it wouldn't stop growing. What started out as a really Punky-looking fluffy mohair jumper ended up tripping me up as it became a D.I.Y Punk special effects prop for the stage version of The Blob!"

Nick Banks: "In 1976, I was 11 and flares and platforms were the norm. I distinctly remember wearing some spectacularly high-waisted flares, but I didn't have much of a clue about fashion: Mam bought it- I wore it. But as I started getting into this new music called Punk around 1978 getting your hair 'spiked' was still a big move (sounds a bit like a surgical procedure) and I was not ready for this yet. Flares were out of course - I guess it's convenient that at 13 you're growing quite rapidly so school uniform trousers can be ditched quite quickly and more 'in' styles can be procured - but the conundrum was what to wear to the school disco? As all the rest of the lads were getting Punky I needed a solution. I had no idea where to get Punk clothes or how to pay for them so I decided to make my own: Get one old black blazer, nick a dozen zips from the sewing box and sew the zips onto the jacket. My experience of sewing was pretty non existent so I can imagine it looked pretty shit. Add safety pins for added effect, mix with yellow 'Strikers' tee shirt and Dad's skinny 'funeral' tie and away you go (let's forget lank greasy hair - over ears not quite collar length, goofy glasses and shoes remaining lost to history). But hold on... my family weren't ready for the new male version of Vivien Westwood to be emerging from the bedroom in a badly sewn zip jacket. I could see them all falling over laughing at my sartorial adventure. Solution 2: chuck new jacket out of bedroom window stroll nonchalantly out of house with standard jacket on, swap to the new look around corner and sorted! Worked for a few times 'til me Mam found zip jacket at back of wardrobe and I was ousted – *'he's a Punk now... ha ha.'*

"I remember buying a pair of army trousers from the army surplus store, as my next fashion statement, but with hindsight they were way too big, almost flares!! I must have looked a right tit. Fashion ideas were sometimes gleaned from mail order ads in NME/sounds etc, usually way beyond any budget we had. I had a black and red mohair jumper that I wore to death, where it came from I can't remember."

What better introduction to the alternative outlook to music and life than living almost next door to one of Sheffield's most innovative musicians of the era.

Jamie 'Headcharge' Smith: (Sheffield Punk) "Well it all started for me at a very early age of around 10 years old as within a 50 foot radius of our house was next door neighbour Richard H. Kirk of Cabaret Voltaire. Then just down the steps was a big old scout hall that the Stunt Kites rehearsed in and just at the top of our road was the early beginnings of Emperor sound system set up by my school mates Vincent, Trevor, Lowgan and Clive. Most of us went to Firth Park school where you also had other school mates getting things going with the music i.e. Richard Hawley etc.

"One of my earliest memories of what was gonna be my chosen path of a crazy music life was one night as a kid falling to sleep in our attic bedroom on Scott Road and being woken by loud sounds n' laughter coming from outside: I jumped out of bed, ran to the window looking down on a crazy crew of people banging away on a white piano, one of which I recognised as my neighbour Richard H Kirk. Years later as me n Rich became mates I reminded him of this party and he just looked at me and said *'fuckin' hell that was my 21st birthday party HAHAHAHA',* I remember seeing Rich at the bus stop outside our house on many occasions dressed in long coat, motorcycle boots, black trousers n weeerd flicked back hair looking very alternative for the time. One particular day after seeing him jump on the number 20 bus I went into our newsagents next door and there he was - right on the front of the NME or was it Sounds? Now I knew what he was about and bought 'Nag Nag Nag' and was immediately hooked!"

But the expression of being alternative did not always see the desired attention for young Punk kids!

Craig Chatterton: "One time I was in Suggs sports shop in Sheffield. I had my Punk clothes on and a padlock around my neck. I was only 11 or 12 years old or so, but this big skinhead came up to me and said *'Can yer Mum sew?'* so I said *'Yeah course she can'* So he went and head-butted me straight in the face and said *'Well tell her to stitch that up then'."*

Left: Craig Chatterton - the epitome of Punk youth

Right: Phil Chatterton with Punk lasses outside Sheffield Town hall

A little coloured vinyl record therapy may have helped blank out the aggressive indifference being vested upon Craig.

Craig Chatterton: "We would always collect the coloured vinyl Punk records too. When 'Warhead' by the UK Subs came out, word got round that there was two copies of it going to be available at Violet May's record shop in Sheffield and these two kids at school who were our rivals said that they were gonna go and get em both. Well I got myself up at 8am on Saturday morning and went straight up there and made sure I got my copy of it before they got their hands on 'em both."

Dally: (Rotherham Punk) "I was 11 years old In 1978 when I bought my first vinyl LP, it was 'Black and White' by The Stranglers and I'd been secretly listening to my elder brother's copy of 'Never Mind the Bollocks' by The Sex Pistols for about a year (it was hidden inside another album sleeve for quite a while just because it said bollocks on the cover!) as well as frantically recording any punk music played on the radio. In 1979 I went to my first Punk gig; it was Devo at Sheffield City Hall. As it was my first gig of any kind I wasn't expecting anything quite so loud. I had never experienced a chest crushing bass drum before."

70's Punk trend setter John Harrison – a Rotherham Punk who bore a striking resemblance to Punk icon Sid Vicious - was an influence, along with Sid himself, on one young Punk convert.

Dave Burkinshaw: "I remember seeing Sid Vicious on the news and my parents and my dad saying what a lout he was! I didn't dress like it straight from the start though; I followed John Harrison's path, as he was always the trendsetter amongst us, and about late 1978 I started going to a Punk clothes shop just off Pond Street in Sheffield (I can't remember its name) but I bought a pair of tartan trousers covered in zips and a string vest. I pierced my ear with a safety pin and put a padlock and chain round my neck. This was it I was a Punk and proud of it. My Mum and Dad didn't like it but I think they just thought it was a phase I was going through. I was listening to groups like The Clash, The Jam and later on Stiff Little Fingers, the Undertones, UK Subs, Angelic Upstarts and more."

Darren Tywnham: "I can remember John: he was the spitting image of Sid Vicious and a top lad. There was a great crowd of us back then. We would spend hours playing all the Punk records in Tony's Mum's front room... music blaring out. Tony's Mum never complained and would always make all the Punks cups of tea. Wonderful times and some right laughs."

Nick Banks: "I had to work on Saturdays at Gainsborough' market for my Mam so I'd slope off to wander round the town during the afternoon. Woollies was the nearest shop to where the stall was so I would peruse the singles in there. Greens as another shop that was a bit like Woolworths but had a record section. I distinctly remember telling me Mam that I was going to buy an LP one day but it had a rude word in the title. I remember that she didn't seem that bothered but was unimpressed. 'Never Mind the Bollocks' always seemed to get put behind Burt Bacharach or James Last although I had been the last to play a record and relished putting 'Never Mind the Bollocks' to the front. Ho hum. *That's not music' 'can't tell a word they are saying....'* etc etc my Mum and Dad would shout! Initial Punk records I bought were 'Live X-cert' The Stranglers, 'Give 'em enough Rope', 'Parallel Lines' by Blondie etc...

"Sometimes expeditions would be ventured on to Circles record shop in Rotherham - *'Is it in the charts'* they would always ask *'err don't think so'* we would reply *'no we only stock chart music....'* they would always reply - so how does music get in the charts then? We would muse.....Sound of Music was always best, racks of Punk singles in plastic bags, but what should you buy? It was always difficult to decide what to buy as you wouldn't want to waste that hard earned pocket money on something duff. Also the real test would be rare trips to Sheffield and Virgin at the bottom of the Moor; dark, mysterious always full of hippies, rockers (Stinking of gyp juice - patchouli oil) and Punks... really intimidating!! Ask one of the guys about a record or ask for it to be played and risk a sneer at something 'uncool'? Don't think so!

"Punk music was the conversational topic of choice in school. I vividly remember Dom Wood recanting his story of visiting this dark, dank subterranean club in Sheffield to see the Skids with a stage so low it cut into your legs. It sounded so very exciting and very cool: So sometime later a plan was hatched for a load of us to go to see the Damned at the Top Rank. Tickets were purchased (how I don't know) and we all piled on the bus (the 287 Maltby-Sheffield?) We knew the gig was an over 18's affair so we needed a plan to get in. New birthdates were memorized all round. What could go wrong?? The concourse outside the Top Rank was packed with Punks- all looking really way out and very cool to see Rat Scabies wandering nonchalantly around was brilliant - pop stars don't do that kind of thing?? We saw other kids being turned away, so we all decide that new birthdates might not be enough Get in plan part 2: send Punkiest looking kid in our group in first and the rest of us will get in unnoticed!! So Graham Torr was volunteered by the rest and we followed close behind in the door crush. *'What school y'at?'* said bouncer *'Oakwood?'* Graham said without thought...'refund at that window son...' we all skipped past as this was happening (great mates eh!!) and once inside were almost sick with laughter at what had just happened.

"The concert was a real eye-opener. Artery first up. Why is he shakin a biscuit tin? Unusual stuff I'm sure but we wanted the real deal. Ruts next: this is more like!! It was absolutely fantastic, Malcolm Owen very impressive. As the Top Rank got fuller and fuller we retreated to the balcony. The Damned were all we wanted them to be, they were brilliant. That night really made an impression on me. Details have been lost to my memory cells after this time but the excitement of the crowd and the music was very special. I don't remember gob so much but I bet there was plenty. Yuck. Sadly we couldn't stay to the very end as the last bus to ours left at 10.35pm or so, so we had to drag ourselves away and get down Pond Street sharpish. So many things to talk about we must have gone over the whole night for days and days after. I don't recall Graham telling us about his night though.

"After that I tried to get to gigs as much as possible, I remember having to go on my own to quite a few (maybe no one could afford it??) The Clash were spectacular, right down the front with my head in Mick Jones monitor (couldn't hear for days) even getting smacked in the head and some get trying to nick my jacket didn't phase me...Siouxsie and the Banshees/Altered Images - I remember Siouxsie flashed her tits to the balcony on the left (I was on the right!!); UK Subs where the guitarist demolished the stage...Adam and the Ants in full 'Kings of the Wild frontier' finery, I even got a bit of his outfit and played the bass when it was thrust in my face... Never got turned away but sometimes had to watch out for marauding skins that seemed to lurk waiting for any passing punks chasing you through Pond Street."

Punk posters from 1977

Tony Beesley: "I always had a lot of time for some of the underdogs of Punk and once I started gonna the big city, I would go and buy lots of singles from Revolution Records on the gallery at the Castle market in Sheffield: bands like Chelsea, Radiators from Space, the Wasps, Saints and the most unhip Punk band of them all, as far as local Punks were concerned – Generation X. My favourite of them all has to be the Adverts though! I started with 'Gary Gilmore's Eyes' and moved onto all of their singles 'Safety in Numbers', 'No Time to be 21', 'Television's Over' and even the much maligned 'My Place' which my mate Andy Goulty bought when it came out and loved it... many punks taking the piss out of him for it too. I love the Adverts and I always will."

Punk Rock must have infiltrated almost every school playground, youth club and disco throughout the whole of late 70's UK. It provided the soundtrack to a whole generation of 13 to 16 year olds, all of whom must have been aching desperately to see these Punk bands in person, but often had to make do with the naïve but fun act of emulating their new wave heroes in their front rooms... for the time being anyhow.

The self expression of one young Rotherham Punk Rocker who had already started seeing the Punk bands up on stage would almost result in a night in the cells. John Harrison had been captivated by Punk since hearing his brother's Sex Pistols and Jam records back in early 77. Spurred on by older Punk mate Bryan Bell, he ventured to a cluster of late 70's Punk gigs at the Top Rank: one of his favourites being the Adverts, at which gig John was thrown onto the stage by Bryan and the rest of the Punk gang landing right at Punk pin-up Gaye Advert's feet. The excitement of this and the euphoria of the gig was still sending adrenalin through him on the trek home back to Rawmarsh.

John Harrison: (Rotherham Punk) "One night coming back from seeing the Adverts in Sheffield, me and my mate Bryan Bell, and someone else who I can't quite remember, we got a taxi to Rotherham and set off to walk the rest of the way home to Rawmarsh. While we were walking through Parkgate, along Broad Street, there was a road up with all those flashing beacons at the side. As we were drunk, we each picked one of these beacons up and walked up the hill with them on top of our heads, the beacons flashing away. A police car came past and pulled up; a cop got out and asked us what we thought we were doing, what's the game lads! Unfortunately for Bry, the policeman was related to my brother's wife and he was no fan of my brother, and then he found out my name from his walkie talkie (after I told him who I was).

The Adverts at Sheffield Top Rank: Is Gaye Advert glancing down at young Punk John Harrison? (Photos: Nick Hawksworth)

"We both got arrested and taken to Rawmarsh police station and were both searched for drugs etc. Because of my age, they couldn't put me in a cell, so I ended up in a detention room, while Bry was banged up in a cell. They discovered a jumping bean I had made myself with a ball-bearing and capsule and they asked me what it was. I told em it was a jumping bean and showed em how it worked. They obviously thought it was a drug or something, so were disappointed it weren't. From there, I sent the cops to my brother's address, and they came back and quizzed me again getting the truth out of me... that I was living at my Mother and Dad's house. An hour or so later my Dad turned up at the police station, after I had my fingerprints taken and photo taken. They then let me go with poor old Bry still left behind in his cell. We got charged and it ended up with me and Bry making an appearance before the magistrate in court: fortunately we were both let off with a conditional discharge. I was told by my Dad to never wear those Punk Rock clothes again. I didn't take much notice of that and continued to be a Punk!"

Nick Banks: "Once I had been to a few Punk gigs it was clear that to look cool/good a leather motorbike jacket was needed... Really needed! So money was scrimped and saved (I was still working on the market stall at this time). I can't remember where the purchase happened; the Market would be a good bet: That wonderful smell, arms as stiff as boards - right proper. My elder brother got a leather jacket at the same time and he got our younger mate Steve Allot's (pictured in Our Generation on page 239) Mum to paint the 'No More Heroes' sleeve on the back. It was photo quality, really impressive (and through a circuitous route got me my first Punk girlfriend.). I also elected to paint the edges of the seams of my jacket red. Subtle like.

"Now the Haircut? This was a bit of a problem area. Quite a few of my contemporaries had gone for the traditional spiky look, but my mum had always cut my hair, how was I going to get round this? - Sound like a right div!!! Well, I didn't really and I guess it damaged my Punk credentials. I could try to say that I was going for the Ramones look but I don't think I would have thought of that at the time."

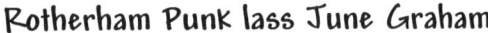

Rotherham Punk lass June Graham

Tony Beesley: "Amongst the growing gang of school New Wave kids I knew were my best mates Andy and Pete, Shaun Angell, Tracy Stanley, Clarkey, Nicky Booth, Lynne Haythorne and June Graham who was mad on Blondie and the Boomtown Rats, amongst others. We all knocked about together and had some good laughs. The youth club nights were great and the closer the lasses got to leaving school, the more the coloured spikes appeared. I think loads of us Punk kids must have celebrated leaving school by having our hair dyed. It was a great time for self expression, that's for sure!"

hair and back-combed

Tony Beesley: "We were buying all sorts of records- us 78-79 Punk kids: I bought the first Squeeze LP, Jean Michele Jarre's 'Oxygene', 'Magic Fly' by Space and singles by Tom Robinson Band, Japan, the Flys, Fingerprintz and all the Elvis Costello and Blondie singles; Andy bought all Patti Smith's LP's and singles by the Tourists etc, Pete was into some of the electronica stuff- M's Pop Musik, Bill Nelson's Red Noise and some more obscure stuff. Of course, secretly I was still listening to Bowie and Bolan singles as well, Pete was still crackers on Thin Lizzy and Andy would buy anything that he liked... Punk or not. The Punk stuff would be our main staple diet but it was not the only stuff we liked... it's just that we didn't go around broadcasting a lot of it."

It was the Sex Pistols powerful wall of sound that inspired this young Punk.

Kevin Wells: (Kilamarsh Punk) (Below) "I will never forget the feeling of hearing Steve Jones's guitar sound for the Sex Pistols; it was the most powerful sound a twelve year old could have ever heard. That got me hooked on Punk Rock and a sound that I have followed to this day. Even though I wasn't old enough to go to gigs the buzz of saving up for the latest 7" vinyl or LP is something that cannot be matched in this day of CD and digital download. A visit to the record

shops, (usually Virgin's at the bottom of the Moor, Bradley's many Sheffield outlets and the very frightening skinhead-dodging visits to Revolution on the gallery near the Castle markets) usually resulted in a good few hours standing with my gob open not knowing whether to go for the latest Stranglers or 999 release and then coming out with the latest Dickies single cos it was on coloured vinyl."

Skinheads, as well as other youth cults of the time did occasionally mingle and forget their differences.

Mandy Taylor: "Where I lived in Sheffield (Richmond) there wasn't usually any trouble between Punks, Mods, Skins and Rockers etc, in fact there was a gang of Mods we knew in Woodhouse that used to have house parties and everyone from all genres would come along. I can't ever recall any trouble at all at their parties. I also used to be so embarrassed as there used to be a gang of prog rockers that used to call for me, nice guys but at the time King Crimson didn't float my boat. I tried to make sure I was out, but my mum would let them all in give them drinks and they'd still be waiting for me when I got home!!

"I did, however, come across trouble once, though, when I went into Sheffield City Centre, it used to be renowned for the Skinheads fighting with everyone. On this occasion I was about 15 and I'd been swimming at Sheaf Valley with my two best mates Ruth and Linda. Some Skinheads from the Wybourn started surrounding us as we were coming out towards Pond St. Knifes were pulled by them and we were threatened. They then recognised me from the shop I used to have a Saturday job in and wanted me to nick stuff from the shop for them. I was so scared but somehow I got the guts to stand up to them. I remember standing there staring them out trying to look cool (but shaking inside), then one of the staff from the baths came out and said they'd called the police, I don't think they had as I don't remember the police coming, but it must have scared the Skinheads off. All I can remember is walking home to Richmond (we must have spent our bus fare or something) constantly looking over my shoulder.

"My first DJ stint was at City School. The first record I ever spun in public was either Devo-'Mongoloid' or Sex Pistols- 'Pretty Vacant'. I was new into the school sixth form and took over the stereo in the common room (interestingly enough the boys took over the tuck shop). I think I really must have annoyed the townies in the sixth form constantly playing Devo, Clash and the Sex Pistols, I wish I'd followed my instinct back then and taken the DJ career path instead of waiting till a few years ago, but that's another story!"

Mandy Alleyne: (Barnsley Punk girl) "I was born in Barnsley which was a mining village in those days and the people tended to be set in their ways. As I was growing up I experimented with a number of looks, which quite often shocked most people. I got into music at a young age, Punk being at the forefront of everything. My mum hated the music I listened to and to her it was a dreadful noise, but to her ears I suppose it must have been."

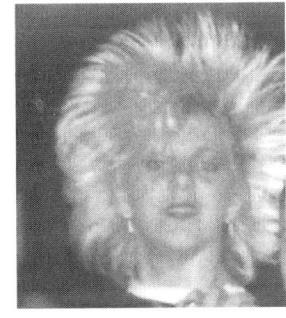

Mandy Taylor: "Music has always been important to me, whenever I hear a particular song it takes me back to either when I first heard it or a specific memory associated with that song. I could go on forever but when I think back to my teens the following are the songs that instantly jump to mind and what I associate with them - 'Janie Jones' and 'Garageland' by The Clash take me back to my Auntie's dining room. The Ruts 'Staring at the Rude Boys' remind me of hockey at school – I was in the school hockey team and one of the team bought me this single for my birthday, we then used to sing this in the mini bus for away games (usually to give us a bit of courage when we played the teams known for playing dirty and trying to get us when the ref wasn't looking!). Devo's 'Whip It' - always makes me want to dance: I remember once at a school party getting up to dance to this crazy Devo style, and everyone surrounding me and this other lad (who was also into Devo) clapping whilst we strutted our stuff. 'I am a Poseur' by X Ray Spex takes me back to hanging around with Ruth and Linda, we'd sing this song to each other when we spotted the townies that really loved themselves.

"When I listened to 'Mary of the Fourth Form' by the Rats I always wanted to be cool like Mary at school, but I was quite a girly swot till I was about 15, I suppose it wasn't till the 6th form that I used to think I was cool, but then my cool was defined as going straight to lessons from clubs and all night parties (usually Steeleys and the Limit) in my going out gear, wagging lessons, swearing at my parents, smoking and drinking. I know I went off the rails somewhat back then but strangely enough my biggest regret is not taking notice of some of the bands that I saw at the Limit and Steeleys."

A trip across the channel saw Mandy come face to face with firstly the uninitiated to Punk and then Punk itself - German style!

Mandy Taylor: "My first memory of a club is a Punk Club in Bremen called something like the Bisbenger. I was 15 and had gone on a school exchange trip. I remember being horrified when I met Martina (sorry Martina) the student whose family I was to stay with, she was dressed like a hippy and had Foreigner in her record collection. It felt like all we did was listen to Foreigner and drink herbal tea. I bought a Devo EP in a local record shop a couple of days after I arrived but she wouldn't let me play it. So I preferred to hang around with some of the German Punks at her school and they took me to the Bisbenger club. I remember hearing some real hardcore stuff and being intrigued by a Punk band called Ideal (pronounced something like e d al). The German Punks did me a tape of them and I played the tape to death. I've tried to look them up on the *internet* since but can't find anything – I've probably got the spelling wrong I know!"

Young Punk kids were appearing from all over the Punk planet from mid 77 onwards, spurred on by the appearance of such TV events as the Top of the Pops appearance of the Sex Pistols with 'Pretty Vacant'; Marc Bolan's Punk showcase acts on Marc; Revolver on ITV the following year; The Jam's frenetic Mod Punk energy and the clarion call of The Clash and 'Something Better Change' by the Stranglers. Even the much fabled and loved Artful Dodger managed to join in with the Punk fun.

Young Punk fan John Ashmore had played the role during long runs of the stage show at school. His enthusiasm for spectacle off the stage spread to the explosive Punk scene! Another colourful Punk character is also remembered in this story.

UK Subs at Sheffield Penthouse (Kristan James Melik)

John Ashmore: (Rotherham Punk fan) "People ask me *'where did we get our clothes from?'...* Well there really was nowhere as far as I knew that sold Punk clothes. The main places were the two Army stores in Rotherham town centre, where I used to buy army trousers and donkey jackets: stick some chains on em and that was the look. One of the craziest Punk kids was Mark Barnet. He got up to allsorts. I remember he had his hair sprayed with jet-black car spray. Can you believe it? At school he kept turning up in jeans and the teacher says *'get yerself home and come back with some trousers on'...* Barnet came back in his Pyjama bottoms. He was going out with a lass called Tracy at the time and the stupid bleeder painted *'Mark loves Tracy'* in massive white paint... straight outside his own house. The cops came straight away and asked Barnet if it was him *'Yeah it was me'* he just owned up straight away."

Jamie 'Headcharge' Smith: "I was so lucky being brought up in Pitsmoor!! One particular memory is of a night that we were playing footy just down the steps outside the big old scout hall, when all of a sudden I heard yet more crazy sounds coming from the hall: I immediately forgot about the game and ran up the grass bank opposite as the widows were far too high for me to see through. I was met with these five guys hammering out an unholy racket and again was hooked. This turned out to be the Stunt Kites and like before (with Rich of the Cabs) I ended up seeing them at the bus top and eventually chatting and becoming friends.

"One of my earliest festy experiences was Western Park with the Stunt kites, 2.3 and Vice Versa but my memory fades a little on that apart from it was a great day out for a young kid inspired by the new sounds I was hearing: I do clearly remember this girl getting up on stage and swiftly going topless so that was it I was most definitely hooked FOR GOOD!"

Valerie Garvey: (Sheffield Punkette) "I first heard the Sex Pistols and thought it was just something different. Then I saw a picture of Billy Idol in Jackie mag and thought he was so nice. I wanted to hear his music so some mates brought a plastic record player to my shed and we listened to some Punk on that with a 2p stuck on the arm to stop it jumping. I then thought well I never fitted in to how everyone else looked so I will be different and turned Punk!

"When I was at school in Nottingham I remember going to have my ears pierced twice and everyone said wow and I felt so good so I dyed my hair with crepe paper - if you wet it the colour came off and I put that in my hair along with food colouring etc. Then it went from strength to strength: I left school; had my nose pierced twice and self bleached my hair topped off with wearing my dads shirts with the collars cut off. The rest is history."

Julie Lee: (Rotherham Punk girl) "I don't remember exactly why I got into Punk – I think it was a combination of things really – the music, clothes, hairstyles, attitude. I was at school when I first got into it so I couldn't do much about my hair but I did start spiking it and I bleached it at the sides – that was about all I could

get away with at the time. I also pierced my nose while I was still at school. I did it myself in the bathroom at home. I think I was the first person at school with a pierced nose. On the day of my last exam – English Literature O level - I went to the hairdressers and had my hair bleached and dyed bright pink. The exam was in the morning and by about 3.30 my hair was pink. I loved that colour!

"Over the next four or five years I had my hair pretty much every colour imaginable but I went back to pink many times. The wildest I had it was violet and pink at the same time – that was a special dye job for a trip to France. My hair was medium length and back-combed to the hilt although I did go through a period of wearing

it in the sun when I had it orange. It looked great but was very high maintenance. I spent a small fortune on hairspray when I was a Punk. In terms of clothes, the trousers were skin-tight, often with bondage straps and zips. I had a kilt, which I wore over the top of my trousers, a bullet belt, Destroy shirt and all the usual stuff. My skirts were very short and tight. I remember when me and two mates went to London for a few days. We got a lift there and slept in a van. We hardly had anything to eat and had to walk everywhere because we spent our money on Clothes from Carnaby Street and Kings Road.

Julie and Punk friends in Soho

"The most important piece of clothing to any Punk was our leather jackets – that's what identified us, you could recognise people by their jackets. On the back I had 'The Damned' painted across the top panel and a picture of Siouxsie in the main panel. I kept my jacket a long time after I stopped being a Punk, I just couldn't part with it, and then I gave it to a guy I was going out with and he wore it for a while before passing it on to a mate. I used to be on the bus in Sheffield and I would see my jacket going down the street on someone's back, still with the picture of Siouxsie on the back panel.

"Mostly people reacted to my hair rather than my clothes or anything else. It was always so bright and therefore so obvious. People stared at me all the time but I didn't care. Sometimes people made comments but if they were out of order I just gave them the finger or snarled at them or something, I didn't waste time getting into anything because I didn't care what they thought anyway – why would I!

"I went to loads of gigs when I was a Punk – there were so many bands around and they were always doing gigs. I saw pretty much every band there was to see but the best gigs were things like Christmas on Earth. That was on in Leeds and it was an all day gig with loads of Punk bands. I think the Damned headlined but I don't remember much more about it. Me and my mate drank a half bottle of vodka each on the train on the way over so we were pretty pissed when we got there and it was only about 10 am.

"My favourite bands included Siouxsie and the Banshees, the Damned, the Clash, the Cure, Stiff Little Fingers and Killing Joke. The Sheffield scene was pretty good because all the bands played there when they toured. Alongside that you had the smaller venues like the Marples and a couple of other pubs where you could see the less mainstream bands and local bands. There were also a few great pubs in Sheffield where Punks used to go and drink, not to see bands. It was good going somewhere where you could just hang out with other Punks over a few pints of lager. It was much harder to do that in Rotherham.

"I was never directly hassled and had a couple of mates who were skins so maybe that helped. I do remember there being a lot of hassle and there were loads of free gigs put on to try and bring Punks and Skins together through music. The tickets were free and the bands were good, people like Killing Joke. I was also friends with a young Rockabilly from Rotherham and never had any hassle from Teds – not sure if being mates with him was the reason. I remember having a great time at some gig on Herringthorpe playing fields where the Specials were headlining. There were all kinds of people there and I don't remember any hassle.

"I don't think I so much got tired of the Punk scene as I grew out of it. There came a point when the Punk lifestyle of not conforming, doing whatever I wanted, seeing loads of bands, not doing much with my life etc. didn't fit any more. I had moved to Sheffield and started to make new friends who weren't Punks and I slowly started to move away from Punk myself."

Tony Beesley: "Around Spring 1979, I had saved up enough cash from my paper round and selling off old Queen LP's I no longer wanted and I sent off for some so-called Punk strides from the back pages of the NME. You could get allsorts from the ads in there back then – there was Punk t-shirts, Punk at Parrot, Bonaparte records and Small Wonder label's listing (I still have an old catalogue of theirs with the records I had all crossed out that I had). Anyway, a red pair of proper punk trousers was on their way to me through the post. It was a Saturday morning and the Banana Splits were on the telly when they arrived: I couldn't wait to open the parcel and try them on... I was sick to death of wearing the D.I.Y sewn up Brutus jeans. When I opened em, the trousers were fuckin' fluffy velvet-type material and looked a right state. What a let down... teach me to consider discarding my home grown Punk attire that one... I looked over at the telly and could have sworn Bingo was laughing at me!

"Even so, I was absolutely immersed in Punk Rock and new wave for around 4 years, it was a 24/7 thing for me, not a uniform or fashion thing at all. It was a complete transformation of who I was and I held on to it hoping that the future ahead was going to be as fixating as I felt at the time: I truly could not imagine a future without Punk Rock, and all of its music, in my life!"

Batty: (Rotherham Punk/Mod fan) "I was never really into the Clash (or the Sex Pistols) that much but it was the Angelic Upstarts, Sham 69, UK Subs, The Jam and a few others that did it for me. I also saw Hazel O' Connor with Duran Duran backing her up early on! My venues were mainly the Limit, Marples, Top Rank, Sheffield Poly and Rotherham Clifton Hall where me and my mate Darren Twynham got backstage and spoke at length to Upstarts singer Mensi and being young 'uns we upset him by calling him a Geordie: he's a Mackem from Sunderland and told us what that meant in no uncertain terms. We also found out where he got his facial scar from too. I can also remember after The Jam gig at the Top Rank when the Skinheads came in through the doors and got chased back out. At the time, I had just managed to get Bruce and Rick's autographs on my ticket but we couldn't get nowhere near Weller for the fans."

Tony Beesley: "I remember buying 'Armed Forces' by Elvis Costello on release and being disapointed by it after that run of singles before it ('I don't wanna go to Chelsea', 'Pump it up' and 'Radio Radio etc) and thinking it would be as good as 'This Years Model', which in its own way it was, but I just couldn't see it at the time, so I sold it on straight away to Stranglers fan Adi Robinson. This was the fold out cover and free post cards and single version too and I later bought it back in standard form. Elvis was great and I came to love his work throughout the 80's and bought a clutch of his albums, but, like many, he craftily rode the rest of the new wave to his own benefit and barely ever gave any credence to it in the years to come."

Valerie Garvey: "I loved being a Punk I felt like I fitted in unlike at school etc. You could always go down town day or night and meet up with someone you knew. Someone would always buy you a drink and on a Saturday night there was always a party to go to. I didn't just knock around with Punks but other people who were different: some had been Punks and had grown out of it but they still dressed alternative.

"It wasn't always nice though: I used to get some right hassle. I walked into a pub once; I think it was the Pump or Royal Standard and the manager took one look at me and said you're barred I was shocked and asked why and he said *'well look at you...!!!!'* Another time I was walking into a pub and a big beer man pushed me into a load of tables *'saying look at that xxxxxx look at the state of her.'* I was so angry as it had taken me hours to do my hair n' make up and he was just a rather over-weight man squeezed into too small clothes. Another time I popped into my local shop and as I went out two women started talking about me saying horrible things. Little did they know my old Sunday school teacher was right behind them and gave them a good talking to. Saying I was one of the nicest people to know. I did get used to it: things would make me laugh like old ladies talking about me in the bus queue I would think I'm Punk but I can hear you. They would be saying look at the colour of her hair disgraceful and they were stood there with their purple rinsed hair...!!! I was lucky that I never got beat up unlike some of my friends did, girls n' boys too- sadly."

Neil Anderson: (Chesterfield Punk) "My first experience of trawling the record shops of Sheffield was finding Rare 'N' Racy on Devonshire Street. I found The Damned's first album there for about £1.50 in pristine condition. It was the best find of my life. I lived in Chesterfield at the time and it was always a bit of a circus getting to Sheffield involving various buses and trains. God knows how I found Rare n' Racy – I am pretty sure it was my uncle's influence who used to frequent it and had told me to give it a blast.

"I gravitated from there to Virgin at the bottom of The Moor: Great shop but they never seemed to turn the lights on - it always seemed to be in permanent twilight but I suppose that added to the aura. They always seemed to refuse to play Punk Rock. I remember a girl pleading for them to play Stiff Little Fingers - it fell on deaf ears as they just carried on playing Yes or something. But for all of its faults they stocked some quality stuff and the place had a great vibe around it."

Too much too young Punk posters

Billy Idol (with Generation X) at the Sheffield Top Rank early 1979, The Police – who managed to arrest and fool many a young teenage new waver with their pre-fame Punk pretences, A tourist (Annie Lenox) at the Limit, Elvis Costello whose aim was true but who rode the new wave for a career kick-start and a 1978 Sheffield University Blondie poster

Annie Lennox photo (Kristan James Melik) Billy Idol (Nick Hawksworth)

Tony Beesley: "I didn't care what limitations were being imposed on me. As a young teenager lots of things are expected of you: be it school, your friends or parents etc. I truly did not care about anything at this time, I just had to shed everything and become a new person. I was confused and frustrated and Punk Rock was the perfect kick off to give me the confidence to be what I wanted to be. It really was like a cleansing of the soul for me, especially the more I became intoxicated with the whole spirit and attitude of Punk. My Mother would say that reading Sounds magazine was corrupting me ha ha!! God rest her soul. My family were saying *'Our Tony is gonna end up to no good'.* The truth is that I was never really any good at much to start with anyway, I was certainly no fucking David Watts thats for sure, but one thing I was good at... and that was expressing myself and sticking two fingers up to the rules being set out. Of course when you get past this point, you have to start thinking about doing something to back up your convictions. Saying *Fuck you* to the system is ok, but if you don't have anything of use to offer in exchange why bother in the first place. So I started expressing myself not just via my clothes and their paint splattered decorations, but with my words and ideals and later on taking up the guitar, writing a fanzine and anything else that came to mind that was positive and expressive!"

Batty: "I went to Wath comprehensive school, and during the dinner hour, there was just enough time to run and catch a bus to Rotherham town centre and get to the Sound of Music records shop and buy a handful of new records from the likes of the Ruts or The Jam: then back to school again."

Tony Beesley: "And then there was that Richard Jobson dance that we used to do at the Youth club when 'Into the Valley' came out: legs kicking high as we could. That used to fucking knacker us kids out something rotten, but it were a right laugh. Most people think that Punk dances meant just jumping up and down on the spot, which it was a lot of the time, especially when we started going to gigs as that was the only real option when crammed into the pogoing mass like sardines, but a bit of effort did go into inventing new and different dances when time, space and location permitted. The robot dance we had seen on Revolver was one; the epileptic shake to the Lurkers was another. I can remember me and Pete Roddis going to a wedding do at Rawmarsh Baths Hall and after a night of the usual crap of the time, the Nolans, Kool and the Gang etc, we managed to locate The Jam's 'All around the World' in the DJ's collection: we got up to that and cleared the dance floor in split seconds, everyone staring in bewilderment as these two quiet donkey jacket-wearing spiky-haired kids in the corner who suddenly had erupted into two frantic vertically-travelling maniacs going crazy to this wall of Punk Rock- Mod assault of a record!"

Andy Coles: (Rotherham Punk fan)"I think the first time I became aware of 'Punk' was whilst waiting for my once-every-three-months 'pruning' in John Bird's Barber Shop on Ship Hill in Rotherham. On a small table, there was a copy of the Daily Mirror that had a photo of 'one of them Punk Rockers' with a pierced cheek and stories about how *bad* these people were. I can remember thinking *'they've made this up: people never do things like that.'* As I started liking the music, I knew that I would never in a million years dare to dress like the older, more-sussed lads at school who were also getting into Punk, I was *far* too shy for anything like that; my hair was side-parted and I wore dodgy cords (but hey, so did The Undertones!). My mate and I had been both into Slade and then Abba, but our musical tastes suddenly diverted; he went off into the world of ELO and Status Quo and I began to like the Punky stuff that was coming into the charts at the time. In 1978 I bought a K-Tel compilation album called 'Action Replay' which had a few new wave songs on it... 'Rat Trap', 'Hanging on the Telephone', 'Radio Radio', 'Come Back Jonee', 'Drummer Man'...and I loved them. I had missed the Sex Pistols boat; they had now split and their barrel was being well and truly scraped. The singles 'C'mon Everybody', 'My Way' and 'Something Else' were doing the rounds. My parents bought me 'The Great Rock n' Roll Swindle' on vinyl for Christmas and I pored over the cover for hours, loving the bright garish colours inside the gatefold sleeve, the 'ransom letter' style fonts and photos of the Pistols in action. Exaggerated rumours of the group's antics circulated round the school... *"One of 'em crapped ont stage and't other 'et it!"* and so on.

"I was in the same form as Phil Chatterton (as in Phil Murray and The Boys from Bury) who raved about Punk bands such as The Damned and The Buzzcocks. I soon had a copy of 'Never Mind the Bollocks', which I reluctantly swapped with John for a copy of The Clash's 'Give 'em Enough Rope'. I wasn't that impressed at the time (though I love it now). I swapped that with someone else for another copy of 'Bollocks'. God knows how many times I've bought that album on different formats; picture disc, remastered CD, re-remastered CD, re-re-remastered limited special edition box set ...*'ever get the feeling you've been cheated?'* indeed. I felt that the lyrics were, and still are, absolutely brilliant!

"Some of us used to buy those ex-army canvas rucksacks for school from Wakefield's Army Stores in Rotherham and write Punk band names on the pockets in felt tip...some of them we'd never even heard the sound of. It just looked good...or so we thought. A book that someone brought into school, 'The Sex Pistols File' by Ray Stevenson, made for essential reading. It was full of music press clippings and photos; *'Where did they get those fantastic shirts from?'*

"Meanwhile, I naively stuck with the dodgy cords and zip-up cardigans, but with luminous green and black striped socks (oh my God) and was unsurprisingly mocked for it...*'Where's thi' bum flap then, Colesy?"*... bastards. I used to have those massive badges from Pandora's Box on Wellgate in Rotherham on my blazer and still have a few of those.

"One thing I THOUGHT that I had picked up from various interviews that I'd read about 'Punk' in Smash Hits, NME, Record Mirror and Sounds was that it wasn't *meant* to be about wearing a uniform... but if Punks themselves were insisting that you had to wear certain items of clothing, then *surely* that was missing the point? In those days, you had to be in one tribe or the other. Towards the end of school, my musical tastes expanded to take in the so-called Post-Punk bands, such as PiL with 'Metal Box', Joy Division (Ian Curtis had just committed suicide) and The Human League, whose first two albums remain on my all-time favourites list. I liked the synthesiser stuff that was emerging; John Foxx, Tubeway Army, the revamped Ultravox (who my ELO-loving mate also adored) and OMD. It was 'shiny' and 'futuristic' and synths looked easier to play than a guitar! Not that I could afford one. 'Smash Hits' held a competition to win a Korg Micro Preset synthesiser, but no luck there... bastard."

Even though Punk was the major influence on Phil Chatterton, he was starting to develop a taste for Rock n' Roll and the fusion of Rockabilly with Punk that would eventually come to be termed Psychobilly. The gig outlook still remained consistently eclectic though.

Phil Chatterton: "I went to loads of gigs: I even went to see Shakin' Stevens and the Sunsets at the City Hall. I saw the Jets and Stray Cats as well. Stray Cats were amazing; to say what little they actually had instruments wise they came out with a fantastic sound. Brian Setzer was a great guitarist. I saw them at the Sheffield Lyceum and Leeds University.

"A while before that, I can remember our Rich taking me to a gig at the City Hall Ballroom which was underneath the City Hall. The bands playing were Clock DVA and Vice Versa. Our Rich was with all of his Punky type mates and I was sat looking around mesmerised by all the strangeness of it all. Back then Martin Fry was in Vice Versa and the band eventually became ABC a year or so later. That night he had a blue tracksuit type thing on and he had a Wedge style haircut, dancing around all over the stage. Clock DVA were... weird! Eventually someone ended up getting me interested in the Meteors by passing the first LP onto me, and I had the flat top haircut done and it all started from there."

It's hard to imagine and visualise nowadays, how a revolutionary music scene and all of its attractions and signals of danger could affect and impress itself on kids so young but obviously receptive to its appeal. Talk about teenage kicks... how about kindergarten under tens Punks! Too much too young personified!

Carl Myers: (Greasbrough Punk fan and Mod) "I was born in 1969 and grew up in a mining town called Rotherham in South Yorkshire. We lived in an area called Rockingham. I remember my eldest cousin Nigel told me he had a new album to play me by one of his favourite bands of the time. We were all sat in the dining room, just after having our pickled cucumber and onion sandwiches when he put on the first track. Blasting out of the speakers came 'Holidays in the sun' by the Sex Pistols. My cousin started bouncing around the table doing this stupid dance whilst ripping off his tee shirt. I remember him wearing his school tie loosely around his neck as he pogoed up and down on the living room floor. *'I've told you before, turn that crap off.'* shouted my Uncle as he lent over to stop the music. *'If your gunna play that shite then get up to your room and play it there'* he added.

"We all retreated to my cousin's room where we continued to play the 'Never Mind the Bollocks' album. I thought, *'fuck this is a cool album'.* With all that swearing and cool music, I need this album myself I thought. I saved up all my pocket money and tried to persuade my mum to get me the album but she refused to go in the shop and buy it due to the swearing on the front cover. She said I would have to go in and buy it myself while she waited outside. I remember the moment to this day going into 'Carousel Tapes' just on the outside of the market in Rotherham and buying it. I couldn't wait to get the tape home so I could blast it out in my bedroom and practise my pogo dance. Me and my mate Andy Fereday were both hooked on the 'Sex Pistols'. We used to walk around Rockingham with my cassette player blasting out the Pistols album. I remember us making our own bum flaps out of some old jeans of my dad's. We hung them off the back of our asses with some old bog chain that I nicked from the school toilets. I spent all my pocket money on music magazines, badges and patches from Pandora's Box in the market. I got my mum to sew all the patches onto my denim jacket. I felt proper cool walking around our streets trying to be all grown up hanging around with the older boys who all had girlfriends."

The inspiration from Punk and consequently some of the bands that had been revitalised by its energy led young Punk fan John Atkin to begin to take seriously the art of playing bass guitar.

John Atkin: "I remember my friend Ian Denham and I sneaked off to see The Who at the Birmingham NEC, we had lied to our parents saying we was stopping at each other's houses as we had to sleep in the railway station as we couldn't get home. Naturally we got found out and were both in the dog house. Around this time, Julian and Gary Davies had decided to form a band, and because I had a bass I was asked to join. Trouble was... that for the first year of playing I was so bad, most of the practices consisted of Julian either pointing at me with his drum sticks or grabbing the bass off me and shouting *'give it me'* or *'Look it goes like this'.* Then after a year it just clicked and eventually it was how I made my living. Nobody in local bands owned a decent guitar (a Gibson or a Fender was a rare sight)... I remember going to see 3D Fiction just because they had a Yamaha DX 7! But, my first band 'Alternative Route' was now born."

Another young kid wanted a part of the Punk band experience!

Dally: "It was in 1979 that I joined my first Punk band. I'd been playing guitar, drums and piano from an early age and when Punk came along it all made sense. The band was called The Social Outcasts and featured Rich Scottrick on drums, the current Boys from Bury drummer. My Mum bought me the bass guitar from the guy who was leaving the band so that I could join. All the other members of the band were my elder brother's age (3 years older than me) but they took me under their wing. I'd grown up living around the corner from a couple of them. I had to get special permission from the school youth club to rehearse there with the band as I was officially too young to join. Slow progress meant that I ended up leaving the band to form a band with my brother on bass, me switching to lead guitar. We practised quite a lot and I started writing the songs. We only played one gig in the main hall at school but most people were surprised by how accomplished I was for someone at that age."

Neil Anderson: "The biggest gauntlet in terms of music was definitely the shop on first floor of Castle Market, Revolution I think it was called. They had The Damned's 'New Rose' poster on the door and I so wanted it (thankfully I managed to buy it at a gig a couple of years later). When I wasn't there I was trawling the likes of Bradley's, Violet Mays and the fantastic Rat Records near the Leadmill - I've still got the carrier bag from there somewhere."

The lure of that most Thatcherite of all youthful dislikes – the Youth Training scheme presented itself to one young Punk kid with an eye for a musical future.

John Atkin: (Rotherham Punk fan) "Punk to me was more than just music: it was who you were! Rotherham in the late 70s early 80s was a bleak place but it was home. Julian Jones introduced me to Punk by giving me a C60 cassette full of Punk music like The Clash, The Buzzcocks and the Stranglers. At dinner time we used to go to the youth club which had a room where we went to listen to Punk records, I think it was the pool room, but we had no interest in pool or getting the highest score on space invaders.

"When we were at school no one expected to get a job but the thought of £25 a week on a YTS was tempting as that meant I could save up and buy a better guitar because I had no chance on my £2 a week pocket money. But that's what Punk was - being part of a community where we felt we belonged: the bands talked our language and sang songs on how we felt. One gig I do remember was The Jam just before they got famous I think the tickets were less than £3.

"I remember this kid who used to play Punk records in our room, I have forgotten his name but he was a Stranglers fan and he said that he played the bass. I had no idea what a bass was and imagined it to be a great big organ type thing but from then on my interest in the bass was born. My granddad had got some compensation from an accident he had while working down the pit so he gave us all £100 each. From this I persuaded him to let me buy a bass guitar and in 30+ years of being around guitars I have never played a bass as bad as the one I started with."

Stephen Beesley: (Rotherham Punk fan/authors nephew) "The clearest memory I have of the Punk days is going down to our Tony's and hanging about in his front room (where he had all his records and Punk mates would be coming and going, though their names now pass me by apart from Andy Goulty and Pete Roddis)... One day Tony had this new record by the Undertones called 'Jimmy Jimmy' and he says *'Have a listen to this'* and before he put it on I was singing the chorus of 'Jimmy Jimmy'... he says *'Well that's how it goes, how did you know.'* I had some Punk

records myself and liked The Clash, Undertones and stuff like The Dickies: I got a clip off our Dave (my older brother) for selling their single 'Nights in white Satin' on white vinyl. I would also go along with Tony to the record shops sometimes and that's how I would end up buying some Punk records as well.

"Another Punk memory is the time me and our Dave went to some do, wedding or whatever it was, in our punk clothes. It was at Rawmarsh Baths, I was about 12 years old. I remember us two walking down there with my Mum and Dad and we were wearing our Dennis the Menace striped jumpers, fake leather PVC trousers with a chain down the leg, boots and our hair spiked up. On the way down we were practising our Punk dance we were planning on doing when we had the chance at the Baths hall. My Dad was taking the mickey most of the way down. There must be other stuff that went on, but it's a long time ago now and hard to remember it all."

Tony Beesley: "I discovered the Damned by reading a Paul Weller interview where he said that the music press had been responsible for the Damned splitting up. I think it was in Rock On magazine. The lasses at school used to bring me loads of colour posters of the Jam that they had torn out of their Jackie comics and this article was one brought along too. The Damned's records were long since deleted and could only be bought in the back pages of the NME for a few weeks of my paper round money combined. As a result, it would be the reformed Damned's April 79 released 'Love Song' that would be my first Damned vinyl purchase: three of four different picture sleeves, but unfortunately not on red vinyl. A Top of the Pops appearance and a chance finding of the first Damned album 'Damned Damned Damned' from Revolution records in Sheffield were pivotal in nurturing my zest for getting into the band and seeing them play live.

"I managed to get to see the Damned at the Top Rank a few times. Their 1979 gig was as chaotic as you could possibly expect from the band. Slaughter and the Dogs didn't turn up for a start! We got to briefly meet the Damned who were as crazy and anarchic in stance as we'd expected. The Captain was mad as a hatter, Dave Vanian as mysterious and vampish as Nosferatu himself and Chris Miller the Punk drummer also known as Rat Scabies told us to *'Fuck off'!* Punk Rock or what?

"The Damned's set that night consisted of all their singles – 'Problem Child', 'New Rose' and 'Neat Neat Neat' included, and if I remember rightly they also did a couple more off their much maligned and self-loathed November 77 LP 'Music for Pleasure'. The greatest response of the night was when they charged through their anarchic anthem 'Smash it up' followed by Rat kicking over his drum kit and throwing pints of beer all over the crowd. A few of the Rawmarsh Comp Punk kids were there that night. I went along with Pete Roddis (as always) and Beanz, but we saw quite a few kids from school there who were sort of floating Punk fans. Original 77 Rawmarsh Punk stalwart Bryan Bell wearing his tartan kilt and bondage trousers was diving around even before the band came on so we joined in with him and his gang and we never stopped all the way through the pre-gig slab of classic Punk sounds and then continued throughout the Damned's set. The pogoing was non-stop and frantic; me and Pete pushed ourselves into an almost frenzied state, we were that into the atmosphere and energy buzzing from around us. We almost crawled out of the venue that night; we were absolutely knackered and no way was I gonna go to school the next day!"

Anarchy, Chaos and Destruction with the Damned at the Top Rank 1979

Damned Photos: Courtesy of Tim Jones

This particular gig was given a firm thumbs down in a 1979 issue of Sheffield fanzine NMX, as was a Generation X gig – attended by hordes of young teen-Punks earlier in the year. The excitement felt by the next wave of gig-going Punk kids was not being enjoyed so avidly by all of the more seasoned Punk gig goers of Sheffield. Understandably what may seem to be leading the way for the 14 year olds was by now, very much almost old hat for the older generation. Still, the chance of actually seeing these much loved Punk bands live on stage for the first time just as the whole era was about to peak... following what had seemed like a lifetime of collecting their vinyl offerings, was clearly a very exciting time.

Paul Simonon and Nicky 'Topper' Headon of The Clash entering the Top Rank for their London Calling date (Debra Marshall)

The Clash - Sheffield calling at the Top Rank

Tony Beesley: "1979 had been a fantastic year for music. I had started it with a seriously obsessed non-stop daily playing of The Jam's 'All Mod Cons' and 'Give em Enough Rope' by The Clash and discovered loads of new bands and records. The fun and excitement was non-stop... this voyage of Punk discovery. The days at the youth club, buying records, parties, laughs and great times with my mates and trying to adopt a new wave look massively influenced by Weller, and also The Clash, were amongst some of my favourite times of my whole life. What could be better than experiencing seeing The Clash live to top it all off!"

The Clash were supported by the late Mikey Dread for this date: previous Clash supports at the Top Rank had been Richard Hell and The Voidoids, Slits, Specials and Chelsea.

All Clash Live at the Top Rank photos sole copyright of Nick Hawksworth Badges courtesy of Pete Skidmore

Tony Beesley: "The Punk gigs that we saw at the close of the seventies and the first few months of 1980 were also the peak for Punk for me personally. A small handful of us mini-Punk kids had been listening to and absorbing Punk Rock for a good couple of solid years: the records, the sporadic TV appearances of our favourite bands on the Marc Bolan show, Revolver, Something Else and Top of the Pops, making scrapbooks out of the NME and Sounds music weeklies (remember the Boomtown Rats one I gave you when 'Rat Trap' came out June?), our frantic pogo sessions at the youth club or the hours of Punk sessions in my front room; the gate-crashed parties along with our ill-informed stabs at Punk Rock fashion – now, though, we had finally seen the Punk experience in real living Day-Glo colour.

"It could get no better than that could it? These are the moments I remember most – The Stranglers playing 'Hanging Around' spitting pure Punk venom our way, Siouxsie getting soaked in spit, the Skids hammering through 'The Saints are Coming', 'Masquerade' and 'Into the Valley'... the Jam's euphoria of 'Strange town' and 'Tube Station', a shirtless Feargal Sharkey rallying us all to the sounds of 'Teenage Kicks', 999 getting 'Nasty Nasty' and us getting covered in spit, Devo asking us 'Are We Not Men – We Are Devo', the Damned instigating us to 'Smash It Up' and The Clash's Mick Jones call to never trust condoms with 'Protex Blue' alongside Joe's retort of 'This is the Punk Rockers speaking' urging us to take 'Complete Control' on the 'London Calling' tour.

"The excitement I felt on the number 69 bus on my way to see The Clash and all those other gigs (usually on a Sunday night at the Top Rank) was intoxicating, scary and gave a hint of danger ahead, but what events. By that time I had hundreds of Punk records – from the Leyton Buzzards to the X-Dreamysts, and as much as I loved the whole Punk thing, just about, the change created by albums and gigs such as The Clash with 'London Calling' and seeing Devo was now paving the way. It's a pity that the decade ahead, once it got past the first two years or so, would never match that feeling!

"There was a time around 1980 that it all seemed to fit into place. The Punk scene may have died down south, and the trendy music press were writing it off as yesterday's thing, but what with the 2-Tone sounds, the best of the Mod revival bands (Purple Hearts and The Chords), the new sounds coming from lots of the bands influenced by Punk but moving ahead (Joy Division, The Fall, Gang of Four, Adam and the Ants, Human League etc), the ground-breaking new records from the likes of Magazine ('Correct Use of Soap'), The Jam ('Sound Affects'), The Clash ('Sandinista') etc and the smaller Power Pop sounds coming out on the Indie labels (Rudi, Moondogs, Protex etc)... and then the delights of the Undertones - it was almost perfect. This is what I had wanted and had been searching for, a new environment of new sounds and creativity with the aggression, energy, idealism and passion of Punk Rock: I had reached where I wanted to be... 1980 was the peak for me: why did it all have to end?"

Too much too young
Part 2 – (Mods, 2-Tone kids and scooterists)

"It was a struggle at first to get hold of the right gear to wear. We were just trying to emulate what the older kids were wearing – parkas, badges, more badges and sewn on beer towels. For me though, there was only one sound that got us all up on the dance floor and that was Ska!" –
Tony Lound (Rotherham Mod)

The thrills of the sounds of 2-Tone when it spread through the school playgrounds and youth clubs of the day would create many memories for a lot of scooter-loving Mod revival young music fans. These were the wide-eyed boisterous lads who had swapped their weekly order of the Beano for a spend at the local record shop on the latest Specials and Selecter singles. Their stories could be representative of any kids their age at any part of the country: their stories contain lots of earthy, yet innocent, humour, rival gang clashes, scooters, pills and the kind of enthusiasm and excitement for life and music that can only be experienced while being young!

The late seventies presented many a local youth with stand-out moments that leave lasting impressions within the memory. The excitement of the fun fair took a more colourful and - at the time - visually outrageous turn as soon to be 2-Tone loving Mod Rob Wasteney recalls -

Rob Wasteney: (Rotherham Mod) "As a kid I always waited for November time and the arrival of the country's largest and finest travelling funfair, know as the Stattis. The fun-fair occupied land off Main Street in Rotherham town centre up until 1978 when the Stattis ended due to the building of the town's new police station and courthouse on the land. It must have been 1976/77 and as per usual the yearly visit came round and me my sister Christine accompanied by my Mum and Dad went to the fun fair. The fun fair had dozens of rides and what seemed like endless stalls and sideshows etc. We were having a great time on the rides and as we rounded a corner and headed towards the next ride we saw a sight which stopped us in our tracks; A group of about six youths containing a couple of girls were dressed in what looked like the remains of ripped clothes. The fabric was held together with various safety pins and chains topped off with studded belts and big boots, one lad even had a studded dog collar round his neck! It might not sound very crude and rebellious today but in that era was causing more attention than any of the fair's attractions. I didn't realise it at the time but I had witnessed my first sighting of the approaching Punk movement. It would be at least a year before I saw the likes of these youths walking the streets of my home turf of Rawmarsh."

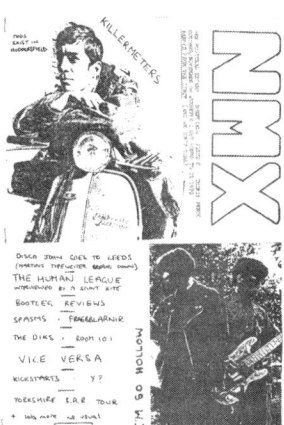

The Punk Rockers Rob recalls meeting would almost certainly have been Tim Jones, Jo Brailsford and their Rotherham Punk gang. A few miles out of town and the number of Punk Rockers in the Rotherham suburb of Rawmarsh was indeed very small in the very early formative days of Punk; only a handful such as Bryan Bell and Ivor Hillman taking the plunge and deciding to wear the shock and outrage inducing Punk Rock attire in 1976. Some early Punk-loving fans were already being noticed as showing the Mod inclined side to the Punk movement.

Tony Beesley: "Back in 76-78, me and my mates used to play football on our old junior school field. The caretaker would chase us off if he saw us but mostly we played along undisturbed. Whilst playing our cheat to win footie matches, we would notice all, anything and anyone that appeared eye catching, but my very limited skills at goal scoring took a side-step when I would notice the bleached blonde hair and tartan kilt of local Punk Bryan Bell walking by as well as the 'In the City' picture sleeve under another local Punk fans arm.

"The Punk in question was nicknamed Zal. He lived around the corner from me, was a good few years older than me and I had seen him scrapping outside Millmoor the few times I went to see Rotherham UTD play around 74-75. As a massive Jam fan myself, I took great interest in Zal's passing records and couldn't take my eyes off his picture sleeve for the Jam's classic first single: mine was in a plain white sleeve and it would take some serious Sunday afternoon record swapping sessions to attain my own copy of it. As the summer weeks passed by in 1978, I noticed our local Punk and Jam fan passing by with all the Jam's vinyl offerings so far released and a more noticeably Weller-influenced Mod barnet gaining prominence. Boy was this guy cool or what?

"As me and my mates made our way to the youth club disco with our clutch of New Wave 45's we would pass Zal's house and by 1979 the sounds of X-Ray Spex's 'Identity' and Vibrators 'Automatic Lover' had been replaced with the dance beat of Secret Affair's 'Time for Action' and 'Gangsters' by the Specials. There was now also the sight of a *cool as fuck* brand new dark red Vespa P200E scooter stood outside his house. The Punk had become the Mod and the transformation was now complete!"

Specials in Sheffield in 1979 by Kristan James Melik

The lure of the swiftly growing Mod revival was now firmly on the horizon as 78 merged into 79!

Jeff Platts: (Barnsley Punk/Mod) "I remember being all of 13 years of age gazing at the older geezers strut across the school playground in their Ex-army parka's, and pod shoes. I remember thinking, *'this could be my next thing!?'* My folks had had a constant battle with me around 78 - 79 over my Punk hairstyles and craving for mohair jumpers with huge holes in them. I'd also made a bloody attempt at piercing my own lip with a safety pin for a school disco...surely mod was safer and more in keeping with the clean cut son they dreamed of being proud of one day! It was around 78 at the time and 'Quadrophenia' hadn't yet hit the high streets. When it finally did, I and a few more of my ilk became fully fledged Ken Dodds (Mods), at least on the outside! The problem was, whilst I'd managed to blag the money from my mum for a new 'sensible winter coat!' in the shape of a US Army parka, she wouldn't be pushed on the Ben Sherman and Fred Perry top, so underneath I was still sporting a ripped Pistols T-shirt and a the afore mentioned holey Mohair jumper. I used to sweat my bollocks off dancing down the yoofy in that parka... but, I didn't dare reveal my Punk under layer!"

Mandy Taylor: "I used to go every Monday to Steeleys with a Mod girl called Jill from around the corner where we lived. I think she was in the year below me at school I can't even remember how we got talking, but I do know it was Jill that got me into Ska and some Mod Stuff, and thinking about it, it must have been Jill that I went to the Mod house parties with. I know we saw some live bands at Steeleys and we must have got served with lager or cider otherwise I would have remembered what bands we saw and definitely saved my tickets and stuff like I do now.

"It was equally the same with The Limit; I used to go with some of my work crowd usually on a Thursday and Friday. I can remember being ill in the toilets once and the floor swimming with God knows what!! I can even remember what I wore on some of the occasions but can't recall who I actually saw play there. Ah the recklessness of youth!"

Specials by Kristan James Melik

Dave Burkinshaw: "In 1979 to 1980 a lot of the Punks started getting into the Mod scene. I followed this too. In 1981 I remember the mass fight at Herringthorpe leisure centre when the Specials played. They refused to play until the fighting stopped. Eventually it did stop and they came on: they we're amazing. Although I never really dressed as a Mod, I was into the music and also got into the sixties stuff because of this. I now often wish I had been born ten years earlier!"

Tony Beesley: "I went to Skegness for a fortnight during the summer of 79. This was the peak of my Jam loving days... you could sense that they were gonna be even bigger than they already were too: up until that point they were a lower regions of the top 20 New Wave band, but all that was soon to change. In Skeggy, there was a notable presence of Mods knocking around. I hadn't seen that many up until that point, apart from some of the Jam inspired Punks we would see on our weekly trips to Sheffield and the few that were starting to appear in Rawmarsh. I had brought my mohair sweater and black n' white Jam shoes along with me to Skeggy and when I wore em one of the nights, I managed to pull two birds in that same night: Two lasses from good old Barnsley... it's amazing what a pair of Jam shoes can do!

MOD PARKA based on U.S. Army Fishtail original, complete with hood and lining. State chest size with order. Please allow ten days for delivery

PRINTOUT PROMOTIONS (Dept. N.M.)
28A ABINGTON SQUARE, NORTHAMPTON
PRINTOUT PROMOTIONS

"The Specials had just brought out 'Gangsters' and that was a big one that summer. Andy Goulty went out and bought that as soon as it came out and we used to play that non-stop. Then, not long after, one of us bought Secret Affair's 'Time for Action' (possibly Andy again?). We played that out too, but by the time it had reached the lunchtime school disco, the whole Mod revival had really kicked in and even though we weren't Mods as such – having a big influence on us though – it was now time for us to play the whole Mod thing down. We didn't get into the whole New Wave scene to be the same as everyone else that's for sure... Mod would have to wait a while longer to get my full attention"

John Quinn: "The Mod revival all seemed to consist of a load of Weller-worshippers without an original idea of their own - with the exception of The Chords, who put out a few decent singles -

and the 2-Tone/Ska scene, which while brilliant in parts, had died off too soon and I could never be arsed with pork pie hats and skinny ties anyway."

Craig Chatterton: "'Gangsters' by the Specials when that came out was great and some of the other stuff. I couldn't get along with Madness and all the stuff that followed though. Our Rich went to the big 2-Tone tour gig at the Top Rank – Specials, Madness and Selecter. Myself, I carried on liking what some of the Punk groups were doing, especially the Stranglers who were still creating brilliant albums and as a budding bass player I was influenced a lot by J.J Burnel's playing. He was probably the best bass player of all the Punk groups for me."

Pete Skidmore: "LONDON early 1980 and I was still at school: the head of the local youth centre Howard Holmes was very good at championing various youth cultures and he had picked up on us lot - there was quite a few Mods and Punks who visited the club but mostly it was just normal kids. I'm not sure how it came about but a trip to London was arranged one Saturday in early 1980 purely for a trip to Carnaby Street and the Kings Road, although later on it was mainly because Sheffield United (who Howard supported) were playing there. We arrived in London and first port of call was Carnaby Street. Howard dropped us and pointed out where it was and a time to be back, so we had all day to ourselves in London. We marched on to Carnaby Street: there was about 10 of us - mostly Mods and a Ted who was a year older than us. Anyway, here we are on Carnaby Street and we went in a couple of shops. The third one we go in has got all the mod gear so we are looking around and working out how much we have to spend when word goes around that a Skinhead about 12 years old has followed us from the other shop and appears to be watching us: So we go to the next shop and he follows us only to disappear once we are in it, so we don't think owt else about it. On leaving this shop, stood in front of us, is about five or six mean- looking Skinheads; we outnumber them but, as we are on their patch, they hold no fear: plus they are older than us or appear to be."

"Anyway we make to walk past them and they block the way, their leader pipes up '*I want some money off you and we will leave you alone*' so we all looks at each other whilst we are all shitting ourselves and Craig being the oldest speaks up '*not a chance mate*' and turns to us and says something like '*they will all want something so no chance*' so the skins turn to each other and start deciding what they are going to do. On this Craig turns to us all and says '*we run but follow me - don't split up.*' All of a sudden we make a dash with about a two second gap on the skins as we successfully make it out on to the main road, where they don't give chase. So that was it... we had come all this way to go on Carnaby Street and we are going to get either mugged or beat up if we show our faces on there, so we ended up on the tube up to the Kings Road, where we find Johnson's clothes shop. Me and John spots these Ben Sherman striped button downs '*how much*' I ask. I get the answer of £4: nice one I will have three then! So I picks em out and goes to the till and the guy then charges me £36 for 3 shirts! '*you said £4 each mate*' '*no they are £12*' so Craig jumps in '*you said £4 why have you suddenly changed it to £12*' '*I never said £4 I said £12*' I was not going to spend all my money on these so put em back. The guy had clearly seen we were young lads not from London and wanted to make mugs of us. We had been in London less then two hours and everybody wanted to take the piss with us: it put me off London for life and I still don't like it and I still don't like cockneys a great deal either. We had a good day out in London with no more grief and didn't come home with owt either. We then went back to have another pop at Carnaby street but no chance; the Skins were still knocking around. We waited in a pub till Howard picked us up. Whilst we were in the pub, the Skinhead leader came past just as Howard was pulling up across the road; so out we walked and Craig walked straight up to the skin and punched him in the face knocking him out as we all legged it across the road and dived in the van!"

Phil Chatterton: "I went to see the Selecter with the Bodysnatchers supporting at the City Hall. I was right at the front of the stage and Selecter singer Pauline Black shook my hand. As for the other Mod music, I thought Secret Affair were too poppy, but Sheffield's the Negatives were good: I saw them at Rotherham Arts centre and bought their 'Money Talk' single which I liked and got signed by the band. I liked the Negatives along with The Jam whose first album I loved as well as 'All Mod Cons'. The Trouble is that often it would be kids into Punk at school and then overnight they would come back wearing a Parka and say *I am a Mod now!* It seemed to be much easier to wear Fred Perrys and be spared the hassle that they would get by being a Punk!"

John Bell: (Rotherham Mod/2-Tone fan) "I remember me and my mate Karl Hemmingway getting our hands on a couple of tickets to see BAD MANNERS in Sheffield. We were about 13 at the time but with shaven heads, Ox blood Dr Martens, bleached jeans, best Fred Perry T-shirt, braces and crombie we were ready to go .We got the 69 bus from Rotherham to Sheffield but as we walked up stairs I remember the distinct jip juice smell of ROCKERS; OH FUCK no going back now. Lets just say they hurled abuse at us all the way to Sheffield *'Wait till you get in Sheffield you're going to get your fucking head kicked in don't you know Gillan are in concert to day'* was one comment I remember. Well we finally pulled into Sheffield bus station to a mass of Skinheads. I have never seen so many; just the confidence we needed. We turned around to the Rockers with huge grins on our faces only to see the lot of them climbing out of the fire exit. We marched to the concert with loads of Skinheads but we must have looked so young so a group of lads and lasses took us under their wing and got us inside. Once inside we went straight down the front and stomped all night long. Well until it was time to catch the last bus home!!!!!"

While John was taking verbal abuse from Gillan fans climbing out of the back of a double decker bus, a friend of his - young aspiring Mod Rob Wasteney - was nurturing the start of a life-long love of that most loved method of transport to a Mod – the scooter!

Rob Wasteney: "I developed a love for scooters, I suppose looking back it was all part of the Mod life style that had totally consumed me, I felt very privileged to live seven or eight doors down from a couple of lads who were quite older than me and already had scooters, they were cousins Zal and Phil Parkinson. Zal had an old scooter that I can't for the life of me remember what it was, Phil had a nearly new Lambretta GP 150, it had the deepest black shine that I had ever seen and he always rode it minus its side panels to expose its chrome engine, tool box and petrol tank. You could hear it from quite a distance due to a large carburettor and big bore exhaust. I'd run to the window whenever I'd hear it start up and watch him ride down the street till he disappeared out of view.

"On another occasion I was in the car with my family driving through Kimberworth, As we passed Peter Frost Motorcycles on Kimberworth Road, I noticed a brand new Vespa scooter parked outside on the pavement, It was obvious that it was brand new and was waiting to be collected or delivered to a new owner, I remember how smart it looked with its deep red paintwork. I got the shock of my life later that same day when I arrived back home and saw the same scooter parked outside Zal's house, he very soon became someone I really looked up to.

"I was now wearing button down collar shirts with Sta-Prest trousers and getting suits made to measure by George on Rotherham Outside Market. I would buy all my shoes from Rebina in Sheffield. I remember wearing a boating blazer which I wore with Levi jeans and red, white and blue bowling shoes. Harrington's in Castle Market always sold some decent gear and I remember you had to try clothes on in the stock room upstairs which was quite amusing."

Batty: "In 1980 I took home £27 a week from work and I paid a mate (John Makin) £15 for a Jam ticket, work out how much that would be today!! Another time I couldn't get a boating blazer anywhere in Sheffield or Rotherham so I went all the way to Leeds for one and was well chuffed when I finally got one."

Tony Lound: (Rotherham Mod/Rude boy) "In 1980 I was 13 years old, in the second year at the Comp (and wagging it already), bored, a few problems at home and no musical tastes to speak of except for a liking for the Stranglers because my mate's big brother liked 'em. Fashion,

for me, simply meant getting dressed in a morning.

"I was in bit of a rut really, no role models to look up to either: until that is... a new family moved into the chip shop next door. Dave Thompson was much older than me, was hard, good with the ladies (including my sister!), had a motorbike and my step dad hated him with a vengeance... instant fucking super hero!!! He must have been around 17 and was well up on fashion, so it wasn't long before the Suzuki was gone and one morning I heard this put...put...put sound coming down the path. Now I knew of this film called Quadrophenia and I had seen all the queues at the cinema of older kids waiting to see it, but the whole Mod thing landed on me that day when a bright red P2OOE with lights, mirrors, crash bars, back-rest, whip aerial with obligatory fox tail... turned up next door being rode by Dave... I was hooked!

"It was a struggle at first to get hold of the right gear to wear. We were just trying to emulate what the older kids were wearing – parkas, badges, more badges and sewn on beer towels, but it wasn't so much the fashion for me – it was the music. It was all a bit confusing at first, what was a Mod band? and what wasn't? With the exception of the Who and a couple of Kinks songs, I couldn't be doing with all of the 60's stuff, nor was I that over-fussed with Secret Affair and the like. For me there was only one sound that got us all up on the dance floor and that was Ska!

"We would wait (not that patiently) for all the usual stuff that the DJ would put on at the school youthy from 'Sunday, Monday Happy Days' to watching the girls line dance and clap their way through Northern Soul fave 'Interplay' by Derek and Ray. Then on came 'Too Much Too Young' and we were up, stomping like loonies! Ska and 2-Tone, that's what we wanted, we weren't so much Mods... we were Rude Boys!

"As time progressed we began to develop our own style. Rob Wasteney, John (Bell) and me had all managed to get two-tone suits by now, but rarely wore them full on. It would either be trousers with Fred Perry polo shirt and loafers, or the jacket with jeans, Jam shoes or Hush puppies (and braces of course).

"For knocking about on the streets or the local park, we would most likely don a crombie, Fred Perry, drainpipe tight Levis jeans (white or red) rolled up to the shins with Doc Martens and topped off with a Dexys hat and Rotherham United scarf!"

Like fellow Mod mate Rob Wasteney, Tony Lound soon felt the need for the Mod method of transport.

Tony Lound: (Right) "Rob Wasteney managed to get his hands on a Jet 200 and John Bell bought a chop down small frame Vespa from some kid at St Anne's flats in Rotherham. We were all only around 14 at the time, so fuck knows how they'd paid for em, but by now I was desperate to have my own scooter. It turned out that Phil Parker – one of the older Mods from our end – was selling his GP 150. I went round with Rob and was gob smacked when I set eyes on it. It was a proper Scooter boys Lami: no bolt on goodies to spoil its lines, just deep gloss black with tons of chrome. It made Rob and John's scooters look pretty bland by comparison (Sorry lads but it did) and I simply had to have it.

"I sold everything I had for that scooter; all my badges, patches, my parka and even my records. I didn't even eat for two weeks... saving my school dinner money to raise the cash I needed... £125.00 (mostly in 10ps and 50ps). I proudly pushed it away down Monkwood Road in Rawmarsh past the school gates at dinner time, perfect timing!

"We'd given up on school by the fifth year. Instead we spent most of our day in a council garage by the bottom school field, fucking about with our scooters. Rob had spotted this garage with its door ajar and peered inside to find it empty so we devised a plan. We stuck our own locks on it, brought up the scooters and kept em in there. Now we had no parental problems whenever we wanted to take our scooters on the road! I'm also pretty sure that my mate John Bell turned up one day with a sofa, so that was it... home from home!

"Another Mod mate Macca (Andrew McEwen) stuck his head over the fence one day and said he didn't fancy school that morning, but needed to be there after dinner time. We decided to go out on my Lamby two up. A 14 and 15 year old with no insurance, no licence but enough dinner money to buy some fuel. We went to Wentworth, Chapeltown, Hoyland and Barnsley and broke down in Wentworth, Chapeltown, Hoyland and Barnsley. Macca didn't get to school that afternoon."

There was also a soundtrack to the lives of the Mods that rode these scooters.

Rob Wasteney: "Like many other Mods I was a massive Paul Weller fan and was buying every single and LP that The Jam released, I was also listening to a fair bit of 79 Mod revival stuff which

I know wasn't everyone's choice but I really enjoyed it and I soon added Secret Affair, The Lambrettas, Purple Hearts and The Chords to my record collection. I'd chosen R.E as a subject option at the end of my third year at Rawmarsh Comp. I wasn't the slightest bit religious but I just thought it would be a bit of a toss off. I sat next to a kid called Pete and every lesson we would just sit and chat. During one lesson he told me he had a Who album and for the remainder of the lesson I put forward one offer after another until a deal was reached. In the end I'd offered 8 Bad Manners singles: I wasn't risking him changing his mind and within minutes of the school bell ringing I was on my way down Kilnhurst Road to his house. That album 'Meaty Beaty big and Bouncy' didn't disappoint and I became a massive Who fan.

"The school youth club had been a large part of my social life for a while, I'd always enjoyed and looked forward to my nights there. It had always been held in the upper school hall which was a well designed building with a raised stage and seating area over looking a large dance floor. After it moved into a colourless drab room at the bottom of the Rosla building it never had the same appeal to me. One night I sat and looked round at what a fucking shit hole it was, I realised it was time to move on!

"Moving forward to the Christmas of 82 and I'd been given a few quid instead of presents. I'd the sole intension of buying a Vespa 50 special and getting it on the road all legal. A bloke who worked for the council in Rosehill Park had promised to sell me one he rode to work every day, I think he was taking the piss and never expected me to turn up with the cash as when I did he basically fucked me off and told me it wasn't for sale anymore. I was bitterly disappointed and rushed into buying the next available scooter a Lambretta Jet 200 from a guy in Quarry Street, Rawmarsh, it was a fucking stupid thing to do because I had little chance of ever getting it on the road legally. I waited for darkness to fall and rode it home with a large smile on my face; I was now a Mod with a scooter.

"John Bell had got his hands on a Vespa 100 and Tony Lound had bought Phil Parkinson's Lambretta GP150 which was a very nice scooter. We had already chalked fuck on the remainder of our education so spent everyday in the garage we had attained tossing it off or tinkering with the scooters. As darkness fell we would dress in all our finery and cruise the streets of Rawmarsh.

"With the distraction of school well and truly behind me I could concentrate on something a lot more important, being a Mod! I still continued to ride the Lambretta well until the inevitable happened when one day me and John Bell got stopped by the police on his Vespa. We ended up having a day out at the old court house on Frederick street in town were I was relieved of sixty quid and my license endorsed with six penalty points *'Bastards'.* I was only riding pillion as well.

Mods Mayday for Tony Lound and friends at Scarborough

"1983 was a real eye opener for me. Id started to hang around town and had met Mods from all over the borough: I was amazed to see how many mods there actually was and gone were the schoolboy Mods that had just been playing at it. These Mods were the real deal. We had started drinking in the Cleaver on Wellgate some nights it was brimming with Mods and the jukebox was forever playing The Jam, The Who and plenty of Motown.

"I can remember when we started the Rotherham Harlequins scooter club at the Station Hotel in Parkgate. Me, Dean Bradshaw, Tony Lound and Paul Critchlow got together to start the club. We had some cracking nights there. We started to meet on Thursday nights and soon progressed to putting a Friday night do on: we produced some flyers and posted them all over town. The night was a huge success and fucking storming, and Mods came from as far away as Worksop. Paul Critchlow was a larger than life character a bit of a rogue and he managed to get a DJ to accept a percentage of the door money in payment for his services.

"The landlord was a right miserable bastard but that night he took a fortune over the bar. I remember at some point in the night everyone was dancing like crazy- really fucking going for it, the landlord ran upstairs screaming to cool it ... Plaster was actually falling off the ceiling downstairs!"

Tony Lound: "Some other mates from school turned up on the scene around mid 83. At the time (together with Rob Wasteney, Dean Bradshaw and Paul Critchlow), I was organising Mod/Ska/Soul nights at the Station Hotel in Parkgate (near Rotherham) with our fledgling club Warriors Scooter club... soon to be re-named Harlequins. Neither of these new lads had been known to be into scooters or Ska or anything but it turned out Jeff Allen had got himself a 50 special and the other lad Huey (can't remember his full name?) had a rather tidy 90. They wanted to do the Skeggy rally but didn't want to go alone (being so green) so it was suggested that I go along with em two up. Another mate, Paul Bryan, had been ear wigging and decided he was going as well – on the back of Huey's 90 (this was probably wise with the 90 having more power as Paul was big and anyway you didn't say no to Paul Bryan did you!).

"The day soon came: we slept on Huey's room floor on the Friday night so that we could be away real early at 4am. Paul had already gone a day early with the lads from 'Sound Alliance scooter club'. He would still need a lift home though. It took hours, two up with tents, bags and all. In Skegness, we met Paul at the clock tower and after only being there for about ten minutes, we witnessed a scrap between two scooter boys.

"Later, we got invited back to the Sound Alliance lads' caravan over in Chapel St Leonard's. En route some git in a car gave us some hassle so we followed the bastard back to his caravan and started riding around it... the whole eight scooters riding around the caravan mimicking Red Indian war cries! The poor fucker shit himself and it turned out later that he had also called the cops. We retreated to the Smugglers and got steadily pissed. Jeff and Huey set off alone to get some fuel and it was then that the cops pounced on them: nothing too heavy – they just read em the riot act. We think it was all a bit too much for the two of em as they then wanted to go... not back to the caravan or to set up tent... no back to fucking Rawmarsh! We tried to persuade em, me and Bry, but to no avail; they were going and that meant that we had no other way of getting home as a result: So home we went. We set off at 6pm and got home around 2am Sunday morning. Fucking excellent day trip to Skeggy that was! We didn't see much of Jeff and Huey after that for a while."

Like much of what had arrived on the cutting edge of music since Punk's arrival, the Limit club in Sheffield also paid its homage to what was happening on the Mod and 2-Tone scenes. The 1979-80 revival had seen many memorable Mod inclined occasions celebrated at the venue, including the legendary March of the Mods tour and early groundbreaking sets from the Specials, Madness, Selecter, The Chords, Sheffield's very own Mods the Negatives and the, much loved by Mods, rhythm and blues of Nine Below Zero, whose singer Dennis Greaves' follow up group The Truth turned to a more Pop approach to entertain Mods with, whilst aiming for the reaches of the mainstream charts.

Rob Wasteney: "The first time I visited the Limit club: it was a Thursday night and, as usual, we were at the Station Hotel for the scooter club meet. Someone came in and told us The Truth were appearing at the Limit that night, twenty minutes later and me, Paul Critchlow and Dean Bradshaw were in a taxi heading up Attercliffe, we were as naive as fuck and thought we would watch The Truth and get the last bus home. Well The Truth didn't come on stage till the early hours and by that time we had spent most our money on beer and didn't have enough for a taxi home , I'd copped off with a pretty Modette that I'd seen a couple of times from Worksop. At the end of the night Paul rang a relative to come and pick us up and when he turned up the daft cunt had fetched his wife with him, three seats and four of us ! I remember the choice was either a lift home and leave the girl or stay with her, easy choice. I got a cab from the Hole in the Road and told the driver I only had about three quid left, the driver was a gem and drove at least a mile after the cash ran out. We had about a five mile walk back to Rawmarsh. She treated me en route which made it all worth while! I think it was about 7am when we reached our house.

Dennis Greaves leads The Truth at the Limit (Heather Quinn)

"Throughout 1982 I'd eagerly listened to all the story's that Zal told me of scooter rallies drunken violence and vandalism. I'd collected all the newspaper cuttings of rampaging Mods and scooter riders causing havoc at various Coastal resorts, and by the time April and Easter of 83 came round me and another Rawmarsh Mod - Dean Bradshaw - had just one thing on our minds- Morecambe Bay! We travelled by train from Sheffield and headed via Manchester arriving at Morecombe Bay early evening. It was a sight I'd never forget with thousands of Mods and scooters swamping the place, we wondered around for hours just taking it all in. I remember that warm feeling and a real sense of belonging! We had planned to sleep rough and save our money but as temperatures plummeted we headed for the all nighter on the pier. I remember us being surprised to find only Northern Soul being played. The following day, after visiting the Rally site and dealer Market, we sat on the sea front drinking beer watching the scooters cruising up and down the seafront and breathing in the two stroke purple haze ...Fucking amazing...!"

Tony Lound: "I still wanted a Vespa 90 like Huey's with its rapid acceleration and small frame handling. It was then and still is the most exciting and fun scooter I have ever ridden. I finally managed to get my hands on it: we agreed a price, but me being skint, I promised to pay in instalments with a tenner down on deposit.

"So began the strip-down, wheels off, bars off, forks out and bits all over the place. I had it all planned – white wheel rims, black hubs, yellow body work with racing numbers on the panels. The fact that I had no money never even came into the equation. Several weeks later there was a knock on the door and there stood Huey and Jeff wanting to know when I was actually going to pay something. I was honest and told em I was skint so Huey asked *'Can I have my scooter back then?'* *'Erm yeah ok then'* I had to admit the obvious. I was never going to make the instalments on it, let alone get the work done on it. So off they went wheeling it away with much of its bits in boxes – poor cunts. I had wasted a tenner though!"

A Mod haunt closer to home than the late night lure of the Limit club was Rotherham's Clifton Hall.

Rob Wasteney: " What a magical place Clifton hall in Rotherham was in the late 70s to early 80s: A majestic building that stood on Wharncliffe Street at the top of town, it hosted some of the country's finest Northern Soul all-nighters. I remember standing for hours on the balcony looking down on a talcum powder dusted dance floor watching in awe as an array of Soulies stomped, did twists spins and executed drops and back flips: some wore coloured vests covered with patches and soul bags with beer towels tucked over the waist band to mop up endless amounts of sweat.

"After been introduced to the Soul nights by a Rawmarsh Mod Paul Bryan, I began attending the all-nighters at Clifton Hall with other Mods from the Rotherham area. Dealers in the back room had boxes full of rare Soul 45s which they sold for large amounts of money: I soon found out they weren't the only dealers working the all-nighters... Id always wondered where some of the dancers found the energy to dance all night. I never realised they were probably full of amphetamine sulphate (speed or whizz). It wasn't long before I wanted to try some, and on another occasion I bought two wraps from someone in the gents and foolishly swilled both down with a beer. I certainly had a great night full of energy! When the hall emptied at 8am on the Saturday morning me Andy McEwen, Dean Bradshaw and Tony Lound headed not for home but to the no.69 bus stop and a day up Sheffield. I don't know if I was just exhausted or if it was the amphetamine but I collapsed on the Moor and had to be carried back to the bus stop and home to Rawmarsh. It scared the life out of me and I never took anything at Clifton hall again."

Robs recreational habits may have ended almost before they had started of his own choice; but a trip to a Mod weekend still managed to inadvertently affect his level of extra hallucinatory perception – potentially dangerously too! Fortunately the lads had a spot of carry on camping Mod style to look forward to.

Tony Lound: "We did Great Yarmouth 1984 in a car: me Rob Wasteney, Paul Bryan and Dave Parkes. It was Rob's car, so he did the driving while we supped the ale and sniffed poppers that we had just bought from a local Sex shop. The fucking car stunk of it and poor Rob kept complaining that he was getting high and couldn't drive straight. Luckily we got there ok.

"Once in Yarmouth, we got the tent out only to discover we'd got no poles. Bry tore down a tree and started making some out of it. The fact that we were pitching up just around from the long bar on Marine Parade in what must have been a small park didn't phase us one bit, but two coppers were having none of it and fucked us off rather sharpish!"

A much anticipated journey to London would change from an exciting sight seeing tour of the swinging sixties capital of the world and its epicentre – Carnaby Street to a more sobering conclusion for one Rotherham Mod.

Rob Wasteney: "The last Saturday before Christmas 83 saw my first visit to Carnaby street London. Me, Shaun Hill, along with a couple of Modettes that we were seeing at the time, boarded a Riley's coach in Corporation Street Rotherham and headed for the capital. On the journey one of the girls happened to say that her mother had warned her to stay clear of any large department stores for fear of any terrorist attacks. Me and Shaun laughed our bollocks off and proceeded to take the piss at every opportunity. I think we arrived at Marble arch around 11am and couldn't wait to get to Carnaby Street. On route we came across Harrods in Knightsbridge and couldn't resist a quick look around. We were amazed by the size and stature of the place.

"Carnaby Street felt great to just be there: visiting shops I'd been buying gear from in the past by mail order and now I was free to browse the racks and shelves at my leisure. I remember buying a Mac like the one I'd seen Weller wear and a nice Ben Sherman shirt. Later we sat in the window of a cafe overlooking the street seeing mods looking cool as fuck walking by. Soon we decided it was time to head back and walking the same way we had come we turned right to be met by what seemed like panic, people running in every direction and police everywhere! It later emerged that just before 1.30pm a car bomb had been detonated outside Harrods killing 6 and injuring 75... It was quite sobering to think we had missed being caught up in the carnage by just one hour! There wasn't any piss taking on the journey home - well not from me and Shaun that's for sure."

Back in Rotherham, Rob and his Mod mates encountered a more common slice of teenage confrontation.

Rob Wasteney: "Just like The Jam record 'Thick as Thieves' the Mods who hung around town were just that. One Mod Dave Evans - who lived up Wickersley was getting hassle on a regular basis from some local straights most nights when he was on route into Rotherham to meet up with us. We were getting fed up with his tales of being punched, kicked and generally shoved about and the final straw came one evening when he arrived in the bus station to tell of his biggest beating yet. We realized that enough was enough and after hearing that they were at Wickersley school youth club we decided to jump on the bus and go give them a good beating. There was about twenty of us that night and we boasted one or two handy lads so we held little fear.

"The door of the youth club was locked before we made it down the school driveway and we were quickly informed by a youth leader that the police were on their way. After a few minutes of exchanging the obligatory expletives and hand signals through the locked door we made our way back to the main road. Just as we came through the school gates we saw the Rotherham bus heading up the carriageway- us being in two minds on whether to head back into town or hang around to see if anything was going to kick off? In the confusion all but four of us Mods jumped on the bus and it pulled away. The four of us that were left crossed the road and headed into the estate opposite (unbeknown to us a call had gone out from the youth club that a gang of rampaging Mods were in the area looking for bother). We had just got to where the Joker pub is when we heard a car being driven at a fair speed with a screech of brakes: we turned to see all four doors open together and like something out of a film four blokes jumped out. I don't know if they were older brothers or fathers of the kids from the youth club but it was obvious that we weren't going to be much of a match for them; so we ran like fucking hell in opposite directions.

"I checked over my shoulder after a few yards to see all four chasing me; fucking great... A fist to the back of the head and I was knocked to the ground where fists and boots rained into me. I realized this was going to be a savage beating unlike anything I'd had before so somehow I managed to scramble to my feet and run down a path opposite only to find myself in a back garden surrounded by a six foot high fence. Behind me I heard a cry of 'got the bastard now' and just as the beating was about to resume, out of the darkness came Eggy who had been hiding behind a coal bunker. He was screaming and swinging around his head the largest coal shovel I'd ever seen. The blokes turned and legged it; probably fearing for their lives. We made our escape and on the way home he told me how he had seen it all unfold and decided that there was no way he could have hid and done nothing, he said he would have rather been beaten to a pulp himself. I couldn't believe he had put his neck on the line to save me from what I'm sure would have been a hospital visit at best. That night I learnt how it's much easier to defend your own turf than it is to invade someone else's."

Meanwhile one young local Punk fan was acquainting himself with 2-Tone at the school disco!

Carl Myers: (Greasbrough Mod) "It was about 1979 -80, all the Punk movement was dying out but the music still remained with me. My mate Ian Coult was heavily into Madness and The Jam at the time and he got me into them too. There was no way he would listen to the Sex Pistols at the time so we used to blast out all his Ska and 2-Tone collection in his bedroom. I remember our Xmas party in the fourth year of the juniors. Everyone would bring in some of their own music for the teachers to play for us at the disco. One track that stuck out in my mind was called 'Needle in a Haystack' all my mates were dancing around doing chest rolls on the hall floor and flicking their legs around as though they were floating. My mate Mat Wilkinson (Tatter) started to teach me the moves. I noticed he always looked smart in his two-tone Sta-Prest trousers and smart shirts."

Along with Mod role models on the dancefloor, young Mod kids could also find genuine diamond geezers on the scene: with a knowledge of all things scooter-wise and an understanding for young and keen minds (a little bit over-keen) obviously not letting an opportunity pass them by.

Tony Lound: "Paul Critchlow (Critch) was one of those kids that would do 'owt for yer, generous to a T, but he had his limits. We hadn't known him that long and one particular day me, Rob Wasteney and Reggie Scott called for him, but he wasn't in. We asked his Mother for the shed key so that we could get on with some work on his scooter for him and she fell for it!

"Critch's shed was an Aladdin's cave of scooter bits and tools and believe me we wasted no time. We were heading down the path, panels, engine bits and tools under our arms when Critch appeared. *'Put em back lads'* was all he said with a smirk on his face. We simply turned around and walked back up the path putting it all back exactly where we found it and nowt else was ever said about it."

Tony Beesley: "Me and a couple of the lads from my Mod band 'The Way' would call on Critch, God rest his soul, from time to time. There would always be loads of Mod kids hanging around and laying about the house, it was like a Mod commune: there was even a scooter in his bedroom. He had a really good record collection too. I can remember him showing em me and I was going through the records and thinking *'I want that single'* and *'I wish I had that record'.* As well as spending plenty of time on scooters and helping organise Mod and scooter events, he had obviously spent some serious time on building up a respectable Mod collection; and we aren't talking the average stuff either – he had some real Soul gems from what I can remember. The last time I saw him, was when I was working in a local factory and he arrived spanner-in-hand to do some contract work. We had a laugh about the old days and I never saw him again. He was a real character that lad."

Tony Lound: "Me and the lads started drinking at the Little Effingham pub just out of town with some of the Rotherham town Mods. We were reminiscing about Scarborough rally 83 when Critch (see photo below on scooter far right) said to me outside *'Fuck it lets go now'.* This was 10.30pm mid week and we were on our own... so we did.

"We were on the A19 between Selby and York and it was foggy as fuck; we couldn't see a thing with those crappy Vespa lights. This car came up from behind with full beam on, then just sat behind us lighting up the road ahead. It stayed behind us right up the A64 until there was better lighting, then flashed his lights, pulled round us and raced off. It was a cop car, proper jam sandwich. There we were two up, pissed up, no licences or owt to speak of for ID, but he didn't give a fuck: he just wanted to see us through his patch safely... top bloke or what!

"When we got to Scarborough we slept in a bus shelter on Marine Drive in our parkas. It was fucking freezing too. We had sobered up and after thinking *'What the fuck had we come for?'* we got some breakfast in a café and set off back. Part-way back and disaster loomed. Critch was a bit of a bodge artist and had not bothered putting a split pin through the castle nut on the back wheel. It came off (the wheel) and so did we. Thank fuck Critch managed to hold the bike up as we slid down a grass verge only coming off as we came to a near stop by some hedges.

"We pushed the scooter to a bungalow and the bloke let us put it in his garage until Critch could get back with a van. He took us to Sherburn and we caught a train home via Leeds. We walked into Rotherham bus station about 10pm that night and bumped into the Mod lot we'd been drinking with in the Effingham. We told em of our adventure but not fucking one of em believed us!"

Tony Lound: "One night when I was in Rotherham bus station Critch turned up on a Vespa 150 super. It was all lights and mirrors and all the younger Mods were fussing round him. I owed him a tenner and he asked for it. I'd got it, but not on me so he said *'Take the scooter and go and get it then'.* Fucking ace! All the Mods were looking on in envy as I put the lid on and kicked her up. *'Watch the clutch'* warned Critch *'It's sharp as fuck'.* Too late... I was off like a rodeo bull, shot off the kerb and glanced the front wing of a taxi. I managed to stop it and looked back to see the taxi bloke climbing out – fists in the air. I shot off again and left em to it. When I got back, I gave Critch his money. He told me he had smoothed things over with the taxi driver, but it had cost him. I still owed him a tenner.

"Another story from my days hanging around with Critch was when he brought some pills out. Don't know what the fuck they were though. We went to the multi-storey car park at Rawmarsh shopping centre opposite the Crown pub and told Brad (Dean Bradshaw) they were blues. Anyway, he took em! After a while he said he felt dizzy. Then he started running about and rolling on the floor screaming out that the car park roof was coming down on him. Without warning he took a run and jumped straight over the edge. We raced over expecting the worse. There he was on top of the shop roofs only about 4 feet down. He knew of course and was sat pissing himself laughing at us. He'd had us hook, line and sinker and we had

Dean Bradshaw

shit ourselves fearing the worst."

Carl Myers: (Right) "When we moved up into Wingfield Comp in 1981 we started to hang around with new faces from the surrounding areas of Greasbrough and Kimberworth. It was a little alien at first getting used to our new mates but eventually some of them became best mates over the years. We had our own little gang of mates from the Rockingham area that we all knocked around with every night: Ian Coult, Daz White, John Hensby (Bimbo), Wayne and Andy Fereday (Fez), Mark Presley (Prez), Wayne Littlewood (Woody) RIP mate. Prez was one of the first to get a video player, a Ferguson top loader. Three of us at a time used to chip in with 33 pence each and hire videos out from a shop that I think was called Milliards in town. I remember watching the films like Jaws, Wanderers, Rocky, Scum, Evil dead, King Frat, and all the Lemon Popsicle films. Ian was the next to get a video player and I remember watching all the similar films, and then out came the movie E.T. We were all hooked on the BMX craze then due to this film. We seemed to have forgotten about music of the time. This was probably because I was still listening to my old Sex Pistols albums and Ian's Madness and Jam albums. The music in the charts at the time didn't really interest me back then.

"One weekend I persuaded Ian, Prez and Woody to watch 'The Great Rock and Roll Swindle' on the video. Ian wasn't too impressed but Prez fell in love with the Punk scene and still is to this day. We used to watch music videos by The Beatles and The Jam and listen to our favourite music until one day Ian invited us round to watch a video he had come across. 'Quadrophenia' was on the kitchen table in its cassette box. I remember asking Ian what it was about. *'Let's bang it on the telly and see'* he said. The rest is history as they say.

"I was now 14-15 and I had got a job on the local milk round with my mate Daz White. It paid me £10 a week plus I got my pocket money off my parents too. I was pretty well off for a school kid who worked two hours a day before school. This was ideal because I was into the Mod scene and I could afford buy Sta-Prest trousers and Bowling shoes and records and other stuff like that with the money. Me and Ian both saved up enough money so we could both buy made to measure suits. We had them made by George from the outside market in Rotherham. So there we were, 15 yrs old and getting our first Mod suits made. We already had parkas that we bought from an army surplus shop next to the Peace Gardens in Sheffield. The first time we wore our suits was to a school leaving party at either Tiffany's or The Tivoli. Can't quite remember which it was but one of the teachers commented on how smart we looked in our suits. He said it reminded him of the 60's when he was into music. I had my black loafers on and Ian was wearing his Jam shoes: and with our smart suits we both felt so smart. We were in the 4th yrs but the leaving party was for the 5th yrs. We always got invited to

the 5th yrs parties which was ace because we used to get kisses from all the older girls.

"We started to hang around in town on Saturdays outside the Bargain Beauty shop. (BBC) I got to know other Mods from different parts of Rotherham. Eventually we had quite a large circle of friends whom we used to have some bloody good laughs with over the next few years. I met lots of new mates who hung around the Rawmarsh bus stop in the bus station. Johno, Rich Fretwell (Dick), Wardy, Jeff King, Steve King, Rob Wasteney, Roy and Roger Mason, Critchlow (RIP), Sarfa, Michelle Green, Pauline, Dave Evans, Dean Bradshaw, Curly, Paul Goldsboro, Carl Smith and many more whose names escape me. We used to meet in the Scala amusement arcade most evenings and every Saturday afternoon. Over the next couple of years I had invites to parties, concerts, piss ups, football matches and stuff like that all of the time.

"Me, Johno and Rich Fretwell used to drive around in his mate's dad's Ford Cortina every Sunday night. He used to charge us 50 pence each to contribute towards the petrol money. Our favourite place was to visit was a pub in a little village called Everton, on the way out to Gainsborough. This was because we could get served with a pint of beer there. It was 1984. The Style Council were huge and I was a big fan of them. One particular Sunday night while driving around I was asked if I wanted to buy Johno's Style Council ticket for the gig at the City Hall in Sheffield as he couldn't make it. *'Jesus'* I thought. I snatched his bloody hands off. We drove over to Rockingham to my house so I could give him the money for it. Five quid it was. I paid him with the money a got from the milk round. One week later on the night of the gig I jumped on the bus outside the Plough, wearing my new Paul Weller mac that I recently bought from London on a school trip. I couldn't wait to see Mr Weller for the first time ever. I was meeting my mate Jeff King in town at the Rawmarsh bus stop, and then we were gonna get on the no.69 bus to Sheffield. I nearly didn't get to see it after leaving the ticket at home and I had to get off the bus at the next stop and leg it all the way back from Greasbrough to the bus stop where I got on. I ran back across the road into our house. My dad's in the kitchen drying out his tobacco on top of the oven grill. *'What time you going to this concert thingy?'* he says. *'And don't forget your ticket off the top of the cupboard'.* For fuck sake I thought. My ticket was here all along. Panic over. I'm just glad I didn't get all the way to the City Hall before realising I'd left my ticket behind. By the way, I still have the very ticket in my possession today."

Rob Wasteney: "Who could forget the legendary 80's Mod nights held right on our doorstep at the superb Assembly Rooms in Rotherham. I think the first one I attended was around 83 when The Scene headlined. We'd heard there was going to be some hassle from the straights so we were a bit anxious. In the end we had nothing to worry about as hundreds of mods descended from all over Yorkshire some big handy lads as well... I'm not sure how often the nights were put on but I remember attending one in 85 and again in 87 when Small World reformed to play a one off sell out gig, now that was a fucking storming gig and packed to the rafters. I was never really sure who was responsible for putting the nights on but certainly none of the Mods I knew had anything to do with organizing them."

Carl Myers: "Me and my two best mates, Ian Coult and Wayne Fez went to a Tiffany's Mod do wearing our suits and parkas. When we got to the door ready to pay the bouncer told us that we weren't allowed in wearing our parkas. I thought, *'what the fuck, it's a Mod do. People are bound to turn up with the dam things on'.* The only way we could get in was if we put the parkas in the cloakroom or if we were to put them into a carrier bag. I wasn't letting my parka out of my sight but we didn't have a carry bag either. It was only then that the girl on the pay booth chucked us a bag and told us to put them in there. When we eventually got into Tiffany's for the first time I couldn't believe it. *'Wow'* I thought. Look at all these people in here dancing and milling about chatting. We got sat at a small table around the perimeter of the dance floor and I noticed that most people had put their parkas on the backs of their chairs. *'Fez, pass me my parka'* I shouts. If they're doing it, then so am I. Unfortunately that day the venue wasn't serving alcohol. The do was a pop and crisp only one. So we were on coke and ice only. Mind you. We were only 15. I was dying to get up and dance but I felt too shy to get up. This was all new to me but I was just loving it sat there watching all the Mod birds walk by. I'm glad in a way that I stayed by my parka because lots of Mods were complaining later on that all their badges had been nicked off their jackets and parkas.

"Throughout 84 -85 we attended many do's in Rotherham either at the Assembly Rooms or at the Clifton Hall venue. Groups that I can remember seeing were The Gents and Makin' Time. It was quite a hairy moment getting to and from the venues in town as most of the trendies used to hassle us whenever there was a do on. One particular night at the Assembly Rooms there was a well-attended Mod do going on. I was there with the usual crowd dancing and getting pissed when I recall one of the lads sitting on the stairway with his face smashed in. *'Who did it'?* Everybody was shouting. It turned out that it was some trendies who were outside near the fountains next to the old C&A. They were the ones that started on my mate and beat him up. A load of Mods piled out for revenge and as they did the trendies all legged it, but unlucky for one of them he got a right beating. He should have been faster on his feet!

"What sticks out in my mind about this particular incident is that the trendy who got beat up was a good friend of one of the Mods that night. When Kingy realised his trendy mate had taken a beating he started to kick off shouting and screaming that it wasn't fair that his mate had been beaten up. He then ripped off his parka and his bowling shoes and chucked them into the fountains before walking off into the night. Now that little fracas always reminds me of a scene from 'Quadrophenia'."

One Punk loving Mod fan set off on his very first Mod rally: little knowing that it would mark a life long love of the whole scooter scene and lead him to perform in his own Ska influenced band many years later.

Jeff Platts: (Barnsley Mod) (Left)
"At around 14 I went to Scarborough on my first ever scooter rally. From what I remember back then there was no distinction between Scooter rallies and Mod rallies, they were one and the same. The majority of the weekend sea-siders were Mods back then, the evolution of the scooter boy began soon after. I remember conversations with mates about our own identity, were we Mods or where we scooter boys?...all these years later I don't think it mattered really, the two common denominators that underpinned everything we stood and still stand for whether Mod, Skin, Punk, Scooter boy, Soul boy etc was and still is our passion for music but most importantly classic Vespa and Lambretta scooters."

Rob Wasteney: "Due to the violence and hassle from the Skinheads that had blighted the national scooter scene of the mid 80s, me along with Russ Smith, Roy and Roger Mason and other Rotherham Mods abandoned the scooter scene and instead started to attend only dedicated Mod rallies and events. I'd joined the Phoenix Society which had brought Mods together on a national level for the first time: the Phoenix Society produced a monthly newsletter 'the Phoenix List' informing us of club gigs and rallies in and around London and throughout the UK. It soon became an important forum for the Mods of Rotherham and surrounding areas."

As the youths of our generation were making their mark within the local Punk and Mod scenes; eventually catching up with the older gig-going, club-attending (in the know) originators, fashion followers and music and clothes obsessed, one local Punk motivated 15 year old, whilst also taking note of the Mod revival, began to notice a shift in the fashion culture of another setting – the football terraces!

Shaun Angel: (Rotherham Punk/Post-Punk fan) "1980 was the year of my first encounter of the so-called 'Casual' era in football. I've read in certain soccer hooligan books that the casual movement in football had its roots in 1977 in Rome when Liverpool played there in their first European Cup Final and fans picked up designer clothes ideas off the Italians. Personally, I think that's a load of bollocks!, because in 77 a lot of the football crowd that went to the games for a tear up had adopted a lot of the Punk look; PVC trousers, fluffy hopped jumpers and baseball pumps.

"Two years later in 1979 with the revival of Mod, Skinhead, Ska and Rude Boy music in the charts with Madness, Specials, Selecter, Secret Affair and others another trend started with the re-introduction of the 60's look of two-tone suits, Sta-Prest trousers, Fred Perrys and Ben Sherman shirts with lots of suede and loafer shoes.

"A year later in 1980, UB40 played at the Birmingham NEC which I went to with a few of the football crowd I hung about with and that is when I personally saw first hand this new exciting look which was later termed casual. Loads of the crowd there were wearing Fred Perrys of course, but with flashy white trainers and faded jeans. What was more eye-catching though were these silly fucking haircuts that a lot of them had – with a long lop sided fringe covering one eye and what looked like a big chunk cut out of the back. I remember thinking *'Is this a fucking gay convention or what!'*"

Youth culture was an ever changing concern for our generation, during a time when Punk Rockers embraced many new looks and movements... be that the 80's Casual; the flamboyance of futurism or the new Mod influenced style!

Tony Beesley: "I can clearly recall the very last time I went out with all my Punk clobber on. I got geared up with my old PVC trousers, leather zip jacket, Clash T-Shirt and jet-black dyed-spiky hair. I called for my mates and we hung around the local shops as usual, pissing about, taking the piss out of each other and passers by. I went home that night, and for some reason, decided that that was it for me with the Punk look. I never wore them again; my next outing was wearing a post-punk/Mod informed look... black T-shirt and red braces, Harrington, Chelsea boots, Levi's and I had my hair razor cut by Vic the barber."

The days of living a young teenage life within the local Punk and Mod circles with all the excitement and danger that came with it, living as fast as the paper round money would stretch and how much you could get for your old bags of toy soldiers to buy the latest records... this could only ever last a season or two before the prospect of becoming part of the larger picture came along. The buzz of actually seeing those bands that you had been crazy about for what seemed like eons, but was actually the space between one recorded album to the other; the difference between not having a real clue as to what to wear to the youth club or what a good Mod suit was to knowing the coolest cut of trousers or realising which Punk band had been riding the bandwagon (too many to mention here) and which ones really meant what they were singing about. The excitement and street-cred level may have increased ten fold with your first Jam and Clash tickets bought and the chance to become part of the real thing; but there can be no beating those days - for many - when the most important and memorable times were spent living life to the full and getting up to far too much too young!

Chapter Five
From Prams, Repulsive Aliens and Plastik Toyz to Brian Damage!

"I think the main thing about The Prams was that we were very very young. We were crap (at least at the beginning) but we stuck our necks out - and got our noses put out of joint by those other punk bands that were around" - **Chris Anderson** (The Prams)

"Sheffield gigs were easy enough to get to. Wander down the hill from the pub and 2p on the 69 bus!" - **Brian Damage** (Rotherham Punk Rocker)

John Flanagan (2nd Prams singer) – "I can tell you how the name came about. We were all sat in the Dickens bar in Rotherham: I wasn't in the band yet, but we were sat talking over a beer, when in came Arthur from Canklow. Apparently at the time he used to go around collecting wood in his pram, set fire to Canklow woods and then call the fire brigade. He came in through the door and shouts *'Somebody's nicked my pram!'* We turned to each other and said *'That's it - what about the Prams'.* There was no need to put it to the vote!"

The Prams were a Rotherham Punk Rock garage band; formed in the true spirit of the Punk ethos, i.e. anyone can have a go! They formed in 1977 right at the height of the nationwide Punk hysteria and continued, with an ever-changing series of varying line ups right up to the very end of the original Punk era – splitting in 1981. Beginning with Punk as their template they eventually achieved a Post-Punk - with a hint of Mod - sound of their own.

Their unstable but dependingly colourful career saw a flux of musicians of varying skill pass through their ranks, including a Rotherham bred member of Mark E.Smith's The Fall. They were also featured in a Rotherham Advertiser newspaper piece assembled by man of the road Jeremy Clarkson whilst  doing his dues working for the paper on his ascent to TV fame. Unfortunately, The Prams never achieved the status they deserved to reach, but had one hell of a great time in trying!

The Prams Chris Anderson with other Punk musicians to be - October 1977

Katherine – Hancock – Peat: (Rotherham Prams fan) "I remember the Prams playing Greasborough Town Hall. The Advertiser did a write up on them and the young reporter who did it was none other but Jeremy Clarkson - yes, of Top Gear fame. He started his career at the 'Tizer(Rotherham Advertiser)."

An early Prams gig in 1977 at Old Hall Youth club Rotherham

The band's early appearances saw literally anyone who wanted to have a crack at performing joining them onstage. It could be said that these early formative days of playing were a bit of a riot.

Simon Ellis: (Prams Bass player) "The full family tree of the Prams was Chris Anderson, me, Billy Burdon, Oz, Caroline Boaden, Peter Birch, Johnny Brown (who also briefly joined the Fall), Brian Pearson, John Flanagan, Graham Saunders, Phillip Wright...I think that's all of 'em."

John Flanagan: (Prams singer) "I can remember one particular gig, and the whole audience seemed to be up there with us. Everyone wanted to have a go at being in the band and to be honest at some points I don't think we ourselves were quite sure who was in or not."

Right: Simon Ellis and Caroline Boaden

Heather Allen: (Prams fan) "I saw the Prams at the Rotherham Co-op near 'the Charade' and had to pretend I was at the school disco as I would not have been allowed to go; though I did get caught out as I missed the bus back!"

Tim Jones: (Prams fan) "I have got to be truthful; the first attempts for the Prams were absolutely crap, but they were fun!"

Carl Eggleston: "The Prams were the very first live music I ever saw, apart from the club acts and jazz bands my Dad had took me along to: so the effect was amazing. I thought umm 'Wow'!"

So how did these young Punk kids get their musical career off the starting grid?

Chris Anderson: (First bass player) "The Prams first gig was at that shed near Clifton Park, was it called Clifton Hall? It was the Thomas Rotherham Summer Dance. I was trying to pull a bird at College called Maria. She had been going out with some jock-type kid called Andy, I think, who was trying to get back with her and he was in charge of organising the dance. He was bleating on about how he needed a band. So me trying to impress Maria goes *'I've got a band. Yeah, they're ace - Punk band.'* And it got all bravado then, so he says *'alright, you can play'.* I knew he knew I didn't have a band, in fact I could hardly play - I had a Woolie's Ovation bass that cost £18. Anyway, the gauntlet was down and The Prams were born."

Brian Pearson's introduction to the delights of Punk Rock is fairly typical of the time, but much more importantly than that – he (along with the rest of the various line ups) got up off their arses, picked up their instruments and joined in with the Punk revolution. Rotherham may not think they needed them, but they were gonna get them anyway!

Below Pram pranksters Brian Pearson and Simon Ellis

Brian Pearson: (Prams guitarist) "The earliest I can remember about getting into Punk was seeing a few articles in NME in 1977 about it and wondering what all the fuss was about (at the time I was into the Stones, Alice Cooper and AC/DC). I then decided to find out for my self and bought the Clash and Stranglers albums – I was blown away with the speed and aggression of it all and got my mates round (David Pratt, Craig Milbourne and Graham Sanders) to listen to them. It had the same effect upon them so, there and then, we decided that we were going to be Punks and nicked our dad's old jackets, got our mums to take in our jeans, cut chunks out of each others' hair and that was it... sorted!

"We were too young to get into pubs at that time as we were in our last year at school so we just hung around trying to look cool. When we had a bit of money we used to go up to X clothes which was on London Road I think and buy what ever we could afford (I wish I had still got the bondage shirt and t shirts by Sex as I bet they would be worth a few bob now).

Prams first singer Peter Birch

"I already had a guitar and could play a few bits by this time and my older sister Julia said she knew a few other Punks who were a few years older than me who had formed a band and they wondered if they could borrow my guitar for their first gig. It was a Telecaster copy with writing on it just like Joe Strummer's. Anyway as it turned out Simon (Ellis) did not get on with my guitar but asked me down to see them rehearse and informed me that their other guitarist (whose name I can't remember – Sorry whoever you are!) was leaving to play with another band and would I like to join the Prams.

"The band at that time (the first stable version) consisted of Simon Ellis – Guitar, Chris Anderson – Bass, Caroline Boaden – Drums, Peter Birch – Vocals and me – Guitar. We did a few gigs with this line up - the most notable being at Clifton Hall in Rotherham where the audience spat at us all the time and threw beer all over the place. I remember one Punk at the front must have cut his hand on something and all the way through our set he threw blood all over me. I was covered in it by the end but it was great fun playing and people enjoying it - when you had only just learnt a few chords.

"We also played at a local club a lot called the Co-op which was a cricket club at Brecks in Rotherham. However, Chris later left the band to move to Brighton with his parents and Johnny Brown then took over on Bass duties and this line up continued for some time recording two tracks on the now famous (Rare) 'New Wave From The Heart' album in 1979, which was recorded at Planet Studios in Doncaster along with other local bands The Diks, The Squad, Subliminal Cuts, Vice Squad, Eyes at Risk and The Negatives.

"We had problems with bass players a few times and at one point we enlisted the help of my mate Graham Saunders to do one gig in Sheffield because he could play guitar so surely he could easily play bass (plus he looked well hard!). He hated bass and vowed never to play it again so eventually Simon Ellis took over bass duties permanently.

"Pete Birch eventually left the band (to go to University I think) and we enlisted the talents of John Flanagan to take up lead vocals- who breathed new life into the band. We also met up with a guy named Marcus Featherby who kind of managed/mentored us a bit and with his help we recorded a double A side single later on in 1979 with us on one side and TV Product on the other (The first time I think this had been done). We recorded our side at Cargo Studios in Rochdale and TV Product recorded theirs at Western Works with Cabaret Voltaire."

Carl Eggleston: "It was at Rotherham Art College, where I first met Simon Ellis and The Prams, how many hours were spent in the Mailcoach front bar? At the time they had a self-styled manager known as Fruits who was a real character! The Prams played a students' union do at the Assembly Rooms, where after playing the entire repertoire of material; the only encore left was Fruits mooning the whole crowd from the stage. It was also at this do where a practical joke was played on one rather gullible student, and everyone who was going played along saying that it was going to be a fancy dress do. It wasn't at all, but this one guy whose father was a surgeon-turned up in full theatre garb; Surgeons suit, white wellies, mask, gloves the whole lot. How ironic that about 6 months later a Punk-styled band called Devo would feature the exact same outfit: Rotherham at the forefront of Punk style or just an accident? Either way it was bloody funny at the time."

Tim Jones: "There was the gig at the Assembly Rooms where the student union bloke kept switching the power off and Oz kept switching it back on. If I remember rightly there were about a dozen folks that ended up on the stage joining in with the singing. Flan was on Oz's shoulders."

Chris Anderson: "Anarchy at the Assembly Rooms! - Yes it was chaos. Caroline's dad wouldn't let her out to drum with us that night so we finally persuaded Billy Burden to drum for us - he was ok but didn't know any of the songs."

Brian Pearson: "We played in quite a few places around the country but my most notable gig was when we supported the Adverts at the Limit. I thought we sounded good and would impress them but the Adverts avoided us all day so we never got to speak to them to find out what they thought. I guess they did not share my opinion as I doubt we stole the show that night. How could we compete with Gaye Advert on bass?"

The Prams in Doncaster 1978

Carl Eggleston: "The Prams were quite a cool crowd to knock around with, Simon the guitarist, and Caroline the drummer, they were quite good. They released an E.P and I had a copy of it, which along with the rest of my hard earned collection of Punk singles was stolen at a party my sister had. At the time there was a party on most weekends, or that's how it seemed, somebody's parents had left them in charge of the house where a whole host of late teens would turn up armed with a party of four, or seven if you'd clubbed together, or some Colt 45. Anyway we would all get drunk and generally create mayhem. It was at one of these parties I was invited and decided to take the whole Prams/Co-op crowd with me. I can honestly say the crowd sitting cross- legged in the front room were not expecting Fruits to stride in, remove the Steve Hillage or some other 70's hippy music and replace it with the newly released 'New Boots and Panties' album by Ian Dury and the Blockheads. And as if that wasn't bad enough, then insist that every last note was played, at least once. A student at college on the following Monday christened him *'that long streak of piss punk rocker'*, a bit harsh really.

"Another member of the Prams crowd was their ex-bass player Johnny Brown, his parents were quite well to do, and lived on the Duke of Norfolk estate. At the time Johnny was dabbling with lots of drugs, and although a brilliant artist, was completely hat-stand, reportedly offering to show his parents' dinner guests his knob whilst off his head. Johnny designed the cover for a single by The Fall, possibly 'Bingo Masters Breakout', but I couldn't be sure. Johnny's cousin was a guy called Pete Short, who at the time was possibly one of the few who could drive, and as the proud owner of a mini pick up (company car), could always be relied on for a lift here, there or everywhere."

In April 1979, the Prams were featured in issue no.3 of forward-thinking Sheffield fanzine 'NME' (New musical Excess) soon to be NMX. Described as being from 'that cultural wasteland of Rotherham', they are compared to Wire and The Cure: their inclusion of the Cure's first LP track '10.15 Saturday night' in their set is commented on as being *'not exactly the best way to build a reputation for original music, but I expect they'll grow out of it.'* The band themselves are mentioned as being not too keen on the finished product of the 'New Wave from the Heart' LP: they had two tracks ('Night Fever' and 'Indigestion') featured on it. Despite these critical points, the verdict was left open for Rotherham's finest Punk band as the writer looks forward to seeing them play at an upcoming NOWSOC gig.

In the May issue of New Musical Excess the Prams' Rotherham Arts centre support to Eyes at Risk and Doncaster's Sublimal Cuts is reviewed and the enthusiasm for the band has stepped up greatly.

Martin Lacey: (NMX writer/editor) "You can tell they don't get many gigs in Rotherham, so few, in fact, that nobody knew what to do. Despite an impressive turn out of Punky looking types, everyone insisted on sitting on chairs and as far away from the stage as possible and when one brave (or drunk) fan, presumably a friend of the band, actually danced the only response was of the *'Get out of the way I can't see'* variety. As avid readers may recall I'm taking up from where I left off in my brief feature on the Prams in issue 3, where I said they were good but sounded on record too much like Wire.

Now let me correct myself: they're VERY good and on stage don't sound overmuch like anyone I can think of. It was a very short set, but at least that meant every song was good. Not surprisingly, the live versions of 'Night Fever' and 'Indigestion' were much better than the recorded ones on 'New Wave from the Heart'. They'd have done better to take a cassette recorder to one of their gigs. They've got plenty of other original songs, such as 'Bourgeois Order', 'Video Video' and 'Here Comes the Modern Men'. You can move to them, but you have to listen as well. Interesting and exciting... and fun!

"Considering the state of the audience, The Prams got a good reception. The Arts centre is a good venue, apart from the fact that the bar shuts at 10pm and they won't let you take drinks out of the bar, and the band looked and sounded perfect. They encored, incredibly enough, with the old 2.3 classic 'I'm so bored being bored about London' (or something like that), which I hadn't heard for ages. It's good to see someone's keeping the spirit alive as this lot piss on most of what's coming from the big city these days. When 2.3 wrote the song they were saying 'Do something HERE'. The Prams have done it – there can't be many more hopeless places to be an artist than Rotherham." **(From NME – New Musical Excess fanzine issue 4 - May 1979)**

By this point in their short career, they were playing with a temporary bassist and in the NME piece left their telephone number requesting a new bass player. A change in vocal duties would also be on the cards not that much further into 1979. One Prams fan recalls here his first initiation into Punk Rock... which would be followed some time later when his ambitions would be met!

John Flanagan: "It was 1977 but I can't remember the date. The last time I had seen my nephew, a few days before, he had shoulder length hair a scoop neck T-shirt and a pair of split knee loons. He showed up at my place sporting short spiky hair, drainpipe jeans and a bike chain around his neck. He had an LP under his arm featuring 4 blokes on the front cover covered in custard pies. He said *'Listen to this'.* On hearing track 1 side 1, I was amazed, shocked and dumbfounded: Total brilliance. What I had been waiting for. My decision to be in a band came within a very short time of hearing 'Neat Neat Neat' on that first Damned album. I had to get my haircut, change my appearance and sing in a band. My existing record collection was now irrelevant and defunct. Instantly obsolete and I needed to form, or at least join a band."

That band would arrive in John's life a couple of years later when his vision of Punk Rock merged with the 'We couldn't care less' attitude of Rotherham's most overgrown Pramsters!

The Prams line up at the time of their 'Modern Men' single – John Flanagan – Vocals, Caroline Boaden – Drums: Percussion, Simon Ellis – Bass: Backing vocals, Brian Pearson – Guitar: Backing Vocals,

John Flanagan: "The Prams? - I was invited to practise with them. Gigs were arranged frantically and life soon became a whirlwind of Drugs, Alcohol, Girls and Fast Cars. No it didn't, I'm lying. I was scared of Drugs, couldn't afford Alcohol, couldn't afford Fast Cars (favourite track off 'Another music in a different kitchen' Buzzcocks LP) and couldn't afford Girls either."

Chris Anderson: "I think the main thing about The Prams was that we were very very young. We were crap (at least at the beginning) but we stuck our necks out - and got our noses put out of joint by those other Punk bands that were around. But in the main, they had been playing Dr Hook covers a month earlier. They could play and we couldn't; but they saw that as an advantage. We knew we couldn't but we could hear the songs in our head - and so could like-minded people - it was like they got the gist and could fill in the gaps for themselves. You must have heard it a thousand times, and it does sound like an excuse for being shit but punk was a state of mind more than anything. And we were babies. I'd bet we were the youngest for miles around."

John Flanagan: "I suppose Simon was the main member of the band but I remember him having no ego whatsoever and everybody's suggestions and input were listened to. We were booed off once at the Assembly Rooms. We were very pleased at this at the time! This was an acceptable achievement. I think musical tastes in the band at the time I was in it were quite diverse but I was into Clash, Damned, Ramones, Sex Pistols and lots of one hit wonder things like Prag-Vec, Eater, Protex etc. I loved Television, Magazine and Wires' 'Pink Flag' LP was on my turntable constantly. I did think that the local Punk scene was a very us and them kind of thing, though.

Brian Pearson - The Mod contribution to the Prams!

"My favourite Prams moment was when John Peel played our single at the very end of one of his 2 hour shows. I was on my own listening to him when he introduced the song and named the band. I remember being embarrassed even though I was on my own. Strange! Recording the single was done at Cargo Studios Rochdale we couldn't afford an A and B side. It was a very professional set up for a very unprofessional singer!! The single has 'dedicated to Oz' on it. (Steven Cruise, an early band member, with an awesome voice, also a very adept drummer): I ran over him in my 850cc Mini van a short time before. I don't think this dedication made up for it really though."

Brian Pearson: "By this time I was getting more and more into the Mod scene and had a scooter and when we were invited down to Brighton to support a band that Chris Anderson (our early bass player) had formed I could not wait to see where Quadrophenia had been filmed (I believe Chris' older brother 'Fruits' was an extra in the beach fight scene). I cannot remember the name of the band but think it was Smegma and the Cheesy Bits! On our return the band seemed to just fade away playing less and us all doing different things. I can't remember when I left but it must have been around this time. The Prams carried on for a bit after this but did not play much as far as I remember.

"I later joined another band called Vitamin Z in around 1980/81who had a horn section and played a kind of funky cross between Dexys Midnight Runners and ABC. We only did one gig in Sheffield with Darrel D'silva - Vocals (Now a very good actor on TV – Prime Suspect, Spooks and a drama about police in Sheffield – If you read this Darrel – Spooky Tooth!), Damien Hand on Saxophone and for a very brief period Simon Bird (Cute Pubes) on Drums. (I cannot remember the other members I am afraid – Sorry to all of you). All in all probably the whole era was the most exciting time in my life and it's nice to have been part of it all. As well as being in a band myself I saw most of the popular bands around at that time but never saw the Sex Pistols which is my biggest regret."

Rotherham's greatest hope for Post-Punk- The Prams

Three of The Prams reflect on what the future holds?

Prams photos courtesy of Kristan James Melik and Simon Ellis

John Flanagan: "What I would change? Seriously, nothing at all: They really were marvellous times I can assure you of that!"

By 1981, unfortunately, Rotherham's first Punk band The Prams were almost at the end of their short but exciting career. The Punk scene, itself, had also changed drastically. Rotherham did not fully endear itself to its most genuine Punk band of the early Punk Rock period; it could be said that Punk itself was more than a bit of a thorn in the side of the general public residence of the town. Yet, the memory of those local Do it yourself garage bands of the Punk era, including the Prams, now seem to far surpass any other local musical offerings of the period. The Prams single (shared with TV Product) 'Modern Men', a superior Post-Punk composition, is now creeping up the Punk collectable vinyl lists. They also had two songs on the 'New Wave from the Heart' LP – 'Indigestion' and 'Night Fever'. The Prams approach to Punk had been untainted by any pretensions and media infiltration and they left behind some colourful and fond memories for their small gang of fans. A Prams re-evaluation is surely well over-due!

Simon Ellis, Caroline Boaden and John Flanagan – Rotherham Assembly Rooms (1980)

Tony Beesley: "Sadly, I never actually heard the Prams properly back then. I think someone brought the single round once, but I can't recall much about it getting played. I put it down to that fateful decision to put the 'New Wave from the Heart' LP back on the Sound of Music's record racks that time in mid 1979."

One Rotherham Punk who did know of the Prams and attend their gigs was Brian Houghton, who due to the intake of some less than healthy medication during the formative years of the local Punk scene does not recall actually seeing the Prams or indeed many others! Here is part of Brian's slightly *damaged* Punk story.

Brian 'Damage' Houghton: (Rotherham Punk Rocker) "I can barely remember a thing, No where's or when's - Nowt. I remember the song 'Indigestion' really well. Marie tells me that we saw the Prams together at least once, and I know I also saw them with Darrel (D'silva) - the latter certainly in Rotherham. But no concrete memories exist. Don't do drugs, kids. It isn't big and it isn't clever!

"As 1977 turned into 1978 I was a few months into my fourteenth year. A rather shy and introspective individual with no older sibling to learn from and having spent every family holiday at the Whitby folk festival, I didn't have much of a frame of reference for Punk. Oddly, but rather sweetly as a memory, my grandmother (Nanna Nell) features twice in this story. The first time is her being tickled pink at the antics of the girl next door, slightly older than me, who had taken to going out wearing whackily garish make-up and very customised, bin-bag-incorporating clothing that covered slightly less than it ought to. If questioned about it today, the girl next door, Lindsay, would simply explain that she only did it to piss her dad off (a particularly severe ex-serviceman kind of bloke), which I'm sure is true. But other than the fact that I'd always been in awe of her, I think it was the nerve and rebelliousness that appealed to me.

Brian Houghton also known as Brian Damage - looking like a 1979 proto-type Kurt Cobain and a later shot during the 80's

"I was a relatively tall and mature looking adolescent and consequently had little problem beginning my underage drinking phase around that time; so by the beginning of 1978 I was rapidly becoming a regular in the Charter Arms above the market in Rotherham - usually downstairs, playing pool and nursing a pint of luke-warm beer trying to make it last as long as possible. I think it was a particularly insipid brand of Home Ales at the time.

"The Charters was always an interesting place with a bit of a reputation for seediness. All extremes of human life were represented there. I suppose it made sense that it would become something of a focal point for the emerging Punky children of the time. During the next few months, the tribe began to coalesce and gather. 'Revolver' was on the telly (I would have to negotiate very hard with my parents to be able to watch it on the one TV in our household). I clearly remember the likes of the original line-up of the Banshees before they signed to Polydor, and the bizarre spectacle of X-Ray Spex having a profound impact on me. I very much liked it.

"It's my belief that it is during those initial and hesitant experiments in developing a social life that people often adopt patterns that become habits of a lifetime. As an underage drinker in Rotherham's town centre pubs, this often meant augmenting the public houses with the attractions of crowd-like behaviour in going to football matches, nightclubs or gigs. For me it was gigs. More than 30 years later it still is.

"My recollections from that time are faulty, fuzzy and fractured. From sometime around my fifteenth birthday onwards I developed what I then regarded as a healthy interest in killing brain cells by consuming as much beer as I was capable of. By the time I left Oakwood School, I'd managed to augment this tendency with an (at-times) almost industrial consumption of speed. A growing interest in drug abuse also saw me freely abusing Dalmaine, moggys, palphium (think pink!) by the time I was 17 and taking A levels at TRC.

"I can recall some events and places well enough, but can't remember in what chronological order they occurred. Some memories seem to begin in the middle and then stop before any logical end. Some things I know I witnessed are lost forever. Did I really see Iggy Pop at Sheffield University in July 1981? I know I intended to. The ticket stub still in my possession suggests that I did, but I haven't got a Scooby! (And I loved Iggy – still do!)

"At an early Cute Pubes gig, rather bizarrely in a church hall near the Stag pub, I got punched full in the mouth. There was a gig by Pulp that I popped out of the Charters and over the road to see that is anecdotally the first they ever played. The Prams and my mate Dazzy playing sax with Clock DVA. But I'm not really sure precisely when any of them were.

"The bigger tours were at the Top Rank: Siouxsie and the Banshees I saw twice and they were magnificent - first with an early incarnation of Spizz (Spizz Oil, I think) then with Altered Images supporting.

Far left: Sheffield's Pink Flag fanzine

"I remember wandering around Sheffield with the lovely Claire Grogan, but haven't got a clue why. Divine at the Top Rank was a truly surreal experience and The Ants were phenomenal! A few of the first wave of American bands played around then too, generally at The Limit. I remember the B52s' first UK gig there well. Those beehives didn't last too well in that claustrophobic sweatbox! Lux Interior put his fist through the low ceiling when The Cramps played. He did it again, more deliberately a year or two later, with the words *'remember this?'*

"There are some occasions that I think I remember, but on further reflection realise are just oft repeated anecdotes from a time when I wasn't there at all. Like the Megalomania gig at The Royal, and us all laughing at one of the pub's locals who'd clearly decided to join in with the spirit of things and whose wig had developed a life of its own as he bounced around.

"Bigger gigs and further away: the second (but not the first) Futurama festival at Leeds Queens Hall (A draughty ex-bus depot, I think that was chilly as hell to sleep in September 1980) The Banshees headlining one night– I was a bit of a fan! The sensational and genuinely terrifying 4be2s – Jimmy Lydon's band with their mob of gangster henchmen were renowned for fighting Northerners and I can clearly see them jumping single-file off the stage into the audience to batter someone they took exception to. They looked for all the world, in my mind's eye, like the froglets off The Clangers. The first incarnations of The Psychedelic Furs and Echo & the Bunnymen just before my 17th birthday were performances that will stick with me forever. Part of Hazel O'Connor's Breaking Glass tour (I seem to remember her band comprised most of Spizz. – the Athletico version that year).

"Futurama was so good that I went again the next year - September 1981 - with my first proper girlfriend Yvette - that time. I'd learned the previous year's lesson and got a room in a B&B nearby. It was called 'Daze of Future Past', which was a bit pretentious as far as I was concerned. I Liked Theatre of Hate and Bauhaus on day one, Killing Joke on day two, and she liked The Thompson Twins, Wall of Voodoo, and Altered Images, so result! I still haven't a clue who headlined day two.

"Marie features again at another early Pulp gig, this time at the Hallamshire with an incarnation of the band that also included Jarvis's sister (Saskia I think). Marie was going out with Dave Kurley, the singer for New Model Soldier at the time, but Dave and Saskia had copped off by the end of the evening. Scandalous at the time!

"The Leadmill opened as a venue in either late 1979 or 1980, holes in the roof covered by parachute material to keep the rain out. My most memorable early gig there was the first visit of the Dead Kennedys. Someone in Sheffield council had objected to their name as offensive so it was deliberately misspelled on the tickets as Ded Kennedys in order to enable them to play.

"Somewhere in and amongst all this lot is The Marples. Often the first stop on a pub crawl that lead up West Street: Hornblower next, then Frog and Parrot, The Hallamshire and sometimes ending at the Beehive (a bit posh for us, truth be told, but The Cabs drank in there and we were still impressionable children at heart). Sometimes we never got beyond the Marples because a band was on.

"Marcus Featherby, who I believe had, for some odd reason, changed his surname from Weatherby, ran nights there and was also the main player in getting an LP together. I suppose it therefore made sense that the same bands would provide entertainment on his nights. I loved a band called Veiled Threat, who I think hailed from Chesterfield and who, after a slight change in line-up, renamed themselves Bikini Atoll... The Scarborough Antelopes, I'm so Hollow, B-Movie, and The Flying Alphonso Brothers always provided fine entertainment, but I admit to being fully befuddled by De Tian and their mosque chanting. The Shy Tots and Pulp (again! How many times did I encounter them in those formative years?) played there too at around the same time. I remember Mark Thingamy out of Artery climbing out of one window and in through another during one of their performances. Y? changed their name to Danse Society during a performance at The Marples. I deduce (but don't know) that this was a Bouquet of Steel showcase because Y?s track on the LP was called 'End of Act One' so the occasion made a fitting beginning to act two."

The party continued unabated for the rest of the late 70's and into the early days of the next decade for Brian, but by 1982 the casualties were coming in from the front line of the Sheffield Post-Punk scene!

Brian Houghton: "By the summer of 1982 things began to get a bit dark. People began dying in uncomfortably quick succession - all from smack. Janine, Marie and me frantically searching the West Gate pubs looking for Speccy to tell him Jud had died is a particularly distraught memory. We were all immortal in our own minds at that age so it was profoundly shocking. First Jud and then Speccy not long after, then Ian - the David Sylvian look-alike who, if memory serves me right (and it often doesn't!) was some kind of secretary for an early version of the Human League. It didn't stop us caning it though. In September 1982 – in a move that in retrospect quite likely saved my life - I vanished off to London for three and a half years, in a move to avoid looking for honest employment and instead study for a degree, which largely took me away from the punky children of this corner of South Yorkshire and into the emerging Temple of Psychic Youth. My memories of a lot of that time are broken and twisted. What a terrifying prospect: trying to access coherent stories from that area of my psyche!"

Perhaps Brian, whilst indulging in his regular assaults to damage his psyche, would have seen a Sheffield Punk band around at the time called Repulsive Alien?

Repulsive Alien were Sheffield's second known Punk band, arriving on earth to create Punk mayhem and entertain John Peel, amongst others, around 1978-79. They featured on the 'Bouquet of steel' compilation LP of 1979 and played at venues such as the Broadfield and the Marples. Their

Repulsive Aliens photos courtesy of Kristan James Melik

reign was short but just as exciting as any other Punk bands: their flame burning brightly for not that much more than a year or so, but the heat was as captivating and inviting as the local Punk temperature would allow!

Nick Hawksworth: (Sheffield Punk and guitarist with Repulsive Alien) "Like a whole bunch of other kids at the time, Punk was our music. The bands were ours, it was loud, it was rebellious, our parents didn't like it and it was glorious. Repulsive Alien formed because of it. We didn't live in Tower Blocks or back alley slums, we lived in Dronfield. I was a huge Bowie fan but then I heard The Ramones in Virgin on The Moor and remember the staff arguing for and against it between themselves. The song was 'I Don't Wanna Go Down to The Basement' and it was 1976. The rest, as they say, is history!!

Alien Didi

"I'd sort of known about Simon (Milner) from a few years earlier when me and a friend used to walk down the path at the side of his back garden and throw stones at him. Sometime later it turned out that he was a school friend of my younger brother and I went along with him to Simon's house one day and sat bemused whilst this group of 14 year old school friends attempted to make some music despite the lack of working instruments. That was late 1978 and they were The Ulcers. I was a couple of years older and had already been writing songs with the guitar I'd bought from a second hand shop in Chesterfield so somehow it was suggested that I join them. We dispatched the guitarist and the singer and set about taking things a bit more seriously.

"The name came from a Virgin Record 7" single bag I had which depicted a Sci-Fi scene with spacemen shooting their Ray Guns at 'those Repulsive Aliens.' Simon and I wrote songs as though they were ten a penny, some survived but others didn't. I had visions of us being the next Strummer and Jones. We just clicked and due to help from parents with equipment and the eventual meeting with our singer, Didi (David Thorpe), via a mutual friend of Simons. We started rehearsing furiously in the Church Hall at Holmesfield. It's now the summer of 1979 and we were true second generation Punks. By this time we were not only seeing all these great bands at places like the Top Rank and The Limit but we were also watching the local bands. There was definitely an outburst of musical and artistic things happening and you really could go out every night of the week and see great bands playing in the upstairs rooms of pubs and clubs.

"Two very important things happened to us at this time, firstly we met the Stunt Kites and

started following them around every time they played and basically tried to copy them, and shortly afterwards we met Marcus. I ended up living with Marcus Featherby at the house on Whitham Road and he opened so many doors for us. He introduced us to people and places, he gave us confidence and I suppose an identity. He might have come in for a bit of stick over the years but Sheffield and the music scene there would not have been the same without him. We played as many gigs as we could. We would play anywhere, and on a couple of occasions we even got paid!! Our first gig in Sheffield was at the George IV and I remember being bitterly disappointed because I wanted it to be perfect. Didi even called the audience a bunch of hippies which was so wrong on so many levels.

"We played The Hallamshire, The Broadfield, The Royal, University, The Marples, and The Leadmill and supported Artery in the corridor of Psalter Lane Art College. It was the best of times and even lugging amps and drums up and down numerous flights of stairs (especially Marples and George IV) didn't detract from the absolute sense of what a brilliant time it was. People recognised us and wanted to talk to us. They wanted to know when our next gig was. We had fans!! Memories of travelling to play the Fan Club in Leeds in a van that might not have been entirely roadworthy and wondering why Didi had missed the pickup in Sheffield, and travelling to Fairview studios in Hull to record 'Say and Do' for Bouquet of Steel. Y? had the afternoon session that day and their mums brought sandwiches. Unfortunately, despite all the gigs, photos and memories, the only recording

Some Aliens and friends

(professional or otherwise) to show for it all is 'Say and Do.' I always thought that was a shame.

"We played our final gig as Repulsive Alien on August 16th 1980 at the local band festival at The Leadmill. Pulp were playing their first Sheffield gig and Artery headlined. It was our drummer Stany's 16th birthday. We threw cake all over the stage. Afterwards, we were asked by a couple of punky looking kids if they could have our songs as they were forming a band. Apparently they became The Mau Mau's. Despite forming Divine Comedy and carrying on in a slightly different musical direction, it was never the same and we drifted off into different directions. At the time of writing, I have no idea of the whereabouts of either Stany or Didi, though Simon still is, and always will be, a great friend."

A Prams 45-sharing band also had a bash at adding some product to the Sheffield scene. Sheffield student and Punk fan Pete Jespersen takes over from where he left off earlier in Punk Rock voices.

Paul Jespersen: (TV Product drummer) "TV Product formed in early 1979, out of the student-house party scene in Hunter's Bar. The songs were surprisingly melodic! Initial influences were the Buzzcocks and Wire, so much so that the penultimate song in our set lasted about 30 seconds, with lyrics consisting of 'Guess what NOWSOC – we're not Wire – one two three four STOP' – immediately followed by a cover of 'Boredom'. The first line-up, whose debut gig was supporting Artery at the Polytechnic, was Ian Bartlett – vocals Glyn Thomas – guitar, Simon Hinkler – guitar, Tony Perrin – bass and myself Paul Jespersen – drums.

TV Product: Glyn, Paddy, Ian and Paul

"Simon was a local lad who, crucially, as well as being proficient on guitar, had access to a van (he worked for a vacuum cleaner business called T L Killi's on Glossop Road, and had use of their transit van). Tony was (at the time) a rudimentary bass player but he was good at making things happen (he later went on to manage Artery and The Mission, I think). Ian was like a more handsome Johnny Rotten, and Glyn could write songs – things were looking good!

"Of course the downside of forming bands with students is that they all go home in the summer, or, worse, go off to do 'sandwich years' or gap years, so the situation became somewhat fluid in the summer of 1979. However, the band had attracted the attention of the enigmatic Marcus Featherby, who facilitated the release of a record on Limited Edition Records. Simon, Tony and Paul recorded 'Jumping Off Walls'/ 'Nowhere's Safe' at Cabaret Voltaire's Western Works studio. This was released as one side of an EP – the Prams were on the other side. A third track, 'Social Psychology', which didn't make it onto the EP, is the great lost TV Product song – I'd love to hear it again. I guess the master tape is out there somewhere.

"We had a rehearsal space in a building called (I think) Britannia Mills, near Gibraltar Street. Other bands, including the Negatives, had spaces there too. We gigged as a three-piece for a while, then Simon left to join Artery. The final line-up of TV Product, which was together under the shortened name of TVP for about a year, was Paul, Glyn, Paddy on bass, and Sheffielder Ian Cutler, a great lad, on vocals. We had lots of strong original songs but it's telling that I haven't seen Glyn or Ian from that day to this – we didn't have that us-against-the-world gang mentality. I guess we didn't want it badly enough! But it was a great feeling to be part of a very special scene.

"Simon of course went on to be in The Mission, and I see from his website that he is still making music today, which is great. I stayed in Sheffield for ten years, and go back frequently (my brother Carl, who attended some of those Jam gigs (77 onwards) with me, moved there in the 1980s and is still there). I'm still playing in bands too – including many years of fun in Glory Days, a Bruce Springsteen tribute band that played at the Boardwalk many times. I know tribute bands are frowned on in some circles, but I like to think that my 20-year-old self would forgive my 50-year-old self, if you see what I mean."

Another Sheffield Punk band making their mark at approximately the same time as Repulsive Alien and TV Product were drawing to a close were Plastik Toyz led by singer Jamie 'Headcharge' Smith. Their influences are cited by Jamie as Stunt Kites, Artery, Cabaret Voltaire, Vice Versa and Clock DVA of the Sheffield bands and amongst many name Punk bands Penetration, X-Ray Spex and The Clash along with reggae inspiration from Lee Perry and Big Youth and classic Post-Punk from Magazine and P.I.L. A listen to late night radio was also pivotal in the creation of Jamie's path to Punk and beyond!

Jamie 'Headcharge' Smith: (left) "At home I found myself tuning in to John Peel late at night - but had to listen at low level in my bedroom due to my parent's awareness that I was getting in to this *weeeerd music* much to their dismay. Around the same time I was given a guitar and amp by an Uncle but did I wanna play it in a normal way - no! I'd fuck around with it trying to get the *weeeerdest sounds* I could; often using different objects around the house to play it. Before long, as and when my parents would go down the pub, a few mates - John Grundy and Dave Johnson - would start coming around and Dave would pick the guitar up and start playing around. He had a natural thing with it so I kind of started with this one drum and doing basic beats. Then the lyrics started coming: I found myself spewing vile lyrics about the vile things in the world. John Grundy soon bought a bass guitar!! That was it; all we needed was a drummer and along came Stevo (R.I.P). We are the PLASTIK TOYZ.

"All we need now is a rehearsal room and as luck would have it our youth workers (one Hippy Dave and Rasta Kung Fu Charlie) gave us All Saints community centre two hours before our youth night started. We'd rehearse twice a week but before long people started coming earlier n' earlier to attend the youth club as they heard us rehearsing and we started letting them in. It ended up like we were doing a weekly gig to about 30 people. I remember looking at the rest of the band and then back at the kids and thinking *'God they like us'* and one of these kids was Soski; a well known character amongst Sheff Skins & Punks alike. Unbeknown to us he had recorded one of our rehearsals and passed it on to Marcus Featherby, which I only found out about one day as I went to pick tickets up for a massive gig at the Nelson Mandela building. Outside the Mandela was a porta-cabin and on entering I was met with Soski

Plastik Toyz Jamie and Stevo

saying to Marcus *'that's Jamie aka Smiffy from the Plastik Toyz.'* Marcus, who I already knew from helping out at the Marples, then reached under the desk pulling out a pile of flyers and I nearly shit myself: "MAU MAUS & PLASTIK TOYZ being recorded live at THE MARPLES. Turns out Soski had passed the recording of the rehearsal to Marcus as a Demo. When I got back home I nipped around to see the rest of the band and show em the flyers; the Looks on their faces were amazing along with comments like *'What have you done ya crazy* fukker' hahahahaha!

"At the gig; Jesus we were so fuckin' nervous. Arriving early afternoon in Stevo's Dads old Commer van, I can remember the looks as we pulled up from the grannies on the way to the bingo. Mau Maus sound-checked then us and it went surprisingly well. We then fucked off to the Wimpy on Fargate (first place I saw Pulp). On arriving back to the Marples (a bit pissed), we couldn't beleeeeve our eyes as it was packed along with the group of kids from the youth club down to support us. I spotted one guy with Plastik Toyz on the back of his jacket!! The DJ was playing and we were due on in about 40 mins just enough time to sink some more Newcastle Brown and calm our nerves even more. Before we knew it we were on!! Ripping though our set like rats on speed!!! I can remember thinking *'Thank fuck for that'* as we came to the end. *'Let me get to that bar'*, I was shaking like a shitting dog but NO!!! Everyone started shouting more and chanting Plastik Toyz n Sheffield - Sheffield. I looked at the rest of the band and said *'fuck it lets do our cover of 'Warhead'* (UK Subs), but I changed it to *'Knob head, KNOBHEAD, KNOBHEAD YOU'RE A FUCKIN KNOBHEAD'* and the kids went mental pogoing while doing the Knob head gesture hahahahahaha. Next on were the MAU MAUS and as per usual they played a blinder and at the end of their set we both got up together and did a cover of *'Motorhead'* by Motorhead, What a night!!!!!

"Several other gigs transpired with Peter and the Test Tube babies, Mau Maus, Cute Pubes and others I forget. Marcus had mentioned if we got things a bit tighter he would possibly look at putting us on tour with the Mau Maus and release our live recording but unfortunately our guitarist left. We did try out the guitarist from Cute pubes, he was really good but it just wasn't the same without Dave and before long we split; missing out on touring and getting our live recording released and God knows what else!"

Right: The face of 80's Punk in Sheffield: Photo courtesy of Karl Lang

The days of Plastik Toyz, Repulsive Aliens and Punks n' Prams and damaged Brian's were almost at an end by the start of the new decade. Sheffield, Rotherham and the local Punk vicinity had given its best shot at creating its own vision of the Punk Rock blueprint: now the time was nigh for a new calling tune, one that was inspired and influenced by Punk, but instead of following the path of 3 chord (or less) garage Punk, the new musical template would be much more considered and open to new sounds; old sounds regurgitated and shifts to the left, right and centre. Punk Rock, at least as a musical force, was dying its last breaths: the remaining death knells for the local Punk Rock scene being played out upstairs at a World War 2 Blitz-wrecked pub. Meanwhile, the rest of the local musical map was awaiting the sounds of Sheffield calling!

Chapter Six

Sheffield calling - Rotherham receiving!

Punks, Goths and Futurists!

"We were well into Crass and their slogan songs, and the message that they were promoting. It seemed the purist 'Punk' line - anarchy, freedom etc (or just hippy bullshit with hindsight?)." –
Nick Banks (Pulp Drummer and Rotherham Punk)

Sheffield Post-Punk fans Simon Milner, Ellie Ford, Robert 'Dingo' Dowling, Michael Day, Simon Ellis of The Prams and Shaun Day (Courtesy of Kristan James Melik)

Sheffield - the new decade and onwards! The mood was an optimistic *steel city* grey. Punk had been the catalyst, the prime mover and the obliterator of any barricades created to prevent the common man of Sheffield from having a taste of whatever he or she wished to achieve – musically and artistically. The raw sounds of Punk were still to be heard blasting out of the Marples and occasionally the Limit club; but this new decade – the 1980's – would be one that took the ethics and idealism of Punk Rock many steps further... and nowhere more profoundly and individually than in Sheffield.

The new bands were already competing in their infant states, so all hopes of a scene with a sense of unity were straight out of the window: perhaps a precedent had been set by the first wave of Punk bands themselves, a few years earlier, with their indifference towards each other? ... or maybe that's the way of all sets of like-minded musicians who manage to be captivated with a wave of optimism and possibilities... it's only Rock n' Roll after all!

And what of the fans? The City of Sheffield's scenesters and the hip teens of Rotherham and other nearby towns all being a mix of sorts: Punk-loving die-hards with a penchant for the new hardcore now fast approaching, grey Mac-wearing forward-thinking Post-Punk fans, Mod revivalists, Rockabilly-loving Punks with flat-top hair cuts and floppy-fringed new romantics embracing the future with a synthesiser. As the decade wore on, the dividing lines would become even more blurred and the confidence of a whole generation throughout the vicinity of South Yorkshire would be smashed to pieces via Thatcherism, widespread unemployment, the miners strikes, the collapse of the Steel industry and the arrival of hard drugs on the streets that would affect whole communities and wipe away the hopes and dreams of our youth... Before then, though, the gates were still wide open, the music was still buzzing and the excitement created by Punk, for the time being, was still in the air!

Photo: Courtesy – Kristan James Melik

The live music venues that had invited Punk and its offspring through their doors had decreased: the days of some of the real earthy down to the roots clubs were on the wane; the glory days of Punk being their flagships. The Outlook in Doncaster and Rotherham's Windmill were long gone... It was now down to a small handful of clubs and pubs such as the Limit, Hallamshire, George IV, the Royal and the Marples to carry the cause.

The local scene ventured into many directions with almost as many varying fans of each splintered style of original creativity. Whilst mainstream Punk Rock began to fade nationwide and Post-Punk took a firm grip on the alternative night life of Sheffield, the last bastions of the hardcore Punk fraternity answered the call of a corner placed pub's upstairs room called the Marples!

The Marples had a notably tragic history. So named the Marples after a previous owner of the premises - John Marples and the licensee's name of Edward Marples - whilst it had been known as The Wine and Spirit Commercial Hotel. Situated on the corner of Fitzalan Square and High Street, the premises became fondly known as the Marples, despite a name change to the London Mart following the outbreak of WW2. The seven-storey high building, along with at least 77 of its clientele, received a direct hit from a high explosive German bomb during the Sheffield Bombing raid of Thursday December 12th 1940, leaving a heap of rubble 15 feet high. The Luftwaffe's journey there was achieved by passing over Rotherham and searching for the tell-tale signs of Hoober Stand and Keppel's column. The tragedy resulted in seven men being rescued from the wreckage during the following day but 70 bodies and partial remains were also recovered or never found. One tragic survivor, as a result of the trauma of the bombing, even took his own life before the wars end.

A pre-Punk era Marples in the background

The site was left undisturbed and derelict for many years, Sheffielders subconsciously respecting it as hallowed ground. The Post-War venue relating to our story emerged right at the very end of the 1950's and was officially named as the Marples for the first time.

By the late 1970's an altogether different explosion hit the venue when Punk Rock arrived in the City. The venue gradually began to book most of the local Punk inspired bands, giving a helping hand to almost-

-all who ventured upstairs to play a live set, although it was the Post-Punk crowd who would mostly play there - Sheffield's most Punk inclined band the Stunt-kites also joining in frequently. By early 1981, with the helping hand of Marcus Featherby, it would be the visiting next generation of Punk bands that would be showing up to perform to Sheffield's new and old hardcore Punk fans.

Brian Houghton: "As a small child, I remember my grandmother telling me about the Marples disaster in the Blitz around 1940 when lots of people, including children, had been killed in the cellar there. I think it troubled me and affected me very deeply, because years later I was always a bit wary of the Marples and didn't feel particularly at ease in there: Until later on … during the nights when I would often be found sprawled out on the stairs, drunk out of my happy little mind. I did spend a fair bit of time in there, but I'm not sure exactly when: pre and early Marcus (W) Featherby times, I think.

"I didn't see a lot of the real Punk stuff there. I think I saw the original Crass there, though I vaguely recall not liking them very much. I definitely didn't go to the one at Christmas where you had to take a toy to get in. I saw the early Cabs there more than once and a very early Pulp, Veiled Threat (who became Bikini Atoll), and the Comsats - I think at the Marples - plus Scarborough Antelopes, Artery and the Negatives. Later on I saw some of the pre-Goth bands there like Wasted Youth and The March Violets, but the first bands I saw there seem to be mostly associated with the 1980 local band sampler called 'Bouquet of steel'."

Lynne Freeman: (Sheffield Punk) "In the early eighties we would often start a night out at the 'Marples' pub in Fitzalan Square. My grandparents and parents had told me about the Marples taking a direct hit during the war and many people had been killed, I always had a quick thought for those poor devils every time I crossed the threshold. We used to end up in there on most Sunday nights, but also when we'd be passing through on any other night of the week! It was great cos there were two bars to choose from, upstairs or downstairs. Downstairs always had a very strange light to it and was filled with the haze of cigarette smoke. It was one of those sort of pubs that you felt that, if it had been in another town, you wouldn't have liked to stumble into it by accident. Actually that couldn't be further than the truth, it was a very matey type pub, no frills, and everyone knew everyone else, unless of course there was a gig on and then it could be an excuse for a bit of trouble!

"Upstairs was also good, although sometimes you had to behave a bit better upstairs, no chucking beer about as it had a carpet and ashtrays! When Punk first started, Landlords believed all they saw and heard in the papers and the minute you walked into their pubs with spiked hair and strange clothes, you could feel the atmosphere change. However, as Punk/Mod/Skin culture all became more popular, landlords citywide decided it was in their monetary interest to let us in! Punk and Punkette? Funny names, but I never thought of myself as a 'Punkette', it was all just Punk to me, no label, not male, not female, just Punk!"

One of the most popular of the new wave of 'real Punk' bands coming through during the Marples heyday were Bristol's Vice Squad. Led by blonde Punkette and pro-animal rights/anti-vivisection singer Beki Bondage (who had recently graced the front cover of Sounds magazine in full colour) they performed at the Marples twice in 1981. Here drummer Shane Baldwin recounts his and his band mate's experience of coming up north and meeting the hard core Punks first hand.

Shane Baldwin: (Vice Squad drummer - left) "Vice Squad's first foray into Yorkshire, a county that really seemed to take to us in a big way, was at Sheffield Marples on 14 September. The Marples was a big pub in the centre of the town that put on bands on its first floor. As usual, the gear went up during the day and the band were picked up from work in Simon's Volvo. We arrived at around eight o'clock and made straight for the bar, of course. Dave describes the sight that met our eyes: *'Three quarters of the audience were women, three quarters of the women were well shaggable, totally unheard of in Punk Rock circles in those days, and the quarter of the audience that were blokes all looked like undernourished rodents or reptiles. To my mind it was heaven.'* One track mind that bloke, always has had. His day was really made when we went into the venue proper to take a look at the local support band, Debar. They were, to be honest, pretty awful, but they had one redeeming feature. They were all girls. We got to know Debar quite well, some of us more than others, and soon found out that they had something of a reputation for their, erm, friendliness, to visiting male band members. Rumour had it (alledgedly) that one of them had given Captain Sensible a dose of what was then called 'The Clap'. How we laughed.

"Upstairs at the Marples turned out to be another sweat-box, and a few songs into the set I was grateful that Igor, with his native cunning and ingenuity, had had the sense to place the drums somewhat off stage-centre, next to an open window. It was still unbearably hot, but at least I could gulp down a few breaths of fresh air between numbers. Though we'd only been in the county for a few hours, we'd found the locals to be friendly (in the normal sense of the word - the other would come later), and helpful.

"They seemed eager to please, and around halfway through our set, seeing that we were suffering a little from the heat, they kindly came to our aid by slinging pints of beer at us. In keeping with the Yorkshire stereotype, when it dawned on them that ale costs money, they switched to slinging pints of water. As we were going down very well, we could only assume that this was their way of showing their appreciation. It was certainly more sanitary than gobbing.

"After a while, though, the sheer volume of liquid being propelled stage-ward became a bit of a problem. Being struck in the face with a full pint of water does, it must be admitted, have a certain refreshing quality, but as the stuff was arriving by the gallon and we were surrounded by electrical equipment, there was also an element of danger. But help was at hand, as Dave, dripping with sarcasm, remembers: *'When we came off our manager was ashen-faced, shell-shocked, having just bridged himself on a 240 Volt mains and formed a human chain between one bit of live and another bit, otherwise all the mike stands and everything else would have gone live and we'd have died. But he took the belt for about forty minutes, as, funnily enough, no other human being on earth would be able to do. I forget what the end result of that was, but I'm sure it cost us a lot of money.'"*

Tony Beesley: "The Vice Squad gigs were met with frantic pogoing from the Punks. One of the few visions I have left of going to the Marples is seeing Beki Bondage bellowing out to a horde of Punk Rockers going crazy...their energy was top class! One of the nights coming back from the Marples, there was a load of us that managed to catch the last bus home and the bus was full of beer-swilling straights – pissed out of their heads. Their faces were a picture of disgust and glee as they saw the multi-coloured hair and spikes galore getting on the bus. We went past em' to lots of the usual abuse and the threats continued on the whole journey. These were big fellas, 20 – 30 something's and they hated Punk Rockers. As it came to the bus stop and our turn to get off, one of the lads, Paul Maiden, made no more to do and leaped up and ran across everyone on the bus's heads and shoulders right to the front of the bus, pressed the door open and shot off. The rest of us were pissing ourselves with nervous laughter and saw our chance and ran down the bus too as the lard heads were agasp at the cheek of our mate. None of us got touched that night."

Beki Bondage and Mark Hambly: Photo credit: Kristan James Melik

Beki Bondage: (Vice Squad singer) "All I can remember of playing the Marples is phoning my Mum up from a call box in there and the constant spitting urrhhh!"

Steve Marshall: "The Marples punk nights started up around 1980 – 1981 and the only few memories I have of those is that it was an otherwise empty room three floors up with a small stage; so you had to go downstairs for a pint!! But it was good beer - John Smiths and Magnet!! It was full of young Punks and sometimes Skins. I remember Crass/Dirt/Annie Anxiety in May of 1981 playing there. I liked the Dirt single on Crass records ('Object Refuse. Reject. Abuse') and I thought they were the best of the 3. Crass were a bit too ideologically heavy and musically avant-garde – for their own good.

"The newer groups like Exploited, Vice Squad, Discharge, Anti-Pasti, and Theatre of Hate etc...I saw them all, but they were the new generation and attracted a lot of younger hardcore Punk followers...and sometimes aggression and trouble too. I liked them, but at 19 or 20, I was now getting to be too old for that kind of stuff already!!"

John Quinn: "My friend Simon came with me to a charity concert at The Marples pub featuring an early line-up of Chumbawamba. The deal was that you took a toy along to gain admittance which would then be donated to a children's charity. Unfortunately the Action Man brought by Simon was snubbed by the right-on doorman who insisted they couldn't accept a war toy. Simon solved the problem by popping home, removing the soldier's uniform from the doll and replacing it with a miniature football kit. He had no problem getting in on his return. On another occasion Simon and another friend, Stuart, were threatened in the Leadmill toilets during a Peter and the

Test Tube Babies show by a gang of Skinheads who demanded 50p. When Stuart explained that the smallest currency he had was a pound note, the head Skinhead reached into his own pocket and insisted on giving him the change..."

Beverley Wilson: (Chesterfield Punkette) "The Marples was a great venue for Punk gigs but not a good place for us to visit as we took our lives in our hands every time we went there. We saw some great bands-Anti-Pasti, Vice Squad, GBH, Exploited and Discharge to name but a few. I encountered my first mosh pit when we went to see Discharge which was a terrifying experience but didn't stop me going back for more.

"We'd get the train or bus over there and then hope to make it back in time for the last bus/train home. We very often missed it though and ended up spending cold, miserable nights out waiting for the first available transport home in the morning.

"On one occasion about 100 Sheffield Skins were waiting for us outside the Marples, (can't remember which band we'd seen) and we had to leg it for dear life down to the train station. One of the Skins got hold of my mate, Vikki, but thankfully let her go when he realised he'd got one of 'the girls'...Very chivalrous! We reached the train station, gasping for breath only for the police to turn up (again) and start questioning us about what we'd been up to: the Skinheads of course had all suddenly disappeared, and we had a job convincing them that we hadn't done anything. Caught the train though!!"

Like more than a fair few young music fans during the original Punk era, Neil Anderson was attracted to the danger and excitement of this new music: though typically it would take a few more years before he would manage to meet the Punk live experience face to face. Here Neil recounts his early memories that lead up to his Marples gig experiences.

Neil Anderson: (Sheffield author) - I remember my Auntie - who was always pretty cool herself - gave me her copy of the first Stranglers album in 1977; it can't have been out very long after it was released. I was eleven. I was totally hooked on it until my dad heard the swearing on it and promptly confiscated it. I remember going to see them a few years later and the band signing an album for my dad and wrote him an apology which he readily accepted.

"But the album that really bowled me over was The Damned's debut - that was awesome. I got into music pretty early on. I had a Slade T-shirt when I six or seven and was well into The Sweet and T-Rex but it was always Punk that really lit up my world like nothing else. The music, the fashion, the attitude - it was fab.

"My first ever gig was Killing Joke at Sheffield Polytechnic in 1981. It was totally rammed. I was 14 or 15. I counted the days down for weeks before. I was living in Chesterfield at the time and caught the train over with mates. I remember my friend Rimmo throwing up out of the window for some reason and agreeing to sell me his UK Subs 'Brand New Age' album for 1p. Killing Joke were awesome, it was their 'What's this for...?' tour. I managed to get on stage with the band for 'Wardance'. I also found £20 which I blew on a load of LPs the day after.

"The Crass gig at the Marples was very memorable. They didn't have to do any advertising as the hardcore Punks arrived from all the four corners of the country. Looking back it's fair to say that half their music was terrible and I'd got absolutely no idea what they were talking about in half their lyrics, but the buzz about the band was amazing and the gig was such an 'event'. Their use of films/backdrops etc was really powerful and you really felt you were a part of something. I remember svengali-style promoter Marcus Featherby taking the cash on the door - he seemed a pretty affable chap.

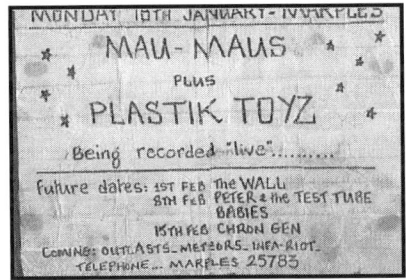

"My favourite Marples gig was probably Anti-Pasti on their 'Last Call' tour or it might have been UK Subs with Sheffield act The Stunt Kites doing some bizarre performance of the Nativity Play as support. The UK Subs were awesome. They had the Harper, Garrett, Gibbs, Roberts line-up and they'd just released 'Endangered Species' - a class album. Steve Roberts was an awesome drummer and Garrett was always impressive with his ability to jump about ten foot in the air whilst playing the guitar. I remember the band were handing out free 'Countdown' badges (their forthcoming single) and photos. I got all the band to sign mine and then stuffed it inside my jacket for safe-keeping whilst I went pogoing mad for the duration of their set. I was drenched in sweat and the photo fell to bits. I'm still traumatised by the incident to this day."

Anon: "I saw Crass at the Marples with the Documentary film as support. Tony was there as well, but he doesn't seem to remember it!"

Tony Beesley: (Right) "I am sure I would have probably moaned like a twat all of the way through their sets. I only went out of pure boredom I suppose: which doesn't seem to have been cured by their minimal talents. In my mind, Crass equals crap wrapped up in a Hippy Punk political propaganda sheet! I mean at least the Clash had style! I never really had any time for all that Anarchy crap. I respect true Anarchists and as individuals it can work but collectively it just doesn't work... there's always someone wanting to be in charge and some of it is just egotistical anyway!"

Phil Chatterton: (Right) "I saw Crass at the Marples who I thought were crap. Discharge cancelled one of their gigs - because of the snow being bad at the time. The no.69 bus was going about halfway to Sheffield and then turning back. I also saw Angelic Upstarts there and went to the 'Fetch a toy' gig when the UK Subs and the Stunt Kites played. We would sometimes go downstairs and have a pint or two with all the Punks on a Saturday afternoon."

Nick Banks: "The Crass gig was a bit of a scary do. I recall them having a reputation as having pretty hardcore followers. I think I went with my brother Richard and mate Steve Allot. The Upstairs was packed and the band had re-decorated the stage with flickering TV's and stuff hanging down etc. We were well into Crass and their slogan songs, and the message that they were promoting. The crowd was a pretty scary looking real hardcore type. There was Punk poetess Joolz doing her thing. I'm sure there was another support I forget, and then on came Crass. It was all pretty intense stuff, and we loved shouting along. I'm sure our 'Punk' credentials (always a big thing, being accused of 'posing' or plastic' was a real no no.) were on the up."

Anon: "I used to love gigs at the Marples. Just walking up those stairs and never really knowing what you were going to find. It was a small & intimate place; you were always on close terms with the band and the rest of the crowd. I think that's why I still love small venues, I can't be doing with big corporate aircraft hangars, and I choose not to go even if it's a band I like. I remember it being quite high though, so it never seemed small in the way that The Limit did – I guess if you'd been you'll know what I mean.

"I used to love second wave of Punk bands there; Anti-Pasti, Discharge, Exploited, Vice Squad, The Wall, Chron Gen, Angelic Upstarts and loads of local bands such as the Injectors who were the perennial support act. *'H Block shock it's a fucking laugh Ha Ha!'* I saw most of the anarchy bands such as Crass, Dirt, and Flux of Pink Indians there as well. Most of the Rotherham contingent used to go up on the 69 bus then we'd leg it down after the gig to catch the last one home!"

Tony Beesley: "It's weird really. I was the same age as a lot of the Hardcore Punks, who were into Discharge etc and they were taking the piss out of the Clash, The Jam etc. I suppose I was old skool (in today's terms) even at 16 fuckin' years old! I went to the Marples, saw *some* good gigs, but to be honest it was just a great place for a 16 year old to be going at the time. It was fun but I just didn't want to be a part of the new tribe!"

Charlie Harper of UK Subs at the Marples 1981 (Courtesy of Kristan James Melik

Left: The Punk Toy event

Craig Chatterton: "I was never that fond of all that *Crash Bang Wallop thrash* of the new side to Punk at the time. I was not that struck with the Oi! bands at all either... a lot of it at the end of the day was just stripped down thuggery. I much preferred the first wave of Punk bands. I obviously missed the Pistols, being so young, and it was like 'Blink and we missed em' kind of thing. We had to make do with the 'Great Rock n' Roll Swindle' and all the singles."

Tony Beesley: "The actual gigs at the Marples are a real blur to me nowadays; I know we had some great times there, but it was mainly a social thing for me, somewhere to go with my mates. I suppose the best gigs, from what I can remember, are the big three of 81 (Vice Squad, Anti-Pasti and Chron Gen) along with the Angelic Upstarts, UK Subs (lots of times), The Outcasts, Chelsea (apart from Gene October's moaning) and Sheffield's finest... Artery! Most of the rest were absolute rubbish and quite possibly more than a little responsible for me getting pissed off with Punk: that and the sheep-like mentality of a lot of the Punk kids around at the time."

Anon: "Some of the Punk stuff did start to get a bit formulaic and, dare I say it, a bit boring! Oi had started to make an impression on me; I loved the rawness, the lyrics and the hint of danger about it. I started going to gigs mainly with Andy Goulty. He always seemed to have plenty of cash and always good for an underage pint in the Globe pub on Howard Street. I could never get served with beer! He was quite tall and looked older than me, even though I was a year older than him! I remember him getting a proper MA1 jacket from an army stores in Shalesmoor that looked the biz, the lining was super bright orange. I went up for one and they were about £20 which was a lot in those days. I ended up buying a Harrington's 'special' for £6 and my Mum stitched me a South Yorkshire logo on the left breast.

Oi! Oi! Oi! at the Marples!

PHOTOS: COURTESY OF KEVIN WELLS

"I also bought some Sta-Prest trousers and got my Mum to shorten them so they looked the bollocks with my 10 hole black docs with red laces! I went to Vic's barbers on Manor Farm for my hair cut and a proper little suede head I looked! I think I looked about 12, though: probably a bit like that little kid in This Is England!

"We both looked part of the scene and were accepted for the Oi gigs now. Some Sheffield skins were always out to cause trouble, though, usually due to a bag of Bostik! We never got any grief off them, but they gave straights & grebo's (Rockers) a hard time – - usually when they outnumbered them ten to one though. Very rare you saw them go one on one, if so it was usually with themselves, over who'd gone out of turn with the glue bag. We once got talking to Garry Bushell who was championing the Oi scene from his London base and had strayed *oop north*. I don't think he had much to say to us from what I recall. I ended up buying Goulty's MA1 off him for a paltry sum when he'd gone off to be a casual. I loved that jacket and it saw me through many sweaty gigs and cold nights. I only gave it away to a mate who was into the ska scene a couple of years ago. It still fitted me as well – yeah right!"

Pete Skidmore: "I went to a few gigs at the Marples when the second wave of Punk bands starting playing there - Angelic Upstarts, 4-skins, Anti-Pasti etc. I saw quite a few of the Oi! Bands; although I could never get excited about them: we went to see Infa Riot who where probably a bit better then the usual Oi! bands but it was fucking spoilt by one of the Pond Street skinheads giving it the Seig Heil bit, he soon got a slap."

Julie Lee: "I virtually lived at the Marples through my teenage years. They had gigs every week and it was only a quid to get in, so I went every week. Marcus Featherby was the guy who ran it and his sidekick was a guy named Jesus. I can't remember half the bands I saw there but I loved

Photo: Beverley Wilson

it. It was a great place to hang out as well because everyone went. I knew loads of people who I only used to see at the Marples and nowhere else. The hard thing about the Marples was getting home – to Rawmarsh. The gigs didn't finish until about 11 and the last bus was at 10.30 from Pond Street bus station. I can't tell you how many times I hitched home, or hitched and walked."

Not all Punk fans followed the route of the average three chord thrash of the second generation UK Punk bands or its Oi! counterparts... such as one ex-Outlook goer.

John Murray: (Doncaster Punk) "After that first wave of Punk, I followed where bands like Wire, Magazine, Gang of Four, and The Fall were going - the first flush of what I guess was to become 'Indie' music. I listened to John Peel right through the early 80's. I never got into the later

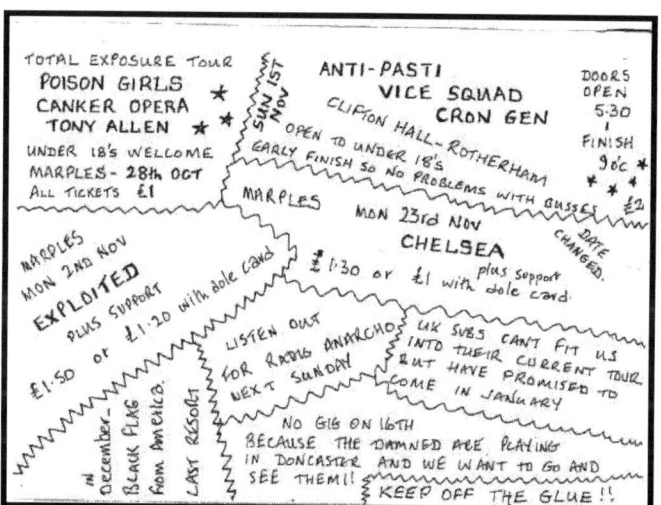

(bristles, Mohicans & studs) waves of UK Punk, but I was re-energized again circa '82 by US hardcore bands like Black Flag, early Husker Du, MDC, and Bad Brains (I went to Sheffield Dingwalls to see them live). I loved their 'non-image' compared to bands like GBH, Discharge etc. I also liked Sisters of Mercy - I moved to Nottingham in early '82 and became a regular at Rock City - the Sisters always seemed to play there. I also really got into Echo and the Bunnymen, Teardrop Explodes etc around that time."

Lynne Freeman: "Punk as I had known it started to fizzle out, not overnight, it didn't just stop, but bands were having rows, people were selling out and everyone seemed ready for the next 'New thing'. However, there were still 'new old things' on the scene...Mods and skins. Both of which cultures I dabbled in! Mod and Skin mixed in quite nicely and my mate Jan and me were often to be found on Scooter runs to the Yorkshire coastal resorts. Again, it was youth culture binding together; it was a wild and happy time, a time when you felt all powerful, a time to just celebrate being alive."

John Quinn: "Meanwhile my tastes had started to diverge somewhat from that of some of my mates. Other Punks of my acquaintance had started getting into The Exploited - who seemed to me like a TV comedy show parody of Punk - or even worse, the Oi! scene, which was far too macho and shouty for a delicate little flower like myself."

Andy Coles: (Left on photo) "Musically, I absolutely HATED the second/third wave groups that were being offered up as 'Punk'. To me, the Oi!/Herbert groups like Sham 69, Angelic Upstarts, Cockney Rejects, The Exploited, Vice Squad and Discharge were just bloody awful. The 'Punk' revolution to me, whether I was thinking naively or not, was supposed to promote some sort of 'intellectual awareness' and 'open-mindedness', but these groups just seemed like a clichéd version of what 'Punk' should be about; nasty and no more believable than Sid Snot from 'The Kenny Everett Video Show' or the 'Gob on You' Punk band sketch from 'Not the Nine o'clock News'. *Anti-Nowhere League*? I don't think so! As an art student, I loved the more 'arty' side of punk; Vivienne Westwood's Sex and Seditionaries designs, Jamie Reid and Malcolm Garrett's groundbreaking graphics for record sleeves of the era and the ultra-cool of bands like Siouxsie and the Banshees."

Nick Orme: (Sheffield Punk fan) "When Nico (ex Velvet Underground member) played at the Marples it was a very surreal experience. Here we had one of music's true legends in the place, and there were lots of older blokes in there stood at the bar oblivious to who she even was! They just stood around with their pints of beer chatting while we were mesmerised by Nico. I saw her again a couple of years later down at the Leadmill, but the Marples one is the one that sticks in my mind."

Nick Robinson: (Sheffield musician) "I remember it (The Marples) as a cold venue, lacking atmosphere and I never really enjoyed playing there. I've got a vague memory of playing downstairs there some years later, but this could be just a bad dream."

Jamie 'Headcharge' Smith: "I ended up getting more involved with the Marples and helping out with Marcus and Jesus; both on the promotion/gigs and Pax records. I can remember being down at the railway station waiting for Marcus to arrive back from London with the compilation album WARGASM. I got the first white label copy which I still have today. The launch for the album saw us on a trip down South spending the day in a government nuclear bunker with all the bands n' press (NME/Sounds blah blah) and, if I remember right, we ended up at Poison Girl's house afterwards!!!!!"

ex VELVET UNDERGROUND
THE LEGENDARY
NICO

PLUS ERIC RANDOM WITH CELEBRITY BAND

MON 26th OCT — AT THE MARPLES
FITZALLEN SQUARE
SHEFFIELD

£2 ADVANCE
£2·50 on door

TICKETS AT VIRGIN RECORDS, RECORD COLLECTOR, RAT RECORDS

As well as visiting Sheffield Marples, Chesterfield Punk girl Beverley Wilson and her kindred Punk crowd realised that, especially during the turn of the decade onwards, they would need to do some travelling for any substantial Punk live experience.

Beverley Wilson: (Left) "Although there were some good local Punk bands we usually had to travel to see anyone. On one well remembered occasion, about 20 of us hired a transit van with the intention of going to see The Insane at Retford Porterhouse and then travelling on to Skegness to spend the rest of the weekend there.

"When we eventually got to Retford I was the only person who actually got to see the band as I paid to get in whilst the rest of the guys tried their usual trick of getting in without paying by climbing through the skylight - only this time they got caught and ended up spending a few hours in the police cells. We eventually set off for Skegness but got stopped by the police again en-route, and when the copper opened up the back of the van there were so many of us crammed into it that we literally fell out onto the road. They let us go on our way in the end and we arrived in Skegness just as dawn was breaking, cold, hungry and hung-over with nowhere to go as there was nowhere open.

"On another occasion we hired a proper 45 seater coach to go to London for the day. We got stopped by police just as we were leaving Chesterfield and asked where in London we were heading. We told him-truthfully-the Kings Road. When we got there a few hours later we got stopped by the London police. The guy in Chesterfield had only radioed through to say we were coming. However, the sight of a gang of Punks on the Kings Road was nothing to the London police and they let us go on with just a warning to 'behave ourselves'. We were always getting stopped by the police as I recall and I don't think we'd ever really done anything wrong - it was just how we looked!"

Perhaps, some of the last words to be spoken on the subject of the Marples Punk era should be left to its mentor, the one man who contributed more to its success and identity within the Sheffield music scene than any one single person; the gigs organiser, manager and in many terms a legend in his own right – Marcus Featherby!

Marcus Featherby: (Right) "I never owed any allegiance to the cliques which ran places like the Limit or the Leadmill, and neither was I a part of the Nowsoc coterie who organised gigs at the university. That's why I had to find alternative places where bands such as Artery, the Negatives, Repulsive Alien and the Mau Maus could play. With the help of a couple of Punks, and Andy Lee in particular, we organised gigs at the Basement Club until the building changed hands - a perverse name considering that it was on the top floor and equipment had to be carried up a narrow staircase.

"We then put on a couple of gigs in the lounge of the Marples and, because the manager was happy with how they'd attracted more customers, he spoke to the brewery and we were moved upstairs. I don't think the room upstairs had been used since the end of World War Two, but I went up there with a bunch of Punks and we cleared all the pigeon shit away.

"Initially it was only local bands which performed there but, because so many punks wanted to see more established bands, I contacted various promoters. They were horrified that we were only going to charge a £1 entry fee - saying that it devalued the groups. So I simply started to contact the bands myself - which pissed off the promoters. It very quickly became an established venue and those very same promoters were soon asking for the Marples to be included on their client's itinerary - which I agreed to, but on our terms. We subsequently had some of the biggest names performing there, and I always insisted that a local group supported them. I got slagged off for letting the Skinheads in, but I'd rather they came in, than waited outside and beat the kids up as they came out. We never really had any trouble at the Marples and I'm glad to report that it helped change the lives of some people. At some other venue in the City, a skinhead came and tapped me on my shoulder, and when I turned around I saw that he was with a black girlfriend. He'd changed his ways, and that is one of the most touching memories I have of those times - along with the UK Subs performing at Christmas, when the entrance fee was a cuddly toy, which were later given to a women's shelter, and embarrassed Skins and Punks were pulling teddy bears from under their jackets - and the time that Crass played there - and then there was the legendary Nico - and one of Artery's best ever performances - and, and, and... so many happy memories!"

Doncaster Punk Wayne Kenyon with the Mau Maus

The Marples Punk days ended during the dismal 80's and then there really was no other live venue based place for the Punk kids to go and socialise. It is more than fair to say that it was an end of an era. The venue continued to trade over the years as a typical City centre pub and gradually the Punk Rockers and Skinheads amongst its clientele faded away. The pub suddenly closed in 2002, seemingly going through a refit and refurbishment and remaining empty until the following year when it was re-opened as 'Hein Gericke' motorcycle accessories shop with the old Punk stomping ground now being occupied by flats for students. Little must any current occupant realise the many wild and explosive memories that the surrounding walls hold silently to themselves and what an historic and colourful past has occurred within its domain.

The impression Punk and the Marples days made upon one of Sheffield's most motivated punk activists would serve to inform for many more years to come and result in adding his punk credentials to the steel city's own Dance and DJ scene... the experiences of Punks D.I.Y sensibilities being the prime motivation!

Jamie 'Headcharge' Smith: "The Punk scene inspired lots of kids to get out there and form their own bands. For the first time they saw that it was possible to get hold of some instruments, start playing together and do some basic recordings on cassette. The equipment could be bought, borrowed or stolen; it didn't matter as long as the kids could be in a band. They weren't really bothered about being able to play their instruments either, it was about being in a band and making some noise and maybe offending a few people in the process. It was also a kind of rebellion, sticking two fingers up to the music industry establishment and showing people how they could do it themselves. There was a lot of independent work going on in Sheffield and motivation by all involved. From renting out local venues and pubs for gigs so their mates could come, selling the tapes recorded live at the gigs or in bedrooms and even screen printing their own shirts and merchandise. There was a tight knit band of Punks in Sheffield and for about a year a large number of them would congregate in the Hole in the Road then wander round the markets and cafes in the town centre. The main 'organised' venue putting on loads of gigs in town was the Marples, with smaller places such as the Hallamshire Hotel and other pubs where local bands would play. More or less every underground Punk band you could imagine was on the bill at the Marples and this was great for the local Punks to regularly meet up and hear some good music. A bit later the Leadmill was born and bigger name Punk bands played there on a regular basis. This all contributed to the local punk scene and the feeling that anything goes, as long as you do what you like have a certain attitude and enjoy it, its Punk Rock."

Punk band dreams continuing for Murray Fenton with a showdown at the old Dusty Miller!!

Murray Fenton: "I spent the summer of 1981 pretty much on my own at home, writing songs on my recently-acquired 2-track reel tape recorder. I teamed up with a guy I'd known in the year above, Karl Clarke, like myself a Clash fanatic. We fast became the Strummer and Jones of Parson Cross (if only...) spending our days writing songs and going to every jumble sale we could find to look for clothes to customise. We used to pin up stuff on the wall in Virgin Records, pseudo-political posters looking for a drummer and generally just to try and instil the name of the band in people's minds in time for when we were actually ready to gig... MEGALOMANIA was born!

"Within weeks we had a set and recruited my old mate Dean Buxton on bass and Cramped Legs drummer Ian Lambert. Our first gig was at The Lion, on the Wicker. It was originally arranged by a couple of lads from Rotherham who were into Anarcho-Punk, for the Dusty Miller in Rotherham. We went down the Saturday before to have a look at the venue, piling on the old 69 bus. We walked in and asked to see the landlord who gave us short shrift. Asking if we could see the room we were booked to play in we were greeted with *'No you're fucking not; I thought you were a reggae band. Fuck off'* and turfed us out, with me protesting our vague reggae connection in order to try and keep the gig alive."

The demise of Murray's Meglomania was soon followed by the sad loss of a friend during the then present conflict out in the Falklands.

Murray Fenton: "We played a few more gigs, The Fighting Cocks in Ecclesfield (where the photo was taken – the only one I have of the band and I'm ducked down behind the PA stack!!!) also with another Ecclesfield/Parson Cross Punk band called The Mix and a few gigs at the

Hallamshire, George IV and the Royal – by this time slimmed down to a three-piece after Karl left. Soon after that I was invited to join Quite Unnerving on guitar and the band played their final gig on May 26 1982 at the Royal Hotel, a pub I was banned from for expressing anti-Falklands War sentiments. I had to sneak in just before the set. On April 12th I had performed and dedicated the last song (an anti-war song called 'kill or be killed') to my old Ecclesfield village friend Shaun Hanson who was killed on HMS Ardent a few days earlier out in the Falklands."

Punk Rock in Sheffield was given a home with the Marples for a year or two, but ultimately the whole local Punk scene itself shot off into so many directions, that by the mid 80's there really was no such thing as a solid and individual local Punk Rock scene. The scene had diversified into Goth, Oi!, synth loving futurists, intellectual Post-Punk, Hardcore, Anarcho-Punk and Psychobilly along with injecting the scooter boy scene with a Mohawk and army trousers and ultimately later on sending a proportion of its followers towards the future early House scene and its even more diverse offspring sounds. The only venues to consistently put on gigs for this array of eclectic Punk after-shock scenes and their associated bands were the Lyceum (during its own short live music venue career), the *as always* progressive Limit club, the fledgling Leadmill and briefly Dingwalls - itself only open for a limited period.

Phil Singleton was from Manchester and enrolled as a student at Sheffield Polytechnic in 1982, spending four years of Punk induced gig-going fun as an alternative to his day-time studying, taking in all of the venues on offer... including an American Punk treat from Jello Biafra and his cohorts in Punk mayhem: with a commendable support cast and ... the still obligatory Punk salvo!

Phil Singleton: (Right) "I was always at the Leadmill, Limit, Dingwalls and the Pond Street Poly etc. I was pretty much the only student at the Poly who looked like a Punk at that time. I never stopped wearing my leather jacket throughout my four years there! I also had a Destroy cheese-cloth which I occasionally was brave enough to wear. One local punk, who I never knew by name, kept spotting me wearing this: *'Look, he's got a Johnny Rotten cheesecloth!'* he would shout, much to my embarrassment.

"The Dead Kennedys show was one of the best shows I've ever attended. Their appearances in the UK were infrequent to say the least, and here they were at the peak of their powers. It was a great bill. Local boys Mau Maus joined Peter & The Test Babies, Millions of Dead Cops, and The Dead Kennedy's. However great the DKs were that night (and they were fantastic), it was MDC from Texas that got me. I bought their LP the week before the show from Rat Records (the record shop near the Leadmill) and listened to it over and over so I would know all the songs. They didn't disappoint - they were the real deal. It was a performance I'll never forget. Gobbing was still a regular pastime for many back in '82, and MDC came in for the usual showering. Their singer, Dave Dictor, caught a big greenie on his hand. He wrapped it around his finger, put it in his mouth and spat it back at the audience. This was the most disgusting act I ever witnessed at a Punk show, or anywhere else come to think of it. They weren't phased at all and played a great set that night. I remain a fan to this day.

Neil Anderson: "Sheffield Lyceum was a fab venue. I remember seeing Killing Joke, The Damned and Stiff Little Fingers there in the same week. The poster still hangs on my kitchen wall. I remember the first time The Damned played there the weather was awful - it was a blizzard and hardly anyone turned up. We ended up bumping into some old woman who turned out to be singer Dave Vanian's mum! God knows what she was doing there. Anti-Nowhere League supported, they were mental and you kind of knew they were going to be big. Damned drummer Rat Scabies handed out free fags to the audience and they had these Damned 'Worlds of Chaos' T-shirts which were the worst design I'd ever seen. I bought it but never actually wore it."

The Lyceum had been infamously bankrolled by the Limit clubs' owners which story is now passing into Sheffield's historical folklore and covered in detail in Neil Anderson's essential read of the Limit 'Take it to the Limit'. The actual Victorian era venue was opened back in 1897 and as well as its original theatre golden years, it was also used as a bingo hall, surviving demolition during the mid 70's and meeting the latter day Punk years and Post-Punk live experience thanks to the renewed interest from over at West Street's most legendary club.

The Damned at Sheffield Lyceum by Kevin Wells

The opening performance was from Disco act Odyssey but the venue also put on gigs from Punk era bands The Clash, Damned, Stranglers, Boomtown Rats, Stiff Little Fingers and Squeeze... Goth Rockers Bauhaus, Southern Death Cult, Killing Joke and Barnsley's Danse Society, Post-Punk acts The Cure, Talk Talk, Bow Wow Wow, Orange Juice and Sheffield's very own Cabaret Voltaire and the Human League. Also, Pop acts of the day Kid Creole and the Coconuts, Thompson Twins, Fashion, Yazoo, Stray Cats, Belle Stars, Ska/Punk from the Beat, sixties greats the Kinks and Joe Cocker along with two momentous Simple Minds outings at the brink of their major stardom and once more (the Limit having secured an earlier tour date as well) catch of the decade - U2. As well as the local venues hosting Punk and its relatives, local Punks also ventured to Punk habitats a little out of town.

Gary Stables: "A lot has been said of the gigs at the Marples and rightly so, but I always preferred Retford Porterhouse because it was such an event, meeting in the Charters, the proverbial couple of jars, then on to the train and more beer and on to Retford: the atmosphere there was brill as it was only a small venue so you were up close & personal with the band & getting backstage was a doddle. Me and a mate of mine called Sam used to buy a tray full of beer; go to the stage door and announce we had got the beer for the band and they would promptly let us in (worked every time). And if we didn't get invited anywhere with the band we used to go back to the train station where the woman in the canteen would give us the out of date sandwiches and pasties which we would take into the waiting room and barricade ourselves in; put the heaters on and get some kip till the first train in the morning."

Bryan Bell: "The Retford Porterhouse was a venue to go to: me and my mate Martin and an assortment of other Punks went to loads of gigs there. It made a change from the Sheffield venues and kept on booking Punk bands throughout the whole era."

Tony Beesley: "That was one venue I never went to at all- the Retford Porterhouse. By the time some of my mates were starting to go there, I was at my last stages of being into the modern day Punk scene, so that's probably why I never went.

"The Punk scene was now the total opposite to everything I had been drawn to in the first place about it. My box of records from 1981-82 has maybe a handful of what the so called hardcore Punks would term real Punk and I was sick to death of the rules and being dictated to by a scene that was as jaded and removed from its original ideals as it could possibly get.

"But, it wasn't all negative. I strongly admired the anti-nuclear ideals (This was a time of West v West nuclear threat and an omnipresent vibe about the inevitable Third World war being imminent was in the air), also the anti-vivisection sentiments and a lot of the political stuff that was being held by the new Punk bands: it was just the music I was bored with. Some great records were being released, however. One band I particularly liked was Product. I bought their LP on Clay records (the home of Discharge). I played that record a lot that early summer of 81, along with some great singles from Rudi, TV21, Moondogs (who played the Limit on 26th Feb and had their own sort-lived TV show 'Moondogs Matinee' that year) and Defiant Pose. I was also listening to a lot more New Wave stuff like Hazel O' Connor, Japan, OMD, TV Smith's Explorers, Pete Shelley's solo stuff, Altered Images and others.

"The Lurkers returned in 82 with a new singer and a couple of decent singles too- 'Drag you out' and 'Frankenstein's Ghost' and not long afterwards the Vibrators made yet another comeback and a new line up of 76 originals Chelsea appeared with a strong new set: so it was not all totally bad on the traditional Punk front of the period, though my optimism was to be short-lived."

217

Some record sleeves of 81-82 from my collection: Defiant Pose, Rudi, Moondogs, Killjoys (minus Kevin Rowland), and the back sleeve of the unreleased second Revillos album

As well as the ever-evolving early 80's Sheffield Post-Punk scene the shape of the steel city centre itself was changing.

Neil Anderson: "A most bizarre memory was the early days of The Moor's pedestrianisation. I'm presuming the Town Hall was looking at a never ending raft of ways to win over the public's support for the project by trying every conceivable type of entertainment. The day I wandered down... there was a radio station holding a disco there, maybe Hallam? And the only people around were a bunch of Punks chanting 'Exploited Barmy Army' (one of the first singles by The Exploited that came out in the early eighties) at the bemused DJ. Anyway, it obviously ground him down as the next minute one of the Mohawk kids appeared clutching the single (I presume he'd gone and bought it from somewhere) and it was suddenly blasting out from the speakers and this massive mosh pit ensued: absolutely quality and argument enough for the pedestrianisation."

Tony Beesley: "When we think of the 80's, it's always the dodgy mullet-led chart crap that people refer back to... at best the New Romantic records, which there were a fair few good ones of; and a lot more crap ones. The start of the 80's was fantastic though and even though the Punk thing had kind of ended, the direct effects of it were still very heavy. People tend to forget that!

"As for Sheffield itself, the live music scene was still alive and kicking, but lacking the vibrancy of the earlier Punk-charged years: new bands were coming through, though, and it sort of felt like this was now time for us Punk fans to think about starting our own bands and doing it proper. I myself was now thinking very seriously about writing some new songs and getting some like-minded musicians along for the ride."

The Post 81/82 Punk bands continued their sonic assault within an increasingly claustrophobic and insular climate. Banging their way into the sounds were bands such as Action Pact, Abrasive Wheels, the Ejected ('Have you got 10p' E.P) and struggling 2nd wave bands such as Charge (who played an impressive set at the Marples around this time) along with Irish Punks with tunes The Outcasts – another good live set performed at the Marples: sadly their drummer was killed in a car crash not long afterwards.

Above: Old Rotherham during the early 80's... also soon to be pedestrianised to make way for pedestrians such as... Punk Rocker Phil and the legendary Bionic Man

Left and below: Dead Kennedys at the Leadmill (Kristan James Melik)

The optimism of early 80's Sheffield Punk resulted in an inspirational springboard for many. Taking in a seemingly relentless assortment of gig offerings at the Marples (with a massive input from the legendary Marcus Featherby), a Punk-endorsed new record shop in Rat Records, the early Leadmill Punk dates and the whole ideology of self identity and a proclamation of individualism was an open door... however that entry would soon be firmly closed as the decade wore on and a jaded and safe conformity to Punk's own expectations became the new manifesto!

By 1982, the peak had certainly been reached and things seemed to be slowing down: the Top Rank cut back its live bookings to a bare minimum and whilst the Limit continued to provide its own special brand of entertainment, the music scene itself wasn't always able to supply the worthy demand. The venue slowly slipped into a little more than conventional club-motivated one, with the emphasis more on the disco than the bands doing the rounds... but is any of this surprising when considering the state of the music scene by 1982-83?

Photos Courtesy of Pete Skidmore (Stranglers by Neil Kitson)

Above: Vic Godard (of Subway Sect) supporting Altered Images at Sheffield Polytechnic and the Stranglers at Sheffield Lyceum 1981

Sheffield Punk and Mod fan (and there was no bigger Jam fan around than this guy!) Pete Skidmore was not alone in feeling frustrated with the course the crumbling new wave was taking in 1982: not only having to swallow the bitter pill that was the news of The Jam's split later in the year, just as the street Punk scene was being overtaken by a new breed of thrash-loving Punk fans but also the remnants of the new wave showing a clear willingness to move ever further away from their fans. Would anyone have guessed that the disenchantment with Punk would arrive so quickly: the idealism, belief and validity had been stripped away down south much earlier, but was now just as evident up north!

Pete Skidmore: "Around 1982 the whole scene was changing, bands that we followed had split or just died off; Punk was changing a lot too and maybe for the worse. Don't get me wrong there was a few who knocked some good tunes out, but come on, The Exploited and Discharge? There seemed to be a hell of a lot of bands calling themselves Punk which to me wasn't Punk at all, it was learn one chord and we can now make 15 albums of the same shite. It was Punk that was also attracting a different audience, kids who would have been 8 or 9 around 77-78, these bands were their bands not ours (thank fuck). There were a few gems hidden in there such as the 4-Skins first album, Infa Riot early stuff, the Business, the Rejects of course and the Upstarts who attracted the cabbages following, which to me was a shame as they had some good tunes.

Altered Images at the Polytechnic 1982

Photos by Pete Skidmore

"The scene in Sheffield was also changing; the gig going West Street crowd were now turning their main attentions to either of the two Sheffield football clubs and fashion and ideals changed; bands we watched two or three years ago were now only doing the odd tour or album; bands were becoming more pop and far more top 40 friendly; bands such as Altered Images, Associates and Simple Minds... now they were

attempting to crossover to a bigger audience... some bands had one or two good albums in them and then called it a day, Teardrop Explodes were one of those bands. Or the ultimate sin - bands that sold out! Simple Minds, U2, Spandau Ballet etc... I was at the Peter Powell road show at Sheffield Top Rank around 81 with Duran Duran on and there were maybe 100 people there, a year later they were selling out every venue they played. I think with the original bands we followed all disappearing we looked elsewhere to make our scene and left the thrash Punk of Discharge, Exploited and Crass to the dumb Americans!"

Tony Beesley: "When the Punk scene burnt itself out and the only remaining Punk crowd was the truly hardcore gang, me and my mates would go to the Lyceum to catch bands such as 'Theatre of Hate', 'Simple Minds', 'Orange Juice', 'Killing Joke', 'Gang of Four' and the odd returning Punk bands such as the Stranglers and the Damned. When the Lyceum closed, it was the Limit, Leadmill or Dingwalls. Dingwalls was great for the short while it was open. I saw some great gigs there: Punk, Post-Punk or otherwise. Every band seemed to play really well there. The trouble is, one minute it was there and the next it was gone!

"By 1982 -1983, my tastes in music had changed so much, that after that, I slowed down on the gig front and spent most of my time trying to get my own band together and going to Mod nights. I was still drawn towards the most interesting music to come out of Punk, but was also becoming more and more influenced by sixties R&B and Mod bands. I did like some of the synthesiser/Futurist records but couldn't really relate to the actual scene. Those two dates Simple Minds played at the Lyceum were well impressive, though. They were at the peak of their most original phase, before they took a U turn and went all stadium Rock. I loved their first run of albums up to 'New Gold Dream'... it's a shame that by the following year the electro-pop thing had gone over to crap like Howard Jones etc.

Photo by Neil Kitson

Teardrop Explodes and Echo and the Bunnymen at Sheffield City Hall 1982 (Pete Skidmore)

"One of the best new bands was Department S. Apart from 'Is Vic there?' I thought those two singles 'I Want' and 'Left Right' were superb: all the energy and swagger of Punk but with a new slant. I also liked Altered Images for a while, early Human League, Ultravox and some of the early Postcard label stuff. Then there was Dexys, who were doing their Irish Gypsy thing... great album 'Too Rye Aye' but it was a bit too much overkill on Dexys after 'Come on Eileen' for a while. As for Punk Rock as a music itself? Dead as door-nails by then for me, I was even selling some of my Punk records by this point, stuff like all the Menace singles, Cyanide's LP and the Vortex compilation LP."

The disenchantment was getting that bad! But the disillusionment with the way Punk travelled its course during the 80's merely served to inspire original Punk Pete Weston to dig his heels in even more firmly to the bands and styles of punk that had taken his interest in the first place.

Pete Weston: "The New Romantic, Mod and Skinhead scene broke in and a lot of the Punks seemed to drift off those ways: the Oi stuff? We hated that shit and all the bands that were playing it like the Exploited. I never felt part of those trends and always stayed true to Punk, It all started to die off then and as far as my musical taste went, I just got really into The Clash, Wayne /Jayne County and Iggy Pop more and travelled all over watching them - picking up on the odd stray new Punk bands on the way. Then to knock a final nail in the coffin all the few bands left seemed to turn up the volume and the speed and it all sounded like the same mess with all the individuality gone. There seemed to be an influx of younger people appear in *off the shelf* Punk clothes and hair cuts that just seemed against the whole movement. We felt worlds apart from them and just used to take the piss out of em but this apparently is what Punk was all about? So I divorced myself from that lot although in my head I have always remained a Punk."

Andy Coles: "The original Punk groups were still doing the rounds and I went to see The Stranglers on Sunday February 13th 1983 with Phil and I can remember him attempting to spit the 30 feet or so to the stage but his catarrh-loaded effort only travelled about 10 feet onto the top of a Punkettes beret. Everyone between us and her turned round and laughed and I often wondered what she must have thought when she got home and found said 'luminous green slug' on top of her hat! I still have a bootleg cassette of that gig."

Tony Beesley: "I remember selling some of my records to Andy's mate Phil: he came up to my Mum's house with Barney Rubble and I got shut of some Punk stuff to him. Everyone was selling records at one point... Punk became almost throwaway for a while: my mate Pete even sold his original 'Teenage Kicks' on Good Vibrations for 20p!!!"

Mark Barnet: (The legendary Barney Rubble) "Tony should have a fuckin' public health warning attached to him ha ha ha!!"

Some other Punk kids took a swift diversion back to the music that they had liked prior to their Punk initiations.

Paul Clarke: (Right) "It was probably always on the cards that I'd be a Heavy Rock/HM fan at some stage. After being a fan of Punk and it being my shop window- for want of a better word, and going to some brilliant gigs, I became more impressed musically by Hanoi Rocks and Lords of the New Church etc along with the youth club Heavy Rock sessions. This was the stuff that was widening my musical radar. So for the rest of the 80's onwards it was Motley Crue (Their Dr Feelgood show at Birmingham NEC was the best show I've ever seen, a sleazy-raunchy-Rock-extravaganza that simply blew me away) also Guns and Roses, Skid Row, LA Guns etc. It wasn't just the music that impressed either: it was the big shows that were just amazing!"

Heavy Rock and HM aside, the alternative to grass-roots Punk, apart from the Mod revival, was the local artier side of the music scene; often influenced by the synthesiser as opposed to a Fender or Rickenbacker and having a fair bit in common with the New Romantics and the sounds and fashion of futurism. The sounds of Electro-Pop and its spin offs would almost dominate the rest of the decade... gradually creeping into some open-minded Punks' musical horizons!

Richard Chatterton: "I saw a variety of bands at a range of locations. The Limit club was the legendary venue in Sheffield which was visited by the Cramps, Teardrop Explodes and the

Bunnymen, Siouxsie, Fad Gadget and Punishment of Luxury among others; Bauhaus, the Clash and the Gang of Four wowed the Lyceum – an elegant newly restored former music hall. Chelsea, Artery and iconic ex-Velvet Underground diva Nico I caught at the more *rough and ready* Marples pub. I also saw the Au-Pairs at the Psalter Lane Art College who were one of the bands that had women not just on vocals but playing bass, drums and guitar – Punk had allowed women to be heard and not just be dormant eye candy. They were fiercely feminist and lesbian. In Doncaster I saw Theatre of Hate and Classix Nouveaux and I attended the Futurama festivals at Stafford, North Wales and Leeds where these bands were collected under one banner."

Andy Coles: "I loved all the synth/ 'New Romantic' stuff that was going on. Local heroes The Human League, Heaven 17 and ABC were making South Yorkshire look cool again and there was a buzz surrounding new Rotherham band Vision, formerly Spiral Visions. I got to know Vision bass player Pete Jackson, who was going out with one of my friends on the Art course and it seemed like things were taking off."

Tony Beesley: "I never became part of the futurist crowd and felt neither a part of the Mod revival gang or the crumbling Punk scene of the time: although there was some fairly decent music coming out, it was a very frustrating and mixed up period for me... the after-Punk period!"

Colleen Allen: "The early 80's saw me march through a wide range of musical loves, from the earlier Punk, new wave, New Romantics to New York Dolls, Bowie of course and Brian Eno: Musical influences during that time were ever changing, I also enjoyed much of the significant local bands, Clock DVA, Cabaret Voltaire, I'm So Hollow, Artery and loads of others.

"My first band Spiral Vision provided an opportunity; at last, to put words to thoughts and action to emotion, along with a small loyal following. I loved the rehearsals, the studio moments, the few gigs and the people. My memory is so poor, but I have affection for band members Rich, Andy (Beaumont) with his originality, Chip and his cheeky raw charm, Pete Jackson and his gentle demeanour and Pete Cooper with his ever smiling sparkle. Spiral Vision and the friends that followed the band prior to and beyond my residence were good people, Yorkshire's best, different people now of course, all of us, different paths, trials and tribulations, I raise my hat to those guys, they looked after me.

"1980 to 81 - I think I must have been angling a little more towards the New Romantic look. My memory rudely awakened today, (whilst vacuuming) revealing a small window and clips of a certain Ultravox gig in Retford. With much backcombing and blondeness, frilly bits and 'Marso Marso' pretentiousness, we stepped into the venue which might or might not have been the Porterhouse.

"My friend used to carry a humungous bag with a FULL set of rollers, hair tongs, hairspray, perfume, make up and God knows what else, the only thing missing and the only thing of any bloody use would have been a condom or two. The gig was ok as far as I can remember, but perhaps appreciating the joys of Midge were secondary for good reason. My friend and her friend decided they would like to go back stage, I didn't want to because, well, I knew the script. The mission was to flirt wildly with the bouncers and then enter an arena where reflected fame was more important than self respect. These girls were bare faced (and probably bottomed) groupies. I have never been one to bow down and lick the feet of someone because they are famous, I can't comprehend that mentality and hey, who knows where those 'feet' have been. However, these 'friends' went ahead with their groupie mission, despite the unwritten law that you do not leave your mates stranded, they left their friend stranded, that friend would be bloody me.

"So, aforementioned girls and insanely big bag went off shagging Ultravox, yes, the group en mass, lock stock and barrel, (no fancy individual stuff). I meanwhile was stuck in Retford without sufficient coinage to get a taxi back home - minus tarts and they clearly weren't coming back, come on, why waste time being a decent human being when there are juicy backstage anecdotes to be had .

"I had the shameful task of having to reveal my plight to this slightly crazed guy who was chatting me up in the audience. So, with limited choices, gritted teeth and a bit of a wobbly lip, I went to stay with this loopy stranger in his strange flat, in this strange town, feeling, well, strange and not in a fashionable Visage 'voguing' way. No, in a totally shitting myself and 'I hate Steve Strange and all that damned pointy shouldered, Pierrot 'stuff' way. It was quite horrible, shaking off the attentions of a man who sort of saved my skin, but also made my skin crawl a tad and was bloody hard work. He was persistent, I was resistant and I survived. Not one word of apology from friends and I never did like Midge Ure much after that."

Punk had only been a side order for Rotherham Hairdresser Christopher Nicholls; a recipe of the Stranglers, Boomtown Rats, Jilted John and Squeeze being the new wave's main intrusion into his musical diet. It would be the synthesiser dominated acts that followed Punk that would gain the interest and attention for Chris... and he would experience first hand (with a pair of scissors) the fashion requirements of others immersed in the delights of the Futurist/New Romantic scene.

Human League at Sheffield Lyceum (1981) courtesy of Neil Kitson

Christopher Nicholls: (Rotherham hairdresser) "The emergence of the new romantics resulted in all manner of innovative hairstyles and having just mastered the conventional haircuts people were suddenly wanting styles which were completely different altogether. I remember spending all day doing wedge after wedge, the one sported by local pop star Phil Oakey of the Human League. This was the full-on advent of men suddenly sporting women's hairstyles. I recall the waiting area of the salon where I worked being split by the short back and side's generation and this brave bunch that were open for ridicule with their audacity to be different. This was also the rebirth of men wearing make up as in the likes of Jim Kerr of Simple Minds early days, Japan, Visage and who could forget Boy George and Marilyn. Men's make up had not been in fashion as much since the

17th century! I must add that anyone in Rotherham at the time willing to accommodate this was exceptionally brave!

"Ultravox were a group I liked, partly due to being brainwashed by my younger sister, and also by the impact of their classic single 'Vienna'. These lads were to blame for the mass appeal of the V shaped side-boards, prior to Midge Ure and Ultravox, the side burn could only be found on the deck of the USS Enterprise as worn by the crew of Star Trek!! Echo and the Bunnymen were also a group I liked along with some of the many electro pop bands and one-hit wonders; Adam and the Ants being another example of male singers donning make up."

One local music fan (not unclosely related to our hairdresser friend!) became intoxicated with the sounds of futurist post-John Foxx band Ultravox: the love of which influenced her first school leaving job.

Wendy Nicholls: (Rotherham Ultravox fan) "I was a youngster in the 70s which gave me a good ear for and love of music from a very early age, having a treasured tiny radio I would take to bed with me. I learnt to play Classical Guitar when I was a teenager: Wanting to play and not just listen to music. Being a teenager in the 80s, for me, was a fabulous time thanks to my favourite band Ultravox! I fell in love with this band when I was only 12 and was totally hooked by their perfect individual style of music and was thrilled when I saw them live.

"It was my love of their records: LPs, limited edition clear vinyl, and picture discs and collecting lots of other bands vinyl also which inspired me to want a record retailing career. The first record shop I worked at was 'The Sound of Music' in Rotherham town centre. I was only 16 and loved every minute of being there. I did actually move to competitor K+D/Roulette Records, when they closed 'The Sound of Music' down the following year."

Photo copyright Andy Coles

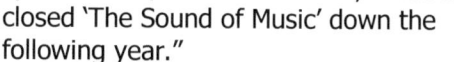

Circles record shop late 1982, near the old Advertiser offices where many a Punk, Mod and Futurist bought their vinyl. Look closely and you can see an ad for The Jam's 'Beat Surrender' single

Tony Beesley: "We were still buying records from the ones in Sheffield and there was also still such a thing as Record shops in Rotherham – the legendary Sound of Music and Circles Records. I must have bought every single Jam single from the Sound of Music and continued to throw my money over the counter right to the very bitter end of this legendary record shop. This was back in the day when buying your music actually meant something. You won't get tripped up and whacked round the 'ead by a skinhead sat at your PC downloading music will you. But it was all worth it."

Sound of music, K&D Records and Circles Records all eventually closed in Rotherham: even the much loved second-hand record shop Backtrack of later years followed suite. Record sleeves led to Punk inspired further Education ambitions for one Rotherham lad. Laser Records opened in 1985 and included a Gothic decorated record bar upstairs, but no record shop ever came close to capturing the magic of the delights of the Sound of Music! Now there is not one single outlet to purchase records or CD's left in the town!

Andy Coles: "After leaving Brinsworth Comprehensive, I decided at the very last minute that I wanted to go to Art College. My long-term plan was to design record sleeves and I had read somewhere that some of The Clash had gone to art college (Bloody Hell what sort of a career plan is that?). Rotherham College of Art and Technology (RCAT) I guess was a gradual awakening for me. A couple of lads took the piss out of my 'straight' clothes and that was it. I kitted myself out in jeans and army shirts and then eventually a leather jacket from Corona Fashions, a shop on Attercliffe in Sheffield. I had a brilliant pair of pointy boots with straps on that used most of my £39 annual local authority grant to buy from Rebina Shoes in Sheffield. Later on, I had a black dinner jacket from Rotherham Market that I used to wear with them and a pair of Doc Martens that I still have.

"In college I came into contact with open-minded people who told me about groups they were into and gigs they had seen. Nicky Booth was a Stranglers enthusiastic who turned me onto many groups such as Cabaret Voltaire, DAF and Kraftwerk. Alan Parker opened my ears to groups I'd never heard of; Pigbag, Orange Juice and Aztec Camera. I have to thank those two in particular for my Post-Punk musical education. 'The Charter Arms' on Eastwood Lane was the college after-hours (and often *during* - hours) meeting place of choice and I seemed to spend loads of evenings there, making £3 last on three pints of snakebite and black. My closest mates were Dave Silkstone, who I had been at school since juniors with and Phil Dodsworth, a Madness fan from Aston who was also converting to a Punkier way of thinking.

Ian Astbury of Southern Death Cult at the Lyceum (Phil Chatterton)

"I bought a Korg Micro Preset synthesiser, like the one in a Smash Hits competition, from Nicky Booth and he demonstrated it to me by playing the bass-line from 'New Dawn Fades' by Joy Division. A few of us practised for a while in various dives but nothing came of it. We toyed with a few band names; two that I can recall were Let's Submerge (from the X-Ray Spex song) and Citizens of the Waiting Grave (*bloody hell, that's heavy!*) and a couple of us once signed autographs for a little old lady who was behind us in the queue for the bus... ha ha!!

"The Lyceum in Sheffield had been re-opened for gigs and put on some brilliant bands. I went to see The Human League in 1981 and can remember watching clouds of fine plaster dust falling from the roof, due to the sheer BOOM of the bass. I walked out from that gig and nearly got knocked down on Norfolk Street because I didn't hear a car coming. I'm sure I've been hard of hearing since that gig! The Star reported that the crowd had not moved much and were just staring. I bet they were thinking that the ceiling was going to cave in like I was.

"Amongst the pretentiousness and posing of the New Romantic scene, the odd-group like Soft Cell were producing brilliant lyrics, but with tunes! I went to see Japan at Sheffield City Hall on my own (*Billy No-Mates*) because I couldn't get anyone interested in going. Shortly after, the band put another date on and the lads, now into them, all went...bastards.

"Over the next two years we soaked up a mixture of what would be considered 'New Romantic' (that *still* sounds bad!), Punk and Post-Punk. In 1982, I recorded the Peel session of Southern Death Cult, which I played until it wound round the heads of my cassette player one day. Between 1981 to 1983 Dave, Phil and I went to see loads of the groups of the era, groups that were being considered as '*Positive Punk*' or '*Goth*'...Killing Joke, Bauhaus, X-Mal Deutschland, Lords of the New Church, Southern Death Cult, etc. The mezzanine area of RCAT was an area where we chatted away, pointlessly eyeing up the hairdressing students and planning visits to gigs with the few quid we had."

The lure of all things futurist was not to all tastes of the ever-changing Punk crowd of Sheffield and Rotherham. There was also the Punk and prototype Goth of Brigandage, Sex Gang Children, Bauhaus and a pre Cult fame Ian Astbury in his early 80's Goth appendage – Southern Death Cult! Times were changing fast and the map was changing with it too!

Phil Chatterton: "I saw Southern Death Cult at the Sheffield Lyceum. There were around 150 people there. A few years later they would be packing out venues. I got into them and Theatre of Hate too, who I just caught the end of their set when they supported the Clash at the Lyceum."

Richard Chatterton: "What I thought was a coup (whilst doing my fanzine 'Act of Defiance'), and turned out not to be so, was the interview I did in a small club in Leicester Square with the singer of Brigandage, who along with Blood and Roses were to be at the forefront of the new Positive Punk movement. They had been on the front cover of the NME in 1983 and were being filmed that night by London Weekend Television for a documentary but they never really took off despite being nice guys."

Tony Beesley: "I got into Killing Joke for a short while after hearing 'War dance' on the John Peel Show in 1980. Some of my mates saw them at the Limit club around then too, but the first of three times I saw them was at the Polytechnic which I think would be the summer of 81. There was some great displays of colour on show that night: multi-coloured hair, leathers, studs and piercings... a real sign of the way things were going fashion-wise on the Punk scene. As much as I thought this all looked great and was well impressed with all the individualism on show, I remember feeling that I wasn't a part of it any more. Killing Joke were good that night: their first two LP's made quite an impression on me, but by the following year and attending a show at the Lyceum, I was well past listening to them, as the band and a lot of their followers set out on their path to Goth-dom!"

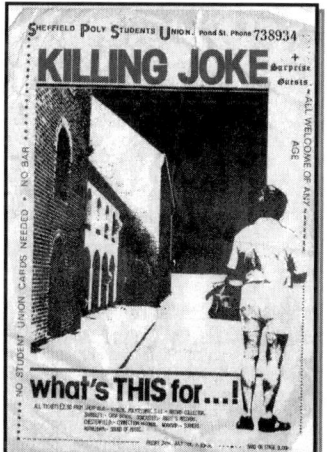

Neil Anderson: (Right) "Maybe it's because Punk Rock had virtually fallen off the face of the earth by the mid-eighties that we tried a few different things to brighten up the nights of discontent. We'd tried the Anarcho-Punk thing for a few weeks but soon got bored with being vegetarian and arguing about politics we didn't understand.

"Anyway, fun time frolics were put back on the menu – much to the disgust of people that were truly serious about their youth genres – by regular theme nights. The Goth nights were definitely the ones that required the most copious amounts of alcohol to oil the wheels of uptown mayhem – especially when there was an hour in make-up to get started. The Limit staff always took it pretty much on the chin. The only time they took offence was when we arrived for a night on the beach. The surfboards were ok but when the beach balls took flight the bouncers had enough and chucked us all out."

Nick Banks: "Early Goth pioneers *Quite Unnerving* were brilliant. Again no drummer but two bassists...they used mesmeric taped percussion with driving bass riffs and proper 'primal screaming' vocals from Dave Loukes (He sadly perished in a motorbike smash)."

John Quinn: "On the subject of Goths we once saw Leeds leaders Sisters Of Mercy play a free concert at Sheffield University, as part of what must be one of the most bizarre line-ups of all time. Also on the bill were Time UK, formed by former Jam drummer Rick Buckler, and a guy called Matt Fretton, who was a Primark version of Howard Jones: if you can imagine such a thing. What happened was that the place was full of Goths for the Sisters, and then a load of Mods turned up and started fighting with them. Then Matt Fretton appeared on stage, wearing a white suit and bow tie and accompanied by two girl backing singers - and the entire place emptied within seconds. In a rare show of youth unity, Goths, mods and innocent bystanders all agreed on one thing - they had no desire at all to see Matt Fretton."

The return of Sheffield Punk Simon Milner; previously repulsing as an Alien arrived with Goth – bringing back memories of being rejected at the Limit!

Simon Milner: "After Repulsive Alien split I bounced from band to band, one of which was Urban Religion, my answer to the Goth bands of the time. I was a mad Alien Sex Fiend, Birthday Party and Bauhaus fan. We had our one and only gig at the Marples. Trouble was, the Batcave tour had hit Sheffield the same night, Alien Sex Fiend, Specimen and I think Flesh for Lulu and they were all about to take to the stage at the Limit. The Marples was empty...the Limit was full."

Nick Banks: (Right) "Eventually me n' some lads went to Margate on our first holiday when I was about 16 and I dyed my hair black and started back combing it as by then I was getting into 'Positive Punk' (proto-Goth really) Southern Death Cult, Danse Society, Sex Gang Children etc.

"I had started hanging out in Sheffield a lot from about '80 - '81 - initially it was moping around the City Centre - but as I acquired my Sheffield girlfriend I would start going out around the town in the evenings, West Street mostly – Hallamshire, Limit etc. I had just joined a new group playing a more poppy kind of sound (Phono-Industria t'was the name). We asked Anne to be the singer and she said ok. We went to get a gig at the Hallamshire – *'no problem'* said the lad who was doing the bookings - Dave Kurley of New Model Soldier – *'but I'm fed up with looking after the bookings why don't you lot do it?'* So in time I became the person whom bands phoned up if they wanted a gig. I had a notebook by the phone in Rotherham with pages dedicated to Thursday and Sunday gigs. No need to send a demo to the upstairs at the Hallamshire as it was the lowest rung of the ladder; just bring your gear, some lights and a PA etc.

"Me and Anne took the 50p entry at the door. I was 17 at the time. All monies went to the bands... we never took a penny!! If there had been a good crowd Jim the landlord would give us a free half: generous. So I got to see loads of new bands of the early 80's, most were pretty ropey but we had Quite Unnerving, Pulp, In a Bell Jar, Party Day (from Barnsley I think) and Mods the Ya Yas. This is where I got to meet many people including Jarvis - He and Tim Allcard (In A Bell Jar) used to piss us off 'cos they would sit at the top of the stairs listening to the groups whilst smoking 'organic roll ups' and not paying the 50p to go in - tight bastards!"

Tony Beesley: "I wish I could re-trace my memory bank enough to recall all the gigs I went to. I saw quite a few at various venues around the city, but have no fixed memories on a lot of 'em at all. I would have seen Pulp a number of times here and there, and also Veiled Threat, Mirror Cracked, They Must be Russians etc... but sadly all is lost. It's mainly the bigger gigs I remember. Of the smaller gigs? some of what I can remember are Artery, Icon, Stunt kites, Vendino Pact and Mau Maus supporting the Angelic Upstarts."

Mau Maus were formed in 1981 and after being spotted by Marcus Featherby were given a support slot at the Marples with Mensi's mob. They followed this up with various gigs around the city and recorded their first demo tracks over in Rotherham at Kaleys 8 track studio... unbelievably the band recorded ten tracks of U.S Hardcore influenced Punk Rock in under five hours and wait for it – for the total cost of a fiver! They also featured on the Wargasm compilation LP and released their first EP 'Society's Rejects' on Pax records followed by two more EP's 'No cause for concern' and 'The Facts of War'.

Mau Maus:
Kristan James Melik

Their debut long playing outing was 'Live at the Marples' which saw the light of day in 1984. After leaving Sheffield's Pax label they toured Germany and Holland, recorded a new EP 'Tear Down the Walls' (its message to bring Punks and Skins together) and became involved in the 1984 Miners' strike: not surprisingly considering that two Mau Maus – Lee and Podge – worked at Derbyshire's Renishaw pit. The band eventually split in 1985. Their dyed back-combed jet-black hair and pre-dominantly black clothing was in contrast to the usual Day-Glo colour of the average Punk Rocker... a sign, and possible influence, that the Punk uniform was changing as a more dressed down, darker, often Gothic looking style began to integrate into the tattered wardrobes of the nations and Sheffield's Punk-spawned crowd.

Nigel Lockwood: "For myself, even as early as late 77, the true excitement of Punk had all but disappeared, and by the following year a lot of what Punk had become seemed like old hat! I suppose 1978 was the year of new wave and the start of Post-Punk.

"Later on I saw Kraftwerk at the City Hall on 19th June 1981: the androids were amazing! Also the Liverpool scene had exploded with Echo and Bunnymen and Teardrop Explodes, seeing them at the Limit and University. Also the Manchester scene had exploded with Joy Division (who I saw with Buzzcocks at the Top Rank) and the Hacienda club. Making an impact too was Gary Numan, who some said was a Bowie imitator. I saw him at the City Hall on October 8th, 1979, billed as Tubeway Army, with support from O.M.D. whose tape recorder they called Winston. Numan's band was all synths and the lighting was a steal from Bowies 1976 'Station to Station' Wembley shows, all strip lights. In my diary of the day review, I stated '*Will he really be the first machine rock star of the electronic 80s'??* I also put that he reminded me of a young version of Larry Grayson!!"

Nigel Renshaw: (The Stunt Kites) "Even though John and myself have been best friends since about 1979 the first couple of years we never saw eye to eye and hardly ever spoke to each other!!! I used to write the music, record them onto cassette tape and pass them to John so he could put lyrics to them!!! There was great respect and friendship between the bands, especially in the early days...Everyone used to attend each others gigs, and you've probably heard this story, but I always remember John reading off a 'Sheffield Band Register' that he'd made up prior to a Saddle gig and calling out each bands name to see who had turned up and ticking them off as he did so!!! The likes of Artery, ClockDva, I'm So Hollow etc. etc... Adi and Clock DVA did one of the first recordings of the original Stunt Kites in Adi's front room.

"I once went down to London with Artery on a week's mini tour of London. On their last night, can't remember where, I was talking to Killing Joke's label secretary at Malicious Damage towards the end of the night, she was fuckin' beautiful!!! Anyway Mark and the guys had packed all their gear into the van and were on the outskirts of London before realising they'd left me and the aforementioned beauty still talking and canoodling in the club!!! They did eventually come back for me!!!"

Klive Humberstone: (In the Nursery) "There were some interesting gigs that I saw at the time. I was also playing concerts with In the Nursery (we played Bar 2 on 8th March 1982). On 12th June 1982, I saw 23 Skidoo & Hula playing at The Royal Victoria Hotel. Great venue for a concert of that calibre. 23 Skidoo were superb. David Tibet was playing with them at the time and I recall him playing his Tibetan thigh bone onstage. The night had a real vibe, Hula performed a great set and the visuals from both bands were stunning."

The Post-Punk period of Sheffield also left behind a very striking visual documentation of the time, helped in no small part, by the enigmatic Marcus Featherby who avidly championed both the continuing hardcore Punk scene and its much more imaginative and forward thinking Post-Punk counterpart. Marcus certainly had a keen eye for photography and capturing the moment!

A Sheffield Post-Punk Gallery

Stunt Kites at the Limit club 1981

John Allen: Vocals, Nigel Renshaw: Guitar, Tony Armitage: Drums, Andrew Young: Bass, Nick Gabbitas: one off keyboards/synths
(Photos copyright: Nigel Renshaw)

Artery take the slide

Jayne Wilson of I'm so hollow

Jarvis at the Limit

The legendary pioneers of Post-Punk Electronica -

Cabaret Voltaire

Mal of Cabaret Voltaire

Pulp's first photo session

Klive Humberstone of In the Nursery

Scarborough Antelopes

Repulsive Alien delivering 'Bouquet of Steel LP to John Peel

Scarborough Antelopes

Divine Comedy's Nick Hawksworth

All Post-Punk Gallery photos kind courtesy of Kristan James Melik except Human League, Cabaret Voltaire, Jarvis, Stunt Kites (Nigel Renshaw) and Colleen Allen (Above)

The surviving colour and spectacle of traditional Punk did still manage to catch the eyes of the uninitiated; especially within the confines of a traditional working men's club.

Fiona Palmer: (Rotherham Punk girl) "Paul Maiden and I ... he was 17 and I was 16: Arrgh young love! We were sat in Denaby working men's club waiting for the 'turn' to appear on stage, though from the looks and stares of the regulars, you would think that they thought we were the turn. It was the day after I'd had my hair dyed for the very first time - electric blue and must not forget crimped too, though I had not learned the art of back combing then. Oh and by the way we were bladdered and we needed to be."

The times were changing even faster, though, and as much as the visuals of the Punk look were still proving to be worth the thousand yard stare of a flat-capped Marlborough smoking dominoes-playing committee man; the demand for something more musically adventurous was becoming increasingly clearer.

Julie Lee: "I started listening to different types of music, looking for something else but I didn't settle on anything for a while. I toyed with the Goth scene but found it a bit bland then ended up getting into bands like the Pixies, the Godfathers, Nick Cave and the Bad Seeds to name a few. I like music played with real instruments, especially lots of guitar."

John Quinn: "I was rather fond of quite a few new romantic and electronic groups, but some of them proved too popular with the public for the teenage musical snob I had become. So I became more indie and underground, spending most of the 80's buying Post-Punk singles on obscure labels - many of them second-rate rip-offs of The Fall and Joy Division - and also becoming more aware of the politics and marketing of the music business which often decided whether an act or style was going to succeed or fail. Punk got me interested in that."

John Ashmore: "Later on I started going to see Sheffield band Artery. I saw 'em at the Marples and the Polytechnic with Tony and the lads. Passing the Marples one night, there was a right load of trouble going on and me and my mates got roped into it and ended up getting chased down to the no.69 bus stop. Walking home from Rotherham we were passing the old Parkgate steelworks and one of the lads (Clarkey) had a poster and was banging the walls as we passed. The cops went past us and I remember us saying *'I bet they turn back round and give us some grief'* and sure enough they did. *'You lot have been smashing windows haven't yer'* they accused, looking at Clarkey with his poster. He couldn't believe it and made his plea *'It's only a poster look!'* It was like that in those days if you looked different."

The drive to create something different and new from the ashes of the Punk explosion had been kicked into motion right from the Buzzcocks 'Spiral Scratch' E.P at the very start of 1977. Sheffield and its closest towns and suburbs had always been imaginative in its version of what the Punk opportunity offered in the form of creating its own musical vision and, from the beginning, almost exclusively concentrated on moving onwards from the pulse beat of straight forward Punk Rock by numbers.

From the early outings of Cabaret Voltaire, Sheffield Punks most idealist and honest Punks 2.3, the creation of the first incarnation of Phil Oakey's Human League and Sheffield Post-Punk personified Artery; the intentions were clear – this was an entirely different kind of Punk tension!

Vice Versa were created in 1977 by Punk fanzine (Steve's papers) writer Stephen Singleton. Stephen, typically for the time, came from a life of Glam Rock gigs at the City Hall followed by the epiphany of Punk Rock. Joined by mates David Sydenham (keyboards) and Mark White (Vocals/Guitar), Steve played bass: they played most of the local City venues (Penthouse, George IV, Limit etc) and released their first vinyl outing , the Music4 E.P in August 1979 after a first gig supporting Wire at the Outlook in Doncaster the year previously. Their music was influenced by Punk, but it was, in true Sheffield form, the synthesiser that captured their imagination and inspiration to create their own brand of after Punk music!

By the time fellow Punk and fanzine writer Martin Fry boosted the ranks, David Sydenham had left and the blueprint was being developed into something that would arrive at ABC and a future of Glam infused Pop for the Post-Punk dandies of the early to mid 80's. In the wake of a series of audience dividing gigs – including a tour of Punk-filled Dutch youth clubs in Rotterdam - a cassette release, a second E.P and interest from John Peel - *'Let's do something more organic (and) more funky'* was the new manifesto for the future. The Poison Arrow was sharp enough to shoot into the air with a new found optimism and will to change. The new ingredients of ABC worked!

Vice Versa had played support to fellow Sheffield Post-Punk band Clock DVA on December 7th 1979... Clock DVA had started out in late 1977: Enigmatic Sheffielder Adi Newton (real name Gary Coates) who, like fellow Sheffield musicians Richard Kirk and Stephen Mallinder, had been a part of the strong skinhead gang of rough neighbourhood Parson's Cross. His Brando rebel spawning Wild One fixation and name change (Adolph Hitler haircut = Adi and Bowie 'Man who Fell to Earth' character 'Newton' = surname) soon coincided with a Stooges/Velvets/MC5 collision with Punk. Joined by future I'm so Hollow Bassist Gary Marsden, mate Joseph Hurst on synths and another character of Sheffield Punk era folklore Stephen James Turner - better known simply as Jud, they played their first gigs at the Limit and Penthouse. Lineups and band relations were volatile and ever-changing; but the band managed to evolve from being one of the most

misunderstood, fanzine disliked and chaotic of the Sheffield Post-Punk bands to be one of the most individual and respected offerings the Steel City had. Cassette releases and ZigZag interviews led to national music press coverage, support slots with Throbbing Gristle and often critically acclaimed albums. Their potential never absolutely reached; the story was interrupted with tragedy when Jud died of a heroin overdose on August 26th 1981.

Guitarist John Valentine Carruthers, from a later line up joined Siouxsie and the Banshees in 1984 – replacing ex Magazine guitarist John McGeogh. Clock DVA influences and band members changed: a loose line up of Adi Newton, Paul Browse and Dean Dennis continue to record albums... one former member -guitarist Dave Hammond was spotted singing on Songs of Praise in 1990!

The Punk explosion sent Martin Lacey (Martin X Russian) to a placing at Sheffield University – one that he opted out of. His friend Russell Davies followed him from their home town of Pinner (Harrow) to find Martin waiting at the steel city train station dressed in full Punk attire; Russell still wearing the obligatory long hair. They soon formed They Must be Russians – Sheffield's proposition of answering to the Ramones. A support slot refusal from the Cabs saw the bands debut in the table tennis room of the students union at Sheffield University. Somehow Chuck Berry (Vocals) had managed to join Russ Repulsive (bass) Hazel of Barnsley (Drums) and Martin (Sparkle/X Russian/Lacey) to play the set of gigs. Later on the line-up was complemented with the addition of Lisa Marshall on occasional vocals (occasional being because a mere 13 years of age, she could only join in when her Mum allowed).

Paul Russian

They must be Russians by Kristan James Melik

Richard Chatterton: "They Must be Russians handed out parcels containing objects as they ironed clothes and made free form jazz on stage (I got some razor blades and an orange)."

There were numerous changes of musicians in the ranks (Martin Lacey being the first to abscond, arriving back on the scene with the highly regarded local scene-chronicling NMX fanzine). Paul Russian replaced Chris on guitar and vocals: the band soon releasing their E.P 'Nagasaki's children'. A support with Throbbing Gristle was followed by regular gigs at the Marples, Polytechnic etc and a second single 'Don't Try to Cure Yourself'. Prog rock influences (very un-hip at the time) paralleled yet more line up changes and the band continued until around 1985; when after 2 album releases and a more funk orientated style, they called it a day.

Amongst the Sheffield Punk bands to bring some of the Post-Punk spirit to their work were the Stunt Kites and the Deaf Aids... Rotherham Punk band Cute Pubes themselves committing some progressive Punk with commendable musical worth to tape; but unfortunately splitting not long afterwards (see Our Generation Vol 1). Singer Dave Spencer was also involved with another budding set of Rotherham musicians that on one occasion determined in true Punk style to add the sound of a drum kit to their ranks.

Gary Stables: "In the early 80's I was knocking around with a few guys who were in bands, John Vernon of L.O.S, and Dave Spencer of the Cute Pubes, so me and a few mates decide to form a band too, namely myself Dave Frost, Neil Creswell and Tony Betts. Any way, Dave had told me of a mate of his in Greasbrough who was selling a drum kit: only trouble was that there was no transport, but good old Yorkshire Traction came to the rescue! So us four Punks set off on a bus ride from my house in Rawmarsh to town then on to Greasbrough to buy the kit for a £25 bargain. Then came the return journey of a full kit, four Punks and arsey bus drivers... but we eventually got it home much to the surprise of Ma & Pa who had no idea of what we were up to."

Another Rotherham band Comsat Angels (formed from the remains of two bands), came to, first Indie and then almost mainstream, prominence during the early to mid 80's. Regulars on the John

Peel show, their first LP was released in 1980 which contained one of their best loved songs 'Independence Day'. Following tours with Siouxsie and the Banshees and U2, they were plagued by an amount of bad luck coming to a bitter end in 1995, leaving behind an admirable collection of music that stands up to much of the Post-Punk 'Bunnymen' stylised rock of the 80's.

I'm So Hollow came from teenagers Rod Leigh (guitar) and Yosef 'Joe' Sawicki' (drums) first Punk band V4. Influenced by Punk, but not rigidly playing it, and buying a synth from the Human League's Martyn Ware, they were joined by guitarist Gary 'Dayton' Marsden and singer/keyboardist (and early Punk style setter) Jane Wilson performing consistently at venues such as the Broadfield, Rotherham's Art centre and Windmill, Sheffield Penthouse, George IV and Psalter Lane art college and all the other accommodating venues of the day along with the Futurama festival in Leeds. They appeared on the 'Hicks From The Sticks' LP (track – 'I Don't Know'), as well as '1980: the first 15 minutes' and the legendary 'Bouquet of Steel' compilation.

I'm so hollow (By **Kristan James Melik**)

I'm so Hollow recorded for John Peel's show, released their first single proper 'Dreams to fill the vacuum' on their own Hollogram label at the start of 1981 and after a temporary split, returned to record company signing with Illuminated records - recording and releasing their first LP (Emotion/Sound/Motion - Oct 1981). They considered themselves to have achieved their own ambitions and had already split before its release.

Rotherham Punk and futuristic visionary Colleen Allen landed on a scantily clad atoll!

Colleen Allen: "I left Spiral Vision and joined a Worksop band Bikini Atoll and we had gigs in Worksop, Retford Porterhouse and one or two other places, again a great bunch of guys. I left this band aged 18/19 to do my art degree in London, later transferring back to Sheffield to complete my degree.

"Psalter Lane Art College was brilliant, the social life great. Living in Nether Edge and a regular abuser of pubs and clubs, The Washington, The Broadfield, Leadmill, 'Jive Turkey' nights, Art studio parties (my studio was Nursery Arts) and we often linked with Blast Lane and other studios to enjoy arty shenanigans'. I also briefly sang with 'The Inhabitants' with my sister Heather, Steve Chapman (Stunt Kites) and Dave. I also did some backing vocals for the Stunt Kites which was great."

One band, along with the Human League, ABC and others, who did achieve household name status were Chesterfield/Sheffield Post-Punk act the Thompson Twins. They formed in 1977 and originally came across as sounding like XTC (playing an early gig at the Limit for £25 as support to Teardrop Explodes), but by the time they reached Pop star status in 1983, the only original member was bass player and singer Tom Bailey. They sold 25 million records ('Hold Me Now', 'Doctor Doctor', 'You Take Me Up' etc) and ex teacher Bailey returned to Sheffield to raise funds for his ex school. He now lives in New Zealand.

Sheffield Post-Punk legends Artery meanwhile continued performing and recording gaining critical acclaim and a new line up, but major success continued to pass them by... the world, shamefully, not having caught up with their particular individual style and unique talent.

The Post-Punk round up of the early to mid 80's Sheffield scene and its receiving neighbouring towns and suburbs included...Vendino Pact, In the Nursery, Hula, The Box, Dig vis. Drill, Worksop's' Bikini Atoll (featuring Colleen Allen for a spell), B-Troop, Cardboard Criminals (Dave Kurley's band pre-New Model Soldier), The Blimp, Best left Dead, An Ordered Life, a pre-Pulp Richard Senior band called Banshees influenced) Choir,

The Bath Bankers, (Wire, Cure and The Corridor, Dachau

sixties/Bowie/Roxy influenced Closet Psychotics from Chesterfield, Defective Turtles (who released a single in 1984 called 'Don't let the Bastards Grind You Down'), God (Nick Banks pre-Pulp short-lived 1983 band – 'I joined a band with Paul and Miggs (God!) while answering an ad in the Virgin at the bottom of the Moor' – Nick Banks), Mirror Crack'd, The Naughtiest Girl Was a Monitor, Psychic Twist, Rapid Eye Movement (another Dave Kurley outfit), proto-Goths Quite Unnerving (song title example – 'Corpse Creeper'), Screaming Trees, Sons and Lovers (featuring for a short while Rob 'Dingo' Dowling' from Tsi-Tsa), the Iggy pop fixated Silent Scream, Surface Mutants (single 'You Take Me Somewhere Strange'), the synth-Pop of Time in Motion, the Richard Hawley spawning Tree bound Story, UV Pop, Vector 7-7, Veiled Threat, Vitamin Z (who snatched a slot on kids TV Show Razzamatazz – remember it?), Psychobilly influenced Zyclones and ex-Repulsive Alien member Nick Hawksworth's band Divine

Comedy! (Not the other one)... Many more served and even many more never got off the drawing board, some loved, some hated, most long forgotten and a few remembered with great fondness... As the 80's progressed Rotherham offered exclusively Red Sector, the Filth Sisters, Suburban Dream amongst the already covered in Our Generation Volume one - 'Cute Pubes, Vision, My Pierrot Dolls, The Way and others featured in these pages!

Nick Banks: (Middle across with friends) "Pulp were one of my faves of this time, great dark songs, intense, shambolic but totally riveting. Toilet roll used as set dressing, tin foil, Russell Senior's Sparks-like image etc. Others were New Model Soldier (I still see Dave Kurley regularly) - one gig that sticks in the mind was at the Crucible Studio: DK came on stage alone and just stood staring at the crowd for about 5 mins (I think a technical hitch but very dramatic) - He went off but then the crowd were assaulted from the sides by two fire extinguishers going off, very startling!! I got it right in the face... the band then took the stage but with a giant stuffed bear where the drummer would be (they didn't have one), and played a blinding set."

John Quinn: "After the musical awakening started by Punk, the urge came to look a little bit deeper, both into musical styles and what was happening in this very area. The only Sheffield groups who seemed to play plain Punk were Stunt Kites, whose (brilliant) name emblazoned many city walls, Mau Maus, and The Injectors, whose

best-known song was the charmingly-titled 'I'm A Rapist'. But what became known as 'Post-Punk' was providing some interesting diversions. The first two local groups I actually saw live were straightforward guitar pop. The Flying Alphonso Brothers and The Tremmers appeared in a tent during The Moor the Merrier week. I watched them and was amazed that they set up and carried their own equipment. These people had been in the paper and regularly performed in front of people. They were pop stars. Where were the roadies, groupies and bodyguards?"

The Flying Alphonso Brothers (Right) included ex Prams guitarist Simon Ellis – nearest leap in the photo - and featured their superb new wave pop track 'Video Date' on the Bouquet of Steel' compilation.

Photo: Simon Ellis

Simon Ellis: "The Flying Alphonso Brothers were formed by two brothers, Mick Limb (guitar, vocals) and Paddy Limb (drums), from Ecclesfield, and Dave Lant (bass, vocals) who lived at Orgreave I think. They were The Squad before I knew them and they had two tracks on the 'New Wave from the Heart' LP...I joined after The Prams split. We did pop songs really, mostly written by Mick, and mainly at breathtaking speed! We did loads of gigs and had quite a following on the Sheffield circuit and it was a great band to be in. We did some recording but never really got out of Sheffield, and eventually drifted apart...I've never seen the others since, no idea what happened to them."

John Quinn: "However, they (The Flying Alphonsos) seemed like the men on the street compared to the likes of the Human League and Cabaret Voltaire. They had strange haircuts and synthesisers and might as well have been from outer space. I once found HL (and later Heaven 17) member Martyn Ware's number in the phone book, rang it and hung up through sheer fear as soon as he answered. I'd have been a crap stalker. Excitingly, they also seemed to be genuinely famous, at least as far as the national music papers were concerned. And there were other acts following in their slipstream such as In the Nursery, led by a pair of identical blond twins, but in no way similar to Bros.

"Compilations such as the 1980: The First 15 Minutes EP and the Bouquet Of Steel album introduced a lot of new sounds - and even more thrillingly the labels seemed to be based near my Hunter's Bar home. The HQ of Neutron Records was actually the home of Steve Singleton from Vice Versa who later became ABC. I know this because I knocked on the door and spoke to his mum. The Broomhill base for Aardvark Records meanwhile, appeared to just be a house with nobody in it. Is that any way to run an international enterprise?

"It could be useful knowing the addresses of the local scene's mainstays. The Comsat Angels lived and rehearsed in a house I'd pass every day on my paper round, and I knocked on their door as well, getting a couple of free singles - including their rare debut 'Red Planet' for my cheek. And when the reformed version of the Human League was big, I impressed a cousin no end by pointing out Phil Oakey's house to her as we went past in her dad's car. What I didn't expect was for her to screech for her father to immediately halt the motor so she could get her photo taken standing on the street outside. I didn't dare knock on the door. He actually was a pop star. He might have had guard dogs...Or a gun? My mate Sid lived just across the road from Oakey and he and my other mate Salt actually knocked on his door one New Year's Eve. A couple of months later Oakey was interviewed in The Face and complained about 'two little prats' who had turned up at his house at Hogmanay.

"Funds permitting, I would purchase as many records by local bands as possible. Some of them were just strange. They Must Be Russians' debut EP consisted of a Beatles-eque love song, a Cabaret Voltaire-alike burst of electronics, a heartbreaking ballad about the Holocaust and a raucous version of 'Nellie The Elephant' - it was as if they realised that this may be their only chance to record and they wanted to cram in as many styles as possible. They were one of the lucky acts in that they went on to put out several more singles and albums, but some others never got beyond the first release. Or maybe their only ambition was to have one thing in the shops and then split up - a laudable aim in itself. I'm So Hollow are still my all-time favourite local act, with a great name, concept, badges...and some excellent songs too. However after releasing one single - on transparent vinyl on Hollogram Records - and an album, they quit despite apparent interest from major labels because by all accounts they just couldn't be bothered. I wasn't aware of this at the time but their drummer lived only a few hundred metres from me. Had I known I'd have knocked on his door too.

"Clock DVA's debut album 'Thirst' had me in tears on first listening, basically because I thought it was so bad. I love it nowadays though. At the time I had plasters on both legs after an operation and had to get a taxi to school, paid for by the education authority and shared with a girl of about nine who had an illness meaning she had to cab it to her place of education too. I took 'Thirst' in to lend to someone at school and on seeing the record bag, the girl went: '*Ooh, what's the record? Is it Duran Duran?*" *Er, not quite...*

"It was hard to get to see these bands to perform live as they tended to perform in pubs and over-18's venues. I wasn't and didn't look it either. One I did manage to

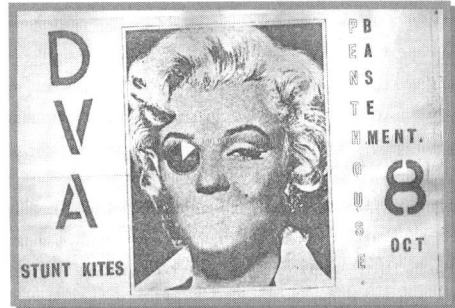

see a couple of times was Artery. The first time was at the Marples pub. Brendan and Plattsy from school had been there earlier in the week for a headline set by Barnsley Goths Danse Society. They had originally thought that pretty boy singer Steve Rawlings was female until the combination of a deep voice and a lack of...er...for want of a better word...tits...convinced them otherwise. There was also much praise for support band Pulp and especially their singer, one Jarvis Cocker, who was variously described as 'tall' 'ugly' 'speccy' and 'hilarious.' He soon became the subject of a graffiti campaign at our school (nothing to do with us of course) leading to the headmistress announcing at Assembly that she intended to find out who he was. Wonder if she ever did?

"Anyway Pulp were playing again a couple of days later at the same venue, supporting Artery, and intrigued, I decided to go, never having succeeded in getting into a pub before in my life - I'd once managed to get a load of mates banned from one simply by sitting in the beer garden with them. I made the mistake of telling my dad where I was going and he threatened to ground me before letting me go on the grounds that I was unlikely to get in anyway. Much to my amazement I did and was amused and entertained by Pulp, (dressed in matching outfits made of curtain material) and entranced by the sheer oddness of Artery.

"Later the same year I saw them again, this time at a John Peel road show at the Polytechnic, where they were supported by the underrated Vendino Pact. I even managed to have a brief chat with the great DJ himself, as apparently did Jarvis from Pulp, who passed on a tape, leading to his then teenage band getting a Radio One session and thinking they were going to make it big. They never did though. Er, hold on....Brendan and I became big Danse Society fans and even got to know them vaguely. Not that it got us any special favours.

"One of the most eventful occasions is when we decided to spend Bonfire Night watching them play live at Birmingham University. Brendan's sister was living in Brum at the time so at least we had somewhere to stay. However when we got to what we thought was the venue, it was completely deserted. We'd only turned up at the wrong campus. And it's a very big city... While we were wondering what to do we spotted a similarly-over coated figure wandering about. He'd made the same mistake as us, but luckily he'd brought his car and kindly offered to give us a lift to the proper place. We had a bottle of vodka with us and offered him some. *"No thanks lads. I don't drink,'* he said and also offered to give us a lift back to the city centre after the show. As this would save us taxi cash we spent most of our money on more alcohol.

"Before they went on stage we had bumped into Danse Society's bassist Tim who seemed pleased

to see us, so after the show we decided to try and get backstage. We were hanging around when their singer Steve spotted us. We expected him to say: *'Thanks for coming all this way to see us. You're great fans. Why don't you come and have a drink'* What he actually said was: *'What the fuck are you doing here?'* before stomping off, shutting the door behind him. Never mind, we thought, that guy from earlier will give us a lift and then we can get a bus back to Small Heath. We waited outside for our chauffeur and saw him - practically unconscious and being carried by what we presumed were his mates. Upon seeing us he said: *'Sorry lads. I decided to have a couple of pints'*... Of methylated spirits by the look of it. We then had to walk back to the city centre. It took about four years. At the end of their tour the band played in Sheffield where our carefully-crafted plan to get free tickets from the manager ended up with him marching us to the box office and watching us pay.

Danse Society's singer Steve Rawlings

"By now I was old enough to get into concerts (although I always carried my birth certificate just in case) and saw shows by the likes of Clock DVA offshoot The Box, funksters Chakk, electonicists Hula and the weirdo Wealthy Texans, who were led by The Star's ex-pop page writer Martin Lilleker and who once did a Fretton job by clearing a venue, although in this case it was because they were determined to keep on playing hours after everyone else had lost interest. Treebound Story (Richard Hawley's first band) were another Sheffield band I saw live. They came up to the Star's office one evening to be interviewed by my predecessor Dom Roskrow, and ended up having a big argument among themselves that almost developed into a fight.

"Then I took over Martin's former job and Instead of me knocking on band's doors, they were knocking on mine. Well it happened once. I was eating my tea - beans and toast - at the time. And to my surprise members of bands seemed to be for the most part normal local beings. It was downhill all the way..."

Tony Beesley: (Right) "I did do a very 'blink and you'll miss it' Robert Smith-influenced Cure look, jet-black hair over my eyes style, black clothes, Chelsea boots (as always) black Grand-dads shirt and faded black canvas jeans around late 1981: my lifetime's contribution to Goth!"

Ipso Facto at Sheffield Marples 16ᵗʰ May 1982 (Klive Humberstone)

Klive Humberstone: (In the Nursery) "Ipso Facto were an esoteric gothic band who formed in 1982 and gigged mainly around Sheffield and the North. They were a fairly short lived affair circulating through line-up changes around front man Eb and releasing 'Noir Doir', 'Mannequin' ,'Give It To Her' and 'Glass Tigers/Apostle' of Sleeze on their own Zodiak Records label. Graham Wrench (who now manages Richard Hawley) played guitar and Ged Warren played bass.

"I went along to the gig, having already met Eb the singer. He used to talk about the band (and his vision) long before they had played a gig. His 'rock' plan was textbook stuff and I'm pretty sure his role model was Jim Morrison. They played a good show on the night - stark and distinct with a heavy drum sound. Minimal white lighting carved out shadows on the venues back curtain drop. Ged looked great playing bass guitar, tall and lean, sporting eyeliner, a mohair jumper and leopard skin hat. I noted in my diary at the time, that although the intention of the show was to confront the audience, it lacked the passion and appeared 'staged' - especially by the antics of main man 'Eb'."

Later that year it was another Gothic leaning band that Klive went along to see...Danse Society and supported by UV POP at the Limit on 9th September 1982.

Klive Humberstone: "I have always been slightly let down by the recorded material of Danse Society. The live show worked a lot better and the Limit gig was a good example of how they worked together as a band with atmospheric and passionate portrayals of some of their best songs. They were a 'Goth' band, but didn't know it themselves, or maybe just didn't care. Great guitar work and powerful drumming, matching the slender vocals of Steve Rawlings."

Above: Danse Society at Sheffield Polytechnic 1982 (Klive Humberstone)

Andy Coles: "As Punk progressed, I felt that it became more diluted and clichéd beyond belief. The Positive Punk/Goth/Psychobilly bands had failed to reach their potential and a lot of the music being produced was duller than dishwater. I mean, how many people still slip a Balaam and the Angel album on for pleasure?

"Southern Death Cult moved through Death Cult to The Cult and later *completely* 'lost it' in my eyes after the excellent Hendrix-tinted 'Love' album. They were saying that their influences were Free, Deep Purple and Led Zeppelin, which was fair enough if they were just going to take inspiration from them, but The Cult eventually turned irony-free into a balls-out heavy rock band and that was it for me. Goth began to become 'crusty' and I absolutely hated this idea. I was never going to go back to having long hair again after it'd taken me soooo long to get away from it! I was sporting a big quiff, jeans and baggy shirt by this time. The line from the Sex Pistols' song 'Seventeen' that goes 'We don't care about long hair, I don't wear flares!' was never more appropriate. The idea of a Punk-based group with long hair was anathema to me and it seemed as if we had turned full circle and were back with boring hippies like 1975! Did Punk Rock really happen?"

Goth may have helped lead the descendants of Punk to present day Heavy Metal saturated Goth-dom – long hair n' all, but its early attempts did manage to bring Rotherham Goth-loving Punk Nick Banks to his rightful place in one of Sheffield's' most interesting and individual bands: they were not Goth, had a direct link to Punk and had a positive and important future in music ahead of them.

Nick Banks: "I first saw Pulp at the 'Stars on Sunday' series of gigs at the Crucible Studio, must have been '81 or '82. I was into Post-Punk proto-Goth Positive Punk, call it what you will, Pulp were none of this. They were doing their first album 'It'. Gentle acoustic 'whimsical' numbers with lots of la la la's. I loved it. I kept seeing Pulp and gradually got on nodding terms with Jarvis etc. They became my favourites really.

"So one day I noticed a small hand-drawn ad on a wall at the Leadmill. *'Can I have a go'* I said to Jarvis. *'Alright come up to ours on Sunday where we practise.'* So I turns up to find Jarvis in his mum's kitchen with a white bulldog going mental. The family dog was in another room going even more mental. *'This dogs' followed me home, we need to get rid of it'.....'* so we eventually did after traipsing round Intake trying to lose the bulldog. We eventually picked it up and put it over a fence and legged it. We never did get to play any music but we got on ok. I didn't get the gig immediately but a couple of months later I started rehearsing with everyone and that was that, first gig at a packed Hull Adelphi, basically a big terraced house with toilets as changing rooms. All went well.

"We played The Adelphi quite a bit in the early days, we used to like to get in the van early and go to Cleethorpes: once we played a game where you would put your money in the hat and the one who got furthest along the breakwater scooped the pot. So Jarv got the furthest but did a beautiful dive into the cold stinking Humber estuary on his return...we all pissed ourselves of course. And with no change of clothes he really made the van stink for the next 12 hours...happy days!"

Right: Debs with Mick Jones of the Clash

Whilst some Punks were taking the path to full time Goth or gaining confidence in some of the best of the upcoming Post-Punk Indie bands, original Punk character Rocka Debs was still loving the sound of the Westway which, at the time was being adapted for the year of 1982 and a more Parisian setting!

Rocka Debs: "One of my best Clash experiences was when we went to see them in Paris. We caught their week long residency at the Theatre Mogador, with The Beat and Wah! supporting. We got to hear tunes from the soon-to-be-released new album well before they were played over in England. It was the first time we heard 'Know your rights' and 'Should I stay or should I go' and we learned them off by heart. Graffiti artist Futura 2000 was also onstage painting a graffiti mural. He had got to know us from hanging around with The Clash and generously added our names to his artwork, along with The Clash's. When I saw him put my name Rocka Debs on the backdrop, I nearly exploded. I would love to see that again!"

Local Punk with a keen eye for colour and individuality in clothes; Fiona Palmer had also tasted the Punk experience, both via the live Punk gigs she had attended in Sheffield, the attention her electric blue hair received and also embarking upon a Punk D.I.Y shopping outlet: well almost do it yourself!

Fiona Palmer: "You could guarantee my mum Elaine (the female equivalent of Arthur Daley, though much better looking) was one step behind me, pushing me into yet more adventures to seek my fame and fortune bless er! My fellow Punk and Punkettes at the time did have lots of fun in that boutique -sod the business and money making!"

Not long after this Punk business venture Fiona returned with a crack at performing. No total stranger to singing (her studio recording of 'Dream World' achieving cult interest over the years). The Punk intoxication had now merged, as the times commonly reflected, into a medley of futurism and synth dominating 'New Wave'. Fiona's version was 3-D Fiction.

Fiona Palmer: "(Describing the photo at left) This is 3D Fiction backstage at Tiffany's (now Liquid n Diva) warming up for our PA in front of an audience of oooh...about erm...well actually I didn't care how many by this stage cos I was rat arsed, a wreck with nerves, and we were only miming.

"Members of 3D Fiction included: Andy Stevenson(keyboards) one with the red hair that looks like he's been stood in a strong westerly wind; Aubrey(lead singer) the one that looks like he's part of the poster decoration stood at the back; Fiona Palmer(backing vocals) another story of Lambrusco anyone? calms the nerves honest. 4th member Spider is either camera shy and taking the photo, or on stage warming up his beloved keyboard revelling in all the fame and glory of being a new wave/futuristic/punk type band in Rotherham in the 80s."

It was an ex Frozen one - Andi Stevenson - that Fiona had teamed up with: Following attempts at recreating a new sound of futurism from the template of their peers Ultravox and early Tubeway Army, Andi had seen the band splinter in all directions, leading ultimately to his journey to 3D Fiction and beyond!

The Pros and Cons of being a New Romantic by Andi Stevenson!

ANDI STEVENSON (MON AMOUR, JULY 1982)

Andi Stevenson: "For me it all started in 1979. I'd been into Punk for two years and couldn't get enough of the raw energy. I was a Punk and loved it. Back then and to this day whenever I go out I always put on Slaughter and The Dogs – 'You ready now?' The ultimate in get yerself up for it. Once a Punk always a Punk I always say. But having spent the previous two years listening to the likes of Buzzcocks, Penetration, The Adverts, the Stranglers, Magazine etc, I was starting to like stuff with synthesizers and keyboards in. Sneaking into the Top Rank in Sheffield aged 14 to watch these bands was an amazing experience, though!

"I was already listening to Tangerine Dream and Kraftwerk and also early Pink Floyd and The Doors, who made great use of keyboards. One of the bands my mates and I were into was Ultravox! with John Foxx on vocals. This was well before

Midge Ure joined and turned them into a pop stars. Ultravox's first LP recorded in 1976 simply titled Ultravox! is still my all time favourite album. They became the first British band to use a drum machine on the classic track 'Hiroshima Mon Amour'. They sounded like no-one else and no-one has ever sounded like since. They were part Punk, part Rock and part Electro and they were the forerunners of what would become New Romantic. Their third and final album in 1978 titled 'Systems Of

FROZEN ONES
THE FROZEN ONES MKII: DECEMBER 1979

LEFT TO RIGHT: PETE COOPER (GUITAR), PAUL RAVEN (VOCALS), ANDI STEVENSON (KEYBOARDS), PETE DAVIES (BASS)

Romance' would be the first true New Romantic album and I would later name two of my bands after Ultravox songs.

"From their demise the phoenix would rise from the flames starting the New Romantic movement that would take hairstyles from the Punk period into a new bizarre level and also take the best bits of the Punk fashion merged with Gothic period costumes and men wearing make-up to create an outrageous new style.

"One of the things that stands out from this period was reading an article about John Foxx the lead singer of Ultravox! On their debut album was a song titled 'I Want to be a Machine' (which incidentally has the most killer bass sound of all time). To write this song he apparently lived his life for a whole year as a Machine!!! No emotion, no smiling, no talking, no laughing, no sex etc, etc but how he got round the no eating thing is still beyond me. But this was the spark that got me into this music and this is still the song I want playing at my funeral.

"The first band to seem to spring up from Ultravox's demise were Tubeway Army with Gary Numan on vocals who cited Ultravox! as his main influence. By 1979 Sheffield's Human League with their debut album 'Reproduction' and Japan with their album 'Quiet Life' kept the movement slowly moving forward gathering momentum until 1980 when it exploded into life. I met Phil Oakey from the Human League that year in Doncaster in the toilets at an Ultravox gig. Well I didn't get to say owt to him cos I was stood next to him in the urinals and he pissed on me foot. I was so amazed I just looked at my foot with urine on it and watched him walk out the door.

"1980 was the year of some of the best stuff. Visage's classic 'Fade to Grey' Japan's 'Gentlemen Take Polaroids' and the emergence of Fad Gadget. John Foxx from Ultravox also returned as a solo artist with an electronic/New Romantic masterpiece in his debut album 'Metamatic'. When I first heard the debut single from this album I couldn't believe all the new and innovative synthesizer sounds I was hearing. It completely blew my mind. I must have played it 100 times straight off on my crappy old turntable. I remember at one point getting so excited I ran downstairs from my bedroom to my mum in the kitchen who was cooking Sunday dinner blurting '*you've gotta come and listen to this!!!!*' I shouted like a 6 year old on Christmas Day. My mum ambled upstairs and I put the needle onto the record and I said summat like '*God have you ever 'erd owt like this?*' She replied '*it's not really Frank Sinatra is it now?*' and left after about 30 seconds muttering '*and turn that racket down*' as the bedroom door slammed shut. Still I reckon she was probably relieved to hear that rather than 'Orgasm Addict' or 'Friggin in the Riggin'. I once had a bloke come knocking at my door complaining from 7 houses down the street cos I was playing 'Oh Shit!' by

Buzzcocks too loud. I think I told him to fuck off and die ha ha! By mid 1980 it seemed right to move over to New Romantic. Most of the best Punk bands had split up, the rest like the Stranglers

had become watered down and nothing new was coming through. When the Buzzcocks folded in early 1981 it was like a dagger in my heart.

"One of the first things you realized when dressing up like a New Romantic was how totally shocking it was for other people to deal with. When I was dressing up as a Punk people used to avoid me on the street cos they thought I was some crazy violent person. That couldn't have been further from the truth. Every Punk I knew wasn't violent but was totally in it for the aggression and spirit of the music. Of course a rumpus would occur sometimes if a group of Rockers or Skinheads came across a group of Punks but mostly Punks were in it for the music. The only time I've felt aggressive towards anyone was the return of the Mod and Ska movement. I hated Mods and their music with a serious passion and wouldn't hesitate for a confrontation. While on the way to Virgin Records and Violet May Records in Sheffield, one Saturday afternoon, we were on the train crossing Norfolk Bridge on Attercliffe coming into Sheffield. The train stopped on the bridge and when we looked out of the window there was about twenty Scooters with Mods on at the traffic lights on the road below. We started ripping all the light fittings out of the train and raining em down on the Mods stationary below.

Bowie/Futurist orientated nights in Sheffield poster (Nigel Lockwood)

SOUND AND VISION

David Bowie
Roxy Music
Ultravox
Joy Division
Gary Numan

NOV. 10
Romeo's & Juliet's
Bank St. Sheffield.

Advance Tickets £1·00
Available from venue
£1·50 on the night
Dress Optional

"Becoming a New Romantic was all about expressing yourself. The more expressive you were the more people would take notice of you. By nature I was a very shy and quiet person but I found myself hooked on the adrenaline of people stopping and staring at you. From this period I developed the name 'Mop' cos of the birds nest I had on my head. I used to use 5 large cans of Boots Hairspray just to get my hair in place to go out on a Friday Night and the same again for Saturday Night. It's probably down to me alone there's a hole in the ozone layer. It used used to take me 4 hours just to do my hair! One day going into town on a Friday night I was so tired from the night before I rested my head against the window of the Bus. By the time the Bus arrived at the Charters Pub I tried to get off but my head was stuck to the window with all the condensation on the window mixed with the hairspray. I had to wait to get off until the bus arrived in the Bus Station and rip my hair off the window!!!! On one other occasion my hair was bright pink and blue and we were loading our van for Band rehearsals with Mon Amour on a Saturday morning outside my house. As I walked round the back of the van, carrying an amp, a car drove past and the driver saw me. His face was a picture as his jaw dropped and he stared at me as he drove past straight into a car coming out of a junction at the front of the van. Luckily everyone was ok but we were laughing like crazy until the guy who owned our van realized he had no tax disc so we had to skedaddle pretty sharpish.

"It was common place to walk into a new pub somewhere and the whole friggin place just stop as one but that kinda gave you a buzz. There was one occasion at a pub in East Herringthorpe that was like something out of an old western movie when even the piano player stops. As we walked in everyone seemed to have tattoos on their faces, 'cut here' on their throats and half the pub were boneheads. Everyone stopped talking when we walked in and the juke box stopped. Not the best place for a band to walk into with the 4 blokes wearing frilly shirts, knickerbockers and full make up. But the more the locals stared the more we would stare back and eventually they all got on with their inbreeding.

"On one occasion in 1981 I went to a New Romantic club in Doncaster with my girlfriend Julie. By this time I had pink back-combed hair, a nose stud, diamond earrings and wearing knicker bockers and a Dracula cape with full make up. We were stood there having a drink minding our own business when two square blokes came over to us. The first bloke said to me *'would you 2 gorgeous ladies like to dance?'* I said *'I'm not a lady and I don't dance now fuck off'*. They were out of the door like a shot! These were some of the good times of being a New Romantic. Some of the bad times included the first time I had my hair dyed pink and my nose pierced in 1981. I met my girlfriend as usual after her work, as always on a Saturday evening, and went to her house for dinner. Her Mum and Dad weren't there when I first walked in so they didn't see my new hairstyle and nose stud. Her mum shouted us down for dinner about an hour later. We sat on the sofa together waiting for dinner and a few minutes later her mum walked into the room with a tray of food for us each. As she walked in she looked up and let out a large scream and dropped the trays of food. At which point she yelled *'you can get out of my house with that fucking thing in your nose and don't ever come back till it's gone'*. After that our relationship was doomed. Her dad refused to let me back in and we eventually spilt up. I did get the last laugh, though, a few years later. Walking back from town with all my glad rags and make up on I walked through Clifton Park and as I was walking past the bowling greens I saw her dad with all his pals playing bowls. So I headed in that direction and walked right past em and said *'Hi John how you doing mate?'* His face just turned to stone and all his pals had eyes on stalks. I just smiled and carried on walking. A couple of years ago I met her Dad for the first time in 25 years since that incident and he called me a few names and said he'd never been so embarrassed in his life but we had a right good chat and laugh about it.

"One Thursday evening I met our singer, and close friend Fiona Palmer, in town and we went for a drink in the Fioffees pub. One of our friends was resident DJ there on Thursdays so we went up to the top floor with our drinks to meet him. I hated going in trendy places cos there would always be some nutter who would start. And sure enough this was to be just the same. As we got up to the top floor there was a table with about 9 or 10 lads on it and, as I walked past, they all started wolf whistling and shouting the usual abuse. We carried on walking across to the DJ box and as we got there I said to Fi and Richard the DJ *'wait here I'll be back in a minute'*. I went back across the floor to an empty table and got myself a chair and walked over to the table of 10 rowdy lads. I pulled up my chair to their table and said *'nah then lads what were we saying?'* They all went quiet and didn't say a word. I just smiled and went back to Fiona and Richard. I thought that

would be the end of it but as we left at the end of the night I noticed the lads had gone, or so I thought. Fiona went out first and came back in and she said they're all waiting for you outside. She said *'don't go out'* but I knew I had to face them so I walked out the door and told em to step back and let me out. They all kinda stepped back then surrounded me so I looked for the biggest and said to him *'what's your problem?'* he replied *'I don't like you'*. At this point I knew I was gonna get a shooing by 10 lads unless I could take out the biggest so I just launched into him. We had a massive scrap for about 10 minutes until we were both so knackered we couldn't stand up. I ended up with a few bruises but it could have been so much worse if they had all joined in.

"It was a similar do or die situation on our bands' first ever gig. My first time live in front of an audience we booked ourselves, My Pierrot Dolls first ever gig at the then notorious Maltby Manor pub in September 1981. A renowned Heavy Metal hangout at the time, we were gonna go there and play a set of New Romantic songs. I was shitting myself as we got ready to go on stage. All 4 of us in make-up, clothes made by our girlfriends and the obvious sign of 'bobbing our pants' wrote across our faces.

"My legs and arms were shaking so much as we went on stage. Nobody even really looked up at us at this point. We gave the signal and the jukebox stopped and we started playing. I dared to look up after about 30 seconds to see a room full of Hairies all glaring at us. I could see a little pocket of our friends huddled together in the corner but other than that we were on our own. The first song was instrumental so Ivor our singer wasn't with us on stage. When the song finished there was total silence apart from the tills and glasses clinking. Even our friends daren't clap, then one bloke shouted *'Is thar it nah are u gonna fuck off'*. Luckily at this point our singer came out and he started the next song. When this finished all the heckling started but Ivor was a dab hand at handling it. He single handedly turned the whole audience from being against us to being on our side with some brilliant wit and poking fun at ourselves. Our bass player Barry Thurman had bleached blonde hair and Ivor told the crowd it was a wig he'd borrowed from his Mam.

Top of page: the face of Northern New Romanticism Ivor Hillman Above: My Pierrot Dolls at their most glammed up, Ivor is in the centre and future Springheel'd Jack bass player Barry Thurman is at the extreme left (Photos courtesy of Andi Stevenson)

The Crowd were in stitches. Then one bloke shouted *'and where did u get your wig from then? 'me?'* asked Ivor. *'I got mine from an old English Sheepdog cos I know a vet'.* Again the audience were in stitches and all the abuse they shouted he turned it back against them playing them all the time until he won them over completely. At one point the crowd were shouting for AC/DC and Led Zeppelin songs. *'ABCD?'* asked Ivor, *'never heard of em'* he joked. The crowd were shouting Led Zeppelin and again Ivor asked *'Lad? Lad Zappalin who are they?'* The hecklers soon went quiet once they realised Ivor had the mic and he was far wittier than they were."

New Romantic Rotherham band My Pierrot Dolls had swapped the glamour and photogenic fashion appeal of Futurism for something far more Gothic by the mid 80's: But as lead spokesman and singer Ivor Hillman once proclaimed *'Yer can take the lad outa Yorkshire, but tha can't take the Yorkshire outa the lad'*... a trip to Preston to play on a stage only very recently graced by then cult Goths- The Cult! was accompanied by every true Yorkshire lad's favourite pastime!

Ivor Hillman: (My Pierrot Dolls singer)
"An early morning start was the order of the day for our Clouds gig at Preston. We'd only got the gig a few days earlier as another band had dropped out. Fruitcake's long term friend Paul (known to us as Johnny Rotten) hired a transit and picked us all up one by one. We'd bought loads of cans of beer and began drinking them at 9am in the morning in the back of the Transit. En-route we picked up Drummer Howard Daniels from outside Huddersfield train station. Once aboard Howard cracked open a can and the party began. At Noon after loads of pee stops over the Pennines we arrived at Clouds. First thing we noticed was two weeks before us the Cult had appeared and now little old My Pierrot Dolls would grace the main stage. After sound-checking we made our way to a local pub in Preston. It was still only 2pm and we weren't due on for ages. Nine thirty came and we stumbled our way to the club, hardly being able to stand let alone play a gig. On stage at 10pm and making ourselves at home we began drinking more and more to the extent we were all virtually paralytic. On we went to a muted reception. The club was packed and waiting for the Goths from Rotherham to open their set.

"We started banging the songs out in what can only be described as awful and we could see the natives were getting restless. Suddenly they began spitting at me as I threw myself in a drunken stupor around the stage. I recall quite vividly a punk at the front filling his gob with beer and then spraying it all over me. At this I threw my Frank Spencer beret at him followed by my pumps from my feet. It began to get too much for the promoter and after about 6 songs he pulled the plug. The sound system we were using was turned off and the club's DJ began playing songs by the Cult to the delight of the crowd as we stumbled our way out of the club. That night was the longest night ever and returning home at 5am, drunk, tired and with virtually no clothes on was a memory I'll never forget."

Andi Stevenson's Gallery of Futurism

My Pierrot Dolls (July 1981)
Mon Amour 1982 below/1983 right

Vision 1981

Andi Stevenson: "The main drawback of dressing like a New Romantic was that it would always attract the nutters to you. You had to be able to look after yourself and I ended up in a lot of close shaves with pissheads wanting to have a pop at me. The best way to deal with it, I found, was to give it back to them and not back down."

Above: 3D Fiction June 1983 and Mark IV with Fiona Palmer (October 1984)

Left: 3D Fiction Mark III with Fiona Palmer

Andi Stevenson: "It's funny but Punk changed everything. Until Punk everyone had to be a super musician playing prog rock or whatever. Punk encouraged people with little or no playing ability to get up and give it a go and thus from Punk sprung up, New Romantic, New Wave, Indie. Just cos you could barely play 3 chords didn't mean you couldn't write a great song. On some occasions though having a distinct lack of talent really did mean you were shit. A classic example of this was in my second band The Frozen Ones. Chip our drummer had left to join Spiral Visions who would later go on to have a hit as Vision with 'Lucifer's Friend'. He was the only one in our band who could play but nevertheless we carried on and decided to do our first demo. We decided to book into the same studio that had recorded The Human League's 'Being Boiled' single and another Sheffield band with a gem of a name called The Naughtiest Girl Was A Monitor also recorded there. We stupidly thought cos we were going to this studio we were gonna be big ha ha! We were recording our second song called 'Images' which was two chords only throughout the whole song repeated over and over again for three minutes. After about 20 retakes the Bass Player couldn't even play these two chords in time without fucking up and the engineer tired of forever rewinding the master tape turned round, took his pipe out of his mouth and sarcastically said *'it's a good job it ain't three chords sonny!'.* Inside I was pissing myself but really I felt so embarrassed that we couldn't even play a two chord song. Happy days and happy memories."

Andi Stevensons' family tree of futurism and new romantic identity included a closely related sequence of musician-sharing bands... From his early days in Punk outfit Grip! to The Frozen Ones and his musical partnerships with other like-minded New Romantics Vision, My Pierrot Dolls and Mon Amour and Divine supporting synthesiser act 3 D Fiction... the road to mid 80's short-term utopia was a busy affair that culminated in disappointment at the last lap!

Andi Stevenson: "Mon Amour would become 3D Fiction and six months later Fiona Palmer joined us. Things rocketed during 1983/84/85 supporting Divine and being invited by Steve Wright to play at his Road show in Rotherham. Unfortunately things turned sour when on the verge of some success Fiona was poached from us by her management in 1985."

The New Romantics (mostly termed futurists at the time) early attempts at upsetting the stereotypical norm of early 80's UK: their effeminate look – often belying a much harder inner centre – along with their flamboyant decadence and often ground-breaking and experimental approaches to music, clothes and fashion was quickly assimilated and integrated into the Media and the clutches of the desperate Post-Punk music industry- spewing out a Top 40 of clones, feeble popsters and ultimately a new hierarchy of pop stars fit only to woo the audience of mid 80's Smash Hits teenyboppers!!!

Jamie Headcharge: "The Punk scene had slowly started to die away with people growing up and moving on and the 80's synth/pop movement took over. Around this time, people started going to clubs a bit more, a notable venue being the Limit Club. The synth/pop genre felt like a complete shift from the DIY style of Punk. It was more commercially orientated and was about making pop songs more than contributing to a life style movement, even though there was a new kind of fashion movement building up around these bands. There were some great synth bands in Sheffield that seemed to carry on the Punk ethos a bit more, like Cabaret Voltaire and Clock DVA, Quite Unnerving and Mortuary in Wax who had much darker edgier sounds. The thing that was missing from the new electronic wave was some kind of scene to wrap it all around."

The original catalysts for the Punk affected generation... the bands themselves, were swiftly becoming as removed from their audience and the real world of Thatcher's Britain than could have been possibly conceived a few years previously... the spirit of 76 had been diluted useless within any obviously evident musical circles... Combat Rock, Strawberry Rock or revitalised Punk Rock... not many of the vast array of splintered Post-Punk musical styles on offer shared much in common with their – now once again disaffected – youth of followers. The mood of the times was one of frustration or self-denial: could our nations youth be back to square one and be no more better musically and idealistically represented than they had been back in the dark days of pre-Punk Britain? Ever get the feeling you've been cheated... indeed!!!

Tony Beesley: "It's weird that before I was even in my 20's I had become so cynical about the whole Punk ideal. I still firmly believed in the ethics and spirit of Punk but couldn't find anything out there that was worth injecting the ideas into: taking a look around, it was as though all the main players of Punk had become exactly what they set out to destroy, and everyone else had almost given up on it all. The whole visual side of Punk had also been diluted so much that it was hardly recognisable... from the peacock flamboyance of the Futurists – whose glam was a kind of escapism to the gloom of Thatcherism, to the crusty hardcore Punk Rockers... none of it resonated with me! For quite sometime during the 80's, it seemed as though Punk had never even happened!"

Chapter Seven

Did Punk Rock really happen?

"We got three days in the nick: one for fighting and two for losing. My first two weeks in Her Majesty's Forces hadn't gone quite to plan, not so much Queen and Country, rather WHAT A TWAT!!" - **Bryan Bell** (Rotherham Punk)

"The Clash were past it. Their time had been and gone. If only they hadn't had to record the abysmal 'Cut the Crap' LP to prove it!" – **Tony Beesley**

Rubella Ballet by Phil Chatterton

There was now a massive void left by Punk and as much as the many facets of the Sheffield and local Post-Punk scene had taken the whole Do-it Yourself aesthetic to its logical conclusion, the whole musical climate of the time, and what it represented to the cast of our generation, was gradually becoming worryingly not that dissimilar to how it all was immediately prior to Punk Rock! What was in store to rival the excitement and life changing experiences of a generation awakened by Punk and its after-shocks? Would the progressing decade present anything new? Would it all have been in vain and be just as though Punk had never happened?

Punk, Post-Punk, US Hardcore, Mod, 2-Tone, Electro New Romantic spin offs, prototype- Goth and now Psychobilly were showing a massive influence on the kids that were feeding off the new music of the time. Often there would be a division between these scenes and cults, but as the 80's progressed, the lines set out between each genre became more blurred and less obvious seeing some of the Punk generation searching for something extra- music wise... and still, occasionally, upsetting the scheme of things!

Phil Chatterton: "About 1983, me and my mate Andy went to the boozer 'Broughten Inn' which was in Attercliffe, near where the Arena is nowadays. They were having regular Rock n' Roll nights there with proper Teds attending... most of em into Gene Vincent etc. We liked the music so would go along.

"One of the times, me and another mate called Tin Tin (who later got into the football violence

scene but is no longer with us)... we managed to get the DJ Roger to put 'Wrecking Crew' by the Meteors on, so we both started doing our dance in the middle of the dance floor. Before we knew it we were surrounded by the older (and much bigger) Teddy Boys. I remember the music suddenly coming to a stop and I looked up and this big Teddy Boy with a bottle of Brown Ale in his hand was just staring right at us. He said *'That's not Rock n' Roll, its Punk and this is Rock n' Roll night!* We were totally surrounded by all these Teds with big quiffs and greased back hair. This Ted bird came over to us and said 'I'd *leave if I were you two'* next minute, the Landlord of the place came running through with a baseball bat swinging it around and mouthing to them all to clear off! Luckily their bus was about due and they left. Not long after that, we left as well. It was time to go back to Rotherham town centre for last orders at the Turf before the last bus home."

Tony Beesley: "I loved that single 'Stamp of a Vamp'/ 'Hey Now I'm in Love' by Vic Godard (Subway Sect) that came out in 1982. The crooner Sinatra style was fantastic: that single must have upset some old Punks, but I loved it and still have the record!"

Andy Coles: "At the end of 1983 I moved to Surrey to study for an Art degree and got in with a different crowd of students. I met up with people of similar tastes, who I went to see bands with like The Cure and Siouxsie and The Banshees. A new mate, Martin Brockman introduced me to the delights of the Medway scene, based around Chatham on the River Medway in Kent, which produced 'lo-fi' rock and roll artists such as Billy Childish and The Milkshakes, who were taking their cues from the raw garage bands from the 1950's and 60's. I liked the raw trashy sound, all twangy guitars and three chords that harked back to the early days of the Cavern and Merseybeat.

"We shared common ground with our love of Link Wray and 50's kitsch-influenced bands like The Cramps and The B 52s and we went to a 'Batcave-revue' type gig at Hammersmith Palais, where Sex Beat played first, followed by The Specimen who basically got bottled off. Then out came The Cramps for what has to be one of the roughest gigs I have ever attended. Singer Lux Interior (bless his soul) came on and immediately jumped into the audience and started attacking someone who had pissed him off. We were near the back and it was rough *there*, never mind at the front! 'Chicken-dancing' and punches erupted all around us and the atmosphere was one of near riot."

Over on West Street in Sheffield, the Limit club was just as popular as ever: the Punk years behind them, the club concentrated on promoting all the latest in cutting edge music, whilst also becoming a haven for aspiring Goths, Casuals, hedonistic Disco Saturday night ravers and good timers all.

Amongst the many bands to perform in the ensuing years of the clubs early 80's to 1991 last laps were Echo and the Bunnymen, Gene Loves Jezebel, Pink Military, Wasted Youth, The Meteors, The

Alarm, Original Mirrors, Modern English, Blue Rondo a la Turk, Animal Nightlife, Wham, Rotherham's Futurists Vision, Sharp Cuts, Pulp, Soft Cell, Vitamin Z, Delta 5, Department S as well as the many legions of long forgotten local bands. The Limit club's reputation has been sealed forever as one of the country's most individual and - often - most fondly remembered clubs of all time: its reputation rivalling the sixties heydays of Sheffield's Esquire and Mojo joints!

Colleen Allen: "The Limit was amazing, we used to get in before 11pm so it was cheaper, always sharing half a lager and 'black', literally just that to feed the adrenalin for a night of fine

music and coy eyeing up. The late night bus home was a nightmare, it was ok for those living in the city, but we had to get a bus with the yokels from Dinnington, it took a thousand years to get home, generally filled with abuse or/and lewd comments.

"We used to spend so much time at the Limit, how the hell we got in I don't know, although copious amounts of make up, alcohol and targeted ego-stroking certainly helped. Although we never had any more than a couple of quid, we spent many hours trudging around numerous 'Towny' pubs to exploit older guys and elicit free drinks, before running for the hills laughing gratuitously and onto more 'respectable' pubs, our pubs, The Hallamshire or The Beehive. Here, we were less likely to trade drinks for a broken promise, with respect and warm welcome from old friends (much older!) and colourful people, a fantastic feeling."

Andy Coles: "I remember going to The Limit, which was pretty Goth-orientated at the time and stuff like The Beastie Boys started to creep into the play list and this got the 'beer boys' onto the dancefloor, often resulting in some 'fisticuffs'."

**live at the limit
sheffield
thursday dec. 16**[th]

Mandy Alleyne: (Below right at the Limit) "I remember the first

time I went to the Limit in 1983. It was awesome - the music they played Dead Kennedys, Alien Sex Fiend, Birthday Party, the Cramps, the Cult, Sex Pistols and that's just to name a few. Finally I could go somewhere where they played music I actually loved. The people were awesome too; we all had something in common. Our dress sense was the same, which seemed like a huge thing at the time, but finally a night club was here that accepted the way we used to dress. Living in Barnsley, we stuck out like a sore thumb, so quite often got a lot of weird looks and comments - even my mum would say I had spoiled my looks."

Gary Peacock: "I worked in Sheffield and had many nights out with the lads from work. A regular at the Limit I saw the Specials, New Order, B-52s, Simple Minds, Joe Jackson, the Skids and many more, my favourite two nights there were the Undertones concert the day after their first appearance on Top of the Pops, they played 'Teenage Kicks' as an encore maybe a dozen times and I've never seen as much sweat in one place, the atmosphere was just the ultimate drunken fun night. The other special limit night came in the mid 80's when the Human league played as a rehearsal for a European tour; I was stood near Lee Chapman and Gary Megson. All hell broke loose when *Sheffield Wednesday good times!* Started being chanted to their song 'Good Times': probably the biggest brawl I've ever seen."

"Another Limit episode that sticks in my mind was speaking to Terry Hall after the Specials concert, he was sat at the edge of the stage and looked thoroughly depressed, not a spark of wit or ego came out in our conversation and I thought *'well he'll not make it as a pop star'*, as I've got older I've come to realize that he was probably just a nice decent bloke. They did a comeback tour recently and a couple of lads in my local saw them at about 75 quid a ticket, I really pissed them off when I told them I'd seen them in 1979 for 50p and 10p bus each way. I also saw them at the 2-Tone Top Rank concert later on, but my memories of that are blurred by another good kicking."

Crazy nights at the Limit – Phil Chatterton and friend

Tony Beesley: "There were some right characters that frequented the Limit club: I hardly knew anyone in the place, but kept myself to myself whenever I went there. I think I went around ten times at the most. It was dark, grubby, smelly, wet-floored, usually an air of danger in the air and claustrophobic... but it was unique and what it did for the Sheffield music scene is almost immeasurable."

Andy Coles: "One 'claim to fame' is that I didn't notice the couple of steps by the DJ booth in The Limit because the place was so full and I fell onto Death Cult guitarist Billy Duffy, who was less than impressed. Peter Hook of New Order was on the mixing desk for them that night. One night, I can remember dancing next to Jarvis Cocker, who was in an early 'mop-hair and National Health glasses' stage, grooving to The B-52's 'Rock Lobster'. He was doing the *'down, down'* bit where you got lower to the floor and I recognised him from The Star (because he had an unusual name) and remember thinking *'With this bloke's image, Pulp will NEVER be big'*...WRONG! I guess the millions of photocopied fly posters that had their name on them around Sheffield in the 80's must have paid off. Pulp went on to headline Glastonbury and became one of my favourite groups ever."

Andy Munday: "By the time I got there (the Limit) I was generally half pissed and by the time they played the track 'Take it to the Limit' to let ya know it was 2 o'clock in the morning and ya had to get out I was generally proper pissed. The bands in there were of a higher grade to the pub bands but I could never hardly see them cos everything seemed to be on one level and I'm only a small bloke. The scene there was just great, but if anything I liked the Crazy Daizy best along with Improvision club at the old Top Rank on a Sunday night where I had seen Slaughter an the Dogs, Vibrators, Adverts, Eater and the Negatives etc."

Andy Coles: "Back home, I would usually end up at The Formula One Club (*still* being called The Charade by everyone) as it was near home and also to The Limit, which seemed to have changed somewhat. There was still the permanently sticky floor and the toilets were no less disgusting than they always had been, but the atmosphere seemed different, not as exciting. I thought that this was due to the different songs that were coming into the club's play list. The place was still pretty 'Alternative' overall, but some of the early House and dance music records were now being played and I hated them. Stuff like The Beastie Boys had come out too and the beer boys would smash into anyone on the flooded dancefloor, all in the name of 'dancing'. Dance floors everywhere were always 'a bit lively' if any Psychobilly records were played but the last time I went to The Limit, some of the people there were out for real trouble and goading people into reacting. I gave the place a wide berth after that and never went again."

Disease photo: courtesy of Kristan James Melik

Richard Chatterton: "Back in Sheffield, Disease stepped out from backstage at their Limit gig before they were on and asked every member of the audience what their names were, and then incorporated this information into a song, to a throbbing bass-line. '*Hello Rich, hello Carol, hello Dave, hello Jo, hello Sally, hello Neil...*'"

Memorable nights out at the Limit, Crazy Daisy or any other venue in the city also meant the hindrance of the return journey home... in those days not always an easy ride.

Gary Peacock: "The last bus was a story on its own, there was a night bus to Brinsworth but not Rotherham and it used to go from outside the Crazy Daizy, about 1.30am I think. There was nearly always an atmosphere of violence waiting for that bus, and knowing that we had to walk from Brinny through Canklow into town and onto our homes, what excitement, used to get in at 3 and up for work at 6.30, great days though."

Tony Beesley: "Gigs at the Limit were always late ones, and the few times that I went were always late returns home. As with the other many gig journeys home, when we set off we would hardly ever have even given a second thought about how we were gonna get back to Rawmarsh. The options were either a whip round for a taxi as far as we could afford or the long trek home by foot: which would be almost certain after a night out at the Limit. Numerous times a gang of us have walked the twelve miles or so from Sheffield to Rawmarsh, risking the taunts, abuse and chase from the various anti-Punk factions on the way."

Murray Fenton: "We used to go to the Limit with 20p in our pockets, would you believe? 2p bus fare to get there and 18p back as it was the late bus and they charged double the adult fare. Can you imagine going out with 20p in your pocket nowadays."

Phil Singleton: (Left) "One incident sticks firmly in my mind, a pre-gig brawl between Sheffield and Lincoln skins at a Peter and the Test Tube Babies show at The Limit Club in 1986. The DJ was running through his Punk catalogue, when 'Holiday in Cambodia' came blaring out of the speakers. The dance floor suddenly filled. At first I thought 'This song is popular!' Then they started kicking the shit out of each other! I was sat at a table next to the dance floor at the far end to the stage, (not far from the door if I remember). I held onto my beer trying not to catch anyone's eye! I'll never forget, a bouncer had two of them in headlocks - one under each arm - and he charged at them head first through the doors! I thought someone might get killed! I remember Peter laughing it off when they came on stage. *'I believe there's been some trouble tonight.'* At the end of the show I bought a copy of the Test Tube Babies single Banned from the Pubs and got Peter to sign it. I think it was at this gig when a bloke proposed to his girlfriend and she said NO!"

The sounds of Punk Rock at the Limit were always in the mix on the dancefloor: even a Saturday night club special for the divas and groovers would also throw in more than a few Punk classics... but other ingredients were entering the melting pot right from the club's inception. Always well recognised for its leaning towards Electro and the local proprietors of that style, the club also gave a welcoming invitation to most cutting edge and new untapped music and styles throughout the whole of the 80's. As a result the clientele could, on a average night, consist of the obligatory Punk spin-offs, Goths, Indie kids, Psychobillys, Rockers, Rastas, casuals and clubbers that preferred the down to earth freedom of the Limit's dark depths than the stifling fascism of the average City centre fashion orientated clubs. In truth, once entering the Limit, you could be relaxed in the knowledge that you could just be yourself with all pretences otherwise left alone. In 1987, afternoon break-dancing sessions were held in the afternoons with DJ Mongoose and others providing the thumping bass sounds that could be heard booming along West Street... If there was a need for providing an outlet to showcase anything new on the scene... then The Limit was always on the ball in accommodating it!

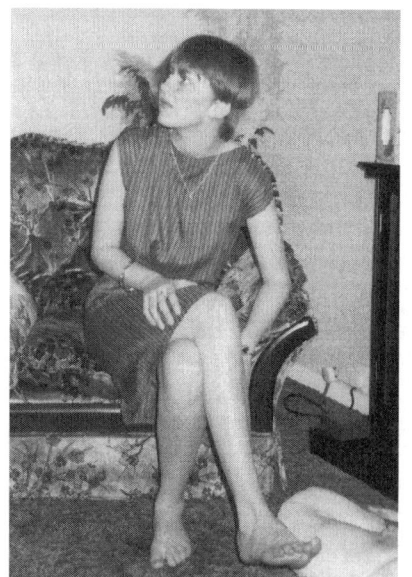

Rotherham New Romantic and ex-Punk fan Tracy Stanley was seeing out the last days of Futurism in 1982 – 83, though her futuristic travels never transported her to the Limit.

Left: Tracy Stanley searching for a visage!

Tracy Stanley: (Rotherham New Romantic) "I never went to the Limit or the Crazy Daizy though my boyfriend at the time Pete used to go: I went to Charades at the stag roundabout and Tiffany's in Rotherham for the New Romantic nights (very cool). We also went to gigs at Sheffield City Hall and the Lyceum and followed a local band called Spiral Vision and then My Pierrot Dolls. I was listening to Simple Minds, Duran Duran, Human League, Ultravox (saw all these live) also loved Japan, Visage, A Flock of seagulls - the list could go on and on and I still enjoy their music.

"It was a brilliant time in music as everyone really went to town with extravagant hair, make-up and clothes (even the lads). Personally I preferred it to punk as the atmosphere when going out wasn't at all threatening and I never got chased by gangs of skinheads like I did when I was into punk, all people wanted to do was dance and pose which suited me down to the ground."

Gary Stables: "Towards the middle of the eighties myself and my mate Sam were getting into bands such as Hanoi Rocks, Cherry Bombs, and Motley Crue: more Glam Punky stuff as apposed to the newer Punk bands as Exploited etc or as Tony puts it Toy Punks. I thought Punk had lost its way a little bit by then and was becoming a bit stale; it was all shout and play as loud and as fast as you can."

It was no easy thing, trying to follow up the excitement of the Punk years; the mid 80's and onwards presented many variations of the original source, but none as captivating as the sounds of a few years earlier!

The colour of the 80's may have been of a sickly garish blend of Day-Glo – but the heart of the decade was devoid of much of the passion or the raw creativity of the years during and immediately following Punk!

Whilst never turning his back on Punk and much of its musical counterparts, Rotherham Punk fan and idealist Richard Chatterton had soon began to look beyond the three-chord metallic thrash (one chord for some) run of the mill Punk. The effect that Punk had on Richard reached out much further than the appeal of Punk's shock and outrage tactics. His story actually began back at the start of our generation's story... but clearly continued with much displays of Punk intent and a nod to the future. As the 1980's were progressing, the future being faced looked more than a little shallow, false and matched with a political bite that managed to sting much of the working class.

Richard Chatterton: "The national music scene was beginning to go downhill at this point. The Human League, OMD, Dead or Alive, Ultravox, Depeche Mode, the Cure and even early Punk rockers Adam and the Ants were among the groups who had 'gone commercial' and *sold out* in my eyes and lost their earlier buzz. Much later, I read a quote from Rick Wakeman... a man much maligned by the Punks for being responsible for a lot of the mind-numbing solos of the pre-Punk Prog-Rock scene, which the new wave did its best to destroy. He said that whereas the Punks did virtually put an end to the self-indulgent meanderings of ELP, Yes and Genesis – the result was that after Punk they were simply replaced by the musical dross of Kajagoogoo, Haircut 100, Howard Jones and Duran Duran, bands who had been signed on the basis of haircuts. Sheffield's own Comsat Angels were told to sound like U2 who, despite having talent, were to become as bloated a millionaire super group as Rick Wakeman was ever part of. I never liked or trusted U2 much, nor the Police either - another band who rode on the coat-tails of Punk to gain stadium success."

Richard's restless Punk spirit led him to have a go at spinning some tunes and a return to his old Punk haunt of Chesterfield.

Richard Chatterton: "I delved too into the dee-jaying and club scene – although this stint was also as brief as my foray into publishing but did last a little longer than my rock star career.

After being asked by Steve (who I had met at the Fusion nightclub) to help out at a Punk 'do' at the Chesterfield Conservative Club, I spun the discs in between local bands the Chaos Brothers and Footrot. Deejaying was hard and tiring but I just about pulled it off. A couple of big Skinheads leaning on my deck were very helpful in advising me what to play near the end – the Jam the Jam the Jam the Jam then Skinhead Moonstomp for the finale. Though I didn't seem to have much choice in this I was lucky in that I had these records and everyone went home happy including myself.

"Later I was with pal Macky trying out a night at a club in Rotherham. The night wasn't the best night – on a Monday I think and despite our best efforts (a coach even came over from Sheffield but was only three quarters full) I decided not to do it again. I seemed to spend most of my time sat on the door missing all the fun – while Macky just played the stuff he was into at that moment which was mostly was neither danceable nor familiar with most of those inside. Fields of the Nephilim, Gene Loves Jezebel and Play Dead were only household names in the darkest houses but at least, again, we had given it a go. I wasn't going to be the Post-Punk version of Peter Stringfellow. Finally doomed to the trashcan was my radio career. I had been given the chance to present an hour long show on a local pirate radio station with buddy Russell and we eagerly planned our play list and chat but the two lads presenting the week before scuppered the pirate after making an offensive joke on air. 'What's pink and hangs out yer trousers?' was the clean part of the gag. The cops shut down the show and confiscated all the equipment.

"In the years 82-85 I did get to see some great bands – Aztec Camera, Monochrome Set, Killing Joke, Dance Society, Southern Death Cult, Spear of Destiny, Sex Gang Children, Gun Club, Bauhaus, Siouxsie and the Banshees, the Sisters of Mercy, Aswad, guitar legend Bo Diddley and Iggy Pop. I was not averse to seeing the raw Punk and Rockabilly bands such as the UK Subs and the Meteors although I preferred the more melodic and/or politically aware Crass, New Model Army, Flux of Pink Indians, Poison Girls and Rubella Ballet (my mate Mark Adams from Chesterfield had recently joined them as bassist.)."

As mentioned in Our Generation volume 1, Richard upped sticks and moved to Sunderland in the early 80's to study – and enjoy football, painting and music!

Richard Chatterton: "One bonus of being in the North East was that it was the home of the Channel 4 music show 'The Tube' and every Friday there was a stream of Mackems across the Tyne. I never got to go but would see some of my friends in the audience every week – Gerry, Jim Tate, Hud, and Melanie from Leicester who actually got herself a job there ushering people around. My reason for not going is that I heard that you had to pass a sort of dance audience in the later series to be part of the crowd. The real reason was that I couldn't be bothered to make the effort.

"After two years of concentrating rather too much on the football and nightlife, I decided to buck myself up. I had to as well, for I was threatened with being thrown off my course, along with quite a few others. I worked over the summer on paintings, and then concentrated on painting Futurist-influenced-football-canvases. I was regularly going to watch Sunderland FC with my mates

Russell and John Graham and I had met up with one of the first football artists in residence Chris Stevens who gave me some tips.

"On the last day I was rather sad – the Art College show was a nervous experience, standing behind the public as they criticised your work. It was perhaps the worst time so far in my life. Up till then I had been in education, I hadn't really been worried about being on the dole and then Art college had given me a chance to be who I wanted to be and do as I liked. I'd really had it now. I had no plans, didn't want to learn to be an art teacher as some of the others had resigned themselves, and hadn't applied to do a masters. I'd scraped a 2/2 and as we cleared out our stuff from our respective rooms Pete Stott, a friend from Burnley who was on the ceramics course, exclaimed '*Right. That's it. I'm gonna be a waster all my life. I just know it.*' And that was exactly how I felt, and still do to some extent!

"Back home, the music (and gigs) hadn't all slipped into lacklustre limbo. Green on Red, Long Ryders and the Cramps at the Octagon, Husker Du, Psychic TV, Suicide, the Men They Couldn't Hang, Big Audio Dynamite, the Membranes and Paul Simonon's Havana 3AM at the Leadmill, PIL, Lloyd Cole and the Cocteau Twins at the City Hall. But the culture wasn't the same. I didn't know what I wanted from the eighties – thought provoking music in the mainstream, a fairer society, the downfall of Thatcher and consumerism, things I definitely wasn't getting."

John Quinn: "In my sixth-form days when I was trying to be as left-field as possible Sounds used to run a regular Obscurist Chart, which featured bands I had never heard of and whose releases seemed only to be mail order cassettes - the likes of Prevent Forest Fires and the Ambitious Merchants. I'd read through it every time it appeared and although I never sent off for anything in it I'd occasionally drop some of the names in it to impress....er....the impressionable.

"I had planned to go to University but applied for a job as a trainee journalist with the old Morning Telegraph - and through sheer charm (not to mention talent) got it, meaning that instead of studying politics for three years in Liverpool I was now going to do a four-month journalism course in Wigan.

"I was the youngest one on the course, the only one with a mullet hairdo (they were fashionable once, honest!) and rather blotted my copybook by getting arrested for the first and only time in my life shortly after starting (drunk and disorderly: fined £25) so didn't feel very confident. However, during a break from lectures one of the other students mentioned The Fall, a subject I knew all about. We began talking and I was thrilled to find out that Paddy from Preston had actually compiled the Obscurist Chart, under a slightly altered version of his surname. Not only that, he had previously published his own fanzine and was a member of the aforementioned Ambitious Merchants as well as boss of the Apple Crumble label, one of whose releases (not music, just Tony Benn talking) had gained a five-star review from Dave McCullough, one of the gurus of post-punk journalism.

"We became friends and still are, although he was two or three years older (something that is still in dispute to this day) and just before the course ended he invited me to a party in London, which he promised would be attended by members of such prestigious bands as Doof and Twelve Cubic Feet. We stayed with his elder sister and on the Friday evening went to see an unnamed band playing in a pub in Islington containing a couple of ex-members of the dearly departed Undertones.

"The next day and before the party we headed to the Rough Trade Records shop to stock up on goodies. Paddy was pleased that his fanzine, A Breath Of Fresh Air, was on sale (I think I bought one) and we set about buying piles of the sort of stuff it was even hard to get hold of in Sheffield, let alone Preston - one of Paddy's purchases was by The Legend, another fanzine writer who he had pointed out at the concert the previous evening. It was the first release on a little label called Creation Records.

"Taking our purchases to the counter, I picked up a Membranes t-shirt, thought about buying it, then decided against it as I'd already spent enough, and I'd have to pay Paddy back anyway, as he had a credit card and I didn't. Upon getting the card back and looking at the receipt we realised that the amount he had been charged was £13.51 - about a quarter of our total spending. Our eyes met and we decided to just get outside as soon as possible. We'd got as far as the door when we heard the assistant say: *'Excuse me mate.'* Oh well, it was worth a try, we thought as we headed back to the counter. But to my surprise, the assistant handed me the Membranes t-shirt, saying *'You forgot to take this'*... Time for a quick getaway. At a nearby bus stop, we pondered how we'd been so undercharged. Then the thought hit us at the same time. It was now just after 2pm. We'd been charged the time rather than the price..."

Tony Beesley: "The mayhem of the Punk years kind of carried on with me and John: not in our dress sense - the zips and PVC was long gone by 1982 – 83 - but this was the start of our drinking lunacy days. Mod and the stylist approach was our outlook by then, but the chaos and nights of anarchic out of hand craziness still hit new heights."

John Harrison: "Tony's Mum had to put up with allsorts with us two. We would come back trollied after a night out and piss about: one night we got hold of a massive tube of talcum powder and threw it all over each other. We looked like Homepride men. We would throw food about and cause a right racket.

"Another night, after a party at our Robs, we set off back to Tony's house; on the way having a run in with a cop in his car... telling him to Fuck off! He followed us round to see if we split up. When we got there, I was that pissed I was feeling sick (them homemade pickled onions were lethal) so I set off home. A while later I was climbing up Tony's Mums drain-pipe shouting *'Let me in!'*."

The mischievous carefree attitude of the Punk years also managed to manifest itself in various swindles and moments of cheeky subversion.

Tony Beesley: "John was a swine for borrowing money off people and not paying it back. Aside from the legendary green tin escapade (see Our Generation Volume 1), he set up gambling syndicates with some of our associates. For a good while he reaped the cash in, which swiftly went behind the bar at the local boozer, but unfortunately for his paying customers, he never (or hardly ever) actually put any of the money into any chances of a gambling win. Their cash never stood a chance. I thought this was funny and would occasionally wind old John up after a few bevies and ask him, in front of his clientele, if there were any winners this week, as it was about time somebody won something. John's face used to be a fucking picture.

"John even wore a Sgt Bilko gambling plastic hat at one point and set up 'Escalado' horse racing in the front room, robbing the gullible punter(s) blind at every disposal while listening to our Mod records. And like I say, back then, it could be a task and a half in getting the three quid you borrowed him for a night out back. He led me (and others) around the trail of the Lonesome Pine many a time whilst trying to retrieve our loaned out readies.

"Another really funny thing that John did was he went for a haircut in town and upped and went half way through it being finished. That night me and Digga (a mate who was always more than fond of taking the piss) went to the pub and stood at the bar was poor old John with his hair half cut: it was long at the sides, in short and long bits all over the top and half shredded at the back: You know those laughs when your belly fucking aches like mad... well that was one of those times. As soon as we saw him, we cracked up laughing and couldn't believe the sight before us. John was as serious as fuck and I reckon he knew he had a right to be took the piss out of, but it made it even funnier that he wasn't laughing either. Digga was actually rolling around on the floor laughing. We christened it the Rupert Bop haircut and we tried to order our pints, but couldn't speak to say what we wanted. Good old John, he was and is a very funny guy. One thing is, though, he can give it, but has always been able to take it too and with that haircut it was a good job as well.

"Around this time, I had a go at my first reefer. I wasn't really that bothered to be honest. I didn't really smoke proper to start with (that habit would snare me some time later), so the appeal of a roll up the size of a needle that you had to suck like the birds eggs we used to nick when we were kids, was not much of an exciting proposition. That is, until, we had thrown enough beers down our necks up at the pub to convince us otherwise.

"One older lad we knocked about with for a while was always on the dope. One night we were in the boozer and after sticking the Jam on the jukebox and a sing-along to 'Town called Malice' followed by an hour of piss-taking out of each other and anyone in close distance of us, the beer talked us into joining this fella in his communal puff and chill routine. He rolled up his reefers right there in the pub; this was a local working men's boozer, not yer average city hove. Then he even has the cheek to light up and smoke the bleeding thing right there with Mrs Miniver and Albert Norton sat at the side of us talking about the day's weather or something!

"We eventually got banned from that particular beer stop off; twice actually but not for our antics that night. No, the sweet smell of marijuana never earned itself a single complaint from the blue rinse and flat capped 'Pint of John Smith's and a half of lager and lime please' gang. Maybe we left them 'tuned in, churned on and teeth dropped out' as we made our way out and back to my Mum's place.

"On the way, the curiosity of the cat managed to paw John into having (not his first I don't reckon) draw of the blow. At the bus stop nearby we huddled together and shared a couple of rather naughty roll ups, and the resulting giggles started to kick in. By the time, we got back to my Mums house and woke her up with our rendition of the Clash's 'Janie Jones', the pangs of late night hunger had kicked in. The answer was surely that relatively new convenience food invention – oven chips! I was so stoned by that point that I couldn't carry out the task of making our late supper. The sounds of oven trays *clanging and frozen chips flying around* were met by sounds of piss-taking laughter from the other room as I accommodated my first experience of smoking dope. The next day I felt fantastic. I had had my best sleep in years.

"You would have thought we had got stoned on one other occasion though! Me and John went through a phase of avidly listening to reggae. I had loads of cassettes of the stuff; Peter Tosh, Mighty Diamonds, Steel Pulse and loads of more obscure stuff. That summer, we would buy some bottles of cider and sit in my Mum's front room winding down to our tapes of reggae, watching it go dark outside. One late summer's night, it got colder so we put the gas fire on. We then started to slumber into a cider induced heavenly state to a soundtrack from the sounds of Jamaican dub. The ambience flowed over us and yet we were dope free. Eventually, after our state of Babylonistic coma almost began to swallow us up, something told me to wake up. I may be wrong, but I think the tape ran to the end and I woke up to proclaim *'Let's listen to the Jam's Modern World' LP John'.* As I stirred and finding myself struggling a little bit to get up, I saw that the gas fire was not even lit. *'Don't turn on the light – or light a fucking fag'* was the only words I could muster as I realised that the sweet smell engulfing the room was not Bulmer's finest but the escaping aroma of British gas. Uhhm the sound and kingdom of Jah was closer than we thought!"

Meanwhile 'class of 76' Rotherham Punk Rocker Bryan Bell had swapped Punk anthem 'God Save the Queen' for a new far more seemingly conformist vocation – 'To serve Queen and Country', though the conformism was not as stiff upper lip as it may appear to be!

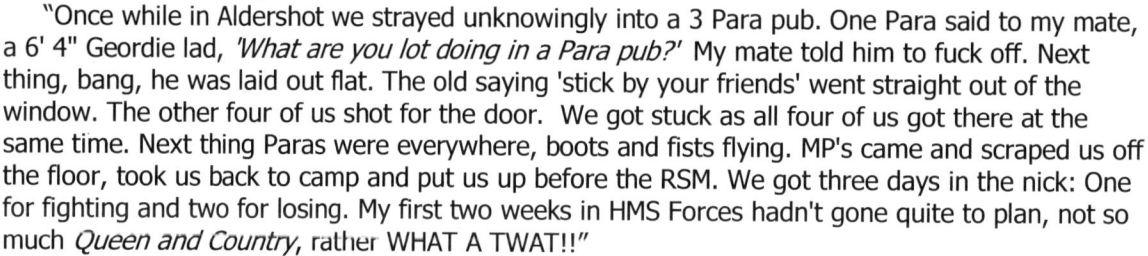

Bryan Bell: "Our first haircut we had to pay for! One lad had a No. 1 all over before he went in and still had to have it cut. Well the bed-pack of the lad in the room next to me; when the Corporal said *'What the Fuck is that?'* Instead of keeping his gob shut, he said *'Is it the content or just the general shape you don't like?'* We were two floors up, the Corporal got the bed pack, opened the window and dropped the bed pack out, and just said 'Fetch it you twat!'

"Once while in Aldershot we strayed unknowingly into a 3 Para pub. One Para said to my mate, a 6' 4" Geordie lad, *'What are you lot doing in a Para pub?'* My mate told him to fuck off. Next thing, bang, he was laid out flat. The old saying 'stick by your friends' went straight out of the window. The other four of us shot for the door. We got stuck as all four of us got there at the same time. Next thing Paras were everywhere, boots and fists flying. MP's came and scraped us off the floor, took us back to camp and put us up before the RSM. We got three days in the nick: One for fighting and two for losing. My first two weeks in HMS Forces hadn't gone quite to plan, not so much *Queen and Country*, rather WHAT A TWAT!!"

Speaking of the Queen a new band had appeared in 1983... The Smiths, led by flower in the pocket singer and poet of a generation – Morrissey, released their first single 'Hand in Glove' earlier that year and had achieved positive and excitable music press reviews. Their late 83 Top of the Pops appearance, along with early John Peel sessions caught the attention of many Post-Punk listeners waiting for something significant to come along and cut through the dross of the 1980's music scene! The band would reach their peak with their critically acclaimed 'The Queen is Dead' LP in 1986.

Andy Coles: "I first heard The Smiths on John Peel's radio show. Their initial sound was slightly reminiscent of The Byrds and in interviews, the outspoken lead singer who was known only by his surname Morrissey would enthuse wildly about 60's pop music and the 'angry young man' films of the time... 'Saturday Night and Sunday Morning', 'Billy Liar' and 'A Taste of Honey'; kitchen sink dramas that I had loved as a kid. Morrissey looked fantastic, a skinny geek unafraid to stand up for the downtrodden, in his National Health glasses and hearing aid. I bet he'd had the piss taken out of him at school like I had. Guitarist Johnny Marr played out 'jangly' delicate tunes on a Rickenbacker like Roger McGuinn. *Fantastic!* I was hooked! The first time that I heard the radio session and the opening notes to the single version of 'This Charming Man' which was a jubilant and catchy tune that still sends shivers down my spine even today. The people who were labelling the band as 'miserable' and 'depressing' were obviously missing the humour in the lyrics and the music was vibrant; taking onboard post-punk influences and stirring in a healthy dose of 60's pop. Morrissey even expressed an admiration for the New York Dolls, who had inspired the Punk scene and drummer Mike Joyce had been in punk bands The Hoax and Victim. For me, The Smiths were a breath of fresh air, miles away from the Goth scene that was becoming more and more patchouli-scented."

The Smiths by Andy Coles

Tony Beesley: "It was the classic music fans scenario: I caught the Smiths on Top of the Pops with 'This Charming Man' late 83 and was won over. They were the first new band that had come along since the demise of the Punk after-shock that did anything for me and left a lasting impression. I consequently bought all of their records for the next year or so, but sadly never went to see them play live. I was too busy active in forming my own band to get to that many gigs at that time; much to my later regret as far as some bands are concerned. To be honest though, I did eventually get tired and bored with the doom and gloom of Morrissey's lyrics and he became a kind of clichéd studenty name to drop in my opinion: once again... time to move on!"

Nigel Lockwood: "1983 saw the emergence of the mighty Smiths: I bought 'This Charming Man' on release although I didn't see them play live until 1985 at the City Hall, on their 'Meat is Murder tour', and at Manchester Palace Theatre the following week. I recall the P.A. during the interval, after James had supported, was all Buzzcocks, so it was all Manchester orientated. The Manchester gig was a triumph, opening with 'William It Was Really Nothing', and encoring with 'Heaven Knows I'm Miserable Now'...At another gig at Preston Guildhall, in 1986, they came on late, straight into 'The Queen Is Dead', then Morrissey got hit on the head with a coin, went off and that was it ..."

Anon: "My music had sort of fell by the wayside but then I heard The Smiths and was hooked. I went to see them on the 'Meat Is Murder' tour and we were down the front along with loads of lasses shrieking at Johnny Marr! I looked like a cross between him and Morrissey but without the flowers in me back pocket! I had a girlfriend's brooch on and a killer quiff held up with Harmony hairspray! It was that stiff that you could go to bed and wake up looking exactly the same. It was a great gig though. I'd got the album 'Meat is Murder' and turned veggie for 2 years. I was an impressionable youth! Bacon sarnies lured me back I'm afraid."

The Smiths may have been the next big thing and gathering their music press applause and front covers, but Punk's greatest rock n' roll band were to gain a few more front covers before their flame was to completely burn to a flickering match-light. The Clash, like the Smiths, may have influenced the resisting of meat consuming for a minority of fans, but their next move would gain both front cover headlines and more than an element of shock for Clash City Rockers far and wide!

Tony Beesley: "I really couldn't believe it. I can clearly remember that day: I was on the way to the dentist and picked up Sounds magazine. Mick Jones sacked! I thought - is someone having a joke or something? It was so hard to believe it. We had only recently lost The Jam and now to kick Mick Jones out of The Clash. That really did truly signify the end of the Punk era for me."

The Clash guitarist's dismissal served to present an opportunity of a Clash fan's lifetime for one Sheffield musician... the outcome being a much more honourable and fitting one – in the end.

Murray Fenton: "AND SO... THE CLASH! ...I made my fortnightly bus journey up to Chapeltown DHSS office to sign on one September morning and made my regular stop-off to read the Sounds and NME. On seeing the front cover of Sounds, I was filled with horror....

The CLASH HAD SACKED MICK JONES! I was stunned!! HOW COULD THEY!!! I walked back to Ecclesfield in disbelief. My grief soon turned to plotting.....

"Having spent most of my teens with a guitar around my neck, relentlessly learning just about every song from every album I owned from the Punk era, I had become quite an accomplished player. I had fronted my own pseudo-Clash (oh OK, 'wannabe' Clash ha-ha) band called Megalomania, so I recorded some demos, using a studio belonging to An Ordered Life and duly posted a cassette tape and letter to Kosmo Vinyl, the bands manager at the time. Then one day out of the blue his PA rang me and invited me for an audition at the Electric Ballroom in London!! So off we set, 6am, almost a family day out in my sisters' boyfriend's green Ford Cortina estate.

"When I arrived, expecting to be greeted by the band or their entourage and spending my day bashing out a few hours of classics, I was met with what appeared to be every guitarist in London queuing down the street. The band had placed an open audition ad in Melody Maker – I'm pretty sure every guitarist under 35 in the city was there! The audition was a roll-on/roll-off, performing to two backing tracks. One was a kind of funky thing, the other more London Callingesque rock. I sat and watched people try-out for about an hour...The funniest one I can still see to this day was a manicured-perm haired young lad in spandex get up and in the intro to the first tune, began wailing and squeaking, two-handed tapping, dive-bombs the lot... in about ten seconds he managed to cram all his trickery in... and they just cut the track and said 'NEXT!'... extremely accomplished for his age and really the birth of all that modern flash guitar playing but as you'd imagine, totally the wrong man for the job.

"Eventually I made my way to the front and having had my name ticked on a list, made my way to the stage. It all seemed to go so fast but I played for a lot longer than most people seemed to – the full 90 seconds or so of each of the backing tracks and when I'd finished I was summoned over to a table in the corner. The whole day had been an exciting experience but as I approached them I realised I was going to speak to Bernie Rhodes and Caroline Coon. They congratulated me on my performance and I apparently made the shortlist of people before receiving a phone call a couple of weeks later to say I hadn't got the job and good luck. That was six weeks later and that night, having gone out to drown my sorrows; I was approached by a heavily bearded man in a duffle coat with the hood up, in the Limit Club in Sheffield. The incognito duffle coated man was Mark Gouldthorpe and that night I joined Artery!"

The next year, 1984, a revamped Clash - with original members Joe Strummer and Paul Simonon being joined with Vince White, Nick Sheppard and Pete Howard re-appeared. Joe and Paul graced the front cover of the NME for the first time in what seemed like a lifetime. The full cover interview inside featured rants from Strummer attacking the Punk bourgeoisie and everyone else he could think of whilst declaring a new Clash manifesto. Somehow these, what should have been promising (on paper at least) declarations, seemed a little tiresome and prefabricated: almost sounding like a premeditated political programme. For the first time in their career the world's finest rock n roll band were starting to sound ideologically spent and more than a little desperate. The Bernie Rhodes influence was also back on board it appeared.

Tony Beesley: "Of course, I still loved the Clash (trying desperately to get over the loss of Jonesy still)...how could I not? They had been such an important part of my life. I was fanatical about the band, but after the initial excitement of reading that feature, I was worried! Here was a band so important to us all - our whole Punk generation - and now they were in a corner having only the weapon of lashing out at their contemporaries at their disposal: there wasn't even any new-recorded material available either. A few months later, they were doing the rounds busking in Leeds and other cities, which I respected as a brave move, assertive proof that they were still close to their roots and their fans. Unfortunately, by that point, there was no turning back: The Clash were past it. Their time had been and gone. If only they hadn't had to record the abysmal 'Cut the Crap' LP to prove it!"

Brian Houghton: "I was more than a bit nonplussed really. Didn't understand why and couldn't see much point in the ranting interview in the NME at the time. Ambivalent and positively underwhelmed!"

Richard Chatterton: "I did miss the post-Mick Jones Clash when they turned up in Sunderland on their busking tour bar at the Mowbray Hotel, the Drum Club. They drank in the nearby Salem pub and played in the Bunker and the Carlton bar, which was basically the Art college bar. One of the band, Vic Sheppard, had a brother who was in the first year and they all crashed at his place, according to a girl who shared the house, and also a very cramped studio space in a corridor, with me and another guy. I was so upset at missing all this."

The Punk days of seeing the likes of The Clash at the Top Rank in 1977 seemed a lifetime away for first wave Punk fan Tony Cronshaw in 1984: but the euphoria soon returned on a trip to see the Clash – this time minus two in their ranks.

Antony Cronshaw: (Sheffield Punk/Skinhead) "I had thought that my gig going days were well behind me as we entered 1984, I'd married Christine some six months earlier and to earn a living I was selling my soul most weekends entertaining the good people of Sheffield as a mobile DJ, weddings and anniversaries but certainly not 18th birthday parties, you avoided them like the plague. My only joy was doing the Old Harrow at Gleadless every Friday where I could play all my favourites, you'd get the odd ball wanting some charts, I used to love it when they'd say this isn't chart music, to which I'd reply well it was in fucking 1977. I was playing the place that some seven years previously, the DJ of the time would rarely play my records, but now I was in *complete control*. With money in short supply I had to convince Christine that a trip to Leicester was affordable, I don't know why I worried as she was 100% behind the idea.

"So off we set to the De Montford Hall to purchase our tickets, no online booking back then, we relied on our battered Ford Escort estate to get us there, some two hours later it limped off the motorway and ventured towards the city centre. With four tickets safely purchased, a kindly mechanic patched up our car for the return journey, we finally returned home some eight hours later but it had all been worth it.

"The gig was on a Sunday so at least I'd not miss out on some brilliant function; making up our numbers were Neil Tolson and Judy Dyson, we arrived in good time and the area surrounding the venue was buzzing, punks, skins and those that had moved their dress sense on, no bin liner and ripped jacket this time. Once we were in we were up in the balcony, how times had changed. The lights went down and this was it, I was on a high and this was the only drug I'd ever needed, 'London Calling' opened the set and the place exploded, Sheppard, White and Howard had replaced Jones and Headon but who cared. 'Safe European Home', 'Rock the Casbah', 'Guns of Brixton' and 'This is England' were moving the night on and we were loving every minute and I was 21 again. Next came the classic 'Police and Thieves', 'Garageland', 'Tommy Gun' and 'I Fought the Law'. I think they finished with 'White Riot' or 'Bank Robber' but I cannot really remember but on their return to the stage, it was back to 1977 with 'Janie Jones', 'Career Opportunities' and 'I'm So Bored with the U.S.A' and then it was all over. My only disappointment was that they never performed one of my favourite tracks 'White Man (In Hammersmith Palais)'. But I'm not complaining, we'd enjoyed our trip down memory lane and loved every minute."

Richard Chatterton: "My Dad called me Johnny Opposite (great name for a punk lead singer) but in the scheme of things I wasn't all that weird... just because I dyed my hair, went vegetarian and refused to watch quiz shows on TV. At this time, I was listening to Eno a lot and Bowie's Low album replaced 'London Calling' and 'Black and White' as my favourite album. An NME ad had read 'There is old wave. There is new wave. And there is David Bowie.'"

Tony Beesley: "There was almost no-one keeping the fire of Punk burning for me. I could never get into Bad Religion, Black Flag and all of the American hardcore Punk, as much as I had respect for it. One of the closest bands to touch me, in their carefree spirit at least, was the Pogues. Their fusion of Irish Folk and other diverse styles played with the frantic energy of Punk was a breath of fresh air. I saw em play in Sheffield and Shane McGowan came onstage with a pint of whiskey!! What a guy. He was pissed as hell surprise surprise!! Great fun though!"

Andy Coles: "I was into The Smiths and groups like New Order, whose sound became less gloomy and more dance orientated with each release. As much as I love The Smiths, I still think New Order's 'Blue Monday' is the best record of the 80's!"

Richard Chatterton: "It was strange how, as the music scene in Sheffield started to rise, worryingly the Sheffield steel industry was also beginning its irreversible descent. My dad's firm, Hayfields, went on strike in 1980 but by 1985 he and everyone else there were redundant and of course the mining industry was also decimated by strike, closure and Thatcher bringing the whole area to its scarred and bloody knees."

Chapter Eight
The splintered generation!

"The rest of the eighties was pretty horrible. Thatcher had defeated the miners and no one had succeeded in wrenching her from power. Big hair, big shoulder pads and big bank accounts were de rigeour and the pop charts were dominated by acts who would reflect this - tanned and shooting their videos in exotic locations" – **Richard Chatterton**

"We had Indie shoegazers, Goths, Psychobillys, scooterboys, Punk injected Hip Hop, Acid House Ravers, and the sound of Madchester: all had their merits, but as a whole our generation was, in a way lost... you could say we were the splintered generation!" – **Tony Beesley**

The decade following Punk's final demise (1985 – 1995) belonged to a whole host of Post-Punk factions and spin off genres and cults: none more so than the wide all encompassing umbrella of

what was/is loosely termed Indie. Punks generation – and the area in question here was no exception – managed to endear themselves to a vast array of musical styles and quite often the fashion and clothes that went along with them. As much as the scope and surface visibility of Punk Rock had become almost obsolete, and in many ways this period showcased inarguably some of the most bland and atrocuous music and fads to ever reach a teenager's attention, the integration and soaking up of Punks influence and idealism was spread wider and wider – some would say ever more distant – as the 80's and early 90's went on.

The year prior to Punk's ten years anniversary did see the emergence of Punk catylised Pyschedelic/Punk fused Indie hopefuls The Jesus and the Mary Chain... whose riot inducing gigs created national and music press headlines echoing the Punk spectacle of 1976. 1985 also saw the re-birth of sacked Clash pioneer Mick Jones with his new landscape of Punk/Funk meets hip hop to an Ennio Morricone film soundtrack-sampling background – Big Audio Dynamite, whilst fellow Punksters the Damned followed the path of Goth! The decade ended with a generation of ecstasy-swallowing ravers embracing Acid House, Techno and the sounds of Madchester, and in-between gave us the Beastie Boys, Sigue Sigue Sputnik, USA hardcore and its many sub-genres, Stone Roses, Paul Weller's new soul vision, the great Kevin Rowland's revised soul vision, C-30 indie guitar bands, the ever-present Gothic vision of The Cure and the mesmerising doom appeal of Morrissey and the Smiths.

Anon: "Shortly after the Punk and Oi days, I ended up getting my first job and earning some proper money, so the glistening lights of Rotherham and Sheffield club land beckoned. I was out clubbing most weekends, so my dress style changed again to made to measure soul bags from dodgy George in Rotherham market, Pod shoes from Rebina, leather box jackets and silk scarves! I ended up working in Romeo & Juliet's in Sheffield. Had some fantastic times there, it was like getting paid to be out on the piss."

King Kurt at the Leadmill (Andy Coles)

Andy Coles: "I was impressed by Punk/Rock and Roll bands like The Cramps, whose love of 50's 'schlock' was to 'night time' what The B-52's were to 'daytime', we would go and see all the so-called 'Psychobilly' bands who were starting to become popular. We went to see King Kurt at The Leadmill in Sheffield (left) and when we arrived on Leadmill Road, there was a mile-long queue of absolutely psychotic-looking blokes who, thinking we were too well turned out, began chanting 'Clean! Clean!' and chased us the full length of the road before catching us up and bombarding us with talcum powder and shaving foam. Once inside, the whole floor was covered in talc and flour. During the gig, one of the blokes with us (whose name I forget) said, with much bravado, that he was going to get to the front, climb onstage and stage dive into the crowd. Off he went, for what seemed like half an hour, as he worked his way to the front before he climbed onstage alongside the band. He then proceeded to dive backwards into the audience and...everyone moved to one side. You could hear him hit the floor above the noise of the band! Another half an hour later, he reached us at the back of The Leadmill; his skin was the colour of chalk; his stomach on the verge of vomiting."

Just around the corner from the Leadmill a political gathering being broken up was witnessed by Sheffield Punk Rocker Debra Marshall. The era of the Miners' strike was upon us... the Battle of Orgreave on June 18th 1984, times of social upheaval for many and further splintering of a whole generation and their families and friends.

Debra Marshall: "Back at the time of the Miners strike, I lived in Claywood flats above Sheffield train station. The view from there was all around the area as it over looked City Road and much more. I can remember one particular time. I could see a Arthur Scargill Miners Rally demo kind of thing going on down at the Labour club. All of a sudden the black Marias appeared and out came loads of police. From this view I could see groups of miners and police spilling all over the place. The police were charging in waves of blue lines trying to catch the fleeing miners... infact it was reminiscent of the back of the first Clash album sleeve."

Shaun Angell: "In 1984 dear old Maggie Thatcher had decided that she was going to shut the majority of pits in Britain down and do what she did with the Steel workers – put them all on the dole. Everyone knew it was just an excuse to crush the unions and fuck us northern scum up and create the North – South divide which has existed ever since.

"Despite all the problems and poverty the strike brought to the mining communities, people stuck together and the whole situation created a siege mentality, a us against them attitude. It also opened up a world of opportunities for a young 'Jack the lad' like myself! Various schemes and scams were launched to bring in much-needed cash. I worked legally for a local Fruit and Veg man and illegally at nights and weekends, robbing and thieving from various warehouses, coking plants who were operating with strike-breaking lorries (scabby cunts!) and steel stock holders. There was also a lucrative line in women's personal hygiene products which I can't possibly discuss!

Above: Punk generation miners Shaun Angell (Rusty Egan quiff 4th from left) and Pete Roddis (Front centre)

"Apart from the obvious hardships, the Miners strike in a strange sort of way, were, for the most part, the best twelve months of my life. The laughs, the cammeraderie, the friendships forged and for a twenty-something-apprentice-football-hooligan like myself, the picket-line violence was something I thrived on and got a real buzz out of.

"The music at the time was Echo and the Bunnymen, Heaven 17, Paul Weller (Council Collective being in aid of the cause – top man) and the aptly named 'Two Tribes' by Frankie goes to Hollywood. It's a generation ago since the strike and young people in the South Yorkshire by and large don't have a clue about the area's proud heritage and historical importance. They leave school, go to college for years on end or work in a fuckin' call centre talking bollocks for 8 hours a day in a building built on the site of a former pit. How ironic that the Tory Government of the time spent millions of tax payers; money to try and break the strike instead of investing in the coal industry... and then successive Labour Governments spend millions more importing coal from other countries when we've got billions of tons of the fuckin' stuff right underneath us! What's that all about!"

In the spring of 1985, nine years after the Sex Pistols had released their debut Punk anthem, 'Anarchy in the UK' the idea of anarchy almost reigned supreme at Sheffield schools Hurfield, Ashleigh, City, Waltheof, Brook and Carter Lodge with a wave of demoralised and discontented kids going on strike, walking out of classes and displaying their anger. Local anarchist groups swiftly recognised the disruption and began distributing leaflets calling for kids to smash up their classrooms! 16 youths were arrested, other pupils expelled and a local vicar hit by a flying brick. In the end, though, order was restored and the Anarchy in the UK tour still did not end up paying a lasting visit to Sheffield after all!

Goth vicar Dave Vanian of the Damned during the band's most Gothic period (Phil Chatterton)

The Damned: Punk's original pioneers of anarchy, chaos and destruction and perfecters of the art of being the first on the block to get things done, continued their fascination with all things Gothic in 1985, even having a top ten hit with a cover of Barry Ryan's 'Eloise'. Punk for the 80's was a very mixed bag and maybe it always should have been, but in becoming so diverse and out of touch with any sense of a movement at hand, the whole concept of Punk became more and more diluted and less visionary as the decade wore on!

Rotherham futuristic Goths My Pierrot Dolls were no strangers to violence and verbal abuse: lead singer Ivor had fought his way through the Punk years and then immersed himself into the glamour and cosmetics of the New Romantics – no easy feat in a South Yorkshire mining town. Following regular positive local press coverage, the band managed to make it to a Battle of the Bands contest to be held at Sheffield University: little did they, or their fans entourage, realise that the contest would end as one won with the strength of the fist and not the song!

Ivor Hillman: "Well this was the one gig that could send us on our way; the gig that would catapult us into national recognition. The band had reached the national heats of the TDK battle of the bands competition where we would battle it out with five other bands to see who would represent Yorkshire in the finals in London. I'd made a big effort to recruit everyone I could from

Dale Farm foods Rawmarsh, all my work mates and colleagues would turn out in force to cheer us on in Sheffield. The response to rallying the troops was excellent and a full coach made its way to Sheffield University - all anticipating a night of beer and music.

"We had been at the venue sound checking in the afternoon and sizing up our opposition, which included mainly Sheffield bands: one which stood out for the name alone and also for having a good reputation were the 'Flying Alphonso Brothers'. The Alphonsos were always going to be our main threat but we felt with the majority of the support we would influence the judges to send the Dolls through.

The battling Hillman brothers Ivor and Ian

"The night started and the bands took to the stage. The first couple of bands were met with little applause as only a few friends and family had made the journey to watch them. When it was our turn to take the stage the Yoghurt fans had had chance to sink more than enough liquid refreshments. All big drinkers - men and women - and all had come for a good night out; little did they expect the night would go with a real bang. After a few songs, I noticed a disturbance in the crowd and to my horror, my brother Ian was flailing arms and reining blows down on to a lad in the crowd. Suddenly it all went up. Unfortunately, for the lads from Sheffield they'd not bargained for the lads from the factory who were more akin to scrapping than the students from Sheffield. Terry Milns, who loved to body build, was hitting one by one and they fell like flies. Terry was aided by two other nutters Tommy Graham and Melv Goulty, they too took no prisoners. Eventually it was left to me while the rest of the band cowered backstage to plea for peace. That night the gang from the factory returned home triumphantly, we were disqualified from the competition and the next day the saga hit the headlines.

"The actual story in the Sheffield Star read as follows: An outing from a South Yorkshire yoghurt factory turned sour when rival fans clashed at a Sheffield pop contest. A coach load of music lovers from Dale Farm Foods, Rawmarsh, travelled to Sheffield University to support local heroes, My Pierrot Dolls in a Battle of the Bands contest. But the heat of the national competition – ran by a well-known cassette company – ended in violence as fans fought in the University's Concert Hall. Today the group's singer Ivor Hillman, who leapt on to the stage to make a peace plea, said, *"It wasn't our supporters who started it: it was a group of lads at the front who were heckling me and calling me a poof when I was singing. My fans were merely protecting my good name."*

"When we weren't placed," Ivor continued, *"it was the last straw for our supporters who were already very angry. I think they took the defeat worse than the band did."* *"There are a few bruised knuckles at the factory this morning.",* laughed Ivor, who, as well as fronting the band, works at the Dale Farm Foods factory."

Another battle was taking place for the author: a cross-roads period where the genres of Punk and Mod, and everything else inbetween, were pulling him in all directions during a very confusing period of music and its culture.

Tony Beesley: "The buzz was still on for what Mick Jones of the Clash would get up to after being ousted from the Clash. I remember buying the first Big Audio Dynamite LP as it was released and being excited about it. I think I got it for Xmas 1985 along with the first and only LP from Big Sound Authority.

"At the time, I was going through my journey out of the narrow-minded end of the Mod scene, having just split with The Way and being pissed off with the sheep-like mentality of certain elements of the Mod crowd. I was just as open minded about the B.A.D LP as I was with the new records from bands such as The Scene (great single 'Something That You Said' though!). I always thought that the whole idea of being a Mod, as well as the obvious obligatary love of black music etc, was to be open minded and look forward as well. Ok, at the time there was not that much to be found that was worth bothering with, but there was stuff out there if you looked hard enough. I kind of took all the best of what I had soaked up from Mod from the last few years, which always remained with me from that point, but also kept a listening ear for anything else interesting. I suppose I came out of the Punk ideoligy too much to be totally tied to the past. Ironically, I soon became obsessed with Sixties Soul and R&B even more obsessively as the years passed."

1986 and the year of celebrating 10 years since UK Punk's inception was upon us and how soon it all seemed! The NME joined in with a 3 part special series, one of which saw John Lydon on the front cover (as well as kids' pop mag Smash Hits). Over at Left Field TV Company Channel 4, there was the 'Way We Were' programme- which was a very entertaining and worthwhile compilation of the best of the Granada TV Punk-showcasing series 'So it goes' series.

The national charts were crap and one of the closest sounds in the charts to Punk was the Buzzcocks-like pop sensibilities of the Housemartins. One ex member of local Mod band The Way recounts a Housemartins related tale...

John Harrison: (Right) "At the Octagon centre, me and Terry (Sutton) went along to see the Housemartins. This was at the time just after Tony Beesley had left The Way. Terry had rung me up while I was in a local pub in Rawmarsh called the Monkwood (ironically the very place where Tony and I had formed one of the very earliest incarnations some years earlier). Terry says *'John, we want you to come back and join the band*! to which I replied *'But I have flogged my guitar!* I rejoined anyway and we did a new Demo tape of new songs that Terry had written. Not long after we were very close to getting a record deal. What happened was we had sent a demo tape to Go Discs record label and it looked like it was between us and the Proclaimers who got signed up. This record label bloke said it was a toss up who were getting signed. We lost out and they got signed up instead!

"Back to the Octagon Housemartins gig: we had free tickets with passes because of the Go Discs connection and we went up and spent all afternoon up there. We were talking to Hugh Whitaker of the band - he was sat there making tea and toast - in the venue. The irony of it all is at the gig the support group were the Proclaimers. The gig was great and both bands were too.

Norman Cook (Fatboy Slim) made a few mess ups on the bass. No one had heard of the Proclaimers back then. As far as I remember, that's how it all went. Regarding the near miss sign up - when I went and told my mum she was terrified cos of all the drugs etc and had visions that I would end up on heroin or something. Who knows...Maybe it wasn't meant to happen."

The Way mark II, went into the studio to record their brand of Politico Pop-tinged with Soul resulting in a classy four-track Demo tape: 'War Hero' echoing the Jam's 'Strange Town' riff with the swagger of Stiff Little Fingers, whilst 'I Won't Give In' showed a new direction with the addition of a brass section and a distinct Redskins influence. Gigs came locally at Mod nights at the Assembly Rooms, amongst others, and a trip down to the smoke followed with an interview with the Morning Star. Original member John Harrison's replacement Jon White's joining also coincided with a change of direction for the band, with new songs and opportunities arriving!

Ian Deakin: "Jon White (AKA Stan, Whitey, Joby) was a breath of fresh air.Totally different. Musically, always pushing to try something more complex. We'd never seen anything like it because he could do all that Mark King slapping shit but far more aggressive which suited our new 'punk-funk' sound."

Terry Sutton: "And at that point things stepped up in terms of the gigs we played, our public profile (i.e. we seemed to be in the papers all the time) and attention from the industry. I put it down to the band rehearsing three days a week. We got really tight and the brass section got better with every gig. Phil Jupitus was the first to get any kind of ball rolling for us regarding getting outside the local scene. Peter Jenner was next to help and he got us our first, admittedly shitty, gigs but they helped us get on the bill at the Alexandra Palace for the USSR 70th anniversary celebrations (which had the added bonus of having a genuine IRA bomber spending the night in our hotel room! We weren't arguing). Then we were onstage with David Blunkett the night before the General Election in '87 (I don't think his dog liked us). Then we headlined the National Anti-Apartheid Conference in Sheffield. I was very proud to be asked to do that and got to meet Oliver Tambo (future South African president)! Soon after we got a great review in the NME, despite us having a bust up with Steven Wells and played some dates with his old mate, Attilla The Stockbroker (who dedicated his live album to us!).The following year saw us play with New Model Army at their Bradford homcoming gig, the Mayday gig on The Moor bandstand with John Prescott, the Rock Against The Rich Tour with Joe Strummer and a very special gig in Rotherham with John Cooper Clarke, a very young Steve Coogan, Tony Capstick and some other Rotherham bands including 'Spring Heel'd Jack' and 'Phil Murray and the Boys From Bury'. It was at this gig that I was approached by SHJ's pianist, Simon Cardie, and found we got on rather well. I wasn't aware what great friends we'd become later on. Out of all the memories of gigging, I suppose the Strummer gig has to be the highlight of my career. I spent pretty much the whole weekend in his entourage but being alone with him backstage in Brodsworth was something I'll take to the grave."

Ian Deakin: "Yes, when I found out we were supporting him I was so nervous but excited to be doing the gig. I know Tel had said many times how much he liked Simon as a musician so a move was now definitely on the cards though it didn't happen for a few months till he'd wormed his way out of Spring Heel'd Jack. I know that, for me, around this time, we played one of our best gigs, at the Mean Fiddler in Harlesden. We brought a full coach-load and were playing with Morrissey's 'fave new band', 'Bradford'. We blew them away.

"Around the end of 1988 Tel had the audacity to phone Weller's Respond offices and asked a bloke called Kenny Wheeler about whether Tracie was available. He told me to send the new recordings and that he would pass them on. Well, we all thought he was crackers but about two weeks later Tracie was on the phone raving about a song called 'I Just Don't Know'."

Terry Sutton: "We'd been in Fairview Studios in Hull earlier that year with Mond Cowie from the Angelic Upstarts producing. It was weird actually. He stayed at my mum's in the same bedroom as me for a whole week. I'd wake up in the morning and Mond would be there with his eyes already open. The freak. I'd love to see him again. Top man. But he delivered the goods for us and we were actually getting invited to meet A&R men at EMI Manchester Square. I went for lunch with Go Discs Head, Andy MacDonald, and The Boy Jupitus to discuss signing but I scared him with all my talk of 'total artistic control'. That's the one thing I've never waivered from; why I've never had 'a deal'; too stubborn for my own good."

PHOTOS: KARL LANG

Above: The Way – Jon White, Tracie Young, Simon Cardie, Ian Deakin and Terry Sutton line up.

The girl next-door beauty and charm of Tracie Young had first been recognised by Paul Weller, earning her a spot on Top of the Pops with the Jam for their final appearance on the show with 'Beat Surrender'. The following year saw Tracie join in with Paul's new Style Council collective on debut 45 'Speak like a child', a hit with 'The House that Jack built' and a run of quality Pop/Soul singles and a criminally under-rated album (recently re-released) 'Far from the Hurting kind'.

Ian Deakin: "So... we went to meet with Tracie in London. We'd had a female American manager - but that didn't work out - and we got landed with these two dicks from Today newspaper for management. Tracie met us outside the Albert Hall and we had a photo shoot right there - even though we'd never met! Anyway, we went for lunch and got on wonderfully."

Terry Sutton: "Thing is, I used to fancy her so much - especially when she was with The Jam on Top of the Pops - that I had to be totally professional and repress any sexual urges I might have had. Once I went to stay at her place in Chelmsford to work out our vocals and we went out for a drink afterwards. We were pissed when we got back and Tracie went and put Teddy Pendergrass on the stereo. Make out music. How I stopped myself from making a move I'll never know. I'm usually such a pushover for such blatant seduction techniques. Our last gig as 'The Way' was at the Hull Adelphi. It was the best gig we ever played musically. A ten-piece band that night. We didn't know it was the end but soon after I began to get feverous about film and acting and had decided to go to University."

Ian Deakin: "The last time we saw each other for a long time was at a party for Jon's sister's birthday. It was a grrrr-eat night which we still have an hour-long dvd of. It's incredibly funny cos Tel has the most exciting perm."

Terry Sutton: "The last shot is of Ian going for the bus in the morning, disappearing into the distance. It's always been a pretty poignant shot for me because I wouldn't see Ian for the best part of seven years bar the odd occasion like his wedding."

The Way's recorded legacy consisted of a number of Demo tapes and live recordings. Amongst these offerings, were a 4 track tape recorded in 1987 with a more brassy sound and yet more rousing political fighting talk with 'Stand Up and Fight', whilst 'England's Glory' saw the ghost of Weller's long-standing influence laid to rest. With a tune not entirely dissimilar to The Jam's 'Just Who Is The 5' O'clock Hero', 'England's Glory' is quality Blue-eyed Soul with a Tamla feel. They then went on to record and create more quality songs such as 'I Just Don't Know'. The songs produced within this period all deserved to have had official releases: it's a shame they were recorded at a time when the average music fan was more interested in the crap that was being fed to them by the music press and charts of the day. A different time and place, maybe a few years back or forth, and the status of the finest Mod band to come out of South Yorkshire may have been somewhat different. Maybe if The Way had carried on a little longer they may have truly made their mark; but the world wasn't listening quite enough! Shame on it too!

Ian Deakin (Right) continued with his love of music and playing drums. His tastes soaked up some of the more contemporary Punk influenced sounds of bands like New Model Army who served up Punk on a crusty template; the new Hip Hop, film soundtrack sampling post-Clash ensemble of Mick Jones's Big Audio Dynamite as well as the Wedding Present and the Pogues. Ian also joined Dave Spencer's Spring Heel'd Jack, but his days with Terry were not really over for good - as the future would indicate some years later!

The mid to late 80's were often a disparate and unsatisfying time for our generation's members.

Pete Skidmore: "I can't remember buying any records whatsoever in this period apart from the Beastie Boys' album and Style Council records although they got played once and put to one side. We went for our first mortgage in 1988 and shortly after bought our first house, music was forgotten about and all my records were left at my parents' house. The Mod scene I had been into was still going and looking back now I wished I had kept up with it all."

It may have been 1986 and ten years since Punk, but its impact, idealistically at least, was still prevalent.

Tony Beesley: "The Do it yourself optimism of Punk influenced me to start my own fanzine in 1986 (the year I got my very first VHS player, a huge top loader thing on rental, complete with dog hairs wrapped inside it!). I had already had a crack at fanzines before, but now I felt I had to get the job done proper. I ran my fanzine 'Populist Blues' between the summer to winter of 86 and enjoyed the experience of creating it. I would bang the words out on an ancient typewriter that hardly printed and had some letters missing from it, leading to me adding them individually by pen, and glued photos and artwork in place. Then, I took the end result to Ratcliffe's printers in Rotherham Town centre and got whole stacks of them printed out. They must have thought I was mad. I did my own distribution and publicising, taking copies to record shops, guitar shops, gigs, mates' houses, the pub and even the 1986 Rotherham show. The fanzine was amateurish, thrown together with crap equipment, but it was my own invention. It was a failed adventure ultimately, but carve it down to experience. I don't regret my attempts at doing that sort of thing. If you don't try you never know? Populist Blues fanzine ran for four issues in 1986 and a *Punk ten years on* special issue."

Richard Chatterton: "For my fanzine I interviewed a pre-stardom Pulp in the Sheffield Hallamshire Pub which was full of jeering Glaswegian miners down for a miners strike rally. During the Pulp interview my friend Darren asked what Jarvis would do when he was famous. I thought that an extremely pointless question as that was never going to happen."

The Fanzine writing may have been influenced by the idealism of Punk, but the sound of the suburbs was long gone and temporarily forgotten for a period of time during the 80's.

Tony Beesley: "In the mid 80's, I was going through my big 'Weller' influenced Soul Boy period. I was amassing boxes and boxes of Soul 45's from the sixties gritty R&B sounds through to the 70's Stax and looser Soul stuff, Chairmen of the Board...also quite a lot of Funk like Beginning of the End's Funky Nassau, Sly Stone, Parliament, some Billy Preston and contemporary 45's from

Black Britain etc. I knew all the decent record shops. In Sheffield there was Record Collector in Broomhill, Amazing Records, Spin City run by Northern Soul connoisseur Andy in the Castle Market and later on Fon records, Warp, Jacks records. Rotherham had Backtrack records run by another Northern Soul face and DJ Snowy (who I got to know quite well due to spending lots of time and cash in there), Circles (10p Indie singles on a Saturday afternoon), Revolver (later K and D), as well as a few 'here one minute and the next they're gone' record shop ventures.

"The best place for second hand records in the mid to late 80's in Rotherham though had to be the Wednesday antique market: that was an absolute goldmine... Small Faces 'Patterns'/ 'E to D' on Decca, The Action 'Baby you've got it' on Parlophone, Willie Mitchell singles and loads of fantastic Soul and Mod 45's usually for well under a quid. One of my Mod mates Ridgy even managed to get 'Shimmy Shimmy Coco Bop' by Chicago Line on CBS from one of the stalls... he later sold it, but at least he had it.

"The lure of finding that rare Mod/Soul/R&B 45 was addictive as well as trying to keep up with anything interesting coming out at the time (few and far between as the decade progressed); along with the gradually increasing Record fairs starting to appear at the Leadmill, Polytechnic and town hall, the capture of interesting vinyl to add to the collection was a weekly ritual. Trips to the coast would also result in visiting down the back street record shops – Smugglers in Bridlington, 2 decent ones in Skeggy (I finally tracked down Manfred Mann's 'Up the Junction' soundtrack for a couple of quid in one of em) and a superb second-hand record shop in Scarborough run by some bikers/rockers where you had to climb up ladders to get a box of requested singles down... Most of my blue label Stax singles came from there. As for the chain stores? Forget em... Virgin was never the same in Sheffield since relocating from the bottom of the Moor to the top of the city centre:

though they did have a US issue of 'The Who Sings My Generation' LP in there. The Punk Day-Glo coloured vinyl of a few years previously, though, was now turning up at the record fairs for - to start with - cheap prices: but for a while the interest in our most rebellious pop culture era seemed to have all but disappeared, only the attitude remaining intact!"

It may have still been music that sound-tracked Shaun Angell's lifestyle, but it wasn't records that he went hunting down when a visit to Costa del Blackpool coincided with some scouser shop training!

Shaun Angell: "Dead or Alive, Echo and the Bunnymen - both Liverpool groups: these scouse bands, in my humble opinion, were the business at the time. Whilst on a weekend jolly to Blackpool, me and some mates met up with some Liverpudlians who introduced us to the fine art of thieving from sports shops to obtain all the latest designer gear like BJ Fila tracksuits, Fred Perrys, Dunlop green flash and Adidas Stan Smith trainers. Friendships were formed that last to this day and many a good night was had in Liverpool's 'The State' nightclub and Sheffield's cult venue The Limit."

The golden era of *Punk* was back on the cards again for some Punk loving fans.

Anon: "I would meet up with some old mates and got going to gigs again. I saw the always-brilliant 999 at Retford Porterhouse a couple of times and in Leeds. Also the Ramones in Leeds and loads of bands at the Leadmill, including Sigue Sigue Sputnik, Husker Dü, Redskins, Gene Loves Jezebel and many others. We used to sleep out most of the time and spent some right cold nights on the street. We were once cabin hopping in Doncaster station and ran across the lines to get to another cabin and away from the guards, when this guy popped up from nowhere and called us *'bloody idiots'* for doing it. I said *'its ok mister, we all looked both ways first'* and every body just cracked up. The guy shook his head and wandered off muttering that we were *'stupid and not funny'*. At least the laughter kept us a bit warmer! Once at Retford Porterhouse we were going mental to 999 when one of those big ceiling tiles got punched out of the roof and landed on yours truly's head! I had a right headache, I tell you! Least it gave everyone summat to laugh at again, it always seemed to be at my expense, though! I've always been a bit of a clown, I guess I'll never grow up but that's not a bad thing in my opinion."

Tony Beesley: "Realistically, on the surface, most of the 80's were atrocious for contemporary pop music. The alternatives were the Smiths (who I quickly tired of), Spear of Destiny, Pogues, Weller, some of the Indie scene bands and the odd Punk stalwart coming up with something decent now and again. Some of those that never made it too... Blue Ox Babes, Armoury Show and a great solo outing from Stiff Little Finger Jake Burns and the Big Wheel with 'Breathless'. Even some of the best stuff that came out, though, still had that horrible over-produced sound and feel to them. There was some good pop music knocking around, but you had to really search through the dross to find it. I suppose it's always been like that: Still you can't help but blame the 80's for being the crassest decade for pop music - and fashion. Thank God I never had a bastard mullet - though I knew some poor fuckers who did!"

Thankfully, there was an alternative to the dire 80's Pop production line: and the music and bands of any worth usually had some link to the original Punk scene. A visit back to Manchester, the scene of a few old Punk memories for one local music fan, was just as colourful and hard edged as always.

Anon: "I then got into Spear of Destiny and me and Stewie (Kerr) used to go and see them all over, kipping out as usual. We used to get on the guest list quite often. I'd met Kirk Brandon when

Theatre of Hate supported The Clash and he seemed a genuine and friendly guy. We once went to Manchester to see them at the Apollo and had a few drinks and experiences in the city centre. We went in a Yates's bar and two women of about 70 were fighting over a bloke of about 80 who'd put his false teeth on the table to watch the fight! I was tempted to lift 'em but thought better of it. We than wandered into China town and went in this pub with 100 year old Chinese men in it just playing mah-jong and smoking yellow fags, not drinking. We then went into what we realized afterwards was a gay bar. Bear in mind this was 1986 and we were straight teenagers. It was just before last orders in the afternoon and someone had told us they would do after hours so we thought we'd stop but I had an odd feeling and told Stewie we should go.

"Maybe it was because all the walls had posters of Rock Hudson, James Dean and the like on them and all the guys (there were no women) had handlebar moustaches. As we left the bouncers (yes, they had bouncers on in the daytime) shouted after us *'don't you want to stay boys?'* We ran down the road and into another pub. The landlord said he called time and we couldn't have a drink. I said *'it's ok mate, but just tell us if that pub down the road is...'* *'What? The gay bar'* he interrupted and laughed his bollocks off. He pulled us a pint then because he said he thought we looked like we needed a drink because we had no colour in our cheeks! Downed in one! A close escape me thinks!

"We then made our way to the Apollo but none of the band was around so we had a little nap on the grass using our coats for pillows. We were woken by them being pulled from under our heads by some urchins of about 8 years old. They were right scruffy and we could hardly understand them because they were pikey types. They were cadging fags, cans of lager and small change off us. We traded some fags for information on where an off licence and chip shop was. They took us into Moss Side and into this precinct where every shop had thick mesh on its windows and it looked like you see in Belfast in the 1970's. I know its very common know, but as I said earlier this was 1986 and it was unknown of in our hometown. Anyway, we got what we wanted, wandered back and met the band, got on the guest list, sold our tickets and had a right good time. We kipped on Manchester Piccadilly station that night. It was nice and warm and we had no hassle.

"It was around this time that I met my wife to be (oh why did I have to go into that bar at that time on that night!!). She liked music so I was able to still go to gigs. We saw Icicle Works loads of times, they were awesome live but it never really came across on vinyl. We used to go to Rock City in Nottingham in preference to Sheffield cos it's a superb live venue. We saw the Ramones, Fields of the Nephilim there. We also got into Rap when it first crossed over from America in 1987. We saw Run DMC and the Beastie Boys at the Manchester Apollo and a triple header at Rock City with Public Enemy, LL Cool J and Eric B & Rakim. They rotated the acts each night and Public Enemy were on first with the S1W's and all the Uzi's, Professor Griff with his propaganda and Flavor Flav hamming it up. They were awesome and the atmosphere was buzzing. We were literally token white guys in there that night and there were some local turf fights going on all night. The bouncers just left it cos it was really nasty but it just centred on those concerned. It really was a hostile night. The other two acts couldn't live with Public Enemy that night and both cut their sets short. We were also into the Grebo scene and saw Pop Will Eat Itself, Gaye Bykers on Acid,

Crazyhead and all the other West Country bands that had a scene going. We also got to see PIL in Manchester in what was part of a mad weekend in Blackpool. The late, great John McGeogh was with them at the time and they were superb. Lydon was on the top of his game then with the mad orange hair and big suits."

As Quadrophenia had spearheaded and popularised the Mod revival a decade previously, a TV film about Estate agents and other respectable workers in the week – football hooligans by the weekend - The Firm (featuring Gary Oldman) would also influence the fashion of the football clothes conscious fan; the Casual!

Chris Nicholls: "I recall the Pringle jumper being the much sought after male fashion item of the day and huge gangs of lads walking around Rotherham on a Saturday afternoon sporting their wedge haircuts. Thus ultimately the new fashion itself becomes yet another uniform."

Shaun Angell: (Left) "To be honest, I'd forgotten all about my experience at the NEC when I went to watch Manchester City play Aston Villa at the old Maine Road ground in Moss Side a couple of months later with a City supporting mate of mine. Villa went 2 – 0 up and there was trouble in the seats behind the goal with dozens of rival fans slugging it out. The fighting went on for only a few minutes but it was really good old-fashioned toe-to-toe stuff. All the lads that were arrested all had the same seemingly homosexual dress sense that I had seen at the N.E.C! These fuckers could scrap though and weren't Nancy boys either, they were soccer's new breed of hooligan – the Casual.

"I was hooked and thought *'I'm having some of that'.* For the next decade or so fashion, football violence and the music scene went hand in glove and became universally accepted with hooligan circles as a golden era which was never quite the same before or since."

Anon: "I always remember Tony once saying to me *'you'll never be able to buy records, go to gigs, play golf, watch football and run a car at the same time'.* Well, I guess he was right, so I dropped everything and got into football!

"I'd been watching Rotherham United since 1978 and I did enjoy going, especially to the night games with all the floodlights on! They had some good times on the pitch in the early eighties and being into the suedehead look, you had a few rucks on the Tivoli. It all fitted in with the music I was still listening to. I'd seen Casuals from other teams coming into town and causing some trouble and was impressed with their look. I happened to bump into Goulty who'd adopted this new look and him being a budding entrepreneur he offered to sell me some jumpers. I took him up on it mainly because I had very little money due to being at college and we followed different teams, so I wouldn't bump into him wearing his 'old' gear!

"They were Lyle & Scott and I thought I looked the biz because all my new mates wore Pringles! I was off to Sheffield and bought some bleached skinny Levis from Western Jean Co. They used to sell seconds quite cheap and no one was the wiser! I then got some Adidas Samba trainers. They were quite expensive at the time but I loved them. I also met up with some old mates who were really cutting edge, going shopping to Leeds, Manchester and even London for their gear. I bought loads of stuff off them including some Diadora Borg Elite trainers ('*I don't care if they are fucking kangaroo skin – you're still not coming in',* I was once told by a bouncer at a

Sheffield pub), Tacchini Dallas tracksuit bottoms, Cerrutti polo's and some other well dodgy pastel coloured tennis related stuff.

"When I started working at BSC and earning some OK money I did blow some serious cash on trainers and clothes. I used to buy Farah slacks from Greenwoods in town and have them made to the exact length I wanted and then have 1" slits cut up the side seams so they'd lay flatter on your footwear! I went to Spain on holiday with my mates and spent my time trawling the backstreets for obscure Lacoste gear and Kicker shoes which were quite rare at home then. I wore it all for a night match with my Farah's and some really soft black loafers and I looked the dogs. I got some right compliments from my mates in the know, which I loved.

Shaun Angell and Rawmarsh casuals at Rawmarsh Baths 1982

"Later on when I stopped going to football I still liked my clothes and used to spend more than I could realistically afford on Stone Island jumpers, Paul Smith & Armani jeans, any kind of Ralph Lauren Polo clothing, Burberry shirts and jackets, Henri Lloyd jackets, in fact basically anything with a label that looked like a football lad would wear. It was a look that I liked. I still love my Adidas old school trainers and have traded quite a few pairs on eBay over the years.

"I'm quite a loyal and honest person and have never really knocked work but I had the chance to go and watch my team in a very special night match. I had on my Henri Lloyd sailing jacket which was lime green and did it stand out in a crowd! It used to get a lot of attention as it was before Henri Lloyd has become what it is now. We won the game and everyone ran down to the wall to congratulate the team. Anyway, I went back to work the next afternoon after recovering from my '24 hour vomiting bug' to be met with cheers and applause wherever I went. *'We all saw you on the telly...we can't miss you in that green coat, can we'* was all I got all shift. I protested that I was bed-bound all night but I think the face-wide grin might have given it away; I've never been able to show a poker face.

"Another aspect of the casual scene was the violence. It was accepted that if you were a dresser you were there for trouble. To be fair, I guess it's why I did it, so I was under no illusion and took what was coming to me and gave as good as I got. I could go into a lot of detail but I don't think that's what this book is all about. The early to mid eighties were a great time to be involved with football if you liked a bit of terrace action and following an average team, it was always entertaining, especially when teams with big reputations at the time like Chelsea, Derby County, Hull City, Sheffield United, Leeds United, Newcastle United and Burnley came to town. I think if they're honest, they didn't get the walkover they expected. No way was we invincible but we were a set of game, well-dressed and loyal lads. The RCM! It did get a bit hairy, especially when you got two Hull City fans pulling Stanley's on you in a confined area, getting fingered to the cops by Muppets who only wanted to talk the talk (well done Donny Rovers fan – says it all really!), smashing a bus up, fighting with 40 year old miners, being seriously outnumbered and still standing, urban vendettas, getting run down the darkest of dark alleys in a strange city and being chased through car parks by cops with batons on horses. I met some really good mates through all this time and that was one of the best aspects of it all, I guess."

Shaun Angell: "You could always rely on the same 20 – 25 lads to back you up. Even to this day, I've never put my trust in any group of blokes like I did with the chaps from Rotherham when involved in any fracas. From 1980 – 1986, when the casual scene was at its peak, everything was booming: the music scene; fashion in general – especially for us young un's – was fantastic. The country, itself though, was fucked up– dear old Maggie Thatcher saw to that... having thousands of steel-workers, shipyard workers and miners end up on the dole."

The Mod scene of the 80's was changing and no finer example of its metamorphism into the scooter scene (a common, but not necessary compulsory move for many) could be exampled clearer than this story from Barnsley Mod, and future Barmy Surplus singer Jeff Platts (above with friends).

Jeff Platts: "It seemed that all East Coast (namely Scarborough) going mods hailing from Barnsley gravitated at the time to The Albert. A pub close to town centre and one where at 15 or 16 you didn't get asked your age, providing you were in the company of bigger lads who would keep you in check. The Barnsley Vikings and later The Barnsley Coasters would hole up there, or at least kick off their tour for the day/night there. Remember back in the day you had till 2/3 o clock in the afternoon to get as much in you as your pocket could afford, or youthful liver could take, followed by fish and chips then back to the digs for an hour on the bed before the 3 s's, shit, shave (if you were old enough!) and a shower. To my memory showers were still a posh extravagance to this council estate working class warrior!

"I remember queuing to get in the Albert from 6.30pm so you could get in and served for the doors opening at 7pm. I forget the landlady's name, but she was the one who dished out the warnings, threats and stares that could have you pissing yourself with fear in a corner of the bar. Anything remotely rowdy, lairy or otherwise was dealt with swiftly with no hesitation what so ever. The landlady kept an ancient peelers' truncheon behind the bar, a foot long and the girth of which any Exmoor pony would be proud of. I say truncheon...the bigger older lads insisted it was a strap on dildo and 'woe betide you young uns if you get out of order and she corners you in the corridor to the bogs!!??' Either way....it kept me in check!!

"The Albert was witness to one of my many epiphanies as a young Mod. I say epiphany; it could have been a caterpillar/butterfly metamorphosis kind of thing on reflection. The bottom line is... I strode into The Albert one sunny afternoon a Mod... and emerged a scooter boy. It was always a struggle keeping up with Weller and his wardrobe for a weekend fruit and veg shop barrow boy. *'Do I buy the new boating blazer or the new single?'*...it was always a dilemma but at the end of the day, it was the music and the mode of transport I aspired to own that won the day.

Well... that and overhearing one of the Barnsley Vikings saying he was probably going to have the 'mods' tattoo on his wrist covered over with something else once he'd got a few pints inside him.

"Aunty Gwen was another Scarborough character from those days. A gentle, homely elderly lady that threw her doors open to us every Easter. A clean pinny every morning and tea so strong you could stand a spoon up in it. In the beginning she didn't know us from the next thug looking bunch of mods/scooter boys the local papers had warned local hoteliers and business people about. In the end she was Aunty Gwen and we were her returning grandkids once a year. It didn't matter how many of us turned up...she wouldn't see us sleeping rough on the sea front, there was always a corner of a rug somewhere in her household. You wouldn't get away with it these days...red tape, fire regulations, health and safety, call it what you will, however I must confess, I do like to stretch out in my own space as I reach my mid 40's. I have many fond memories of Aunty Gwen, not least her acceptance of younger people and their lifestyles. I guess the old girl is dead and gone now? God bless her."

Changes in the form of bereavement, a new relationship and 80's fashion for Tracy.

Tracy Stanley: "By the end of 1985 I had lost my dear mum and was also in a new relationship that was tempestuous to say the least. I spent most of my time intoxicated trying to forget my traumas and spent my leisure time either in the Monkwood hotel or the Adam and Eve in Rotherham, going there at least two to three times a week. I loved dancing and as they played a mixture of old and new I would never leave the floor. I was really into Talking Heads by then

but my love for the likes of Simple Minds and Depeche Mode never dwindled. My dress sense was becoming more grown up and I started wearing things that were more feminine but still keeping my individual style. Shoulder pads and clinched in waists featured strongly and I remember bright colours like cerise, yellow and orange were very fashionable."

Ex Punk Rocker Tracy Stanley still in Post-Futurist attire at the left and at right shortly afterwards

The love of clothes would be a constant throughout any Mod, Futurist, Casual or stylist; the trashiness-inflicted 80's mainstream not even dissuading any decent clued in individual, but most of the participants of our generations cast would at some point take a step into club land utopia!!

Andy Coles: "We used to try and extend our nights out after The Charters by trying to gain entry to the Adam and Eve, a nightclub based in Rotherham Market. The bouncers were famously acerbic and nasty and to get through the door was always a miraculous event. I went to an afternoon Christmas 'do' and watched disbelievingly as a bouncer dragged a kid out of the fire exit and smashed his face on the railings...his crime?...whilst in Yuletide high-spirits, he didn't put his shirt back on when first requested to! Once when refused entry, we asked one of the Neanderthals why, to be told *'Hang on, I'll fetch you a mirror'*...sarcastic bastards. We used to try and persuade the DJ to play a few 'alternative' songs. A number of songs that were always popular amongst us were 'The Passenger' by Iggy Pop, 'No GDM' by Gina X Performance, 'Homosapien' by Pete Shelley and 'Clash City Rockers' by The Clash. Anything by The Banshees always went down well and we were open-minded enough to appreciate Gay Disco like Divine too.

"One night after dancing, an out-of-breath Phil Dodsworth sat down hard at the edge of the metal dancefloor and smashed through one of the surrounding glass panels. He was shitting himself for the remainder of the evening as the DJ was saying that the manager would like "a word" with whoever had done this and we were winding him up, saying "Here you are, mate, they're here for you", every time one of the glass collectors walked by. I once slipped on the dancefloor and went flat down and thought that I'd broken my wrist. The girl I was trying to get off with was less than impressed and off she went with someone else. Funny that used to happen all of the time!"

Shaun Angell: "When I was on strike (with the pit) a dozen or so Scousers came over and stopped at me Mam's and at our next door neighbours. We went to the Adam and Eve nightclub in Rotherham, which was popular at the time. Despite hardly having any money, I had a great weekend thanks to the lads from Liverpool. I remember trying to dance to King Kurt, The Clash and the Style Council! As always I looked a complete twat, but really couldn't give a fuck. Although we had a bit of a set to with the doormen at the end of the night, it didn't really spoil our fun!

After the tragic event of May 85, when fighting broke out and a wall collapsed killing dozens of Italians at the European Cup Final between Liverpool and Juventus, a couple of my scouse mates were locked up for five years following a fitted trial."

Two pop culture films arrived in 1986, both carrying high expectations. The Colin Mcinnes novel loosely inspired 'Absolute Beginners, starring Eddie O' Connell and Patsy Kensit with appearances from David Bowie, Sade and the Kinks' Ray Davies, was directed by Julian Temple and was hyped to great levels ultimately failing to live up to barely anyone's expectations and losing a considerable amount of money in the process. Attempting to present Mcinnes depiction of early Modernist London as a musical 'Absolute Beginners' ranks amongst the worst flops in British film history. The other film of 86 was the Alex Cox directed bio-pic of Sid Vicious and his tempestuous affair with the much maligned Nancy Spungen, taking in the rise of the Sex Pistols and Sid's spiralling fall into junkie hell and the alleged murder of Nancy. Far better received than 'Absolute Beginners', Sid and Nancy boasted a fantastic portrayal of Sid from Gary Oldman and a respectable Nancy from Chloe Webb (Courtney Love aspired to the role but played a smaller part). 'Sid and Nancy' was derided by John Lydon, applauded by Joe Strummer (who contributed to the soundtrack) and opinion was divided between Punk fans the world over.

Above: film poster 1986

Tony Beesley: "For what its worth I don't think 'Absolute Beginners was all as bad as it was made out to be. True it was flawed, often poorly acted and blandly scripted in many ways, but it was a very visually attractive film with some excellent music. I suppose it was doomed to failure from the start and had so much to live up to: unfortunately, for many, it didn't do much at all. I saw it at the old Rotherham Classic cinema, now long gone as the town hasn't even had a cinema for many a year and I remember there wasn't that much of a turn out for it. I did buy the soundtrack album though. Working Week was on it whom I loved at the time and bought all of their records. They were a superb Jazz/Soul outfit!

"Now 'Sid and Nancy'... I thought was atrocious. The second half with Gary Oldman's accurate portrayal of Vicious and the New York setting was commendable, but the first half was an *absolute beginner* for Pistols fans. The band was shown to be as cartoon like imbeciles and there was so many errors in it its unreal. It did nothing for me at all. Alex Cox was sat near me at the Joe Strummer after-show I went to and I had to stop myself from expressing my great disappointment in the film. But, I did have lots of respect for the man as I avidly watched all of his Moviedrome film showings on Sunday nights and listened with great curiosity and interest in his knowledgeable seminars on each coming movie. A couple of years later he did 'Walker' which was very satirical (a helicopter in 1840's Nicaragua??) and I also bought that soundtrack too, as it was written and performed by the one and only Joe Strummer."

Above: Film Poster 1986

Batty: (Left) "As the Punk and then Mod scenes had faded earlier in the decade; I left music behind and opted for football. Whereas before it had been the music of The Jam, Sham 69 and Angelic Upstarts that gave me a buzz, from then on it was all football. I never got into the Human League and all that at all. I did make a return to music around 1986, though, when I started getting into the Housemartins."

The approaching House scene resulted in a change of look and location for one Punk free-thinking individual: ex of Spiral Vision and the Inhabitants.

Colleen Allen: "Around 1986 and just prior to me leaving for Manchester for the next 16 years, I remember having a radical change, both in look and musical taste. I cut my hair off, lost about 2 stone and became funky and fresh and into Chicago House, 'House Nation', 'Jack My Body, and the wonderful Farley Jackmaster Funk's 'Love Can't Turn Around. This music saw a different route for me, I moved to Manchester to study my Masters degree in Sculpture."

Even one of Rotherham's most idealistically minded Punks began to merge back into the mainstream for a very short while by the mid 80's. Thankfully help would arrive just in time from some old school acquaintances and his younger siblings.

Richard Chatterton: "I even started going to 'townie' nightclubs where you had to wear a tie and jacket to get in: woeful. The geeks inside danced to the offensive dirge served up by no-talents Stock, Aitken and Waterman and they pretended to row boats on the dancefloor, before having a smooch at the end. My saviours were a bunch of ex-school friends in nearby Whiston who had formed their own pub team. My brother Phil and I joined in with and their company and this made dole and the mid-eighties tolerable. Without them I think I would have gone mad. By this time, our kid and my youngest brother Craig had formed Phil Murray and the Boys from Bury and had made their debut at the Rotherham Art centre in 1985. The football team, along with many of the regulars of the 'Three Magpies' public house in Brinsworth would become their unofficial following."

Years before the Gallagher brothers pulled themselves up from their Madchester-obsessed humble beginnings to be, what seemed like at the time, the biggest band since the Beatles, two Rotherham Punk fans made their first fun-filled brotherly attack on the music scene. It wasn't Oasis mania nor was it that serious: but with Phil Murray and the boys from Bury, you were guaranteed to have a good time. It wasn't Manchester or trendy Camden town – or even trendy Sheffield for that matter. The location for this dose of Punk-influenced Psychobilly madness with a dance for the Turtles was the many and varied clubs, pubs and rock venues of Rotherham.

Rotherham band Phil Murray and the boys from Bury were formed in 1985 inspired by their experiences and influence of Punk along with a strong Rockabilly/Psychobilly edge. Starting out as what was (and in their own words still is) a hobby, their very first outing in front of a paying public was at Rotherham Art Centre. Since that debut performance they have played around 150 gigs mostly local to begin with at venues such as Shipmates, Elliot's Bar, the Travellers, BJ'S Bar, Brinsworth community centre, The Charters Arms and the old Rotherham Windmill Punk haunt later renamed the Tivoli.

In later days their gigs spread further away as well as adding support sets with The Damned, Vibrators, Sham 69, John Otway, John Cooper Clarke, Dr Feelgood, UK Subs, 999 and the Members and two of their own tours being named 'No sleep til Canklow' and 'Shurrup mi Dad's in bed'. The Chatterton brothers and their motley crew of musicians have always retained a strong and loyal local following; enough to instigate an exclusive dance 'The Dying Turtle' devoted to them. Their input to the Rotherham

and surrounding area has been constant (apart from a break up around halfway through their career) and recent days have seen them release an anthology album - of sorts - of all their most loved and popular self composed songs. Their musical outlook has more often than not been on the lighter side of the agenda and pretentious leanings have never been allowed to creep into the scheme of things.

Phil Chatterton: "Our very first line-up was me on vocals (I never could be bothered to learn to play an instrument), our Craig on bass, Lloyd Gregory – lead guitar, Chris Brown – rhythm guitar, Andrew Sunderland – keyboards and Andy Bower - drums (for the first gig only before he went to University). We had about 8 or 10 songs back then which were influenced by classic Punk with a strong Ramones sound, but also a Rock n' Roll influence... some of our early sets included old Rock n' Roll songs. The first gig at the Art Centre was supporting another local band called A Load of Shits who played Punk covers: They included Graham Torr and John Vernon. The other band playing were local Punk Dave Frost's band Fat Bellied Rat Thieves. We pulled a right crowd for that one."

Craig Chatterton: "From playing with cardboard guitars (a few years earlier during the Punk era) to this gig was my dream come true. To see our mates all dancing to us... well we had made it and I thought *'This is what I wanna do'.*"

Phil Chatterton: "When we came off stage we went back in and as I looked around there was Load of Shits getting plastic cups thrown at em and there was John Vernon swearing at everyone whilst Spencer and Torr were slogging it out arguing! From getting our Rich in on his one-fingered one-note playing synthesiser, our Craig starting to pick up and learn a bass guitar to Monday nights in the bedroom while the neighbours were out to playing gigs with local legend Tony Capstick... this was the life for us. Above all though, it was our hobby and that's why we are still doing it, we enjoy it!"

An early gig for the boys was at the little recognised Rotherham Live Aid event which took place not long after the national one at Wembley stadium at Herringthorpe Stadium on 25th August 1985. Amongst the local bands to play were Red Sector, Kid Salami and the Carboni Brothers, Ivor Hillmans' Futurist turned Goths My Pierrot Dolls, Mod influenced Revolver, Mods The Way, Traces of A, 3-d Fiction, New Pop Romantics Turn the Key, the events organising band Mark Lynham and Karl Hague's' Suburban Dream and the Boys from Bury themselves.

Phil Chatterton: "I remember that morning for the Live Aid gig, I was working. Another thing

was that we were announced as BILL! Murray and the Boys from Bury. Not having enough time to practise, we had to start a song again after half way through playing it."

Left: Rotherham Live Aid

Craig Chatterton: "It was freezing cold for August. We came on around 4pm and in no time we had a few fans doing the Dying Turtle in front of the stage which ended up getting recorded on video. As for the other bands playing that day... we didn't really know or get on with any of 'em."

A line up change put a halt to Murray proceedings, but this temporary pit stop didn't put an end to the sounds of Bury Psychobilly!

Phil Chatterton: "After the first few gigs Chris Brown had also left to go on a 3 week holiday to the USA and never came back. As a result, we didn't do much band wise for a while, but six months later we were back with a regular drummer Mark Mills (also handy cos he could drive too). We started getting it together properly from then on writing loads of songs and managing to get a regular rehearsal room at the Royal Standard in Masborough. At last we had a proper line up with a Rock n' Roll type drummer. I remember us writing 3 songs in one night. After Lloyd left we had a bit of a change in style for a while; playing some Hendrix covers and also a back to the roots Punk covers set with Damned songs etc.

"We did lots of good and enjoyable gigs in Rotherham: when we played Elliot's in the town centre on Thursdays it was busier than on the weekend nights. We had a big following from Brinsworth and Whiston who would come along and support us."

Memorable supporting roles for the Bury boys would come in all shapes, surprises and experiences... Punk Poets and Dustbin men from soap land descended into Bury land with unexpected and humorous results.

Craig Chatterton: "One of our support slots was with Punk Poet John Cooper Clarke. He was surprisingly coming out with loads of sexist jokes, reading out of a big fat folder, no backing tape as he sometimes had and to be honest he was not quite what we had expected of him.

"A really funny thing was when Coronation Street actor Kevin Kennedy was playing with his band (A Bunch of Thieves) at Rotherham's Sub Club. He wasn't due to play until 11pm, so someone brought him up to Elliot's where we were playing to see us. As soon as he arrived in the place the chants were 'Curly Watts is at the bar... *Curly Watts is at the bar'* etc etc. This kid came in the door too and he looked like Curly and everyone started chanting '*Curly Watts is here'* to him as well... the false Curly Watts got the right face on!

"At the Tivoli (with Tony Capstick), we were having a good night until this big fat woman fell over and couldn't get back up. She had a big Hattie Jacques frock on that was showing more than we wanted to view and Capstick came out and looking the sight up and down politely says *'WHATS GOING ON HERE'.* What a line up, Rock n' Roll with Chuck Fowler, a disco, Capstick at his best and then the Hattie Jacques special... how could we top that?"

Phil Chatterton: "Chuck Fowler rang Lloyd up and asked us to do a gig as he was double booked... the gig was upstairs at Rotherham boozer The Fuljambe. We got there and the place was full of drunken Irish and Scots and as we got our bearings a little lass approached us and gave us a request to play some Michael Jackson! Umm a good night was ahead of us then eh. Towards the end of the night a load of bikers turned up and one started messing about picking me up and banging my head up against the ceiling while we were performing. It certainly livened up our song 'Murray blues'.

"One gig at the Charters got a little heated when some of our fans were enjoying themselves doing the Turtle while we played and these two lads started flagging them off. They had already been having a go at my girlfriend at the bar so as we finished, I put the Mike in the slot and I went over to one of them and punched him. This was a one off as I am not usually violent. His mate came running over and all hell broke lose. It was like a Bash Street Kids fight. I remember is of the landlord pulling me to one side as I grabbed the mike and said into it *'Well that's showbiz!'* Towards the very end, though, all the UGLY! families started rowing so we collected our £50 and scarpered. A tenner apiece seemed alright under the circumstances."

Scooter events also featured in the bands itinerary in the late 80's.

The boys from Bury playing in 1989 Craig showing his Blakey from 'On the Buses' look

Craig Chatterton: "We did a scooter night at Clifton Hall in 1988 and some of the lads were jumping off the balcony; some getting caught and some not. There were a few that got hospitalised. We also played one in Glasgow and the place was full of skins, scooterboys, Punks and psychobillys, but there was no trouble that I saw. One funny thing was when they had this competition for who could drink the most beer through a straw the quickest. This big fat skinhead, who had known of the competition beforehand, brought his own big fat straw and beat em all hands down. He got the fat end of the straw I suppose!"

ROTHERHAM SCOOTER CLUB

9th ANIVERSARY DANCE

At The CLIFTON HALL Rotherham
Saturday 12th March 1988
7-30pm Till Midnight
Featuring PHIL MURRY And The BOYS from BURY

Tickets £1-50

By 1987 it was time to hear the sounds of Rotherham's unique blend of Rockabilly, Punk and Rock *with a little bit of Screaming Lord Sutch's madcap musical humour* thrown in for good measure on a studio recorded work. The subsequent release was an 8-track tape called 'Blimey' followed six months later by a follow up 'Songs from the Schlong'. The sets included songs such as self-penned songs 'My baby left me for a buck toothed bastard' and 'Shut up my Dad's in bed'. The Boys from Bury met the Damned when they supported them on a date in Sheffield.

Craig Chatterton: " Me and our Phil were having a fag near the backstage door and Dave (looking like Count Dracula as he does) came by and I said 'Not tonight son' in a joke to which he replied 'Very funny' and walked past us and into the backstage area."

Phil Chatterton: "Captain Sensible was right nice, but singer Dave Vanian kept himself to himself. All those bands that we have supported are some of the many we had been listening to over the years. We never dreamt that we would be playing with them all those years ago. It was really weird when Charlie Harper of the UK Subs rang us up personally."

Craig Chatterton: "It's now 25 years since we started and we just want to carry on gigging and any money that we make put back into the band. We play more places now... Derby, London etc and when we get the time we try and get more songs written. It's taken 27 years to get our first proper album out on CD, but it does contain a lot of the best songs from all those years."

Throughout the years of Bury Rockabilly Punk fun and mayhem, members of the band have come and gone: some others that also served are Darren Bayliss (bass), Neil Jones (rhythm guitar), Lindsey (sax), Shaun Parkin (bass), Warren (drums), and Andy Sunderland (keyboards).

Dally: "In 1989 Lloyd, the guitar player with the Boys from Bury, left to join the Happening Men and so I was asked to take his place. My playing style was quite different from Lloyd's, being rawer and punky, so the band sounded quite different from before. We started writing songs straight away with numbers like 'Saturday Night' (originally called 'it's Halloween') and 'Sanatorium' coming along quite quickly. We were still producing the more bluesy numbers like This Town but with my playing they had a harder edge."

The current line up of Phil Murray and the boys from Bury is Phil – Vocals, Craig - bass guitar, Dally – guitar and Richard Scottrick on drums.

There was another major Punk-inspired Rotherham band to make their individual mark on the Rotherham and local music scene. Fronted by ex-Cute Pube and Clash fanatic with a musical heart big enough to encompass everything that is exciting, fast and energetic enough in Rock n' Roll– Buddy Holly meets Joe Strummer: Dave Spencer!... the band Spring Heel'd Jack!!

Named after a mythical Victorian boogieman, Spring Heel'd Jack's sound merged the speed and energetic style of the Clash and (amongst other Punk influences), Buffalo Springfield, Lovin' Spoonful, The Doors, Beatles, Stones and Bob Dylan and co/vocalist Jackie Ineson's Soul and Jazz tastes. Formed in 1985 their original line up comprised of Dave Spencer - Vocals/Guitar/Songwriter, Jackie Ineson - Vocals, Barry Thurman (ex-My Pierrot Dolls) – Bass, Rob Bellis – Guitar, Simon Cardie – Keyboards and another ex-Cute Pube Simon Bird – Drums.

The Punk meets Rock n' Roll power pop of the band could be heard all throughout the locality of Rotherham, Sheffield and the music-starved towns and villages of nearby. Although the influences may have been indistinguishable, the main strength of the band lay in both the song writing of Dave Spencer and the energy and accomplished musical skill of the rest of the band.

Interestingly, when asked (a full ten years exactly since the Punk of 76) what the key spokespeople of the band Dave and Jackie thought of the celebrations surrounding the Punk era, their response was dismissive of its nostalgia circus...Jackie replied with *'it's hypocritical to try and revive Punk. The Clash were the perfect Punk group, but they were also an example of Punk going wrong. My idea of Punk was change and that is missing in music now'*. Leader Dave Spencer spoke excitedly at the time of a need for change and creating something new, and felt that Spring Heel'd Jack was the band he had been aiming for, all his previous groups leading the way to this one. He went on to declare... *'Springheel'd Jack offer NO NONSENSE!!, NO BULLSHIT MUSIC!!* This is a chapter in their illustrious and Rock n' Roll fun-filled career!

Damon Cardie: "I first met Dave (Spencer) sometime in the spring of 1984.I had somehow blagged my way into playing guitar with Turn the Key a few months earlier and had done a handful of gigs with them .They were far more musically accomplished than myself at that time, but I quickly realised that this wasn't the musical path I wanted to take, having grown up on a diet of Led Zep and Deep Purple, along with a smattering of my younger brothers' choice of Dead Kennedys and The Plasmatics.

"Whilst in Turn The Key, I distinctly remember sharing the bill with Dave's Band The Fury at a gig at The Arts Centre and thinking they seemed to be having a far better laugh than I was and had the kind of swagger and energy that was much more up my alley. I became friends with Dave and Dom over the next few months as I flitted from Turn the Key to Kid Salami and the Carboni Brothers, meanwhile spending every free evening in The Charters where, invariably, Dave and Dom were fixtures, discussing their plans for world domination."

Simon Cardie: "I met Dave Spencer round at my parents' house in early '85. I think he'd come to see my brother as they were playing together for Rotherham Live Aid. I was outside in a neighbour's garden at the time when he walked down our path. He didn't know who the hell I was. I remember the first thing that he said to me was *'Have you got any honey or lemon for my voice?'*

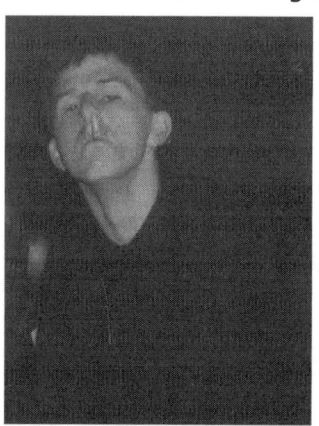

I said *'Fat fucking chance in this house'.* Dave got his guitar out and started playing something with my brother Damon, who mentioned that I played keyboards. I got the keyboard out and Dave showed me a song he'd written called 'Desperate' and I played along with him for the first time. I'd never actually thought of playing in a band as I was supposed to be going to Music College or something. It was either that or if my music teacher had his way, I'd have been playing in the clubs. Probably backing strippers on a Sunday lunch time: great in one respect, total shite in another. I don't remember our first rehearsal much, which was in the basement at Peter Bird's hairdressers. As I couldn't afford a decent keyboard, I'd bought one that the band took the piss out of. It was wholly inappropriate and they said it sounded like a 'fucking ice cream van'."

Rob Bellis: "It was around 1980 and I knew of Dave from Oakwood School, although I was a few years below him. He was a Cute Pube and I remember him going to Graham Torr's house across the road from me. Graham was a fellow Cute Pube and a 'kid on the street' kind of friend of mine, although he was a little older. We used to ride his Dad's Honda 50 around the field behind our houses in the late 70's. The Cute Pubes were like a famous Punk band to me, being maybe 13 years old and a hugely impressionable kid. When Dave came to Graham's he never had a guitar case and would carry his guitar under his arm. I found that quite odd as I had a case for mine, I thought it was very Rock n Roll."

Dave Spencer: "By the middle of the 80's, I had sort of pushed myself into a kind of social corner: I was bewildered by anyone who hadn't been into Punk, but equally, I had no time for anyone who was still a Punk, as, in my eyes, it was all over and had been for years. Rob, Simon Bird and Simon Cardie, and later, Damon, were all what you could call Punk sympathisers and Jackie and Barry had been Punks anyway... so it was perfect casting I suppose.

"As far as influences go, at that time (1985), I was more interested in 1966 than 1976 - Dylan's 'Blonde on Blonde', 'Aftermath' by the Stones and Buffalo Springfield were an indication of where I was wanting to head writing wise. I wanted a sound of more acoustic guitars with more depth and harmony than I had been able to achieve before, but of course it didn't turn out like that. Not for a long time."

Damon Cardie: "Both The Fury and Kid Salami had fizzled out by the winter of 84/85 and a few abortive attempts were made to get something musical together, which culminated in Dave and myself joining with a couple of friends, Jackie Ineson and Trev Houghton, to create an ad-hoc group called Safe as Houses, doing old cover versions with Dave and me on acoustic guitars, four part harmonies and Trev playing the vacuum cleaner on a spectacular rendition of 'Leader of the Pack'. I think this must have been the spark that initially ignited the idea of Springheel'd Jack in Dave's mind as a kind of Crosby, Stills and Clash. Jackie would go on to be a part of the Jack.

"We carried on playing through the first half of 85' but, it was more about the drinking and partying at that time. I think the crunch came when; somebody had the idea of putting The Cute Pubes back together for a reunion gig. Although I hadn't even been a member of the band, nor could I play drums, someone thought it was a good idea for me to fill in on drums! In the end, I switched places with a very generous and multi talented Graham Torr and he played drums for the gig on my 19th birthday at the new Rotherham venue of BJ's (formerly The Alma Tavern), on Westgate (in Rotherham). The gig was a one off but, Dominic Wood, who by this time had got his own band together, came back into our lives and, asked if I would like to join his band, the fantastically named Dominic and the Derekoes, on guitar. I jumped at the chance of playing some loud guitar and, Dominic had a great presence of his own, speaking in an American accent and sporting a cowboy hat and bootlace tie. We played mostly original Dominic-written songs in a Stonesy, Rn'B' B style and gigged prolifically around Sheffield and Rotherham.

"By this time, Dave and I had decided to rent a house together in Rotherham which was the most squalid shithole imaginable. This wasn't helped by the fact that we didn't clean it once in all of the six months we were there. By the time we left, the kitchen floor was an inch thick in grease, surprising really considering I can't recall eating anything but takeaways. The only home cooked meal I do remember having there, was a shepherds pie our girlfriends had cooked us when we moved in .When we moved out, the same shepherds pie's remains were still in the oven covered with what looked like a rain forest. This house was where Spring Heel'd Jack finally started to take shape and I remember feeling a little jealous when I heard some of the new songs drifting through the wall from Dave's bedroom. Of course I had already thrown my lot in with Dominic so had no cause for complaint, but if Dave had asked me to defect to his band, I would have been in like a shot. Strangely, along with Jackie and Simon Bird, an old ally of Dave's from way back, my brother Simon joined them on keyboards.

"Dave had met Simon round at my Mum's some time before and then Simon had started to come out to The Charters where he had made his face known, usually on the end of someone's fist, as he had the unnerving knack of saying whatever came to mind before he engaged his brain. Dave remembers reacquainting himself with Simon as he was recruited to sell tickets for the Rotherham Live Aid spectacular. Some supposed hard nut had been trying to nick tickets from Simon, and when Simon stated this fact, the hard nut accused Simon of calling him a wanker and it looked like it was all going to kick off. The situation was calmed down but, as the hard nut was walking away, Simon muttered something just loud enough for the guy to hear...wanker: It kicked off and Dave had to step in to pull the hard case off Simon. It was fate, Simon was in and Barry Thurman was recruited from My Pierrot Dolls and Spring Heel'd Jack were born.

"Spring Heel'd Jack's first gig was at The Hallamshire in Sheffield on the 23rd January 1986 with Dominic and the Derekoes. I don't remember any discussion over who would headline, it just seemed right and proper that Springheel'd Jack would be topping the bill; even then, there was a natural pecking order that we adhered to. From the off, there was a quality there in the songwriting that was impressive. 'Desperate', 'Cold Silhouette', 'It's Gonna Rain', songs that still stand up to scrutiny even now. The harmonies weren't quite there at that stage, but a couple of months later, Rob Bellis joined on lead guitar and added an extra voice to the mix. Again, when Rob joined, a little jealousy set in on my part: I felt I'd missed the boat again."

Rob Bellis: "It wasn't until maybe 1985 that myself and Dave spoke to each other. I was in the Rotherham Music Library with friend and musician Dale Richardson. Dave knew Dale, I knew Andrea, Dave's girlfriend at the time. We probably discussed relative issues but I remember Dave asking me if I was *'some sort of Punk Rocker'*. I didn't really know what to make of the question.

"My hub of the universe at that time was The Charter Arms. I was just out of college and was guitarist in Punk band R.I.P. with Andrew Staveley, Rob Hardwick and Mark Hinch. We were playing very few gigs, merely youth clubs and for poor sods who didn't know what they were letting themselves in for. With Frankie Goes to Hollywood and Wham in the charts, we were reviving Sex Pistols' Bodies' and Adverts 'Gary Gilmore's Eyes'. We were okay, in tune and in time at least. Andrew was a fantastic front man, very inspiring and talented.

"R.I.P. didn't materialize into much, floundered and failed as many do at that age. I chatted to Dave a few times in the Charters from our brief encounter in the library. I was obviously selling my skills as a guitarist, trying to get in his band. Eventually we got together in a rehearsal room I rented above my Dad's workplace. We worked through harmonies and guitar parts of Springheel'd Jack songs. Dave was already into the vocal harmonies reminiscent of the Beatles, Beach Boys and the Byrds and, although I loved the Beatles, harmonies were something I'd not attempted. It couldn't have been too bad as Dave invited me down to rehearse with the rest of the band in their room underneath the Rotherham Markets, just steps away from the Charters, how convenient."

Damon Cardie: "Through the first half of 86, Spring Heel'd Jack were becoming a force to be reckoned with despite, and probably because of, the disparate personalities involved. All of them had opinion. This was no dictatorship, although Dave was in the driving seat, the passengers were all asking *'are we there yet?'* Meanwhile, The Derekoes were disintegrating. The other members were all a lot older than me and Dom and had responsibilities. And, they were from Sheffield, we were far more civilised! We limped on as a three piece, but we were on our last legs. Dominic eventually moved to London and it was over."

Rob Bellis: "My first gig with Spring Heel'd Jack was an all day event at BJ's on Westgate, Rotherham in the summer of 1986. It was a dirty old drinker formerly known as BJ Mash, and prior to that the Alma Tavern. It was probably a CND or Anti-apartheid event, as was the trend in those days. We played well and I felt proud to be part of my first *real* band. With alcohol calling, we decided to leave the equipment up on stage until the next day only to find microphones stolen.

"We began recording late 1986 at Input Studios on or around Division Street, Sheffield prior to coming third in the battle of the bands 1986 at Sheffield City Hall. With a keyboard player discharging himself from hospital that day after appendicitis and drums falling off the riser, I'm surprised we even came third. The recording was fantastic experience for me as an 18-year-old wannabe. We ended up with what I thought was a great demo but it did not quite capture that live energy. Spring Heel'd Jack recordings never did portrait us at our best, our live best."

"In those early rehearsal sessions I worked musically as I'd never worked before, so enthused, just realising some sort of dream for a kid just out of college wanting to pursue music. It just fell into place personally: I grew as a guitarist, as a backing vocalist and as a live performer. It truly formed the foundations of what I do today."

Simon Cardie: "We rehearsed in Peter Bird's basement for about 18 months. In the end, we left there. Either because Peter was sick of us never paying any rent to him, breaking his coffee machine, stealing hair appliances or eventually kicking the door off the hinges when we couldn't get in one night. It was that or the smell of fish and rotting meat coming from the outside market. Next, we moved upstairs in the loft of a dentists. We got that place because the guitarist Rob Bellis's dad was a dental technician there. I remember one night that Rob's amp had broken and we had to fix a new socket on the back. We had no tools so we just stuck his amp in the dentist chair downstairs and tried to drill the old socket out using all the dentists drill bits supposed to be used for fillings. It must have been fucking horrendous for the next patient as the bits were all bent. I think we had to leave there as well."

Dave Spencer: "From us starting in January, we were gigging and writing very rapidly. I remember writing '51st State' around the time of the Libyan bombings. One of the broadsheets published had something to the effect that Britain was in danger of becoming little more than an aircraft carrier for United States, and I just thought, 'SONG! From the bombing, to performing the song, it was only a matter of three weeks. We were very focussed. We were constantly song-writing, rehearsing and gigging. It did get to a point where we felt we were actually beginning to achieve something. Considering we had only been together about nine months. For some, though, it was a bit of an anti-climax when things didn't happen straight after that, resulting in Jackie leaving the band. Then Barry Thurman left and we had less than a month to find a new bass player."

Damon Cardie: "Dave and myself had given up the shithole in early 1986 and moved on. After The Derekoes, I got the offer of reuniting with two members of Turn the Key, Gary and Julian Jones and the bass player from Kid Salami, Mick Gregory. We formed a band called Cat Ballou and I was the vocalist, another role I was far too under-qualified for. We played a kind of complicated quirky pop, a world away from The Derekoes. Never let it be said that I don't rise to a challenge. I coasted along, still very much in the Spring Heel'd Jack world, but one step removed as all of my social life was with Dave and the gang. Then it happened! *'Barry's leaving the band, do you want to play bass?'* I had about a week to learn all the songs, I'd never played bass before, didn't even own one or an amp... no problem."

Dave Spencer: "By December 1987, the priorities of some members of the band were beginning to change. Barry had left, not because he wanted to play 'Smoke on the Water' for some dodgy working men's club turd... er turn, but because he needed the money... simple as that. Within days of Barry announcing his departure, Simon Bird said that he was quitting his job working at his brother's hairdressers to open his own hairdressers, but

that meant he would not be able to dedicate any more time to Spring Heel'd Jack. Fortunately, for us he said he would wait until we found a replacement. It was only then that we realised how lucky we had been to have a drummer as good as Simon. We auditioned a fair few drummers before we chanced upon Ashley Hyden. Ashley was 17 years old and was *almost* good enough to join a band. Being a novice meant that he did yet not have the stamina to play a full rockin' set with the band. Simon bird was as good as his word and stayed with us until Ashley was ready.

"In early 1988 we managed to scrape enough money together to record a four track E.P. But by the time we had the cash to press a thousand copies; we were thoroughly disillusioned and disappointed with it. It sounds like we didn't know where we were going, and we didn't. Simon Bird played drums on it but Ashley was the drummer when it was 'released'. Although John Quinn of the Sheffield Star gave it a great review in the Sheffield Star, we had no idea about distribution and I ended up with boxes piled up around the house. After the initial round of gigs to promote it, we ended up forever thinking up scams to get rid of them. We gave them away at some shows and threw them, Frisbee style, into a particularly unresponsive crowd at gig in Worksop. How we got out alive that night, I'll never know... I ended up dragging them around with me for decades like a great black plastic Albatross, before I managed to think of one last great idea to shake them off."

Simon Cardie: "As a band we got on really well and it was all just a big laugh. The only competitiveness in the band used to be between me and Rob. If he turned his amp up, I'd turn mine louder so you all you could hear was us. I was the youngest and Rob was the next up. The rest were a couple of years older but we all hung around the pub together. Everyone that played in Rotherham bands used to go in the Charters and it was a fantastic (though occasionally violent) place to be. I've been thumped on several occasions in that pub: Usually my fault.

"After a gig down in London one night when everyone was a bit pissed or, we decided to go and get something to eat from a takeaway. Everyone's at the counter ordering food but I was so pissed I'd got my back to them trying to read the menu above the counter in the mirrored wall at the back. I couldn't work out what it said as it was backwards, so I just asked for a kebab. Then the guy at the counter said *'I'm behind you, you fucking moron'.*

"We turned up one night at the Wakefield Rooftop Gardens to do a gig, and had been double booked with 'Hitman and Her' that were filming there that night. We went backstage into the corridor and there was this strange bloke practicing his dance moves in a mirror. We tried to speak to him but he wouldn't stop dancing. Dave said 'what are you doing?' and he said 'I know what I'm doing but do you?' It was a strange place and a shit gig. After the gig, we spotted a wooden box that looked ideal to put some gear in, so we nicked it. It was only in the van on the way home that Rob decides to open this box and discover that there's a heavy industrial drill in it that's worth a fortune. So he just opens the window and throws the drill out onto the road and keeps the box.

"We did a gig at a place called the Welly Club in Hull. As no one in the band at that time could drive, we used to hire a van and driver called Mick and he took us over there that night. Thing is, while we were playing he started chatting up two women, one of whom was a teacher and the other her nanny I seem to remember. At the end of the gig, he was incredibly pissed and said he wanted to stay over with them both in Hull. It was pointed out that if he did that then we couldn't actually get home as none of us could drive. Mick came out with a fantastic idea of teaching Neil Jackson, who was our roadie and also our friend, how to drive the van in the car park. Thing is, Neil was as pissed as him and had coincidentally failed his driving test that morning. Not only that, he'd also got his arm in a pot because he'd broken it a few nights before diving over a wall when he was pissed. Mick, still undeterred decides it's a good idea, so we have to stand watching Neil hit things in the car park. It was a fucking joke. Eventually Mick agreed that maybe this wasn't such a good idea after all, but then gets the arse on because he's got to drive home and won't get to spend the night in Hull. We were so stupid at that time. We got in the van to and Mick was all over the road. He eventually managed to hit the central reservation on the motorway at about 90mph and we thought 'goodbye everyone!' He got it under control but we were covered in all our gear in the back of the van. I was gripping the seat with the cheeks of my arse. When we eventually got back to Rotherham, a massive grinding sound started coming from the engine and all of a sudden, it fell out onto the road under the van. We didn't use that van anymore. It was a death-trap."

Dave Spencer: "We played everywhere we possibly could; spreading our wings further and further we spiralled away from South Yorks. We became harder and cooler. At one gig we did in Scunthorpe a scrap kicked off with people smashing each other in the faces with ashtrays. This was as we were loading our gear IN! At an all day event at Leeds University we came on at 6pm and the crowd was already hammered. A fight broke out in front of us and we just did our set laughing at the mayhem, hitting the chords and trying to reach the harmonies. The people in the audience who weren't fighting were staring open-mouthed as we ignored the riot in front of us. We played our set, had a laugh at some idiots and were back in the Charters by 9:00pm. BUT at one gig at Hull University, we had to flesh up our set to a 60 minutes one by covering 'Teenage Kicks' and 'Anarchy in the UK' as well as a 100 mph version of 'Please Please me'. We started to do this far too regularly and the covers became a horrible soul-destroying template for the next six months or so. Then Rob left and in hindsight I can't blame him."

Rob Bellis: "I left Spring Heel'd Jack in 1989. I'm not sure what really happened. I was introduced to a couple of songwriters who drove for us one weekend to a gig in Saxelby in Lincolnshire. I was asked to play for their band, Gasoline Party, a few weeks later. I accepted and I don't know why. I left Spring Heel'd Jack and I don't know why. I can't remember a discussion with Spring Heel'd Jack on my leaving, it just happened. It seemed to be a seamless move from one band to another. I must have told someone in Spring Heel'd Jack I was leaving."

Dave Spencer: "Towards the end of summer 1989, everything went haywire. Rob left, then we pushed Simon Cardie out in a childishly sloppy, 'we're splitting up, oh and now we're getting back together – without you', load of bollocks. We drafted ex-Cute Pubes guitarist Graham Torr in to play guitar for a couple of gigs, before we realised what a mistake it was to get rid of Simon and I phoned him up and literally begged him to rejoin. Simon had been without a band for about half an hour before Terry Sutton had contacted him and asked him to play keyboards in The Way. This was to prove fortuitous for Spring Heel'd Jack. With Simon Cardie back in the band, we started gigging with renewed vigour and enthusiasm, but for Ashley, it only took a few missed rehearsals and one late arrival at a gig, and he was out! In came Ian Deakin who we dragged from the clutches of Terry Sutton. Terry lost a great drummer, but at long last we were about to find our way. After about two years of instability Spring Heel'd Jack might have ground to a halt out there and then, but this bunch of Herberts was about to be revived by a couple of Charlies!

"My old mate and ex-Cute Pubes Bass player, Dominic Wood was by now living in London and liberated from the confines of small town Rotherham was beginning to move in lots of new artistic and social circles which would have been inconceivable up north. He was helping to run a Community Arts Centre near Regents Park which had a club night every Sunday. Charlie Gillett of Capital Radio was a regular DJ there. Charlie had managed Ian Dury and discovered Elvis Costello and was in my eyes something of a legend. Dom told him about the band and played him a couple of demos and one Thursday night Dom drove him up from London to watch us at Elliot's bar in Rotherham. He was very supportive but said that we sounded like ten bands rolled into one and that we were stylistically too diverse. His advice was to write as many songs as we could and as quickly as we could and the songs would find a style of their own. We did exactly as we were told and he was absolutely right! We ended up with a set of songs with a common musical theme and at last we sounded like we were the same band. Charlie Gillett made us sound like the band we had always wanted to be and at last we were able to capture the sound in the studio.

"We started sending out demos of the new Spring Heel'd Jack and it wasn't long before the phone rang. It was a guy called Charlie Pinder from East West Records. At first I was a bit cynical, but as the conversation went on, it turned out he knew all the songs on the demo we had sent, and he was guessing at our possible influences. This Charlie said he wanted to see us live so we set about organising a gig the Powerhaus, in Islington. We hired a coach to drag as many people as we could away from Rotherham for one Sunday to come and support us. We spent weeks honing every last nuance of our half hour set, to make sure we made the right impact, as we knew this was our 'Big Chance'. On the Friday before the gig, Charlie phoned to say that his boss had insisted that he had to go and check a band out in Dublin that weekend and that he couldn't make it and that he was very, very sorry. We dragged ourselves down to London and turned in the most miserable and dejected performance imaginable. As I shuffled through the crowd after the gig, saying halfhearted 'Thanks' to the half hearted 'Well done's, someone stepped toward me from the bar and said 'Dave! I'm Charlie! I managed to get here after all! My heart sank, as he said that it wasn't quite what he expected and blah blah blah and he wanted to see us on our home turf etc.

"He did keep in touch and we organised gigs in my new home town of Sheffield. The Leadmill started giving us support slots. We did a cracking gig supporting Pete Wylie and Wah the Mongrel. Not only did Charlie's boss send him somewhere else that night, but the NME's Sheffield reviewer Johnny Thatcher arrived about 10 minutes after we came off and missed us. Bastards! I do recall, though, Charlie getting in touch and saying that he was in town one night and we went out and had a great night, but he never got to see us live again. He eventually called us to say that his boss had decided that they were going to sign Jah Wobble and the Invaders of the Heart and he wished us good luck for the future.

"Maybe if we had only been going for a year or so, we might have viewed the experience in a more positive light, but after six years of hammering away, it just seemed like the final nail in the coffin. At least, though, thanks to Charlie Pinder and the late Charlie Gillett, we were inspired to write and record some great material in the last two years of the band. I feel honoured that the late great Charlie Gillett spared us the time to come and see us and advise us and I feel lucky that we met the Charlie Pinder, the only A&R man I ever met that actually did his job, but I still fucking hate his boss. We didn't 'make it' - whatever that might have entailed, but the time we had driving round the country in those horrible transits had a massive impact on all our lives, and I am immensely proud of the band and every single person who was involved in it."

Simon Bird: "I was previously the drummer with Cute Pubes and when I think back to the Spring Heeled Jack years, the memory of the band is a bit of a blur for some reason, but I know for definite that I enjoyed it to the max. This gives rise to a disturbing thought for me, what did I do, how much did I drink, have my brain cells suffered as a consequence, probably, but I seem to be able to function in normal society with a modicum of efficiency, so that's ok, yes... Ahh, that's better now I've got that disturbing thought out of my system. Now let's think now, Spring Heeled Jack? Mmm...Punk? Country? New wave? Pop? God Knows!

"I remember the battle of the bands thing and Ashley the new drummer we were phasing in to replace me was preparing to do a last minute stand in and was not quite match-ready, worried, poised with sticks in hand to do the job. I felt a bit bad when I arrived as if by magic, I virtually snatched the sticks off him and appeared behind the kit to count them in. This, it seems to me is how things usually went with SHJ. I wonder what Ashley thought of this new band he was joining, we must have looked somewhat dysfunctional to him, but the music was good and well rehearsed what ever happened otherwise. I seem to fit my time with Springheel'd Jack in to my mind as my main music and early friendship experience *and* I think the music still stands up for itself in even in today's mush."

Rob Bellis: "Some of the most distinct memories of my days with the band are playing at the Stage Door venue in Scarborough, in the middle of winter. They forgot we were due to play, no prospects of an audience so we returned home, crashing the van in snow, impaling it on a no entry sign. How ironic. Damon playing most of a gig (Collegiate Crescent Sheffield) with one leg through the stage after jumping though it; Or the time we played a nurses party at Rotherham General Hospital, Simon Cardie passed out on the keyboards mid gig, drunk of course... also Leeds Duchess of York: we played to one man and his dog in the audience. It must have been the same man and dog that Oasis reminisce about at the same venue."

"If you consider Spring Heel'd Jack's original personnel, there was some great quality and musicianship: Dave had such a strong tenor/alto range; Simon Cardie could emulate Dave

Greenfield of the Stranglers with amazingly fast arpeggios, Simon Bird is the most solid drummer I have played with, period; Barry Thurman's bass locked in fantastically with Simon Bird. Jackie Ineson offered that folk, Eddi Reader-esque backing vocals. When Damon Cardie replaced Barry in 1988, it was the start of the next creative phase, along with creating the rhythm section with ever changing drummers. It really was an eclectic, non-mainstream genre that formed. Spring Heel'd Jack could not be pigeon holed, and that, unfortunately, was our nemesis. It seemed that although we offered a great live performance we could not transfer that into a saleable commodity. I still have the rejection letters from record companies. At least they bothered to write back.

"Live work however was always the way Spring Heel'd Jack felt they should sell their wares. We were energetic, ballsy, loud and very 'fuck you'. Well that's how it felt at the time. Please tell me different. There are many stories to tell about Spring Heel'd Jack's encounters attempting to reach rock n roll stardom and I'm sure many youthful bands can tell a similar tale. Many are drunken tales involve shoplifting, engines falling out of vans, gigs with one man and a dog in the audience, all of which were experiences that every budding musician should enjoy."

The sound of Spring Heel'd Jack still cut through the mediocrity of the vast majority of the music of the day. It may not have been Punk, but it was a distinct relative of the old bastard! Songs such as the punchy 'Good Psychology', Cold Silhouette', 'TV', '51st State' and 'God Knows' led the way through storming live sets when if you closed your eyes, the return of prime Joe Strummer in Punk rebel spirit was back in the building! Punk Rock Power Pop with a healthy dose of classic sixties pop sensibilities was the order of the day! Sadly, as Dave now recognises, like many others, Springheel'd Jack were unfortunately a good few years too late and more than a few too early. The world wasn't quite ready to fully embrace the talents of the band and after the usual musical disagreements and the stress of continuing to write and perform during a very hard time for music; the band went their separate ways, leaving a 7" E.P and piles of recorded work as their legacy.

Dave Spencer went on to write and perform solo and in other various band line ups eventually teaming up with Sheffield band Cool Canasta (Formed from the ashes of a band called Y and its members being Chris Lawrence – drums, Tony Crooks – Keyboards, old Punk friend Adrain Carver on bass along with Dave on Vocals and guitar duties). They released a superb tune called 'Hard Times a Coming' in 2008, Dave finally giving up the fight to stop sounding like and being influenced by The Clash. Last year he got back together with ex Punk band Cute Pubes fellow member Graham Torr (over from the States where he moved to) to perform a rendition of the Clash's 'Death or Glory'. Rock n' Roll and the Punk spirit will always flow through Dave's veins. In 2008 he reacquainted himself with the Punk day's legacy and became one of the major forces and inspirations involved with the Our Generation Volume 1 book!

The remaining cast of Springheel'd Jack also performed for a while as Beaker, which was basically the same band minus Dave Spencer. Jackie Ineson left performing altogether and moved to Wales. Simon Cardie joined The Way and still works with Terry Sutton and Ian Deakin of The Way who are now the Special Guest Stars. Barry Thurman left the HM band he joined and is still good friends with all the members of Spring Heel'd Jack. Neil Jackson is the best roadie the world has ever known. Spring Heel'd Jack reformed to perform a final gig in Rotherham in December 2009.

As Spring Heel'd Jack were flexing their Rock n' Roll muscles across an ever-expanding radius of clubs, bars and Casbahs, Andi Stevenson was producing a new 'rocked up' vision of his new romantic futurism!

Andi Stevenson: "I formed an unsuccessful band called Steel in 1986 doing rehashed versions of Mon Amour and 3D Fiction stuff but more rocked up. I then joined a band called The Gasoline Party in 1989. At the time the Rotherham press called it the Rotherham super group as it contained Chip from Vision, Mark Love, Ian Elsom and Phil Foster from Rotherham Band Roache 5, Rob Bellis from Springheel'd Jack and myself. To be honest the band would have gone all the way but Mark and Phil uprooted to London and the band only lasted from 1988-1989. Mark Love had the most amazing voice ever and should really have been a massive star."

Whilst it was certainly true that the first wave of Punk and even its follow up flotsam had been rendered totally redundant by the mid 80's, if not earlier (a certain Mr Lydon almost ending his days on the ill-fated Lockerbie flight a couple of years later...a change of plans being his saviour), a few Punk leftovers remaining determined to carry on the pro-active idealism of the cause. Only a handful of Punk era musicians managed to retain the true spirit of those times by moving ahead with new sounds and styles such as sacked Clash member Mick Jones with his new Big Audio Dynamite venture and the occasional show of solo genius from his nemesis Joe Strummer. Billy Idol's (by now a MTV HM icon) old Gen X cohort Tony James also caused a few minor ripples with his new 'Punk for the future' band project - Sigue Sigue Sputnik.

Bryan Bell: "Sigue Sigue Sputnik were Tony James out of Generation X and Martin Degville was the lead singer: he tried to be a bit like the Sex Pistols, controversial and though it didn't quite work, some of the music was quite good."

Nigel Lockwood: "I was at the Leadmill when B.A.D in 1985 were playing their first date there, supporting The Alarm, and Tony James (who was helping Mick Jones with his guitars) was going round the audience telling everyone about his forthcoming band and how they were going to be really big – the next big thing in music! I said to him *'what do they call your new band then'?* And when he said 'Sigue Sigue Sputnik, I thought... *'What a strange name'.*"

The manifesto for the Sputniks was to create and court controversy in a similar manner as McLaren had guided the Sex Pistols ten years earlier. The media hype was in gear and anticipation was high, but ultimately the Punk years had hardened our resolve as well as the general Punk indifferent public to something as fabricated and ill conceived as this latest ploy for headline-grabbing attention. Even so, the state of the charts that spring of 86 was harbouring so much dismal over produced rubbish that the sounds of the Sputniks taking off sounded almost positively refreshing!

Tony Beesley: "Sigue Sigue Sputnik? - Style over substance as far as I was concerned. A mirror to most of the whole decade in music! I preferred Derwood's (Gen X guitarist) band

Westworld who seemed to have some promise and then just disappeared off the scene. I remember being a little interested in the Sputniks to begin with, and some premature excitement about what they were gonna come out with, as I have a lot of time and respect for Tony James and was and still am a fan of Generation X, but when I heard Love Missile F1 -11 I thought it was weak: Better than 'We've got a fuzzbox and we're gonna use it' though! I remember bumping into ex-Punk Bryan Bell at a do at Rawmarsh baths hall and he was raving on about em, but they never impressed me one bit to be honest."

Sigue Sputnik at the Leadmill ... ex Generation X and future Carbon Silicon member Tony James at far left. (Photos courtesy of Nigel Lockwood

Tony Beesley: "We all went our own ways musically, during the 80's (I walked straight into the window of Laser records shop for a start). The unity of our Punk generation had totally disappeared too and I don't know of anyone who I knew that I could relate to on musical terms back then, weird as that is: only a few years ago, we were virtually inseparable in our love for Punk and its many offshoots. Now the only thing we had in common was what lager we may have drunk. We – the supposedly blank generation? – were really were becoming a splintered generation!"

If any venue in Sheffield (and a fair few miles surrounding as well) could lay claim to being the most influential, cutting edge and important one on the map of the mid 1980's right through to the recent local live music scene... even giving the legendary Limit club a good run for its money (which eventually gave way to club nights as opposed to gigs) then it would almost without a shadow of a doubt be the Leadmill!

The Leadmill had been Mojo club competitor The Esquire back in the sixties heyday: all the best (and sometimes worst) bands of the era played there as well as local talents such as Joe Cocker. Ironically the King Mojo reunions of the 80's and recent years have been held on the premises of the Leadmill – once its main contender. Post-Punk and the last bastions of Punk came to the newly opened, but not quite refurbished, Leadmill in 1980. Hundreds of upcoming bands passed through the Leadmill's entrance helping gain prestige for Sheffield's live music scene. By the mid 80's the venue had built a solid reputation as one of the country's best live music venues: many fondly remembered memories of sweat soaked gigs there are shared by our generation's 80's crowd!

The 'one & only' LEADMILL

6-7 Leadmill rd S.1.

Richard Chatterton: "On a Saturday afternoon at the Leadmill, the Scarborough Antelopes played while sitting in armchairs and one band amongst a line up, which again included Pulp, had a cyclist in the line up who rode through the crowd as they played."

Andy Coles: (Right) "I'm sure it was at a Killing Joke gig at The Leadmill that we went to that someone climbed up onto the roof beams above the main room, made their way to the front and dropped down besides singer Jaz Coleman on the stage, much to his surprise."

Anon: "I loved that band (The Clash) like no other and still play their music today. I was gutted when they sacked Mick Jones and, to be honest, wasn't all that impressed when they released Cut the Crap so I guess it wasn't really a bad thing when they called it a day.

Sponsored by Marston's

"I remember reading about a new band called Big Audio Dynamite in the NME. They had an article headlined Bomb Culture and I always thought if I ever formed a band that'd be a cool name! Anyway, the band liked to be known as B.A.D. and were fronted by Mick Jones, once of The Clash. Gotta hear these, I thought. I checked out the gig guides and saw they were playing Sheffield Leadmill in a couple of weeks. Quick phone call to Stewie and it was on. They were brilliant and were what I always imagined The Clash could have been with all the sampling they'd already experimented with. The image was really good with loads of nods to New York graffiti art and baseball caps. It was a great gig and we ended up sleeping in a car park stairwell that smelt of piss because we couldn't afford a taxi home! It was all worth it though! I went out and bought the album which was as good as I had hoped.

"They toured pretty much non-stop for a couple of years and we saw them on every tour and they were really good. They never once played any Clash songs though as the pain was still a bit much for Jonesy, I guess. On one tour they were supported by Chiefs of Relief who had ex-Sex Pistol Paul Cook on drums. Me and Stewie were sat in the pub near The Leadmill and the band walked in, along with a certain Mr. Cook. *'Bloody hell'* I said to Stewie, *'it's Paul Cook'*. Never one to miss a chance to mingle with the stars, I went and sat next to him when he'd come from the bar. *'Alright Paul'* I said, *'do you miss being in the Pistols'* and he just looked at me with an *'oh no not that question again'* look on his face. After a string of one-word replies I returned to Stewie thinking *'he's a miserable twat'* but on reflection I couldn't really blame him. I probably asked him all the same questions as everyone else.

307

This is Big Audio Dynamite calling – Sheffield Leadmill 1984

All B.A.D photos courtesy of Nigel Lockwood

This is Joe Strummer calling – Sheffield Leadmill 1988

All photos taken by the author

Anon: "Joe Strummer was my hero but I loved Paul Simonon's coolness and style. When I heard he'd formed a band called Havana 3AM I just knew I had to see them. They weren't really a Punk band and were quite influenced by Latin sounds but their album was good. A trip to The Leadmill beckoned when their tour was announced. I went with a student lad called Stu who was on a work placement with me and who I owe a lot to for getting me back into music and for keeping me pretty sane in what was a pretty low point in my life. He now runs No Rules Promotions in Sheffield and is still really into the Punk scene. The band was good and the place was packed. They did all of their own material but between each song there were cries for Guns Of Brixton, arguably Simonon's finest three minutes! At the end of the set he strode up to the mike with that big gap-toothed grin and said '...this ones called...Guns of Brixton'. The place went mental with the crowd just dancing wherever they could. I think everyone in the place sung or shouted every word, it was brilliant, a proper special moment."

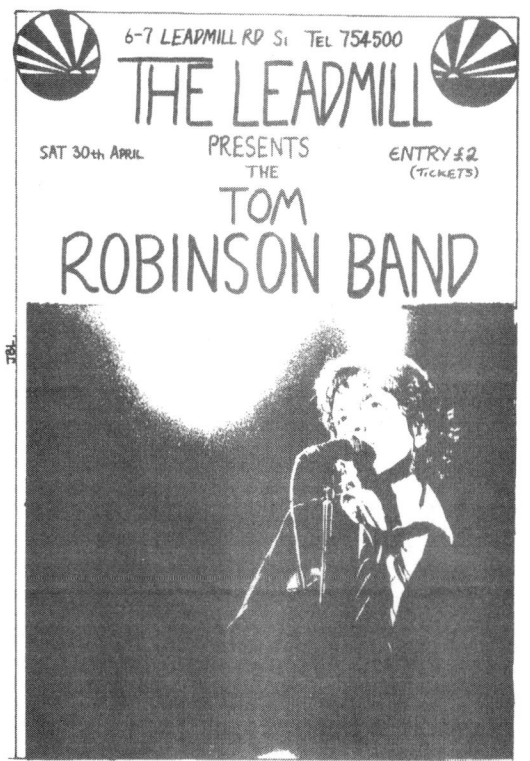

Tony Beesley: "I managed to see a fair few good gigs at the Leadmill during the early days and throughout the rest of the 80's. I had seen the last dregs of Punk Rock perform their increasingly repetitive sets occasionally... being dragged by my good mate Gaz Stables along to yet another UK Subs gig amongst others. Others I saw play there such as Tom Robinson and Lords of the New Church sort of bridged the gap left by Punk, whilst a late 1980's visit by ex Clash front man Joe Strummer and his Latino Rockabilly War managed to increase the live gig experience up a good few notches.

"I saw some good contemporary Punkish type of bands at the Leadmill. I went through a phase of digging all those Punky garage-sounding bands. That was refreshing for a while. Some other gigs I went to see at the Leadmill, that I can remember anyway, were mid 80's Indie hopefuls Hurrah (whatever happened to them– 'Big Sky' was a great single), New Pop/Punk Peroxide wonders the Darling Buds - who put on a fantastic and energetic gig after the pre-gig queue witnessed a punter unable to resist the temptation of driving the un- manned Double Decker bus over the road. He ended up driving it up and down Leadmill Road much to the amusement of us all."

Pete Weston: "Mid to late 80's I was still big into Spear of Destiny, Iggy Pop, Big Audio Dynamite, Bob Marley, Dillinger, Mano Negra, The Pogues and any stuff that took my interest. I had bought the first two Elvis Costello singles and liked them but never bought any of the albums then some one told me to listen to Spike when it came out and I was to become a big fan of all his future stuff. Nobody does bitter and twisted like him! Joe Strummer coming back gave us a new focus and we just loved that period. We liked the music and as usual he had a lot to say."

Tony Beesley: "Then there was a brand new Blues influenced Rock band with a name taken from the South West of America - Texas. There was a buzz about them already. The single *'I Don't*

Want a Lover' had just been released and I, along with a good few others, liked what I had heard. I went on the night, concerned I wouldn't be able to get into the gig without a ticket, but me and my girlfriend scraped into the heaving venue.

"The place was its usual hot, sweaty, dark and sticky and exciting self as Sharleen and Aly McErlaine hit the stage. I can't recall if their first number was the single, but they obviously played it; which was great. The rest of their first album 'Southside' was performed really well. The blues influence mixed with more than a bit of Ry Cooder-flavoured Rock as well as the sweet and soulful vocals from Sharleen. Soon to be single 'The Thrill Has Gone' and another of my faves 'Every Day Now' were all played and from what I can remember the crowd loved it. A few weeks later I went to see them again at the University's Lower Refectory. I took some photos at that one, but got bollocked by the security, so only ended up with three shots. This was the start of the new rules and regulations of concerts being introduced: Christ what had we been through Punk Rock for then?"

**Texas at the Leadmill
March 1989**

A Leadmill gig roster

An incomplete but illustrative listing of some of the many bands to have played the Leadmill (Thanks to Nigel Lockwood for his extensive collection of Leadmill flyers, posters and memorabilia)

Dead Kennedys', Chelsea, The Meteors, Crass, Cabaret Voltaire, Aswad, Exploited, Mau Maus, Chakk, Misty in Roots, Anti Pasti, Culture Club, Richard Strange, Rip Rig and Panic, Animal Nightlife, Blue Rondo a La Turk, The Fall, Jah Wobble, Tom Robinson, Lords of the New Church, Vendino Pact, Kissing the Pink, 23 Skidoo, Test Dept, The Gymslips, Killing Joke, UK Subs, They must be Russians, Amazulu, Divine, Clint Eastwood and General Saint, Nico, The Cult, Inca Babies, Hurrah, Waterboys, Blow Monkeys, Shriekback, John Cooper Clarke, Jonathan Richman and the Modern Lovers, Tracie and the Soul Squad, Skeletal Family, JoBoxers, New Order, Mighty Wah, Difford and Tilbrook, Marc Almond, Everything but the Girl, Red Guitars, Simply Red, Alien Sex Fiend, Pete Shelley, Sid Presley Experience, The Pogues, Joe Strummer, Subhumans, the Men they couldn't hang, Redskins, Prefab Sprout, Easterhouse, Sigue Sigue Sputnik, Treebound Story, Dr and the Medics, Big Audio Dynamite, Floy Joy, Primal Scream, Julian Cope, Martin Stephenson and the Daintees, Mighty Lemon Drops, Stump, The Godfathers, The Shamen, Band of Holy Joy, Green on Red, Zodiac Mindwarp and the Love Reaction, The Fields of the Nephilim, Weather Prophets, The Bodines, Go-Betweens, Voice of the Beehive, The Proclaimers, The Housemartins, The Replacements, Goodbye Mr McKenzie, Pulp, Edwyn Collins, Biff Bang Pow, The Extras, Pop will Eat itself, Microdisney, The La's, Andy Pawlak, The Warhols, 9 Below Zero, Jools Holland, Kirsty

MacColl, Dr Feelgood, The Jack Rubies (Supported by the Stone Roses), Half Man Half Biscuit, Mega City Four, Mercury Rev, A Certain Ratio, The Hypnotics, Gary Numan, Slowdive, Paris Angels, Pete Wylie, Mudhoney, Blue Aeroplanes, Babes in Toyland, Texas, Manic Street Preachers, Bassomatic, Chapterhouse, Cud, My Pierrot Dolls, Teenage Fanclub, Flowered Up, The High, Spiritualised, St Etienne, Buzzcocks, Stranglers, The Damned, Stiff Little Fingers, Boo Radleys, Soup Dragons, Havana 3am, Happy Mondays, Geno Washington and his Ram Jam band, The Sundays, Loop, James, Gaye Bykers on Acid, Inspiral Carpets, Jesus Jones, Darling Buds, House of Love, EMF, Massive Attack, The Verve, Tom Tom Club, James Taylor Quartet, The Wonderstuff, The Primevals, Blue Ox Babes, Luxuria, Stereolab, Blur, Powder, Catatonia, Mansun, Travis, Moby, Coldplay, Muse, These Animal Men, Elastica, Shed 7, Supergrass, Longpigs, Echobelly, Oasis, Sleeper, suede, Gene, My Life Story, Mother Earth, Cast, Marion, Bluetones, Charlatans, The Hives, Groove Armada, Doves, Feeder, Drugstore, Black Grape, Ocean Colour Scene, Paul Weller, Tricky, Stereophonics, Bad Manners, Gil Scott Heron, White Stripes, Echo and the Bunnymen, Jon Spencer Blues Explosion, The Alarm, Libertines, the Strokes, John Squire, Yeah Yeah Yeahs, Richard Hawley, Jet, The Coral, Babyshambles, Arctic Monkeys, Kaiser Chiefs, Wreckless Eric, Desmond Dekker, John Foxx, Wedding Present, Athlete, Franz Ferdinand, Arthur Lee, Kasabian, The Killers, Snow Patrol, The Ordinary Boys, Jimmy Cliff, Cornershop, Milburn, Graham Coxon, the Chords, Twisted Wheel.

And so the venue continued throughout the remaining years of the 80's careering through the following decade and beyond with an enviable roster of live acts and always carrying the call for new music!

The Leadmill

6/7 Leadmill Road
Sheffield S1 4SF
(0742) 754500

SATURDAYS ⟫⟫⟫
Main band on stage at 11pm.

A ten-minute swift walk from the Leadmill and on West Street's Limit club forward thinking Punk Richard Chatterton's trip there created an issue with self-identity: something becoming very familiar to Punk loving 20-somethings.

Richard Chatterton: "I once went to the iconic Limit club in Sheffield on a Monday night and instead of the post punk and funk they were playing House, Hip Hop and Techno. Where was this music coming from? I couldn't really identify with it. There was becoming nowhere in Sheffield for people like me to go – I was being ghetto-ised and was forced to go to Rock Night every Mondays at the Roxy, and I hated bands like Bon Jovi and Foreigner as much as I did the crap in the charts. I think 1987 was my 'annus horribilis' to quote her majesty. If in 1978 I had my 'road to Damascus' eye opening moment when I understood Punk for the first time, then 1987 was when I had my Samson experience and had my locks cut off. It had been coming, when once I was out with the lads on a Thursday I alone was refused entry to the Stonehouse. I had never felt so dejected and I sat in the Sheffield Nelson Mandela bar in the afternoon after my power was removed. After a short while I even had the mullet at the back shaved off which had been there as some kind of memorial to my lost locks. With my hair seemed to go most of my attractiveness to women. I hadn't done badly for a few years but soon my brother would christen me Mr Push – who doesn't pull. The hairstyle would never return – after that my hair didn't so much as recede but recline then decline."

A new venue merely a bus ride away from the City Centre of Sheffield opened in 1989 and catered for the cutting edge, the ramshackle and the ugly of Punk and its offspring underground. Take Two was situated at number 54 Staniforth Street in Attercliffe and its gigs were once again run by Marples legend and one of Sheffield's greatest musical promoters - Marcus Featherby.

Simon Milner: (Sheffield musician)
"As Timberwolf we played many times at Take Two, a fantastic venue on the edge of town...great facilities but not much in the way of management organisation. We started life as the Singing Stars of Texas, changing our name to Timberwolf halfway through a gig. We were a mish mash of all sorts of influences which made it exciting and edgy; unfortunately no one seemed to get it, including us at times. We had a following of denim-clad AC/DC type rock folk. I never understood that, as we bore no resemblance to any of the hair bands around at the time...we split just before a label came into being for us... Grunge!"

Mark Hilton: (Sheffield student) "It was the way it (Take Two club) opened up the farther out reaches of Attercliffe for us students (at the time) really - and realising the No.52 went beyond the City centre. Its biggest drawback was timing - pre-World Student Games, trams, etc. pre- modern licensing laws, therefore you went for the band you were seeing (usually your mates) then you got back to town ASAP to get some drinks in (usually the Limit). So ironically it became the pre-Limit bar for some of us! Oh and Marcus would never shut up but his enthusiasm was amazing."

The Take Two venue also provided a good run of Punk originals performances: The Lurkers, Chelsea, Wreckless Eric, The Mekons, and ex-Advert TV Smith's new band Cheap all playing in 1988. Even one of New York's finest Punk exponents Wayne County (minus the original Electric Chairs) arrived to spread some 'Toilet love' there.

Pete Weston: "It was a small but homely venue with a proper stage. I remember seeing Jayne County and local band Phil Murray and the boys from Bury there and them both being good gigs. As previously mentioned we saw Wayne/Jayne County 3 times and they are definitely in my top 10 of bands to see live. With classic dirty rock tunes and songs with titles like 'Fuck Off', 'Bad in Bed' and 'Fucked by the Devil' what's not to like! They always did an extended and dramatic version of 'Rock n' Roll Resurrection' which, given Wayne/Jayne's talent for raw obscenity, never failed to please.

"The Take Two club went on a bit longer and a then friend of ours called Kev became the booking manager and quite a few good Indie bands played gigs there but as per usual it ran on a tight budget and as with most local venues it struggled to get people in so it folded."

Neil Anderson: (Right) "I remember Take Two because it was such a nightmare to get to. You had to hand it to the owners though - opening an alternative club in Attercliffe was one brave move or just a simple case of a wish for commercial suicide. We somehow managed to get there from Chesterfield on a regular basis. I remember it being a nice, friendly place except for the time the Macc Lads played and it was full of football hooligans everywhere. I remember seeing a great UK Subs gig at the Take Two club. Drummer Steve Roberts was hanging off the ceiling by his feet and still playing: Very impressive. He was such a lovely bloke too. I can't actually remember who else I saw up there... Peter and the Test Tube Babies and probably GBH. To say it was such a nightmare to get to I've no recollection of the route we took or transport mode. I think we might have ended up at The Limit after!"

Rob Dowling: "I played there with a band called Traces of A. The Take Two was a nice little venue. I'm not sure if the buildings still standing it's been years since I was down that way!! Marcus could talk for England as I remember, though."

Phil Chatterton: "I saw loads of local bands at the Take Two. I remember when we (Phil Murray and the Boys from Bury) played Marcus liked us as we brought a right good-sized crowd in. We did two gigs with Dr Feelgood there, who were fantastic, especially the first time – the second time they seemed to be in a bit of a rush. Lee Brilleaux the Feelgoods' singer was great too. The band arrived in their denims and Lee changed into his (trademark) suit before coming on stage."

Craig Chatterton: "During the Feelgoods set, Lee was hanging upside down from a beam near the front of the stage, with his legs wrapped around it whilst playing his harmonica.

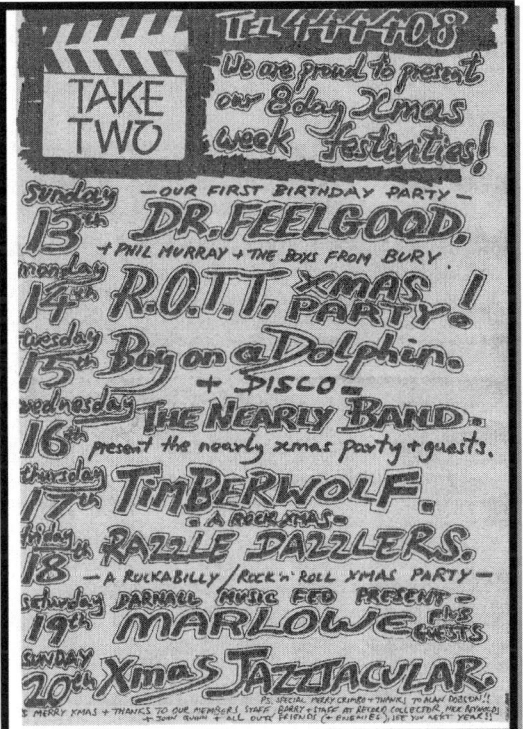

Afterwards they were very generous with us, the support act, sharing their rider. We were all helping ourselves to their big stash of booze. Lee had a pint pot and kept filling it up with Gin and tonic."

Ironically, original Dr Feelgood guitarist Wilko Johnson also performed at the very same venue and stage that his previous band-mates had set foot on.

Punk stalwarts the UK Subs played the Take Two venue five times between 1988 and 1990 with support bands such as The Corpse Grinders (themselves regulars at the venue) and The Bland. Other Punk and thrash acts to take the stage of Take Two around the time were GBH, D.O.A, Penetrators, Dr and the Crippens, the delicately named acts Slopdosh and bobbar and Gas Police along with the kings of Anarcho Punk- Conflict. A live Psychobilly album was recorded at the venue and released in 1989... the venue being a popular haunt for Psychobilly fans, of which bands such as the Krewmen, performed to the enthusiastic gravity defying quiffs of the Take Two wrecking crews!

Tracy Pidd Smith:(Sheffield Rockabilly fan) "I came across the Take Two and Marcus when it very first opened and I was advertising the venue in my 50's retro clothes shop. I was into the Rockabilly/Psychobilly scene. The first time we went up there, it was the afternoon I think... it was light anyway. The clothes I would have worn on my Take Two escapades would have depended upon the mood and could have been 40's suits, heels and a hat or leggings and a Basque ha ha!! Along with big belts and big hair! It was always a good

atmosphere and a real melting pot of styles with people dressed between being quite normal to being well ... not normal at all. It didn't matter as it was neutral ground. Marcus was brilliant with all of us. He was so normal but, no matter what, he accepted what we looked like. We in turn respected him and the place and I never saw any fights or trashing of the venue. The music would have been the Epileptic Hillbillies, Cramps, The Jets, B-52's and maybe The Clash. I lost count of how many times I went there, but it really was like home... but much noisier!"

The venue also had an underneath dungeonesque setting in The Dark room which was located immediately beneath the Take Two and launched nights of Psychobilly madness and mayhem with bands such as Tracy's faves the Epileptic Hillbillies playing sweat and beer-soaked sets there!

The Take Two Psychobilly Gallery

A special thanks to Tracy Pidd Smith for Take Two flyers and posters

Seasoned gig goer and veteran of the Glam Rock era and the Punk Rock wars, Nigel Lockwood, soon picked up on the prospect of a new Rock venue in town.

Nigel Lockwood: "The first time I went to this new interesting venue, was to see Dr Feelgood, on December13th 1987. It was a poky little place, don't know what it was before Take Two, but it didn't stay open that long as a venue, and although by the time of this date, it had already been open a year or so. Lee Brilleaux and his band got paid £ 1000 for this gig, a fair amount back then. It was also a great gig... I'd seen the Feelgoods regularly since 1975... and this didn't disappoint!"

Take Two flyers courtesy of Tracy Pidd Smith, Paul and Steve Oxley

Left: Psychobilly takes the Take Two (Paul Oxley)

Nigel Lockwood: "My other fave gigs at Take Two include Robyn Hitchcock in 1988, then for my 32nd birthday, I had my own gig there. Some mates from an old local band called the Cardboard Criminals, along with Rollin Thunder, who later became the Harbour Kings, played it. They did loads of covers of Johnny Thunders/the Only Ones/R.E.M/Stones/Patti Smith/Sex Pistols etc, which I still, have a tape of. Another great night.

"I also saw (ex-Feelgoods guitarist) Wilko Johnson there on July 1st 1988, but, by far the best was Primal Scream, who played the venue on August 12th 1989. Their set included their classic singles 'Velocity Girl' and 'All Fall Down' and they also did a cover of the MC5's 'Ramblin Rose'. I also saw Wreckless Eric there but he hated the place, and Bradford, who had previously supported Morrissey. Loads of others played there, including the Charlatans and Carter the Unstoppable Sex Machine. The audiences were always a curious blend, especially as it wasn't that easy to get to, being a bus ride away from town: I don't think it stayed open much longer after that..."

On one occasion, the Take two was visited by local Mod and Ska fans from Barnsley.

Mel Rhodes: (Barnsley Mod girl) "We arrived early at the venue, so decided to visit the Dog and Partridge pub across the road. As we walked in, a hush descended over the customers already in there. A large group of pyschobillys and a couple of punks stared back at us. But all ended well, with us having a few games of pool and a good bit of friendly banter.

"The Take Two was an odd place. It was always cold and dark with white walls and very low seating areas and tables all round the room. On this occasion, the Doncaster skinheads made an appearance and an Australian Bonehead we called 'Aussie' but his real name was Jason. The band on that night was called Outer Zeds. The lead singer seemed out of place and looked like Rod Stewart and wore very loud stripy trousers. The music wasn't particularly good and no-one could tell much of what they were singing, but the turnout and the atmosphere was good."

SHEFFIELD'S BUSIEST LIVE MUSIC VENUE

Owter Zeds

SAT 25TH FEB

TAKE TWO

54 Staniforth Road,
Sheffield, S9 3HE, ENGLAND
Telephone 0742 444408

The venues in Sheffield were scattered and spread around the City limits... from the outer reaches of Attercliffe's Take Two, the Leadmill and the Limit at each corner of the City centre to the bus ride away location of the University's Lower Refectory and the Octagon centre... but in most cases a sense of a close-knit scene was long gone by this period in time. Bands were getting bigger and the fans were becoming less directly involved.

Chris Nicholls: "I remember being dragged along to the Octagon centre at Sheffield University to witness the unknown INXS and being blown away by the group playing to a crowd of barely 50 people! It would still be a little while before the group were to explode, and it's also hard to believe that 20 years or so later I am now living in the band's home town of Perth in Australia."

Neil Anderson: "I think the local scene ended in the early to mid-eighties. I ended up growing my hair and de-camping to Rebels for a few years but never really liked the metal music that much. My dress sense didn't change a deal - I just grew my hair. I still went to loads of gigs when key bands were doing the rounds. I used to go to a lot of stuff in London when gigs weren't happening in Sheffield."

Right - Neil Anderson taking a breather from Punk

Tony Beesley: "On the way to see Post-Undertones band 'That Petrol Emotion' at the Polytechnic, me and my girlfriend were on the no.69 bus when a scene what seemed straight out of John Carpenter's 'Assault on Precinct 13' occurred. As the bus emerged out of the Wicker Arches Bridge, a volley of what at first seemed like bullets came crashing and zooming through almost every one of the bus windows. I grabbed my girlfriend and pushed us both down into hiding position on the floor of the bus between seats as brick after brick after brick came smashing through the windows missing us by mere inches. The volley seemed to last for eternity, but was most likely only a 40-second assault at the most. There was only us and the driver on the bus, which came to a grinding halt half way up the Whicker. We got off the bus just as shocked and bewildered as the bus driver. I was well pissed off and shouting at the dark shadows rapidly disappearing down the road as police officers arrived on the scene. A few details were taken, I complained and protested and accumulating contact details, dragged us both into the close by little dark and dismal boozer for a swift trauma soother in the shape of a pint of Carling. We then made our way down to the Polytechnic to see if the adrenalin of the band would match our 'Assault on Precinct Wicker Arches' experience.

"Around this time, me and John Harrison ventured into the Falstaff boozer in Rotherham town centre. This was the opening setting for my Punk years beating from those over-sized Teddy boy bullies all those years ago. Expecting to see ageing Teds and Rotherhamite bruisers wanting to still beat me up, who should I see propping the bar up... Punk legend Barney Rubble. I had not seen him for years. We had a pint or three and some catching up. Then we parted our ways, me and John escaping the Dickensian clutches of that old Rotherham boozer and into further binge-drinking oblivion elsewhere. It would be many more years before I saw Barney again. Another place that me and John visited was the Rawmarsh Baths Hall, the scene of our Mod gig in 85 (and John's green tin episode) and other Mod nights. That gig had ended up with fighting and the police arriving. This visit did too and we nearly were arrested again... with no green tin in sight!

"To be perfectly honest, during the last couple of years of the decade, I was probably slightly more interested in films as I was music. Don't get me wrong, I was still buying lots of records and going to gigs, but not that much was captivating me. I had always been a lover of the cinematic experience, but after gelling with The Way drummer Ian Deakin's passion for the acting of Robert De Niro, became just as intoxicated with his movies as music.

"Ian had just about every film of De Niro's on VHS and was a real obsessive of him and we would spend hours watching everything from 'The Gang that couldn't shoot straight', 'Bloody Mama' and 'Bang the Drum slowly' to 'Raging Bull' and 'Once upon a time in America'. I had the classic 'Travis Bickle' with Mohawk poster up in my bedroom at the time and even went almost full tilt for the hair cut. Also, around this time, the value of Punk vinyl was starting to increase: I remember selling my Ramones 'Blitzkrieg Bop in picture sleeve for £60... I only paid 40p for it anyway. Other items I sold were my ultra-rare Sex Pistols poster mag for an unbelievable £12; signed fanzines, posters (including my beloved Gaye Advert poster and Clash in Ireland and first LP ones) and all of my badges: I was now amassing lots of films on VHS and to subsidise this I did sell some good records and memorabilia."

Back in 1976 'Taxi Driver' had been a groundbreaking film and appeared almost exactly at the right time – parallel to the emerging Punk movement. Its tale of De Niro's Vietnam vet character living on the edge of society with an underlying disgust at the low life of New York's nocturnal world displayed a tension, anger and sense of 'something's got to change' not dissimilar to how the first prototype cast of Punk were feeling at the time. The intended targets may have been at opposites, but the films penultimate moments and following conclusive burst of *Out of Control* violence certainly resonated with more than a few of the Punk fraternity. Four years later at the very start of 1981, the film hit the headlines and earned life-time notoriety when US president Ronald Reagan was the target of an attempted assassination and the assailant cited Scorsese's 'Taxi Driver' as his motivation and influence.

The days of the Punk and Post-Punk era Casual and their rucks on the football terraces were now slowly coming to an end, as far as the – so far - almost unlimited freedom of the terraces and outer areas of the grounds were concerned anyway.

Shaun Angell: (Far left on photo) "With hooliganism at an all-time low in the football world, the Government of the day (Dear old Maggie Thatcher and co) decided enough was enough and after the events of the Heysel stadium at the 1985 European Cup Final between Liverpool and Juventus, plans were put forward to smash the organised football firms once and for all. Operation 'Own Goal' was launched and turned out to be a massive own goal for the authorities!

"Undercover police were infiltrating the larger football gangs of Chelsea, Millwall and particularly West Ham. They wore the same clothes as the lads in the firms – Tacchino tracksuits, Adidas sweatshirts, bleached jeans and expensive trainers: even the same wedge haircuts that all us silly cunts had at the time! Somehow though, something wasn't quite right and the active hooligans became highly suspicious of these strange faces within their ranks as paranoia swept through the gangs up and down the country."

Like a vast proportion of the rebellious Punk rockers, Mods, Skinheads and any other anti-authoritarian youth gang with an identity and scene at their disposal, the glory days were now the past for the grown up Daddies of the Casual scene too. The football hooligans and fierce fighters who loved nothing better on a Saturday afternoon than a few pints with a good soundtrack, wearing top class clobber and a damned good organised scrap at the end of it... and a football match in-between of course. Sure, the casualties were to be counted and the taste of blood may forever be smeared in the minds of some of the most over-indulgent and over zealous participants - but like all things good or bad... the Casual scene had had its day. Some of the terrace warriors of yesterday were now leaving behind them often more than reputable street fighting CV's – in exchange for big money and prestige... not too dissimilar to a kind of Punk subversion from the inside!

Shaun Angell: "I personally knew several top boys from West Ham's Inter City firm who went to prison on remand whilst awaiting trial for various violent offences including wounding, GBH, and possession of offensive weapons. One of them is now currently a high ranking officer in the RAF, and another is a multi-millionaire who owns several management companies looking after the interests of many of today's Pop artists, along with promoting dinner events with boxing legends."

As the heyday of the Casuals, and with it the full on days of football, clothes and fighting (not always in that order) came slowly to its conclusion, one Sheffield Mod was being influenced by another new mix of sounds and musical approach.

Lee Radforth: "The Acid jazz scene evolved in London in the late eighties with DJ's Gilles Peterson and Chris Bangs, who were, as far as I am aware, credited with naming scene which was an amalgam of Jazz, Latin, Hammond grooves and hip hop with the Sunday afternoon Dingwalls Talkin' Loud and Saying Something sessions and Soho's Wag Club being something of focal points for the movement. That old mainstay of the Mod scene Eddie Piller was in the thick of it trying to get bands together to try and get a live element the scene. It was really a hotch potch of Jazz dancers, funk enthusiasts and Mods all searching something new, with the term Acid Jazz a somewhat hilarious way of trying to tie all the disparate parts together. An article in ID magazine talking about Acid Jazz Mods probably brought it to a wider audience. But it was a good time.

Acid Jazz - James Taylor Quartet perform at Gorleston- on-Sea's Ocean Room August 87

"Clothing, as far as I was concerned, involved vintage Levi cords and slim fit cord jackets sourced from Aflex Palace in Manchester or a number of great vintage stores in Nottingham. Gabicci tops and roll neck jumpers worn with beads, bass weejun penny loafers and vintage trainers. Music, as far as new sounds were concerned, revolved round Eddie Piller and Giles Petersons Acid Jazz records, and later Talkin' Loud records formed by Gilles Peterson after leaving Acid Jazz. To say the out put on the labels was eclectic would be an understatement but I guess that reflected the fact that it was a very loose collective on every level, but to me the highlights were Galliano, early Brand New Heavies, The Young Disciples, The James Taylor Quartet, and The Jazz Renegades. As far as original grooves went if you couldn't find the money or time to search out the 60's and 70's issues you were well catered for with a number of excellent compilations; the best of the bunch in my opinion being the Bazz Fe Jazz and Giles Peterson inspiringly named Jazz Dance, Jazz Juice, and Acid Jazz series plus a whole host of Latin and Boogaloo compilations on Charly and not forgetting some excellent Blue Note reissues."

Tony Beesley: "By 88-89 I had emerged back out of my almost puritanical anti-white boy rock stance attitude and Soul overkill phase. I was still listening to Soul, contemporary Mod sounds and some early House music, but by 89 I was also entranced by the sudden influx of classic singles coming out. It was one of the best years in ages, with the Stone Roses 'Made of Stone' and 'She Bangs the Drums' along with Diesel Park West 'Like Princes Do', Wire's 'Eardrum Buzz!', 'Londonderry Road' by His Latest Flame, The House of Love's 'I don't know why I love you', Darling Buds and the Primitives and old new wavers turned Psychedelic maestros XTC who released their greatest album 'Oranges and Lemons' that itself spawned a series of sublime 45's 'King for a Day', 'Mayor of Simpleton' and 'The Loving'. There was also the sounds of US band Sonic Youth emerging and the buzz-saw garage Punk of The Jesus and the Mary Chain. Things became interesting again for a while. In 1989, I lived for modern music and films!"

Ex Doncaster Punk/Skinhead and Skin-Deep singer Wayne Kenyon found that his after-Punk career was being overshadowed by the latest music press darlings and scenes!

Wayne Kenyon: (Doncaster musician) "After Skin-Deep split the other lads in the band formed ska band 100 men... Mik and Stig later moved to London and Mik now plays guitar for Babyshambles. I went my own way and formed the Ferrymen... I was basically on my own and had to find new members and start writing new songs from scratch: I even started learning the guitar as I was only the singer in Skin-Deep. This was around 1989-90. It took me two years to get the band together and we played our first gig in 1991. The music was similar to Skin-Deep but

more towards the Housemartins and the Cure and Billy Bragg. After Punk I got more into bands like The Housemartins, The Smiths, The Cure, Bradford, Redskins, The (early pre-dance) Farm and was big into Billy Bragg and Canadian band Bare Naked Ladies. I never liked the Madchester scene or the grunge thing and think that Nirvana are one of the most over rated bands of all time.. Kurt had a lot of interesting things to say but the music was crap in my opinion.

"To be honest we were a bit late, as the Madchester thing was just hitting it big and the grunge scene was on its way, but being a stubborn twat I just carried on doing my own thing... It's such a pity that music is led by fashion. If it's not the 'in-thing' then people don't really want to know... which is why we had much more success in Spain and Germany than in the UK. We released records/CDs and toured in both countries to promote them.

"It was amazing how differently we were treated in both countries compared to the UK. In The UK it was set yer gear up in the corner lads and don't make too much noise... *'Here's yer money, now fuck off...'* In Germany and Spain it was proper venues, back stage meals, hotels paid for, paid well for the gig etc."

The Ferrymen played quality Northern Pop and thousands of stickers saying so could be spotted spread across Europe during 1991; one even found its way onto a camera shot in the Full Monty film. Unfortunately, the band had split by that time... their appreciation being fully recognised with the release of a 20 track compilation CD on German label Fire station records in early 2009: 12 years later... including faves 'Whole world', 'Green eyed Monster' and 'All For Nothing'.

In 1989, it was an unbelievable 10 years since the Clash had released 'London Calling' and the promise of a new decade of optimism had been upon us. Little had we known back then that the 80's would be so devoid of much of any true substance? The Thatcher years had seen a complete U turn from Punk's initial idealism and explosive effect. The New Romantic new pop that was given birth with the help of more than a few of Punk's original faces was a true sign of the times that we were living in as Conservatism and complacency ruled for most and the politics of rebellion were thrown out of the window. Luckily there would be some who would continue to fight the cause. Newtown Neurotics, Billy Bragg, Paul Weller, the Redskins and others would pick up the baton left by the Clash: though the much maligned Red Wedge Musicians and politicians gang that sprung up in 1986, although trying hard and earnestly to connect with people, did very little to endear any left wing manifestos to the average pop music listener. As the 80's ended, many would fail to see any relevance in the little that was left of Rock n' Roll's political and rebellious nature. The spirit of the times instead, was focussed on escaping from the realities of the decade and having a good time: some records and scenes having the most particular impact!

Tony Beesley: "The big record at the end of the decade was the Stone Roses first LP: I fell for that record hook, line and sinker and bought all the singles too, including the 12" ers with extra tracks. The tunes were superb, the swirly guitar and spaced out vocals were very much of the moment and seeing as there was a clear Byrds influence – who I was a massive fan of – that just sealed the deal. By the time 'Fools Gold' came out at the end of 89, the bubble of the Madchester scene was ready to burst, and when it did there would be enough drugs, arrests, crime, hedonistic casualties and strait-jacketed inmates to fill the whole of Spike Island ten times over... on a quiet day that is as well! The others were Inspiral Carpets – 'Move' was a late 80's classic, I loved that Farfisa organ sound and they were clearly influenced by The Seeds and maybe the Standells and all that sixties USA garage music – also for a while I was digging the Happy Mondays: Ian Deakin had been raving on about them to me for a year or more."

Gary Peacock: "I thought the late 80's were a right load of shit! I can only really remember seeing New Order, Style Council, Prefab Sprout, Eurythmics (I liked Annie Lennox right from her days in the Tourists) and Billy Bragg. I mainly went to comedy clubs at the weekends, which were generally quite good 'the new punk'. A few mates were into the Smiths/Wedding Present/the Fall, but I never really saw much in them."

The Madchester 'Baggy' scene seemed to appear out of nowhere in 1989, but in fact it had been gradually coming together, from a variety of different scenes for a good while. Bands such as the Happy Mondays had been slogging away for what seemed like eternity; the Stone Roses themselves had already been Clash copyists The Patrol and had also dabbled with Goth, but the merging of the sounds of Acid House being played at the Hacienda and the Dance sounds coming in from the states, crossed over with the tuned in Indie kids of the city – who were turned on by New Order and Indie Rock - resulted in a new musical phenomena and a scene that would spread across the Pennines and beyond.

Andy Coles: (Right) "After the Smiths split up, there was a short interval before their influence spread and bands like The Stone Roses and Happy Mondays came along. I loved these and went to see The Stone Roses at Spike Island in 1990; a 'legendary' gig that although good, wasn't quite the Woodstock it was made out to be... the sound was poor and the supports were crap. New Order's Hacienda nightclub was seen as the Mecca at the time for fans of dance music and the so-called 'Baggy' or 'Madchester' bands, although I never went."

Kevin Wells: "The 80's obviously started off well with bands from the late 70's Punk/New Wave scene still carrying the torch, but with the invention of music-television bands started to get more polished in the way they looked and most of the music spiralled into middle of the road drivel."

Gary Peacock: "At one point I lived in London near Holland Park and used to go to the Slug and Lettuce in Westbourne Grove, which was very trendy at the time: I used to see Martin Fry in there quite a bit. It was at the Slug that I heard the first Stone Roses LP. It got played it over and over again and for me that LP changed music again; I still listen to it now and cannot believe that it's over 20 years old, it was a brilliant record."

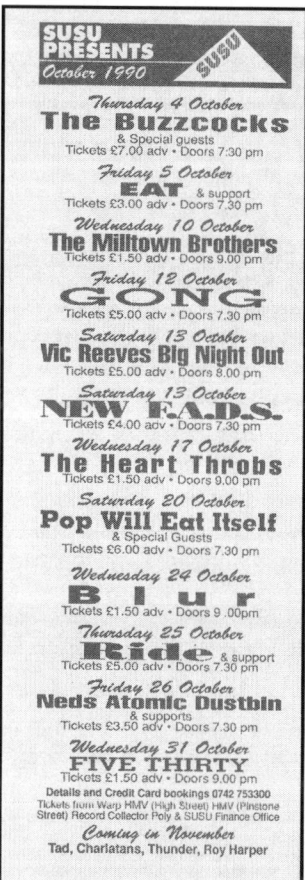

SUSU PRESENTS
October 1990

Thursday 4 October
The Buzzcocks
& Special guests
Tickets £7.00 adv • Doors 7.30 pm

Friday 5 October
EAT & support
Tickets £3.00 adv • Doors 7.30 pm

Wednesday 10 October
The Milltown Brothers
Tickets £1.50 adv • Doors 9.00 pm

Friday 12 October
GONG
Tickets £5.00 adv • Doors 7.30 pm

Saturday 13 October
Vic Reeves Big Night Out
Tickets £5.00 adv • Doors 8.00 pm

Saturday 13 October
NEW F.A.D.S.
Tickets £4.00 adv • Doors 7.30 pm

Wednesday 17 October
The Heart Throbs
Tickets £1.50 adv • Doors 9.00 pm

Saturday 20 October
Pop Will Eat Itself
& Special Guests
Tickets £6.00 adv • Doors 7.30 pm

Wednesday 24 October
Blur
Tickets £1.50 adv • Doors 9 .00pm

Thursday 25 October
Ride & support
Tickets £5.00 adv • Doors 7.30 pm

Friday 26 October
Neds Atomic Dustbin
& supports
Tickets £3.50 adv • Doors 7.30 pm

Wednesday 31 October
FIVE THIRTY
Tickets £1.50 adv • Doors 9.00 pm

Details and Credit Card bookings 0742 753300
Tickets from Warp HMV (High Street) HMV (Pinstone Street) Record Collector Poly & SUSU Finance Office

Coming in November
Tad, Charlatans, Thunder, Roy Harper

Nigel Lockwood: "The first time I saw the Stone Roses was supporting James at the Manchester international 2, on 30th May 1988, which was a benefit gig for clause 28. Also on the bill were the Happy Mondays, but we only caught the tail end of their set... then I saw James again at Sheffield University with the Mondays supporting: this time I saw the whole set, great dancing n' all !! Of course into 89, they all went mega, and great headline gigs at University and the Poly etc, I never did get the mutation into the dance and drugs side of it all though..."

Janine:(Rotherham Indie fan/Mod) "I was mad on the Stone Roses and all the Indie stuff around that time; Inspiral Carpets, Charlatans and Primal Scream. It did lead me onto the Mod scene too, especially after picking up on Paul Weller and The Jam and all of his solo stuff."

Pete Weston: "I did get into The Happy Mondays and Stone Roses as well as all the other stuff I was into."

Nigel Lockwood: "And then all of a sudden, it was the end of another decade, which for me, had also taken in the advent of Arena shows and outdoor stadium gigs including the Stones, Springsteen, Michael Jackson, Madonna, Bowie etc. THE ultimate stadium show I went to that decade was Live Aid, at Wembley stadium in 85, but enough has been written about that already, but it is still one of my all time live experiences. Also special 80's gigs mentions must go to Johnny Thunders, Hanoi Rocks, and The Lords of the New Church, the Cramps, Cherry Bombz and the Alarm: all of you who made me cream my jeans often, God bless you all..."

John Quinn: "As the eighties moved into the nineties, this is when I began thinking I'd parted my ways with youth culture. Madchester had its moments - especially Happy Mondays - although all that stuff about the Stone Roses' debut being the greatest ever made left me completely mystified. And still does. I bought it shortly after it came out and filed it under *'not bad but certainly not brilliant'* - and then I started hearing about how wonderful it was. Repeated listening (and it was hard to avoid around that time) still didn't unlock this supposed wonderfulness. I began to think that maybe I was just too old to appreciate it. It was obviously for the young. I was in my mid-20s at the time. Not down with the kids anymore. To this day I still think that the 200-year long *'we can really play our instruments'* bit at the end of 'I Am the Resurrection' is one of the most irritating things ever committed to vinyl."

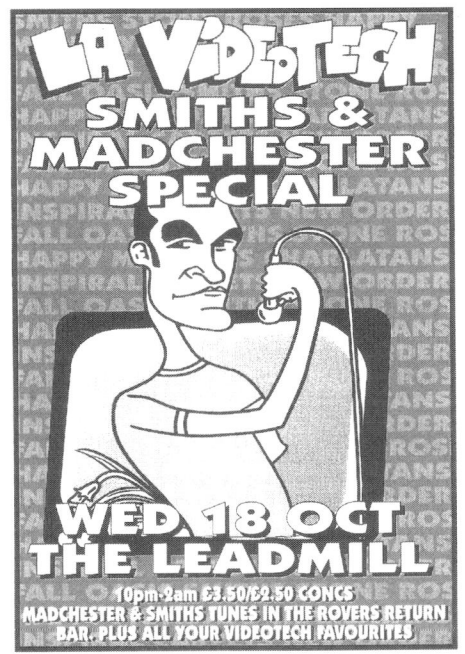

John Atkin: "I have to say; though I was not a massive fan at the entire Madchester thing at the time, I kind of liked it in one way as it did feel British. I do realize more now that some of the bands were actually quite good, but back in the day, it felt more like it was music aimed at townies! I suppose when you feel like you had already been part of an era (Punk for example) a lot of the latter-day scenes to follow seemed a bit false. Also, I had started to grow musically and become a fan of other styles other than the usual Indie stuff… Soul, Disco, Jazz and Funk."

In no time at all, every Indie band wanting to be noticed were jumping on the bandwagon of the new Rave explosion of Rock meets Dance culture via the 12" remix. Perhaps the most innovative and respected of all the 80's guitar bands to drop a psychedelic tab and turn on and drop out was Primal Scream.

The local club scene was also motivated greatly by the new Indie/Rave cross-over: Sheffield Leadmill being already on the ball with early House nights and the booking of almost any Indie band worth plugging a guitar into an amp. By the height of the whole Madchester period, club and Baggy themed nights were rampant and Rotherham was no exception. The onset of club culture, via the Acid House scene was now upon us!

Above: Stone Roses play a support slot at the Leadmill

Andy Coles: "I guess we stopped clubbing as we took up with regular girlfriends and the music scene changed around us. At the Peppermint Park nightclub in Rotherham, we used to shout at the DJ, a smashing bloke called Emmanuel to *'Get this House music shit off!'* and *'Put some decent fucking music on!'* but after a while it was futile: Dance music was talking off."

Shaun Angell: "1988 - Acid house and the rave scene-all loved up! That was the year that was! It was the start of the 'Acid house' scene with thousands of young men and women getting completely off their heads on mind blowing substances at dodgy venues up and down the country. These were usually old farm buildings, warehouses, and disused aircraft hangars etc that were commandeered by the organisers of the said events.

"It was also a boom time for many football hooligans like myself (allegedly) as many of these 'loved up' events needed security, ticket sellers and middle men to help things run smoothly and promote these popular happenings. It was a licence to print money to be honest and all the major football firms around the country from West Ham and Millwall in London to Hibernian and Aberdeen in Scotland, had the lads on the doors-all of them on the make and take with the amount of drugs and money going through the entrances."

Tony Beesley: "My most unusual diversion away from my Mod and Punk leanings has to be when I immersed myself in the House/Acid House/Rave music and club culture for a while around the end of the 80's to mid 1991. Yet again, there was a bit of a Weller-inspired thing going off, as I had been impressed by Joe Smooth's 'Promised land' that he had covered on one of the Style Council's last vinyl offerings. I started to root out quite a lot of Chicago House records, compilation LP's and then some of the Italo House that was around and to begin with it was quite refreshing but very soon became boring and repetitive. One biggie I bought was 'Voodoo Ray' by A Guy called Gerald... that was a superb record at the time and really influential and groundbreaking! I went to a couple of the early House nights at the Leadmill, but didn't really go full-on into it at that point.

"The real buzz came with the onset of the whole Madchester Baggy scene around the last half of 89. I had been buying the Stone Roses records and one day went on a Happy Mondays 12" buying rampage (Happy Monday on a Saturday afternoon!)... The buzz was on for something about to happen in music again. The pivotal moment for me was that classic Top of the Pops episode with Happy Mondays doing 'Hallelujah', 808 state with their Club anthem 'Pacific' and 'Fools Gold' by the Stone Roses. Next thing the whole thing went bananas!

"For a while I totally immersed myself in this new scene. Here I was, my first kid on the way, and I was growing my hair into a Shaun Ryder curtains style and wearing baggy-flared jeans topped off with those nightmare-ish hooded tops with an almost Egyptian looking design to em'. I then started to seriously uncover the real underground stuff of the new Rave culture... loads of records from Fon records which then became Warp and some crazy nights out to match. My good mate Andy Morton went over to Manchester and I gave him a huge list of records and he brought me some of them back. One of them was an early 808 state 12". I was crazy about them for a while and we went along to see them at the Octagon centre which was great. There I was in my tie dye shirt, baggy jeans: pissed out of my head and intoxicated with this new scene. Me and Andy were also planning a trip to the Hacienda in Manchester. Again Rotherham, just as it did back in the Punk era with the Windmill Punk nights, joined in with the scene putting on some superb

Raves at Pachas nightclub and even the Art Centre doing a couple.

"I can't remember all of the clubs and Rave nights I went to, but some events seem to be more prominent enough. Shipmates, or Horatios, in Rotherham held some fantastic nights around this time. It was out of the centre of town so mostly avoided all the townie idiots. The music was spot on with lots of the Stone Roses, Primal Scream (Christ 'Loaded' was never off the turntable back then was it, everywhere you went it was on), 808 State, Soho (Hippy Chick), Happy Mondays, Blur – with 'There's no other way' the sounds of LFO with smoke being pumped out all over the dance floor was intoxicating... Shades of Rhythm, Altern 8 and so on. Great nights, some right laughs and the dancefloor was always full. Drugs were on the go, for sure, but it wasn't at all heavy at that time. That was to come later.

"Another crazy night was the LFO rave at the Polytechnic. That was a superb night. I was well into the Sheffield sounds of LFO and their self-titled track LFO was as representative of the time as 'Loaded'. At the LFO Rave, I remember one lad in an anorak speeding off his head and just running all around the place non-stop. He was dripping buckets of sweat and eventually just collapsed in a heap in a corner. I was so pissed I fell down all of the fucking stairs which were so slippy from all the condensation and spilled beer. I went on my backside from the top to the bottom and just got up as though nothing had happened. My missus was absolutely crying with laughter at that.

"One night I remember going along to one of the Sheffield clubs, which was a backstreet one and as we entered it was like being transported to a seedy club in Chicago. It was completely full of, what looked like gangstas and dealers... looking as mean as you could imagine and wearing more gold than I had ever seen in my entire life. This was like gangsta turf and I was a bit concerned we were going to get done over... but in all fairness, apart from the looks up and down as we walked in, we never got one inch of grief off anyone. I even managed to be given a bit of space to do my crazy Acid House freaky dancing stuff... and no-one even offered me any drugs. They most likely assumed I was sorted!

"I went to lots of club nights in Sheffield: Cuba at Occasions, the Leadmill's House nights, Raves at the Polytechnic and later on some fantastic euphoric Rave nights in Rotherham at club Pacha: It was great for a while and everyone was well loved up with all the ecstasy doing the rounds. Believe it or not, I never touched the stuff, preferring to stick to my beer and the occasional spliff if any was being passed around. The whole euphoria of the Raves themselves was enough for me. I did do one bout of free-basing one stupid night and was sick as a fucking dying dog... so never again for this soft-core raver I'm afraid. I saw lots of lads (and lasses) becoming drawn into the scene and its darker side though. They started on the soft stuff, but soon descended into much heavier means of recreation. Some went down a very dark and one way path and have never come back from their journeys: Sad, but true!"

Ex Punk Rocker and Mod John Harrison had seen much hedonism and youthful exuberance throughout his teenage years, but the local rave scene was simply not his cup of tea – or pint of water either!

John Harrison: "Tony took me along to a rave. One thing I do remember about going to that rave is that they had turned all the cold water taps off, so that you had to buy a pint of water for 50p. It was red hot; you didn't even have to move to get a sweat on. Luckily, I had just had the skinhead after one of my mates – Gary – had cut my hair all over the show whilst I was asleep, leaving me with clumps of hair sticking out all over the place and bald bits at random... so I had it all shaved off. We went up to the top tier of this place and sweat was just pouring off us, and all that you could get to drink, apart from alcohol, was either warm water or pay for a pint of cold water. To be honest, the Rave thing was not my scene at all. Everyone was high as kites on ecstasy and acid, which was not for me!"

Richard Chatterton: "Acid house was storming the country but more importantly to me bands were picking up their guitars again in response to the Stone Roses, Happy Mondays and Inspiral Carpets, heroes of the 'Madchester' scene. It was almost 1990 and although things would never be the same again and I would be out of touch with 'the kids' and in my thirties, Sheffield United were at last making their way into the top division and within a few years we would again have a Labour government. Well if you had offered me these things at the time I would have snapped off your hands!"

Colleen Allen: "Madchester was at its height, Acid House, and 'Black' music. I recorded and performed with our band 'Ache' with my partner at the time Mark Miller, Patrick Simmonds and Adam Piper. I became pregnant but that didn't stop me from rehearsals in dodgy Hulme flats and all night studio sessions. With my baby in hand I went for rehearsals, gigged at the Hacienda, and continued life in the studio, brilliant times with people I adored and of course my growing family. My role model for the time was Neneh Cherry, who I saw live when I was 7 months pregnant at some venue in Central Manchester, I loved Neneh for giving pregnancy the cool factor, independence and the right to be a mother and more."

Tracy Stanley: "In the late eighties to early nineties music was changing and I got really into Stone Roses, The Farm, Inspiral Carpets, Happy Mondays etc and used to go to Club Pacha in Rotherham and Josephine's up Sheffield. Fashion became more relaxed and anything went: basically going out in jeans was unheard of for me but there I was, and it was liberating. I loved the Acid House scene although I never dabbled myself. It was just the atmosphere; it was a complete change from what we had experienced. It went from tension, constant fights, and bouncers knocking drinks out of your hand to get to their subjects, to what they called the *second summer of love*. Instead of fighting, footie fans were listening to music and popping a pill. The music was the Shamen, 808 State, D Mob, and KLF to name but a few. Compared to Punk it was similar in some respects as it was brand new and exciting and changed things."

Tony Beesley: "I was fast approaching my 30's and trying to hang onto some sort of hedonistic fun. Rave was dangerous, new and exciting, and for me fit the bill for a short while! It was totally different from Punk and the rest of what I had been into since then... some of my craziest nights out were around that time. Maybe I was trying to subconsciously shrug off my responsibilities as much as anything else? I really would not recognise myself then nowadays."

Lynne Freeman: "As we moved on from the eighties, people again wanted something NEW, not something which was reinvented. This time it came in the form of acid house and rave culture. I quite liked the Manchester bands, and although by this time I was married with a child, I couldn't let that freedom and wildness of spirit go. Even so, just because I wasn't out every night didn't mean I had to turn into a dead head; here was music again that unleashed something in me. I was often to be found, leaping around my kitchen while making tea to the sounds of the Happy Mondays and Stone Roses."

Pete Skidmore: (Left) "There was no bands around that I liked: the Style Council had split up and the onset of 'baggy' was approaching, bands like the Stone Roses Charlatans, Inspiral carpets, Happy Mondays etc. I never got into them at the time, even now I think it was over-rated, but it kick-started a stale music scene again. I love the Rose's second album though, as it's so heavy and also some of the Inspiral Carpets stuff along with the Charlatans who I've seen a few times."

Andy Coles "Sometimes we would go to Peppermint Park in Rotherham and get them to play some 'alternative' stuff but when the DJ, a black guy called Emmanuel, began to introduce 'house' music we would be shouting *'get this shit off'.* I saw him a few years after on my stag-do and he said *'this guy used to give me some right abuse."*

Tim Jones: (Right) "As time went on my interest in music remained, always looking for something new. I listened to bands like Gang of Four, the Cramps, the Smiths, Wedding Present, Pixies and then into Inspiral Carpets, Happy Mondays and the Stone Roses. Then it was dance music with bands like the Orb, Orbital, Leftfield and Chemical Brothers. I started to go to Festivals, starting at Reading and then Glastonbury where dance music seemed to be the music of choice, and remains a firm favourite today."

Shaun Angell: "The music was a thumping, pumping mix of Marrs, Yazz, Inner City, Mica Paris and early stuff from Inspiral Carpets, The Charlatans etc. The atmosphere at these illegal gigs was electric but there was very rarely any trouble because everyone would be dancing, prancing, hugging and kissing-all the usual bollocks. I really didn't give a fuck because I was only bothered about making money!

"At the time I was working as a lorry driver after the local coal mine closed down courtesy of Maggie Thatcher- this of course opened up all sorts of financial opportunities for me and as a 20 odd year old daft cunt like me wasn't about to let any chance of earning a few quid pass. I used to do a regular run up to Glasgow on Monday and got myself acquainted with some nice local chaps at an engineering firm near Ibrox Stadium in Govan. This was next to the river Clyde and for a small fee (as you would expect) I used to make a couple of trips down to the docks loaded up with steel tubing which was used to erect the big marquees for the raves which were going on in various parts of Scotland at the time. Once at the docks at a prearranged place the lorry load of steel would be transferred to barges or small trawlers and taken to their various destinations via the waterways and river networks to places like Ayr, Edinburgh, Dundee and Aberdeen. Never any hassle, just an innocent little sideline. Good fun had by all."

Anon: "I remember a few Rave associated nights I went with Tony to. The main one and maybe the best was the 808 State one, which had a really cool lightshow - strobes and that. Some others were the Flowered Up gig at the Leadmill who were also quite good. They got tied in with the whole Rave and Madchester thing that was going on at the time. They played a decent set to my memory. It was all ok and quite exciting, but things started to turn sour after a while."

Me, Andy Morton and Paul Clarke – 3 ex-Punk Kids at Paul's wedding in 1990

Fast forward a few years and one ex Punk and Marples gig goer turned to chronicling the local Dance scene in the mid 90's -

Neil Anderson: "Bizarrely I wrote a guide to clubs called the 'Dirty Stop Out's Guide to Sheffield' in 1995 and became an authority on the night scene - which included House/Rave etc and I suddenly found myself in the likes of The Face, Mix Mag and DJ magazine. Sheffield became a clubbing Mecca in the mid-nineties but - even though I had to visit venues like The Republic for 'research' purposes I still preferred a good punk gig."

Jamie 'Headcharge' Smith: "In America around this time House Music and later Techno were becoming big in clubs and were more about what was happening on the dance floor instead of people going to see a band on stage. The UK wanted a piece of this and local artists began to appear. In Sheffield, Warp Records set the standard for UK Techno and electronic music with many ground-breaking releases. The ethos shown by many of the new electronic artists was similar to the way that the punks had thought back in the late 70's. It was the case that with some simple electronic instruments and a computer once again anyone was in a position to make their own music and be as experimental as they wanted. Alongside these music releases people were looking for outlets to hear good quality underground dance music without going to the town centre club venues frequented by 'towny' types. There wasn't really much alternative but for people to organise their own Raves in warehouses and other unused buildings. They didn't need a regular venue with a stage, just a room where they could put the record decks and PA and a space for dancing. This later developed into what was known as the free party scene where every Saturday local sound systems such as Smokescreen and D.I.Y Sound system would find a quarry or field out in the countryside, leave directions on an answering machine and people would meet up for all night parties. This immediately had a connection with the Punk ideals about doing it yourself, just getting out there and having some fun and being anti-establishment. The sounds of Sheffield were emerging too: The Forgemasters, LFO and the eclectic and experimental sounds of the Warp label!

"The organised club scene in town was about conformity, big businesses and making money. The rave scene was about like minded individuals getting together and creating a place where people could meet up, listen and dance to some great music without feeling ripped off."

Tony Beesley: "By the middle of 1991, the whole Rave thing had become massive and the hard drugs had infiltrated so far into it: I was becoming very disenchanted by it all. Our earlier idea of visiting the Hacienda (the Rave Mecca) was now the idea of a nightmare as stories began to filter through of guns and very heavy dealings. Also the earlier optimism of the House nights and the new Dance experimentation had almost disappeared. The music coming through was Belgian Techno, which to begin with was fantastic with Joey Beltram's work etc, but was now being churned out on non-stop compilations of repetitive rehashes of a winning formula. You could buy a bag of records one week and the week after they would be classed as outdated. Things were moving too fast to retain any true element of quality. The fashion was Joe Bloggs and everyone and their kid brother was now on the scene. It was time to move on and forget all of this. I sold all of my records of that era and now I just look back on it all as just a temporary diversion away from the real me that

produced some great records, especially the early Detroit stuff and our own Sheffield pioneers and some of the more recent offerings from Underworld, Chemical Brothers and Leftfield (I just had to buy 'Open up' when that came out in 93)."

As the 90's picked up the pace, with Indie shoegazing the only real antidote to the increasingly dominant profile of the sounds across the Atlantic, one local musician entered his most successful period after attempts at Punk (Grip), Post-Punk futurism (The Frozen Ones), the New Romantic synth sounds of the early Vision and that bands spin offs and the Gasoline Party.

Andi Stevenson: "From the ashes of the Gasoline Party I formed probably Rotherham's most successful live act called Carnival of Thieves in 1990. From 1993 to 1998 we performed over 1,000 gigs with the pinnacle performing in front of 55,000 people at the 10th Anniversary Hells Angels Bulldog Bash in 1996 (The one where Eddie Kidd crashed his bike and ended up crippled and brain Damaged) ... so sad really and it happened not long before we went on stage). The band did two albums: the first one amazingly getting in Kerrang's Top Ten albums even though it was a self-financed album. The second album, though musically much better, didn't do much because I split the band almost immediately after its release."

The early 90's was a strange time for music: the much derided 80's were waved away with little fondness (a decade that in truth did produce a lot more interesting music than it is given credit for, especially the book-ending beginning and ending years)... the future for music seemed stale: an endless production line of Industry produced pop music, the new dinosaur bands (U2, REM etc) and an alternative band scene that offered nothing more interesting than the length of the guitarists fringe... as for the alternative nightlife of the Steel City- Even the Limit club had closed its doors for good by now! What was there in line for the restless spirits of our generation?

Richard Chatterton: "Work wise I again spent time signing on. I went on a Thatcherite community programme working as an archivist in the Bretton Hall Drama department based at the Yorkshire Sculpture Park. On my first day I found myself alongside other art school casualties, mostly from Leeds, who also didn't know what to do with their lives. After six months the travelling by bus became too much and I reluctantly left. Soon afterwards I decided to pick myself up and start the long journey towards art tutoring. I spent six months in the US working on a kid's camp and then travelling cross country to LA. I got an office job - at last - at the Manpower Services Commission and temped for a while, did voluntary work in Youth Clubs and then was offered a place at Birmingham Polytechnic to study for a Post Grad in Art and Design Education. I also met my future partner Joanne, who had served behind the bar at the Limit Club for years without us bumping into each other. We shared a love of Bowie and the Velvet Underground and she owned a jukebox and the only juke box engineer in town called her the 'Rockola Lady'."

Tony Beesley: "Everything became boring again: Indie music became so so repetitive and snobby. I was just buying Dance and Indie records as a matter of repetition, but I had lost all real interest and enthusiasm for it all: if this is the future we were yearning for, give me a taste of something from the past. I started to listen to my old singles boxes again for fresh inspiration... Punk Rock, The Who, proper Soul and Rhythm and Blues... the bleeps had become redundant, give me back some passion, some real grits and soul... and let's get those guitars plugged back in!"

Madchester and its accompanying Rave scene had burnt itself out into a thousand varying and disparate paths by the middle of 1991. A second generation of bands appeared – Northside, Paris Angels etc, but the scene was dying! The Happy Mondays had met their drugs and Bellyache nadir; Inspiral Carpets now knew how it felt to be lonely; the post-Spike Island Stone Roses virtually retired from their recording career for another long and bitter four years whilst The Hacienda and many more once exciting and challenging clubs of the era succumbed to hard and dark crime-ridden times along with more than a few of the scene's more adventurous types... Ecstasy was made illegal and the side effects of a loved up generation of ravers created a new decade of psychosis and character self-assassination for many. Smiley was no longer smiling!!!

On a positive note: for Sheffield innovators Cabaret Voltaire (Right) the sounds of electronica and Techno - and its many spin off genres of the time - had finally caught up with their particular musical stamp. In 1990 they released some of their most accessible (but still adventurous) records to date and met the burgeoning Dance music scene head on with club favourites such as 'Easy life' and 'Keep on' and their extended 12 inch mixes. Their involvement with the Warp label and their own linked studio, along with their Sweet Exorcist projects, saw the Sheffield pioneers finally being credited as being the true musical visionaries that they had always been.

Tony Beesley: "By the early 90's, I had started to settle down, in a sense, and after getting married we had our first son Dean in 1990 followed by Sean two years later. Having kids puts all things in proportion and suddenly that latest record by that latest band that you are into, just doesn't seem as life-defining. I still went to see bands occasionally and was as mad about music as ever, buying vinyl by the bucket load when I could afford it and selling stuff too: If you saw that fella outside the Charlatans Octagon gig selling Charlatans live tapes - that was me (the returns paid me into a House club after the gig!). For a while, though, it was hard trying to juggle bringing two little kids up and maintaining my love of music and going to gigs, but I somehow managed to balance the two. My love of Soul and Mod returned back in my life as well- after a few years away from it: The Indie haircuts and baggy jeans now being replaced with Mod clobber and a Weller style haircut again. I saw some of my old Punk mates now and again, but totally lost touch with most of them. The Punk era really seemed like a lifetime away at that time!

"I remember tuning into John Peel during the early 90's and it was all Jungle, Drums and Bass being played, along with the obligatory The Fall session. As much as I still greatly respected Peel's massively eclectic tastes and forward thinking approach, I had to turn it off: it was boring and going nowhere for me personally. The same with Grunge and most of the shoegazing Indie bands of the time. Apart from the odd band such as Ride and the false start of the Stone Roses etc, there was nothing new coming along for me that hit the right buttons.

"Towards the end of my Rave days, I was starting to pick up lots of the new underground Soul sounds coming through the club and House scene - Alison Limerick's 'Where Love lives', 'Olympia's 'I want your love' and Frances Nero's 'Footsteps': another great track was 'Unfinished Symphony' by Massive Attack. I had been collecting all the Warp and Network label dance 12"singles and some of those later ones were heading towards Soul and Disco, one E.P even being called the Discotheque E.P. From there I dabbled a little in the Acid Jazz stuff with early Brand New Heavies and a bit later Mother Earth etc.

"Then there was the whole sixties thing again: which never seems to truly go away once you uncover it all. I started re-listening to the Byrds (who I love to this day), Arthur Lee's Love, Buffalo Springfield, Beach Boys (Pet Sounds era), Zombies, The Move and the Doors. I also collected all of Bob Dylan's best albums and became an enthusiastic fan. I still dig a lot of his stuff, but my affection has always been tainted ever since he came out with that statement of saying all of his songs such as 'Times they are a changing' etc never meant anything to him! Of course throughout, I always kept my love for the Small Faces and the Who close to my heart. By the early 90's I had ended up with literally 1000's of records, a mate of mine went over to the states and came back with a garage full of 45's and I bought loads off him. I soaked up lots of different sounds and Mod-inclined music: eventually I just had to sell off lots of them as there just was not enough space to keep them or time to listen to them. It had been a really golden era for listening to music for me though.

"Uncovering lots of rare stuff from bands like the Standells, Richard Kent Style and lots of Soul etc inspired me to go much deeper and before you know it, I was hooked on the truly obscure Mod sounds again. It was all retro before that word even existed as an everyday term, as far as I knew anyway, but it was all cool stuff and still sounds the biz to this day."

It was clear that a clean sweep of the UK music scene was soon about to take place... and it would involve a respectful nod to two previous decades of British flavoured Rock and Pop!

Before the re-evaluation of British Pop music could take place, there was an invasion from over the Atlantic to bridge the gap... Grunge careered out of Seattle, USA, from a music scene that was influenced by, amongst other sounds, the UK Post-Punk sounds of the late 70's to early 80's. Often referred to as Lo-Fi (due to its muddy dampened sound) and much of its releases being brought out on the Sub-Pop label, the Grunge scene's adhered title was also in reference to its dressed down slacker look.

John Quinn: "I could never really get a grip on Grunge. A lot of it just sounded like heavy metal and as far as I'm concerned that type of music begins and ends with Motorhead. Some shoegazing stuff around that time was okay, but not exactly dynamic. We wanted action."

Nigel Lockwood: "The Grunge scene and all associated bands were really pre-dated by Sonic Youth, who I incidentally I saw at Manchester University in 1989, supported by like-minded band Mudhoney, who also were an influence on the Seattle bands. I was actually intending to see Nirvana on their last tour and had the tickets and then the inevitable happened."

The Grunge hero of the hour was Nirvana's Kurt Cobain: the band racing to the fore of the 1991 music scene following their albums 'Bleach' and the seminal 'Never Mind' – the latter of which, along with an 'of the moment' Top Of the Pops appearance with single 'Smells Like Teen Spirit' captured the spirit of the times and the attention of every aspiring music fan with a taste for guitar driven Rock music with guitar to the fore and memorable riffs of repetition that they themselves may aspire to learn. For the next 3 years or so, along with Pearl Jam and others, Nirvana and Grunge and the universities of the Slacker generation X held the music scene by the length of their crusty long hair.

The era of slackerdom and Grunge came to a close with the suicide of Kurt Cobain in April 1994: just as a new generation of English pop musicians were starting to rebel against the American Grunge invasion. The previous year had seen post-baggie revitalised Blur decide that *'there's no other way'* but to call for the yanks to go home and re-evaluate our English Pop music heritage instead. Blur were going through a re-evaluation of sorts; presenting an anti-Grunge agenda with their new Mod-enthused classic British Pop-loving outing 'Modern Life is Rubbish'. A band soon to seriously rival Blur also released their first single -'Supersonic' almost in direct conjunction to the demise of Cobain and Grunge!

Socially... of course, much had changed locally, as well as nationally, too. The towns of Rotherham, Doncaster, Barnsley and their immediate suburban relatives, were quickly losing their Post-War character and Northern grittiness. The closure of the pits, the ever-increasing Steel Industry privatisation and job cuts, Thatcher being superseded by a replacement puppet helping to kick the last of Northern independence into the history books... the creation and subsequent opening of the huge Meadowhall shopping Mall in 1990 signed the death knell for much of the local businesses and the CD had replaced the record, heralding a new era of music as a commodity to be created, sold and consumed with about as much identity as a box of Cornflakes... Marion Elliott (Polystyrene of X-Ray Spex) had screamed to us in 1977 about *a consumer society* and now in this new decade of divided affluence and privatisation... that very future had arrived!

Back to the music! In 1991 Paul Weller arrived back on the live circuit as the Paul Weller Movement: his Mojo being revitalised by the revisiting of his old Small Faces and Who 45's amongst other influences – Acid Jazz, Traffic, Tim Buckley and Neil Young included. Joe Strummer was also not too far from rediscovering his muse and presenting his brand new world vision of a Global sound system. There was even talk of a fully-fledged Dexys Midnight Runners re-emerging. As it happened, Kevin Rowland followed his half-hearted solo album of 1988 with a mere taster of what his large and unique talent was capable of.

Nigel Lockwood: "I went to see the Dexy's reunion in the mid 90's and I was amazed and intrigued by the amount of Kevin Rowland look-alikes."

Tony Beesley: "I have a massive amount of respect for Kevin Rowland, and let it be said, his once right-hand man Kevin Archer who himself wrote some superb contemporary post-Dexys Soul with the Blue OX Babes... strictly speaking, though, Archer was just as much of a visionary as Rowland and there has been more than a element of *who came first* debate regarding the two's musical ideas. The singles Rowland put out 'Manhood' and 'My life in England' were good enough, but it could have been so much more. The real Dexys vision was never truly re-ignited, I am sad to say. The man has enourmous talent, so I still live in hope for the true return of Kevin Rowland."

The rebels of the 80's were long gone – though not forgotten – by 1992. The short lived pro-feminist Riot grrrl period passed: apparent leaders of the gang being Huggy Bear, but it was L7 who famously presented a waist down full frontal display of Riot grrrl nudity on late night Channel 4 music and culture show The Word.

Parallel to this, a new line up of kids were forming bands: kids who had missed Punk by, in some instances, the best part of a decade or so, but were as deeply affected by, and inspired by the possibilities of taking Rock music back to its most basic, and often rudimentary form, as the kids of 76 – 79 had been. Following Suede (whose frontman Brett Anderson was old enough to have caught first hand the tale end of Punk- Anarcho Crass style Punk in this instance) – a small - but significant enough - certain kind of new noise was being produced. The nods toward Wire, Adam and the Ants and other left-field Punk era acts, along with the pop sensibilities of The Jam, and in Elastica's case ... the Stranglers - were being formulated. By 1993, the songs were written and the music papers were starting to take notice.

Modern Life is not so Rubbish!

The Indie Kids, the bored and restless Punk generation and retired Mods all, were now being swept along atop a wave of new music that was looking back for its inspiration to the Mod sounds of the sixties, the new wave craft of Punk song writing and a positive nod towards the future!

Tony Beesley: "Around this time, I bought myself a guitar and an amp again and started to play once more, after a period of around four years of not even owning a guitar. I had sold all my amps, guitars and equipment around 1989 and lost all interest. Still, even now, my days of performing to an audience were a thing of the past, but I did feel a great urge to play again and learn some new songs. I started to play along to Blur, Paul Weller, Elastica (who had just released their first single 'Stutter') and to no-one's surprise, I suppose, the old Punk records."

First, though, there was the music press invented New Wave of New Wave that helped pave the way for the next musical phenomenon: The loose movement of associated bands, those Punk inspired kids we speak of - a selection of whom graced the 'Shagging in the Streets' E.P - were thrown together to inject a dose of excitement into the tired out Grunge inflicted UK music scene.

Tony Beesley: "I saw the very first live reviews of this new wave of new wave thing, which would be around late 1993. At first I was sceptical, but after checking out the first few records from the bands, I was converted. Yes, yet again it was a media created movement, but the music was right up my street and a welcome antidote to all the crap that was being served up at the time. These Animal Men were a much under-rated band and appealed to me with their almost Mod take on new wave mixed with a kind of New York Dolls style of trashy Rock n' Roll. The records were exciting again and on vinyl: Smash were much better live though.

"It wasn't just a case of regurgitating the old Punk stuff as there were new themes and contemporary angles in the songs and some great new charismatic personalities emerging... Sonya of Echobelly, Louise Wener – who often spoke a load of crap, but was always engaging and came across very un-PC, which is no bad thing... Shed Seven made a good start but, for me, became bogged down in the straightjacket of Indie land soon after their first album.

"I was buying lots of the records amongst many long forgotten ones, but there were some true classics that are amongst the very best of the years since Punk. Sadly doomed by the time Oasis made their mark, and the music press had a new toy with the squabbling Gallagher brothers (who themselves hated the new wave of new wave)... this was a brief golden period of music and fondly remembered by myself."

At the very start of a year that saw Manic Street Preacher Richey Edwards disappear never to be seen again, the Charlatans Rob Collins emerge out of prison (to be met with a tragically premature death the following year) and Kurt Cobain pass into Rock's fatalities history... the NME front cover gave us Elastica jump-starting the New Wave of New Wave. The scene was set and very soon it would be time for Britpop!

Chapter Nine
Britpop and the revitalisation of Mod!

"For a short while it seemed like the war was won... or so we thought!" - **Andy Coles**
(Rotherham music fan)

"After many years of playing crap gigs getting fuck all recognition, and almost breaking up many times, eventually Pulp started getting a bit of attention and seemed to be in the right place at the right time for once: payback time. It was very gradual, you didn't wake up one day and it was all flashing light bulbs and Peter Stringfellow buying you champers the next... but the rest is history so they say" - **Nick Banks** (Pulp)

The advent of Britpop was just what the British music press were waiting for at the time. With more than a vested interest in the creation of a new scene that would not only take front cover precedence and boost sales, but at the same time also earn them reappraisal and street credibility after almost a decade of introspection and dwindling relevance in the eyes of the music buying public. The scene was set with Suede's Union Jack flag draped front cover of Select magazine... a band possibly as much responsible (by proxy) for the ensuing Britpop fever, without wishing to be a part of it, as Dr Feelgood had been with paving the way via Pub Rock to Punk 20 years previously.

The NME's new found love of all things British in contemporary pop music would manage to encompass a vast array of greatly talented and less than truly talented bands and artists from the Post-Madchester meets Sex Pistols *wall of sound* of Oasis to the newly revamped career of Mod God Paul

Weller via a catalogue of new bands that fit the genre. For a while during 1995 and into 1996 if it was British and registered as pop music, with even the vaguest nod towards recreating the classic sounds and styles of our own swinging sixties boom... then it must be Britpop!

Apart from the Blow up club (where the Mod element to Britpop came into full force), the so called epi-centre of the Britpop scene was credited to Camden Town, London, where members of Elastica, Menswear and Blur rubbed shoulders with, and partied along with, celebrity hangers on and fellow musicians in the Good Mixer - a run down Irish pub. Each week a brand new band would grace the Indie hopefuls sections of the music weeklies, whilst a new wave of Britpop-devoted music programmes hit our TV screens almost relentlessly. Friday night's 'Something for the weekend' preceded by the infamous CH4 extravaganza 'The Word', itself a left over from the 1990 Baggy scene days, set the ball rolling, followed by the White Room and the Chris Evan's hosted irritation of T.F.I - that seemingly aimed to try and recreate the 'weekend is here' euphoria of mid 60's Redifusion stalwart 'Ready Steady go', but ultimately served merely to entertain us with some fantastic live bands in the studio whilst annoying many of us with its repetitive moronity. A certain proportion of the memory of the Britpop years will be forever tainted by that programme!

Throughout a period of the Britpop era, towards the end of 1995, when classic British Pop was being re-evaluated and appreciated and long forgotten Brit-Mod rockers such as the Creation were finally being applauded, the Beatles anthology albums, and more notably, the accompanying TV series meant that the days of Beatlemania were being re-awoken. That Christmas period, as the last Beatles anthology episodes were broadcast, everyone with a love of all things cool and sixties orientated were asking friends and immediate elders *'Just who was your favourite Beatle?'*. Cynics have even suggested a Beatles connection with the actual creation of a movement called Britpop? What is sure, despite its often annoying 'catch all' title, the period spawned some fantastic new music! Finally, and coincidentally, the antithesis of the Beatles reappeared in 1996 with the re-imagining of the original Sex Pistols – complete with Glen Matlock back on bass. A Melody Maker front cover revived a whole new series of live dates around the world and open debates on their modern day relevance, many declaring profound positive opinions on Punk Rock's naughtiest band!

The newly found enthusiasm for quality British (often Mod inclined) Pop music was not lost on the City of Sheffield, its gig-going student population and some of the Punk generation's thirty something gang. The Leadmill venue, as always, provided the live setting for many of these upcoming 'music press-applauded' bands (Oasis played a legendary career starting-point gig there on April 9th 1994 following a Take two appearance under their earlier name of Rain), with landmark appearances from all of the key participants of the scene. Close by, the Octagon centre and lower Refectory also catered for many memorable outings from tours such as the Bluetones/Supergrass double venture, Elastica, Blur and Sleeper, Teenage Fanclub and in-between their Leadmill and Arena shows, the 'Definitely Maybe' touring Oasis. Britpop even afforded finally, the well deserved acclaim of Sheffield's finest – Pulp. The Modfather himself even chose the Leadmill to play a low-key 'Stanley Road' promoting set at the Leadmill in June 1995. A new Labour government was just around the corner and all appeared to be perfectly timed for a brand new hopeful future. The new positivism of the new era would also turn out to be a perfect opportunity for revitalising some Mod inclined Britpop-loving music fans!

Tony Beesley: "Just prior to Britpop, I would be wearing lots of Mod looking clothes...Prince of Wales check trousers, hipsters, Paisley shirts, Ben Sherman's (which were so hard to track down back then before all of the High Street versions reappeared with Britpop etc), Levi's, Sta-Prest trousers, Suede western jackets, two-tone shirts, Clarke's original Desert Boots (which I had to order from a shoe shop in Rotherham). My hair would be short Mod crop with triggers (usually during the summer) and the longer more Bouffant Weller/Marriot style. I was totally intoxicated with the whole sixties Mod thing. In those days, Punk seemed such a long way away. I still loved all the best Punk bands and would go and see the Buzzcocks and Joe Strummer, but for a while during those days, it seemed as though the Punk thing had all been a dream. I was so far removed from what I saw as modern day Punk like all the Hardcore American sounds that no one would have even guessed that I had been so affected by Punk back in the late 70's. Then came Britpop!

"I loved Britpop, despite its title. It was a fantastic time for British music. The feeling in the air was very Positive and that here we were in the middle of a new golden age for Pop music... which of course for a while we were. Anything seemed possible. I became a regular gig-goer once more too. Of course, in essence, it was a media created hype- as always, but the music was great and I felt a part of something again!

"Immediately prior to Britpop, there was the 'New Wave of New Wave' thing, with its Retro 70's Punk and New Wave influence. I was quite excited about that and went straight out and bought all of the records as they were starting to appear. Despite the music press invention, there were some superb records coming out and I saw some great gigs too. I think the first one was Smash at the Leadmill who were being touted as the spiritual leaders of the movement? They were good that night and it did remind me of some of those old Punk gigs. Blessed Ethel were support who also got tied in with the New Wave scene. Then I saw These Animal Men, Echobelly, Elastica, Sleeper (every other week it seemed at the time), Powder (superb under-rated band), Tiny Monroe and Shed 7 (supported by Supergrass at the time of their classic Punk 45 'Caught by the Fuzz' - one of the best records ever). I remember at the These Animal Men gig at the Leadmill, meeting up with Terry Sutton and we went backstage. The band were hanging out and playing table football with their girlfriends. They kept giving me a shifty look as if to say *'who is this fella?'* I was wearing a Polka dot shirt and cream Levi's jean jacket topped off with a Punky Mod hairstyle...which I think may have confused them as the standard attire of the average Leadmill Indie gig goer was not yet Mod influenced in any noticeable way. Around this time Oasis played at the Leadmill with their first single 'Supersonic' just out, quickly followed by Blur at the Octagon centre (Sleeper supporting) and the Britpop era in Sheffield was born!"

Steve Gledhill: (Doncaster music fan) "1986-1991 is pretty much a desert for me, in terms of music - I completely missed out on a lot of stuff, probably linked to a lot of turmoil in my private life. I started getting interested again at the turn of the 90s, with the Acid Jazz and House movements, but didn't really get really back into things until the emergence of Oasis and Radiohead."

Like those long forgotten bands of the Punk era (who but the truly faithful can recall Venus and the Razorblades, the Users, Rikki and the last days of Earth and Neon Hearts?), so Brit-Pop had its unfortunate stragglers – Mantaray, Whiteout, Rialto, Speedy, Sussed and Posh - that would be largely erased from most musical memories before the 90's ended: It was a step back to another golden period of British Pop music that would inspire the sounds and look of much of the era's fans.

Inarguably, Britpop brought to the fore many Mod influences and associations (along with Punk and the Casual look). The song writing of Kinks songwriter Ray Davies was being re-applauded and Paul Weller was displaying just as much excitement with the new mood in British pop music as anyone else. A good section of the fashion of Britpop lifted much of the Mod cut of clothing, and the classic British Pop song was once more being celebrated.

Tony Beesley: "I had bought 'Modern life is Rubbish' by Blur in 93 and again there was the Mod influence. It had been a great poke in the eye to the Grunge scene that was massive at the time and a scene that never touched me at all: the only concession being Nirvana's unplugged set and LP and their 'Never Mind' LP. Then came shoegazing band-come-good Ride's 'Carnival of Light' album... which I loved. With Blur's 'Park life' LP in 1994 and the rest of the new bands coming along this was a very exciting time. You could still buy vinyl back then, even though

339

CD'S were available as a mass market thing. I would go to Circles in Rotherham town centre and buy loads of this new music coming out. Elastica (I saw these 3 times and I have to say they are up there in my best gigs ever: I just couldn't resist the temptation to racing to the front for a good old dive around to 'Vaseline' and 'Annie'...perfect Punk Rock for the 90's), Action Painting 'Laying the Lodger' (what a great Punk Rock single for 94 that was, very Subway Sect sounding), Teenage Fanclub, Heavy Stereo, Pulp, Mantaray ('Adoration' was good; my eldest son wore the free T-Shirt that came with the first LP, it was that small), Thurman (their single 'English Tea' is a Mod/Britpop classic, even though they had jumped on the bandwagon, previously being long-haired rockers ahhhhhh!!!!), the Weekenders (Blow up club spawned Mods), Powder, Suede, Bluetones and loads more. I loved both Oasis and Blur. I remember when all the battle of the no.1 spot fuss was going on, that some people regard as the high water tide for the Britpop scene: even my young five year old son Dean, knew about them both. Then there was that Melody Maker front cover with all the bands displayed on there: it seemed like a proper music scene in many ways, but there was also a sense of 'Here we go again, the media are taking a grip of things again'... still it was great while it lasted!"

Heather Quinn: "I first got into Blur around 1993/94 after reading an interview with Paul Weller. He cited Blur as one of his current, favourite bands. I hadn't really taken much notice of them, but thought if Weller likes them I'd better check them out! 'Modern Life is Rubbish' had been released a while. I remember watching the video of 'Sunday Sunday' and the lyrics reminded me of the Kinks. I bought a copy of 'Modern Life' just as 'Park life' was about to be released. Being a fan of 'Quadrophenia' (the film), I thought it was a brilliant decision to feature Phil Daniels.

"The first time I saw Blur live was at Sheffield Uni and I thought they were fantastic. The energy of the band (and the audience) was electric. They stormed through the set-list. It was obvious they would go on to bigger things. Although not strictly Mod, I loved Britpop for the style of music which came out of it, plus the fashion was not so far removed from the Mod ethos. You could see that many of the Britpop bands were influenced by the likes of the Jam, the Who, Small Faces etc.

"I was watching 'The Word' with Terry Christian, when this band called Oasis came on singing "Supersonic". They looked spot on and really grabbed my attention. The singer oozed attitude, as he snarled his way through the song. I instantly became a firm fan and as with Blur, you just knew they would become big. I was disappointed that I never managed to see them live until they played Sheffield in '97, by which time they had started playing arenas. I took my teenage nephew to see them at Sheffield Arena and it was around this time I started to feel really old. Bands had always been older than me and now it was in reverse, plus here I was chaperoning my 14 yr old nephew who was crisply dressed and the spit of Liam. As well as Weller, Blur and Oasis, I was also listening to a lot of Ocean Colour Scene, the Seahorses, Mother Earth and JTQ. I was really into bands on the Acid Jazz scene too."

Anon: "I had been through a few wilderness years musically. I was bringing up my young family and working shifts, so didn't really have the time or money for gigs or vinyl. I remember watching the Word late one Friday night and this band came on who looked cool; had some attitude and sounded great. They were Oasis and they sang 'Supersonic'. I then tracked it down and loved the B-sides as well. I found out they were playing at the Leadmill in a week but because my youngest daughter was only a few weeks old, we decided not to go. That's one of the few gigs I regret not going to. I bought the album on its day of release and played it non-stop. We them went to see them at Rock City and they were awesome. It was rammed and condensation was just dripping off the ceiling and running down the walls. It was when they did 'I Am The Walrus' as their last song and just walked off one by one to just leave a wall of feedback. I had the misfortune to stand behind 'Nottingham's Tallest Man' for most of the gig – why does that always seem to happen to me! So that was it, live music was back in my life. I had a mate at work that was also into Britpop and we saw most of the main bands from that era either at the Sheffield City Hall or the Leadmill and Rock City."

Wayne Kenyon: "I was cool on Britpop at first... didn't really get the name, Britpop? I wasn't too keen on Oasis after only hearing the singles but I borrowed the album from a mate and loved it. I was more into Oasis than blur; being an old Punk Rocker their music appealed to me more, more of an edge and attitude about it. I also got into Shed 7... I didn't really go for the girl bands like Elastica etc... not really my cup of cha. Loved the Manics, though and I still do!

"The good thing about Britpop was that it brought back guitars, after the early 90's Techno dance shit that filled the charts... anyone remember any of those bands? No didn't think so... I had arguments at the time with people who said that shit like 2 Unlimited would be remembered as long as the Smiths...really????? Oh shit! I remembered 2 Unlimited....

"The bad thing that came out of Britpop for me was that it paved the way, in the UK at least, for the poncy American so called Punk bands like Sum 41 and Blink 182 and, dare I say in the UK, for even softer versions like Busted and Mcfly. There is a generation of kids who think that these are Punk bands. No time for Green Day either, I don't wanna be an American idiot, ha ha. One of the bands I got into which kind of came out of the Madchester scene but stayed through Britpop was James. Still love em, but wish radio DJ's would realise they have more songs than 'Sit Down'."

Andy Coles: "Eventually, during the 90's the music scene changed again and after Grunge (*urgh, horrible!*) completely passed me by, along came the Britpop bands. Oasis and Blur fought it out for top band status and Sheffield's own Pulp managed to finally take off! Jarvis Cocker's lyrics filled me with the same excitement that the lyrics of John Lydon and Morrissey had previously and often had me laughing out loud with their references to places and things that were familiar to me. It seemed somehow at the time that 'Indie' had taken over the charts, even being taken up by the white-shirted beer boys who had previously made going into Sheffield such a pain in the arse. The video for Pulp single 'Mis-Shapes' even took revenge on the townies that had made Cocker's life such a misery around the City Centre. The Tories that we blamed for screwing up our area went into opposition (thank God!) and in came New Labour, who were going to lead us to a better future (yeah, right!). For a short while it seemed like the war was won... or so we thought!"

Speaking of Pulp and the new optimism of the times; the effect of Punk also contributed to much of the cutting edge and idealism of the key players of Britpop; its direct links too many to explore in detail here – suffice to say that the Sex Pistols coincidentally reformed in 1996: Punks influence being omnipresent and vise versa... most visually obvious when Jarvis did his infamous Michael Jackson protest at the Brits!

Nick Banks: (Pulp drummer) "I suppose the Britpop times were great really, it may be a cliché but we just got on with our stuff. It was a laugh in the main...Pulp were in essence - in my opinion - a Punk band. We always approached songwriting and stage shows with the attitude of try to be different. Be entertaining. Be new. Having punk as my formative musical experience really instilled the idea that the attitude of go against the mainstream was the way forward. Be different."

John Quinn: "It was a very mixed bag and it of course it depends what you define as Britpop. Supergrass for instance were often lumped in with it, although, their music always seemed like it could have come out any time in the previous 20 years, while Suede, who according to some started the whole thing, were never really connected in my head with what followed.

"The likes of Elastica, Echobelly and the sadly-not-as-successful-as-they-should-have-been Rialto put out some fine material. But of course the three bands that everyone remembers and connects with Britpop are Oasis, Blur and Pulp. I'd interviewed Noel Gallagher on the phone before Oasis headlined The Leadmill. Apart from saying that I sounded drunk (I wasn't) he came out with all the *'we're the best band since The Beatles, we're going to be huge'* stuff. Yeah, right I thought, having not been too impressed with their first single. But I went to see them anyway and was told beforehand by a fellow crowd member with Manc connections that they were really going to blow my mind. Then they appeared on stage and started with 'Shakermaker', which Noel had told me was going to be the next single. *'What a load of absolute crap,'* I thought after about a minute and went and stood in the bar where it sounded much the same, but just a crucial bit quieter. Nothing else they did that night dragged me back into the main room, so I wrote them off as another bunch of blowhards who thought too much of themselves. I later found out that they had played Sheffield before that, unannounced on the bottom of a bill headlined by fellow Creation Records act BMX Bandits. I was at that concert too, but this time didn't even leave the bar to see what they were like. You can see how I got my reputation as a music scene star maker.

"As they say, the rest is history. They ended up being very good: For a short while anyway. I finally got to see a full set by them at Sheffield Arena during the 'Be Here Now' tour, by which time it's fair to say their best days were behind them. The strange thing is that I quite like 'Shakermaker' now. Compared to practically everything else they've recorded since 95 it's a masterpiece.

"Blur meanwhile were much more inventive and have released some fantastic stuff. They can probably rest assured that they will always be considered legends. But I just don't like Damon Albarn... at all. This also stems from a telephone interview early in their career. Like Noel he bigged himself and his band up, but unlike his Oasis rival who, at least seemed to have a sense of humour, Albarn had an air of extreme condescension about him. There have been very few occasions when after interviewing someone my first thought has been: 'What a tit,' but the Blur bloke is one of them. I could be wrong about his personality (as it says in John Harris's excellent Britpop book The Last Party, Damon's speciality is certainly not good first impressions) but he just struck me as someone with his head fully inserted up his own arse. He's extremely talented though. In fact probably a genius, but I still don't like him... So there.

"Morrissey once put out a single called 'We Hate It When Our Friends Become Successful'. I've never been friends with Blur or Oasis, in fact never spoken to a member of them since those interviews, but Pulp are a different matter. I'd known their drummer Nick since schooldays and had become acquainted with Jarvis, Russell, Steve and Candida through regularly going to see Pulp and writing about their various exploits - one of the first pieces I wrote for The Star's pop page was on their 'Death Comes To Town' single, which to this day still hasn't been officially released. Great band but they're just too quirky (and unlucky) to ever make it was what I thought. Wrong again.

"We might not hate it when they become successful but it certainly changes things. The band themselves were always friendly and polite but you could see people treating them differently because they were now pop stars. Of course Jarvis got most of the attention and the fact that I knew him and also worked for the local newspaper led to an increase of attention for me. There was even a particularly creepy tabloid reporter who came up to Sheffield and tried to get me to tell him about Jarvis's secret life. I ended up explaining that if there was a secret life I didn't know about it. That's the point of having a secret life, I should imagine.

"But tabloids are used to famous people. The general public is a different matter. A relative in Scotland actually asked me if I was on first name terms with him. Of course not, I refer to him as Mr Cocker Sir and doff my cap every time we meet...

"It got worse. One female friend living in Liverpool begged, nay demanded, that the next time I met him I should get his autograph for her. So, on seeing him in The Leadmill around the time of 'Common People' I asked for his signature. It was one of the most embarrassing moments of my entire life. He sneered at me, and rightly so, even if to his credit, he did write a few words which I passed on. I stayed at my friend's place recently. She still has it pinned up on her wall. The next time I saw him he apologised and explained that he'd been hassled all night and for someone he'd known for years to treat him like some sort of awesome star was the final straw. Fair enough. I've made a point of never asking for his autograph since then."

Tony Beesley: "One of the downsides to Britpop was all the casual Joe Normals who suddenly jumped onto the lad image with Oasis and started to think they were Mods. The lazy looking over-sized Ben Sherman shirt-wearing brigade was here and suddenly they had been Jam fans all their lives. Even so, I suppose, as a generation of a certain age, we had grown up from laughing at the Likely lads in the 70's to behaving badly under the influence of this new lad culture. We were all, in some way, affected by that mentality and swept along for a while, I suppose."

Mandy Taylor: "When I think of Britpop I automatically think of Oasis and Blur and the mid nineties. I was however surprised to learn that Pulp are also classed as Britpop and therefore I was one of the very first people at a Britpop gig! I was at the same school as Jarvis Cocker and attended the first Pulp gig in the school hall. I think it was around 1979, and I'm sure that they were called Arabicus Pulp back then as I remember a badge I had saying something like '*Arabicus Pulp are damned good.*'

"I wouldn't say I'm a massive fan of Oasis (my son is) and I think that at times their lyrics can be lazy- what's that one that goes something like 'there's lots and lots for us to do' that reminds me of a theme tune to a kids programme. Personally for me, Oasis don't evoke that Brit feeling. I much prefer 'Song 2' by Blur but mainly because it's a good bouncing around song, again I don't get that sense that their songs reflect for me that Brit feeling. For me Pulp did do this, I think it's because they have reflected some of my Britain from when I was growing up, I can certainly identify with 'woodchip on the walls'. I know where Stanhope Road is and I have a good idea who Deborah could have been."

Tony Beesley: "Again, as back in the Punk era, some of the support bands of the Britpop era were exceptional: Sleeper supporting Blur played a fantastic set at the Octagon, and Louise Wener was... well 'Delicious'; Powder (with Elastica I think?) loved them too... they reminded me of Penetration and all the old new wave bands; Supergrass with Shed 7 at the Leadmill were outstanding as were 60 Foot Dolls who I saw supporting someone? They were really energetic. That period 94 to early 96 was a fantastic time for me: I was overwhelmed with the whole 24/7 appeal of music... gigs, records, playing guitar (I was only a bedroom musician by this time!), clothes, Northern Soul do's, a bit of Acid Jazz (Phaze did a stomping version of Julie Driscoll's 'Indian Rope Man')... even the music on the telly was much better. Being used to seeing Punk bands dive around, I did find it strange, though, to watch Oasis stay almost motionless during their whole live set."

The Britpop era also spelled the end of a more personal time for one local Mod and fan of the scene.

Pete Skidmore: "We had lived on the outskirts of Sheffield for a while and to be honest it was shit I hated it, I had become everything I hated when I was younger. I lost touch with mates although I made new ones but not the same. I dropped football; only going to big games, we even went to see Simply Red! What was I thinking? Although seeing Stevie Wonder was good. I got to see Weller again on some of his first solo dates, got married in 1994 what a mistake! In 1995 we moved back to the Woodseats area and Britpop was happening! I was back into music in a big way, was back drinking in Woodseats; seeing old mates and going to gigs, it was heaven. I got to see Blur, Oasis, Charlatans, Inspirals, Pulp and Weller etc.

"Around this time, I was buying records or CD's every week we even had a record room in the house! I was well into Cast and discovered the Real People- a truly awesome underrated band. My relationship with my wife was falling apart and I had other distractions such as Woodseats pubs, concerts and music and football. I started looking around for another scooter and started buying Scootering magazine and going to a mod night in a bar up near where the West One complex is now on West Street. My old mate Russ Sutton owned it, and they had a mod night every month or so, plus I was starting going to Brighton beach at the City Hall which played a lot of Indie, old sixties and Mod stuff. I was having a fucking great time; it was that great that I was chasing women although I was married! My marriage started to crumble at the start of 1996 and we split the following year.

"I had made new mates and was back going to gigs: at the Leadmill I saw bands such as Ocean Colour Scene, Paul Weller, Black Grape, the Verve, Cast, the Real People... Pulp at the City Hall and Super Furry Animals and Oasis at the Arena, all great bands. I had a room full of CD's all on shelves and I spent most of my time in there. I bought my wife's share of the house and had loads of fun. In 1997 I got a scooter and with a couple of work mates went to a couple of rallies; I was really hooked again!"

Tony Beesley: "I loved the new material from Ocean Colour Scene. I had bought 'Sway' from their baggy era days, but by that point it sounded really dated, whereas 'The Riverboat song' and 'You've got it bad' sounded fantastic. I caught some of their early gigs at places like the Leadmill and they were fantastic. It all tied in perfectly with my tastes in the Britpop stuff and my on-going love of Mod Music. There I was a thirty something with two kids and having a fantastic time again going to gigs, buying loads of vinyl and wearing all the Mod clothes I could get my hands on. Back then, there was hardly anywhere to buy the cool clobber around here, apart from the charity shops and the usual rip off mail order places. You really had to search hard for Italian Knitwear (sometimes I would find something right under my eyes in one of the fashion catalogues) or a decent button down shirt. The only place to get a decent pair of trousers in Rotherham, apart from Mallinsons, was having them tailor-made by George at the top of the Market... but he had pissed off around this time too."

Jeff Platts: "Oasis – Mod? To me they were just casuals trying to make out they were Mod."

Heather Quinn: "When the Britpop/Adidas fashion craze started, I'm afraid I jumped on the bandwagon. As the 1980's had progressed I had found it increasingly difficult to find the right style of clothes. I often made my own clothes, or hunted in charity shops - which in those days stocked all sorts of things, unlike today's versions of charity shops. Occasionally I would take a trip to London to visit Carnaby Street or Portobello Road market. However, as mortgages and kids came along, all this started to grind to a halt."

Tony Beesley: "I took on board some of the fashions that came with Britpop at the time; mostly the Mod influenced styles. I was wearing the go-faster Adidas trackie tops, Fred Perry's again, Harrington's as always and a bit of a Mop top hairstyle. I was still in my 30's and in touch with the scene: even buying all the music weeklies every week again. It was a really exciting time."

The best of the late 80's Indie bands such as Primal Scream (whose 'Screamadelica' was a much loved Indie Dance crossover LP), Teenage Fanclub, Lush and even the constantly absent Stone Roses managed to stay in favour during the emerging Britpop era: in some instances, it was a case of the music scene finally catching up with them, rather than vice versa... a case in point – The Charlatans: and not forgetting the Mod icon Mr Weller!

Tony Beesley: "One of the massive LP'S for me at the time was the Charlatans 'Tellin' Stories'. The other exceptional LP's of the period were the first ones from Supergrass and Elastica, the first two Oasis ones, obviously, and then there was my old fave Mr Weller!

"I had been a massive Jam fan and was also big on the Style Council. I don't care what any of those post- 'Wild Wood' 'bandwagon' revisionists say nowadays, Weller's songs with the Council were still, for the most part, top-notch stuff. True he went off the boil around the 'Cost of Loving' LP, but some of his best songs were written back then:' Man of Great Promise', 'Blood Sports', 'Head Start for Happiness', 'How She Threw It All Away', 'Spring Summer Autumn' being a mere few examples. The critics and some fans had been dissing Weller after that but the true Weller fans had always been there regardless!"

Weller fanzines and Day at the Races ticket

One such true Weller fan was Sheffield Modette Heather Quinn - who (like ardent Weller/Jam fan Pete Skidmore) had followed the Modfather right from his Jam days.

Heather Quinn: (Left) "When The Jam split, I was gutted. I thought the early Style Council was good, but wasn't so bothered about their later material. I went to see them a few times, but for me they lacked that spark of the Jam. Towards the end of the 80's there was hardly any new music around that I liked. I rarely went to gigs, with the exception of seeing Steve Marriott, who was still doing the pub circuits.

"Fast-forward to '91 - I remember being on the bus on Snig Hill and spotting a fly-poster advertising the 'Paul Weller Movement' at the Octagon. I bought tickets as a surprise birthday present for my other half. When the night arrived, I remember arriving at the Octagon to an eerie emptiness. After being used to sell out venues and chants of WELL-ER, this seemed odd. There was no crush, no fighting to get to the front, just a handful of people awkwardly milling around. They ranged from aging die-hard Jam fans (us) to Style Council fans who had no interest in the Jam. Slowly the venue began to fill. I felt for Weller - it was like he was starting at the bottom all over again. Weller and the band came on stage. He looked nervous. The band was ok, but somehow seemed disjointed. The female backing singers looked uncomfortable and out of place. Weller played the Small Faces' 'Tin Soldier', as a tribute to Steve Marriott, who had just tragically died.

Paul Weller at the Octagon (Heather Quinn)

"Maybe it was my imagination, but the sorrow of Marriott's death hung over the evening. Weller played well though, getting better as the night went on. You could detect that spark and little did I realise that the spark would light the blue touch-paper and we would all have to stand well back, as Weller made a triumphant return to lead the way for Britpop through the 90's and beyond."

Pete Skidmore: "I (also) got to see Paul Weller's new band at the Octagon in 1991... £14 a ticket and not a lot of people there! Still it was good and I started showing an interest in music again especially with the new CD format, I bought the first Weller album, which was a Japanese import before it came out here, which I loved."

Every now and again during Rock n' Roll's illustrious and ever-changing spiral of events, a special and pivotal moment arrives that proves to be, not only a lifetime rewarding memory, but also creates a feeling of belonging and being at the right place at exactly the right time. For the Punk cast of our generation it could have been any one of a mixed bag of enticing experiences... from the secret Sex Pistols gig at the Outlook in Doncaster during Punk's summer of hate, The Clash proving their worth beyond the Punk Rock blueprint at the Top Rank during their London Calling tour, Ramones on one of their few visits to these inland shores, the Specials at the Limit club through to Oasis at the Leadmill! Not long after the gobs from Manc land played their career kick-starting performance at Sheffield's most visited alternative club, another often heard voice of the people decided to take a journey through Stanley Road via the Sheffield Leadmill.

Tony Beesley: "One of my favourite gigs ever is when Paul Weller played at the Leadmill. That was a corker that one and I only just managed to get hold of a ticket. The place was packed out, it was red hot and the atmosphere was electric. From the moment Weller picked up his guitar, the place was alive with a massive surge of excitement. It was really obvious that Weller was genuinely enjoying it too. I mean the old lad don't often smile for nothing does he? All the classics were played, though this was at a stage in his career that he had not seriously re-visited his back catalogue. But, to be perfectly honest, there was no need for the old Jam and Style Council nuggets... this was here and now – 1995 and the sounds of the era were being performed up there on that stage: I was loving it!

"I remember chatting with Dave Spencer at that gig. It was the one that we both realised that we were both born on the same exact day as each other: we always seem to meet up for important occasions that's for sure. What a gig that was too. A couple of years before I had been to see Weller play in Sheffield and it was a very low key affair. I don't think many could have predicted how big he would become after those wilderness years. Yet again, the Mod stylings were an influence on me. This time, it was a more pastoral late 60's kind of influence - the stripy ribbed tops and all that. I saw Weller numerous times throughout the 90's and beyond and his influence continues to this day."

Sheffield Modette Heather Quinn – one of the most consistent Mod obsessives of our generation – caught another act at the Leadmill who were very much respected by contemporary Mods.

Heather Quinn: "I first came across the Prisoners in '82 when they released 'A Taste of Pink'. I thought they were a great band and very underrated. When they briefly reformed around '96, I was pleased they were to play the Leadmill. I remember the gig was a late start and the night seemed to be never ending. The Leadmill had a fantastic club straight afterwards, which really made the evening. The place looked sold-out; it was absolutely heaving with bodies. The Prisoners were unbelievably good, especially as it was about ten years since they'd last been together, their playing was so tight. They played like men possessed - the sound of that Hammond organ just filled your soul. Everyone was

exhausted by the end of the gig. The Leadmill ceiling dripped its usual mixture of sweat and condensation and your feet stuck to the floor so badly it was almost impossible to dance, but no-one cared; it just added to the fantastic atmosphere."

As the Britpop era unfolded, Mod connections and all, the stirring of all things Mod returned to reaquaint themselves to original Mod revivalists from the area!

Rob Wasteney & Scooterist pal Wayne Ridge 1996

Rob Wasteney: "There are always times in your life when you sit and think of good times that's been and gone; people and friends who you haven't seen in a long time and the like! On one of these occasions - on a winters night in Jan 94 - I listened to some music I hadn't played in a while enjoying a few cans of beer and reliving a few happy memories. I realised just how good and how much bloody fun I'd actually had over the years, but apart from buying the odd scooter mag I'd done very little on the scooter/mod front for four or five years and I know you can't turn the clock back but I couldn't help but wonder if anything was left of the scene and if so if any of my old friends were still involved in it?

"Most people when looking back on their youth are embarrassed to look at photos of how they looked and what they had worn: even what records they have bought and listened to. I felt nothing like that and could only look back with pride - for me being a Mod had been a fantastic experience and something I would never change or do differently. They were days of great excitement and I really lived everyday on a high, looking forward to the next gig, night out or a scooter ride."

"Before Feb 94 was out, I had bought another Lambretta scooter: it wasn't anything special but more important for me was that I'd found my way back into the lifestyle that had given me so much pleasure in my youth. It had changed greatly and gone were the thousands of people and scooters on rallies, I rode to Southport in May of 94 and there was only a few hundred people present, no trade stalls and an average 3/4 full night time do. To be fair I think 94 was around the time when the scooter scene really bottomed out. Today, though, the scene is once again buzzing, vibrant and full of activity.

"Later that year I joined the Sheffield Travellers scooter club and started to attend the CCI Mod rallies put on by Tony Class and Emma Cox: numbers again were not great but the people and night dos were pure quality... be it Rhyl, Scarborough or the Isle of Wight - a great time was always had. I'd also discovered Roy Mason (Rotherham's Ace Face) and his brother were still involved in the scene and riding scooters - well some thing's never change."

A year later and Rob's old scootering pal Tony Lound was once more bitten and subsequently intoxicated by the whole scene again. There was proving to be plenty of life left in these old 2-Tone, Mod-loving Scooterist kids, and now with far more responsibilities in their lives (and that's only the scooter parts).

Tony Lound: "20th Dec 1995, The Scene were appearing at the Theatre Royal, Barnsley organised by the Barnsley Vikings Scooter Club. I had recently purchased a Vespa T5 classic,

simply to use to and from work and the odd nostalgic blast. It was on one of these 'nostalgic blasts' that I bumped into my old mate Rob Wasteney riding an ochre yellow GP200. It was surreal, having not seen each other since our late teens, here we were nearly 30 both reliving our youth!

"It was Rob (Wasteney) who introduced me to the Barnsley Vikings. They were quite a big concern on the scooter scene running events, rallies, ride outs and so on and were touting for new members. Apparently they hosted members who were cast in the film 'Quadrophenia'...no question then, where do I sign!

"The scooter scene had come on some from where I had left it in the early '80s. Ska, Mod and Northern Soul were still the main but Brit Pop and The Manchester sound had given things a new edge bringing with it a fresh influx of younger faces following the likes of Oasis, Stone Roses, Blur and so on. The Britpop scene brought more variation to the music being spun at the Club do's and on the National Rallies. Many large venues were promoting the scene as a whole, in particular Brighton Beach and it brought in many a younger face through the doors of our club swelling the ranks. It wasn't long before they were up on the dance floor to

Northern Soul and Ska with the rest of us old gits! Live Ska was still very much available, with Pauline Black and the reformed Selecter still doing the rounds. The Specials were soon to reform with Neville Staple on lead and pretty much an original line up albeit minus Jerry Dammers.

"The most prevalent of them all though were Bad Manners, still knocking out the original stuff at scooter rallies, club Do's and night clubs all over the UK. I managed to see them probably more than a dozen times during '96 & '97. The best gig I can remember was June '96 at Whitby Esplanade it was just a local Scooter Club do but the smaller the venue the better they were.

"I had been *'bitten by the bug'* again pretty bad. What was meant to be a way of re-living my youth on the odd weekend with some like minded mates had by the end of 1997 culminated in over 30 Rallies and Events plus Club Do's and countless Club meetings: I'd got myself a double page spread in our 'Bible' the Scootering Magazine which featured my custom Vespa and I also become the Number-1 (chairman) at BVSC! It then resulted in it becoming like a second job and was putting a strain on things at home: all the fun had gone out of it. Something had to give, so in typical drastic fashion I resigned as Chairman, quit the Club, while the good times out weighed the bad, then sold the Scooters and called it a day (never to look back)!!!"

Below: Tony Lound and scootering mates in 1998 just prior to packing the scene in. Brighton Beach flyers picked up by me during my visits there

In 1996 the effects of Britpop created) scene peaked and optimism. Oasis and Blur the 90's, Jarvis was a celebrity and many of the great hopes overnight.

were slowly fading as the (media lost much of its initial spark and were the new Beatles and Stones of – which he always deserved to be – of the era seemed to disappear

The local Mod scene had yet again been revitalised with the opening of Leeds and Sheffield's Brighton Beach nights: which presented a monthly dose of a late night swinging sixties theme playing the best in Britpop and contemporary Indie music with a passionate injection for the real rootsier and cooler sounds of Mod, including classics of the day and a consistent supply of newly uncovered Mod sounds – on vinyl. Sheffield's very own monthly Mod event took place beneath the City Hall in the Ballroom with its expanse of rooms, corridors and dancefloor(s). To begin with the venue would whet the appetite of many local Mods and serve as a regular meeting place with the very best in cool Mod music being sound-tracked... obscure and newly discovered or commonly loved classics.

Tony Beesley: "Brighton Beach started at the City Hall Ballroom in 96 and I started going there about the end of the year. There was a gang of us that used to go, not all Mods but certainly influenced by it and the Britpop scene. There were friends of mine Phil and Paula (who were mad on Oasis, Ocean Colour Scene and the Kinks, Small Faces etc) who used to go regularly. It would be us, a couple of Mods and a mix of curious mates who were on the fringes of the scene who would tag along. We had some fantastic nights there. To begin with it was a very Mod event… Christ, I once had to rub my eyes in disbelief when I spotted a true 100% dead ringer for Pete Townsend circa 1964 – he even had the big nose too.

My mid 90's Britpop Mod era

"In the small room, there would the place, all dressed to the very Hammond/Jazz influenced, sixties R&B 45's. The music in the other side was more be loads of Mods from all over nines. The music in there was mixed with lots of really obscure mainstream Mod like The Kinks, Small Faces, Tamla, Booker T and the MG's, the Stax sounds mingled with the very best in contemporary music like Primal Scream, Charlatans etc. I remember the 'Blow up a go go' track by James Clarke being massive in that side. At the time there was a kind of revival of the Hammond organ instrumentals and all the 'Blow up' compilation CD's started coming out: once cheesy instrumentals now sounded pretty cool. I would look forward to the Brighton Beach events… Great times!"

Neil Anderson: "I went to Brighton Beach a couple of times and saw Paul Weller at Don Valley Stadium but I always preferred The Jam."

Janine: "To begin with, Brighton Beach was fantastic! It was a real get together for Mods and the music and atmosphere was top quality. Eventually it all went downhill and became a place where hangers on would just go along to freshman's and pick up a retro shirt to go in there. The student lot ruined Brighton Beach, without a doubt."

The excitement of the times inspired some 70's Mods to reacquaint themselves with scooters and scooter clubs.

Pete Skidmore: (Right) "Some lads who I had known in the early 80s were starting up a scooter club: there seemed to be loads of scooters around Sheffield again and we finally got a few interested and various names were banded about namely 'Bitterness Rising Scooter Club' which didn't happen until one of the lads came up with Northern Line SC? He had been a member of it when it was around in the early 80s. I didn't see the point in reforming a club that most of us hadn't been in anyway but the name stuck. We met on Wednesday nights at the Wentworth pub across from Sheffield Arena, I was a founding member along with Martin, Simon, Jayne, and Gary who came up with the name, and we started to get more and more members and at one time could probably count a good 30 or so scooters on a Wednesday night. I had a Lambretta GP 175 which later became a 200: it was a mix of Lambrettas and Vespas. Around this time (1998-99) a lot of scooters appeared: this was mainly due to lads leaving the scene in the early 80s due to families and now they had grown up and were getting back into the scene, plus a lot of younger lads who were into Mod and Britpop. My mate Martin had a lovely Lambretta GP 175 in gold which he later had murals painted on of scenes from the film 'Lock Stock and 2 Smoking Barrels'. He won a few trophies as well for this

Pete at the Weller Don Valley all-dayer in 1997

scooter. We did quite a few rallies in that first year.

"Further afield, we went to Cleethorpes, Mersea Island Skegness, with always something daft happening due to masses of beer. We went to the St. Georges club in Scholes near Holmfirth which I was one of the best I ever went to. I was dancing and Martin and Simon were battling it out behind me with some Rotherham lads. We went up to Bridlington in October to the custom show, setting off at 3 in the afternoon, my scooter was flying by this time after having spent a lot of cash having a rebuild at RS Tuning in Doncaster which was owned by Ralph Saxilby top lad! I brought Selby town centre to a standstill when the lights at a junction suddenly changed to red and I had to stop- leaving a 20 foot skid mark on the road and people were looking around to see what had happened. The next day saw me and Gary put all our bags in a shopping trolley and pushed it across Brid to another B&B.

"The scene around this time was the best, we went to Skegness and there must have been 100 scooters in a lay-by - just before the A1 - waiting for us Sheffield lot. What a sight to see- all those scooters rushing the barriers at Dunham bridge with the poor guy inside trying to get the barrier down: he must have lost at least £100 on that day!"

Tony Beesley: "The end of the Britpop era came and it was a case of where to next... yet again! The optimism of the mid 90's and the ousting of the Tory government had now subsided and it all became a bit depressing to be honest. There was even a slight New Romantic revival in 96 with the new short-lived Romo thing, I bought the Plastic Fantastic single to check it out but it didn't do much for me. For me personally, 1998 was a bad year all round: I found out my Mum had got advanced breast cancer, I took a kicking in a Rotherham boozer from four hefty blokes (a fight that also resulted in my mate getting bottled and my other mates girlfriend being kicked in the stomach whilst pregnant by those same big and very brave fellas)... and to top it all off I ended up with serious pneumonia not long after and nearly ended my days: the hospital thought I had bleedin' lung cancer n' all. I have the scarring on my lungs for life too to show for it. I also stopped buying the NME in 98 after twenty odd years.

"The music scene was being drained of all excitement too. Cornershop were ok, Beck got my interest for one single only... Ocean Colour Scene, my big Mod hope of a couple of years earlier were now playing Arenas along with Oasis, Blur and Pulp and the rest. Even Weller seemed to have hit an artistically-low point in his solo career (in my opinion anyway) with a luke-warm continuation of his heavy soul which culminated with his worst solo album two years later with 'Heliocentric'. Thankfully he came storming back in 2002 with the outstanding 'Illumination', but in 1998 most of my musical comfort came from my ever dependable boxes of Mod/R&B 45's."

This was also the advent of the tribute bands. At the end of the 90's the first attack of tribute mania was starting to take a hold on some disaffected music fans: early ones of note being the Australian Doors, the long standing Bootleg Beatles (who understandably had seen greater fortune on the back of the Beatles Anthology interest and Britpop itself) and clones dedicated to the sounds and styles of the Stone Roses and the Jam. Not that many years later the fascination for this sort of almost cabaret fans indulgence would grow into a very lucrative business with some touring name-sakes commanding more revenue than the acts they were copying.

Pete Skidmore: "We were also regulars at the Boardwalk whenever the Jamm played who were a tribute band probably going longer then the original Jam. Cleethorpes was always a good rally: we would meet up with Phil Deakin and the Rotherham lads- a cracking set of lads as well! A daytime session and then out at night and into the winter gardens for the evening do. It never ceased to amaze me the lengths people would go to look good at these rallies, some would have spent all

The *North* of Englands Premier Modernist Event.

S h e f f i e l d

day riding and then dressing up at night in suits and stuff. I take my hat off to them. Our lot it was all about the beer and getting there ASAP and hitting the pubs.

"We went to the IOW in 2001, although cheating we chucked the bikes in a van. I had only just got back from Zane the night before and I was sat in the back of the van with a big bag of weed and a beer! Munchies at the service station! I was thinking of going a bit further and doing my scooter up even more. I had a few themes I wanted to put on it but settled on my love of Punk picking out my favourite Punk records and having the covers scanned and printed on to vinyl stickers. Derek at 'Absolute Scooters' did a great job with putting them on and lacquering them in. I added a name to my scooter calling it 'VIVA LE ROCK' after the old Punk T-shirts. It looked well and I was well pleased and I did some miles on it over a couple of years; using it everyday for work as well. On Sundays it would be parked outside Nonnas the Italian coffee bar on Ecclesall road whilst Karen my girlfriend, and now my lovely wife, would pass the day away with coffees and buns! It got some serious looks and people would always stop and look at it!

"To be honest I didn't really get into Northern Soul until I was in my 30s; probably around 1997-98 and it kinda stuck with me from then. Now I'm no expert on this genre of music but I went mad on it for a while, mostly the well known stuff. Some of my favourites are 'Too late' by (I think) Johnny guitar Watson?, the Frankie Valli track 'The Night' is awesome, Nolan Porter 'If I Could Only Be Sure' which I liked before Mr Weller covered it, plus 'Come On Train' by Don E. Thomas which has recently been used for a credit card ad, I could go on and on as the thing about Northern is that there is that much that you can always find something new to listen to.

"During this period we had trips to see Paul Weller, Bridlington was one where Martin pestered Weller's dad for autographs which he got, also Manchester Apollo and Sheffield City Hall where we had a huge turnout meeting in the nearby Wetherspoons pub. We went to see Ian Brown at the Octagon with me and Martin pissing everybody off around us by moon-walking during Ian Brown's version of 'Billie Jean'. I also went to see the Charlatans at Doncaster Dome and The Fall at Sheffield University where me and Karen had been on space buns and joints for two days and we just stood laughing all the way through the gig."

Kevin Wells: "The 90's and the formation of the Britpop movement saw bands embracing their guitars once again and a lot of bands getting their inspiration from the Punk and Mod bands of yesteryear. Oasis were the front runners of Britpop and when they hit stardom with all their swagger, even though it was nothing new, it was still like a breath of fresh air. I remember seeing them on the 'Definitely Maybe' tour at Sheffield University and thinking *'wow' this is back on, a band that connected with the crowd,* it was as though they could have been any one of the crowd getting up on stage and just doing it (circa '76). The only trouble with the Britpop era, though, was the amount of crap bands that jumped on the band wagon and that's why I lost interest with music towards the end of the 90's."

John Quinn: "And that was that. Oasis have finally split up - at least a decade too late - the original Blur line-up played a series of rapturously-received shows recently, and Pulp are no more either, although I have heard very vague rumours about a possible reunion. And nowadays I don't even know what's in the charts and don't care either. I'd rather stick to my old stuff. That was when bands wrote proper tunes. Maturity, it gets us all in the end..."

The Mod scene had changed drastically since the revival of the late 70's and the underground years of the 1980's. Organised clubs and rallies split and formed new societies as the emphasis on the differing notions of what Mod meant to them became too wide to seal the cracks.

The music and code of dress also saw a dividing of the Mod inclined. Original early to mid sixties loving Soul and R&B suit loving Mods with short hair and a purist outlook to Mod saw little to relate to in the new swiftly emerging Swinging Sixties Regency jacketed, Yardbirds/Brian Jones Mop-attired Freakbeat fans. Organisations such as the New Untouchables (previously the Untouchables) endeavoured to bridge these differences with a hip mix of all that sounds cool on and off the dance-floor. They continue to do so to this day. Manchester's Hideaway club sought to create a melting pot of late 50's R&B, Rock n' Roll, Blues, Hip Jazz and obscure soul and became highly respected for its exceptional standard of quality sounds. What is for sure is that during the 90's and onwards, the meaning of Mod meant a lot more variable things to more and more people!

Tony Beesley: "I suppose I went through a bit of a Psychedelic phase, looking up old obscure UK Psych, Freakbeat and the Nuggets stuff. My hair got longer and the clothes took a more late sixties look for a while... suede, paisley, polka dots and again-Chelsea boots. Amongst the present bands I liked were Psychotic Reaction and Big Boss Man (who played some seriously funky Hammond organ-driven instrumentals), along with some of the really obscure funky Mod stuff that was coming through during the late 90's onwards such as Sugarman 3, Brothers Seven, Charles Bradley, Nick Rossi Set (the sound of Georgie Fame for the 90's and beyond – proper Mod for the present!): I also bought all those Blow up style lounge-sounding compilations too. The ever-progressive Primal Scream did a really cool B-side – the giveaway titled 'Hammond Connection'. As much as I loved all of this, I feel it was a case of me branching out and absorbing more varied sounds as opposed to a conscious decision to change my tastes. The classic Mod look soon reappeared and I got my hair cut in the really short Mod style again – moving back onto the Soul and R&B sounds."

As much as Mod is about the music of Black R&B, Soul, Mod Jazz and a portion of related Beat music being spun on original vinyl for Mods new and old to show their affection for on the (talc strewn) dancefloor, the influence on musicians throughout its long history has never been something to be ignored. Much has been said and written on the sixties bands and possibly more about the 79-81 Mod revival period: but the following decade quite possibly introduced the most actively pure Mod live bands scene since the sixties themselves.

It would be more than a fair task to try and document every Mod inclined band and the job will be done in a more dedicated volume elsewhere... but it would be only right to try and mention at least a good few of the bands that were trying to impress ardent Mods and swinging sixties Freakbeat fans during a golden period of Mod – the 90's.

Along with the Prisoners, The Clique come close to being one of the most revered Mod acts of the time: their line-up fluctuating a little through the period, they released a much loved LP 'Self Preservation Society' in 1995 and performed at many rallies and Mod vents of the time. They, like most of the Mod bands of the era, were signed on Detour records, whose founder David 'Dizzy' Holmes can be thanked most of all for keeping the contemporary scene alive on vinyl.

Knave included Go Go dancers and a Hammond organ onstage, The Apemen (from Germany) and The Jaybirds (from Austria) both frequented the big weekenders, Mustn't Grumble were a Small Faces dedicated band, the Solarflares were ex-Prisoner Graham Day's 'powerpop evangelists', The Risk from Guernsey also produced powerpop sounds and also serving their dues were The Hoodwinks, The Mystreated (psychedelically inclined), The Surrounds, The Phrogs, The Direction, Hipster, Psychotic Reaction and The Aardvarks and many more. Popular music history does not record all of these bands, but ask any self-respecting Mod of the time and they will have seen or bought records by at least some of them.

One devoted Mod, who has been dedicated to the cause right from the first stirrings of the Mod revival of 1979, is Stewart Hardman.

Stewart Hardman: (Barnsley Mod) "I remember back in the days when I was first starting out on the scene, and having a badge that said 'Mods into the 80's', so this would have been late '79, and I was thinking that was like some far off time and place, and here I am in 2010 and still doing the same scene....

"As we moved into the 1990's things opened up in a big way really, we had dual rallies at the start of the decade, firstly the Phoenix Society rallies of the mid 80's had phased into the C.C.I. – Classic Club International, and then we had The Untouchables start up, bringing a more purist Mod sound, away from the Revival and slight Indie sounds which were been played on the CCI. They later had a split themselves and became The New Untouchables, which is still going to date. There were also at various times The Rhythm and Soul Set, Hipshakers and then towards the end of the 1990's The Underground which ran for something like three to four years, I'm almost certain that I attended all at various times throughout the years.

"It was also a time when Mod became more accepted; in the press; on the High Street and even for Mods and Scooters to be featured in adverts on the television - probably the most famous one being for Lucozade and then the Walkers crisps ad with a voice-over from non other than 'Jimmy' Phil Daniels. Even the bands of the time were talking about their Mod leanings/influences without (in most cases) being too tongue in cheek.

"After a couple of *dark* years at the start of the decade, with the Grunge era, the scene suddenly got a jolt of fresh blood when the early Blur/Charlatans released singles that got lots of playing time at Mod do's and rallies up and down the country. I suppose this was fully realised during the 'Brit Pop' (hateful name) years of 94/95. Then when a totally revitalised Paul Weller was back with some of his strongest material in years, with the Wildwood/Stanley Road LP's, the music press heralded him as the 'Modfather.'

"The scene got a much needed influx of new blood, drawn in by the likes of Oasis, Mantaray, These Animal Men, Ocean Colour Scene, Menswear, Blur, Charlatans, and Supergrass to name but a few... Which is needed every so often, otherwise it's just gonna stop with the old guard as we are now! Every so often, some new blood comes through, and they find a whole new world of the sights and sounds of Mod: some stay and explore, some for a while, some for a short time and then jump off the ride into whatever else is about, but so long as we manage to keep attracting new people, we may just progress the whole scene... Who knows?

"So what else came afresh during that time? Well I attended that first foreign rally, going to the likes of Spain, France, Germany, Italy and America... and suddenly finding a whole new crowd of people into the same sort of things, and feeling like the new kid at school on your first day at school again, having to make new friends, hearing and seeing new sights and sounds, hell, even the food is so different. Friends I made in early 1992-93 on these rallies abroad have become really good friends that I still have today, and in some cases are the first people I contact when I get to that particular country.

"It's such a culture shock that first rally in another country, (for most people the most foreign rally was the Isle of Wight!!!!), even down to the actual greetings when you see other Mods in the street. Here in the UK we tend to just *'Hello'* or *'Hi'* or the head nod, but when you get the European greetings of handshakes/hugs or the double peck on the cheek (mainly with the Girls !!!), you can see that *'Ah, English'...* look on people's faces. I can remember one such occasion when I had been over to Leon in Spain for the Purple Weekend, and had gone all through that first initial day of awkwardness at such greetings, to being quite into all that by the end of the stay - to the point of, when I returned home and attended a do a few days later, and tried to greet some of my friends in the same manor – the response from many was like *'gerroff, what you up to...'*

"Towards the end of the 90's we had 60's band The Action reform in the original formation for a rally on the Isle of Wight. I had just bought my very first scooter and with friends we headed off travelling overnight, down the A roads (me with L plates, you see), and some hours later getting there and seeing the band perform was a very special moment.

"As I said here we are now in 2010, where do we stand? Well the numbers may have gone down a little, and for some the waistline and hairlines are now not what they once were, but the love of all things connected to the Mod scene still draws us: that special something, you can't just put your finger on the what or why at times, but once you get that bug, it's got you for good. I am looking forward to another year of rallies and events as ever, last year (2009) was a really good year! I got to see a reformed Purple Hearts, Secret Affair, Small World, Pope-Chords, and Long Tall Shorty etc. A 30 years of Mod anniversary with gigs at various places throughout the year, which is pretty much where I first started... Mods into the 2020's .... You never know...?"

Lee Radforth: (Right) "Well as I fast head for my mid 40's can I really still be so obsessed with a so called youth cult? Well in a word, yes. The beauty of the way Mod has evolved from those few visionary kids back in the late 50's in London is that the clothes, the music, the attitude, knows no age limits and encompasses the way you live your life and the way you see life. Mod style and influences are all around us in advertising, graphic design, architecture as well as the obvious style magazines and recurrent music trends. So I, like many other like minded souls, will continue ploughing my own furrow and living my own vision of the Mod lifestyle. The clothes may well be tailored a tad more English Gent, and the days of white Levis are long gone, the all-nighters get fewer and take longer to recover from, but in Sheffield we are blessed with three of the scenes best DJ's and record collectors in Graham Wright, Gav Arno and Mik Parry and a great bunch of people in whom the flame still burns brightly."

1977 era Punk and passionate Mod and Jam fan Pete Skidmore takes us almost up to date with his more recent escapades in the world of our generation's culture and some insightful views on contemporary pop acts and gigs!

Pete Skidmore: "Up to 2003 I did loads of rallies and was having a great time doing them, the smaller ones seemed better; one at Scunthorpe in 1999 was a very good one. We also had our own rally event at Davy's club on the Prince of Wales road, Martin who organised it managed to get Jack whom the Who's 'Happy Jack' is based on, he was a fucking lad and a half and he turned up pissed and sat in a corner telling stories about the Who, surrounded by loads of young mods. At night he came and stood at the bar with a few of us, I had been smoking joints all day and started with the giggles to which Jack took offence and was about to stick one on me when I got dragged off. I was laughing my bollocks off and couldn't stop; anyway Jack disappeared into the night and resurfaced two days later in Manchester. The last rally I did was in 2003 we had just got back from France me and Karen and our 8 month old son, it was run to the shires out near Derby somewhere. I got hammered and we sat out till five in the morning- drinking and chatting, but I wasn't all there so I was off home at first light. I still went to meetings at the club and had my scooter but with a young family and I worked nights something had to give so it was the club. I had some good times and the club is still going but I don't think there is any of the original members left.

"Once our son came along, like thousands before, us our life changed: we stopped going out as much and we didn't go to a concert for a couple of years. One of the first we went to after a while was the Arctic Monkeys at the Leadmill, supported by Reverend and the Makers, the Harrison's and Millburn. It was a good night out, we went to Nottingham Rock City to see the Monkeys again and what I noticed was all these young kids with their mobile phones in the air. It was just when cameras on phones started coming in and was so annoying. There was a lad at side of us who spent the entire concert on his phone telling his mate what they were playing! It was completely different from the old days.

"We also went to see the Monkeys again at Manchester old Trafford where there was 49.998 dickheads: big concerts don't do it for me at all. I'm big on Richard Hawley as well and we have seen him in Sheffield plus Buxton and York. Jarvis Cocker is another one we like - having seen him at the Plug where we got filmed for the South Bank show. I think we were the only working class Sheffielders there that night. We also saw him at the old Sheffield Top Rank where he did a brilliant version of the Human Leagues' 'Being Boiled'. Richard Hawley gigs are full of the middle classes? What's that all about? I think they are trying to be Sheffielders but a couple of Hawley CD's and a McKee on the wall don't make you one sorry!"

Kevin Wells: "A band that grew out of the Britpop scene was the Libertines, who became the new scene setters, even though I never saw them live, I know a few people who did and they all said the same thing, it was chaotic, messy but exciting to watch with Carl Barat musically being the perfect foil for the drug-fuelled poet Pete Doherty. Pete became the icon for a generation mostly for the wrong reasons; can you see the pattern, a drug addict jail bird playing for a band that inspired a generation? It felt as though Sidney was alive and well (not well, but you know what I mean). I personally don't like the messages that he gives out to younger people, I favoured seeing Carl Barat's band the Dirty Pretty things, who were good musically but lacked that edge of the Libertines. What did surprise me was when I went to see the Babyshambles at the Plug in Sheffield and how much Pete Doherty put into it. He, to me, still had the edge. The band came on borrowing the backline from the support band and it was as though they had just walked off the street and straight on stage. Pete then asked the crowd if anyone had a fag so someone chucked on a full packet and a lighter onto the stage which he took one out, lit it and put the rest into his pocket as though he'd never seen a full packet in his life. Pete jumped into the crowd after the third song and continued to sing another couple of songs while he was still in there. The band played for about two hours with Pete treating us to renditions of football songs between songs. For a bloke who had so much disregard for himself he put on one hell of a show for his fans."

Murray Fenton: "After Punk, a few bands revived my enthusiasm for music over the years with their energy and attitude... Nirvana were one, early Oasis another. Having a son too young to attend gigs on his own, I found myself seeing many of the modern day American 'Punk' bands in the late 90s/early 00s and there were some really good bands amongst that genre, especially live. But the band who really stood out for me were The Libertines. I'd seen them on the bill with the Pistols at Crystal Palace and thought they were interesting, decked out in the red guardsman jackets and thrashing about the stage not unlike The Clash. A few months later, I was driving back from London when I caught their debut single 'What a Waster' on the radio. I was hooked immediately. It reminded me of The Jam and The Clash, and the good old days! I saw them live properly for the first time in early 2003. They were raw and exciting and the songs were fantastic. It really did feel like 1977 again. Sometimes I'd travel to London after work to see them in some dingy venue, many special, secret gigs here and there advertised on the 'net on the day, despite by now, the band being one of the most popular and successful new bands in Britain. One night, having burned too many candles at both ends, I dipped out on the chance to see them on a Love Music Hate Racism gig in London, only for Mick Jones to come on for the encores and play guitar with them and sing 'Should I Stay Or Should I Go?' too... gutting!!!

"The band had a faithful following and I forged a lot of friendships at Libertines gigs all over the country and met a lot of people who promoted gigs. I was playing in the Fuckwits at the time and we somehow managed to become a bit of a pet band for a while on the scene surrounding the band, playing support gigs to many of the bands who had supported the Libertines, or at some of the venues I'd been fortunate enough to see them play in. I think one of the saddest things ever to happen to British music was Pete Doherty's sad decline into heavy drug addiction (and his even sadder decline into tabloid newspapers favourite Z-list rent-a-junkie), they were a band who really could have done anything they wanted."

Tony Beesley: "As soon as I heard the Libertines I knew they were something special. It didn't take me much persuading to buy 'Up the Bracket' seeing as Mick Jones of The Clash had produced it anyway, but when I played it I was swept away with the pure Rock n' Roll spirit flowing through the album. Great things were gonna come for the band for sure, I thought.

"I made a tape for our car of all the bands of that time- Strokes, White Stripes, and The Hives etc mixed with some old Punk tunes. The big band at the time was the Strokes: again I had been hearing all these great things being said about them so decided to check them out with their first album... which was a great set of songs too. One very fond memory that I have is of us going to the coast and listening to this tape I had made... my two young sons Dean and Sean, who would be around 10 and 11 or so, would be in the back singing along to 'The boy looked at Johnny' *na na na na na*. Our Dean also loved the Strokes as well and was by now well on his way to liking a lot of my old Punk records... the Saints 'Know Your Product', 'Sound of the Suburbs' by the Members being two of his faves along with all the Clash and Jam stuff. This was like a bridge being crossed between mine and his generation... and importantly it was being re-affirmed- music still mattered.

.

"Musically it seems that every few years a new flux of really interesting bands come along: it was just so refreshing to hear these new bands taking the spirit of Punk and all of the other influences they had and mixing them together to create something entirely their own. Along with Weller and all my Mod sounds, these were the sounds of the early Noughties decade for me."

Mod for the Noughties by Tony Beesley - "During my Punk years I was always a massive Jam fan. My initial attempts at the Punk look were as much influenced by Paul Weller's spiky Mod haircut, Jam shoes and off-stage knitted jumpers as the typical Punk style and my home-made Clash zip shirts and PVC attire. As well as being a Jam obsessive, I was really into The Jolt, The Boys, Rich Kids, the Moondogs and other power pop bands that fell into the Punk/New Wave scene. Later on, I bought singles by the Chords and Purple Hearts and a pre-Secret Affair band called the New Hearts ('Plain Jayne' and 'Just Another Teenage Anthem' singles are two shamefully ignored new wave singles). Strange as it may seem, but when the Mod revival did finally kick in, I almost ignored it: maybe it was something to do with Weller's distrust and open condemnation of the Post-Quadrophenia Mod fad? I am not sure? The uniform element of it seemed to crush my idea of what an individual (Mod or Punk) should be. It was all part of the new wave, as far as I was concerned.

"By the time all the 79-81 Mod craze was over and done with, the Punk scene was also finished for me too. Not long after, I joined up with fellow Punk dissenter John Harrison (who had fully embraced the Mod revival himself) and we determined to put the fire back into our hearts with our Punk idealism and love of cool sharp Mod clothes. Along with a heavy Clash influence, our musical template consisted of sixties Mod bands the Small Faces and the Who, The Creation etc and boxes of Mod/Soul/Rhythm and Blues.

"Following our Mod venture as The Way (see Our Generation Vol 1 for the full story), I turned more to the European Mod stylist look and a musical diet of Jazz, contemporary Funk, Soul and the best of Modern cutting edge pop such as Orange Juice, Faith Brothers ('Country of the Blind' was a classic 45) and others. A massive LP for me on release was 'Don't Stand Me Down' by Dexys Midnight Runners. Hardly anyone, at the time, could see its worth and what it was all about, but for me Kevin Rowland's vision was as clear as daylight. It's still one of my favourite LP's ever and it has truly stood the test of time. Somewhere along the line, though, I lost my way by constantly searching for something new and interesting in music... be it the latest Indie band at the Leadmill, a new Soul act, Acid Jazz or the fledgling House scene and my delving into obscure 70's Disco, Funk and Soul, it took a few years to return to my roots: although the Mod attention to detail and love of Mod music never went away as I continued to hunt down obscure Soul singles. As the 80's turned to the 90's and the decade wore on a more Modernist look crept back in and my old Who, Action and Georgie Fame singles started to get played on my turntable again more and more. Before long this, later to be termed retro, approach to music would coincide with the early days of the pre-Britpop era and the whole Mod thing had come full circle for me.

"I had some of my best times in the mid to late 90's and the Noughties on the local mod scene. I had made some great new mates and got to know some of the local hardcore Mods who I had only known by face back in the 80's. My best mate at the time was Martin Ridgeway (a true Mod music obsessive) and between us we truly reignited the Mod spirit and obsession with music and clothes again. We were hunting for clothes all over the place, charity shops (some top class Harrington's and knitted Italian style tops), the Merc catalogue (before it went crap) and having suits tailored at Darnall and Keith's in Rotherham town centre (where's my cloth-covered button spares?). The music became obsessive too. As well as vintage and original 45's, we started buying the dreaded CD!... primarily because we were discovering heaps of superb cool Rn'B and Blue-eyed Soul on the massively increasing volumes of Mod and Soul collections coming out.

"Along with the monthly Brighton Beach event at the Sheffield City Hall ballroom, we would go to Northern Soul nights (when they took our fancy as often the older Soulies weren't all too keen on us Mods invading their space)... also some local ones around Rotherham, Conisbrough etc. There were still Mod nights now and again at Rawmarsh Baths Hall before they knocked it down, though they had subsided to a lot less regularly long before then. Also scooter dos at the Effingham Arms would be on the calendar now and again: though I recall one particular one when four of us Mods went and we felt like outsiders. There we were in proper Mod threads and the crowd were almost to a man comprised of camouflage clobber, denims, piercings galore and more of a taste for the Stone Roses than the classic Mod sounds. Everyone to their own though.

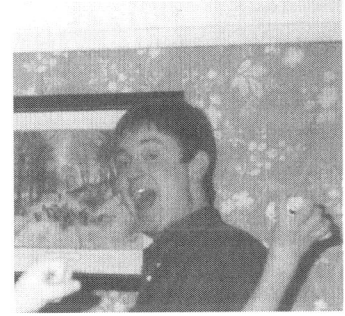

"After a few years, me and Martin (Right) drifted apart and went our separate ways. I kept up the Mod obsession for another two years or so: aimlessly dragging people along to Mod nights: people who were really not that interested in the scene as such: being much more of a novelty than anything for some (but not all) of em. I gradually slowed down the obsession for new clothes, paced my obscure vinyl buying and within time, the triggers (Mod term for the long side bits of hair extending in front of the ears– see Weller, Marriot circa 66 etc) were shrinking pitifully and it all seemed time to take a back seat.

"A year or two passed and a lot of changes (including a divorce) occurred in my life: resulting in a new outlook to life and with it a new freshly charged-up zest for all things Mod again. Coincidentally, my mate Martin was driving the bus I caught to work one morning, and before you knew it, a different kind of drive was back in our veins than the 109 bus he was driving. Clothes, records, compilation CD's galore matched the searches for good authentic Mod nights out. We lost our beer bellies; re-acquainted ourselves with made to measure suits and classy button-downs again and for a short while, yet again, we had some cracking times: and the Mod barnet was back in full force!

"In 2006, the Pow Wow Wow club opened in Sheffield. This soon replaced the ever increasingly-studenty-themed Brighton Beach nights – both myself and Martin still attending now and again clinging on with hope (the final straw for myself was when the smoking ban came into place, which was all good and well, but when I went out for a fag at 1.30am the bouncers said I couldn't come back in! what!) Was it any wonder that the only Mods in the place seemed to be myself and the two

DJ's? But, salvation Mod style had arrived with this new club, originally on Snig Hill in an upstairs location around the corner from the Boardwalk. The atmosphere of the club was fantastic – it actually felt like you would imagine the Scene club in London would have done in 1964: the place was crammed to the hilt with Mods, suited and meticulously dressed to the core! The music was absolutely spot on: the very best in Mod R n' B, Soul and a snatch of ska (Christ how my legs ached after those sessions of Bluebeat). Many of the old faces turned out... but more importantly there was a healthy appearance of young Mods... all looking the part and really knowing their stuff. The drinks flowed, the tunes just got better, we were buzzing and on a massive high... smiles all around.

Various Mod events

"Those few Pow Wow Wow nights were amongst my favourite Mod nights of all time: matched only with the some of the mod Way (Assembly

Scarborough weekends and nights I played with The Rooms, Clifton Hall etc). The same year a gang of us went to the annual New Untouchables Rally weekend at Scarborough. There was me and my girlfriend Vanessa who got there for the Friday night do underneath the Pickwick – meeting up with a few friends like Stuart (ex Barnsley lad) and Miki from London: Martin and Nic followed the next day by car and Roy and Rog Mason and others came on their scooters in the afternoon. The night do was at the old Lemon Tree club where the 80's ones used to be. The venue had changed that year from the Spa Ballroom on the Esplanade, which I preferred to be honest.

"I had a new suit tailored for the weekend, which I wore on the Saturday night: wearing my casual Polo tops and Harrington for the day wear. We all met up on the way down from our B and B's across from the train station and in the corner boozer and on the way down there, we got some right looks. Maybe the townies can't handle some real cool and smart clobber... weird though, cos it reminded me of all those years ago getting strange looks from straights when I was a Punk kid. Fucking hell though, 40 something years old and getting attention like that... what a buzz!

"Inside the club, the place was swarming with Mods and sixties types (a few too many swinging sixties Austin Powers throwbacks for my liking but everyone to their own). Anyway there was plenty of friendly faces to talk to... Gary and Carol from Nottingham, Julie (who - owns the Mod clothing shop Ready Now in Derby) and some lads I used to know from Donny years ago, along with all of our crowd. The live band were great too – 5 Aces (formerly Boogaloo Investigators... I bought their CD and had a chat and a whisky with the guitarist). Amazingly, I got chatting to a lass from the states who lived in Tennessee of all places and when we got talking it comes out that I had spoken to her already a while back via email about Mod etc. She says *'Are you Tony from Rotherham?'*... Apparently I had helped talk her into taking up a career in journalism... what a small and strange world we live in eh?

Back to the Roots on the dancefloor

Janine and Alex DJ ing

"4am next morning and we all stroll back to our B&B's... buzzing again. Next day and the comedown was horrible. A stroll across the beach in my parka to bring me back to earth didn't do the trick. That's the only trouble, when you have great times like that... the comedown! Train home on the 2.15 (not 5.15) and back to the grind! Oh well I had a pile of CD's I had bought from Rob Bailey's stall at the afternoon session to look forward to playing. There's nowt like some good music to sooth the frayed senses!

"2007: and I decided to put on my own local Mod events. I called them 'Back to the Roots'... in the intention of bringing more of the original spirit and music back into the equation. I sorted all the music from my record collection and Martin donated some cracking tracks too.

"We went through a lot of stuff; I did some flyers and took em all over Rotherham and Sheffield. We held them upstairs at the Queens Hotel in Rawmarsh and charged two quid entrance. The first one was a decent attendance and everyone had a great time: Roy Mason, Carny, Joe and Lynne off the Market, Jimmy from Greasbrough, the two Jamies (Kennedy and Risdale), Gareth and Janine (who also put some great Mod nights on in Rotherham later the same year), Martin and Nic, Andrew from Donny, big Dave Gooderham, our lass and my eldest son Dean on the door with the legendary green tin: no John in sight... what could go wrong eh! (See Our generation Vol 1 for green tin story). We put another one on a couple of months later too.

"I now think of those times as my kind of swan-song for my Mod days. My dedication to the whole ethos of being a Mod – from obsessively buying scores of rare quality Mod 45's, compilation CD's, checking out the new contemporary music that was worth listening to (be it the Arctic Monkeys, The Bees, the Boogaloo Investigators or Weller's latest material) right through to getting every tiny detail exact with everything I wore. I had some fantastic times mixing with Mods at Mod events and made many great friends. A Mod will always acknowledge a fellow Mod (whilst checking out your footwear and the cut of your clothes) and I am on nodding terms with many Mods I don't know the names of. I had also noticed a new breed of young Mods appearing and that pleased me no end. Maybe it was time to hand over the baton?

"In 2008, I started to tire a little of the local mod scene: or rather *I started to tire* - I stopped smoking, put on weight and the grey silver streaks in my hair were now real, unlike the ones I had during my mid 1980's Soul stylist phase. It's no fun getting older, especially when you are totally committed to trying to look your best, and we can't all be as cool as Paul Weller can we!

"I still love my Mod music and have kept my core collection. My clothes will always retain that subtle, yet distinct Mod style: but in my opinion it's a scene that should evolve and be prepared for change. It's the way it's been marginalised recently that does me. The Mod scene is a British institution and its influence will always remain; but it's been over commercialised and rendered almost meaningless in its media image. You can't go in a shop for target emblazoned stuff – mugs, T-Shirts, key rings, regurgitated Mod compilations with all the old usual stuff every self-respecting Mod would already have... you name it its available with a fucking target or scooter image on it! It's been sold out. I had my taste of it, may not have been the 'proper authentic Mod' some aspire to be and admirably achieve, but I loved it (and still do) and became who I am thanks to many aspects of it. Its influence, like that other massive influence in my life - Punk Rock, will never leave me: That same year, I started to write a book about mine and our generation's experiences!!"

Mods getting   **back to the Roots**

Life's ever-changing-intertwining-paths eventually brought two ex Mods (also members of The Way); back together after some years apart... eventually becoming special guest stars of their own!

Terry Sutton: "During those intervening years I spent at Drama school till 1992 and then I returned to Doncaster. I had been going over the 'Sgt.Pepper' recordings with George Martin (who was at that time Patron of the music degree at Salford University but somehow I had convinced the Principal to let me attend) and this made me long to get into the studio again. I had a great new band, Speedway Kick, making modern sounding music with all the latest technology (synths, drum machines, samplers) and Jon White had come back to help us realise the live sound. He had a friend, Keith Angel, previously from the Doncaster band 'No Man's Land', who had a basic eight track recording set up and 'did I want to do something?' This, to me, was perfect. I could have a go at doing my very own Sgt.Pepper!

"I'd always hated the synths and wanted to get back to using real instruments so immediately the rule was 'no synths'. I was writing songs all the time. Much faster than we could record them (the rate was about one a month because of all the bouncing and overdubbing). Anyway, we were called 'The On' and had an amazing, intense year. We lived together. Slept by day, recorded by night."

Ian Deakin: "The next time I heard from Tel he had just returned from doing his music degree in Los Angeles. He'd had a short-lived project, 'Beaker', but now had a new band, 'Bullrush', and Tel asked me if I wanted to go see them play in town. To cut a long story short, earlier that day, the headline on the cover of the NME had read *'Why I've Quit The Roses by John Squire'* and whilst we were watching Bullrush in this empty pub, Tel turns his head and who should be standing next to him? John Squire in person."

Terry Sutton (centre), Ian Deakin (far left) and their Electrascope runners

Terry Sutton: "Anyway, I turned to him and asked if he was indeed whom I thought he was and did he need a new drummer, bassist and singer? I was a bit up front I suppose and scared him off. Thing is, the bassist I was going to suggest was Whitey who - after Squire had formed, had success with, and finally split The SeaHorses - went on to record two albums with him and be his closest musical confidant. The payoff, for me, was at Jon's wedding when I ended up going up to Squire and whispering into his ear, *'Remember me?'* We ended up having a great night and I can honestly say the best part of the evening was watching my brother fall asleep whilst Squire was talking to him, so rivetting is the man's charisma. In fact I suppose we should mention my brother Paul. He was roadying for us from the age of twelve! That's where he got his 'education'. My family have always been most supportive."

Ian Deakin: "So... towards the end of 1996 I'd been rehearsing with Simon Cardie and Rob Bellis. Tel called and asked if I was doing anything, said he'd written a load of songs. I said to come to our new room in Sheffield. And with that we formed what was originally known as 'Beaker' but soon became 'Electrascope'. It was the beginning of getting attention like we'd never had before. People just seemed to love it straight away. We played it to the Longpigs in Axis Studios and they we're full of praise."

Terry Sutton: "We played a gig at the Charter's Arms and it was filled to the brim. Our new manager, Joe Davidson who used to manage The Las, came down and the next morning we were in Eden Studios in London recording for Parlophone. The demo went down well and we were invited to showcase for the MD at Nomis Studios. When we got to London we found out the studio had been double booked and then we were put in this horrible dive with a shitty Carlsbro 100W PA system. It was horrible. Things turned ugly when Keith Woozencroft tossed the compliment our way that we 'sound like Jefferson Airplane'. He thought that was a compliment! As John Shuttleworth would say... Ooof!"

Ian Deakin: "Once Rob was fired and Phil Gardiner and Jonathan Lord were on board we were flying. Great gigs all over the place. Invitations to mad parties. Frequent recording was the best perk and spending a week in the Kinks Studio, Konk, was a highlight for me. We worked our way up from being a support band in London to having our own nights at the Barfly. Radiohead, Travis, Mansun... just some of the bands that came to see us play."

Terry Sutton: "And, of course, there's the notorious Coldplay incident when they supported us at the Borderline. It was our night. We'd set it up thinking a deal with Food/Parlophone was all but done (as our new manager, Cerne Canning, had made clear we'd already got one from East West if we wanted to go with them) and, somehow, stupidly, due to several rounds of whiskey with the roadies, took our eyes off the prize and Coldplay walked away with the spoils. The rest is history. We never had any luck. When we were supporting Mansun on the 'Six' tour we had all the magazines coming to review us but thanks to Mansun's equipment breaking they cancelled the gig and it threw all the timings and, as a result, Cerne went bust (all his other bands were dropped - The Warm Jets, Strangelove, Tiger and Jack - in the same months). Of course he went on to help break The Libertines and Franz Ferdinand and now co-runs one of the biggest management companies, Supervision. But we did have a 'last stand' as it were."

Ian Deakin: "The last gig was at the Leadmill supporting Stiff Little Fingers and, irony of ironies, Bruce Foxton was on bass."

Terry Sutton: " For me, it was like I had come full circle and I told this to Bruce. Told him about Tracie and our past etc. He listened respectfully and, so I was told, watched the gig from the side of the stage with Jake Burns (who paid me a nice compliment afterwards). The whole night was extremely emotional because we knew we were splitting. I wasn't even sure I would play again. I was so spent. I'd just had a larynx operation after getting polyps on my vocal chords and my voice was weaker than ever. I'd given everything to that band but somehow it wasn't enough. A break was essential!

"It was like dealing with three bereavements at once. I spent the next three years depressed and had a nervous breakdown, though I didn't know it at the time. What held me together was seeing my music spread throughout the internet in the early part of the Noughties. I was getting fan-mail from all over the world asking what I was going to do next. Then, Jon White, who had been having enormous success with Groove Armada, released a solo album. I thought 'I can't be having this - I'm the songwriter'. Petty, sure, but it was the kick up the arse I needed. Then, in 2004, I went on holiday to Lanzarote, spent two whole weeks relaxing by a pool, getting a great tan, and bought myself a digital camera with a dictaphone built in... within a year I had over fifty ideas. Within two years over two-hundred ideas! I decided to start buying the bits for a studio and very slowly got there. It took me over two years. Then I gave Ian 'the call'. He hadn't even touched the drums for six years but I'd put the track together before he arrived and then, in about five takes, he got the most complicated of tracks down in perfect time with the click-track - 'Omega Man' - and with that 'The Special Guest Stars' were born."

Ian Deakin: "I can't think of a time when we've been more fired up than the early days of TSGS. It's like we have something to prove all over again. Not to industry or the public, but to ourselves. That we can still 'do it', and do it better than we've ever done. With the same energy."

The way ahead sees a nod to the past for Special Guest Star Terry Sutton – a homage to his Mod past and his days with The Way!

Special Guest stars Ian Deakin and Terry Sutton point *the way* to the future!

Terry Sutton: "After having long hair for the last two years I've just had it cut back into a Mod style so some of that styling may come back into our look in future. I had my three button pinstripe out the other day. And The Future..? I've written about twenty new songs for our next album, 'Computer Town: An Electropera'. Stylistically, it's somewhere between Robert Altman's movie 'Short Cuts' and Kraftwerk's 'Radioaktivitet'. I have a song called 'Send and Receive' that is possibly the best I've ever written. Whatever I do, I'll never stop working with Doink. I couldn't imagine he and I not being in a band together and I hope I'm around to see him still beating the skins in another twenty-five years. He should be completely shorn of body hair by then and, hopefully, like in Kubrick's 2001, we'll go back to the beginning and do it all again. Except next time I'll be the cool-looking drummer and Ian can sing and book the gig."

So the demise of Britpop as a cultural pop phenomenon had been reached; the assimilation into the pop world of great British pop... Oasis, Blur and an eclectic cast of the most talented or luckiest to have gained prominence from the era... be it Portishead, the Charlatans or the Prodigy had also been set in motion. The recognition of all things Mod had also been approved by the music press, musicians with a certain leaning and a general public who now wished to find out a little bit more about this thing that appeared to involve parkas, scooters and Desert boots. But what now for the ones who had been travelling down this long and unwinding road of Punk Rock and Modernist discovery; of suddenly realising that they were no longer the exuberant teenagers of 1977 or 1979 and that they had somehow reached a point beyond the ages that their parents had been when they had started their journeys. The prospect of reaching their 40's now hit the cast of our generation smack between the eyes: but to the true music fan age shows no measureable influence in its effect on the passion of music and its culture.

Tony Beesley: "I got to 40 and couldn't believe that I was still as passionate about music as ever. I had seen so many of my mates down the years almost completely disregard their love of music. It had merely served as a temporary phase to support their youth for some of them I suppose. Although I did, and still do, have some hang-ups about getting older and all of its pitfalls, I still feel pretty close to how I used to feel all those years ago, and whenever I forget that buzz, that eternal adrenalin boost of Rock n' Roll fervour. I only have to listen to the first Clash album again and it all comes flooding back... Punk Rock and the sound of fast and frenetic Rhythm and Blues, raw passion-injected Rock n Roll with a kick that just won't go away. It's truly in my blood!"

Jamie 'Headcharge' Smith: "Being in my 40's??No change for me I just love it and I am always thinking *'right what can I do next'* Ive not made a living out of music but the experiences I've had and the people I've met and the places I've travelled out-weigh any payment, SEX N DRUGS N ROCK N ROLL !!!!

"I remember when my band Plastik Toyz used to do cover of UK Subs 'Warhead'. Only a few years ago a few of us went down the Casbah to see UK Subs, I ended up chatting to Charlie Harper and mentioned what we used to do with Warhead and he pissed himself. Anyway they played and when it came to doing Warhead, next minute I know Charlie's shouting out for me, Oh shit!!! He wants me on stage with him singing our version called 'KNOBHEAD' and yeah we did it together much to the amusement of everyone one. After they'd finished Charlie came and found me and mentioned that they were putting together a 25 years of UK Subs album and if I could find the recording of 'knob head' he would put it on the album. Sadly it never happened mainly down to me being busy with Headcharge and things, what a bummer!!!!"

John Quinn: "Well lots of people I know lost interest in music in their 30s, taken over by families, careers etc. But somehow it stuck with me, and thanks to better technology I could not only look back (which I did a lot, finding things I'd missed first time) but also keeping up to date with what's happening now."

But taking a look around clearly indicates that much had changed since the late 70's and also in the social circumstances of some if not a good proportion of a certain age!

Tony Beesley: "In my early 40's I started to question the relevance of a lot of my past ideals: do they mean anything any more? How do I maintain a good balance of what I believed in back in my youth and still integrate it with my present self? I was a different person and felt different, but no surprises, I was just as mixed up and angry as that 13 year old Punk kid all those years ago: I tried being chilled out and it didn't suit me... IT WAS FUCKIN' BORING!!

"It's amazing how many people I know from our generation that got divorced in later years... their late 30's to early 40's. Almost all of my crowd did so, including myself. I'm not saying that divorce and separation is something anywhere near to being exclusive to the Punk and Mod generation, as its clearly not and is very common, but that aside, it says a lot about the restless characteristics of the Punk era kids such as myself and many I know.

"There was also a sense of our own mortality creeping in: the loss of Ian Dury in 2000, Strummer a couple of years later and many others from the era was a constant reminder that we were ourselves getting older. Looking around, we were also visibly appearing to age... fuck!!"

The extension of the Punk look through an individuals own interpretation led to a dilema for one Punk mum.

Valerie Garvey: "I changed my appearance because of the comments I heard from other kids (on the way taking mine to school) like *'Theo's mums a witch'* etc. I didn't think it was right that my kids got stick because of how I looked. Maybe if I had lived in another part of Sheffield it would have been different but not round here. So I toned it right down, but some times kids still said things. Through the 1990's I don't remember what music I bought... nothing really, I suppose, as most of my money went on the kids."

Right: Valerie and her young daughter

In 2005 a new band from the steel city picked up the baton of Punk-influenced Indie Rock and took it to places that the music had not really been before. It was born of the internet medium and gained a snowball effect momentum via a collective of young music fans tuning into the unique sounds of the band. With a voice of Yorkshire dialect and lyrics of coming from Rotherham the Arctic Monkeys played ferociously in parts; retaining great melodies and gentle subtleties and gave hints of classic Buzzcocks and the Jam amongst other influences. Through the world of downloading and Youtube the new medium for young Indie Rock took shape and was changed forever. The Arctic Monkeys saw the opening and wasted no time in gaining a massive foothold in the nation's musical agenda. A blistering debut album 'Whatever It Is People Say I Am, I Am Not' at the start of 2006 catapulted the Sheffield band into major stardom and the admiration of many including some of the musicians that they had been impressed by during their formative years.

Tony Beesley: "My son Dean introduced me to the Arctic Monkeys. He was an early fan and was banging on about em all of the time. When he showed me one of their videos, I have to admit I was hooked straight away. I loved the first album. We were always playing it. 'Tales of San Francisco' was one of my favourites, but to be honest there isn't a bad track on the whole album. There was a lot of anticipation for their second album, but it was also a good collection of songs. Their third album 'Humbug' is exceptional too. They have done Sheffield proud. It wouldn't be long before me and Dean would be going to gigs together either. Now there's a first for my Punk CV!"

John Quinn: "Good band, The Arctic Monkeys: Only ever spoken to Alex Turner once. At a Richard Hawley concert. He said *'excuse me mate'* and I got out of the doorway. If he'd been a proper rock star he'd have shoved me out of the way."

Kevin Wells: "Another band who have reached the heights of the music industry are Sheffield Arctic Monkeys, they were obviously looking for inspiration from bands such as the Libertines and the Strokes. Alex Turner is a very talented lyricist who observed the world around him and turned them into songs, they got on about their business using the punk ethic of 'Do it yourself' and made sure that everybody got to hear their songs for free by using the internet, building up a growing fan base which made their live performances very exciting. I saw them at the Leadmill when they first started and then I went to see them at the Plug in Sheffield the same weekend that 'I Bet She Looks Good On The Dance Floor' went to number 1. The gig got the adrenaline pumping, everyone was going for it and the band was having a great time. However, I saw little things in the crowd that to me seemed a little out of order: for one thing nobody had any regard for anyone's safety, kids were getting knocked over, women were getting hit etc. It seemed to me that there was a new hooligan element creeping into gigs, too many people getting drunk, causing arguments that escalate into fights and pint glasses full of piss being chucked about. I don't know whether it's me getting older but I like to go out and have a good time, enjoy the band, have chat with old friends and also make some new ones, the last thing I want is to come back home with my clothes wet though with piss.

"Anyway back to the Arctic Monkeys, I have seen them loads of times since they first started and I can see how the band are growing and changing with the times. Some people think the band have sold out and have no connection with fans, but this is always going to happen. As soon as a band gets popular, their outlook on life changes and they move in different circles, so it was no surprise to me that lyrically and musically they have changed. I for one quite like the latest album 'Humbug': you can see they are trying to grow and introduce new sounds to their records; ironically I went to see them on the last tour at Leeds Festival and at the Sheffield Arena and a lot of people were complaining about how much new stuff they played. Don't know why, it was a tour to promote the 'Humbug' album! If the band had played 'Mardy Bum' (full version, instead of the intro) and 'A View From The Afternoon' everyone would have left the Arena saying it was the best show ever, it's that fine a line."

Alex Turner at the Sheffield Arena (Kevin Wells)

The Arctic Monkeys sign-posted a new era for Sheffield bands and music. The forming of new young bands in the city and surrounding area has increased massively following their breakthrough. The signs have been good in recent years; but the world doesen't need a thousand Arctic Monkeys imitators, just like it didn't need so many Sex Pistols sounding bands back in 1977. The agenda is Do it yourself, but do it with your own style and take on music, nothing wrong with influences but no copyists please!!

Along with the rest of the voices of modern dissent, the Punk-injected rock n' roll spirit of bands of today or tomorrow's next Punk-influenced Indie kid who picks up a guitar and forms a band... these voices of rebellion - be they aspiring young musicians, the remnants of the Punk generation itself or the kid who says NO! to the rules and regulations of the system because he has his own take on what he wants to do and create in life... all of these and more indicate that the rebellion may not yet be over!

Chapter Ten

Mandy's Rebellion

"I'm not ready to hang up my Dockers and hand Punk over fully to the new generation yet. I've got gigs planned, new bands to discover, new outfits to make and improvise, new CDs to spin, new friends to make and old friends to get drunk reminisce and go wild with. I'll just have to be continue being a Punk mummy for now!" – **Mandy Taylor** (Punk Rocker)

So here we are – in the present: it's almost 35 years since Julie Longden, Steve Mushroom, Pete Weston, John Flanagan, Simon Ellis, Bryan Bell, the Stunt Kites and all the other members in our generation's small but creative Punk tribe began their journeys of rebellion. The first generation and their younger gang of second generation Punk rebels - who came charging through a year or so afterwards - are now spread across the country, and in some cases in different corners of the world.

Our Punk ideals and attitudes may have mellowed somewhat over the years, but our hearts and minds are still infected with the chaos of those early years of Anarchy and freedom to do as we chose!! The liberating feeling of shedding the expectations of society and the looks of shock upon the stiff upper lips of the normals when the Punk conversion had been fully realised ... well it can never be forgotten can it? The rebel may (or may not) now look smart and integrated into everyday life, but the attitude of a true Punk Rocker can never be crushed... be it 1977 or 2010: the rebellion is still alive... but it may not always show itself with an easily recognisable display of Punk rock visuals.

Mandy Taylor has embraced Punk Rock for the best part of four decades and is still a Punk Rocker and by day she works for the system! You could say she subverts the system from within nowadays: manipulating the corporate company she works for to achieve the Punk Rock lifestyle she desires... whatever, at heart she is still a Punk Rock rebel... throughout our generations' story and beyond!

Mandy Taylor: "Debbie Harry just told me she loves my Dockers and where could she get a pair!! Who'd have thought it... me giving fashion advice to Debbie Harry? Debbie then came to join me and Sarah on the dance floor for a very energetic dance to 'On My Radio' by The Selector. And

no I'm not dreaming or hallucinating this is now and in Rotherham in 2010. What a night! Proof that Punk still lives in Rotherham at least. OK this was not the real Debbie Harry but an excellent tribute band (Blondie UK) but incidentally I have seen the real Debbie Harry live supported by Squeeze at Sheffield Arena sometime in the late nineties. I'm sure had I got close enough she'd have still loved me Dockers and if I'd have asked she would have given a great performance to 'On My Radio'.

Mandy, Blondie and Sarah dance to the Selecter!

It's now 2010 in Rotherham, and there have been some great gigs this year, building on the punk revival of the last few years in Rotherham. I'm not going to say that the full revival was down to me, but I feel that I certainly played a part in bringing Punk and Ska to the fore at the Dickens's Bar No 10 Wellgate Rotherham. Had I not introduced Punk and Ska to the No 10 we wouldn't have had the likes of UK Subs, 999, The Lurkers and The Vibrators (to name but a few) playing over the last few years in Rotherham.

"I started to DJ at the No 10 in either September/October 2005 as a result of Daz pushing me in into a challenge with Mick and I've DJ'd for Mick ever since. (Mick Hill- Rock Promoter and director at Live@Dickens Rotherham). Mick and Bott (Mark Sherman director at Live@Dickens Rotherham and both formally The Metal Gurus) had set up a regular rock night as Dickens at No 10. This was usually every Saturday and did start off as a specific rock night often with a live tribute band supported by a local band.

"Mick and Bott were (and are both still) passionate about live music, but their focus was rock. I had started to slip some classic Punk stuff into my sets Ramones/Clash/Stranglers/Blondie/Damned etc. Whilst I enjoyed DJ'ing in the early days I preferred the thrashier/metal type rock opposed to classic rock. I also loved listening to the up and coming local bands and loved some of the raw energy that they displayed and particularly watching them grow, many local young bands played their first gig at the No 10. I particularly remember Descent to Cocytus not only because I had great difficulty pronouncing their name (I was so relieved when they changed their name to DTC) but when they played their first gig at the NO 10 the venue was full of excited expectant family members including Mums and Dads along with their friends. Their friends obviously knew what they were about, but there was at first a look of shock across some family members, which then settled into relative discomfort and then by the end of the set they were joining in with the crowd. DTC have played many times at the No 10 and I have really seen them grow and develop over the last few years.

"In the early days we had many tribute bands play at the No 10 ranging from Guns2Roses (Guns N Roses cover) to Seyes (Yes) to Green Bay (Green Day). My personal favourites were Rebel Truce (The Clash) and not forgetting our very own Motorheadache (Motorhead) with Lemmy Rob. I have mixed feelings about tribute bands. I have seen some fantastic tribute bands that've put on a great show, but even so, it sometimes feels weird watching them acting like your hero or heroine and singing your favourite tunes; but I think the key you have to remember is that they are tribute bands and are putting on a show. I have seen some people get really serious and analyse every note and pose the bands make. I have also seen some of the tribute bands take themselves really seriously.

"There are a couple I remember where I was convinced that they thought they were the real thing, and a couple of others where I wondered why on earth they were playing rock, I won't mention them by name but their alter egos were quite rock n roll and I doubt the real thing would have asked for the lights to be dimmed so they didn't hurt their eyes, the dry ice to be turned off and the music to be turned to a whisper!! The hardest nights though were a couple of tributes we had that were quite frankly a joke, it was very difficult to try and get the crowd going and ask for an encore when all I wanted to do was giggle! They were dressed like your Dad going to a fancy dress with crooked wigs, awful costumes and karaoke voices.

"Meanwhile, I continued to sneak some classic Punk stuff into my play lists and eventually some of the crowd started to take notice, and often would get up and dance to my stuff. In the meantime I'd been telling Mick and Bott about Phil Murray and the Boys from Bury, and persuaded them to go and see them at the Fairways, at Brinsworth with me and Daz. I'd known Phil Murray and the Boys from Bury (mainly Phil and Richard) since the late eighties when I worked at the Three Magpies at Brinsworth, I saw them many times and particularly remember their 'No sleep till Canklow' Tour with various gigs around Rotherham (I can clearly remember the Charters and Three Magpies gigs). I even had the legendary T shirt but my friend borrowed it and never gave it back – wonder how much it's worth now!!

"Not long after seeing them at the Fairways, Mick booked them for the No 10. I personally see this as a real turning point for Punk and Ska at the No 10. It was also the night when Mick and I had a disagreement over my musical choice (sorry Mick but it is funny looking back now) I had started the night off DJing and really was enjoying the set with all the classic Punk stuff, the crowd was enjoying it too, (a couple of guys even came up to say it was a top set). Phil Murray and The Boys from Bury did their set (as good as always) and I went back to close the night with some more classic Punk. Mick then came up to ask for Whitesnake, and I said *'no don't be silly this isn't a rock night'*. I thought he was kidding at first, but he wasn't and said that I should still play them, eventually after further debate I still refused to play them and I had a proper DJ paddy and turned off the music, packed up my CDs and went and sat at the bar with Daz. We did make up and although we have had a few artistic differences since (shall I mention Toyah???) Mick now leaves me to do my stuff on Punk and Ska nights.

"This was 22/10/2005 and the gig was part of Phil Murray and The Boys from Bury 'Shurrup Me Dad's in Bed' Tour, Mick did book them again, and also started to book more alternative bands now and again. Unfortunately I have misplaced my gig lists and memorabilia from 2006, but certainly from looking at my gig list for 2007, the tribute bands started to get interspersed with alternative bands and Punk nights.

"One of the most unusual gigs I did in 2006 was in Cuba on my hols. On the first Saturday night in our hotel I set up my I-Pod through the speaker system and played a selection of music: Punk, Indie and Rock, the tourists and especially the staff really enjoyed the night, and we all danced till the early hours. The next day the staff kept coming up to me *'Hey lady we really liked your music when you play again?'* I would have thought that this was a bit strange had the staff not explained to us the night before that western music is censored and Bob Marley and John Lennon are really the only artistes from outside Cuba that get played on the radio. This was repeated again the next Saturday and I must admit the staff trying to show us to salsa to some of my tunes was good fun, though I have visions now of the staff still singing 'London Calling' or even 'Neat, Neat Neat' or 'Shurrup me Dad's in Bed'.

"Since then I am proud to say I have started to go global: I have DJ'd twice in Crete, once to a load of German teenagers in an hotel bar – some of my thrash knowledge came in useful and I was able to practise my German (many years after learning it a school). The other was a bit more laid back at a local Taverna. To top off my now international status I have also DJ'd a few times in Barnsley (The Sturdy Lads & The Locorum).

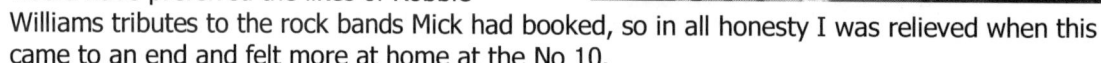

"Anyway back to the end of 2006 Mick booked a series of gigs at the Rotherham United Suite every Friday night; I think we must have done about 6-8 gigs or so. Looking back now I didn't really enjoy these gigs, it became a chore- I was working full time and still DJing on a Saturday night at No 10. In addition I personally felt that, although it was a big purpose built venue, it was more geared up to the cabaret scene, and would have preferred the likes of Robbie Williams tributes to the rock bands Mick had booked, so in all honesty I was relieved when this came to an end and felt more at home at the No 10.

"By this time I'd also been DJing well over a year now at the No 10 and loved it, I had really started to get back into music, (I'd not felt like this since my teenage years) me and Daz were still going to other live gigs and eventually I had started to get Daz to come to a gig of my choice in return going to one of his (Most of the time I enjoyed his choice too, after all prog-rock did influence some Punk bands). I started to replace all my back catalogue of vinyl with CDs and build my CD collection, in addition if anyone asked me for a track I hadn't got I would always make an effort to get it for them. (I still do this and always have a notebook with me which I refer to at music shops and record fairs). As a result I have got into some newer Punk and Ska bands.

"Another great showcase of new stuff is the Rebellion Festival (formally Wasted) now at the Winter Gardens in Blackpool. This is normally held August time every year and has at least 170 bands playing across four days at different venues in the Winter Gardens, this is my favourite time of the year, and the list of bands playing normally ranges from the Sublime to the Hardest core Punk and Oi!! New and Old. Just looking at the bands I saw in 2007 with Daz what a selection! we started with Chas & Dave and finished with the UK Subs, in between we saw The Damned, Slade, Conflict, John Otway, TV Smith, Neville Staple and Sonic Boom Six just to name but a few.

"I absolutely love the Rebellion Fest, as soon as the line up is finalised, I turn into an anorak: and I devour the set list from the web site before we go. However the set list normally isn't in chronological order and so it's quite hard to see which gigs clash, so I take ages and build a spreadsheet with all the times aligned so I can see where I might have a clash, I then highlight all the bands I want to see and then prioritise them in order of: *'I would rather die than miss'* to *'if we've got time I'd like to see'*. The only trouble is we end chatting to fellow Punk fans in the bar or catch up with the Rotherham Crew (in the bar) and before we know it we're running to catch the last gig. I normally start off with about 40 bands I want to see on my list but normally end up seeing about 20, though last year was a record we got to see 27 in total.

"Prior to the Rebellion, I never liked Blackpool, but then before I'd only been on hen nights in cheesy Fun and 80's pubs. I just love the buzz now though as soon as you get checked into your digs, unpack, and have a wander up to the Winter Gardens and get your weekend wristband. I have my printed out timetable in hand and will have planned it so we have a couple of hours till we see the first band, so we'll probably hit the bar, savour the atmosphere then wander around the multitude of stalls (me with my CD notebook in hand, now with a list for the more obscure stuff to add to my collection). I normally end up spending a fortune on the first day on all sorts – CDs, shoes, clothes and jewellery even some art last year. The first time I went I kept looking at the stalls and decided to wait a couple of days but by the time I went to buy them they'd all gone. Unfortunately my mad first day shopping ends up being another reason we miss a band as then I want to take everything back to the digs and then we come back to see the rest of the bands planned for that day.

"And talk about people watching!! It's fantastic to see everyone dressed up; there are people of all shapes and sizes dressed up in their Punk gear. The younger Punks tend to be from Europe and it's almost like looking back in time at a mirror of your former self with the way they are dressed up. I also like to look at people of my generation looking brilliant in their get ups, and wondering what they do for their day jobs. The atmosphere is usually really good and everyone is really friendly, and whatever bar in or around the Winter Gardens you go in, you normally end up chatting or having a good crack with someone. You also meet some strange people too, a couple of years ago, there was a bloke outside walking a rabbit on a lead, Me and Daz had gone out for something to eat and bumped into this bloke, he'd come on a day trip to Blackpool on the train with his rabbit on a lead!! I ended up posing with the rabbit feeling a bit of a prat, what's ironic here is that there were people round about staring at me not because of the way I was dressed but because of the white rabbit. It goes without saying that I've seen some brilliant sets over the years at Rebellion. I can't decide which have been my favourite as they've all been different in some way but these are favourites that stick in my mind

"The Damned 2007, I love seeing the Damned live and each time I see them they bring something different to the set, this particular night they finished off the Friday Night spot in the Ballroom. I remember them playing their classics and then played some of their more psychedelic set, the atmosphere was electric. It was one of those gigs that you walk around after with a big massive grin on your face. I managed to sneak quite an arty shot of the Captain.

"Random Hand 2008 & 2009, this is a new Yorkshire band that I saw first in 2008, I had read a small article on them in the Big Cheese magazine, so they had been highlighted on my spreadsheet as would like to see if possible! When they started their set they blew me away, they played Ska in a way that totally blew your head off, I think if I were to summarise what they are all about it's Ska mashed with heavy thrash, 'Play Some Ska' really got the crowd going, and it was good to see when we saw them again last year that their following had grown and the crowd recognised their music. I have played their stuff quite often at the No 10 (As a result Andy Morton is now a big fan) and I've had no end of people asking who they are especially saying 'Play Some Ska' is brilliant

"Another new young band we saw in 2008 was Outl4w. When we saw them I think the oldest band member was about 15. They are a very talented bunch of lads, and to me despite their age, their music had a mature edge whilst retaining their raw energy. I was really impressed that they also put on brilliant performance to a crowd that contained some hard-nosed Punks and seemed quite experienced in dodging the plastic glasses and beer!

"Neville Staple's Specials every time: I've seen him do the full energetic set a couple of times and an acoustic set on a couple of occasions. One year, I think it must have been 2007, I saw him do a full performance in the Ballroom followed by an acoustic set. In the Ballroom he was bouncing around all over the stage getting all the crowd going. The floor in the Ballroom is a sprung dance floor and with all the crowd dancing it felt like you were on a trampoline. Some of the crowd got him to jump into the crowd, which he did, everyone was going mad and the crowd were loving it, the only thing was he had real difficulty getting back on stage due to his dodgy knee (I think he said arthritis). Not long after when he did the acoustic set I felt a bit sorry for him, I think he wanted to do more of a chilled laid back set, but the crowd wanted all the energetic stuff again. He was a real trooper and gave another brilliant performance and still had the floor bouncing up and down. That night The Beat also played: I tell you Neville & Ranking Roger can give some of the younger bands a real run for their money

"I have also been surprised at the Rebellion to find myself enjoying some of the more *different* acts. In 2007 we saw John Otway, I thought he was really good and funny and he also played his big hit 'Really Free'. John Otway played again this year with Wild Willy Barrett, This time the act was quite frankly bizarre I don't know if we just didn't get it, but Wild Willy Barrett had a wheelie bin on stage and kept opening and closing the lid? We just couldn't understand why but then Jack (one of the Rotherham crew) had us in stitches by shouting *'that's not very wild Willy'* so we just went and got even more drunk! I still can't understand what the bin was about

TV Smith by Mandy

"Another 'different' act was The Crazy World of Arthur Brown whom I saw last year. He kept everyone waiting for ages and kept getting the sound checks to be redone, I think he was about an hour late on stage but talk about a brilliant entrance, he came on stage in a cloak with a full face mask holding a massive big stick (it looked like a tree trunk to me) and just kept banging the stick on stage in a menacing way. This went on for a few minutes and he then sang his first couple of songs still wearing the face mask and holding the big stick. He then pulled off his face mask and threw the big stick into the audience, a guy with a massive Mohican caught it, which I don't know if he regretted as he then spent the whole night at the front holding Arthur's big stick (oh err Mrs that sounds a bit rude!)

"TV Smith & The Bored Teenagers was another favourite gig of mine, it was actually on the acoustic stage, but even so there was a great performance of 'Bored Teenagers', as well as TV Smith showcasing some of his more recent stuff from 'Misinformation Overload'. I remember buying this CD from the gig and me and Daz playing it on the way home, wishing we were still at the festival. I love the picture I took of TV it looks like the gargoyle thing is looking on disapprovingly whilst he is drinking

"It's also great at the Rebellion to wander round and see some of acts milling around with the crowd. You see guys like Charlie Harper and Arturo working on their merchandise stalls, always taking time to talk to their fans, have their photos taken. To be honest I think they are great work horses and I genuinely admire how they are with their fans. Last year though, there was a pretty scary fan incident. We were sat in the Galleon bar in the Winter Gardens having a drink with the Rotherham crew and Animal from Anti Nowhere League walked past, the next thing a fan stupidly went up to him with a glass and started to pretend to fight him, this fan was quite small and Animal is massive – he had the fan on the floor in seconds!! I'm sure if the fan had not been messing with the glass Animal would have took it in good spirit and had his photo taken with him but I'm sure the fan learned a valuable lesson that day- never mess with Animal.

"As I've said I love DJing and have been lucky enough to play some great gigs with some of the best at the No 10. Mick continued to book the alternative bands and have local bands playing Punk nights, we started to get some quite good crowds on these nights and Mick started to look into booking some of the more well known bands.

"One of my most favourite gigs ever at the No 10 was when the first of these bands played. On 07/06/2008 UK Subs headlined at the No 10 supported by Riot Squad and Phil Murray and the Boys from Bury with myself DJing.

UK SUBS AND FANS IN ROTHERHAM 2008

I was so nervous I got myself so hyped up that day: I think I took all afternoon getting ready and all week planning my set list. I remember it was quite an early start so I'd gone down on my own to get everything set up, Daz was coming down later. I was amazed to see how busy it already was outside the No 10, it was a warm June night and the yard was already starting to get full.

"I got to meet Charlie early on, and what a great guy. I started playing my set and I was chuffed to bits when Charlie came and asked about a track I'd just played: it was Jeffrey Lewis with a version of 'Do They Owe Us a Living?' from his album '12 Crass songs'. That really made my night (incidentally we went to see him play the next day at the Leopard in Doncaster where I gave him the album, we also spent a great couple of hours with him after this gig, listening to some of his tales from over the years). Phil Murray opened the night up and by now the atmosphere really was electric, I was now a bit more settled with my set and we had a brilliant set from Riot Squad. Once The Subs came on though the place went mad, it was really hot, the place was packed so

377

shirts came off and the mosh pit started.

"I can't remember their set list, the evening seemed to go so fast and didn't seem real, I don't know if it was because I knew that this was really big for Rotherham and I was a part of it. Whatever the next thing I knew they'd finished their encore. I honestly couldn't stop smiling for days after this gig it was an absolutely brilliant night.

Above: Mandy with
Captain Sensible, Arturo Basic (Lurkers/999), Ed Tudor Pole, Knox
(Vibrators), Charlie Harper (UK -Subs) and Eddie (Vibrators)

"I think that this night gave Mick the reassurance to book other big names and the next big act we had was The Vibrators 01/11/2008. Another cracking night with Leather Zoo and the X Rippers supporting them. Mick had managed to get an announcement on Rotherham FM advertising this gig, and the DJ had given some spiel saying The Vibrators, Leather Zoo and X Rippers playing tonight with the Minx at the No 10, and then went onto to comment *'don't know about a gig this sounds more like a porn night!!'* The X Rippers and Leather Zoo were great; both putting on brilliant shows as always. I enjoyed The Vibrators despite Knoxy being absent (I think he was ill) but I must admit I enjoyed their recent gig more at the live@dickens 14/12/09 when they were reunited with Knoxy.

"Another of my favourite gigs was the Rother Punk Fest in 2009 at the No 10; to me this was our very own little Rebellion Fest and was a fantastic day. I think I started about 12:00 lunchtime on Saturday 09/05/09 and finished about 2:00 AM the next morning. The line up was Riot Squad, Leather Zoo, X Rippers, Graveyard Johnny's, The Arguments, The Hyenas and By Default. I have to say the generosity of some bands is just overwhelming. Leather Zoo provided all the basic equipment, which meant that the stage didn't have to be dismantled and reset up for each band, they had also done the same the week before for an all day charity gig we'd done at the No 10, in addition Riot Squad were there from the start to support all the other bands. Most of the bands really enjoyed the day too: I know By Default couldn't wait to come back and play, I was also impressed by Graveyard Johns as I'd not seen them before, I think that they are doing quite well now, as I often see them mentioned in the Big Cheese Magazine.

"I can't write about the No 10 without mentioning the final gig on 05/09/09, for me it was a night of mixed feelings. Sons of El Roacho supported Ed Tudorpole. The gig itself was great, both acts did a cracking set, but it was also quite sad knowing that this was the last gig at the No 10 and not knowing if I would be involved in anymore gigs, or what would happen to some of the gigs Mick had already booked in (The Vibrators, Becki Bondage, Anti Nowhere League and another mini punk fest) and what would happen to the Punk and Ska scene in Rotherham?

"In 2010 there have been some great gigs but the gigs still need to be supported by the folks of Rotherham. I know from all the gigs over the last few years there that some of the new generation of kids do support the scene, and both old and new bands. Indeed I am surrogate Punk Mummy to one of them: Jaydee. She used to work behind the bar at the No 10 and we had such a great time working together, we used to improvise silly dance routines and dance like crazy to the ska stuff. We still go to some gigs together, Madness was crazy last year and at Sham 69 last January I was a bad influence on her as I got us both thrown off the stage by the Sham!

"The online dictionary definition of Punk is *'a youth movement of the late 1970s, characterized by loud aggressive rock music, confrontational attitudes, body piercing, and unconventional hairstyles, makeup, and clothing'.* I agree with some of this statement and certainly there are still youths from the 70's that still carry the flag for Punk, but I feel that it can be a youth movement of any decade since.

"I do feel however that now perhaps the confrontational attitudes of my generation have since mellowed. When the smoking ban came in I emailed my local MPs and also Parliament complaining about taking our rights away. A few weeks later it was the Rebellion Festival and I was outside puffing away moaning with all the other smokers. I was talking to a gang of Punks round about my age, and told them about my email campaign, they congratulated me and said that it's reassuring to know that there are still some rebels out there. I went back inside thinking about their words and it made me think how sad we've all become. I'm certainly not condoning violence but had the smoking ban been introduced in the late 70's then there would certainly be a proper rebellion, possibly with even riots in the street. But now I'm classed as a rebel for sending a few emails!!

"I feel, though, that Punk is more about attitude and belief, if you look at the online definition again it mentions unconventional make up and clothing, I certainly subscribe to that with clothes-especially when I'm DJing or going to gigs, but nowadays what exactly is unconventional? Just visit any retail outlet or shopping mall and the majority of clothes shops will have many unconventional outfits and looks ready-made and off the shelf. Girls from as young as six have clothes that certainly Punks of my generation would have worn (for example ready-made ripped jeans and attitude t-shirts) yet they watch programmes like X Factor and Hannah Montana! Don't get me wrong there was the cheesy stuff too when I was young, and my most embarrassing fact is that my first single which I was given one Christmas when I was about six or seven was Jimmy Osmond 'The Long Haired Lover from Liverpool'... even at that young age it made me feel sick and I didn't play it! But I really wish that Mummies and Daddies would not buy their little princesses the 'unconventional stuff' just because it's designer or trendy.

"People may think I'm being hypocritical with these views given that I work in a corporate environment and therefore have to subscribe to a set of rules and routine, I have to tone my clothes down for meetings and any work nights out, indeed some of the people that have been to gigs in Rotherham haven't recognised me at the train station when I'm on my way down to London, all suited and booted. To me, though this is a compromise, we all have to be realistic and bills need playing. If I didn't work I wouldn't be able to afford to go to gigs or buy my CDs and clothes, so work funds my lifestyle choice. Plus I also think it's good to keep work as work and separate from my private life. At work I am Amanda and no one even calls me Mandy! Though I must admit I do listen and plan play lists on the train to and from meetings, and if a meeting's not gone so well, a good selection of loud fast music with as much swearing as possible can make you feel so much better!

"My son was recently best man at his best friend's wedding, me and Daz were invited and after the meal we were sat with all his friends. I was really flattered when one of the girls told me that she and her friends used to wish that their mums dressed like me, she told me that when I used to pick my son up from school that they used to think I looked cool. It's a bit ironic really as I used to feel that the other mums were looking down on me, given that they were all dressed as though they were going to a nightclub!

"I'm not ready to hang up my Dockers and hand Punk over fully to the new generation yet. I've got a full year of gigs already planned for this year, new bands to discover, new outfits to make and improvise, new CDs to spin, new friends to make and old friends to get drunk reminisce and go wild with. I'll just have to continue being a Punk mummy for now!"

So Mandy's rebellion continues: the pure unadulterated joy and zest for Punk Rock lives on for Mandy and many others. The attire may not be for shock and outrage anymore; the tastes in music may have expanded much further than the first earfuls of the Clash, Sex Pistols and the Boomtown Rats, but the love of anarchic Rock n' Roll, thinking to the other side of the spectrum ... the need to be different and being yourself has never been more valid!

In recent years, the class of 76/77 Punk (and afterwards) threw back some of its most interesting and, often innovative, bands... to re-create those classic Punk sounds, present a damned good time; and hopefully bring something new to the table. The Punk Rock circus may get a little tedious and smack of *cash from Punk cabaret* occasionally, but the intentions are often genuine and sod the critics!

Tony Beesley: "I have to admit, I was more than a little sceptical when all the old bands started to re-appear again: it just seemed like those old Rock n' Roll revival shows or something. Although I have now amended my views on the whole notion of *some of the originals* still banging away after all these years, I really have no time for some of the obvious money makers and fakes: the business orientated lot! All credit, though, must go to Mandy, Andy Morton, Mick Hill, Jamie Kennedy and all the rest who have helped to keep Punk and live Rock music thriving in Rotherham during recent, and often hard, times.

"Amongst the good Punk gigs I have seen in recent years have been the Buzzcocks, Rezillos, Magazine, Penetration, 999, Lurkers, Slits etc plus locals Artery. We have all had some great times watching these bands: it won't ever be the same as when we were young, but it gives me a right fucking buzz when some of the bands play... It may be many years since those days in the late 70's when we were introduced to Punk Rock, but at times it also seems like yesterday!"

Chapter Eleven
This is Our Generation Calling!
(The Conclusion)

"This may sound like a grumpy old woman but now the Punk look is laid on for everyone, it's so High Street and everywhere you look you see kids and their parents wearing stuff we used to wear years ago (and most have no idea who Joe Strummer was!) and they pay a fortune for it. I still love snipping clothes here and there and adding bits and pieces and coming up with my look for when I'm DJing now. (So different to my day job: the suited and booted corporate look!!)" -
Mandy Taylor

Our Generation 2009 – Dave Spencer, Pete Weston, myself and Carol Weston

The Punks, Mods and futurists of the late 70's and 80's of our generation's story are now fast approaching the 50 mark (and they are amongst the youngest of the bunch). The days of youthful abandon and the care-free approach to life have now been replaced with responsibilities, mortgages, tied down jobs, family and relationships: all the things our parents and peers were aspiring to and that we rejected the very notion of- all those years ago. Before we knew it, though, we too had become a part of society (often begrudgingly) and the trials of age and normality were at our door steps. Was it all worth it though?

Taking the Punk party into the 21st Century? Captain of the Damned at the Sheffield Plug (Debra Marshall)

Debra Marshall: (Below) "There was so much change in the seventies musically. It was a great time to be a teen and Punk gigs were the most memorable for the pogo-ing and gobbing from the fans and the raw energy coming from the bands on stage...it was good to be around at this time. For a generation that was so inspired by Punk and with a newly acquired attitude, we all thought we could change the world. When it came down to it some of us didn't really achieve that much. It's only now looking back that I realise this."

Lynne Freeman: "For me personally, punk was a coming of age, it was an open door to a new way of living. It made you be creative, it made you think for yourself and it made you more tolerant of other people's lifestyle choices. It was at last easy for people to admit to being who they were, be that sane, crazy, gay, black or white. It was a brave time, a time to stand up and be counted. I didn't have to try to conform, here was permission not given, but taken. However, for all of us, youth can be a dangerous time, so while we lived it to the full, some of our friends got lost along the way. We mustn't forget them or their part in our story, so RIP Ian, Specky, Deano and Judd and all the others who are just partying in another dimension."

Nick Banks: "Punk is an attitude not a safety pin; a bondage trouser; a spiky hair do; a motorbike jacket; a pair of Dockers; a Mohican etc. Punk existed before the Sex Pistols/the

Damned/the Clash... it was there with Elvis shocking the Yanks on the Ed Sullivan show, the Beatles and their outrageous 'long hair', Led Zep, Jimi Hendrix. Even Acid House of the late 80's was Punk. If it made your old man kick the telly in, or the press splutter with outrage... it's Punk. I'm not sure where the 'Punk' is today... ask a fifteen year old! I guess many from the Punk era thought that this music could change the world. I always thought that this was a load of bunk - Punk bunk? But later the penny dropped whilst listening to Charles Fox's marvellous theme tune 'Wonderwoman'. Verse two ends with the line *change their minds and change the world.'* and this is how 'Punk' did indeed (or will do) change the world. It made kids realise that being different and original and doing it yourself is the way forward, and can be carried over into all aspects of life, once being leather jackets, gobbing and putting your hair into spikes with glue pales. All in all, though, it was a great time to start getting into music, a really exciting era that produced so many classics: Couldn't have asked for more really."

Tony Beesley: "Sometimes, I have to pinch myself to get to grips with how many years have actually passed. When we were kids, the Second World War was like 30 years since... and that seemed like an eternity: now its well over 30 years since I walked up that ramp to the Top Rank to see The Damned in 1979... where has it all gone? In recent times, the Punk cast seem to have been passing away with an alarming rate: Malcolm McLaren and Steve New in just a matter of weeks. You get to thinking; *'we best hurry up and get done what we need to get done, before it's too late'.* If its one thing we need to do it is to leave behind some sort of mark; a legacy of sorts, something that will state that, in some ways, we did make a difference. The only thing I can do is write about it... and I don't know if that's enough? 40's and 50's we are now? It seems a million years away when we were young and full of ourselves. What we weren't gonna change ain't worth knowing. One minute we were daft kids living for music and the next we were just like our parents had been. I hate the word mortgage, it sounds like a prison sentence... maybe it is?"

Gary Stables: "It was hard being a Punk in South Yorkshire back then with the bastard Teddy boys always on yer back, but I would not have missed it for anything, the excitement of putting on yer Punk gear and heading out into town to meet yer mates, the gigs, the music, but most of all the friends you made: it was like being part of an exclusive club. It was like you belonged somewhere- with people that had the same ideas and thoughts, even today living in a coastal town in South Wales I still keep in contact with a lot of the people I met through Punk Rock some 30 years on. It was and still is fantastic.

"I was devastated when I heard Joe Strummer had died: I was working (driving the buses) and had to stop the bus and try and fight back the tears. I still miss the fella and his loss was a massive one for all of us Punk generation!"

Richard Chatterton: (Right with Joe Strummer) "I understood that the Punk movement was in no way the first to rattle the establishment. I knew already of the tremors Blues and then fifties Rock and Roll had caused in society, and that the Beatles and Stones had encouraged kids to form bands in much the same way as the Pistols did in '76. But Art movements, especially at the turn of the twentieth century had done exactly the same and then some. Dada and its offspring Surrealism was to shock and shake society and issued manifestos to this purpose. The first was an anti-art of nonsense and used painting, text, photomontage, film, assemblage and non-poems to confuse: and the artists often faced arrest. Marcel Duchamp created ready-mades which included a urinal which he signed R. Mutt and he drew a moustache on a copy of the Mona Lisa and wrote that she wore hot pants upon it, Kurt Schwitters made collages from litter and one early Dada exhibition was held in a men's public toilet, and visitors were given an axe to destroy the exhibits (now where did I experience that before?).

"These pioneers were to inspire Art Punks and Post-Punks alike, fifty years later, such as Jamie Reid who defined the Pistols cut-up style and Malcolm Garrett who designed early Buzzcocks covers such as 'Orgasm Addict' which could almost be a John Heartfield collage circa 1919. Italian Futurists declared all Art was redundant and proclaimed their aims to tear down the old Italy and create year zero, just as Punk did. Bands were also taking ideas from this period: Cabaret Voltaire were named after a Swiss nightclub pivotal to the Dada movement, Siouxsie and the Banshees 'Mittageisen' was inspired by Heartfield's collage work 'Hurray, The Butter is Finished!' Adam and the Ants sang 'Futurist Manifesto' before they went panto and two of the Art-Punk Skids and two of the group Magazine formed a new band called the Armoury Show named after a seminal 1913 New York art exhibition in which pride of place went to Duchamp's Cubist Futurist style 'Nude Descending a staircase.' Through Punk I also learned about and became excited by Art history."

Andy Coles: "I look back on the late 70's and 80's with affection, as there were some bloody good records amongst the mountains of crap, bound-for-the-bargain-bin vinyl. A lot of the drum sounds on songs of the 80's sound like they are being produced by hitting a biscuit tin full of marbles with a metal coat hanger and the songs are so shallow and dated. I recall getting soooo angry if a DJ played what I considered to be a crap record, usually something produced by Stock, Aitken and Waterman, but this was usually because I was full of Grolsch. I guess I've mellowed somewhat with age, as some of the records I hated at the time I *can* tolerate now, as they remind me of a particular night out or someone I knew!

"Although I can't say that I was ever what would be considered at the time as a 'Punk Rocker', Punk/Post-Punk is something that did influence my life in a positive way and made me a more open-minded person. Who knows what half the people that I lost touch with over the ensuing years are up to these days? Facebook is helping me to put that right, but there are people I haven't seen for years who I bet will still be raving about most of the same songs that they liked all those years back. The music scene of the 70's and 80's has long gone...but it gave me a bloody superb record collection!"

John Murray: "I still buy loads of stuff - got about 2500 CD's these days - but those first 8-10 gigs at the Outlook in 76/77 have never left me - I think about it all the time. I was so lucky to be in the right place at the right time - that early: the *'question everything, think things out for yourself'* ethic of early Punk has stayed with me throughout my life. I think the DIY spirit of the Buzzcocks 'Spiral Scratch' EP summed it up.

"It was really interesting to hear Devoto interviewed on the Jools Holland show recently when he talked about the 'discipline' of those early days - I understand what he means. I hated it when the spitting and the smack and the glue vibe moved in - that second Pistols gig at the Outlook and the herd who followed Sham 69 really killed it off for me - so I moved along with the bands that I thought kept that 'questioning' and open-minded spirit' going."

Anon: "After Britpop died so did my love of music again. There was nothing coming through that caught my ear so I went back to my first love, 1970's Punk and re-discovered the bands I'd loved and through compilations (and Tony) bands that'd passed me by. Rotherham had a lively little scene going and local Punk bands, along with some of the first generation ones, were lured to play in town and some great nights were had by all. Through a series of unfortunate events, I ended up out of work for five months and I asked the local promoter if I could help out with flyers and stuff, mainly so I could see the bands for free and fill up some of my long days. We have promoted local original bands and have booked many original Punk bands, such as The Vibrators and UK Subs. I also got to see my heroes, 999, play in my home town and The Lurkers, featuring all time good geezer Arturo Bassick, dedicating one of mine and Tony's favourite songs, 'Richmond' (the Pinpoint classic) just for us! Oh how we danced!!

"I'm right happy with my life at the moment. I've got some great mates who I can really rely on and I love my social life doing the gigs. I always have a word for everyone who attends the gigs and like to think it adds to their night that there's a daft lad on the door taking their money! I do all the flyers and have done them as homage to the old Marples ones! I hope people who remember them appreciate this little bit of nostalgia!

"As a final note, I'd just like to say RIP to Joe Strummer. He was my true Punk hero and I saw him with The Clash, The Latino Rockabilly War and The Mescaleros and loved every gig. I was lucky enough to have spoken with him and have my own memories of someone who I consider to be a true legend. I'll always remember the day he died; I was driving over the Woodhead on the way to Manchester with my family to go on a Christmas shopping trip. I felt like I'd lost a friend and was really quiet all day. I remember texting all my mates who were into Joe and we all felt the same. I saw him at the Leadmill exactly a month before he died and was privileged to do so. Oh and by the way, I was stood behind the Sheffield cousin of Nottingham's tallest man at the gig! You just know there's one in every town and city."

Jamie 'Headcharge' Smith: "I look back at my time as teenager in the Sheffield Punk and alternative scene with great fondness in the people, artist, gigs and experiences and most of all making me think outside the box!!! Which I have carried on to this very day and many more people out there have done the same. Today you can find a whole load of people from the Punk/Alternative scene involved in arts projects/free parties and underground events etc...The Punk attitude is still alive and kicking that's for sure!"

Right: Jamie 'Headcharge' Smith (Founder of Headcharge, Dubcentral & Rave against racism and ex Plastik Toyz singer)

Mandy Alleyne: "The best band I have ever seen live was actually the Cramps. They were awesome and I still love their music even today (R.I.P. Lux). In summary if I could choose a time of my life that I could go back to, it would be my Limit days; they were the best times of my life."

Neil Anderson: "I review quite a lot of gigs for various titles these days so I go to allsorts. Recent gigs include Little Man Tate, Rancid and Goldblade. I've been liking Sheffield band Oblong lately. There really are too many bands I've been into/am still into today. Everything from those that were there at the beginning like New York Dolls, Ramones, The Damned, The Clash and Sex Pistols to newer bands that keep the flag flying today like Billy Talent and The Briefs."

Colleen Allen: "The Hacienda was my second home right up to its death in 97. I went on to sing with 'Boom Sound' which was just me and my boyfriend, we had two children at home in Moss side and our own little recording studio. I then joined 'Urban Cookie' (around 96) as a singer then dancer performing in PJ Bells (Jazz club) and on BBC's Hangar 17. Typically, not long after I left 'Urban Cookie Collective, they had a number 2 hit in the charts with 'The Key'.

"I finally hung up my microphone when I split up with my first two children's dad aged 34; instead I became an avid socialite in every cool club in Manchester and was often to be found in Latin bars and underground R & B clubs with metal detectors and constant police presence, dangerous but exciting times. I went on to have my youngest daughter in 1998. In 2002 we moved back to Sheffield and then last year (2009) moved to Hertfordshire where I now live and listen to my girls playing 'my' music from the 70's and 80's."

Dave Burkinshaw: "Punk still lives on loud and proud. I am very proud to have been part of the Punk scene and love to dig out the old music and listen to it. As for the young Punks I see now I think good on you for keeping it alive."

John Quinn: "When I did a degree at the start of this century I did my dissertation on the politics of Punk, kindly helped by members of Crass, Buzzcocks, The Undertones, Sham 69 and even Bob Geldof, who people may not remember was once singer with the Boomtown Rats. I got 75% for it you know."

Gary Peacock: "The bad memories are all death and violence as a couple of mates were killed during that time. But there was no CCTV and United, Wednesday, Rotherham and Barnsley were all in the same division. Punks, Mods, Hippies, Skinheads, the National Front, Teddy boys and Travolta look-alikes too, there's little wonder that there was so much aggro, anything like that mix will never happen again."

Tracy Stanley: "To summarise my years through the decades, I don't feel I could have been born at a better time (apart from the fifties maybe and the explosion of Rock n' Roll). I wonder if there will be anything else that will give us the same reactions as Punk/Acid House and the drama and theatrics of the New Romantic Movement did: I hope so but I doubt it!"

'Out of Control' ex-Outlook Punk club-goer Steve Gledhill speaks of his favourites of the era and beyond.

Steve Gledhill: "In terms of my favourite bands during the Punk years, The Damned were pretty much always the top band for me. For the image, and impact, the Pistols are up there too - less so musically though. I saw the Clash a few times, and though they were great, it was difficult to take them to heart. The Banshees were also big favourites. Of the smaller bands, I liked Subway Sect, and also the Drones (from Manchester). Of the US acts, Johnny Thunders and Richard Hell were great, and the Ramones were pretty much unbelievable: One band where the records most definitely didn't do justice to the live experience. I also remember a pretty amazing night watching 999, though they don't seem to have aged well.

"One constant in music for me since 1977 has been Reggae - I picked up a love for it at that time that has never waned - although I still pretty much stick to 70s Reggae - there's so much of it that discovering new things today is still possible - I do like a lot of the Dubstep that is being produced today though. After Punk I got into a lot of the music coming out of the Sheffield scene - Cabaret Voltaire, Human League, Clock DVA, etc, as well as other Industrial music (Throbbing Gristle in particular) - but also the 2-Tone movement - I followed the Specials/Madness/Selecter tour around on a few dates in the South. Also trekked around watching Devo and The Tubes (who were pretty much the only pre-punk band I remained faithful to). I moved to the South of France around 1984 so that restricted to a large extent the amount of gigs I could go see - there were usually only two or three gigs a year locally anyone would want to see - nowadays it's even worse if anything.

"Today I consume more music than I ever have, and have wide tastes - for the last five years I've also been travelling to go to gigs - festivals in the States most years, and trips around France but also to Amsterdam, London, etc to see bands like Coldplay, Radiohead, Oasis, Elbow, Massive Attack, Tom Waits... I also regularly rediscover the old stuff - The Damned and PiL have both been getting heavy airplay recently."

Julie Lee: (Left) "I still like bands that are quite raw, such as the Arctic Monkeys and the Fratellis to name a couple I've been into recently. I think I will always like that type of band/music. There was a time when I was a huge Prince fan and I got into more funky stuff. I have also been a fan of Acid Jazz – Brand New Heavies, Young Disciples etc. That led me into an appreciation of Blues and Jazz, which I listen to fairly regularly now. My tastes have definitely mellowed over the years! I am still a massive disco fan – I love the seventies stuff. I remember lots of it from when I was a kid but I don't think I fully appreciated it back then. My musical tastes now are really quite broad and always changing. I listen to a lot of music but what I listen to depends on where I am, what I'm doing and what mood I'm in.

"What I loved about being a punk was that there was always something to do and people to do it with. It was an exciting time. I saw more bands in a couple of years than I've seen since. I went all over the place to watch bands and never worried about not having enough money or how I would get home – it didn't matter. It was all about being there."

Mandy Taylor: "In 2008 the Boomtown Rats (without Johnny and Bob) played at the Rebellion Punk Fest at Blackpool. I dragged my fella Daz to their set early to make sure we got to the front, and as their set got going, I decided to relive my teenage days and try to get on stage with them. There was a woman of a similar age nearby who was up for this so we sneaked to the side; their roadie gave us a can of beer each. I was so giddy and I ran on stage, unfortunately I got dragged off straight away (Daz has this all on video) and was basically told by the roadie that I was being allowed the beer and to see them backstage if I wanted to join them all for some fun later!!! I was off like a shot; though I never saw that woman again all weekend!!"

Beverley Wilson: "The Punk years were great times and if I had my life again I wouldn't change a thing. We're all still mates 30 years on and they're the nicest bunch of people I've ever met. Not everyone agreed though, and we got insulted and beaten up more times than I can remember; usually by the Sheffield Skinheads after gigs at the Marples."

Tony Beesley: "Nowadays, my record collection (and yes I do still have a vinyl collection) contains all the greats from over the years. There are all the usuals - Bob Dylan, Neil Young, Beatles, Byrds, Love, Small Faces, The Who, New York Dolls, Patti Smith, Otis Redding, Jimi Hendrix, Oasis, Rolling Stones, Clash, The Jam and so on, along with a very healthy dose of Punk, Soul, R&B, select Little Richard and Rock n' Roll 45's, Electro, Indie, Psychedelia as well as some of what I consider the best of what's come and gone throughout the years since Punk through to the present day.

"I go through many different phases of listening to music, but always return to Punk Rock (and Mod R&B) eventually. The buzz of Punk Rock will never go away, and though I may criticise the merits and failed idealism of the music and its politics: along with its relevance in the modern world, the love of Punk Rock and the vibrant energy and urgency it instilled and captivated me with all those years ago is still firmly intact... no matter what!"

Tony Lound: "Jan 2010 (present day)... Just thumbing through a copy of Scootering Magazine while in Smiths, there's a lovely restored GP200 in the small adds...the wife's looking worried!"

Tony Cronshaw: "I am now 54 and in the past few years have seen Public Image Ltd, Siouxsie and the Banshees, Lou Reed and Hugh Cornwell of the Stranglers. As they say Music is for Life."

Simon Ellis: "I'm just so glad I was around when punk happened...to experience the excitement, the adrenalin, and to be part of what was a huge explosion of talent, ideas and a desire to create something new: It definitely changed my life; all our lives and we were lucky to be there at the right time...A magic time."

Nigel Renshaw: (Right)"For me, as with all of us in the 'Punk Movement' anything was possible and the icing on the cake was us all being as one and in rebelling and sticking two fingers up at society and conformity. Being brought up on Classical Music (still love it to this day!) and to be be able to write my own songs and thrash them out on stage with a bunch of Stunt Kite mates and be appreciated was the penultimate!!! I look back on those days with a great deal of affection and reverence and thank *whoever?* for being in the right place at the right time!!! Musically there were special moments in time... You had the Swing era, Rock 'n' Roll 50's, Beatles and the 60's, Glam Rock and then us lot!!! We, like our predecessors, were lucky... Being that age, that feeling of belonging, the Sex Pistols 'Never Mind the Bollocks' (still sends shivers down my spine!), drugs and alcohol and the many, many experiences I had (and friends I have made) will be with me forever!!! What a Jammie Bastard'!!!"

One Sheffield band who really should have made it much bigger during the fall out of Punk were Artery: They are now back performing!

Murray Fenton: (Artery) "Having joined Artery in the closing years of their (original era) career 1983-1985, the band were asked to reform at the request of Jarvis Cocker, who curated the Meltdown festival in 2007. The band was made up of ever-presents Mark Gouldthorpe and Garry Wilson and three people who had all been members at different times throughout the bands history. I was lucky enough to be one of the three, along with keyboard player David Hinkler and bass player John Clayton."

Artery 2010 at Sheffield 02 Academy: Murray Fenton (Left) and Mark Goldthorpe (Photo copyright Peter Bargh www.bargh.co.uk)

The love of music always comes through in the end, be it via listening or performing.

Wayne Kenyon: "I am probably the wrong person to talk and write about music now as I am as jaded by it all as is possible... To be honest the only reason I am in a band is cos I love the whole gang mentality behind it all. When I am with the band, for those few hours etc, I am 18 again... I couldn't really give a toss about music. My big passion is travelling and seeing fantastic places round the world. I have never owned a CD player or i-pod or whatever and the last album I bought was in 1995. I don't listen to music: It just happens that I have an ear for melody and can put words to those melodies... I can't play guitar or sing for toffee!"

Jeff Platts: "Having participated in the ever changing moods of the scooter scene over the years, whilst there are some constants in terms of the music, 2-Tone/Northern Soul/60's and revival Mod etc, I do witness the music policies becoming a little more relaxed and daring in recent years, all for the good in my opinion. You're not likely to hear Saxon or Def Leppard (Thank God) but the Baggies and Ravers are catered for on occasion, particularly the Baggie crowd. When the Madchester/Rave scene boundaries crossed over via Mr Wilson's careful hands and the Hacienda became a car park/Kwik Save/modern apartment block...many of the kids gravitated towards the

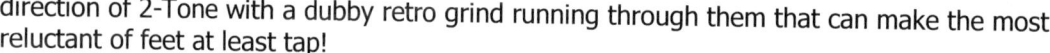

Scooter/Mod scene. It has survived...just, and in my opinion makes up a part of modern British Culture as we know it today. It's not just for the kids anymore, generations of families are involved, Mods are greyer, skins are balder (by default) Punks are less spiky but none the less as passionate about the scene as they ever were. Scooters are embedded in the psyche of modern Britain. TV ads are awash with classic Vespas, pop videos are littered with Lambrettas (a bit like the A64 of an Easter weekend!) and has anyone else heard the Lambretta sound bite on Eastenders!?...not that I watch it!!

"The scooter and Mod scene makes up a huge part of (my band) Barmy Surplus' gig history. Hopefully what we deliver is a potted history of Ska. Our self-penned tunes take a firm nod in the direction of 2-Tone with a dubby retro grind running through them that can make the most reluctant of feet at least tap!

"Any covers put in the set are carefully chosen for the audience so we like to gather as much information as possible about the venue and the expected clientele prior to us performing. Its not unusual for us to be catering for a mixed bunch though, the times many Mods, Punks and Skins have shared the floor, they might dance in different ways...but they dance, and that's the point!... Making people dance is one thing...making your own peers dance is another. I love it!!

"Ska has been written about for years and if you buy into the three waves theory i.e. Old school, (the likes of Prince Buster, Laurel Aitken etc) being the first wave, 2-Tone (and associated labels) being the second wave, and bands such as Spunge, Catch – It – Kebabs and Rancid making up the third, then Barmy Surplus can be deemed as all-rounders. Without making this sound like a blatant plug, we do what we do because its in our bones, we grew up with it, the labels, the scene,

the people, the do's and parties...we are IT!! and with 2 stroke oil running through our veins, it makes for a fantastic weekend with fantastic folk... Mod or not!"

Carl Myers: (Left) "Without the Mod scene through the mid 80's I wouldn't have met so many nice people, most of whom I still keep in touch with to this day. No matter how many times I hear 'Tin Soldier' by the Small Faces I still get that buzz and reminisce. As the 80's came to an end and all my old Mod mates faded away until later years to come, I started dating a girl who thought the mod scene had died in the 60's. So I found it pretty hard adapting to what felt like starting a new life without the mod scene and the music that went with it. I did have a smile on my face when Weller made his come-back a few years later, though."

Shaun Angell: "Personally, I think all the social unrest, back then, led to an *us against them* attitude amongst 16-25 year olds. I also think that the way young men dressed at the time – in expensive jeans, cords, trainers and track-suits etc gave them a sense of identity and showed (clearly) their rebellious streak." (Speaking on the Casuals)

Colleen Allen: "I am not sure if it was Punk itself or the type of person that gravitated to the movement that formed its steely bollocks, but I have never and I won't ever grow up from the need to rebel, to think 'out of the box' to remould life my way, with my set of rules and in my bubble. Doing 'it,' not Sinatra style, but with Sid - 'My Way'. Asperigers, Tourettes-like in compulsion– the art of Punk and its mentality were almost painful, idiosyncrasies and urges so deliciously alienating, yet overtly celebratory of the outsider within. I wouldn't be surprised if every last one of us falls within the mid to higher functioning range of 'the spectrum'.

"And so, to date, the bi-polar-embracing and divorcing of social subcultures has been my personal platform for challenge, always searching for the answers. Every transformation from the age of 13 and Punk, to present day and 46 marks my journey of discontent, my mission to challenge the attitude of mainstream society towards 'difference'. Perhaps this is why I lost myself in Art and music and thereafter the development of alternative education for excluded kids, prison teaching and therapeutic Art delivery. I feel I did and do live this life hard. From singer, hip hop dancer, exhibiting artist and feverish socialite, to Roma advocate, prison lecturer, researcher, manager, semi-reclusive and most importantly mother to my girls Raine-20 (Artist/DJ), Beri-16 (developing writer/photographer) and Millie-11 (budding actress).

"Punk made me stand up and be counted as the 'freak' I felt, I refuse to judge others as I have been judged over the years, I won't be guided by stereotypes, I value people BECAUSE (not in spite) of their difference. Thank you to Tony for urging me to reflect on, rummage in and rekindle fond memories, we still can't remember if our paths actually crossed but they certainly have now and with everyone else recapturing their moments within this third book, I feel part of that bigger family again, despite being 140 miles away in Hertfordshire!"

Tony Beesley: "What is it that brought all of us disaffected and largely un-hinged kids together via this enormous avalanche of music and culture? We can't have been normal can we? The ones truly affected by Punk and its after-shocks, us who took it all on board with nothing spared: not the fashion victims and fashion followers and certainly not the Mohawk brain-numb cider and glue wallowers without a clue why they were rebelling! No, the ones who went for the Punk ideal full on and carry it on in their whole personal psyche right through to this day.

"We must have been waiting for that extra focus and motivation in life, the missing piece of the shattered and disjointed jigsaw… we must have been in some kind of limbo waiting for Punk to arrive in our lives… maybe we didn't realise this until the time came and then it was obvious something was right and the void was full and almost complete. We knew who we were at last and, even though we may have been unsure exactly where we were heading, we knew we were going somewhere at last. Maybe that explains why, that during the many years following, we have gradually succumbed to that restless unfulfilled void again. Like I say we weren't normal… who wants to be normal anyway?"

Julie Longden: "Throughout the years since Punk I have been into and seen gigs by the likes of Rage against the Machine, the Verve, Fun loving Criminals, Foo Fighters, the Killers and yes even Take That who put on a great show. Still, to this day though, there is nothing like 'Never mind the Bollocks' by the Pistols to lift the mood.

"On the subject of the Sex Pistols, I think it's as though those days of our revolution and anti-establishment - two fingers up against the system - have now almost been turned upside down. We now have John Lydon (Rotten) who has gone from public enemy number one to advertising good old English butter on the telly. This, along with the so-called Godfather of Punk Iggy Pop doing his bit, advertising insurance on the telly, is also a sign of a world gone mad to me. The conciliation of recently seeing Rage against the Machine get the Xmas number one spot makes up for it: I had a smile watching the Xmas Top of the Pops knowing that at least there are some signs of the old rebellion alive and kicking!"

Pete Skidmore: "It was my 30th time of seeing Weller when he played Sherwood Pines in 2009. With Weller you know what you are getting, ok he is not ground breaking anymore but still a legend and can still blow a hell of a lot of these new young bands away. Music and youth culture has changed so much now and it's not tribal anymore, youths are not angry anymore they have no attitude whereas we had it by the truckload, we got out and we made our own scene. Kids don't talk, they text or facebook or twitter i.e. they talk a good time but don't actually have one. We had what we had in our pocket- no overdrafts credit cards etc... if you were skint you still went out, it costs nowt to dance! We had 3 channels on the TV; 1 radio station, pubs closing at 10.30, no downloads and no mobile phones; we had to search out for clothes, we didn't buy the look in one shop like you do nowadays, stuff like Sherman's and Fred Perry's were even hard to find but now you are spoilt for choice with them. We bought jeans and trousers upstairs in Harrington's and got changed in front of other lads and we had to climb a set of fucking ladders to do it! Imagine the health and safety Nazis with that one! Its 24 hour Rn'B on M ''FUCKING' TV the usual crap music with no tune, what did we have? The Old Grey Whistle test! Thousands of youths across the country would have been late for school the next day after stopping up late just to catch a glimpse of the latest Punk band shoved in between endless videos of Meat fucking Loaf screaming about a bat, and these so called Punk bands i.e. GREEN DAY? The film *High Fidelity* sums it up where Stiff Little Fingers are playing in the background of the record shop and a guy asks if this is the new Green Day album!

"You can't get within 100 metres of a band nowadays, not even sound checks; it was the normal thing for us to do. We got into the Ramones sound check at the Sheffield Top Rank and I got 'Rocket to Russia' signed by the band (I still have it) they spent ages talking and signing stuff, just ask WESTFUCKINGLIFE or COLDPLAY - that's if you even get near to em.

"I was in our local a few weeks ago and watching some young lads taking the piss out of each other about music and it was tragic: Three lads all with the tattoos and designer gear arguing about who was the best on X Factor? You fucking serious lads? That's how bad music and youth culture has become. One of them was banging on about Robbie Williams and about how good he is; well to me he has got it made, got 100.000 kids parting with their hard-earned £75 and getting them to stand in a field singing the songs for you while you freak out on stage like Norman fucking Wisdom on acid; what bollocks! I remember me and my mates running the gauntlet of daring to be different when we were Punks or Mods. Even, when in the mid 80s, we went to Manchester to buy Lacoste and Ellesse stuff, you had all the Mancs checking you out as you came out of the train station In other words the 40 something's laid all the foundations for the youth of today to take advantage of and they haven't at all, instead a bedroom culture has evolved around not having the skills to socialise and actually go out! We have lads where I work at 20 years old wanting to work nights all the time, are you fucking serious? you should be out at a gig or a pub or a disco or something instead of working!"

Luckily, the love of the Punk era of 30 odd years ago has been passed on to a much younger NEW GENERATION! The legacy of Punk and its spirit, along with its Mod relative, have been passed on to at least some of today's youth.

Dean Beesley: (Age 20 years Rotherham Born: son of the author) "From a very young age, I would even go as far to say the age of six, I can distinctly remember my dad listening to The Clash and The Jam. Ever since then, I have liked and listened to and loved bands like these two bands. Having been exposed to this sort of music from a young age, you begin to get to know the songs and want to find out more about them and the scene. I think the main thing that attracted me to Punk music is the fact that it was so different and original. I would never experience the excitement and mayhem of the era but listening to it and going to gigs would get me as close as possible.

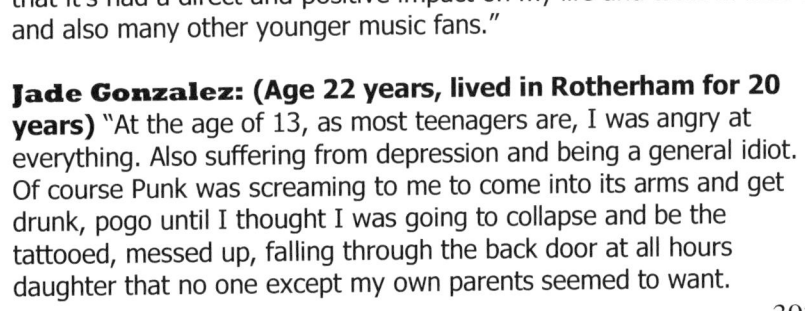

"The first gig I ever went to was Paul Weller at the Octagon in Sheffield in 2006. It was an experience I will never forget...he was absolutely fantastic: such passion and energy for his music and I would say from then on, I really properly got interested in Punk and wanted to find out more about it. Since that gig, I have been to see bands such as 999, the Vibrators and the Rezillos all of who were great. In my eyes, Punk music is way better than a lot of the rubbish out now. A lot of the commercialised crap forced upon people's ears these days is pathetic, it has no meaning and I am glad that I have had someone to open my eyes and show me what true music is.

"There are some cool bands out there nowadays, though: I am a fan of bands such as Hard-Fi, early Kaiser Chiefs, some more cutting edge Dance music and Hip Hop and the Arctic Monkeys and more recently The Violet May: I remember listening to the Arctic Monkeys demos what my mate had and really getting into them

before their first album came out (Alex Turner's Dad taught both me and my Dad at school, probably glad to see the back of the both of us as well!). I used to (and still do) like the Libertines too as my Dad bought their first album and I got hooked on that too. Punk music will always have a special place for me no matter what, so it's fair to say that it's had a direct and positive impact on my life and taste in music and also many other younger music fans."

Jade Gonzalez: (Age 22 years, lived in Rotherham for 20 years) "At the age of 13, as most teenagers are, I was angry at everything. Also suffering from depression and being a general idiot. Of course Punk was screaming to me to come into its arms and get drunk, pogo until I thought I was going to collapse and be the tattooed, messed up, falling through the back door at all hours daughter that no one except my own parents seemed to want.

"It wasn't until I started work at No10 pub in Rotherham, though, that Punk really mattered to me. We put on Punk bands from all over and soon had the Yorkshire Punk scene bursting through the doors every weekend, which I loved. My bosses Ricky and Joanne were really relaxed as long as we got on with the work and respected them, which we all did. So they let me run riot in between serving behind the bar and dance around to bands and hijack the stage. I was joined in all of these shenanigans, naturally, by my 'Punk Mummy' Mandy Taylor who was our D.J. Together we sang into mops devised stupid dance routines and made lots of really amazing friends. I seemed to adopt a whole Punk family through working at the pub because I am the little one everyone wants to look after.

"I am also the landlady along with my friend Carly of 'The Punk Rock hotel' where we lived in Herringthorpe, and put up the bands that played the 10. Sadly we only had three guests, The Vibrators, who I have gone on to stay in touch with and went to stay in London with their bassist Pete for a Camden pub crawl, and in the spirit of all things Punk we got royally pissed!

"Along with Mandy, Mick, Daz and Mandy's embarrassed son Steven we went to see Sham 69. To cut a long story short, I drank my body weight in Newcastle Brown, got covered in bruises in

the mosh pit and stood on by a Skinhead when I fell over. Me and Mandy also jumped on stage for a dance before being picked up and thrown off the back of the stage by two big men, it was an all round hilarious night, made all the more brilliant by the fact that we could see Steven begging the floor to swallow him up because he was mortified that his mum and her mate had got up on stage with Sham 69!'

"Sadly Ricky and Jo shut the pub for good and thus my reign behind the bar was over. But along came Mick, Bott and the others from Dickens and they opened Live @ Dickens, so punk still lives on in Rotherham, and we love them for it.

"My mum or 'Mummy Debs' as she's known as by most of my friends has always been a bad ass Punk at heart. She's my hero and I love her to bits, she grew up wearing tartan drainpipes had a skinhead and lived in her Docs. This year I took her to see Madness in Sheffield as she hasn't been to a gig in years and I wanted to thank her for everything she's done for me. We joined Mandy, Daz and Mandy's brother Pete and his wife Jo, who are all superb company. Donned in our Madness fez hats we had a good old knees up.

"And it was through my drunken haze at this gig that I realised how amazing the punk and ska scene really is. I was with my friends who were the same sort of age as my mum, and next to us there was a guy my age with his son who looked about 5 years old, and all those generations were all united for that one night by the music that we all love so much, and the Punk and Ska we all live sleep and breathe. I am so happy that I was asked to write a bit for this book as I want people to love this scene as much as we do and keep it alive. It's been an amazing part of my life and I don't intend to grow up and stop being a twat anytime soon!"

What does Punk mean in the present day? Here are some next generation views on what it means!

Magda Knight: (Editor of Mookychick.co.uk) "Punk is about attitude more than a look. If you wear cardigans with holes in and second hand shoes that's more Punk than wearing pink neon. Don't be a poseur. Don't listen to anyone who tells you you're a poseur. Fuck them. Labels aren't for people any more than they are for clothes. Re-engage with that person when they say something interesting. Or say something interesting yourself. Apathy won't cut it when you're a

Punk. You're bored when you're boring - you're boring when you're bored. That means direct action - protest in the streets, do bizarre acts of social non-conformity, have sparky conversations where you test the beliefs of people around you - and expect to be tested right back. Get head over heels into veganism, feeding the homeless, whatever. 'Food Not Bombs' is great because it's considered a 'terrorist organization' by the government. Or celebrate 'Buy Nothing Day'. Just get a passion: A passion that you have chosen for yourself, and thought about. Don't shut up about it either. Why is individuality important? Because it hasn't been branded, it hasn't been sold, and it can't be bought. You could be Punk who never washes their hair and wears hiking boots and men's jockey shorts and loves the work of Walter de la Mare. It may not fit the stereotype - but if you're that person, and you're still a Punk, you'll know it. It's about knowing who you are. And if you want to shove that in people's face, or just show who you are by a guiding example, that's up to you. Don't be a follower. Be a pioneer."

A trio of New Generation Punk influenced siblings speak here, of how the sounds of the past generations managed to infiltrate their own!

Robert Jenkinson: "In my teens I was obsessed with Oasis. In the NME Noel Gallagher stated that the early-Punk sound of Oasis was influenced by the Sex Pistols so I went out and bought 'Never Mind the Bollocks'. I couldn't believe that the sound I was listening to was 20 years old. It had so much energy and substance. To me Punk means *fuck you*. I enjoy listening to it to let off steam. Punk has a do it yourself attitude- anyone who knows 3 chords could (and can) be in a band- you don't need to have a Music Theory degree. It made me form my own band and the wall of guitar sound we play on pissed up nights is all thanks to Punk. I think that Babyshambles and The Strokes are currently carrying the torch for Punk in both their music and attitude. Punk has so much of an influence in modern music it's become hard to avoid!"

Robert's brother, Des, was lucky enough to come into contact with two of the key figureheads of the original new wave... a two for the price of one intro to the ideals and sounds of Punk!

A cheers gesture to Punk from Des!

Des Jenkinson: "I remember attending a festival at Manchester Old Trafford Cricket Ground on 12th July 2002. This is the date I really started to get into Punk properly - Joe Strummer was performing with his band The Mescaleros. As a young 19 year old obsessed with Oasis (at the time), I had not really listened to much Punk music at all, and in truth would not have been able to tell you who Joe Strummers first band was! This obviously pains me to say now!!

"On the same day, at the same festival, I also saw Paul Weller perform. I knew a lot more about Paul Weller but had only really been interested in his solo career. The gig potentially changed the way I looked at music from then on. I started to listen to the likes of The Jam, Joy Division, Sex Pistols and of course The Clash.

"Now significantly more educated in the ways of Punk I have come to realise that it is music of its time that will probably never be recreated like it was before, however the menace in which lyrics are delivered and the messages it sends can still strike a chord with young fans now. I believe that because of the gig I attended in Manchester and especially because of Joe Strummer, I have been given the gift of Punk music, and I am truly thankful for that."

Jayne Jenkinson: (20 years old Punk fan from Rotherham) "I spend many Saturday nights in the Leadmill and on the DJ's playlist you can expect to hear music from the likes of The

Jam and The Clash. The DJ is potentially just wanting to re-live his youth again but those on the dance floor are going just as wild and 'singing' along. I ask my friend Rosie how she knows all the words and she replies *'it's cos er... me Dad.'*

"I personally first tuned into Punk when I went to The Casbah in Sheffield and 'Rock the Casbah' was blasted into our ears prior to a local band coming on stage. The next day the parents' Motown CD had been put to one side and the brother's Clash CD was spinning around instead. It soon become noticeable that present day bands such as The Libertines, The Strokes and Arctic Monkeys had been somewhat influenced by punk. I think it's safe to say, though, that Punk will never be lost in time because youths will continue to seek to be part of a scene that is characterised by non-conformist behaviour."

The spirit of Punk inevitably led to Des Jenkinson forming his own band.

Des Jenkinson: "I currently play drums in a band called 'The Magi' in Sheffield. I have a hand in writing the songs for the band and would say that both my drumming and song writing is influenced by Punk. Our band were formed around three years ago, in a tiny attic room in Sheffield. I had been playing drums since I was 8 and moved into a house with my brother (Bob) and two close friends some time in 2005. My brother had been learning guitar for a few years and we decided to start writing our own music with our friend Mark. We soon found ourselves with plenty of songs but no band to play them in. This is when we decided to recruit Ed Watson on bass and brother Andy on Guitar, who had both only just started learning. We also got cousin John-Paul to take up the lead singer role. We didn't know what to expect, what with John-Paul having never sung before and with half of the band struggling to play their instruments. After a few months of hard practice, we soon started to sound the part and secured top gigs at all the main venues in Sheffield. We have also played venues in London and even the famous Cavern Club in Liverpool."

Back to our generation's cast: one particular Sheffield Mod veteran has now been faced with the paradox of the Modern World and all of its Pros and Cons: the need for Modernist progression also leaving a distinct yearning for the cut of the chase as opposed to having music handed out on a plate for modern day consumption!

Heather Quinn: "Hmm... what's it like to be a middle-aged Mod? I'm not sure many people would know that I was. In my head, I'm no different. (At least I don't think so.) On the outside though, I do find it harder to keep true to the faith. My clothes may not be nearly so cool and I'd certainly look a prat if I tried to wear a mini-skirt, but the Mod code is embedded in my brain and there's no getting away from it. Shouldn't I have grown out of it by now? Well, Weller once said that Mod was like a religion and I agree. I still look for that attention to detail and vintage is still more appealing than High Street. Youth sub-cultures don't exist in the same way anymore. Most music nowadays is slick and soulless. Records have been replaced by downloads and record fairs are virtually extinct. I never imagined things would be so different. These days I miss the excitement of discovery - that elusive single you've been after for ages and the smug satisfaction when you know it's finally yours. Bidding for it on eBay just isn't quite the same.

"Mind you, imagine 30 years ago if there'd been the internet as we know it today. Would I have really turned down the chance to have instant access to a virtual jukebox such as Spotify and what would I have given to be able to source an original Biba bag without even having to leave the house? Imagine if there'd been social networking - how easy it would have been to keep up-to-date with the latest in everything Mod. I could have watched footage of the Small Faces 24/7 and researched anything and everything about the rarest of tracks. So, as I'm writing this it's gone midnight, the kids are tucked up in bed, the volume's cranked up and I have the difficult decision of which playlist to listen to next....choices, choices. Maybe the *modern world* isn't that bad, after all."

"Now around fifty years old, 'Mod' is suffering from something of an identity crisis. It means so many things to so many people the term is largely meaningless. To some, its jazz hipsters prowling the Soho streets at dawn looking for a caffeine fix. For others, it's the amount of targets and arrows you can cram on any available surface. Some want Rickenbackers and windmills; some to brush off the talc from their midnight and six shoes; and to others it's simply Indie guitarists with half decent hair." **(Mark Raison - Modculture site's Georgie Fame CD review Jan 2010)**

Tony Beesley: "Even though Mod now has been split up into so many differing factions, there are still some great young people on the Mod scene nowadays: Janine and Gareth (Gareth at left) are a great couple... a breath of fresh air to the scene and their passion and enthusiasm for Mod is inspiring, as are some of the other young faces knocking around that are keeping the faith and making sure the Mod scene survives and moves on with their zest for music and clothes: dig the new breed!!!"

And where has this spirit of the new breed emerged to music-wise? The sounds of blue-eyed soul- that great love of all Mods tastes crossed over into the mainstream with Tabloid-hugging tortured Queen of modern *white projected Soul* Amy Winehouse whilst 2008 saw the talents of a new voice in modern day Soul come through with the help of ex Suede maestro Bernard Butler with his production of the sounds of Duffy.

Tony Beesley: "Duffy has a superb voice, but to me has been under-used material wise. Can you imagine hearing her fronting a proper grass-roots R&B band? I like her album, but it really could have been a stormer."

Duffy at the Leadmill 2008 (Kevin Wells)

The wheels of motion sped into Sheffield at the Leadmill with a new band from Oldham in 2010 with perhaps one of the greatest cross-genre influenced bands of many years. Taking the speed and style of The Jam, Clash and early Punk Rock, the songwriting crafts of the Kinks and the visuals of early classic Who and blended with an appreciation of the best in Britpop, a nod towards the Arctic Monkeys and beyond, Twisted Wheel present a sound as refreshing as anything heard in recent years. The new breed has arrived!

Kevin Wells: "A new band that has excited me recently are Twisted wheel from Manchester; who for a three piece really do get a powerful sound and look as though they really enjoy playing live unlike a lot of bands who suffer from not being able to capture that excitement of their live performances on record. To me it would be an injustice if they didn't go on to bigger things because as a live band they grab hold of the crowd and throttle them into submission, you can't beat that 'in your face' confrontation."

Tony Beesley: "Twisted Wheel are outstanding! I love the band. Their album is the best debut since the Libertines one. They are the sound of Punk 2010 and not the thrash Metal of the typical hardcore lot. It's fantastic to see young musicians taking the spirit and energy of Punk, the sensibility of Mod and the influence of the best in modern music and making it their own. They get the adrenalin flowing big style for me... All credit to them: one of my fave bands in years."

Twisted Wheel at the Leadmill steel stage 19th February 2010

Photos by Kevin Wells

Recent years have seen a revival of sorts for the sounds of Punk, Mod and the Electro Post-Punk sound. Britpop may have been soaked up into the mainstream of the late 90's pop culture, but the influence of that most British of quite recent musical trends and all the other most significant genres to have emerged after the Punk era can be heard in the aforementioned Arctic Monkeys, Franz Ferdinand, Kaiser Chiefs, Hard-FI, Dirty Pretty Things, the Enemy alongside the new Mod expressions of The Moons, The Rifles, The Sons, Twisted Wheel and more. The sound of 'Setting Sons' era Jam could be heard from the Ordinary Boys who themselves spawned a fifteen minute celebrity in lead singer Preston...

Meanwhile one of the few surviving musicians of the whole Punk band explosion of 77 to stick rigidly to his principles and retain his own individual musical vision (and stylist credibility) – Paul Weller - continues to stir up an exceptional and credible mix of classic and contemporary sounds spat out in his own exclusive brand of Modernist flavoured Rock... and also urging the nation to wake up! He has also managed to renew ties with former Jam bassist Bruce Foxton: joining together to perform Jam classics, including first LP Punk fave 'Art School' onstage to celebrate.

Paul Weller at Sheffield Octagon 2006 (Lee Dyson)

Others of his generation of musicians admirably plough through doing what they do best – some retaining the Punk spirit of 77 to invigorate and excite new generations of Punk loving enthusiasts alongside the mixed opinions of their one time fans. New musical approaches and ideas are respectfully presented by the talents of ex Clash man Mick Jones and ex Gen Xer Tony James with Carbon Silicon, whilst the revived Magazine and Slits (amongst others) bring their sounds up to date for modern consumption... throwing in new ingredients along the way. The Buzzcocks still remain one of the greatest pop bands of all time and in recent years have created work ('Flat Pack Philosophy' – 2006 being one) to match the best of their original Punk era classics. Their one time support band Penetration are once again producing some fine quality tunes to stand alongside their two much loved original albums 'Moving Targets' and 'Coming Up For Air'.

Tony Beesley: "When Weller played 'Eton Rifles at the Doncaster Dome, I am not kidding the hairs at the back of my neck stood up and I was transported back to 1979 instantaneously. Ok so this sounds like a nostalgia trip and to a point it was, just like when he played 'Running On The Spot' at the Octagon a couple of years earlier... but what the fuck, why should we get hung up about feeling nostalgic about something so fantastic and memorable. There's a time and place for everything and in these times a dose of good old Punk era nostalgia can be the exact medicine required."

Pete Skidmore: "To me Weller is everything that a musician should be, bags of attitude, great style, speaking his mind on today's so called *Rock stars* and making music that he wants to make and not following music fads to please music journalists. Even after 33 years he is still making music that pushes the bar even higher: by his standards it would have been quite easy to keep making 'Stanley Road' every year or so. Then there's the awesome clothes! Weller is the longest relationship I've had or ever will, barring my wife, son and family: his music has picked me up when I've been down, given me songs that I can put a good time or bad time to, inspired me to search out clothes that nobody else is wearing, sat in barbers shops with a picture of Mr Weller asking for a similiar haircut and wondering especially in my younger days... *'do I look a dick wearing this?'* I could have chosen Bono, Sting or Bruce Springsteen, but no I went down the path of Strummer, Lydon, and later on Jarvis and Richard Hawley, proper music that I can identify with. I and thousands of others come from a similar background as Paul Weller, we have been there, lived those songs, had those feelings and lived that life. With Weller he says what he thinks and stands by what he says, I love the guy for that. A man after my own heart!"

Weller at Doncaster Dome 2008 (Kevin Wells)

Tony Beesley: "If any musician epitomises the longevity of the Punk-instigated generation, it has to be Paul Weller. He is the only one (of the major players) to still have his feet firmly on the ground and still be able to carry that Punk attitude and swagger off. He was upsetting The Clash and most of the Punk elite back in 77 and he is still upsetting people to this day. True he may have the career of a Eric Clapton of Punk, but that's just a measure of his success. I have been influenced and inspired by Weller since the late summer of 77 and am still taking note of his stance to this day, be it his cocky arrogance and digs at the Rock aristocracy or his latest threads: though I have to say its getting a bit tedious the number of Weller wigs you see entrenched on lots of the middle of the road Mod worshippers nowadays, c'mon Paul, give us back your suedehead cut and wash the country clean of far too many post-1966 make-do Mod barnets!"

Kevin Wells: "I have been a gig photographer for a few years now and can be seen 'camera in hand' at many of the gigs in and around Sheffield, always capturing the action from the crowd rather than the photo pit. It's always nice to see a band live and some of the younger bands seem to be carrying on the tradition playing raw, catchy music that gets the crowd going. Following on from the success of Arctic Monkeys, Sheffield produced loads of great guitar bands, two I would like to mention are Little man Tate and Millburn who really ought to have been bigger than they

were. Listening to these bands especially, you can hear a lot of Mod/Ska influences that have stood the test of time. Cruelly these bands are no more- having fallen foul of the corporate record company demands, but both were thrilling live performers and their final gigs at the Sheffield Academy still rank up there with some of the best I've seen.

"Bands such as the Enemy and the Rifles (left) are having great success marrying up to date indie/guitar music with sounds from bands such as The Specials and the Jam and continually fill large venues all over the country. Also it is nice to see a few influential bands such as The Specials getting back together and proving that they can compete with anyone live, it was a great vision from 2009 seeing a room full of 40+ year old mods and skins skanking to the 2-Tone sound of the Specials and loads of young un's joining in as well, and you never know some of the younger element of the crowd might be tempted to form bands to keep the flag flying even longer.

"Kid British rely on a Ska influenced sound coupled with the beats of today's music, a great live band who went down well supporting The Enemy and the Specials on tour. Not so much powerful or in your face; they are more laid back with a sound you can lose yourself in and great to dance to too. Also, Detroit Social Club from the North East are a six piece band that create a sonic psychedelic sound coupled with the guitar edge of the Stooges and the beats of Primal Scream."

Primal Screams' Bobby Gillespie and Mani along with Jarvis Cocker at two Carling Academy 2008 gigs (Kevin Wells)

**Babyshambles at the Leadmill
December 2009**

**Madness at the O2 Academy
December 2009**

Kevin Wells has retained all of his initial passion for music to this day and continues to take outstanding snap-shots of live shows, capturing many new and exciting bands as well as the more established ones. His work is a shining example of the Do it yourself ideology of Punk!

Above: Cool Canasta and singer Chris McClure of The Violet May

Local bands and acts such as Dave Spencer's Cool Canasta, Richard Hawley, Little Man Tate (who unfortunately split in 2009), Monte Carlo Safe Crackers, Barmy Surplus and more recently Special Guest Stars, the unbelievably youthful 'Searching 4 Evidence', The Cartels, the Monicans and The Violet May (named after the legendary Sheffield record shop owner and whose singer is the smoking guy on the iconic cover of the first Arctic Monkeys' album) also continue to show the talent is still intact within the cast of our generation and its descendants! Upholding a great tradition of Sheffield bands – though distancing themselves from their contemporaries – bands such as The

Violet May are taking the best of the past, mixing up the ingredients with a wide cluster of influences and presenting something new and undefined... and the attitude thrown out is pure Punk Rock!!!

Punk - itself - as a musical style, however, has been diluted and categorised to many extremes: its sound being plagiarised by a new generation of skateboarding-slacker-influenced American upstarts. Even though Green Day may have regurgitated the sound of Buzzcocks meets the Clash via The Jam, they lack the suss and attitude of the best UK Punk of the late seventies... and they perform in over sized ROCK Arenas that spew out over-priced tickets, glossy programmes and an ideoligy that Punk was/is something to be marketed in the same way as Take That and the X Factor's cast of wannabee disciples. For many, Punk was meant to eradicate all relevance of the Arena concert and the gigantic gap that exists between performer and the paying fan... it seems that we have come full circle and the taste is bitter, maybe its time to re-awaken the rebellion!

Dave Spencer: "I have seen the future of Rock n' Roll - The Violet May."

Chris McLure: (The Violet May) "I suppose the band were made from the remnants of a low-key Sheffield band called The Barricades which was formed by TVM guitarist John Kubicki with TVM drummer Alan Whittaker. I met John Kubicki in an office; we were both disillusioned with the current crop of bands both locally and nationally. In my view, everything had been diluted and I wanted it to go straight from heart, to practice room to the stage.

"John recruited Alan again, our bassist Dan Booth (unemployed, also miffed at modern bands) and Jono How. I think we all thought that if we were all to form and play live then we had to come in all guns blazing, I personally believe you have to believe that you are the biggest and best band in the world if anyone else is to believe it.

"I suppose every band members ambitions vary. I think collectively, at the start, you concentrate on getting your sound perfect and then it is how the fuck to quit the day job. I feel if everyone is concentrated on getting to one place and does not really want anything else as a career then the force can sometimes be unstoppable: You need the fuckin' tunes though.

"In terms of the current musical climate, personally I cannot see any band at the moment that will inspire a 15 year old boy to go out, buy a guitar or start singing and think *'fuck it, I'm going to be a rock star'*, there seems to be a distinct lack of honesty, sincerity and quality within rock music. I don't think this current generation have any true idea of what the feeling of punk brought with the feeling of rebellion, we are the karaoke generation, fed on a constant supply of fifteen-minute fame pop stars. The internet as a medium etc means that no bands are given chance to progress as artists and people, they are chucked in to a make a quick pound and thrown out the other end wondering what the fuck happened."

Dave Spencer: "They (The Violet May) have that cocky attitude without being arrogant: a little intimidating and confrontational, which I like. It reminds me of when I saw the Sex Pistols a few years ago. I had never realised and truly got how intimidating they were. Even as far ahead as when they reformed and going along to see them, after all that time I suddenly got it. It was like something dangerous was being presented and that's what I see in The Violet May."

Tony Beesley: "Dave rang me up way back at the start of the year (2010) and told me all about them, I had read their feature in the Star and knew about the record shop connection (The Violet May was the old Ted shop we speak about in Our Generation volume 1). Dave was really enthusiastic about them after just seeing them and I took serious note of this and planned to check em out. Missing their Stockroom gigs in Sheffield I got in touch with the band and finally got to see them in Rotherham after recommending them to the venue. Dave was right about them in every way. They are something special."

The Violet May at Rotherham Live at Dickens venue May 28ᵗʰ 2010

Chris McClure: "Did Punk change anything? I never viewed Punk as a sound. However, I always thought Punk was a spirit!!!!!!! I suppose for a working class person growing up in the late seventies and the early eighties it changed everything, but sadly as said before it seems to be lost on this generation, maybe it is time it reared its ugly head again. For example, last Thursday I sadly learnt about the death of Malcolm Mclaren, four hours later I was told never to enter a music venue again after smoking a cigarette on stage. It hasn't changed a single thing for a man in their twenties growing up in Sheffield in 2010. For me The Violet May represent The Violet May: Five men who don't want to work for a living and want to be in a rock band. We have been getting people saying guitar bands are on the way out? All we want to do is get up on a stage and play some fucking Rock n' Roll and then fuck off!"

The Violet May Live at Dickens (Courtesy of Live at Dickens venue)

Tony Beesley: "Every now and again a new band comes along and cuts through the crap. With plenty of attitude, stage presence and tunes to back up the front, we need this to happen every so often: someone to shake up the conceited and bland music industry and all of what it represents. For me The Violet May are one of these bands. And it's so refreshing to see a band not give two fucks about the present day pathetic climate of the nanny state ideology. Fag in hand, mike stand as his weapon, singer Chris McClure couldn't care less about the health and safety issues and the smoking ban. When he's up there, and especially when he comes barging into the crowd swinging his mike and stand, he looks like he could really harm someone... its dangerous, its fun, its exciting, it gets the adrenalin going and its downright dirty fucking Rock n' Roll and I love it."

Heather Quinn: "Most music these days is slick and soulless. However, I've been really impressed with bands to come out of Sheffield since the rise of the Arctic Monkeys. The Violet May caught my attention by their name alone, before I'd even listened to them. As someone who remembers the real Violet May and her Sheffield record shop, this was a band I had to investigate - and I wasn't disappointed. They have that raw energy and certain something which I haven't heard in many bands over the past 30 years."

In 2010 Rotherham band The Tivoli collaborated with Sheffield musical pioneers Cabaret Voltaire, sealing the city and town's musical heritage, past, present and future together. The two places have always shared a constant link and belonging with regards to the Punk scene and beyond. The days of Sheffield Punk Rockers travelling down to the Rotherham Windmill for punk gigs are long gone, but the bonds between the grey Steel City and 2010 shattered Rotherham remain just as strong – music culture-wise - as ever! August 2010 saw The Tivoli perform with The Violet May at the Boardwalk. The Violet May have been asked to leave numerous venues due to their confrontational approach and refreshing indifference to the safety and PC correctness of some modern day Rock venues. The Violet May represent all that is, dangerous and exciting about modern Rock n' Roll.

The influence of Punk, and in particular The Jam, have also now reached the songwriting creativity of young Rotherham band Spiders. The original four piece of brothers Rob Tingle Vocals/Guitar and Adam Tingle (Drums) with Nick Monk on bass guitar and Danny Outram on guitar (who has now left the band) have been together for five years, forming in March 2005 and initially known as the Subs until 2009. With their main influences being a mix of old wave originals The Clash and The Jam along with the Smiths and Robert Smith's Cure topped off with the more recent sounds of the Libertines and their vision of rock n' roll hedonism, Spiders were also inspired by the advent of locals the Arctic Monkeys and Milburn's breaking out of the Indie niche. Another inspiration for the members of the band was BOREDOM!!! Sounds familiar don't it?

Adam Tingle: "We write about the everyday stuff, along with the usual teenage angst and even romance... all of this and other beautiful cliches all rendered with a Punk sensibility."

Typical song titles in the now three-piece band's set include 'Our Wasted Days', 'Nothing To Lose', 'Panic and Emptiness', 'Romance Is In', 'Dangerously Close To What I Want', 'Everytime You Look At Me' and 'Darker Days'. Gigs started off with the obligitary Leadmill experience.

Adam Tingle: "We played the Leadmill and then some festivals – Music in the Sun festival and the Hallam FM Acoustic one as well as playing the Cavern and all manner and number of dodgy venues in and around South Yorkshire that have existed over the last four or so years. Like any band who decide to be honest with themselves – we crave world domination and in Noel Gallagher's words *'it's all about the chocolate brown Rolls-Royce man'.* We started out of boredom, a slight talent for our instruments, a love of Rock n' Roll and the need to be bigger than Jesus!"

Meanwhile fellow new generation Punk-inspired musicians the Magi also look to the future with optimism.

Des Jenkinson: "After a few months of hard practice we soon started to sound the part and secured top gigs at all the main venues in Sheffield. We have also played venues in London and even the famous Cavern Club in Liverpool. We are influenced by many bands including, The Smiths, Oasis, The Clash and The Who. These bands have helped us to write songs such as 'Sexual Tension', 'Voodoo Taboo' and 'Blue Eyes (In the Smoke)'. We hope to carry on gigging, especially in Sheffield where we have a loyal 'mad' following, and who knows what could come our way in the future. One thing...'The Magi' is the future for us!"

The Violet May, Spiders, Twisted Wheel, Cyanide Pills (From Leeds) and The Magi, amongst a growing handful of great new bands, offer a recipe of hope for a new generation of music fans that just can't ignore the presence and influence of the new wave sounds and approach to song-writing of yesteryear... re-designed and created with a modernist new twist taking the ghost of Punk into the future!! Meanwhile Punk at its most basic form continues unabated and much loved with 100's of street core, Ramones, hard core and Oi! fueled bands all over the many reaches of the globe bashing away reviving and re-injecting the energy and fun into Punk Rock, but sadly often doing so without the true idealism and adventurism of Punk's original creativity and self identity!!!

The idealism and D.I.Y approach of Punk in Sheffield has also spread avidly into the Dance music scene. The founders of the Warp label (and before that Fon records) were a crucial catalyst in the promotion of new contemporay cutting-edge Dance music and produced a whole catalogue of groundbreaking new music from many diverse artists of the scene (Nightmares on Wax, Forgemasters, Sweet Exorcist and the Aphex Twin amongst them)... all mostly created with a firm nod to the *get up and do it* attitude of Punk Rock. The label has, in recent years, moved into the world of Independent film making with a string of admirable and critically valued films to its name.

Unbelievably four decades have passed since the mid to late seventies that our story really began: much has come and gone, immeasurable changes have occurred in all of our lives. From being embarrassingly young Pop goers at our local youth clubs – relishing the sounds of Suzi Quatro and T-Rex, our, very often, ill-informed initiations to Punk Rock and the even more misinformed but equally magical first forays at dressing like what we thought looked Punk to the never forgotten first time we all heard the Specials and 2-Tone, the dissension as sides were chosen between each splintering New Wave cult, the disappointment with it all as it all turned sour... we have heard and seen every notable and significant progression in the Pop world and the world we live in and our local surroundings have changed beyond recognition: most likely to all and sundry we too have likewise changed too, though inside we are mostly the same... if a little older and possibly wiser!

Valerie Garvey: (Left) "Punks are some of the nicest people you could ever meet and there is a strong bond between them: not all are good people as there are good and bad in all people but mostly I have found that they are people who think *'live and let live.'* They take care of their mates and family and many care about animals and the environment. So even though I did change when I had my children I will never regret being a Punk... it was one of the best times of my life and I think there will always be a little bit of a Punk in me (much to my kids' distress)."

Tony Beesley: "Yes! Some of us have managed to reach being older and questionably wiser... or at least older, but sadly so not all of our gang – our bunch of little rascals and outsiders who said piss off when asked to be normal – not all have managed to survive with us. How have we that are still around changed? Personally, I still have the Punk rebel streak in me: I think I always did have it, even before Punk. If someone makes the rules, I wanna break 'em... and if somebody says I can't do something or achieve anything, then I will go all out to prove them wrong. I was told I would never have a book I had written seen on a shop's book shelf, people laughed when I told them I was writing a book – just like they did all those years ago when I dyed my hair, plastered zips all over my clothes and decided I just didn't want to be like them! They laughed when I said I was gonna teach myself to play guitar and form a band too... No one believed, when our sixties-born Punk gang decided to turn the tables over and start our own thing, that we could actually achieve anything... But we –

our generation – proved them all wrong: we stood up and did something and it's what has made us who we are today!... I am now hungry again and wanting to get lots of things done and discover new bands, revisit some older ones and celebrate today with a hint of the past for added flavour. Without our past we have no future... it all links together!"

Murray Fenton: (Right) "It's a great feeling to still have the hairs on the back of your neck stand on end when you hear an exciting new band. Same with gigging, it's still exciting to get up on stage and give it some, despite being well into my 40s!!"

Steve Marshall: (Below) "After my Polytechnic course fell through (unsuccessfully) and the relationship with (my girlfriend) Angela ended, I was down and heartbroken back in Sheffield and working in steelworks and power stations earning good money to pay off my thousands in gambling debts. I still gambled a lot of it but left a bit left over for drinking and footy matches, but I didn't pay my rent or any bills if I could help it. So, for the next fifteen years or so, I was a lone wolf; never got married and I lived a meagre but materialistic (TV/video/records) life in a high rise flat in Sheffield centre for 17 years or so. I was - and still am - an anarchist and into that Punk/rebel/Crass alternative society and ideology, but at that time, I was a very lone and mixed up one.

"Most of my mates in that time were square, and apart from the occasional Leadmill one I didn't go to gigs anymore. I became bored and unemployed and a bit depressed – well a lot depressed sometimes. The funny thing was though, I was also fairly insular and kept myself at the edge of things a lot; my parents had been through a big split up, which probably affected me, and I spent time visiting and staying with both of them at their different houses in Sheffield too.

"I count myself really lucky, in many ways. Although I didn't go on to get married, have kids, house and good holidays, like most adult people, I had then (and still do) some strong self-anarchy and autonomy... FREEDOM... in my life and belief that has stayed with me; from the Punk music and ethics of the era right through all my dark and dreary days of gambling problems and poverty. I knew several friends/mates who sadly died. Duane Willey (RIP) from the Limit Club – Wire's 'I am the Fly' was his and our DANCE song. Duane sadly died, I think in 1983/4 after falling from a works roof only just after his girlfriend had had their first child too. Then Jud, Ian Williams and Deano all died from heroin overdoses during the 1980s. They, and others like Laura Deeley - who died of cancer a few years ago are NOT FORGOTTEN.

"So, although I gave myself a tough time, and life didn't really turn out for me the way it could perhaps have done, in a way, I wouldn't swap the experience and certainly not the fantastic - if crazy and manic times - I had as a young Punk from 1977 onwards which were amazing and fabulous experiences. My life was exciting, fun and full of adventure, music, mates, gigs, smokes and booze. I had brilliant times, I was really happy, and still am, to have been a part of that."

Ex Outlook goer and Vice Squad singer Phil Tasker started back on his musical path in Nottingham in 1990 as guitarist with Degree 33. Linking up with two members of The Basking Sharks, Adrian Todd and Martyn Eames (an early 80's electronic synth band) and vocalist/performance artist Graham Elstone to produce original material. Using a heady combination of analog synthesizers, drum machines, heavily treated guitar sounds, samples from cult films and video footage plus a Punk philosophy of one take live recording and performance, no overdubbing, what you hear is played live straight in to the mixing desk. In 2009 an unofficial bootleg was released of Degree 33 on Retro records but an official CD is soon to be released with tracks recorded from the master tapes and extra tracks from earlier recordings. Degree 33 was a combination of electro and guitar fuelled experimentational space rock! All a long way from Phil's days at the Outlook and performing to local and nationwide Punk crowds of the late 70's... but most importantly taking the agenda forward in to the future! He currently plays guitar, sings and writes new material with an un-named band, with other members Adrian Todd and Martyn Eames, this music is also based around analog electronic music and guitar, which seeks to push the boundaries of Post-Punk music and song writing.

You could say that the memories of Punk have many songs to sing, chords to thrash and words to express. Before he indulged in the Max Factor and crimpers of the New Romantic scene and along the way experienced enough vision to become a doll of Pierrot standards and proclaim 'Mon Amour'... Andi Stevenson soaked up a whole DJ's box of Punk.

Andi Stevenson: "Ladies 'n' Gentlemen how do? Are you ready now? Then I'll begin. Maybe back then I was just a bored teenager, an orgasm addict eating Mars Bars everyday, which didn't help my public image. I had no time to be 21 cos the boredom came every 5 minutes and every Wednesday week would be dole day but in the meantime I was killing time cos I had no career opportunities. Somehow I always felt on the eve of destruction, hanging around Mary of the 4th form who had a stranglehold on me like I was a fly in the ointment, but in those strange times Punk became my life.

"But Mary's love was a charade, a masquerade and I said I can't control myself anymore, I love you, you big dummy as I felt myself breakdown. But she laughed and said boys don't cry and I said shut up! But this was the beginning of the end. She said I just can't be happy today its another Sunday morning nightmare you're putting me through and I've gotta getaway from this before I lead a wasted life. I asked if it was something that I said and she said you've broken all your promises and I said so what! What do I get?, all you do is nag! nag! nag! but I just can't get over you: so was it all a fiction romance? She was a backbiter and one of those typical girls with perfect peaches who'd do anything you wanna do to get you those teenage kicks. I often caught her staring at the rude boys and I'd say who you looking at? But all she did was lie, lie, lie but now our time's up and everybody's happy nowadays. I said if things change you've got my number but remember you've also got my telephone girl so give it back before you leave and don't smash it up either. I thought to myself was it just lust so I phoned some friends of mine to help me cos I always need to be looking after no.1 but Johnny was out. So I called his brother and said Jimmy, Jimmy you've got to come to the pub something's gone wrong again but don't bring Harry cos he's a basket case. He said don't dictate to me and I heard him say don't just sit there come on, hurry up Harry we're going down the pub, Go buddy go! I went in the city and they met me down at the tube station at midnight.

"We went to the Chelsea nightclub cos you can drink till late with all your mates and I started feeling all right with the crew but it was there they told me to get a grip of myself. But for now that's all nostalgia cos here comes the summer and I'm gonna suss out a holiday in the sun or maybe I'll just go into the valley racing fast cars with a pretty vacant expression on my face putting my life on the line. I just know I've gotta getaway so maybe soon I'll travel all around the world and see a Hong Kong garden or take a holiday in Cambodia. But she's not there now and it's a happy house I live in when I don't live in a car. I don't mind I'm now an old codger, a fat bastard and that I was once in a rut cos everything's now running like clockwork and London's calling so soon. I'm gonna straighten out myself and live in the modern world. So this is Remembrance Day and it has made me realise they were the best years of my life and Oh Shit! They're gone and I feel hollow inside... but they're never forgotten. Maybe looking back Mary of the 4th form is with a better man than I and maybe in my dreams I can be sixteen again one day! One day the saints will be coming but I've realised until then our memories of our Punk days are everything cos we're all of one skin!"

Kevin Wells: (Below with ex-Jam bass player Bruce Foxton) "As you get older some thing's never leave you, one being the sounds of certain songs and the magic of favourite bands. It's nice to know that the music that affected my generation is still affecting bands today. Having been a

regular gig goer for many years you still feel the buzz when you see a new band doing something special, you know the feeling, hearts starts pumping and the hairs on the back of your neck stand up."

Nigel Lockwood: (Below) "One of my most memorable experiences was the first time I went to New York, in the late summer of 1980, I stayed with my friend, David Webster, at Eddie and Karen Massiminos' house, off Jamaica Avenue, Queens, NYC, for three weeks. Whilst there we went to see the Members, the Plasmatics, Mink de Ville, the Plastics, Johnny Thunders and the Heartbreakers at Max's Kansas city, the Soft Boys at Danceteria, coming on at 3.30 am, meeting Frank Infante from Blondie, seeing Madness do a P.A at club Hurrah, but best of all was seeing my old mate Glen Matlock, who was doing a PA visit for his band the Spectres: he was staying at the Iroquois Hotel on West 44th Street, and that night took us up to Iggy Pop's room... also with him was Mick Ronson, wow! Ive still got the great photos from that night!!

"It's June 2010 and I'm listening to the best of the Charlatans: they are survivors, and like many others, have never really pandered to the clichéd expectations of the music industry, which is how it should be. The likes of Neil Young, Mark E. Smith, Morrissey, Elvis Costello, Iggy Pop, etc, should remain in our hearts forever. Nowadays I have even more eclectic tastes and listen especially to Americana music (Fleet Foxes, Band of Horses and The Low Anthem), along with NY. musician Jesse Malin, who I feel is a missing link to the original Max's Kansas City/CBGB's scene of the late 70's. I also still have full admiration for one of the true innovators of the essence of Punk John Lydon. From a recent John Lydon quote,

referring to being on the same bill as the Police at the Isle of Wight festival – *'Bands with gymnasium bums, its nothing short of preposterous'...* what a quality statement, from the singer who had *green teeth and threw chairs at people."*

One time Cute Pube Punk band member and Springheel'd Jack (and more recently Cool Canasta) leader Dave Spencer had his life take an unexpected and almost fatal turn in 2007... with the discovery of something in his head that really should not have been there!

Dave Spencer: "Wednesday March 28th 2007 after a band rehearsal, I came home and crept into bed as normal, only to be woken up at about 3.00am with the headache from hell. It's hard to describe it now, but there just weren't enough tablets in the house to clear it. It fluctuated for the next couple of days and by the weekend it had calmed down somewhat. On Sunday night it returned with a vengeance, so Monday I thought, *'there's more to this than meets the eye'* and went to the doctors.

"The doctor couldn't find anything wrong with me, but considering the severity of the pain I was describing she asked if I minded going to the Hallamshire Hospital. She said she'd sort it out and call me when she'd arranged an appointment. I'd only been home about five minutes before she rang and said I could go to the Hallamshire right away. Basically, I went to the hospital and time stood still... I was there all day and all they did was ask me some questions and give me a scan and in between, I read the paper.

"About 6 o'clock, a doctor came along and explained that they had spotted an Acoustic Neuroma, which is a benign brain tumour. I was a little shocked, to say the least. It wouldn't kill me, he said, as long as they operated within the next couple of months. Otherwise, I'd be dead within a year or two, although the pain would have sent me barmy first. So, I went in on the 16th May and they operated on the 17th. I started to recover very quickly. A lot faster than the staff said I would, in fact. I looked like I'd been hit by a truck, though.

"As the name implies, an Acoustic Neuroma grows on the acoustic nerve. To cut it out, the surgeon and his team had to drill through the cavities behind my left ear (I now have no hearing at all in this ear) and slowly zap the tumour out. The operation took 16 hours! In fact, about 5-10 per cent is still there, because as it's been growing for such a long time the other nerves have sort of become entangled with it and come to rely upon it for stability. It's caused by something called the Schwann cell reproducing too quickly. Nothing I have ever done (or indeed, not done) has made this thing grow - it just happened. It's probably been growing for about 15 years. It's not all bad though. Now I look at life so much differently. It's a case of *'Hey isn't that grass so green over there'.*"

Dave moved to Spain in May 2010 and continues to write songs and perform as well as working on book cover design and websites.

A near miss for another member of the ageing fraternity of our generation – John Harrison!

John Harrison: "After The Way split up, my life went into a gradual downward spiral: I became a nervous wreck and a virtual agoraphobic and I ended up homeless and living from place to place, anywhere that I could find a bed. My life deteriorated fast! Just when I thought it couldn't get any worse... it did!

"I was stopping at someone's flat and one day I awoke to find myself with a terrible pain in my abdomen. Thinking it was nothing too serious, and typically me, I stupidly took no notice. Time passed and my physical condition got much worse, yet I still persisted to ignore it. Cut to the chase, it was a Tuesday morning and I woke to find the situation was now intolerable, so desperate measures had to be taken. I ended up crawling (literally) to my Mothers house and knocked on the door. She saw the state of me, and luckily my brother Mark was in, and quick as a flash 999 was called. The next thing I knew, I was in hospital, not that I remember all that much. Through a kinda hazy fogginess I remember being whizzed on a stretcher to surgery.

"I came round after four days and was incoherent and soon realised that I had a Colostomy bag attached to my stomach! After a few days, I asked my Mother what the surgeons had said and she replied *'They said if I had left it 24 hours longer, there would have been 'no later'.* I would have died from septicaemia.

"I spent one and a half months in Hospital and then went home to my Mothers for a while. I soon fell back into my old ways, before finally realising that I had to change. I managed to get my own flat and start again. The Colostomy was reversed after a year and a half... thank God! It has left me with some problems, which will be with me for life, but still, I survived a near-Death experience and now I appreciate every waking day, along with all the family and friends who wouldn't let me go. I would like to say cheers to all those that never left me during my darkest hours."

Left: Three quarters of The Way in 2009 Ian Deakin, John Harrison and myself

Tony Beesley: "I have known John right from us being kids but more closely from our late 70's Punk days and onwards, forming a band together etc, but most importantly developing a great and long-standing friendship with him. We were the very best of mates and shared so many great times together... we were young and daft and often up to no good, but we were in it together, through thick and thin. I too saw John's life start to go hay-wire... he had that self-destruct button pressed firmly down for many years. I tried so hard to help and inspire some hope and confidence in him, but nothing seemed to work. By the 90's our laughs and good times were far and few between and eventually we sadly drifted apart for some years. I think I may have seen him on rare occasions from the 90's until 2008, with a space of around six years of not seeing him at all. When I found out he was in hospital I went straight away to see him. I think it was a Sunday afternoon by the time I had found out and got there and when I saw him laid in that hospital bed, looking just like a little kid who had been rescued from starvation or something, it was absolutely heartbreaking. I tried to lift his spirits, but I am not entirely sure that he even knew I was there, even though he was talking to me. When I went home that night, I cried for maybe only the second or third time since I was a kid.

"John came out of hospital after all of his ops, and he came round to see me one night. He did seem a changed person: he had stopped smoking, no drinking and unbelievably brought some caffeine-free coffee with him. He was just like the alert young teenager I had first became great friends with. When I saw him slipping back into his old ways, it was so maddening and frustrating to see. I didn't see, or hear from John, until I started to write my first book 'Our Generation'. Since then we have rekindled our friendship and make sure we get together every few weeks or so and catch up and have a good laugh. He has now got himself more sorted than he has done for a long time. He has mended many of his ways and I value his friendship greatly. I would even trust him with the green cash tin nowadays... I think ha ha!! It's been a long journey and one that has seen some hard times, but our being mates has survived it all."

Inevitably, the whole settings and surroundings to our story have changed, often unrecognisably so!

Sheffield, like Rotherham, has changed almost beyond recognition since the start of our generation's story. Back in the late 1970's, the city was only relatively recently recovering from its Post-War years... indeed the rubble of some of the old bombed out buildings and areas had only been re-built upon during the previous decade. The sights and sounds of Sheffield change regularly: it is always a city on the mend and its landscape is forever being re-designed... not always to everyone's liking. Gone is the old Pond Street bus station where skinheads once chased school kid Punk Rockers to their bus stops and where a young Paul Weller strolled down, meeting the requests of non student Jam fans eager to find a way into see The Jam perform their 'All Mod Cons' set. Replacing the old Pond Street bus station is a modern *'shopping mall inserted'* contemporary interchange with little soul and even less recognition of its concrete-slab-adorned predecessor. The Polytechnic's Nelson Mandela building no longer holds concerts or record fairs either.

The Limit club is long gone, but manages to live on in the much loved memories of the hundreds of Punks, Goths, Mods, Rude Boys, electro fans, New Romantics, psychobillys and clubbers who walked into its dark pleasure. It now has its legendary story told in print and has greatly attended and much loved Limit reunion nights held at the city's Casbah club. Local artist Paul Staveley himself an old Limit goer, has even painted his own individual impression of the Limit nights capturing the colour and wide variety of styles and fashion on offer.

Bruce Foxton returns to the old Top Rank (now the O2 Academy) minus Weller... and Jam influenced The Enemy play the same venue (Right)

Below: Little man Tate also at the O2 Academy

The Top Rank completed its original Punk-motivated flow of gigs by 1983 and metamorphosed into mid 80's haven of Saturday night clubbers the Roxy, before being resurrected in recent years, first as the Carling Academy and then the O2 Academy. As well as contemporary bands, the venue has also seen the revisiting of old Top Rank performers Foxton and Buckler (From The Jam), The Dickies, the Stranglers and Sheffield's finest Artery (now back on form and in motion). Maybe, if you listen very quietly – when the place is empty – you may hear the call from Joe Strummer proclaiming 'This is Joe Public speaking' or 'This is the Punk Rockers!' Recently it has seen the return of the Specials as well as Mod faves Ocean Colour Scene and contemporary Mod influenced Indie styled bands.

Photos by Kevin Wells

Specials at the O2 Academy 2009

The Specials first performed in Sheffield as support to The Clash on their 1978 'Out on Parole' tour. Their next visit was for a packed out Limit club performance the following year just on the cusp of the 2-Tone explosion of the summer of 1979. Later that year they returned yet again to perform at the Top Rank as part of the 2-tone package tour with Madness and the Selecter: a gig marred by sporadic outbursts of violence and right wing intimidation from a proportion of the bands followings.

In 2009 the Specials finally settled their differences (bar Jerry Damners) and after 28 years of absence from being a band they returned triumphantly to the Steel city for a sell out date at the O2, gracing the very same stage that they had trodden as a young Punk inspired ska/Punk band many years earlier!

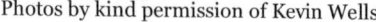

Photos by kind permission of Kevin Wells

Over at the Millennium Galleries in March 2010, legendary Punk visionary/poet/singer Patti Smith performed an intimate talk and concert in celebration of her book 'Just Kids'. Following this the grandmother of Punk, wearing an old black overcoat and Beanie hat, strolled off up Fargate in the centre, unrecognised and untroubled by anyone... a symbol of Punk's assimilation into the steel city's landscape!

Patti Smith at the Sheffield Millennium Galleries by Kevin Wells

The Marples is now partially a betting shop; the Penthouse is derelict as is Revolution Records on the Gallery (though its front shop logo is still intact). The record shops, even the ones of recent years, are long gone: only the Record Collector out of town in Broomhill managing to brave the storm of recent years and the many and varied challenges faced.

The Punks and Mods of the late 70's and early 80's would all have, at some point, travelled through the Hole in the Road in the city centre, using either the crammed escalators or one of the many walk-out exits. The actual Hole in the Road was a great meeting point for the different gangs and crowds of young rebels: there was even a record shop to accommodate... Like much of the city from back then, the Hole in the Road is now also gone, filled in and boasting a tram-way, that passes through a portion of a much rearranged traffic system – *'What a great traffic system'*!

Bernard Sumner of Joy Division/New Order/Bad Lieutenant at the Leadmill March 2010 (Kevin Wells)

The Black Swan, the venue partially responsible for kick-starting the paths of many within our generation's story – via its proto-type Punk offering of The Clash and Sex Pistols way back in July 76 - re-opened, after many years, as the Boardwalk and continues to showcase live music to this day.

The Leadmill continues to hold ground-breaking concerts and popular club nights: the Beat club was a popular haunt for sixties influenced music fans, though it never managed to draw quite as many of the serious Mod crowd as the City Hall ballroom's Brighton Beach nights of 96 – 2000.

Brighton Beach moved first to the University, a move never popular with the dwindling Mod attendees, then back to the City Hall Ballroom for a soul-less attempt to re-capture the Mod glory days of its past. In a curious twist of fate, the night is now held at the O2 Academy; itself previously the Top Rank suite... the scene of many new wave, Mod revival and 2-Tone events. The City Hall itself still holds concerts there, including now and again the Modfather himself! The most authentic local Mod night is the irregular Pow Wow club nights, which sees Mods from all over the country; make it their business to attend. 'Mod for it' also successfully manages to capture the whole spectrum of the Mod scene in a way that Brighton Beach used to do so well and easily!

Rotherham down the road has little left over to boast of, not even having a music store left within its midst at all. On a positive note, for local live music, its live venues bravely attempt to put the heart back into the local music scene, with original 70's Punk bands returning to play at the now defunct Blues Café (999, UK Subs, Eddie and the Hot Rods), NO.10 club (Vibrators, Lurkers, Tenpole Tudor, X-Rippers and a whole host of modern day Punk influenced bands – thanks to the promoter Mick Hill and the guys who persuaded him – Mandy Taylor and Andy Morton)... Those two venues may also belong to the past as well, but the Dickens venue now holds Punk Rock within its walls... where once the very notion of even playing a Punk record in 1977 had been banned. The future is uncertain but the venue and its collaborators work steadfastly to keep the local live music scene alive!

Doncaster has its own vibrant Punk revivalist scene with young and old Punk Rockers alike sharing their love of the music and its scene. The Leopard and Hallcross hold Punk gigs and regular Punk nights and weekenders... the days of the Outlook club being fondly remembered by the older of the fold.

Barnsley has its own original Punk era band the X-Rippers still performing to this day and keeping the fun in Punk intact... the town's Barmy Surplus also play their own unique brand of Ska and Punk to appreciative fans of the local area, and mighty fine they are too.

In recent years the advent of the tribute acts growth has taken over in all genres of music: much of it being sad money-spinning cons to get music lovers to shell out their cash on something not quite the real thing. Punk was never about apeing your peers, but doing your own thing. So much has to be questioned in the merits of copying your musical heroes... go and do your own thing is the echo to much of the mindless copying of many of Rock n' Roll's greatest talents. If any tribute bands come even close to the real thing within Punk revival circles it appears that the two original instigators of the class of 76 are the ones most respected by our ageing Punk generation! Rebel Truce (The Clash) and the Sex Pistols experience!

The Sex Pistols experience at Sheffield Boardwalk December 2009(Kevin Wells)

Tony Beesley: "I have always made it perfectly clear that I have little time for tribute bands, but seeing the Sex Pistols Experience in 2010, all my pre-conceptions about the whole tribute thing went straight out of the window. They completely won me over."

The future of the local Punk and Mod and off-shoot scenes is now in the hands of those who choose to be involved in their making: the music will always be loved and the memories are still being made, a welcome antidote to the gloom and frustrations of living in so-called Broken Britain... whilst finally the memories already created from the past are now firmly set in print...

Tony Beesley: "From the 90's onwards, there have been countless tributes paid to the Punk era and beyond: there have been stacks of Mojo, Q and Uncut etc specials and there are numerous DVD's and some fantastic films revolving around the era ('This is England', 'Control' and 'Away days' etc) as well as books and articles spread around that almost all focus on the bands and their contributions. The whole period has been analysed, chronicled and dissected scrupulously to every fine detail... apart from the viewpoint of us lot – the fans, the kids, the ones who supported the revolution, bought the records and paid for the tickets to go and see the bands. Apart from the odd piece here and there and a couple of accounts, John Robb's excellent coverage of the Manchester scene 'The North will rise again' being one of the very few, the coverage from our Northern viewpoint has been minimal - Sheffield and the region just about non-existent even. I aimed to put this straight and with these volumes of books that I have put together, with the help of all involved, want to finally tell our own stories and let history decide if what we aimed to achieve, what we felt, what we experienced, our mistakes and our greatest moments were of much worth and of any use for future generations to read about... so let the story read of how important its all been... cos for me its been the greatest part of my life!

"It is weird though, ain't it, that I now chat to Geoff Deane (the singer of the Leyton Buzzards), Rusty Egan of the Rich Kids and, on occasion, Damned drummer Rat Scabies, on that symbol of modern living – Facebook. Well over 30 odd years ago, I was going out and buying their records and watching these guys perform on Top of the Pops, now I am asking 'em what kind of a day they have had via the internet!"

And finally how have those twin loves and influences of The Clash and The Jam- Punk Rock and Mod lasted for the author?

Tony Beesley: "I suppose now, in 2010, the twin schizophrenia of having the two most influential music scenes of all time and all that goes with them – Punk Rock and Mod - in my life for so long... has seen a total immersion of them both within my own personal psyche. The two influences battled for many years to gain dominance within this particular atypical Gemini being and have now become almost inseparable with the result that, I suppose, if I 'had' to be pinned down and labelled, you could say I was a 40-something Mod with a Punk Rock attitude!"

In 2010 a change of government brought back the Tories. It seems to have come full circle again, but maybe the desperation from a harsh new political and social climate may encourage the next generation of youth to create their own attack on the system... Time will only provide the outcome and the future is unwritten- as the saying goes.

Our Generation *took it to the Limit* and at times got unequivocally *out of control...* we spat at the system, kicked the fucking doors down and screamed to be let in and have our say...we were gonna change so much and maybe we did change some things - or at least we tried to. We certainly aimed to make a difference, that's for sure, and that's what it's all about - having a damned go at it all... and having a good time at the same time... nowt wrong with that is there?

That was Our Generation calling!

VOLUMES ONE AND TWO OF THE 'OUR GENERATION TRILOGY AVAILABLE FROM THE OFFICIAL WEBSITE

www.ourgenerationpunkandmod.co.uk

And all good book stores

VOLUME 1

VOLUME 2

Further reading

Take it to the Limit (Neil Anderson)
Fat Bloke, Thin Book (Arturo Basic)
Route 19 revisited: London Calling and The Clash (Marcus Gray)
I'm not like everybody else: The 1990's British Mod scene (Enamel Vergern)
It makes you wanna spit (Sean O' Neill and Guy Trelford)
Beats working for a living (Martin Lilleker) – (The Bible for Post-Punk Sheffield bands)

ACKNOWLEDGMENTS

DAVE SPENCER FOR THE FANTASTIC COVER (YET AGAIN).
SIMON CARDIE FOR THE FRONT COVER PHOTO
ROB WASTENEY FOR HELP AND INSPIRATION
PAUL JESPERSEN FOR SUPERB PROOFING
KRISTAN JAMES MELIK FOR INTEREST AND ENCOURAGEMENT ALONG
WITH A FANTASTIC SELECTION OF HIS EXCEPTIONAL PHOTO COLLECTION
KEVIN WELLS FOR HIS SUPERB PHOTOGRAPHIC TALENTS AND KIND USE
OF SOME OF HIS VAST OUTSTANDING COLLECTION
JENNIFER JONES FOR SUPPORT

ALSO

NIGEL LOCKWOOD
SHANE BALDWIN
DEBRA MARSHALL
LOUISE MCKENNING
JULIE 'JOOLS' LONGDEN
STEVE 'MUSHROOM' MARSHALL
COLLEEN ALLEN
JOHN QUINN
MANDY TAYLOR
HEATHER QUINN
JOHN HARRISON
SALLY BURTON
MARTIN LACEY

AND IN NO PARTICULAR ORDER: NEIL ANDERSON, STEVE METCALF, NICK BANKS, PETE SKIDMORE, CHRIS MCCLURE AND THE VIOLET MAY, ARTURO BASSICK, TONY CRONSHAW, ANDY GOULTY, PETE RODDIS, TONY LOUND, CARL MYERS, PHIL SINGLETON, HEATHER ALLEN, SUE BUTCHERS BERRY, LOIS WILSON (MOJO), RACHAEL CLEGG, NICK WARD, TIM JONES, PETE WESTON, ANDY MUNDAY, DIZZY HOLMES, DAVID DUNN, BEKI BONDAGE, GERRY LAMBE, BRIAN HOUGHTON, PHIL SINGLETON, JOHN FLANAGAN, KATHERINE HANCOCK PEAT, SIMON ELLIS, TIM JONES, CARL EGGLESTON, CHRIS ANDERSON, BRIAN PEARSON, PETER BIRCH, LEE DYSON, NEIL KITSON, JIM GATUS, NICK HAWKSWORTH, SIMON MILNER, DIDI, ROB 'DINGO' DOWLING, ELLIE FORD, MICHAEL DAY, SHAUN DAY, LYNNE FREEMAN, BEVERLY WILSON, JOHN MURRAY, STEVE PARKIN, PETE EASON, NICK ROBINSON, NICK ORME, LYNNE HAYTHORNE, DAVE RODDIS, IVOR HILLMAN, FIONA PALMER, TRACY STANLEY, IAN DEAKIN, WENDY NICHOLLS, KLIVE HUMBERSTONE, NIGEL HUMBERSTONE, MARK HILTON, ANDI STEVENSON, STEVE GLEDHILL, JANINE AND GARETH, MEL CARTER RHODES, WAYNE KENYON, MARTIN LILLEKER, JADE GONZALES. CAROL WESTON, MICK HILL, BRYAN BELL, GARY PEACOCK, RICHARD CHATTERTON, PAUL MORTON, PHILLIP WRIGHT, BOB ROBERTS, KEVIN MUNDAY, LEE RADFORTH, NEV QUINN, TERRY SUTTON (PHOTOS AND WORDS), IAN DEAKIN, JULIAN LEUESBY, DAVE BURKINSHAW, PETER BRAUGH, CRAIG CHATTERTON, PHIL CHATTERTON, GARY STABLES, JAMIE 'HEADCHARGE' SMITH, EVE

WOOD, RICHARD WOOD, ANDY HUNT (HMV), ROSS BENNETT (MOJO), KARL LANG, DAVID DUNN, DARREN TWYNHAM, DALLY, JUNE GRAHAM, JOHN ATKIN, PAUL OXLEY, LIZ PRESTON, TRACY PIDD SMITH, PAUL OXLEY, JOHN ASHMORE, JOHN BELL, ANGELA ADAMS, BATTY, JO CALLIS, VICKY BEARD, KAREN STEELE, LORNA HOOD, RICHARD AND EVE WOOD, MARSHA AND ROB ARMITIGE, KID REID OF THE BOYS, MARK RAISON, ROTHERHAM TRAVEL CENTRE, JAYNE JENKINSON, ROB JENKINSON, DES JENKINSON, ADAM TINGLE, ROB TINGLE, NICK MONK, DANNY OUTRAM, JAMIE, BOTT, MICK HILL, ANDY AND LIVE AT DICKENS VENUE, JIM, LYNNE AND STAFF AT RAWMARSH POST OFFICE... SOUTH YORKSHIRE TIMES, SHEFFIELD STAR, SHEFFIELD TELEGRAPH, ROTHERHAM ADVERTISER, RECORD COLLECTOR, MOJO, BIG CHEESE, ROTHERHAM NEWS. OUR PAUL, MEGAN AND MICHELLE FOR PHOTOS, ALSO EVERYONE WHO BOUGHT AND SHOWED INTEREST IN THE FIRST TWO BOOKS.

For un-ending support - My close family, Vanessa, Dean and Sean and not forgetting Charlie the cat!

Those who have sadly left us we remember –

John Peel, Jo Brailsford, Laura Deeley, Darren Marsden, Rob Ely, Paul Critchlow, Dave Bateman (Vice Squad), Tim McCall (a true talent and guitarist), Stevo (aka Paul Stevens) of Plastik Toyz, Pete Boam, Paul Critchlow, Chris Long, Rob Harrison... a much missed Rich kid - Steve New and also Malcolm McLaren who gave us the Sex Pistols and helped to set us off on our many journeys- R.I.P all of you!

Author's notes: The opinions expressed within the pages of this book do not necessarily represent those of the author or any other person or persons within these pages. All effort has been made to contact all persons involved with any copyright acknowledgments and related and if anyone feels that they have been overlooked, please contact us and all due amendments will be respectfully acknowledged and fully respected in further editions of this work.

Sites
www.ourgenerationpunkandmod.co.uk

www.myspace.com/skunksukofficial

www.sheffieldvision.com

www.retro-records.com

www.mudkiss.com

www.sexpistols.net

www.theboys.co.uk

www.detour-records.co.uk

www.punk77.co.uk

www.modculture.co.uk